The Victoria History of the Counties of England

EDITED BY WILLIAM PAGE, F.S.A.

A HISTORY OF
KENT
VOLUME II

THE
VICTORIA HISTORY
OF THE COUNTIES
OF ENGLAND
KENT

PUBLISHED FOR
THE UNIVERSITY OF LONDON
INSTITUTE OF HISTORICAL RESEARCH
REPRINTED FROM THE ORIGINAL EDITION OF 1926
BY
DAWSONS OF PALL MALL
FOLKESTONE & LONDON
1974

Published by the
St. Catherine Press
in 1926

Reprinted for the University of London
Institute of Historical Research
by
Dawsons of Pall Mall
Cannon House
Folkestone, Kent, England
1974

ISBN: 0 7129 0607 X

Originally printed in Great Britain by
Eyre & Spottiswoode Limited, London
Reprinted in Belgium by Jos Adam, Brussels

INSCRIBED
TO THE MEMORY OF
HER LATE MAJESTY
QUEEN VICTORIA
WHO GRACIOUSLY GAVE
THE TITLE TO AND
ACCEPTED THE
DEDICATION OF
THIS HISTORY

EDMUND RICH.
(Reverse.)

EDMUND RICH,
ARCHBISHOP OF CANTERBURY.
(1233–40.)

JOHN STRATFORD,
ARCHBISHOP OF CANTERBURY.
(1333–48.)

WALTER DE MERION,
BISHOP OF ROCHESTER.
(1274–77.)

ST. ANSELM,
ARCHBISHOP OF CANTERBURY.
(1093–1109.)

THE
VICTORIA HISTORY
OF THE COUNTY OF
KENT

Edited by WILLIAM PAGE, F.S.A.

VOLUME TWO

PUBLISHED FOR
THE UNIVERSITY OF LONDON
INSTITUTE OF HISTORICAL RESEARCH
REPRINTED BY
DAWSONS OF PALL MALL
FOLKESTONE & LONDON

CONTENTS OF VOLUME TWO

CONTENTS OF VOLUME TWO

Religious Houses (*continued*)—

CONTENTS OF VOLUME TWO

LIST OF ILLUSTRATIONS AND MAPS

EDITORIAL NOTE

OWING to the many difficulties occasioned during the war and post-war periods when all work on the Victoria County History had necessarily to be in abeyance, eighteen years have elapsed since the first volume of this county was issued. Parts of the work here published were finished and in type before the war, but such standing type has been revised, and any additional information that has been brought to light by the Calendars recently issued by the Public Record Office, and by the work of local historians, has been added.

The Editor wishes to thank Mr. M. Oppenheim for his help in the production of this volume.

ECCLESIASTICAL HISTORY

PART I

THE local history of the Romano-British Church is obscure. *Cantium* must indeed have enjoyed the privileges of Christianity in common with the rest of Roman Britain, but, in the absence of local records and of monumental relics of any importance,[1] it is left to conjecture to throw a dim light upon questions of local ecclesiastical organization. The signatures of the British bishops present at the Council of Arles in 314[2] suggest that at that date there may have been a single bishopric for each of the four parts into which Britain was divided in the arrangement made by Diocletian in the year 297.[3] *Cantium*, in *Britannia prima*, would form part of the diocese (*paroichia*) of Restitutus, bishop of London. Beyond this there is no evidence of any real value. Three or four bishoprics in *Britannia provincia* would compare favourably with the number of continental sees existing early in the fourth century.[4] Thenceforward the organization of sees advanced rapidly, and the British Church was represented somewhat more numerously at the council of Ariminum in 359, when three of the attendant British bishops were too poor to pay their expenses. No names, however, are recorded ; and on the whole it is not unreasonable to endorse the opinion that in the Romano-British Church 'the present diocese of Canterbury' with that of Rochester 'must have been a sort of *ecclesia suburbicaria* to the metropolis of London.'[5] It is significant that Gregory the Great, in his instructions to Augustine,[6] contemplated the establishment of two metropolitical sees, one at London and the other at York, making no mention of Canterbury. In fact Canterbury

---

[1] Haverfield, in *Engl. Hist. Rev.* July, 1896.

[2] 'Eborius Episcopus de civitate Eboracensi provincia Britannia.' 'Restitutus Episcopus de civitate Londinensi provincia superscripta.' 'Adelfius Episcopus de civitate Colonia Londinensium.' Haddan and Stubbs, *Councils*, i, 7. Mr. Haddan adds in reference to Colonia Londinensium 'read, probably, Legionensium, Caerleon on Usk.' Prof. Knight (*Chapters of Engl. Ch. Hist.* 9) quotes an alternative reading, Lindensium, pointing to Lindum Colonia, i.e. Lincoln. Mr. Haverfield (op. cit.) says : 'The reading Londinensium is plainly wrong. It is possible that a copyist confused Lindensium with the somewhat similar Londinensi preceding it. Lindum (Lincoln) was a colony and, as existing remains show, was prosperous in the fourth century. The suggestion Legionensium (Caerleon on Usk) is wholly inadmissible, for (1) Caerleon was from first to last a fortress and never a colonia ; (2) there is no proof that its inhabitants were styled Legionenses in the fourth century ; the military character of the place renders it a very unsuitable centre of early Christianity.'

[3] These four parts were : Brit. prima, Brit. secunda, Maxima Caesariensis, and Flavia Caesariensis ; but their frontiers are wholly unknown. See Haverfield, *Roman Britain*, in Poole's *Hist. Atlas*, pt. i. The see of Brit. secunda is unknown. The sees of the other three provinces would be London, York, and Lincoln.

[4] Cf. Bishop Browne, *The Church in these Islands before the Coming of Augustine*, 68.

[5] Jenkins, *Diocesan Hist. of Canterbury* (S P.C.K.).   [6] Bede, *Eccl. Hist.* i, 29.

in the Roman period was important only as a military station, guarding the crossing of the Stour at the point where the roads from the coast fortresses of Reculver, Richborough, Dover and Lympne converged to run on by Watling Street through the 'open country' of *Caint* to London, and so to the north and west.

The Romano-British Church, whatever its organization in Cantium may have been, was but a poor thing at its best,[7] and Romano-British civilization, weakened by the withdrawals of the legions forty years previously, quickly disappeared before the invasion of the English in the middle of the fifth century. For a century and a half Kent was a heathen land, and British Christianity during that time, driven by successive waves of Jutes and Saxons and Angles further and further away, finally took refuge in Wales and Cornwall and Cumberland, and made no attempt to convert the conquerors. At the close of that period, when Kent again came under Christian influence from another source, the only traditions that remained of British Christianity in Kent were connected with two old buildings of which it was said that they had been Christian temples when the Romans were in the land.[8]

The ecclesiastical history of the county, as distinct from tradition and conjecture, begins with the reign of Ethelbert and the coming of the Augustinian mission sent by Gregory the Great, with a view to the realization of his long-cherished desire to bring about the conversion of the English people. The story of Gregory and the English youths whom he saw exposed for sale in the slave markets of Rome is too well known to tell again at length : the fair faces of the Angles seemed to him to point to their joint heritage with the angels in heaven ; the name of their country, Deira, begat in him a longing that they might be snatched from wrath (*de ira eruti*) ; and that of their king, Ælla, prompted a resolve that Alleluia should be sung in their land.[9] Gregory's elevation to the see of Rome made it impossible that he should carry out his resolve in person. His choice of an agent fell upon his intimate friend, Augustine, prior of the monastery of St. Andrew, which he himself had founded upon the Coelian hill. Augustine is described as a man of commanding presence and lofty stature, thoroughly trained in the monastic discipline, and well versed in the study of Scripture.[10] He arrived in Kent with a band of forty companions early in the year 597,[11] and he died in 604 or 605. A man of somewhat ordinary character, in those few years he did an extraordinary work : by the earnestness of his preaching he converted the men of Kent to the faith, and by the excellence of his organization he laid firm foundations for the future Church of England.[12] It is true that circumstances existed which were favourable to his mission. Ethelbert was a great king; he came to the throne in 560, and reigned gloriously, as we are told, for fifty-six years. In spite of early defeat at the hands of the king of Wessex, his strong character raised him in course of time to the proud position of Bretwalda. His *imperium*, which made him leader of the

---

[7] Haddan, *Remains*, 216 et seq., quoted by Collins, *The Beginnings of Engl. Christianity*, 39–43.

[8] Bede, *Eccl. Hist.* i, 26, 33. Perhaps the nave of St. Martin's, Canterbury, is a Roman building. The most recent expert opinion holds that no Roman work now exists *in situ* in any other Kentish church, though Roman materials re-used are found in abundance.   [9] Bede, *Eccl. Hist.* ii, 1.

[10] Goscelin, *Vit. Angl.* 49, quoted in Dudden, *Gregory the Great*, ii, 105.   [11] Bede, *Eccl. Hist.* v, 24.

[12] For an estimate of Augustine's character see Dudden, op. cit. ii, 146, and Collins, *The Beginnings of Engl. Christianity*, 71.

united hosts against a common enemy, reached to the River Humber. Among the East Saxons his influence was increased by his blood relationship to King Sebert, who was his sister's son. About twenty-five years before his conversion he further strengthened his position by his marriage with Bertha, daughter of the saintly Ingoberga, widow of Charibert, king of Paris. This royal house of the Franks had long been Christian, and it was made a condition of the marriage that Bertha and her chaplain, a see-less bishop named Liudhard, should be allowed to exercise their religion without interference.[13] The condition was respected, and it is said that 'by the counsel of the said bishop, Queen Bertha had all her servants and household "chrysten persones" although the land was then heathen.'[14] The church of St. Martin, one of the churches which, according to tradition, had been built while the Romans were in Britain, was assigned for their use. It is not unlikely that before the coming of St. Augustine King Ethelbert's attitude towards his wife's religion was sympathetic, but there were difficulties in the way of his accepting it. Conversion for the king was not merely a personal matter : he could not act alone ; he must carry his wise men and his people with him. His country was surrounded by paganism. He had before him in the neighbouring maritime districts of Gaul examples of the evils of a relapse from Christianity. The task of organizing and establishing the Church in his kingdom was manifestly beyond the power of Liudhard to accomplish single-handed. It is not improbable that the king was privy to, if he did not prompt, an application for help [15] which seems to have been made to the bishops of Gaul, and which met with no response.[16] The coming of the Roman mission removed all difficulties and chased away all scruples. The king immediately made opportunity for his wise men to hear and consider the story of the new religion. Without unwise haste or hesitancy he himself led the way by submitting himself to baptism in St. Martin's church [17] on Whitsun Eve,[18] and the people readily following his example, England was thus launched into that 'stream of civilization' which has made since then the history of the world.

Bede tells the story of the arrival of Augustine in these words :—

> Upon the eastern coast of Kent there is an island called Thanet . . . separated from the mainland by the River Wantsome, which is about three furlongs broad and only to be crossed in two places ; it pushes both its heads into the sea. Upon this island Augustine . . . came ashore with his companions. . . . Ethelbert . . . ordered them to remain in the island . . . and necessaries to be supplied to them until he saw what to do with them. . . . After some days the king came to the island, and taking his seat in the open air he ordered Augustine with his companions to come and confer with him there. . . . At the king's bidding they sat and preached the word of Life to him and to all his courtiers present . . . He gave them a lodging in the city of Canterbury, which was the capital of the whole empire. . . . As they approached the city, according to their custom, with the holy Cross and the picture of the Great King, our Lord Jesus Christ, they intoned in unison this litany : 'We beseech thee, O Lord, in all thy mercy, that thy fury and thine anger may be taken away from this city and from thy holy house ; because we have sinned. Alleluia.'[19]

---

[13] Bede, *Eccl. Hist.* i, 25. [14] The *Martiloge*, May vii, Add., quoted by Collins.
[15] So we interpret Gregory's statement that the English people had desired earnestly to be converted to the Christian faith. *Epistles*, vi, 58, 59.
[16] Ibid. [17] Bede, *Eccl. Hist.* i, 26. [18] Collins, op. cit. 66, note.
[19] *Eccl. Hist.* i, 25. Bede's authority for 'what was done in the church of Canterbury by the disciples of the blessed Pope Gregory' was Albinus, who gathered his materials from written documents and from 'the traditions of older men.' Bede, *Eccl. Hist.* i, Preface. Albinus became abbot of St. Augustine's in 709. Bede's work was finished in 731.

Several questions of considerable interest arise out of this narrative. Perhaps the most interesting is that which relates to the identification of the landing-place.[20]

Ebbsfleet, identified with 'Ypwines or Heopwines fleot,' on the shore of which Hengist and Horsa 'sought Britain' in 449, seems to be out of the question, though advocated by Stanley[21] and many later authorities ; for, though suitable for the beaching of pirate vessels, the fleets or creeks of the Wantsum on the shores of Thanet could not have been navigated by a large trading vessel such as Augustine and his companions might be expected to use, even under the most favourable conditions of tide.

A Canterbury tradition points to Richborough, which in Roman times was called *portus Rutupis* or *Rutubis*.[22] Both the place and the port were then of great importance. Bede, in his opening description of the island of Britain,[23] quoting the accounts of Pliny and Orosius, tells us that to ships making the shortest crossing from the nearest coast of Belgic Gaul, *Gessoriacum* (the port of Boulogne) on that coast 'lay open' to *Portus Rutubis*, a passage of about fifty miles. The *Itinerary* of Antoninus[24] in like manner shows the close relationship of these two harbours, and there can be no doubt that the ports of arrival and departure commonly used by travellers and traders in Roman and early Saxon times were Richborough and Boulogne. The place which gave its name to the port of Richborough was situated on an island crowned with a fortress which guarded the southern entrance to the Wantsum, just as the fortress of *Regulbium* (Reculver) guarded its northern entrance. Though separated from the Isle of Thanet by the main channel of the Wantsum in Roman times, in its earlier history it seems to have been more closely associated with Thanet (called by the Britons *Inis Ruim* or *Ruochim*) than with the mainland of Kent. A tradition of such association probably underlies the unhesitating statement of Thorne, the fourteenth-century chronicler of St. Augustine's Abbey, in which it is said that Augustine and his companions—

> came to land in the island of Taneth at the place called Retesbrough where father Augustine in the act of disembarking happened to slip upon a stone, which took the impress of his foot just as mud and clay would have done. Whereupon the stone was taken and set up with all honour within the chapel of the saint that was built there ; and year by year, on the day of his burial, for the purpose of devotion and of recovering health a crowd of people there assembled, saying 'we will worship in the place where stood his feet.'

So far Thorne ; and Stanley, without realizing the importance of his research, tells us that remains of the chapel existed in comparatively recent times ; they were shown to John Leland, the antiquary, in the bank of the north wall of the fortress by an old hermit who lived there in the time of Henry VIII.[25] Thus the identification of Richborough with the landing-place of the Roman mission seems to be well grounded.

[20] See 'A Dissertation' by Prof. T. McK. Hughes, published in Prof. A. J. Mason, *The Mission of St. Augustine*, with a map showing the features of the Wantsum and the land adjoining as they existed in the sixth century. The highly interesting but less accurate map of the Rutupian ports published in Hasted, *Hist. of Kent*, is reproduced in Prof. Montagu Burrows, *Cinque Ports*.

[21] Stanley, *Mem. of Cant.* 13, 14.

[22] Richborough is connected etymologically with Rutupis ; Bishop Browne suggests that Rutupis was probably pronounced Richubis. *Aug. and his Companions*, 28. In the *Itinerary* of Antoninus it is written Ritupis.

[23] Op. cit. i, 1.   [24] Dated A.D. 300. Pliny wrote in the first, and Orosius in the fifth century.

[25] Stanley, *Mem. of Cant.* 19 n.

The character of the early English Christianity was determined partly by that of the Roman mission and the ideas, the prejudices and prepossessions which its members brought to their task, and partly by the earlier religious beliefs and customs of their converts. We know little of the *personnel* of the mission, but we are on safe ground in saying that, though on setting out from Rome it may have consisted merely of a band of twelve monks under Augustine's leadership,[26] it was certainly reinforced during its passage through Gaul, and on arriving in Kent it comprised Frankish presbyters, deacons, and clerks in minor orders as well as the Roman monks—all the elements, in fact, that were required to reproduce in completeness the organization of the Church according to the custom of the age. It is not an easy task for us to release the mind from its modern environment and to see things as they were many centuries ago. The parochial organization of the Church is so prominent a feature in the present day, especially in our own land, that it is difficult to imagine the conditions of a period when there were no parsons or parishes in the modern sense of those terms, and when the worship, the teaching, the discipline and the administration of the temporalities of the Church were corporate acts of a bishop and his clergy living together in the episcopal city. This was the principal feature of early Church government: its force was not centralized, gathered from scattered points to a centre, but centrifugal, exerted from a centre. Such was the character of the constitution of the Church at Rome, whence came Augustine and his original companions, and where the government was long-established and settled.[27] In Gaul, whence he collected the rest of his band, and where he found Christianity not as yet occupying the whole field and therefore still missionary in character, the system was practically the same. The chief towns were the episcopal sees and missionary centres. There is evidence of the early part of the sixth century that the clergy sent to preach in the country villages did not go far afield : they had to return every Saturday to the city church to take their part in the corporate act of worship on the Sunday. Even as late as the middle of the seventh century the presbyter and deacons who were then detached from the staff of the city church to serve country churches were retained on the roll of the city clergy, receiving their allowances from the common fund, and being liable to recall by the bishop.[28] Such was the organization which Augustine would feel he had to set up in England. There was one other feature of Church organization with which he was familiar, and which he would certainly try to reproduce. He himself was a monk, called to his task from Gregory's monastery of St. Andrew at Rome, of which he had recently been installed prior. Gregory was a lover of monks, and carefully fostered the system which Benedict had inaugurated in his monastery of Monte Cassino some seventy years previously. The rule of the order as revised by Gregory was strict.[29] It concerns us here only in so far as it deals with the interchange of the secular and the regular life. Once a monk always a monk, except in the case of a man who, being found fit, might be ordained, or being already in orders might be released for outside work as a minister of the Gospel. But in such a case he would

[26] Collins, op. cit. App. B.   [27] Eusebius, *Eccl. Hist.* vi, 43 ; Reichel, *Rise of the Parochial System*, 11.
[28] Smith & Cheetham, *Dict. of Christian Antiquities*, ii, 1555.
[29] Dudden, *Gregory the Great*, Bk. ii, chap. ix ('Gregory and Monasticism.')

no longer have any power in the monastery : the two things were kept quite distinct. A man might not be at once a beneficed priest and an abbot ; and again, an abbot who was elected to be a bishop must forthwith cease to be an abbot.[30] This being so, it may seem strange that monks rather than secular priests were selected to go from Rome with Augustine as his companions. Probably Gregory looked upon them as the men best fitted for the task, and doubtless he gave them temporary release from their rule. However that may have been we may be sure that Augustine and his companions, having mastered misgivings which caused temporary delay in Gaul, came to England with ideas and hopes that included the establishment not only of episcopal sees as centres of missionary work in the several capitals of the country, but also of monasteries in which, according to prevailing ideas, the Christian life might find its ideal expression: to them ecclesiastical organization without monastic institutions would be inconceivable.

For a clear understanding of the conversion of Kent it behoves us not only to realize the ideas of Church government which Augustine and his companions brought with them from Rome and Gaul, but also to gauge, if possible, the religious character and habits of the people to whom they came. The religion of the pagan Jutes, judged by the little that is known of the religion of the Teutonic tribes generally, was essentially a nature worship, based on the belief that divinities resided in lake and spring, in mountain and in tree. The *religio loci* lingered in the land long after the acceptance of Christianity, and indeed we may still see traces thereof in the folklore and superstitions that survive in remote corners of the country. It was the most potent and persistent opponent of the new religion, and to this bear witness numerous enactments in Anglo-Saxon canons and laws even up to the time of Cnut, forbidding well worship and tree worship, the sanctification of places, spells, philtres, and witchcraft.[31] Now this worship of nature needed neither temple nor priest.[32] That both temple and priest are mentioned, though rarely, in Bede in reference to Saxon paganism is due to the fact that on this religion of nature was superimposed another form of religion : to the local and family form of worship was added one of a national character. The two forms may have become mingled in idea, but remained in some degree distinct in practice. With the worship of Thor and Frea, the gods of storm and produce, of destruction and fruitfulness, was associated the worship of Woden, the All-father, the god of war and victory, and the divine ancestor of the Saxon kings. The national religion thus became heroic as well as natural in character, central as well as local in organization. At the great festivals of winter, spring and harvest-time, the people would flock to the district temples of the hero-gods, to make their offerings, to witness the sacrificial rites performed by the national priests, and to share in the sacrificial feasts ; while the ancient rites and sacred places of the older paganism, meeting daily needs, would lose nothing of their influence. As in Norway, so in England, those temples, comparatively few in number and erected at convenient centres, were structures of wood, not of stone ; they contained altars

[30] Gregory's Epistles, quoted by Collins, op. cit. App. F.
[31] Kemble, *Saxons in Engl.* i, 334, App. F.
[32] Tacitus ('Germ.' ix, quoted by Kemble, op. cit. i, 332) says the Germans had neither temple nor image. This however, as will be noted in the text, must be received with caution.

and idols ; and were surrounded by a grove of trees within an inclosure which was probably stockaded.[33]

In this picture there is much that is suggestive of the organization and worship of the Church in the early days of English Christianity. It had more a national than a personal character. The adoption of the new religion must have been formally considered and decided upon by the king and his thegns in council assembled. The change was readily accepted by the people, who offered themselves in thousands for baptism. As the centre of national worship the cathedral church (Christchurch), established according to custom in the king's capital, took the place of the heathen temple, that usually stood beyond the walls of the city. There would the people assemble at the great festivals to witness the sacrifice of the mass instead of the abandoned pagan rites. Thus Yuletide became Christmas, and Easter took its name from the goddess of springtide. These, with Whitsuntide, became the great baptismal festivals of the Church. It is true that there was nothing in the old religion to prepare the way for the monastic institutions of the new, but the life and prepossessions of the members of the mission made such institutions essential to its needs, and the establishment of a monastic church and conventual buildings (the church of St. Peter and St. Paul— St. Augustine's Abbey) on the *fundus* or glebe of the old national temple beyond the walls of the king's city doubtless appealed to the sentiment of the people and inspired respect for a religious organization that was not quite strange. The missionary activity of the body of clergy which formed the staff of the cathedral church, acting under the bishop, afforded the people opportunities of receiving instruction in the new faith ; and gradually the need of a settled local ministry was realized. Going from settlement to settlement to teach and to baptize, the missionaries took up their preaching-stations perhaps on the spots that aforetime had been held sacred to the heathen divinities. This would be in accordance with the spirit of Gregory's instructions : superstitious rites were to be abolished, but the associations of faith were to be preserved. Such associations English paganism in both its aspects presented to Christianity.

But the parallelism that existed between the customs and organization of paganism and early Christianity, and facilitated the transition from the one to the other, does not account for the suddenness with which the people of Kent were apparently weaned from the old and won to the new religion. There was something in the new faith that corresponded to what must have been a need deep-seated in their consciousness. Was it not the hope of a future life, of which paganism offered no promise or prospect ? A glance through the pages of Bede proves that the refrain of the teaching of the Augustinians was like that of the Apostles of old—'Jesus and the Resurrection.' The old faith suggested to them no hope of a hereafter. It was imbued with fatalism, though it were a manly fatalism. The doom of death, 'that Weird that is every man's lord,' must be faced when it comes ; meanwhile, let every man work high deeds, avenge his friend, and win good fame : so, when he lies helpless, will it be best for the warrior. To this spirit of manly struggle in life, henceforth inspired by higher motives, Christianity added the hope of eternal reward after death. Thus

[33] Cutts, *Parish Priests and their People*, chap. i, ii.

the scale was turned in favour of the new faith. In the council meeting that debated at Godmundingham [34] the preaching of Paulinus, one of Edwin's thegns—comparing human life on earth to the transient flight of a sparrow through the supper-hall and confessing himself ignorant of all that went before and followed after—declared that if the new teaching brought them anything more sure it would justly deserve to be followed. And the high priest Coifi, proclaiming the impotence of the gods whom he had long and faithfully served and dwelling on the new prospect of gifts of life and health and eternal happiness, clinched the debate by desecrating the national temple, hurling the king's spear thereat and calling upon his companions to destroy it and all its inclosures by fire.[35] It is clear that the sentiment of the English peoples was now ripe for the acceptance of the religion which had already been embraced by the majority of the kindred peoples of Gaul, and which offered them an eternal hope such as found no place in their worship either of Woden or of nature.

Bede's story of the conversion of Northumbria, with the details of which he was well acquainted, illustrates the sentiments and circumstances connected with the conversion of Kent and other English kingdoms. The movement was a national one, led by the well-considered policy of Ethelbert and his thegns. After the king's baptism great multitudes of his subjects assembled to hear the word, and forsaking their heathen rites attached themselves to the unity of the Church.[36] After Augustine's consecration at Arles he baptized, it is said, 10,000 people at Christmas.[37] Bede makes no mention of the public desecration of a national temple. He is content to quote Gregory's general instructions to Augustine. The heathen temples, if they were well built, were not to be destroyed; the idols were to be demolished and the temples cleansed by the sprinkling of holy water therein; altars were to be built and relics placed there. Thus the temples would be converted from the worship of demons to the service of the true God, and the people would assemble together at the familiar places with a feeling of being at home in them.[38] Gregory, who was not altogether well informed upon such points, probably did not know that the idol temples were usually, if not always, structures of wood. Such buildings would certainly not seem to Augustine to be worth preserving for Christian worship. He was accustomed to worship in churches of stone, and we have evidence that the churches which he and his successors built were erected in stone on a plan which he introduced, and which in some respects is peculiar to the early Saxon period. In spite of Bede's silence on the point all the evidence we have points to there having been at Canterbury an idol temple of a national character which Ethelbert, at Augustine's instigation, replaced by a Christian church. The well-known ruins of the church of St. Pancras in the grounds of St. Augustine's Abbey may confidently be regarded as the remains of the church which was built on the site of an ancient wooden temple. It is undoubtedly a church of 'Augustinian' type and date, and there is no other satisfactory way of accounting for its existence: apart from its erection as the visible sign of the abandonment of the old religion and the reconsecration of its site and surroundings to the use of the new religion it

---

[34] Near York, the capital of the kingdom of Northumbria.
[36] Ibid. i, 26.   [37] Gregory's *Epistles*, viii, 30.
[35] Bede, *Eccl. Hist.* ii, 13.
[38] Bede, *Eccl. Hist.* i, 30.

would seem to have had no *raison d'être*, to have been superfluous to the needs of the establishment of the new faith. Having been built for the reason suggested, we may possibly be not far from the mark in suggesting further that it served the purpose of the king's private chapel, his chapel royal so to speak, just as St. Martin's was reserved for the private use of the queen and her retinue. Bede's unaccountable omission to mention the church of St. Pancras, to which a unique interest seems to be attached, is supplied in the chronicle of Thorne.

Writing under the year 598, after giving an account of the foundation of Christchurch and before mentioning that of the monastery of St. Peter and St. Paul, Thorne tells us that

> there was not far from the city towards the east about midway between the church of St. Martin and the city walls a temple or idol place where King Æthelbert, according to the custom of his people, was wont to pray and with his nobles to sacrifice to demons and not to God; which temple Austin purged from the defilements and impurities of the heathen, and having broken in pieces the idol that was in it he changed it into a church and dedicated it in the name of St. Pancras the martyr; and this was the first church hallowed by Austin. There is still [39] an altar in the south porch of the same church at which the same Austin was wont to celebrate, where the image of the king formerly stood.[40]

It is important to note the fact that St. Pancras is herein mentioned as being the first church which Augustine dedicated, and that Thorne immediately proceeds to tells us that it was in the *fundus* or glebe of this church that Ethelbert, at Augustine's suggestion, built the church of St. Peter and St. Paul, which we now commonly call St. Augustine's.

In later history the church usually described as the chapel of St. Pancras within the cemetery of the monastery of St. Augustine played an insignificant part.[41] Not so the two important foundations of Christchurch Cathedral and St. Augustine's Abbey. To these we turn.

Bede [42] tells us that the king gave the mission a settlement in his capital, and Thorne [43] locates it at 'a place called Stablegate in the parish of St. Alphege, on the opposite side of *regia strata* towards the north, along which runs the wall of the archiepiscopal palace,' adding that it had formerly been a place of pagan worship for the king's household.[44] After his conversion the king, according to the same writer, gave up his royal palace to Augustine and his successors, who there established their metropolitical seat in perpetuity. Hard by, perhaps on the site of the present cathedral, there was an old Romano-British church, disused or desecrated, which Augustine with the king's help restored for use as his cathedral church, appropriately dedicating it in the name of the Saviour Christ. It lay, not in the heart of the city, but in the northern part of it, probably outside the original north wall of the Roman *castrum* and within an extension of the city made in Roman times. Here the mission established itself with plenty of space to the north of the church for their domestic buildings, where Augustine could live, so far as was compatible with the nature of their work, with his presbyters, deacons and clerks in common,[45] anticipating in some measure the life according to

---

[39] The remains of the altar still exist.

[40] Thorne, *Chron.* (Twysden), 1760.

[41] See a paper by Mr. St. John Hope in *Arch. Cant.* xxv.

[42] Op. cit. i, 26.

[43] Op. cit. 1759.

[44] The borough of Staplegate has always been accounted as lying in the liberty of the archbishops; Hasted, *Hist. of Kent*, xi, 291.

[45] Thorne, op. cit. 1760.

rule which Chrodegang, archbishop of Metz in the middle of the eighth century, framed for his secular canons.

Bede, after telling the story of the foundation of Christchurch, records that of St. Augustine's Abbey in the following words :—

> Moreover he made also not far from the city towards the east a monastery, in which at his instigation Ethelbert built from the foundations and enriched with divers gifts the church of the blessed apostles Peter and Paul, in which the bodies of Augustine himself and of all the bishops of Canterbury (*Durovernum*), as well as of the kings of Kent, could be placed.[46]

As we have already seen, the necessity of making provision for the regular life of monks of the mission must have been in the mind of Augustine from the first and must have supplied the most important reason for the foundation of the monastery. The active life of the church, its ministrations and its administration, radiated from the cathedral, served by the staff of secular clergy, working under the archbishop ; its contemplative and devotional life centred in the monastery, the retreat of the monks. But the use of the monastic church as the resting-place of the bodies of a succession of kings and archbishops was doubtless a subsidiary reason for its erection, and it might well appear to Bede and his authorities to have been the most important reason, considering the fame and the riches which on that account attached to it in course of time.

It also has a special interest for the modern student, inasmuch as the custom of burying in churches which became common at a later date, though not unknown at this time, was not usually viewed with favour by ecclesiastical authorities. The practice of burial in the *exedrae* or out-buildings of a church was then creeping in, but it was still the more usual custom to bury the dead in consecrated *areae* situate beyond the walls of a city or monastery.[47] It is therefore interesting to realize that the infant Church of England was able to break through the traditional prohibition of intra-mural burials which the church catholic inherited from Jewish custom and Roman law alike,[48] and to initiate a custom which in course of time became associated with those doctrines concerning the repose of the departed which in the Middle Ages brought immense accretions of wealth to the church.

We have spoken of Christchurch as an establishment of secular clergy and the centre of diocesan organization. After Dunstan's revival of mon-asticism Archbishop Elfric, in the troubled time at the end of the tenth century, replaced the seculars by monks, but the seculars were again in possession before the Norman Conquest. Monkish chroniclers of later times glozed the early history and represented the church as having been monastic from the first, but it is now clear[49] that in the early period the church was presided over by a dean and not by a prior, and that undoubtedly there were secular clergy there. A cathedral church served

---

[46] Bede, *Eccl. Hist.* i, 33.

[47] The Council of Nantes, held probably towards the end of the seventh century, in the sixth canon permits burials in the atrium or forecourt, in the cloister, and in the exedra of a church, but utterly forbids them in the church itself. The same precept is repeated in the canons of later councils, as in the fifty-second of that at Mentz in 813, which, however, expressly excepts bishops, abbots, worthy presbyters and faithful laymen. Smith and Cheetham, *Dict. of Chr. Antiq.* i, 392.

[48] Cicero, *De Legibus*, ii, 58 ; Somner, *Antiq. of Cant.* vi, 1.

[49] See A. F. Leach, in *Guardian* of 12 Jan. 1898, quoted by Boggis, *A Hist. of St. Augustine's*, 5.

by monks would have been entirely at variance with the usages of the Roman Church in all lands, in which ancient cathedrals are, and always have been, served by the secular clergy only.[50]   Thus, like London with its secular clergy at St. Paul's and its monks at Westminster Abbey, or like Dublin with its seculars at St. Patrick's and its regular canons at Christchurch, or like Rouen with its cathedral almost rivalled by the conventual St. Ouen, Canterbury had its secular clergy at the cathedral and its regulars at St. Augustine's.[51]

The next step in the progress of English Christianity carries us along the Roman highway of Watling Street, from Canterbury to Rochester and London, where Augustine, shortly before his death, in 604, the year also of Gregory's death, with the help of Ethelbert established two outposts of the Church by the creation of two new sees and the erection of two new cathedral churches, Justus being made bishop of Rochester and Mellitus of London. Gregory's great scheme of dividing England into two provinces, each to contain twelve sees with archbishops at London and York,[52] conceived in ignorance of the conditions that prevailed in Britain, was never realized. Paulinus,[53] indeed, effected the temporary adhesion of Northumbria, but the success of the Roman mission was in the end limited to the kingdoms of Kent and of the East Saxons, where Ethelbert's influence remained dominant. London was then the capital of the East Saxons, over which Ethelbert's nephew, Sebert, reigned.   The arrangement by which a second Kentish see was established at Rochester suggests that West Kent was then regarded as a sub-kingdom of Kent, and that the later division of the county into ' East Kentings and West Kentings,'[54] with distinct jurisdictions in ecclesiastical and judicial affairs, which has prevailed to the present day, is reminiscent of very early times when Jutish Kent was split up into two, or perhaps into several, petty kingdoms.[55]   A feature of Church organization that stands out prominently in the history of the seventh century is that each several kingdom on conversion to the faith became the ' parish ' or diocese of a bishop whose see was placed in the king's capital.   Thus Rochester, as the capital of West Kent, a sub-kingdom of Ethelbert's realm, became a bishop's see and a fresh centre of missionary effort, with a cathedral served, like Christchurch at Canterbury, by a staff of secular clergy.   The propagation of Christianity among the English peoples depended as much upon the goodwill and decision of kings and their witan as upon the zeal of the missionaries.   Kings and thegns adopted the new faith, and the people followed suit.   Leaders relapsed into heathenism, and the old superstitious beliefs and customs quickly revived. The spiritual level of Christianity in Saxon England remained a low one.   The strength of its organization in Kent lay in the two capital cities and in the monasteries and nunneries established by royal munificence in various districts, chiefly in the eastern and southern parts of the county ; but it is doubtful how far they escaped the general secularization and demoralization of monastic life in the eighth century.   In addition to the abbey of

---

[50] Boggis, *A Hist. of St. Augustine's*, 5.   [51] Walcott, quoted by Boggis (ut sup.).   [52] Bede, op. cit. i, 29.
[53] Paulinus, with Mellitus, Justus, and Rufianus, joined the mission in 601.   Bede, op. cit. i, 29.
[54] Kemble, *Saxons in Engl.* i, 78.   Cf. Larkin, *Domesday Bk. of Kent*, 157, where the mention of ' the four lathes ' of East Kent, as distinct from the men of the two lathes of West Kent, is discussed.
[55] Ibid. i, 148 note.

St. Peter and St. Paul, the *mater primaria* of English monasteries, a list of seven establishments is given in the 'Privilege granted to Churches and Monasteries of Kent by King Wihtred at a Kentish Witenagemot at Baccanceld,' or Bapchild, near Sittingbourne, and confirmed in 716 at Clovesho : namely, 'Upmynster, Raculf, Suthmynster, Dofras, Folcanstan, Limming, Scepeis et Hoe.'[56] Of these monasteries, Sheppey, Lyminge, Folkestone, and Suthmynster (Minster in Thanet) were under abbesses ; Hoe or Hoo was under an abbot. Upmynster is perhaps St. Peter's in Thanet.[57] The foundation of Dover appears to have been the result of the conversion of Eadbald by Archbishop Lawrence after a brief relapse into heathenism on the death of his father Ethelbert (616). The nunnery of Folkestone also owed its foundation, *circa* 630, to Eadbald, whose daughter Eanswitha became its first abbess. It was destroyed, and its site covered by the sea, in Saxon times. Lyminge, said to have been formerly a royal residence, was granted by Eadbald to his sister Ethelburga, who had become the wife of Edwin of Northumbria, and who on Edwin's defeat and death returned to Kent with her chaplain Paulinus, first bishop of York, and founded the nunnery at Lyminge in 633.[58] The Saxon charters bear witness to the ample endowment of the monastery with lands in southern and south-western Kent, including a large tract of land in Romney Marsh,[59] described in the charter of Wihtred (700) as *Rumening-seta*. The origin of the name possibly lies in the original grant of the land in the middle of the seventh century to one Romanus, by whom it was given to Lyminge. Romanus was a Kentish priest who at one time was chaplain to Eanfled, daughter of Ethelburga and wife of Oswy of Northumbria, the foundress of a nunnery at Gilling in Yorkshire.[60] In the nunnery of Lyminge Ethelburga's niece, Mildred, found a home. This Mildred was probably the daughter of Eadbald by his incestuous marriage with his father's widow, the second wife of Ethelbert, and is not to be confused with the Mildred of Minster in Thanet (Suthmynster), who was the great-granddaughter of Eadbald in the line of his second wife Emma, and the daughter of Eormenburga (Domneva), the foundress of Suthmynster and wife of Merewald of Mercia. Minster in Sheppey was founded by Sexburga, the wife of Earconbert,[61] son of Eadbald by his second wife Emma. Lastly, Reculver, formerly a Roman station, the walls of which in part remain, and said to be a royal residence of the early Kentish kings, was given by King Egbert in 669 to Bass, the mass-priest, that he might build a minster thereon.[62]

All these monasteries, with the possible exception of Hoo, were founded in the seventh century, and nearly all of them by members of the family of King Ethelbert. They formed natural centres of missionary work and spiritual ministrations, which extended over the lands far and near with

[56] Haddan and Stubbs, *Eccl. Councils*, iii, 238, 239.

[57] Ibid. 242. For details of the foundation of these monasteries and references to Saxon charters see Jenkins, *Dioc. Hist. of Canterbury* (S.P.C.K.).

[58] Paulinus became bishop of Rochester in the same year ; Bede, *Eccl. Hist.* ii, 20.

[59] Probably 'Romney Marsh' proper, which had been inclosed possibly by the Romans by the building of the Rhee wall, which ran south-west from near Appledore to Romney, cutting off the waters of the estuary of the Rother, from thence gradually turning east and north as a sea wall. The estuary entered the sea by a narrow mouth, and was bounded on the south by shingle-banks and marshes, which (according to Furley) were 'inned about 774,' the date of a grant of land at Old Langport in Lydd from King Offa to Archbishop Jaenberht ; Furley, *Hist. of the Weald*, ii, 763. [60] Bede, op. cit. iii, 25.

[61] The first English king who ordered the destruction of heathen idols throughout his kingdom ; Bede, op. cit. iii, 8. [62] *Angl.-Sax. Chron.*

which they were more or less richly endowed. Later on, when their evangelistic work was done and their moral tone, like that of the numerous later establishments of a more or less private character, had become somewhat corrupt, they encountered the special hostility of the Danes, with the ultimate result that their lands in the case of Lyminge (965), Folkestone (927), Reculver (949), and Dover, were granted to Christchurch, Canterbury, and in the case of Minster in Thanet, to St. Augustine's Abbey (1025).[63]

In passing from the early place-associations, the possible identification of Clovesho or Clofesho with Cliffe at Hoo ('Clive' in Domesday Book) demands a brief reference. It is significant that the origin of the only manuscript of the Anglo-Saxon Chronicle which contains an entry concerning the great council of 742 is assigned from internal evidence to Canterbury, as containing many details of special Kentish interest. In early times Cliffe was not so much an out-of-the-way place as it now seems to be. It lies not far from Hoo St. Werburgh, and near a route that was much used in early times. The road ran from Rochester, past Higham, to the Thames at Tilbury, and so into Essex and East Anglia. Ethelbald of Mercia is supposed to have marked his conquests by dedications in honour of St. Werburgh; and Hoo St. Werburgh is the only dedication of that name in Kent. There is mention in 823 and 824 of a royal vill called Werburghwic. A council would be convened at any suitable place where the king might for a time be resting on his line of route; such a spot was Cliffe. Nor is it impossible that the Council of Cealchythe (787) may have been held at Chalkhythe, near by, and not as usually assumed at Chelsea; and that the Council of Aclea (789) may have been held at Oakley, a farmstead at Higham, and not at Ockley in Surrey. The church of Higham belonged to the convent of St. John at Colchester till Stephen's reign, and the prioress of Higham, in 21 Edward I, was found liable to maintain a causeway running to the Thames and a bridge over the river. These facts and assumptions have a combined force which gives to Cliffe at Hoo a claim of identification with the famous Clovesho which no other place has.[64] Its councils coincide with the overlordship of Mercia.

The county of Kent is peculiarly rich, not only in place-associations, but also in architectural remains illustrative of its ecclesiastical history during the seventh century. To that date may be confidently assigned the foundations recently discovered of churches at Rochester and Lyminge, the ruins of St. Pancras at Canterbury and of Reculver church, and the western part of the chancel of St. Martin's, Canterbury. Other churches of the same period have been destroyed or replaced by structures of later date. The early church of Folkestone has been swallowed up by the sea. Minster in Sheppey and Minster in Thanet both contain early masonry, but nothing so early as the seventh century. The existing church of St. Mary in the castle at Dover, which may have been a Roman foundation, was until recently regarded as the original structure, but it is now thought to have been erected at a late date in the Saxon period. It is possible that the foundations of the original church of the monastery of St. Peter and St. Paul at Canterbury may be discovered as the work of excavation proceeds, but it is hopeless to expect the discovery of

---

[63] Jenkins, *Dioc. Hist. of Canterbury*, 48, 49.

[64] Kerslake, *Vestiges of the Supremacy of Mercia in the South of Engl. during the 8th Century*. The writer is indebted to the Rev. E. J. Nash for this reference and for notes from which the text has been compiled.

any remains of the original building of Christchurch Cathedral. The remains of another early example, of which there is no documentary record, apparently exist in the north aisle of the nave of Lydd church, in Romney Marsh.[65] Possibly the church of Eynsford in West Kent may be yet another example ; it has no stones that can be assigned to an earlier than Norman date, but its plan is suggestive of growth round a church of the early Saxon type. This completes the list of early Saxon churches in Kent, though there may be others awaiting recognition.[66]

The Augustinian influence in the matter of church building seems to have exhausted itself early in the eighth century, the Saxons probably reverting to the use of wood, and when, two or three centuries later, they resumed the use of stone, a native plan, with square-ended chancel, had supervened. But the use of stone did not become general before the second half of the eleventh century. Comparatively few existing churches contain structural evidence of later Saxon work. It may be seen here and there, as at St. Mildred's and also at St. Dunstan's, Canterbury;[67] at East Farleigh, which has long-and-short work in the north-west quoin of the nave ; at Darenth, which has a double-splayed window in the nave ; at Whitfield near Dover, which has a similar feature ; and at St. Mary's in Dover Castle. The inference is that a great majority of the numerous churches of the late Saxon period were wooden buildings, like the church of Greensted in Essex.

A great wave of church building in stone passed over the land after the Conquest. In planning their cathedrals and conventual churches, great and small, the Norman builders re-introduced the apsidal termination with which they had been familiar in Normandy ; but in their parish churches they adopted the native Saxon plan, giving them a square east end. The only instance in Kent of a Norman parish church with an apsidal ending seems to have been that of Sutton, near Ripple, rebuilt on the original lines (it is said) about fifty years ago. Gundulf's cathedral church at Rochester, with its square east end, was a remarkable exception to the rule, which, however, was observed in the chapel attached to Lanfranc's lazar hospital at Harbledown, and in the chapel[68] of St. Bartholomew's Hospital at Rochester.

The Danish invasions, the destruction of churches, which the lesser monasteries failed to survive, the decay of learning, and the general sense of insecurity brought the Church into a parlous condition in the ninth century. We may notice a double result. The destruction of the monasteries robbed the people of their baptismal churches, and so promoted the transition from the older order to a parochial system : this will be touched upon again later. And, ultimately, the lands of the lesser monasteries, as we have previously observed, were absorbed by the great churches. The cathedral churches and St. Augustine's Abbey had from the first been richly endowed with lands by

---

[65] Its early character was first recognized by Mr. J. T. Micklethwaite. See *Arch. Journ.*

[66] St. Peter's, Ythanchester, in the parish of Bradwell in Essex, now in ruins, has a plan which shows affinities to the Augustinian type. It is claimed as the church said by Bede to have been built by Cead *c.* 653. Peers, ' Saxon Churches of the St. Pancras Type,' in *Arch. Journ.* Dec. 1901.

[67] Saxon quoins of long-and-short work in these churches are figured in Cox, *Cant.* (Methuen, ' Ancient Cities ').

[68] Traditionally ascribed to Gundulf, but really built by Hugh of Trottescliffe, monk of Rochester, temp. Bishop Ernulf, and afterwards abbot of St. Augustine's ; *Reg. Roff.* 119.

royal charters.[69] Successive kings confirmed and increased their endowment.[70] The Privilege of Wihtred exempted the lands of the cathedral churches from tribute of secular burdens. This relief, already secured in the case of bocland, gradually became customary in the tenure of all church lands— excepting only the *trinoda necessitas*, 'fastness and bridge and the common host '—'in order that service might be rendered to God.' The famous grant of Ethelwulf was of this character: it had nothing to do with tithe; it simply relieved the tenth part of all the unenfranchised folcland in the hands of ecclesiastics and laymen of all public burdens.[71] Domesday Book shows that while Bishop Odo, earl of Kent, held one-half of the county outside the Weald, of the remaining half fully three-fifths was held by ecclesiastics: the archbishop and his monks and his men, the bishop of Rochester, the abbot of St. Augustine's, the canons of St. Martin's Dover, the abbeys of Battle and Ghent, and Albert the king's chaplain. The abbot of Battle held the manor of Wye. The manor of Lewisham had been granted in 1044 by King Edward to the church of St. Peter of Ghent, together with the manors of Greenwich, Woolwich, Mottingham and Coombe, and five denns in Andreda, appertaining to the said manor, to wit, Æschore, Æffehaga, Wing-indene, Scarendene, Sandherste.[72]

The parochial system in its beginnings was independent of the early central organization of the Church. In the eighth century 'there were two sorts of clerks, one of ecclesiastics under the government of the bishop, the other headless—married and receiving their stipends apart.'[73] These headless, unattached or local priests, were appointed and maintained by thegns, to serve the churches or oratories which they built on their own estates. Herein lay the germ of the parochial system. In course of time laws were passed by which private patrons were allowed to divert towards the maintenance of their churches a certain proportion of the tithe which had previously been paid in its entirety to the cathedral or baptismal church of the district.[74] We may imagine cases in which not only the lord's men but also the freemen of the township were allowed to worship in his church, and by adding to the endowment to obtain prescriptive rights therein. In some cases in Domesday Book churches seem to have been treated as belonging to the men of the vill who subscribed to erect and endow them.[75] Gradually and by varying means a parochial system with a settled local ministry was established, and gradually the bishop established a right to license an appointment and to institute to the cure of souls. This position, however was not reached in this country before the twelfth century. In tracing the growth of the system we have in Domesday

[69] See the charter of Ethelbert to Rochester Cathedral, dated 28 April, 604, one of the few undoubtedly genuine early charters, quoted by Haddan & Stubbs, *Councils*, iii, 52, from Textus Roffensis, a twelfth-century MS. in the possession of the D. and C. of Rochester.

[70] Private persons also left lands to these churches, for the repose of their souls. See the tenth-century will quoted from Reg. Roff. in the *Roch. Dioc. Hist.* (S.P.C.K.), 29, by Canon Pearman.

[71] For the nature of these burdens see Allen, *Inquiry into the Rise and Growth of the Royal Prerogative in Engl.* 143–9, quoted in Selborne, *Anct. Facts and Fictions Concerning Tithes*, 197.

[72] Kemble, *Cod. Dipl.* 771. But the charter speaks of 'manors,' and is therefore adjudged spurious.

[73] Egbert's *Excerptions*, 159, quoted in Reichel, *Rise of the Parochial System in Engl.* 2.

[74] Edgar's Ordinances (A.D. 970). Thorpe, *Ancient Laws* (fol. ed. 1840), 111.

[75] Maitland, *Domesday and Beyond*, 144. This may help us to understand such an expression in Dom. Bk. as 'half a church.'

Book an uncertain guide. For some unexplained reason, the commissioners appointed to carry out the survey in Kent were more careful than those of many other counties to note the existence of churches. 'There is a church here' is a common formula. There are about 360 places named, and about half as many churches. But this must be far below the number of churches then existing, for there must have been churches in many places under which none is mentioned. Lydd and Darenth, both having in their present structures evidence of Saxon work, are cases in point. In the eleventh and twelfth centuries, before and after the date of the Survey, church building was being carried on to such an extent as to be subversive of Church government. In 1064 a law of Edward the Confessor protested that in many places where there had been only one church there were then three or four, and that in order to maintain them tithes were being wrongfully detained from the baptismal churches.[76] After the Conquest the same thing went on, until in 1138 the Council of Westminster ordered that no man should build a church on his own estate without his bishop's licence.[77] In the *Taxatio* of Pope Nicholas, 1291, by which date the parochial system had probably become fairly well settled except in the more densely wooded parts, many places which in Domesday are noted as having several churches are returned as having only one. Hence it is quite clear that the ultimate organization of parishes was evolved by a reduction where necessary in the number of churches, and that this was brought about in the general interest of the community by the pressure of ecclesiastical influence.[78] The people of a group of vills or of small manors would be called upon to support and to resort to a selected church, and other churches in the same area would fall into disuse.

The following notes will sufficiently illustrate these remarks. Elnothington, now partly in Hollingbourne and partly in Bearsted parish, had a church in 1086 (Domesday Book) but none in 1291 (*Tax. Eccl.*). The same note holds good of Bewley in the parishes of Boughton Malherbe and Harrietsham. In Domesday Book, Dartford had a church and three chapels, of which the latter cannot be identified in the *Taxatio*. Norton in Faversham Hundred had three churches, and only one in 1291. In Domesday Book, Lyminge had a church and two chapels, in the *Taxatio* a church and one chapel. Postling had two 'ecclesiolae' in 1086, one of which had disappeared in 1291, the other surviving as a parish church. Similarly Eastling had two manors and a church in each, one of them eventually surviving as the parish church. Of two churches in Eastbridge in Dymchurch, only one (now a ruin) remained in 1291. In 1086 there were two churches at Eynsford, Orlestone, Orpington, Petham, and Yalding, and in each case only one remained in 1291. Marley in Harrietsham had a separate church in 1086, and none in 1291. Palstre in Wittersham had a church in 1086, none in 1291. Tinton in Warehorne had a church in 1086, but possibly Warehorne church now stands on the same site. Goldwell on the Quarry Hills in Great Chart parish had a church in 1086; by 1291 it had disappeared and the existing church at Great Chart had been built. Lastly, Folkestone had eight churches in 1086 and only one in 1291. These reductions show that in the interval the parochial organization of the Church received careful attention and any undue increase in the number of licensed

[76] Thorpe, *Ancient Laws*, 191 (8).   [77] Reichel, op. cit. 17.   [78] Capes, *Rural Life in Hants*, 21.

priests, or in other words of churches with burial grounds, was jealously guarded against.

A study of the map of the county is instructive, in showing how profoundly physical features influenced ecclesiastical development. Throughout the Saxon period the royal forest of Andredsweald, the almost impenetrable borderland of Kent and Sussex, bounded on the north by the Ragstone or Quarry Hills and on the east by Romney and Guldeford Marshes and the estuary of the Rother, was very sparsely inhabited. The place-names indicate its early character, the -leys and -fields showing its glades and clearances, and the -charts and -hursts and more numerous -dens its more densely wooded parts. The Saxon charters granting estates in other parts of the county almost invariably included a right to pasture hogs in denns or denes (i.e. swine pastures) in the Weald, the denes being in some cases specified by name. These charters were drawn for the most part in favour of ecclesiastics, who do not seem however to have paid much attention to the spiritual needs of their swineherds. After the Conquest the opening up of the forest seems to have gone on apace, the denns being converted into manors. But in Domesday Book only eight manors wholly within the Weald are mentioned by name, four of which (namely Benenden, Hadlow, Tudeley and Palstre) had churches.[79] In the *Taxatio* thirty-three places in this district are returned as having churches, and all may be identified with parishes still existing.[80] These Wealden parishes are comparatively large in area.

The boundary of the forest is well defined by the line of villages situate on or outside it, most of them credited with churches in Domesday Book.[81] Eastwards of the Plaxtol valley these villages lie on the slope of the Ragstone Hills and to the north of the escarpment. Westwards they rest on the escarpment, commanding fine views of the central hills across the Weald clay. In their shape and 'lie' these parishes present a remarkable uniformity. They form long strips running north over the top of the escarpment and extending south into the forest area. They have the advantages not only of a rich and varied soil, but also of accessible swine pasture on their border. An east and west road runs along the top of the hills to the north, but all other roads run south to cross the Weald clay, which has no main east and west roads other than the iron road of the South Eastern Railway. The fact that almost within living memory these roads were often impassable in winter shows that the Weald must have been cut off from civilization in early times.

Another line of early settlements ran along the outcrop of the springs from above the clay at the foot of the escarpment of the Chalk Hills. The parishes to which they gave their names generally run over the top of the escarpment and embrace a small portion of the high land. The churches,

[79] Leeds Priory was endowed by its founder in 1119 with the advowson of Goudhurst. The church of Marden was granted to the Black Canons of Lesnes, temp. Ric. I. Smarden church was in existence before 1205, and Westerham with its appendant chapel of Edenbridge before 1213. Furley, op. cit, i, 399, 400. The student may profitably study Furley's Domesday Tables (i) and his excellent series of maps.

[80] There are now thirty-nine ancient parishes (counting Tonbridge with Tunbridge Wells as one) wholly situate in the Weald. Of the six extra parishes Capel was a chapel appendant to Tudeley, Ebony to Appledore, Edenbridge to Westerham, and Shipborne to Tonbridge. The two unaccounted for are Ashurst and Bidborough. Furley, ii, 22. Capel, returned as a rectory in the *Valor Eccl.* (temp. Hen. VIII), is now held with Tudeley.

[81] Of nearly forty ancient parishes (counting Sevenoaks as one parish) which cross the old boundary of the Weald, twenty-eight take their names from places mentioned in Domesday Book, and of these as many as twenty are credited with churches.

many of them mentioned in Domesday Book, are situate about half a mile below the line of the old British track called the Pilgrims' Way.

Bound up with the origin and growth of the parochial system in the rural districts is the question, suggested by the foregoing remarks, of the delimitation of parish boundaries. The final settlement lies far beyond the limits of our period. Kemble says that the boundaries of modern parishes may often be found to be coincident with those of estates given in early charters. In some counties the manor of Domesday seems to have become the parish.[82] In some cases several small manors may have been grouped to form the parish.[83] Furley cites cases to show that in Kent the parishes are often co-extensive with a group of boroughs, or (as they are called in other counties) tithings.[84] Materials for a satisfactory solution are still a desideratum. We may notice that in this county, while the Pilgrims' Way played no part in the formation of such boundaries, they are in several cases continuously coincident with the main Roman roads, particularly in the south-eastern part of the county, the part first settled. Detached portions of parishes, and the eccentric position of churches, are important factors in the consideration. A survey of the structures of existing buildings proves that the great majority of the parish churches outside the Wealden area grew up round a Norman nucleus;[85] but the great impetus given to church building by the example of Lanfranc and Gundulf only serves to complicate the problem which the modern historian has to solve; for the same indications of Norman date are observed in a majority of the disused chapels, which in some cases (e.g. Dowde and Paddlesworth, both now in Snodland) were, and in other cases (e.g. Newlands in Charing) were not, the churches of separate parishes.

Of the thirty-two successors of St. Augustine in the archiepiscopal see very few stand out in the history of the Church as men of commanding character or great achievements. Even less can be said of the twenty-seven occupants of the suffragan see of Rochester during the pre-Conquest period. The memory of St. Paulinus is preserved in the dedication of the parish churches of Crayford and St. Paul's Cray.[86] He was canonized in 1087. His successor, Ithamar, described as equalling his predecessors in piety and learning, was the first Englishman to be raised to the episcopate, and consecrated the first native archbishop, Fritonas or Deusdedit, in 655. Both were buried in the cathedral church. Putta, skilled in music after the Roman style, could not face the Mercian invasion which desolated his see in 676, and he retired to Hereford. The learned Tobias grappled with poverty and occupied the see for thirty years; he was buried in his church, in the *porticus* of St. Paul which he had erected therein to receive his remains.[87] The later history is merely a record of names and of alternating endowment and spoliation, closing with a story of miserable impoverishment. At the Conquest there were only five canons, who lived on what they could beg from the faithful.[88]

[82] Jones, *Wilts. Dom.* Introd. 27.   [83] Capes, op. cit. 21.   [84] Furley, op. cit. 806.

[85] This fact is often revealed by the plan; moreover blocks of wrought tufa and Caen stone, the materials commonly used for cut stone by the early and later Norman builders respectively, may often be found in the rough walling of churches from which all other signs of early date (apart from the plan) have disappeared.

[86] Variously written *Paulynescraye, Creypaulin,* and *Powle's Cray.* Pearman, op. cit. 20.

[87] Bede, op. cit. v, 23.   [88] See Pearman, op. cit. 24, 25.

Turning to the see of Canterbury, we read of two men who shine conspicuously in its annals, Theodore (668–90) and St. Dunstan (960–88). Under Theodore Canterbury became in reality as well as in name the centre of English Christianity. While kings were fighting, their kingdoms were being welded together by the strong hand of the Greek monk of Tarsus into a united church, precursor of a united nation. In his person an archbishop of Canterbury for the first time asserted his primacy throughout the whole of his province [89]—for the see of York was not raised to metropolitan dignity until 735. His first action was to make a complete visitation of the Church throughout the land. His second was to assemble the first English provincial synod at Hertford (Herutford). It was a council of bishops : the bishops of Lichfield (Mercia), Winchester (Wessex) and Dunwich (East Anglia) were present in person, and Wilfrid of York (Northumbria) was represented by his delegates. The council began by affirming the unity of the Church as based upon the ancient and canonical decrees of the fathers ; and it ended in an agreement that a provincial synod should be held once a year at Clovesho (Clofeshoch). A proposal to increase the number of bishops from time to time in proportion to the increase in the number of the faithful was deferred, opposed doubtless by the delegates of York. But Theodore did not wait for synodical authority for the execution of a policy which was dear to his heart and which in all succeeding ages has proved to be essential to the well-being of the Church : East Anglia was divided into two dioceses in the same year ; six years later, in collusion with King Egfrid, and in the absence and without the consent of Wilfrid of York, Theodore split the Northumbrian diocese into four ; and in the following year, at the request of King Ethelred, he divided the Mercian diocese into four or five.[90] Following this reorganization of the dioceses of his province the archbishop, in 680, appointed a synod at Haethfeld, which, Canon Bright remarks,[91] may perhaps be identified with Cliffe at Hoo, the Clofeshoch selected in 673 ; and there the assembled bishops of the island of Britain (their names are not recorded) subscribed to a statement which gave proof of the ' Catholic belief of the English Church.'

Such was the work of Theodore.[92] It formed the framework of the diocesan constitution of the English Church.[93] But in the unsettled relations of the English kingdoms in the eighth century it could not remain unimpaired. The province of York, as we have seen, was constituted, by the gift of a pall to Egbert, its first archbishop, in 735. Later in the century King Offa, jealous of the influence of the archbishop of Canterbury and thinking to strengthen the Mercian overlordship, took advantage of the presence of the only legatine mission sent to England previous to the eve of the Conquest to bring about the creation of a metropolitical province having its head see his capital, Lichfield. Archbishop Jaenberht of Canterbury was

[89] Bede, op. cit. iv, *passim.*

[90] H. & S. op. cit. iii, 125. Wessex was not yet ready for such development.

[91] Bright, *Chapters of Early Engl. Ch. Hist.* 326.

[92] Mention must be made of the famous school of Canterbury (prototype of the yet more famous school of York), which Theodore with the help of his friend Abbot Hadrain established, in which he himself taught, and which produced such men as Bishop Aldhelm and John of Beverley.

[93] In the time of Bede, and much later, the word *parochia* was used of a bishop's parish, i.e. his diocese. There is no record that Theodore attempted anything in the way of a general parochial settlement of the land in the later sense of the term. The times were not ripe.

forced to consent to the scheme and, surrendering the greater part of his province, was left with only four suffragans. This led to a revolt in Kent under the leadership of an apostate priest named Edbert Praen, whom the Kentishmen set up as their king, and to the flight of Ethelheard (Jaenberht's successor and a Mercian) from his see. King Cenwulf (Offa's successor), having suppressed the rising, saw fit to restore to Canterbury its former metropolitan dignity ; and the restoration was formally ratified by Ethelheard and eleven (out of twelve) of his suffragans in a council at Clovesho, in 803, at which the king and his thegns with certain presbyters were present. This same Cenwulf, however, a few years later, seized the monasteries of Southminster in Thanet and Reculver, holding them till his death. This act of spoliation illustrates the uncertain tenure of ecclesiastical property which marks the whole of the early period of the history of the Church.

For two and a half centuries, from the death of Theodore in 690, the history of ecclesiastical progress in Kent is obscure. The fitful incursions of Mercian kings were succeeded by the ravages of Danish invaders. Kent now came under the supremacy of Wessex, and Alfred the Great, who with his son Edward the Elder owed much to the wise counsel of Archbishop Plegmund (890–914), saved the county from any permanent settlement of the heathen within its borders ;[94] but it was not till the whole land became settled and the nation united under the rule of Edward's sons that ruling spirits appeared in Church and State able to promote a spiritual revival and ecclesiastical reformation. The moral and spiritual tone of the Church and of society in general was deplorably low. The lesser monasteries had disappeared ; the rule of the greater houses had become lax ; and the conduct of the secular clergy, both in cathedral city and country parish,[95] did not rise above the standard that was generally accepted.

It was on monastic lines that Archbishop Odo (942–958) conceived revival and reformation to be possible. He had learned the value of a reformed Benedictine rule, the rule of Benedict of Aniane, at Fleury, near Rouen. The revolution (for such it was, so far as it went) for which 'Odo the Good' prepared the way was carried out by his disciples, of whom Bishop Stubbs says that Ethelwold (of Winchester) was the moving spirit, Oswald (of Worcester and York) tempered zeal with discretion, Dunstan's hand may be credited with such little moderation and practical wisdom as can be traced.[96] The general aim of the 'triumvirate' was to restore monks to the houses of which they had been dispossessed by secular clergy, to reform the houses in which the monastic rule had become lax, and to establish new houses. In the reign of 'Edgar the Pacific' (959–75) more than forty Benedictine monasteries were founded. In some cases, however, secular clergy were ousted from their rightful heritage. The extreme party, led by Ethelwold, took as their motto the choice, 'Begone or become monks,' offered by that prelate to the clergy of his own cathedral church, which had been served by seculars since its foundation. Dunstan's discipline was milder than that of

---

[94] The Danes had ravaged Sheppey as early as 832; twenty years later they wintered in Thanet and took Canterbury ; in 855 they wintered in Sheppey, and again in Thanet in the following year, when they ravaged Kent. Such are the brief records of the *Angl.-Sax. Chron.*

[95] The growth of the parochial system was now becoming sufficiently advanced to call for regulating ordinances. See especially the laws of Kings Edmund and Edgar in Thorpe, *Anct. Laws*. Synodical action had now ceased : the witenagemot legislated for Church and State. [96] *Mem. of St. Dunstan* (Rolls Ser.), xcviii.

Ethelwold. In earlier days, as abbot of Glastonbury, his reform of that house was on the lines of a school rather than a convent. As bishop of Worcester and London successively he did not eject the clergy of his cathedral church, and as archbishop of Canterbury he retained them at Christchurch. If his co-reformers had possessed his wiser statesmanship and his juster judgement the continued struggle between seculars and regulars would have been less bitter, and the influence of the monastic movement more general and effective.

Ethelred the Redeless acceded in 979, and St. Dunstan spent his remaining years in comparative retirement, exercising his spiritual functions and working in his famous school in Canterbury. He died in 998, having lived ' pre-eminent above all others during the reigns of six kings.' The nation now entered upon another period of misfortune, aggravated by a recrudescence of Danish invasions. In Kentish annals one name is honourably treasured, that of Archbishop Alphege, who ' houselled ' and otherwise encouraged the defenders of Canterbury in the siege of 1011. The city was betrayed (by Archdeacon Almeric, according to the monkish chronicler, Thorne ; by Abbot Elfmer, according to the *Angl.-Sax. Chron.*), taken and burnt ; and, a few months later, Alphege earned a martyr's death and a saint's fame by refusing to purchase his liberty at the expense of his Church.

The closing years of the Saxon period formed an era of national decay. Simony and intrigue grew apace. Offices of state were filled by the appointment of secular clerks who received rewards of ecclesiastical preferment. Hitherto the Church, if isolated from the rest of western Christianity, had yet been truly national. A process of denationalization was now begun : a foreign element was introduced, and papal legates reappeared. Robert, abbot of Jumièges, was duly appointed by the king and witan to the archbishopric. A struggle between the national party under Godwine, earl of Kent, and the foreigners ended in the flight and deposition of Robert and the appointment of a schismatical archbishop in the person of Stigand. Constitutional government seemed to be impossible. Church and State were ripe for revolution. The death of Edward the Confessor opened the way for the coming of William the Norman.

William was crowned in Westminster Abbey on Christmas Day, 1066, by Eldred, archbishop of York. Stigand was allowed to take some part in the ceremony. The king did not finally break with the schismatical archbishop, the nominee of the national party, until four years later, when he felt his position to be sufficiently secure. In 1070 the first of a series of national councils assembled at Winchester at the Easter Festival. On taking his seat the king allowed three papal legates to place the crown upon his head. Before the same legates Stigand was tried on definite charges of schism and simony, and his deposition was confirmed by the council. William had gained his crown under papal sanction and blessing, and the king's bearing towards the legates of Alexander II showed how far he was willing to go in the expression of gratitude and goodwill. Later on he paid Peter's Pence, but refused to do fealty to Gregory VII for his crown.

William's initial policy was to replace ignorant English prelates by Normans of piety and learning, and when Egelsin, abbot of St. Augustine's, deemed it prudent after the council of Winchester to vacate his post by flight, his place was forthwith filled by the appointment of a Norman named Scotland, who won the regard of his resentful brethren by the vigorous policy whereby he recovered many estates which had been seized by the Normans, and set himself to replace the old church and domestic buildings of the monastery on a much larger scale.[97]   Nine bishops took part in the consecration of Lanfranc in Christchurch Cathedral, 29 August, 1070, and of those nine only one, Siward of Rochester, was an Englishman, three were Lotharingians, the remaining five being Normans.

The first meeting of William and Lanfranc is characteristic of the men. Lanfranc, who was Pavian by birth and a lawyer by education, had migrated to Normandy and established a school of some fame at Avranches before he took the cowl, became prior of Bec, and there established a school of still greater fame, numbering among his pupils men who were afterwards known as Pope Alexander II ; Archbishops Anselm and Theobald, his successors in the see of Canterbury ; Bishops Arnost and Gundulf, his suffragans in the see of Rochester.   While he was prior of Bec, Lanfranc was reported to Duke William as having denounced his marriage with Matilda.   The duke thereupon issued an order that he should quit Normandy and that his monastery should be burnt.   Lanfranc took his journey on a lame horse, with a single attendant ; and passing near the court one day he met the duke, who stopped and asked him whither he went.   'Out of the province by your command ; and if you will give me a better horse I will obey you more quickly.'   Thus two strong men took measure of one another, and the way in which they afterwards worked together was regarded as a 'miracle of the age.'   The duke's marriage was condoned by the erection of *l'Abbeye aux hommes* and *l'Abbeye aux dames* at Caen ; and Lanfranc, in 1066, became first abbot of the former, dedicated in the name of St. Stephen.

When Lanfranc was called to Canterbury the see of York was vacant. The new metropolitan saw the necessity of ensuring the subordination of the northern see.   The struggle centred round the consecration of Thomas, archbishop-elect of York, who refused to make profession of obedience to Lanfranc.   The matter was compromised by the king, who at first regarded Lanfranc's action as high-handed, but a hint that an independent archbishop of York might promote the cause of an independent king of Northumbria induced the king to require Thomas to go so far as to make profession of personal obedience to Lanfranc without binding his successors in the see. Thus the matter rested until the following year, when both archbishops went to Rome to receive their palls.   The story is told at length by William of Malmesbury.   A charge of disqualification against Thomas, on the ground that he was the son of a priest, caused the archbishop of York to throw himself upon the mercy of the pope, and gave Lanfranc an opportunity of interceding on his behalf.   The pope thereupon handed the archbishop of York's episcopal ring and crosier to Lanfranc to be disposed of according to his good judgement for the welfare of the English Church, and Lanfranc immediately reinvested Thomas with them.   With regard to the general relation of the see of York to that of Canterbury, the pope decided that the question should be considered and determined in a national council in England.

Successively at Winchester and Windsor, in 1073, Lanfranc argued his cause with an array of learning and a legal acumen which was irresistible,

[97] Thorne, op. cit. 1788–9.   The foundations of the east end of Abbot Scotland's church have recently been excavated, and will be fully described in a forthcoming number of *Arch. Cant.* by Mr. W. H. St. John Hope.

and gained a decision entirely in favour of Canterbury. The province of York was limited to the country north of the Humber ; in national councils the archbishop of Canterbury was to preside, the archbishop of York was to sit on his right and the bishop of London on his left hand, Winchester was to sit next to York, and other bishops in precedence of consecration ; and the archbishop of York was to make profession of obedience not merely to Lanfranc personally but to him and his successors in the see of Canterbury.

In his attitude towards Rome Lanfranc's policy reflects that of the king. In his endeavour to raise the tone of his adopted church and to conform its organization and spiritual life to the higher level of continental christendom he did not scruple to appeal to the pope from whom he had received his pall, and to seek the advice and co-operation of papal legates ; but his relations with them implicitly showed that neither king nor archbishop would brook uninvited interference. Summonses to Rome remained unobeyed.

In his home policy also the archbishop was at one with his king. The most important and far-reaching constitutional measures of the reign were those which separated the civil and ecclesiastical jurisdictions. The bishops and mitred abbots sat as of old in the great council of the nation, as barons ; as prelates they now sat also in ecclesiastical councils under the presidency of the archbishop. Hitherto bishop and earl had sat side by side in the shire moot to expound God's law and the world's law ; henceforth bishops and archdeacons had courts of their own in which ecclesiastical causes were settled in accordance with canon law. The immediate effect was to strengthen immensely the hands of the bishops ; the ultimate effect, separating lay and clerical interests and weighting the balance in favour of the Church, is beyond our present scope. The position of the bishops was further strengthened by the removal of sees from villages to towns. In one direction, however, their authority was curtailed : the exemption of Battle Abbey from episcopal jurisdiction formed a precedent which was largely followed in later times. The reform and the revival of monastic life, in accordance with the Benedictine rule, which was doing much for the revival of spiritual life on the continent, constituted a chief aim of the heads of both Church and State. Many cathedral churches which had hitherto been in the hands of secular clergy were now entrusted to the care of monastic bodies ; while in some others that remained in the hands of the seculars the clergy were required to live the regular life of ' canons.' ' Let no canon have a wife,' was the rule laid down in the council of Winchester, 1076. Country clergy who were already married were allowed to retain their wives ; but thenceforth no married man was to be admitted to orders. Cathedral and monastic churches were rebuilt on a scale befitting the reconstitution of the bodies that served them, and ' all noblemen vied with one another in building churches on their estates.' [98]

The story of the trial on Penenden Heath near Maidstone, the customary place of the Kentish gemote, whereby Odo, the king's half-brother, bishop of Bayeux and earl of Kent, was made to disgorge Church property belonging both to Canterbury and to Rochester, is a memorial of the justice of the king and of the solicitude and sagacity of the archbishop who argued the case for three days before the king's justiciar, Bishop Geoffrey of Cou-

---

[98] Quoted by Dean Stephens in *The Engl. Ch. from the Norman Conq.*, from William of Jumieges, in reference to Normandy. It is clear that the Norman nobles brought their building passion to England.

tance, in the presence of the sheriff of Kent and leading men of the realm. Having rebuilt his cathedral church and added the necessary domestic offices,[99] and having recovered alienated property, Lanfranc made a division of his episcopal estates, retaining some himself, allotting some to the monks and surrendering to Rochester some which belonged to that see.[100]

On many of his manors he built houses of stone for the accommodation of himself and his retinue on the occasion of his periodical visits. This is the origin of the many so-called palaces possessed by the archbishops of Canterbury. Domesday Book indicates that at the time of the Survey the following manors were held by the archbishop in demesne : Darenth (afterwards exchanged for Lambeth), Otford, East Malling, Northfleet, Norton, Bishopsbourne, Bolton, Charing, Pluckley, Wingham, Mersham, Aldington, Lyminge.

Lanfranc also built[101] outside the north gate of the city a hospital of stone for poor and infirm persons of both sexes, properly segregated ; and on the other side of the way he built a church, in honour of Gregory the Great, in which he placed canons to minister to the spiritual wants of the inmates of the hospital. At the church of St. Nicholas, Harbledown, to the west of the city, Lanfranc made a hospital of wood for lepers, and instituted clerks to minister to them. Reference to the plan of this church has already been made.

Siward of Rochester died in 1075 and was succeeded by Arnost, a monk of Bec, who died within a year of his consecration. The next occupant of the see was Gundulf,[102] who had been with Lanfranc successively at Bec, Caen and Canterbury. With the help of Lanfranc he rebuilt his cathedral church, and in 1080 he replaced the five canons whom he found there by twenty-two monks, the number rising to sixty before his death in 1108.[103] He also founded a hospital for lepers in honour of St. Bartholomew on the borders of Chatham to the east of the city. Like Lanfranc at Canterbury he divided the revenues of his see between himself and his convent, confirming the same by charter temp. Henry I.[104] The manors which he assigned to the monks were Wouldham, Frindsbury, Stoke, Southfleet, Denton, Lambeth and Haddenham. Gundulf was a great builder as well as a great administrator. It is not an unreasonable conjecture that he had a hand in the building of St. Stephen's, Caen, and Christchurch, Canterbury, for his skill as a master builder caused William I to set him over the work of the Great Tower of London.[105] He also founded a house of Benedictine Nuns at West Malling.[106] Nearly the whole of the remains of the ruined abbey church are assigned to Gundulf's date, only the upper portion of the west front being later work. Of his cathedral church two entire bays of the crypt remain, and considerable portions of his work appear incorporated into the later Norman reconstruction carried out by his successors, Ernulf and John.

[99] Milo Crespin, Lanfranc's contemporary biographer, tells us the archbishop brought squared stones from Caen for the purpose. He also used Kentish *tufa*. Considerable remains of his work exist in the south transept of the nave and in the ruins of the dorter adjoining the chapter-house. One of his western towers was pulled down about seventy years ago.

[100] Gervase, *Opera* (Rolls Ser.), ii, 64. This division of episcopal property, which led to cathedral bodies, both monastic and collegiate, becoming independent corporations, in course of time reduced the authority of a bishop in his own cathedral church to that of a mere 'visitor,' called in to settle disputes and reform abuses.

[101] *Eadmeri Hist.* (Rolls Ser.), 15.   [102] See Hook, 'Life of Gundulf,' in *Arch. Journ.* xxi.
[103] *Textus Roffensis*, ed. Hearne, 143.   [104] Thorpe, *Reg. Roff.* 33.
[105] *Textus Roffensis*, 212.   [106] Thorpe, *Reg. Roff.* 486.

ECCLESIASTICAL HISTORY

PART II

For nearly four years after the death of Lanfranc in 1089, the king kept the archbishopric vacant and held possession of the property of the see, granting out lands for money or military service. The diocese was administered by Gundulf, bishop of Rochester. This prelate, who had been consecrated in Canterbury Cathedral in 1077, had come to Canterbury with Lanfranc at his elevation to the see. Famed for his architectural skill, his diligent administration, and his learning, he had received his monastic training at the abbey of Bec, where he laid the foundation of the enduring friendship that existed between himself and Lanfranc, as well as with Anselm. But although he had made his own chapter at Rochester monastic—in the place of five canons putting in sixty monks, and securing to the monastery a separate share of the possessions of the church, in order to make it in money matters independent of the bishop—at Canterbury he found himself in spite of his monastic sympathies in collision with the monks of St. Augustine's, whom he had to punish for raising a riot in conjunction with some of the inhabitants of the town.[1]

Anselm, abbot of Bec, in 1092 visited England to get the oppressive exactions levied upon his abbey's property there lightened. On reaching Canterbury, where he had been held in high esteem ever since his first visit to Lanfranc in 1078, he was hailed by monks and laymen as future archbishop. He refused in consequence to tarry there, and pressed on to Hugh of Avranches, earl of Chester, who had been urging him for some time to come to him. On his way he had a private interview with the king, and remonstrated with him on his iniquities. When, five months later, he wished to return to Bec, the king refused him licence to travel, and this refusal was followed by his appointment to the primacy by the king,[2] whom he had been summoned to attend on what was thought at the time to be his deathbed.

The narrative of Eadmer,[3] whose acquaintance he had made on his first visit to Canterbury, when the youthful Christchurch brother had become the devoted friend of Anselm, to whom he was afterwards appointed chaplain, shows that Anselm carried to almost incredible lengths his resistance to this appointment. He infuriated not only the king, but the bishops and his own followers, by refusals which persisted even to physical struggles against the consecration ceremonies then performed in a neighbouring church,[4] from which he returned protesting that he had not consented.

Rufus, after his recovery, again begged him to accept the primacy, and at Windsor assured him that he was called by the choice of the whole nation.[5] But it is remarkable that there is no distinct record of any formal election by the monks of Canterbury or by the witan, though there are innumerable references to the unanimous desire for his appointment.

---

[1] *Angl.-Sax. Chron.* App. 389.   [2] Wm. of Malmesbury, *Gesta Pontif.* (Rolls Ser.), i, 48.

[3] In *Historia Novella* and *Vita Anselmi*, both in Rolls Series.

[4] 'It would have been difficult,' he wrote, in a letter to the monks at Bec (*Epist.* iii, 1), 'for a looker on to say whether a sane man was being dragged by a crowd of madmen, or whether sane men were dragging a madman along.'

[5] Eadmer, *Hist. Nov.* (Rolls Ser.), i, 371.

The king and Anselm met again in the summer of 1093, at Rochester, when Anselm made it clear that he would accept the archbishopric only on three conditions. These were: [6] (1) That all the lands belonging to the see in the time of Lanfranc should be restored without dispute ; (2) that the king should see justice done in respect of any lands upon which the see had a long-standing claim ; (3) that in matters pertaining to God the king should take Anselm for his counsellor and spiritual father, as he on his part acknowledged the king as his earthly lord. At the same time Anselm informed the king that he himself was committed to the side of Urban, the pope elected by the cardinals in opposition to Hildebrand, who had been appointed by the Emperor Henry IV. Though the king consented to restore all the lands that had belonged to the see in the time of Lanfranc, difficulties arose concerning certain lands held by English thegns before the Norman conquest which had lapsed to the archbishopric for want of heirs, and which had been granted out as military fiefs during the late vacancy of the see. But Anselm's hope that he might thus after all escape the primacy was frustrated by the summoning of a special council at Winchester to exact the performance of the promises made during the king's illness, when he was at last persuaded to accept the archbishopric, and did homage for the lands of the see, the king bestowing on him the archbishopric with all the rights, powers, and possessions which belonged to the see, and with all liberties over all his men, and over as many thegns as King Edward had granted to the church.[7]

It seemed, therefore, as if Anselm had won the day. But his enthronement in Canterbury Cathedral, 25 September, 1093, in the presence of a rejoicing multitude, was marred by an ominous event. Ralph Flambard then served a writ in the king's name for a suit against him, apparently concerning a matter with which the king's court had properly nothing to do.[8] His consecration on 4 December by Thomas, archbishop of York, assisted by all the bishops of the southern province except three, who signified their assent, was made the occasion for a protest from the northern archbishop, whose objection to the title 'metropolitan of all Britain,' used by the bishop of London, the dean of the province of Canterbury, in reading the formal record of his appointment, was allowed, and the term primate substituted in its place.

The king had declared war with Robert of Normandy at his Christmas Council, and Anselm's contribution of £500 in silver, with difficulty collected from his diocese, though at first received with a good grace, was afterwards rejected by the king on the suggestion of the enemies of Anselm that it should have been at least £2,000. February, 1094, saw Anselm at Hastings, where William was waiting for a favourable wind. The archbishop had been summoned to invoke a blessing on the expedition ; but contrary winds delayed its passage for a month, and Anselm, who seems to have had daily interviews with the king, incurred his further displeasure by his faithful admonitions. The king in a rage sent him a message that he need 'tarry no longer to bless my voyage,' and Eadmer tells us 'we left the court with all speed' ; the army departed from the Kentish port without his prayers.

[6] R. W. R. Stephens, *Hist. of Engl. Ch.* ii, 91.
[7] Eadmer, *Hist. Nov.* (Rolls Ser.), i, 372 ; Rymer, *Foedera*, i, 5.
[8] Eadmer, *Hist. Nov.* (Rolls Ser.), i, 372.

A year later Anselm applied for leave to go to Rome to fetch the *pallium*, the indispensable badge of metropolitan authority. Although at Rochester Anselm had expressly told the king that he had already, when abbot of Bec, promised obedience to Urban, to whom, therefore, he was pledged, the king now declared that as it was not lawful for an English subject to acknowledge anyone as pope without the royal permission, and as he himself had not acknowledged Urban, Anselm should not make his application to Urban. At Anselm's request the great council of the realm was convened to consider the question, 25 February, 1095, at Rockingham. Here Anselm was basely deserted by the bishops, who formally withdrew their obedience from him, the only prelate who refused to disown him being the faithful Gundulf.[9] The lay lords, however, showed more independence, and at their intervention a truce was arranged, and an adjournment until Whitsuntide. The king made use of the interval to send envoys to Rome to find out who was there held the real pope, and then to persuade this one to send the *pallium* to himself. The journey was made in great secrecy, and the envoys returned with the information that Urban was the real pope ; they were accompanied by Cardinal Walter, bishop of Albano, who brought the *pallium*, and whom they escorted, as legate, with all speed to the king, not allowing him to tarry at Canterbury, or hold any communication with Anselm. The king had to order a formal recognition of Urban as pope, but he endeavoured to procure the deposition of Anselm. This he failed to do, and had therefore to go through a form of reconciliation with Anselm, which took place at Windsor at Whitsuntide.

On the third Sunday after Trinity, 27 May, 1095, the cardinal legate brought the *pallium* with great pomp to Canterbury in a silver casket. He was met by the monks of Christchurch and St. Augustine's and a vast concourse of clergy and laity. Near the cathedral the procession was met by Anselm, barefoot but in full pontificals, and attended by his suffragans. The *pallium* was laid on the altar, from whence it was taken by Anselm, who presented it to the bystanders to kiss ; after which he robed himself in the sacred vestment and celebrated mass.[10]

A short breathing space was secured to Anselm after this by the king's absence in the north to put down a revolt there ; it was thought that this opportunity would be utilized for an attack from Normandy, and the city of Canterbury, and even apparently the whole county of Kent, was entrusted to Anselm's charge for defence against such a contingency.[11] Anselm stayed at Canterbury, and was so faithful to his trust that he refused to leave the city even for a day to confer with the papal legate on the reforms he had so much at heart.[12]

His letters to the legate show that he believed that reforms of any permanent value could only be achieved by constitutional methods, that is to say, by a council at which the king, bishops, and lay lords were present. But as time went on, and all his appeals to the king proved fruitless, he at last sent to him for leave to go in person to Rome. This was not only refused, but he was threatened with a fine for renewing his request. His persistence this time brought on him the hostility not only of the bishops, but of the

[9] Eadmer, *Sti. Anselmi Vita* (Rolls Ser.), ii, 24.
[11] R. W. R. Stephens, *Hist. of Engl. Ch.* ii, 103.
[10] Eadmer, *Hist. Nov.* (Rolls Ser.), ii, 390–2.
[12] *Epist.* iii, 35, 36.

lay lords ; at last, however, the king told him that he might go, but that he was not to take anything with him belonging to the king, to which ignominious prohibition was subsequently added the command to be at Dover ready to cross in eleven days, and to submit himself before leaving to a messenger from the king, who would meet him there and tell him what he might take with him. Anselm took leave of the king 15 October, 1097, at Winchester, and immediately left for Canterbury. On the day after his arrival there, he took the pilgrim's staff and scrip from off the altar and set forth for Dover. Here he found the king's messenger, his chaplain, William of Warelwast. When at last the wind was favourable, and Anselm and his party hastened to the shore to embark, every article of their luggage was opened and examined, the bystanders protesting angrily against this outrage. As soon as the archbishop had departed, the king not only confiscated the estates of the see, but cancelled all acts and decrees made concerning them during his primacy.

The story of Anselm's sojourn on the continent, his flattering reception by Urban, his speech at the council of Bari, held 7 October, 1098, on the 'Procession of the Holy Ghost,' which was pronounced a masterpiece of learning and eloquence, and his defence of William Rufus against the decision of the assembly to excommunicate him, are all to be found in the pages of Eadmer. The matter of greatest importance to his diocese, since it furnished later the main subject of his disputes with Henry I, was his presence at the great council held at St. Peter's in April, 1099, at which the seat of honour was assigned to him ; for at this council anathema was pronounced on any layman who should bestow investiture of an ecclesiastical benefice and on the clerk who should receive it at his hands and become his man, and this decree was opposed to the custom of England and Normandy.

The death of the king was the signal for his return, and already before his landing at Dover, 23 September, 1100, he had received urgent messengers pressing him to hasten, from the monks of Canterbury, the lay lords, and from Henry himself. Henry, who declared that he would rather have been blessed and crowned by Anselm than by anyone else, but that he had not dared to delay his coronation ceremony owing to the activity of his enemies, gave him a cordial welcome.

It was not long, however, before the unfortunate consequences of the decree concerning investiture began to be felt. According to the ancient custom of England, the temporalities of the archbishopric were in the hands of the king, and it was necessary for Anselm to do homage for them at their restitution. When he declared to the king his intention of abiding by the canons recently promulgated, Henry proposed to leave the matter in abeyance until the following Easter, and in the meantime to send envoys to Rome to induce the pope to relax the canons in favour of the ancient customs of the realm. To this Anselm gladly assented, and was in the meantime reinstated in all the possessions of the see.[13]

Negotiations with Rome were protracted and unsatisfactory, and at the king's suggestion Anselm himself went to the pope. While he remained abroad awaiting the papal decision, Henry confiscated the revenues of the see, and Anselm was the recipient of many reproachful letters and appeals from

[13] Eadmer, *Hist. Nov.* (Rolls Ser.), iii, 424–5.

his clergy. Anselm wrote a severe letter of reproof to Henry for punishing priests, a duty which appertained only to bishops,[14] but at the same time he wrote to his archdeacon, and the prior and chapter of Canterbury, ordering the penalties of deprivation or excommunication to be enforced upon those clergy who broke the canons concerning marriage.[15] Henry sent a courteous reply, promising to make amends if he had offended, and that archiepiscopal property should not be molested.

The envoys, on their return in April, 1106, brought instructions from the pope authorizing Anselm to release from excommunication those who had broken the canons concerning investiture and homage.

Anselm then started for Dover, and was received with enthusiastic greetings in which Queen Maud took part. Owing to various causes, including the serious illness of Anselm, the public settlement of this long dispute was delayed until 1 August, 1107, when it took place at a large council held in London.[16]

Anselm, now aged and infirm, survived but eighteen months, dying 21 April, 1109.[17] In spite of repeated illness, he laboured incessantly to the last to enforce the canons of London against simony and marriage. Gundulf, his lifelong friend, had died 7 March, 1108, and was buried by Anselm in his cathedral church. On 9 August, 1108, Anselm consecrated at Canterbury Gundulf's successor, Ralph d'Escures, abbot of Séez, whose appointment had met with universal approval. He was the intimate friend of Anselm and of Gundulf, who, in dying, had placed the episcopal ring on his finger.

The king kept the primacy vacant for five years, during which time the diocese was administered, at the request of the chapter, by Ralph, bishop of Rochester, who to some extent also was responsible for the province, and the king confiscated the revenues of the see, though the property of the monks of Christchurch was not molested.[18]

At length, on 26 April, 1114, Ralph was unanimously elected by the king, the bishops, and the prior and monks of Christchurch, to the primacy.[19]

He was succeeded at Rochester by Ernulf, abbot of Peterborough, appointed, according to the Anglo-Saxon Chronicle, at the personal intervention of the king. Trained at Bec, he had been the friend of Lanfranc, Anselm, and Gundulf, and when Anselm appointed him prior of Christchurch, he carried on with skill and untiring diligence the work on the cathedral begun by Lanfranc. Not the least of his achievements is the valuable collection of documents he made at Rochester, known as the ' Textus Roffensis,' dealing with the church of Rochester, papal decrees, and other materials for English and ecclesiastical history and for an account of English and canon law, concerning which his authority was held in high repute.

---

[14] *Epist.* iii, 109.   [15] Ibid. 110–12.   [16] Ralph de Diceto, *Op. Hist.* (Rolls Ser.), i, 236.

[17] Before his death he addressed a mandate to the bishop of Worcester, requiring him to treat the archbishop of York as a person under the ban of the Church, because of his attempt to throw off his subjection to the church of Canterbury. Cath. Lib. Cant. Y. 57, *c.* 1100.

[18] By liberal gifts of money and land, and by the settlement of the whole oblations of the high altar (of which Lanfranc had retained half) and of the Easter and Christmas offerings on the convent, Anselm, according to Eadmer and to Gervase of Canterbury, had provided against their estates falling into the king's hands during the vacancy of the see. By renouncing all interest in these revenues, he left himself little more than a nominal supremacy in the chapter, with what fatal results the history of his successors shows. *Epist. Cant.* (Rolls Ser.), i, p. xxx.

[19] Eadmer, *Hist. Nov.* (Rolls Ser.), ii, 489–90.

Notwithstanding the eminently satisfactory character of both these appointments, the pope wrote to the prior and monks of Christchurch that the translation of the bishop of Rochester to the metropolitan see without his knowledge and consent was a very serious act of presumption, only condoned in consideration of Ralph's high reputation. His feeling against the English Church was still more strongly displayed by his refusing at first to send the *pallium* to the archbishop, when Ralph, who was ill, sent messengers to fetch it. Owing to the good offices of Anselm, abbot of St. Saba, nephew of the late archbishop, it was finally dispatched by him instead of by Ralph's envoy, his nephew John.

The death of Thomas, archbishop of York, in 1114, had been followed by a renewal of the disputes as to the supremacy of Canterbury, in which the king supported Canterbury, and the pope York.

The king gave effective support to Ralph in 1115, in his demand that Bernard, bishop elect of St. David's, should be consecrated nowhere but at Canterbury. Though, in the end, to allow the queen to be present, the ceremony was performed at Westminster Abbey, Bernard made profession of obedience and subjection to the see of Canterbury.[20] The refusal of King Alexander of Scotland to allow Eadmer to be consecrated bishop of St. Andrews by Ralph at Canterbury, and Eadmer's refusal to receive consecration from anyone else, ended in his not becoming bishop of St. Andrews. Shortly before his death, the archbishop consecrated Gregory to the see of Dublin at Lambeth.

Ralph died in 1122, and the consecration of his successor, William de Corbeuil, was performed by his own suffragans, the bishops of London and Winchester and others, it being impossible to accept Archbishop Thurstan's offer to consecrate unless he would make profession of obedience to the archbishop of Canterbury. This Thurstan not only refused to make, but he carried on such an active campaign against William at Rome, that it was with difficulty the pope was persuaded to bestow the pall on William, and the king had to expend much gold and silver to obtain it for him;[21] as a result of Thurstan's representations, moreover, the pope decided to send a legate, John of Crema, to England. Though Calixtus died before he started, his successor, Honorius II, renewed John's commission, and he was received with great honour by the archbishops; he incensed the church and nation, however, by taking precedence of the archbishop of Canterbury, and by his usurpation of the place of the primate in his own cathedral at the celebration of mass on Easter Day, a scandal, wrote Gervase of Canterbury, that convulsed the public mind with anger. The feeling against him was so strong that when he was detected to be flagrantly breaking the canons passed at the council held at Westminster in 1125 at which he himself had presided, he was treated with such scorn that he hastily left the kingdom, leaving the rival claims of the two metropolitan sees unsettled.

The two archbishops then repaired in person to Rome, where William was well received by Honorius and won an important victory. By a bull dated 25 January, 1126, the pope appointed him papal legate in England and Scotland,[22] and by this proceeding not only appeased for a time the anti-

[20] Giraldus Cambrensis, *Opera* (Rolls Ser.), iii, 49.
[21] Angl.-Sax. Chron. *anno* 1123.
[22] Wilkins, *Concilia*, i, 409.

foreign feeling, but secured to William personally an immediate precedence over York, and made a precedent for the later custom of making the archbishop of Canterbury the *legatus natus* of the Roman see.[23]

This achievement alone would have made his archbishopric one of importance, but it is memorable also for the activity with which he carried on building operations both at Canterbury and Rochester. He took a very active part in the rebuilding of Rochester Cathedral,[24] and was present at the dedication ceremony in May, 1130, in the presence of the king and a vast concourse of bishops, on which occasion the rectory of Boxley was granted to the monastery, with all its rights and liberties as enjoyed by Jeffrey, the king's chaplain.[25] To the see of Rochester, always so intimately connected with that of Canterbury, he had appointed John, archdeacon of Canterbury, bishop, May, 1125.

The dedication of Rochester was immediately preceded by that of the glorious cathedral at Canterbury begun by Lanfranc ; the kings of England and Scotland and a brilliant assembly were present, and Henry signalized the event by giving the collegiate church of St. Martin, Dover, to the church of Canterbury.

The archbishop's scheme for a reformation of this college and for removing it from the old church within the town to a new and sumptuous structure outside, roused the opposition of the monks of Christchurch, who claimed that the church was theirs, not the archbishop's, and appealed to Rome, succeeding on his death in securing St. Martin's as a cell of Christchurch.[26] His restoration of the abandoned nunnery at Minster in Sheppey proved more fortunate than his attempt at Dover.[27]

His last years saw an improvement in his relations with Thurstan, archbishop of York.

Although he took the oath in 1126 to respect the succession of Matilda, after considerable delay he yielded and crowned Stephen, who at his coronation was lavish of promises to the church which he never kept. The partisanship of contemporary historians has in consequence affected their estimate of William's character. The author of *Gesta Stephani*[28] denounces him as avaricious and a hypocrite ; William of Malmesbury says that he was very religious, rather affable, and neither inert nor imprudent,[29] which would seem to show that he found favour rather with the party of the empress than with Stephen's adherents.

After his death in November, 1136, the see remained vacant for two years, when Theobald, abbot of Bec, and a worthy upholder of its traditions, was elected by the monks through the influence of Stephen and his queen Matilda. A man of deep religious feeling, liberal and charitable, and a lover of learning, he endeavoured to remain faithful to Stephen as the king recognized by the Roman see, but against his will was driven more than once into the opposite camp, and in the end worked hard to ensure the succession of the house of Anjou. Throughout the civil disorder he endeavoured steadily

---

[23] This prevented the frequent intrusion of foreigners as legates *a latere*, and though the supreme jurisdiction of the pope was thus admitted, in English hands it assumed its least offensive form. Stubbs, *Const. Hist.* iii, 229.

[24] Gervase, *Op. Hist.* (Rolls Ser.), ii, 381.   [25] *Reg. Roff.* (ed. Thorpe), 179.

[26] Gervase, *Op. Hist.* (Rolls Ser.), i, 96 ; ii, 383 ; Dugdale, *Mon. Angl.* iv, 528, 544.

[27] Dugdale, *Mon. Angl.* ii, 50.   [28] *Op. cit.* 6.   [29] *Gesta Pontif.* 146.

to administer his diocese and improve its condition ; he attached to his house-hold many young men of legal and political talent, and made his palace the training college of a new generation of English scholars and English states-men ;[30] at Canterbury he established a law school which counted among its lecturers Roger of Pont l'Évêque, archdeacon of Canterbury, afterwards arch-bishop of York, the famous John of Salisbury, the disciple of Abelard, whose letters throw so much light on this period, and the celebrated jurist Vacarius of Mantua ; but his primacy displayed many of the characteristics of 'the Anarchy' with which it coincided, and neither the abbey of St. Augustine nor his own monastery of Christchurch were slow to avail themselves of any opportunity that offered of setting his authority at defiance.[31]

From the first, in matters connected with his province he had a formid-able opponent in the king's brother Henry, bishop of Winchester, who had been disappointed at not being made archbishop, and whose appointment as legate by the pope was a direct slight to Canterbury. It was not long before Hugh, abbot of St. Augustine's, appealed to the pope against a citation from the archbishop, and the case being referred to the legate, the result was very unsatisfactory to the archbishop. Jeremiah, the prior of Christchurch, then appealed to Rome against him and gained his cause. The death of Innocent in September, 1143, took both the archbishop and Bishop Henry to Rome, but this pope's successor, Celestine, does not appear to have granted the legation to either. Lucius II succeeded Celestine 12 March, 1144 ; he refused the lega-tion to Bishop Henry, and decided the case between the archbishop and the abbot of St. Augustine's in Theobald's favour, and Jeremiah resigned. Lucius died 1145, and the new pope, Eugenius, appointed Theobald legate.[32]

The see of Rochester also had a troublous history during this period. Disastrous fires had burned many buildings in Rochester in 1137 and 1139, and as a consequence the monks were dispersed for a time among other abbeys. Bishop John, who died in 1137, was succeeded by John, bishop of Séez, who is said to have treated his diocese ' rather as the robber of a strange flock than as a shepherd.'[33] He was succeeded in 1142 by Ascelin, late prior of Dover, who had a long dispute with Pullus, on whom the archdea-conry had been bestowed by Bishop John, together with several churches.[34] On the death of Ascelin, Walter, archdeacon of Canterbury, brother of Theobald, was appointed to succeed him, the election being made at Canter-bury, and he lived on friendly terms with the monks until his death in 1182, only one serious dispute between them being recorded, that concerning the appointment of a vicar of Dartmouth about seven years before he died, which was finally settled by mutual arrangement.[35]

Theobald consecrated his brother 14 March, 1148. When Stephen forbade the bishops to attend the council held at Rheims by Eugenius 21 March, he secretly embarked in a crazy boat, and was present in spite of

---

[30] Norgate, *Angevin Kings*, i, 352.

[31] It is interesting, however, to notice the number of religious houses founded in spite, or perhaps in con-sequence, of the national disorders, including that of Boxley, the Benedictine nunnery at Lillechurch in Higham, and the Cluniac priory of Monk's Horton.

[32] The exact date of his appointment is not known, but in default of finding him described as legate before 1150 that year has been assigned for the grant (Stubbs, *Const. Hist.* iii, 299 ; Norgate, *Angevin Kings*, i, 364). The historian of St Augustine's Abbey, however, speaks of him as papal legate in 1148 (Thorne, *Chron.* col. 1807).

[33] *Reg. Roff.* 8.   [34] Wharton, *Angl. Sacra*, i, 343 ; *Reg. Roff.* 9, 10.   [35] *Reg. Roff.* 10.

the prohibition.[36] On his return to Canterbury the king ordered him to leave the kingdom, and confiscated the temporalities of the see. He hastily returned to France, but though the pope suspended the bishops who had not attended, conferred the legatine office on Theobald, and wrote to the bishops directing them to demand the immediate restoration of the primate, threatening to lay the kingdom under an interdict if the king remained obdurate, the bishops now sided with Stephen. Theobald published the interdict, but it was unheeded except in Kent, and even there a party among the monks of St. Augustine's, led by the prior, Silvester, and the sacristan, disregarded it.

Mainly at the request of Stephen's queen Theobald was induced to return, and after being reconciled to the king took off the interdict, and received the submission of the bishops, but it was not till the following year that the monks of St. Augustine's made submission to him. Thorne, their own chronicler, excuses them by saying that though Theobald had published the interdict in virtue of his legatine authority, they did not know that he was legate. They were made to feel the full weight of the pope's displeasure, the services of their church being suspended by the archbishop for a time before the convent received absolution, and the prior and sacristan being only absolved after receiving a flogging.[37] When Silvester was elected by the monks in 1151 to be their abbot, he refused to make profession of canonical obedience to the archbishop, though he was willing to receive benediction from him. Finally he had to make profession in the same form as his predecessors had done,[38] but not until various appeals had been made by both sides to Rome.[39]

In the meantime a struggle of even greater severity had been going on with his own convent, where the brethren, after begging Theobald to administer the property which had been granted to them by Anselm, resented the economy of his management to such a degree that they accused him of exercising it for his own benefit, and even appealed to Rome. Theobald took vigorous measures to punish them, and at the mediation of other prelates the convent withdrew their appeal, when Theodore restored their estates, though he insisted on the resignation of the prior.[40]

His refusal to crown Stephen's son in 1152 led to his being imprisoned by the king, but he managed to escape to Flanders. Stephen then confiscated the estates of the see, but being threatened by the pope with excommunication and an interdict he recalled Theobald, who returned to Canterbury,[41] where he laboured to reconcile Stephen and Henry, receiving them both there in Lent, 1154.

The coronation of Henry II was followed by changes in the diocese. The aged archbishop, being too infirm to accompany the king on his rapid journeyings, before long recommended for the chancellorship Thomas Becket, then archdeacon of Canterbury, and John of Salisbury became his own chief adviser and official. In spite of absence Becket continued in possession of the archdeaconry, and Theobald, when very ill and expecting to die, wrote to him in Normandy, where he then was with

---

[36] Gervase, *Op. Hist.* (Rolls Ser.), i, 134 ; ii, 386.   [37] W. R. W. Stephens, *Hist. of Engl. Ch.* ii, 153.
[38] *Lit. Cant.* (Rolls Ser.), i, p. lviii.
[39] Thorne, *Chron.* cols. 1810–14 ; Gervase, *Op. Hist.* (Rolls Ser.), i, 76–7, 147–8.
[40] *Epist. Cant.* (Rolls Ser.), Introd. p. xxxiii.   [41] Gervase, *Op. Hist.* (Rolls Ser.), i, 151 ; ii, 76.

the king, letters full of his longing to see once more both the king and his chancellor, 'the foremost of my counsellors, nay, my only one,'[42] as he calls him.

He died 18 April, 1161, with this desire unsatisfied, and it was more than a year before the accomplishment of his supreme work was secured, in the elevation of Thomas Becket to the primacy. During this interval the chancellor had been foremost in every fight in the expedition against Toulouse, and now protested with vehemence his unsuitability, but in vain. The justiciar, Richard de Lucy, went to Canterbury, accompanied by Walter, bishop of Rochester, and two other bishops, to urge the monks to elect Thomas. He was ordained priest in Canterbury Cathedral, 2 June, by Walter, bishop of Rochester, and consecrated archbishop next day by Henry, bishop of Winchester, assisted by thirteen bishops. At the king's request the pope allowed him to send for his *pallium* instead of fetching it in person. Henry also secured a dispensation for him to retain the seals, and was much annoyed at his refusal to do so. The archdeaconry he did not resign till he was asked to do so by the king six months later.

If the life of the archbishop had hitherto been unclerical, it had always been upright and pure. The consistency with which he now withdrew from affairs of state, living at Canterbury a life of austerity, his principal joy being to sit among the brethren reading in a quiet corner of the cloisters, was the cause of his undoing with the king, not only because of Henry's vexation at the loss of his services, but because it left the way open for his enemy, Gilbert Foliot, now translated to London, and the confidential adviser of the king. He added to his adversaries also by the vigour with which he set to work to recover all property that had been alienated from his see or let on lease.[43]

The history of the disputes with Henry that ended in his murder at Canterbury is of general rather than local interest. Kent witnessed the last stages of his secret flight in 1164, when after his haughty resistance to the Constitutions of Clarendon, and his defiance of the king at Northampton, he determined to escape to the pope. After being concealed by a priest at Eastry he reached Sandwich, and embarked in a small fishing boat there for the continent.

One of the immediate results of his stern fight for the privileges and immunities of the clergy, and the withdrawal of them even in criminal cases from the civil tribunals, was to deprive his diocese of his presence for considerably more than six out of the nine years of his primacy.

It was not until 22 July, 1170, that the reconciliation at Fréteval took place, and the meeting was no sooner over than difficulties arose about the restitution of the archbishop's property, and his reconciliation with excommunicated bishops. Becket embarked in the face of universal warning. All the way to Canterbury from Sandwich, his landing place, as it had been his point of departure, he was greeted by enthusiastic crowds; the cathedral was decorated in his honour, and he preached in the chapter-house from the text, 'Here we have no continuing city, but seek one to come.'

---

[42] John of Salisbury, *Epist.* (ed J. A. Giles), 48, 54, 63, 64, 70, 71, 78.

[43] After being present at the great council at Tours in 1163, at which a severe canon was made against all who usurped the goods of the Church.

It seems evident that he felt he had come back to die. The immediate cause of his murder was his unrelenting refusal to remove sentence of suspension and excommunication from the archbishop of York and the bishops of London and Salisbury, who crossed to Normandy, where the king was keeping Christmas, to invoke the protection of Henry.

Whatever may be the estimate of his life, or of the effect his long, fierce conflict with the king had on the history of the Church for whose rights he so stoutly contended, there can be no doubt that the history of Kent would have been very different but for his murder in the cathedral that followed the king's outburst of rage against 'the turbulent priest,' since this was to make the county for years to come the resort of pilgrims from the whole of the western world.

The king's remorse over his murder, so publicly expressed at the tomb, did not prevent him from keeping the see vacant for more than two years. At last the young King Henry was directed by his father to take steps for the election of a new primate, and finally, after a considerable period of discussion,[44] the bishops, the monks, and the king agreed in electing Richard, prior of St. Martin's, Dover. He took the oath of fealty to the king, 'saving his order,' and nothing was said as to his observance of the 'customs of the kingdom,' or, in other words, the Constitutions of Clarendon.[45] Alexander III confirmed his election 2 April, 1174, not only giving him the pall, but also the legatine office, and a letter confirming the supremacy of his see.[46] He consecrated him himself at Anagni, 7 April.

Richard returned to England to hear that a terrible fire had occurred in the cathedral, destroying the whole of 'Conrad's glorious choir.' He was received at Canterbury with great rejoicings, and enthroned 5 October, 1174. Later he accompanied Henry and his son on a pilgrimage to the tomb of Thomas Becket, at Canterbury, where the work of restoration was being prepared for by William of Sens.[47]

Before his death, 16 February, 1184, the old dispute as to supremacy had been renewed by York, and was left unsettled when that occurred. Another, with the abbey of St. Augustine's, had been arranged the previous year.[48]

He enjoyed the friendship and support of Henry, whom he entertained on several occasions, among others at Canterbury in April, 1177, after which he kept Easter with him at Wye. In August, 1179, he entertained the French king, Louis VII, on the occasion of a sudden and unexpected pilgrimage he made to the tomb of Thomas Becket. Henry II hastened to Dover to receive Louis on his disembarking, the archbishops and all the prelates who could be hastily assembled formed a grand procession to the door of the cathedral church, and three days of fasts, prayer, and vigils followed, accompanied by fabulous oblations, and a charter granting for ever 100 *modii* of wine, about which there was much subsequent negotiation.[49]

---

[44] Gervase, *Op. Hist.* (Rolls Ser.), i, 239.   [45] Ralph de Diceto, *Op. Hist.* (Rolls Ser.), i, 369.

[46] Ibid. 388–90 ; *Gesta Henrici II* (Rolls Ser.), i, 69, 70.

[47] The vast expenses of rebuilding were mainly defrayed by the generous oblations which poured in at Becket's tomb.

[48] Gervase, *Op. Hist.* (Rolls Ser.), i, 275–6, 296 ; *Gesta Henrici II* (Rolls Ser.), i, 209.

[49] *Lit. Cant.* (Rolls Ser.), i, Introd. p. lxvii ; *Hist. MSS. Com. Rep.* v, App. 460–1 ; Gervase, *Op. Hist.* (Rolls Ser.), i, 293.

The last Christmas of his life saw him at Caen with the king, pronouncing sentence of excommunication against all who disturbed the peace between Henry and his sons.

Mistrust of the regulars was shown by the bishop of Rochester, Waleran, who succeeded Bishop Walter in 1182; and at the time of Waleran's death, 29 August 1184, he was preparing, at the desire of the king, for a journey to Rome, where, it is supposed, he meant to solicit the pope to sanction the removal from his cathedral of the regulars by whom Gundulf had super-seded the seculars of its former chapter.[50] This bishop was the archbishop's own clerk, and his appointment to Rochester, according to Gervase,[51] took place in a fashion which exasperated the monks of Canterbury. In the end peace was restored by Alan, the prior of Christchurch. By his arrange-ment Waleran swore fealty to Christchurch in the chapter-house at Canter-bury in the presence of the archbishop. The senior monks not only declared that they had seen this done by Ascelin and Walter, but that it was customary for the bishop, before consecration, to do homage to the arch-bishop for the baronies held of him, and that on the death of a bishop of Rochester, immediately after his funeral his pastoral staff should be publicly carried to Canterbury and deposited in the cathedral until the consecration of his successor. A procession, therefore, was formed to the altar; Waleran read his profession in the presence of people, clergy, and archbishop, then laid the document on the altar, and took from it the staff and mitre. The archbishop having placed the mitre on his head, the new bishop dismissed the assembly with the episcopal benediction.[52]

The pacification of the monks of Christchurch resulted in the dis-satisfaction of those of Rochester; and the election of Waleran's successor, Gilbert de Glanville, which took place 17 July, 1185, was made the subject of a double protest from the monks of Christchurch,[53] because they considered that their rights had been infringed by the withholding of the staff, and because the election had taken place at the archbishop's manor-house at Otford. Deputations from the monks both of Rochester and Canterbury waited on Richard's successor, Archbishop Baldwin, previously bishop of Worcester, and a compromise was arrived at by his decision that the monks of Roches-ter should deliver the staff to him, and that he would then deliver it to the prior of Canterbury, who should carry it to Canterbury.

The primacy of Baldwin lasted barely six years, but was made memor-able by the bitter struggle it witnessed between him and his monks, in which he received loyal support from Glanville of Rochester, engaged at the same time in a contest with his own monks hardly less severe.

That Baldwin's policy was looked upon at the time as an attempt to restore the balance in favour of the parochial clergy seems clear from the words of Gervase, the Canterbury chronicler, who, in condemning the con-duct of Baldwin, says that he was 'seduced by the clerks.' Baldwin, a devout and learned man, was horrified at the secular mode of living adopted by the monks, and he was compelled to neglect the promotion of the learning he loved,[54] while the rich revenues of the monastery were expended upon

[50] *Diocesan Hist. of Rochester*, 77.
[52] Gervase, *Op. Hist.* (Rolls Ser.), 306, 307.
[54] Cf. *Epist. Cant.* (Rolls Ser.), Letter clxx.
[51] *Op. Hist.* (Rolls Ser.), i, 302, 306–7.
[53] Ibid. 324.

worldly magnificence, seventeen dishes being served up daily at the prior's table.

The first measure taken by the archbishop was to procure from Pope Lucius III, 15 March, 1185, a commission to reclaim the property alienated by his predecessors, and to reform the church of Canterbury.[55] The commission was renewed on the death of Lucius by his successor, Urban III, and in December, 1185, Baldwin came to Canterbury and confiscated the *xenia*, and his clerks took possession of the churches of Monkton and Eastry, and certain of the vills of the convent were seized. The monks appealed to Rome, but a mediation was effected, after which he restored the estates upon the convent renouncing their appeal, Baldwin retaining however both *xenia* and disputed churches. He gave Eynsford to John of Poictiers, archbishop of Lyons, a native of Kent.[56]

The monks of Christchurch maintained that as Canterbury was the mother church of England, the profession of obedience made by the suffragan bishops on their consecration was made rather to the convent than to the archbishop,[57] and the bishops were ready to co-operate with the archbishop in his scheme for establishing a collegiate church of secular clergy in his diocese, whose existence should counterbalance the undue power of Christchurch. Archbishop and bishops on 1 October, 1186, obtained from Urban III licence to found a college of clerks in honour of St. Stephen, and endow it with the churches in the archbishop's gift.[58]

In the last week of November, Baldwin and his clerks came to Canterbury to instal his new foundation for a time in the parish church of St. Stephen at Hackington, its northern suburb. The convent united in a second appeal, but on 17 December Baldwin proceeded to Hackington and instituted his canons, after which he returned to Christchurch and suspended Honorius, the prior, and the appellant brethren, closing the monastery and ordering the monks to stay within.

Not only all England, but all Europe took sides in the quarrel,[59] and though Henry II came in person to Christchurch, and begged the monks to renounce their appeal and accept arbitration, they refused to do so.

Emissaries from both sides started for the pope at Verona. Mandates adverse to the archbishop were issued by Urban, who died 19 October, but the new pope, Gregory VIII, annulled the mandates against him.

---

[55] Cf. *Epist. Cant.* (Rolls Ser.), Letters i, ii, pp. 2, 3, 4, 5.

[56] Another Kentishman who rose to high dignity in the French Church was Ralph de Serra (Sarre, in Thanet), dean of Rheims, who had been the friend of Thomas Becket, and warmly espoused the cause of the convent in their quarrel with Baldwin.

[57] By ancient custom in the first place, put on record by the great charter of liberties propounded by Archbishop Becket, it was required that every suffragan of the province should receive consecration in Canterbury Cathedral Church, unless he previously asked for and obtained from the chapter and prior a licence to be consecrated elsewhere. The importance of this is shown by the archbishop's obtaining a renewal of the privilege in a charter dealing not with the whole liberties, but this one only. *Lit. Cant.* (Rolls Ser.), Introd. xlviii. This was confirmed by the action of St. Edmund Rich, when he was opposed by the monks in his project of consecrating Bishop Grosteste at Reading ; he thereupon obtaining their consent, and making acknowledgement that the consecration of a suffragan should be celebrated nowhere but in the cathedral, unless by the dispensation and common consent of the whole convent. The privilege remained inviolate as long as the priory existed, and many of these licences for consecration elsewhere exist. Hasted, *Hist. of Cant.* i, 475.

[58] *Epist. Cant.* (Rolls Ser.), Letter vi. In this grant the pope regulated the disposal of the oblations at the tomb of St. Thomas, giving one-fourth to the monks, one to the poor, another to the fabric of the cathedral, and another to the archbishop to be used at his pleasure. Ibid. Letter dlxi. Another letter of the same date gave him power to build at Lambeth. Ibid. Letter dlx.

[59] St. Augustine's, however, hating impartially both archbishop and convent, held aloof.

Henry ordered the justiciar to take the new college under his protection,[60] and Baldwin issued injunctions for thanksgiving at Hackington for the annulling of the papal mandates.[61] But Gregory died in less than two months, and was succeeded by Clement III.

Baldwin, in concert with the king, sent the bishop of Rochester with a proposal to the convent, 9 January, 1188, and directed him to place under seal the treasure of the church. The sub-prior declined to receive restitution of the estates of the church on the archbishop's terms, and appealed to Rome. Steady opposition was offered to Baldwin under the leadership of the sub-prior Geoffrey, who suspended divine service; and by Baldwin's orders the monks were shut up in the convent for eighty-four weeks in a state of siege.

On the king's return, he sent orders to the sub-prior to resume divine service,[62] and summoned him with six brethren to a council on 11 February, but owing to the obstinacy of the monks, whose emissaries were busy at Rome, proposals for arbitration came to nothing before the archbishop left for Wales to preach the Crusade there.

On 26 January a papal mandate re-affirmed the last letters of Urban;[63] on 17 March orders were sent that persons who had violently entered the convent should be excommunicated, and a messenger bore instructions from the prior to the sub-prior to resume divine service.[64]

The archbishop's reply to the mandate of 26 January was to write to the college directing his servants to intrench the new buildings and put them in a state of defence.[65] When the prior of Faversham proceeded on 23 April to execute the mandate of the 17 March, this produced a riot, in which a nephew of Thomas Becket took part, and was committed to prison, with several other partisans of the convent.[66]

Before Baldwin's return on 31 July, after more than a year's absence, King Henry II was dead. The day after his arrival the archbishop summoned the officers of the convent to Wingham, but the messengers who were sent declared they had no power to make terms. On 5 August he came to the cathedral and subsequently, by the intervention of Queen Eleanor and the justiciar, the convent, after angry discussion, consented to receive restitution, the rights and privileges on both sides being reserved.

Richard was crowned 3 September, and refused to allow the legate appointed by Clement to enter England, bidding him leave the monks of Canterbury for himself to deal with. He confirmed the convent charters on 17 September, and desired the monks to accept the arbitration of a committee appointed by him. At last arbitration was accepted, and final judgement was pronounced in the chapter-house by the archbishop of Rouen, who declared that it had been adjudged by the king and the bishops that the archbishop had power to build himself a church wherever he pleased. The next day Baldwin, in the chapter-house, restored the estates of the convent which remained in his hands, and relieved the prior against whom the monks had objected, from his office; a deed was drawn up, and attested by the king and arbitrating prelates, recording the termination by compromise of the whole cause.[67]

[60] *Epist. Cant.* (Rolls Ser.), Letter cxxxiii.
[62] Ibid. Letters clxxvi, cclxxvi.
[64] Ibid. Letter ccxvi.
[66] Ibid. Letters ccxviii, ccxix, ccxxxvii.
[61] Ibid. Letter cxl.
[63] Ibid. Letter ccxiii.
[65] Ibid. Letter ccxxiii.
[67] Ibid. Letter cccxxxv.

Richard then left Canterbury, and the legate, who had been waiting at Dover for ten days, was allowed to visit the church. Before he was re-conducted with great reverence to Dover by the archbishop's clerks, he executed a secret deed declaring that the compromise had been extorted by fear, and was null and void of any effect prejudicial to the rights of the monks.[68]

The archbishop, who had decided to seek a more peaceful atmosphere by going on crusade, left England on 6 March, 1189. Before doing so he had directed that the collegiate buildings should be destroyed, and the material removed to Lambeth. He died at Acre in November of the same year. Before his successor was appointed, a letter of 20 May[69] following shows that the sub-prior Geoffrey had already returned; at his instigation the prior Osbert was driven to resign, and Geoffrey elected in his place. The monks sent to Rome for an injunction for the destruction of the remaining Hackington buildings, the confirmation of the secret act of the legate, John of Anagni, and the renewal of the acts of Popes Urban and Clement, all which were readily granted by Celestine III.

They petitioned the king for a free election, but finally on the pressing recommendation of Richard, then in captivity, chose Hubert Walter, bishop of Salisbury, whose election by the monks took place 30 May, 1193, before his election by the bishops, who were much displeased at this slight.

The buildings at Hackington were then already demolished and the chapel destroyed. Hubert, however, told the monks he felt bound in honour to complete the work of his predecessor, and in the hope of compromising matters proposed removing the college from Lambeth to Maidstone, and building there on the estates of the convent.

The king on 7 April, 1195,[70] and 13 June, 1196,[71] confirmed an exchange between Hubert and the church of Rochester, of Darenth for Lambeth, and this was again confirmed by him April, 1197.[72] Hubert then procured from Celestine a letter which placed the collegiate church of St. Stephen and St. Thomas at Lambeth in his hands.[73] He was now, by virtue of the exchange, lord of the manor of Lambeth, and had by the common law the right to build a religious house of any order he chose on his own estates.[74] He sent envoys to the convent, 16 November, not to ask the consent of the monks to his foundation, but to lay before them his scheme for securing their rights.[75] The monks rejected his proposals,[76] and a fierce campaign was carried on by both parties,[77] in which the king supported the archbishop, and the pope the monks, until at last it seemed as if the archbishop had won the day when the delegates appointed by Pope Innocent, 19 May 1199, to adjudge the case, gave judgement in favour of Hubert. The monks, however, prevailed on Innocent to rescind the powers of the delegates, and call the parties to Rome.[78] But the country was saved from further indignity by Hubert's coming to Canterbury to propose that the convent and himself should agree to elect delegates to arbitrate. This was done, and their decision pronounced 6 November, 1200, and ratified by the pope

[68] Gervase, *Op. Hist.* (Rolls Ser.), 481–3.
[69] *Epist. Cant.* (Rolls Ser.), Letter cccliv.
[70] Rymer, *Foed.* i, 65.
[71] *Epist. Cant.* (Rolls Ser.), Letter dlxvii.
[72] Ibid, Letter dlxviii.   [73] Ibid. Letter ccccxiii.
[74] Ibid. Introd. p. xciv.
[75] Ibid. Letters ccccxvii, ccccxviii, cccclxv.
[76] Ibid. Letter dlvii.
[77] Ibid. Introd and Letters ccccxiii, &c.
[78] Ibid. Letter dxlv.

30 June, 1201.[79] It was highly favourable to the monks, and Hubert lost all he had contended for.

It says much for his magnanimity that when once his great quarrel with the monks was settled, he seems to have lived on the best of terms with them.[80] He was careful of the temporal interests of his see, obtaining from Richard a renewal, afterwards confirmed by John, of the long lost privilege of the archbishops to coin money at Canterbury, and the restoration of property which Becket had claimed without success. He kept the buildings at Christchurch and on the archiepiscopal manors in good repair, and exercised a splendid hospitality at Canterbury. At his death he bequeathed a mass of treasures, including valuable books, to the cathedral, as well as the benefice of Halstow, whose revenues he directed to be appropriated to the precentor 'for the repair of the books.'[81]

John exclaimed ' Now for the first time I am king of England,' when he heard of his death, which occurred in July, 1295, at Tenham, when he was on the way to Boxley to compose a quarrel between the bishop of Rochester and his monks.

Gilbert de Glanville had given the same loyal support to Hubert as to his predecessor, and in the quarrel with the monks of Christchurch appeared again and again as mediator, and as champion of the archbishop. His claim, as chaplain of the province, to act for the archbishop in his absence, was disputed by the bishop of London more than once. At an assembly of clergy at Westminster, 1193, in the absence of the primate, he defended the dignity of Canterbury against the pretensions of York, and when Geoffrey, the northern archbishop, a natural son of Henry II, entered *quispiam crucem bajulans*, he admonished him that though they would have gladly greeted him if he had entered as was fitting, since he had entered in such presumptuous fashion, they would show him no reverence.[82]

Bishop Gilbert, who was learned in both canon and civil law, frequently acted in a judicial capacity, and in his long quarrel with his own monks it was he who came off victor, so that Edmund of Hadenham, the Rochester chronicler, after denouncing him for depriving the monks of many of the possessions Gundulf had bestowed on them, declared that it was a token of divine vengeance that he was buried without the rites of the church, his death in 1214 occurring five days before the removal of the interdict. The award, which deals with the presentation to several churches as well

[79] He was empowered to build at Lambeth, though not on the forbidden site, a church of canons to be endowed from the archiepiscopal estates or churches, but not to the extent of more than £100 a year. No church of secular canons was to be built by the archbishop without the consent of the convent. The alienated churches were to be held by their present possessors at a small rent for life, and when vacant to be apportioned between the almonry and archbishop. Hubert was to have the *xenia* for life.

[80] In his report to Innocent III announcing the terms of peace concerning the chapel at Lambeth, he asserted that there had all along been no real difference between himself and the monks. Cath. Libr. Cant. L. 133.

[81] In the period immediately following the Conquest Canterbury was one of the most important literary centres of England. The cathedral priory of Christchurch and the abbey of St. Augustine had two of the largest libraries in the country, and St. Martin's, Dover, was also generously endowed, as will be seen from the account of their possessions given in *Ancient Libraries of Canterbury and Dover : Catalogues of the Libraries of Christ Church Priory and St. Augustine's at Canterbury, and of St. Martin's Priory at Dover*, by M. R. James, Litt. D. *A Catalogue of the Library of the Priory of St. Andrew, Rochester*, A.D. 1202, described by W. B. Rye, in *Arch. Cant.* iii. 47, &c., shows that Rochester at this date was extremely rich in valuable works, and that though the monks had by this time declined in learning as well as devotion, they still possessed within their reach a storehouse of wisdom to consult at will. [82] *Lit. Cant.* (Rolls Ser.), Introd. i, p. xliii.

as with the *xenium* is given in *Registrum Roffense*.[83] A considerable part of the last years of his life was spent out of England in consequence of the interdict imposed 23 March, 1208. It was not till the year preceding his death that Kent was able to welcome the successor of Hubert Walter to his see.

The night after Hubert's death, the younger monks had secretly elected the sub-prior, Reginald, a vain, rash man, and dispatched him to Rome to seek consecration and the pall. The bishops and senior monks, who had not been consulted, appealed to Rome. John meanwhile got the bishop of Norwich, John de Grey, elected, and put in possession of the archiepiscopal estates, but Innocent, in December, 1206, declared the election of sub-prior Reginald to be irregular, and that of John de Grey equally so. When he ordered a fresh election to be made on the spot by the sixteen monks from Christchurch, who were at the papal court with full powers to act for the whole chapter, they had to confess that they had made a secret compact with the king to elect no one but John de Grey. The pope scornfully absolved them from their agreement, and recommended to them Stephen Langton, an Englishman, a cardinal, and one of the greatest theologians of the day, whom they then elected with but one dissentient voice, and Innocent wrote immediately to John requiring him to receive Stephen Langton as archbishop.

John refused, but the pope consecrated him at Viterbo, 17 June, 1207, whereupon John, finding that the monks of Christchurch adhered to Stephen, seized their property, expelled them by an armed force from the monastery, and committed the care of their house to their ancient enemies, the monks of St. Augustine's. The pope retaliated by commissioning the bishops of London, Ely, and Worcester to lay the kingdom under an interdict if the king would not give way. Their efforts at persuasion were unsuccessful, and in March, 1208, they published the interdict and fled.

For the next five years Stephen remained abroad, obtaining by his intercession with the pope some delay in the excommunication of the king, to whom he addressed warnings and remonstrance.[84] Envoys sent over to try and arrange terms of peace in 1211 failed in their mission, and in 1212 Innocent pronounced sentence of deposition on John and invited Philip of France to expiate his own sins by executing it. Preparations for invasion began at once, and John collected a large force which he posted at Dover and other ports and on Barham Downs, near Canterbury. Then followed, either at Swingfield preceptory, or, more probably,[85] at the church of the Knights Templars formerly existing on the west cliff of Dover, the surrender of his crown to the pope on 15 May, after which Pandulf, the legate to whom it was made, immediately returned to France, taking with him £8,000 of the £12,000 which John was to pay as compensation to the archbishop and the monks of Canterbury.

The papal protection which John had thus secured resulted in Philip's being ordered by the pope to desist from the invasion, on his preparations for

---

[83] Op. cit. pp. 52–5.

[84] In 1209 he came as far as Dover, with the bishops of London and Ely, under letters of safe conduct from the king and barons, for an interview. But the king, who would go no nearer than Chilham Castle, sent a demand for agreement to articles it was impossible to accept, and the exiled ecclesiastics returned.

[85] *Arch. Cant.* xiii, 231. This charter of vassalage given by John to the legate, was dated 'apud domum militum Templi juxta Doveram . . . xv die Maii anno regni nostri decimo quarto.' Matt. Paris also says that it was made 'apud domum militum Templi juxta Doveram.'

which he had already spent £60,000. John, not being yet released from excommunication, had to recall the primate, who landed at Dover 16 July, and at once proceeded to a reconciliation.

From this moment the archbishop appears as the champion of English liberties not only against John, but against the pope. He is said to have protested publicly and privately against John's homage to the legate,[86] and he lodged an appeal against the legate because he had used his office to support the king in filling up vacancies in the Church without regard either to its general interests, or to the diocesan and metropolitical rights of the primate and his bishops. It is to the credit of the Rochester monks that when the legate came to urge them to elect his candidate in succession to Gilbert de Glanville, they resisted his arguments, and deferred taking any steps until they received a letter from the king directing them to look to the archbishop, as they had been accustomed to look to the king and his predecessors. This was in consequence of the grant made to Stephen Langton, by charter of 26 November, 1214, of the advowson [87] of the church of Rochester, from which it resulted that the royal assent was no longer required in the election of the bishop, who would receive the temporalities of the see from the hands of the archbishop, and do homage to him for the estates belonging to the see. The monks were probably afraid to act, lest any steps they took might be to their prejudice in the future, and the archbishop paid several visits to the convent to urge an election, before this took place, 13 December, 1214. Though Stephen himself attended and took his seat in the chapter-house to admonish the brethren to provide a pastor worthy of his office, he and his brother Simon withdrew before the monks made their choice, which fell upon Benedict, precentor of St. Paul's, at that time presiding in the schools at Paris. With the king's concurrence the legate opposed the appeal at Rome, where the archbishop's case was so hotly upheld by Simon Langton that the legate was recalled.

By 1220 the archbishop had so far reasserted his position as to crown the young king on 17 May at Westminster Abbey. He presided, 7 July, 1220, at the magnificent ceremony of the translation of the relics of Thomas Becket, who had been canonized by Alexander III. It was one of unprecedented splendour, twenty-four prelates taking part, and mass being celebrated by the archbishop of Rheims, who had the day before dedicated the altar in front of the gorgeous new shrine. The concourse of pilgrims was enormous. Soon after, he went to Rome, where he obtained three important privileges : (1) That the archbishop of York should not carry his cross outside his own province, (2) that the pope should not appoint twice to the same benefice, (3) that during his own lifetime no resident legate should be sent again to England. As a result of the last, Pandulf resigned his commission in the summer of 1221.[88]

In December, 1226, Benedict, bishop of Rochester, who had laboured assiduously to repair the losses and damage inflicted on the cathedral and priory by John when he was besieging the castle,[89] died, and the election of his successor, Henry de Sandford, caused a renewal of the quarrel between the monks of Rochester and Christchurch.

[86] Matt. Paris, *Chron. Maj.* (Rolls Ser.), ii, 546.   [87] *Reg. Roff.* 56.
[88] Matt. Westm. *Flores Hist.* (Rolls Ser.), *anno* 1221.
[89] Edmund of Hadenham, *Angl. Sac.* (ed. Wharton), i, 347.

Henry de Sandford had been archdeacon of Canterbury, where he was succeeded by Simon Langton,[90] and was known as the 'great philosopher.' The beginning of his episcopate was marked by the use for the first time of the new choir of Rochester Cathedral.

Archbishop Stephen Langton died in July, 1228. The monks, having obtained the king's licence for election, then chose Walter de Eynsham, one of their own body, a man so unlettered and of such low morals that Bishop Henry de Sandford was sent with other royal envoys to Rome to oppose his appointment. Richard, chancellor of Lincoln, was appointed in his place, and consecrated 10 June, 1229, at Canterbury, by the bishop of Rochester. He died in August, 1231, on his way home from Rome, whither he had gone to appeal to the pope concerning the action of Hubert de Burgh, who had taken possession of Tonbridge Castle, the custody of which the archbishop claimed to belong by ancient right to the see of Canterbury. The pope had given a favourable hearing to this matter, and to his complaints concerning the system of pluralities, and the employment of bishops on secular affairs.

It was at this time that the Kentish ports, which had so long witnessed the departure of the Crusaders for the East, began to receive the friars, who were to carry on their work of revival in England. The order of Friars Preachers or Black Friars, known in later times as Dominicans, entered England in 1221, when a band of thirteen religious passed through Canterbury on their way to Oxford. At Canterbury, by the command of Stephen Langton, their prior, Gilbert de Fraxineto, delivered his first sermon to the English in a church where the archbishop had himself intended to preach, and they enjoyed Stephen's lasting friendship. The first band of Franciscans who arrived in England landed at Dover, 11 September 1224. They were penniless, and asked for nothing but the coarsest fare and meanest lodging. Five of the nine remained for a time at Canterbury, where they slept in a building which was used as a school by day. They were at first entertained by the Benedictines in the priory of Christchurch, and afterwards by the Poor Priests' Hospital, whose prior, Alexander, granted them the ground on which they built their first convent in the name of the corporation of Canterbury, they being by profession incapable of holding it in their own right,[91] though afterwards they acquired much property. One of these first Franciscans to come to England was a Kentishman, Haymo of Faversham, fourth general of the order, who died 1244.

The reforms successive metropolitans had at heart took effect at the earliest date in the county of Kent. At the synod of Westminster, held by Anselm in 1102, a canon was passed that parish churches should not be appropriated to monasteries without the consent of the bishop, and efforts were made both at Canterbury and Rochester to deal with this evil of appropriation. It was one of universal character, and a decree of the Lateran Council in 1179 empowered bishops to make arrangements for the due pastoral care of appropriate churches. After this decree the bishop generally required the monastic house to which an advowson had been

[90] The church of Teynham was appropriated to Archdeacon Simon Langton in 1227, in order to enable him to support the dignity of his office ; Cathedral Lib. Cant. E. 119 S., as also that of Hackington, H. 99.
[91] Hasted, *Hist. of Cant.* (ed. 1801), i, 165–6.

granted to nominate a clerk, who, if approved by him, was instituted to the living as perpetual vicar at a sufficient salary, 5 marks being the minimum allowed in England. Hitherto the monks had discharged their duty either through some member of their own community, or by appointing as vicar a stipendiary priest who was often sadly under-paid,[92] and sometimes churches had been farmed by the monks to the clerks for a small rent. It was in Kent that some of the earliest vicarages were established. Grants made by Bishop Ascelin, who died in 1158, include the free disposition and presentation of the vicarages of all churches, as well as references to 'John, vicar of the church of Southfleet.'[93] The collation of the perpetual vicarage in the church of Halstow, 'ad firmam annue pensionis unius marce,' must have been made about the year 1185.[94] A deed, bearing the seal of Archbishop Richard, in the Cathedral Library, Canterbury,[95] confirms an agreement made between the convent of Christchurch and Roger de Toftes concerning the vicarage of Toftes. When the award of Gilbert de Glanville, already referred to,[96] appointed a perpetual vicar at Sutton and the chapel of Wilmington about the year 1208, he endowed the vicarage with all the altarage, small tithes and offerings, and all lands then belonging to the church or in future to be bestowed on it, except the yard with the houses and meadow belonging to the monks, and the tithe of corn.[97] Another perpetual vicarage is referred to by Gilbert de Glanville in 1207 at the church of Yalding in the deanery of Malling, confirmed by him to the parish and church of St. Mary Magdalen, Tonbridge.[98] Among other early references to perpetual vicarages in Kent may be mentioned those of Coldred, 1206;[99] Adisham, 1207;[100] and Saltwood in 1219.[101]

Archbishop Edmund Rich, the nominee of the pope, was consecrated 2 April, 1234, and immediately gave valuable support to the national party against the king's foreign favourites, which action may have influenced Henry when he sent to Pope Gregory a request for the dispatch of a legate to execute necessary reforms in the church. The archbishop reproved the king for inviting the legate's presence without the knowledge and consent of the kingdom, but received him with respect. After long contests with the monks of Christchurch and Rochester, with the king, the pope, and even the archbishop of York, who did not spare him a revival of the old quarrel about supremacy, the archbishop retired to Pontigny, where he ended his days in the same year as a simple monk. He was canonized 1 January, 1247. The contest with the monks of Rochester had occurred through his refusal to consecrate Richard of Wendover, rector of Bromley, as bishop of Rochester in succession to Henry de Sandford. But when he pronounced him unfit the monks appealed to Rome, and their choice was confirmed 20 March, 1238. The consecration took place at St. Gregory's, Canterbury, and was followed before long by a dispute between the new bishop and Simon Langton, archdeacon of Canterbury, as to the duties to be respectively performed by the archdeacon and by the bishop of Rochester (who by ancient right and custom was the 'vicar' of the archbishop) when the see of

---

[92] A dispute between the convent of Christchurch and the vicar of Deopham showed that in 1177 they paid him but 2 marks yearly; Cathedral Lib. Cant. D. 7, S.; D. 13, S.

[93] *Reg. Roff.* 39, 40. [94] Cathedral Lib Cant. H. 89. [95] Ibid. T. 35.

[96] See above, p. 40. [97] *Reg. Roff.* 52. [98] Ibid. 46.

[99] Pat. 7 John, m. 6. [100] Ibid 8 John, m. 2. [101] Ibid. 3 Hen. III, m. 12.

Canterbury was vacant. It was settled that the archdeacon, whose jurisdiction was not to be interfered with, should give notice to the bishop as often as it was needful to dedicate a church, to hold an ordination, or to consecrate holy oil. If the archdeacon omitted to give notice the bishop might announce his intention of visiting the diocese, but if the bishop should be unable or unwilling to perform these offices, the archdeacon might secure the services of another prelate.[102]

The queen's uncle, Boniface of Savoy, was nominated by the king in 1241. It was not till the end of 1243 that the election was confirmed by Innocent IV, soon after his own accession, and in 1244 Boniface visited England for the first time. He obtained from the pope a grant of the first-fruits of all vacant benefices within his province for seven years to pay off the debt on the archbishopric, and instituted a rigorous visitation of his diocese, the monks of Christchurch being made to pay for deviating from their rules, as also were the monks of Faversham and Rochester.

When he died, 18 July, 1270, he had paid off the debts of his predecessors and built a hospital, afterwards converted into a college, at Maidstone. As the result of disputes as to feudal and other payments which Boniface had with Bishop Laurence, consecrated to Rochester 9 April, 1251, the bishop found himself much embarrassed for money. He added largely to the revenues of his church by procuring the canonization of Saint William, a Scotch baker who was murdered not far from Rochester when on pilgrimage to the Holy Land in 1201.

On the death of Boniface the monks elected their prior, Adam of Chillenden, to succeed him, and Prince Edward wished Robert Burnell to be appointed. Adam went to Rome to appeal, but the pope appointed Robert Kilwardby, a Dominican, who had been chosen provincial prior of his order in England in 1261, and who was a celebrated grammarian and theologian. His nomination to the cardinal bishopric of Porto and Santa Rufina by Nicholas III, 12 March, 1278, necessitated his resignation. He carried off with him 5,000 marks in money, as well as precious vessels, church ornaments, and manuscripts belonging to his see, and all the judicial records and registers of Canterbury, which his successor, Peckham,[103] endeavoured in vain to get back, with the result that the Peckham registers are the earliest now to be found at Canterbury.

John Peckham, the Franciscan friar who was appointed to the archbishopric by the pope to succeed Kilwardby, in spite of the wishes of the chapter and of King Edward, had won a brilliant reputation at Rome as *lector sacri palatii*: he was consecrated 19 February, 1279, and celebrated his entry into Canterbury in King Edward's presence on 8 October. Vowed to poverty by the rules of his order, he had to borrow 4,000 marks from Italian money-lenders to meet the heavy expenses at the papal court of his installation and to pay for his journey home, and when he arrived found that owing to the action of Kilwardby he had to beg for contributions from his suffragans to keep his household supplied with food at the beginning of his residence. It was so difficult indeed for him to pay back the debt he had been forced to incur that for some time he lived in fear of being excommunicated for default.[104]

[102] *Reg. Roff.* 60. [103] Cant. Archiepis. Reg. Peckham, fol. 17, 227, 550.
[104] *Reg. Epist. J. Peckham* (Rolls Ser.), i, Introd. p. lxviii.

His record in his diocese is one of single-hearted, unflinching reform, and searching visitations were carried out, resulting in severe dealings with cases of plurality and non-residence, invariably frequent where English benefices were held by aliens. His register shows that he even remonstrated with the pope for urging the appointment of one Bartholomew de Ferentino, whose ignorance of the English language, he maintained, disqualified him from serving a cure; he issued a commission to inquire by what right the monks of the abbey of St. Mary de Gloria in the diocese of Anagni near Rome held the church of Lydd as appropriated to their uses, and by what authority they were in the habit of 'demising the church to farm' without the archbishop's licence;[105] he called upon the non-resident and pluralist Petrus de Albi to take an early opportunity of visiting his cures and to distribute forthwith a sum of ready money to relieve the temporal wants of his long-neglected parishioners at Lyminge and Wrotham.

The first year of his archiepiscopate was spent mainly in Kent, where he made a progress through all the manors of the see, which must have resulted in a minute inspection of its churches; he made another, 1281–3, of equal thoroughness. His ordinations were solemnized at various of his own churches or chapels in the diocese, and he seldom delegated this duty to another bishop; his register shows that in April, 1284, he caused sequestration to be made of the income of the rector of Staplehurst and of that of thirty-three other churches in his diocese for failing to appear at the ordination held by him at Croydon in 1284.[106]

He was equally strict in his dealings with monastic houses; his ordinances of 1282, and the injunctions at his visitation of Christchurch in 1282, show him endeavouring to reform the monastery both as to the management of the temporal affairs of the house and as to its internal economy.[107] At Rochester in 1283 he found that the prior had not only wasted convent property, but that he had laid up a hoard for himself; this he was ordered to restore in three days.[108] Regulations were issued by the archbishop for the appointment of treasurers and rendering of official accounts,[109] and at Christchurch a strict rule was laid down that no presents were to be given except in the name of the prior and convent. Orders he gave at Rochester, where the people of St. Nicholas parish, having no church of their own, had the right of hearing mass at the altar of St. Nicholas in the cathedral,[110] that a parish church which had been begun and subsequently destroyed should be completed, were, however, disregarded. He made alterations also in the parish of Wingham.[111]

---

[105] Cant. Archiepis. Reg. Peckham, fol. 150a. The abbey, however, established its rights and exercised them until it delegated them by lease to Tintern Abbey in 1326; Cant. Archiepis. Reg. Reynolds, fol. 102b, 200a, 289b. [106] Arch. Cant. ix, 189.

[107] Reg. Epist. J. Peckham (Rolls Ser.), i, Nos. cclxi, cclxii.

[108] Ibid. No. ccclxxxvi. [109] Ibid. No. ccclxxviii.

[110] Ibid. No. ccclxxxvii. The new church was not completed until 1423; at its consecration the vicar and parishioners resigned their rights in the altar.

[111] On account of the number of inhabitants and widely scattered population he divided Wingham into four parishes in August, 1282: i.e. the church of Wingham, parish of 'Esse' (Ash), the church of Goodnestone, and the church of Nonington with the chapel of Womenswold. Reg. Epist. J. Peckham (Rolls Ser.), ii, No. lxiii. His completion of the foundation designed by Kilwardby for a provost and six secular canons in the church there shows him personally endeavouring, as far as his limited means allowed, to repair the state of neglect into which this large parish had fallen, by his private munificence. Cal. of Pap. Letters, i, 548.

His reforming zeal made it necessary for him to interfere more than once in the affairs of Rochester. When the famous Walter de Merton,[112] whose foundation at Oxford marks an epoch in English university life, died in October, 1277, the monks elected John of Bradfield, a monk of Rochester, to succeed him, and he was consecrated by Archbishop Kilwardby, 29 May, 1278: the registers of Archbishop Peckham show that Prior John of Rainham was deposed in December, 1283, by the primate on account of dishonourable practices in promoting the election of the late Bishop John.[113] On the death of John de Bradfield in 1283, Peckham opposed the election of John de Kyrkeby, archdeacon of Coventry, on the ground of his notoriously holding several benefices with cure of souls, and he was forced to resign.[114] Although the right of election had hereby devolved on the archbishop, he allowed the convent another choice,[115] and they elected Thomas de Ingaldsthorpe, dean of St. Paul's, who was consecrated at Canterbury 26 September following. The bishop, who is described by the Rochester chronicler as worthy of all praise, a man 'who deserved to have his place among the blessed,' was yet [116] when he had been a short time in office, according to the same chronicler, complained of by his monks. Peckham, on being asked to mediate, after a careful examination on the spot, reprimanded the bishop, replying to his plea that he had but done as his predecessors had done, with the retort, 'By St. Francis, if an angel had done it he had done ill!' It would appear that excellent relations existed between the bishop and monks after this intervention, or perhaps as a result of the 'perpetual silence' as to the matter in dispute enjoined on the prior and convent by the archbishop, when he pronounced his final decision in 1284. This established the authority the bishops claimed in the appointment of officials, and confirmed their right to the payment of the *xenium* on St. Andrew's Day, whether they kept the festival at Rochester or not.

In 1290 the final order was given for the expulsion of the Jews, and must have led to a considerable enrichment of the monastery of Christchurch, as the king made a grant to the prior and chapter of their houses in Canterbury;[117] an inquisition as to the property thus acquired mentions ten or twelve households and a synagogue, which was sworn as worth 18s. 4d. a year.[118] This was probably the remnant of considerably more extensive property previously owned by Jews there, as they must have been expecting such a culmination and preparing for it. There were jewries also at Faversham and Rochester, and the Pipe Rolls for the twelfth and thirteenth centuries show that Kent was the home of some of the richest of the race in

---

[112] In addition to his great educational work, he is remarkable for the important offices, including the chancellorship, which he had filled when he had accepted the bishopric of Rochester. It is characteristic of the monks of his day that all they could find to say of so noteworthy a bishop at his death was that he 'neither did himself, nor procured from others, any good thing for the prior and convent.' *Angl. Sac.* i, 352. He had, however, obtained for them the manors of Middleton and Cobhambury.

[113] On the other hand he is said to have resigned, cf. *Cal. of Papal Letters*, i, 487. Id. June 1286. Commission to the bishop of Norwich, at the request of John de Renham, priest, monk of Rochester. He had a papal dispensation as the son of a priest, and thereupon was ordained and held the office of prior for twenty-four years, with consent of the archbishop of Canterbury and the chapter of Rochester, but afterwards on better thoughts resigned the priory, and now begs a dispensation for having held it so long. This was granted.

[114] *Reg. Epist. J. Peckham* (Rolls Ser.), ii, Introd. ci.

[115] Ibid. Nos. ccccxliii, cccclxvi.

[116] Edmund of Hadenham; *Angl. Sac.* (ed. Wharton), i, 353.

[117] Cath. Lib. Cant. C. 1213.

[118] *Hist. MSS. Com. Rep.* ix, App. 77.

England.[119] In the quarrel between Archbishop Baldwin and the monks, Gervase says[120] that 'the Jews' sent both food and drink to the convent, and prayed in the synagogues for the continuance of the convent. Jury Lane, opposite All Saints' Church in Speed's map, was probably the site of the jewry in Canterbury, the synagogue being where the Saracen's Head Inn now is, according to Somner.[121] Of the gift of the Jews of England to King Richard, 1194,[122] the Jews of Canterbury contributed £241 12s. 4d. Rabbi Aaron, one of the most learned rabbis of his day, had his home at Canterbury. The Pipe Rolls as well as the chroniclers of the monasteries tell their tale of the part played by money-lending Jews in the county in these centuries ; now in an entry giving the heavy payments made to Ysaac of Rochester, or Benedict, Jew of Canterbury ; or again in an inquisition which sets forth that the 'Abbot and Convent of St. Augustine's were in nought bound to pay anything to any Jew . . . neither for themselves nor for any other abbot.'[123]

At Queenborough an act of peculiar villainy is recorded in connexion with this exodus. The proclamation gave the Jews the choice of quitting England within four months or of becoming Christians, but permitted them to carry away their movable property. The passage of the poor was to be at a moderate fare, and the sheriff of Kent was to see that no one was plundered. Some of the wealthiest secured a vessel and took on board their most valuable effects. They proceeded as far as Queenborough, where the captain allowed the vessel to drift on the sands, and then enticed the Jews to land and walk upon them. The tide turned and the captain left them to their fate, telling them to call upon their prophet Moses, who had brought their fathers out of the Red Sea. Rapin[124] says the vessel belonged to one of the Cinque Ports, and when the king heard of this he caused the master and several of the mariners to be hanged. Hemingburgh and other writers say that the captain obtained favour and reward.[125]

The Canterbury possessions of Aaron, son of Vyves,[126] were on too large a scale to be allowed to fall into the hands of the monks, and were assigned to the brother of the king himself. The Patent Rolls since the beginning of the reign of King Edward had contained repeated orders to the sheriff of Kent for scrutiny of the Jews' chests in his bailiwick.[127] A mandate to John of St. Denis, chaplain to the king, and archdeacon of Rochester, in 1280, directing him, as warden of the House of Converts in London, to see that certain regulations were carried out there, refers to convert fellow priests, and to the tenure of ecclesiastical benefices by converts.[128]

At this time, when the clergy were at last being called upon to contribute to the national burden of taxation, the question of money must have become one of pressing importance to them. A thirteenth-century archdeacon's memoranda of offences and deficiencies in the churches of Herne,

[119] *Vide* references given in *Jews of Angevin Engl.* (edited by Joseph Jacobs), 72–3, 82, 90, 93, 192.
[120] *Cp. Hist.* (Rolls Ser.), i, 405.
[121] *Antiq. Cant.* 124–5 ; cf. Brent, *Cant.* 116, 357 ; Hasted, *Cant.* i, 61, 126 ; ii, 364.
[1.2] P.R.O. Misc. R. 556, 2. Quoted in Jacobs, *Jews of Angevin Engl.* 162.
[123] Pipe R. 10 Ric. I–1 Jn. 164*a* ; quoted ibid.   [124] *Acta Regia*, i, 364.
[125] Furley, *Weald of Kent*, ii, 218.   [126] Close, 18 Edw. I, m. 4.
[127] Pat. 4 Edw. I, m. 35 ; 5 Edw. I, m. 11 ; see also Close, 12 Edw. I, m. 8.
[128] Pat. 8 Edw. I, m. 15, 17.

St. Nicholas, and All Saints, complains not only that books are deficient and chancels out of repair, but that executors are remiss, and that one parishioner has been allowed to die intestate,[129] thus reminding the modern reader of the importance of probate fees to the ecclesiastical courts, and that the parson, whose signature is nearly always affixed to wills as soon as these begin to be attested by witnesses, did not fail to see that the interests of his church were recognized by a number of advantageous bequests.

A grant of the tenths of all ecclesiastical benefices was made by Pope Nicholas IV to King Edward I in 1288 for six years towards defraying the expenses of an expedition into the Holy Land, and this taxation, finished in 1291, known as the *Taxation of Pope Nicholas*, is a most important record, as all assessments of the clergy, both to the king and pope, were regulated by it until a fresh survey, the *Valor Ecclesiasticus*, was made by King Henry VIII. It furnishes evidence as to the value of many benefices in the county at this time, although it is an incomplete account, the value not being stated in a considerable number of cases. The spiritualities of the diocese of Canterbury are valued at £4,733 6s. 4d. ; its temporalities, exclusive of the temporalities of the archbishop, at £2,753 4s. 5¼d. ; while the temporalities of the archbishop yielded a tenth valued at £135 10s. 9¾d. The value of the manors of the archbishop of Canterbury in Kent is given as £1,500 10s. 7d. The temporalities of the prior of Christchurch are valued at £1,066 8s. 1d., those of the abbot of St. Augustine's at £808 1s. 0¼d. The spiritualities of the diocese of Rochester are valued at £1,838 10s., its temporalities at £554 19s. 2d. Of these the temporalities of the bishop are worth £143 12s. 3d., those of the prior of Rochester £95 7s. 4d. On incomes below 10 marks no tenths were charged, and in Rochester a separate list is made of such benefices whose rectors are not beneficed elsewhere. Only seven out of a total number of forty-six such benefices are valued at less than £5 ; of the seven, six are valued at £4 13s. 4d., and one at £4 6s. 8d. These benefices appear also with the others headed 'Taxation of the Churches' in the bishopric of Rochester, where their values are also set down, though in many other instances the value of a benefice is omitted, only the total for the deanery being always given. As far as these figures go, they show no benefices in Kent with an income of less than 5 marks a year, which was the minimum stipend allowed in 1179 for a vicarage, and, except Teynham, with its chapel valued at £133 6s. 8d., no benefices are mentioned as being of very high value, though the totals show there must have been many such. Several vicarages are valued at considerably more than 10 marks. In the diocese of Canterbury the vicarages of Lydd and Reculver rise to £16 13s. 4d. each ; Wye is worth £10 13s. 4d. ; Tenterden, Helham, Tilmanstone, and Woodnesborough £10 ; Charing church and chapel, £8 13s. 4d. ; Lyminge church and chapel, and Benenden, £8 each. In the diocese of Rochester the vicarage of Wrotham is worth £13 6s. 8d. ; those of Green, East Greenwich, and West Greenwich, £10 ; and that of Petham, £8. It is clear that careful supervision had attended the institution of the ninety-one vicarages then in existence in Kent, and insisted on the assignment of a suitable income for the vicar.

[129] *Hist. MSS. Com. Rep.* v, App. 437.

The total number of churches and chapels given in Kent is 353. Of these the eleven deaneries of Canterbury furnish 243, the four deaneries of Rochester 110.

At the death of Peckham in 1292 the papacy was vacant, and in consequence of the delays which resulted at Rome, his successor, Robert Winchelsey, was not consecrated until 1294, when the ceremony was performed at the papal court at Aquila,[130] his enthronement taking place at Canterbury 2 October, 1295, before Edward I and a brilliant gathering. He had been unanimously elected by the chapter, and the king approved their choice ; the new pope before confirming him offered him a cardinalate, which he refused. In spite of his open rupture with the king on the question of clerical taxation, and of the disabilities this imposed on him, he was most active in administering his diocese. He strove to increase the number of monks and improve the discipline in the convent of Christchurch.[131] An attempt to deal with the convent of St. Augustine led to their appealing to Rome, and in March, 1300, obtaining exemption from archiepiscopal jurisdiction.[132]

Against this the archbishop appealed, on the ground that it had been procured by fraudulent misstatement ; and his suspension of the rectors and vicars of the churches on behalf of whom the abbey claimed privileges led again to their appeal to Rome.[133] In March, 1303, the pope delivered his final sentence,[134] that in all churches and parishes where the abbey had only the right of presentation, the archbishop should have the privilege of institution ; that in the other churches appropriated to the abbey the abbot and chapter should have the enjoyment of the temporals, but the archbishop should exercise spiritual jurisdiction.

In 1305 he was cited to Rome by Clement V, who had suspended him from office, and he left William de Testa and Peter Amaluina administrators of the diocese in both spiritual and temporal matters during his absence. The king declared that no foreigners should control the profits of English benefices, and replaced them by Humphrey de Walden ; but though the temporalities of the see were taken out of the hands of the *nuntii*, the king had to acquiesce in their continuing to exercise spiritual jurisdiction until the suspension was removed.[135] This was not until after the death of Edward, and was at the urgent request of Edward II.

Winchelsey was prominent as a member of the party opposed to the Despensers, and they demanded his canonization, but without success, when he died, 11 May, 1313.[136] In the preceding April the pope had issued a bull reserving to himself the appointment of the next archbishop. The monks elected a member of the prominent Kentish family of Cobham, but King Edward II wished Walter Reynolds, a favourite and confidant of his, to have the primacy. The young king wrote of him to the pope as ' not only useful, but indispensable,' and accompanied his recommendation of him with large presents of money.[137] These procured him not only the pope's confirmation,[138] in a bull published at Canterbury, 4 January, 1314, but also the grant of other

---

[130] Wilkins, *Concilia*, ii, 198. [131] *Hist. MSS. Com. Rep.* v, App. i, 446.
[132] *Cal. of Papal Letters*, i, 585.
[133] *Cal. of Papal Letters*, i, 614–15 ; *Lit. Cant.* (Rolls Ser.), Introd. i, p. lxiii.   [134] Ibid.
[135] *Lit. Cant.* (Rolls Ser.), Introd. i, pp. li-ii.   [136] Ibid. iii, 398–402.
[137] Ibid. 257 ; *Flores Hist.* (Rolls Ser.), iii, 156.   [138] Rymer, *Foedera*, iii, 228–9.

bulls conferring on him rights of visitation, absolution, dispensation, reservation, and other concessions. The king was present at the splendid ceremony of Reynolds's enthroning at Canterbury, and received much support from him.

That the primacy of this court favourite, so simoniacally appointed, should have been one showing an endeavour to limit the abuses of pluralities and ordination of unfit persons, and to reform the ecclesiastical courts,[139] may have been partly owing to his bestowing the fullest confidence on Henry de Eastry, the shrewd and experienced prior of Christchurch, whose advice he asked on every occasion,[140] as well as a consequence of the issue of the bull *Execrabilis* issued in 1317.[141]

The appointment of a successor to Thomas de Wouldham at Rochester, on his death in 1316, was delayed by the conflicting claims of Haymo Hethe, the choice of the monks, and John de Puteoli, whom the pope had provided ' out of his paternal care.' In this case the king urged the pope to ratify the choice of the convent, and after a delay of two and a half years Bishop Haymo obtained confirmation. Bishop Haymo is described as ' indifferent to preferment or wealth,' and behaved with great generosity to his monks, his many gifts to them including a magnificent mitre of St. Thomas of Canterbury which he had purchased, though the heavy expenses of his consecration at Avignon in August, 1319, forced him to depend at first on voluntary contributions from the clergy of his diocese, who rated themselves for his assistance to the extent of a shilling in the mark, besides offering a gift in kind during his first year.[142] The registers of his see, which date from his tenure of it, beginning at 1319, show him to have augmented and endowed several vicarages, and to have been active in building and regular in visitation. But the complaints preferred against him to the archbishop by his monks [143] include the general accusation that he was impatient and hot-tempered, changeable in word, and that he did not fulfil his promises.

He tried in vain to persuade the archbishop not to desert the king ;[144] but the archbishop ' feared the Queen more than the king in Heaven,' and, moreover, Henry de Eastry, who had been urging him to temporize, had hinted at the advisability of this desertion. His nerves also had been shaken by an encounter he had had with the mob in London, although Bishop Haymo, who seems to have had much more insight into the popular feeling, had warned him not to venture into the City, as all men hated the bishops.[145] Archbishop Reynolds had then fled in hot haste, borrowing without leave the horses of Bishop Haymo, who was forced to make his way to Rochester on foot with his household, well aware of the danger he ran, though he would have risked greater danger if he had remained. He reached Rochester in safety, but even there a riotous mob forced its way into his cathedral,[146] and talked of pillaging the convent, where for a week he had to lurk in shelter.

---

[139] Stubbs, *Const. Hist.* ii, 48–9.   [140] See letters of H. de Eastry in *Lit. Cant.* (Rolls Ser.).

[141] By this bull John XXII ruled that all clerks who held more than one benefice with cure of souls should within one month after notice resign all but one of their benefices. The immediate result of this was that the pope, who reserved to himself the benefices thus left void, had so large a number at his disposal that in spite of his active endeavours to bestow them to the best advantage, the bishops in 1318 wrote to him complaining of churches left without a parish priest, or with only an alien. The papal registers show that as time went on it became only a matter of form to obtain dispensations for plurality in Kent.

[142] Wm. of Dene, *Angl. Sac.* (ed. Wharton), i, 365–6.   [143] Ibid. i, 370 ; Wilkins, *Concilia*, ii, 556.

[144] Capes, *Hist. of Engl. Ch.* (ed. by Dean Stephen and Rev. W. Hunt), iii, 59.

[145] Ibid.   [146] *Angl. Sac.* i, 368.

To the Parliament which deposed the king the archbishop preached from the text ' The voice of the people is the voice of God,' and was commended by Prior Eastry for his desertion to the queen. But Bishop Haymo refused at the risk of his life to lend his voice to what was done, and stoutly braved the threats which followed his refusal.[147]

The new reign was inaugurated at Canterbury by a fierce dispute between the citizens and the convent, when Prior Eastry, supported by the archbishop, refused to contribute to the expense of providing soldiers required by the king in Scotland, and a royal writ was sent down to protect the monks.[148] General contempt for the clergy was characteristic of the period, and was an inevitable result of such conduct as the archbishop's, and of the insubordination displayed in the church. In 1336 one of his own monks preached against Bishop Haymo in his very presence, on the occasion of his visiting the chapter at Rochester,[149] and at the visitation of 1329 John of Frindsbury, rector of Bromley, whom he had deprived of his benefice for disobedience, expelled by force the incumbent instituted in his place by the bishop, and sent a chaplain to the cathedral church, where, abetted by the monks, he excommunicated the bishop by name at the altar.[150]

This insult may show that it was believed the bishop could not reckon on the support of Archbishop Mepeham,[151] who had succeeded Archbishop Reynolds in 1328. The archbishop had endeavoured to bring about a peace between the king and his own patron the earl of Lancaster, and alarmed the king by his presence at a meeting of the discontented barons, 18 December, at which Bishop Haymo refused to be present, though he incurred the archbishop's anger by this independence. But though Bishop Haymo was fined in consequence of the investigation of the charges made by his monks against him, he became the firm friend of Mepeham, and was the only bishop who supported him when he reopened in 1330 [152] the old contention about the right of the archbishop of York to bear his cross erect in the southern province.

The archbishop exhibited an extreme care for the rights of his see, and such anxiety to be surrounded by a reputable household that it was said that his brothers Edmund and Thomas were seeking for angels rather than men to be his servants and clerks. In 1329 he refused to institute the Cardinal Annibale de Seccano, archbishop of Naples, on whom the pope had conferred the church of Maidstone, and John XXII cited him to the papal curia and suspended him from office.[153] His activity in visiting his diocese involved

---

[147] Capes, *Hist. of Engl. Ch.* (ed. by Dean Stephen and Rev. W. Hunt), iii, 60.

[148] Ibid. 63.   [149] *Diocesan Hist. of Rochester*, 165.   [150] Ibid. 166.

[151] This archbishop was a native of Kent, where his family had held various clerical positions, and at the time of his election he still held the rectory of Tunstall near Sittingbourne, where one Edmund Mepeham had been appointed rector in 1286, and to which he himself had been instituted by Archbishop Winchelsey. During his absence at Avignon, where he was consecrated 5 June, 1328, he nominated his brother Edmund and William of Fishbourne his attorneys ; *Cal. Pat.* 1327–30, p. 199.

[152] Wm. of Dene, *Angl. Sac.* i, 370–1.

[153] *Chron. Edw. I and Edw. II* (Rolls Ser.), 347. The action of Pope John XXII in dealing with Kentish benefices strongly suggests that the bull *Execrabilis* was designed rather to place them at his disposal for distribution among his countrymen than to check plurality. Cardinal Raymond de Farges, cardinal deacon of St. Mary in Cosmedin, was inducted to the archdeaconry of Canterbury by papal mandate, 19 Nov. 1324, after it had been conferred by Edward II on John de Bruyton, and Archbishop Reynolds had collated him. The bull revoking the collation rebuked the archbishop for having performed it. John XXII also thrust into the rectory of Lyminge, which John de Bruyton held, his nephew Gaucelinus de Ossa, who came to England as legate, and obtained and held simultaneously three prebendal stalls in England, and the rectories of Hemingburgh, Stepney, Hackney, Pagham, Hollingbourne, and Lyminge, holding also that of Northfleet from 1320 to 1324. *Arch. Cant.* xv, 224.

him in the same year in disputes with the priory of St. Martin and the abbey of St. Augustine.

His short but troubled tenure of the archbishopric was followed by that of Archbishop John Stratford, who had been chancellor since November, 1330, and was until 1340 [154] the king's principal adviser, doing honest service in both posts.

He died in the year that saw the beginning of the great plague, 23 August, 1348 ; and before little more than a year had passed, three archbishops in succession had been appointed to the throne he left vacant. John de Ufford, who was provided by the pope in November, was carried off by the pestilence in the following June ; his successor, Thomas Bradwardine, died of it in August, and Simon Islip was elected 20 September, 1349. Bishop Haymo, who is spoken of as 'aged and decrepit' in 1349, withstood its ravages, and did not die until 1352.

The numbers of the secular clergy were so thinned by death that the services were with difficulty maintained in the parishes, and those who came forward to fill the vacancies were often illiterate men. To remedy this, Archbishop Islip, ten years after his election, founded Canterbury Hall, Oxford ; it does not appear that he intended it to be a place of education for Benedictine monks only, but disputes between the seculars and the monks during the archbishopric of Simon Langham ended in the expulsion of the seculars in spite of his statutes, and until the college itself was swallowed up by Cardinal College it was esteemed a daughter of the monastery and a training place for monks.

The decimation of the population produced by the Black Death meant a serious falling off in offerings given to the clergy, at the same time that the cost of living was enhanced by the scarcity of labour. Archbishop Islip tried also to supply the lack of priests by stringent legislation, and directed that ' if any priest of our province, under any colour whatsoever, receive more by the year than 5 marks without cure of souls, or 6 marks with such cure, let him *ipso facto* incur sentence of suspension from his office, unless within a month he pay what he received over and above that sum to the fabric fund of his church.' [155]

This canon, which is said to have driven priests to theft,[156] inevitably led to reluctance to accept such cures, and in 1352 the archbishop drew up other constitutions ordering the deprivation by the bishops of those who refused to undertake the pastoral functions when called upon.[157]

Bishop Haymo showed a better appreciation of the situation in his dealings with the beneficed men who had left their cures, and with those who refused to perform their office at the usual stipend. By an order of the archdeacon, dated 27 June, 1349, he commanded them under pain of interdict and suspension to return to their parishes, but for the present gave permission to rectors and vicars whose incomes fell short of ten marks to receive such fees as would raise their benefices to the normal value.

How many of the secular clergy were carried off it is impossible exactly to say, but the diocesan registers prove the number of institutions in these years to have been enormously increased, while these ordinances show that

[154] He resigned the seals 20 June, 1340. *Foedera*, ii, 1126.
[156] Walsingham, *Hist. Angl.* (Rolls Ser.), i, 297.
[155] Wilkins, *Concilia*, iii, 1, 2.
[157] Wilkins, *Concilia*, iii, 50.

the pestilence, as would be expected, raged heavily in Kent. The bishop of Rochester, out of his small household, lost four priests, five esquires, ten attendants, seven young clerics, and six pages, ' and so there did not remain any to serve him in any office.' At Christchurch, on the other hand, the records state that only four of the brethren died in 1349 of the plague, then at its fiercest. This has been attributed to the great drainage works then existing there, but at a subsequent visitation before the century was out the monastery suffered severely.[158] In 1390 an indult to the prior and convent of Rochester directs that they may have six monks ordained deacon when they have arrived at their eighteenth, and priest when at their twenty-third year, the number of monks of sufficient age having been diminished by pestilence and other causes.[159]

In other directions Archbishop Islip showed himself active in maintaining church discipline, and in 1353 arrived at a settlement of the age-long dispute with York. By this the northern archbishop was allowed to carry his cross erect in the province of Canterbury on condition that every archbishop of York within two months of confirmation should present to the shrine of St. Thomas a golden image of an archbishop or jewels to the amount of £40. This decision was confirmed by Clement VI.[160]

His enthronement at Canterbury was private, on account of the Black Death, and the monks, who resented the absence of the usual lavish festivities accompanying the ceremony, ever after described him as niggardly. The vicars, condemned to starve on 5 marks yearly, might have done so with more justice, for to the monks of his own cathedral, in spite of his poverty, he behaved with generosity, restoring to them the churches of Monkton and Eastry in his lifetime, and leaving them magnificent bequests in his will. To Dover Priory he gave Buckland parsonage and Bilsington parsonage ; and the monks of St. Martin's, Dover, he released from their old dependence on Christchurch. By a charter dated 1363 he restored to the monks of Rochester the church of Boxley, which since the time of Theobald had been in the hands of the archbishop.[161] Dean Hook [162] thinks that this last concession may have been previously held out to induce the monks to accede to his wish that his nephew, William Whittlesey, should succeed Bishop John de Sheppey at Rochester. He had consecrated him at Otford, 6 February, 1362.

The fourteenth century witnessed a growing jealousy of alien influence in the church,[163] and when Simon Langham (who succeeded Islip in 1366) after showing his sympathy with the regulars at Canterbury College accepted a cardinal's hat offered him in 1368 by the pope, without consultation with the king, Edward's wrath drove him hastily from England, after his temporalities had been confiscated without delay.

Simon Langham was succeeded by William Whittlesey, who had been translated to Winchester two years after his appointment to Rochester, where he had been succeeded by Thomas Trilleck, dean of St. Paul's, consecrated to Rochester by Cardinal Guido, 26 May, 1364. Archbishop Whittlesey had been long and closely connected with Kent since he took his doctor's degree

---

[158] Hasted, *Cant.* iv, 366.   [159] *Cal. of Papal Letters,* iv, 366.
[160] Wilkins, *Concilia,* iii, 31-2.   [161] *Reg. Roff.* 180.   [162] *Lives of the Archbishops,* iv, 225.
[163] Inquiries as to aliens holding benefices were made at Rochester and Canterbury at this date. *Hist. MSS. Com. Rep.* v, App. 427.

in canon and civil law at Oxford.[164] At a council held at Westminster in 1374 to debate Pope Gregory's demand for a subsidy as lord paramount of England, after much pressure he was induced to declare, 'I am of opinion that the pope is not lord here,' to which all the prelates agreed, and the pope's demands were disallowed.[165]

He was succeeded in 1374 by Simon Sudbury, translated by papal bull from London to Canterbury. Attached to the interests of John of Gaunt, Sudbury was suspected of sharing the heretical proclivities of the Londoners, and was urged by his suffragans to take action against Wycliffe, whom he summoned before him in 1378. He bade Wycliffe keep silence on the matters in question, and allowed him to end his days in peace at Lutterworth.

In 1376 he made a visitation of his diocese, and another in 1378, when his authority was resisted by the abbey of St. Augustine, which appealed to Rome on the ground of its exemptions. A bull of Urban V against pluralities called forth returns during the primacy of Archbishop Langham which show this evil to have been widespread in Kent, and both his register and that of his successor contain numerous entries of licences for non-residence, its invariable accompaniment, but these grow less numerous in the register of Archbishop Sudbury. One of the greatest pluralists of the age was Audomar de la Roche, archdeacon of Canterbury, who was finally deprived of all his benefices and dignities by the archbishop in 1379 for complicity in a dangerous political plot in the interests of the French king ; and the king thereupon granted to Archbishop Sudbury the profits of his archdeaconry, of his rectories of Lyminge and Teynham, and of his vicarages of Hackington, St. Clement in Sandwich, and St. Mary in Sandwich, to carry out the great work he was engaged on in the nave of the cathedral. In 1378 the archbishop had called for voluntary contributions for this work of building ; he spent on it large sums of his own, and did very valuable work also in rebuilding the west gate and a great part of the north wall of Canterbury.

The sermon preached at the coronation of King Richard II by Thomas Brinton, the monk appointed to succeed Bishop Trilleck at Rochester[166] in opposition to the wishes of the chapter (who had chosen their prior John of Hartlip) by Pope Gregory XI, shows that this bishop realized the conditions which were to bring about the Peasants' Revolt of 1381, a revolt which had its starting place in Kent. He exhorted the people 'cheerfullie and without grudging to put to their helping handes for the aide of the king and realme,' but also 'admonished the lords not to be so extreme and hard towards the people.'[167] The Lollardy then taking firm hold in the county probably helped to incense the Kentish mob in London against Sudbury, as well as the fact that John Ball, whom he had imprisoned at Maidstone, where he was released from gaol by the rebels, had for some time excited the people against the clergy in churches, churchyards, and market-place, and now, when he accompanied the Kentish men to London and met with enthusiastic receptions at Canterbury and at Rochester, stirred up his hearers everywhere against the archbishop, at whose murder he was present. The records dealing with the

---

[164] He had held the benefices of Ivychurch and Cliffe, and his uncle, Archbishop Islip, had made him his vicar-general, and then dean of the Court of Arches, before he was elected to Rochester.

[165] Capes, *Hist. of Engl. Ch.* (ed. Stephens and Hunt), iii, 98.

[166] In 1372.

[167] Holinshed, *Chron.* iii, 417.

insurrection, which seems to have affected the whole of Kent, show that while some of the clergy in the first place assisted Wat Tyler to proclaim that the commons should rise, the clergy and their parsonages were in many others made the subject of special attack.[168]

The murder of the archbishop on Tower Hill by the Kentish rioters, 14 June, 1381, was followed by the transference of Bishop Courtenay from London, where he had already shown his aversion from Lollardy, to Canterbury. In Kent, in order to protect himself from such a fate as his predecessor's, he obtained the licence of the king and of the monastery to pull down his less necessary residences, and built and embattled a great castle at Saltwood, which he made his principal residence in the county. He made a visitation of his diocese in 1393, beginning at Lenham. Though his primacy witnessed much legislation in Parliament against heresy, his registers do not show that persecution had yet begun in his diocese.

He died in July, 1396, and his successor, Thomas Arundel, showed at once that he was determined to resist innovations. The following year Arundel's connexion with the house of Lancaster led to his disgrace and banishment, but he returned with Lancaster in 1399, and Richard's death was followed by his restoration to the archbishopric and to the possessions of the see, which during his exile had been in the hands of Roger Walden, dean of York. Early in 1401 the statute *de Hæretico Comburendo* was passed ; to the end of his life he waged furious warfare against Lollardy, and the dungeons of Saltwood were employed in housing his victims. Among these one of the most notable was John Purvey, the intimate friend of Wycliffe and translator of the Bible, who, after being grievously tormented in the prisons at Saltwood, was brought before Convocation, 1400–1, just after William Sawtrey had been burnt for heresy ; when, terrified by this grim example, he recanted at St. Paul's Cross.[169] He was rewarded with the vicarage of West Hythe in 1401, but resigned his living in October, 1403, and under Archbishop Chicheley was imprisoned again in 1421.

The bishops of Rochester meantime had been employed by their archbishops in investigating heresy, and both Thomas Brinton and his successor William of Bottlesham [170] were included among the jurors who pronounced against Wycliffe when an inquiry into his tenets was ordered by Archbishop Courtenay, and William of Bottlesham was also appointed to inquire into heresy at the university of Oxford. John of Bottlesham, chaplain to Archbishop Arundel, who succeeded William of Bottlesham at Rochester in 1400, attended on the primate at the degradation of William Sawtrey. Bishop Richard Young, who succeeded John of Bottlesham in 1404, was translated from Bangor by papal provision.

---

[168] Cf. 'Presentationes de Malefactoribus qui surrexerunt contra dominum regem,' 4 & 5 Ric. II. Quoted in *Arch. Cant.* iii, 66, &c. According to No. 2, the jurors say that William the chaplain, officiating in the church of St. John in the Isle of Thanet, and Stephen Samuel made proclamation there enjoining the breaking open of the house of William of Medmenham at Manston, which was done, and books and muniments burnt. No. 3 gives evidence to the same effect, implicating John Taylor, sacrist of the church of St. John, and John Bocher, clerk of the said church, in the making of the above proclamation 'by commission of John Rakestraw and Watte Tegheler.' Insurgents also broke into the parsonage house of Staplehurst and trod underfoot and destroyed the goods and chattels of John Granton, the parson there.

[169] Capes, *Hist. of Engl. Ch.* (ed. Stephens and Hunt), iii, 179.

[170] Bishop of Llandaff when he was translated to Rochester, 1390 ; he was a friar of learning and eloquence, and in a sermon preached before Convocation in 1399 he admonished the clergy at court to return to their benefices and reside on them. He preached strongly against pluralities. He died Feb. 1400.

In 1409 Kentish heresy received a powerful impetus from the marriage of Joan, Lady Cobham, a Kentish heiress whose estate roll included Cobham Manor and Cooling or Cowling Castle, with Sir John Oldcastle, a prominent Lollard of Herefordshire. His knightly prowess and uprightness had won him the affection of King Henry V, whom it is said he did his utmost to convert.[171] In April, 1410, Archbishop Arundel laid the churches of Hoo St. Mary, Hoo St. Werburgh, High Halstow, and Cooling, all on the estates of Lady Oldcastle, under an interdict because of the unlicensed preaching in them of 'Sir John the chaplain, staying with Sir John Oldcastle,' and the chaplain was cited to appear in his court.[172] In the first meeting of the Convocation of March, 1413, John Lay, chaplain, was denounced as a heretic, and confessed to having celebrated that morning in the presence of Oldcastle, though unable to produce the licence of his ordinary.[173] Convocation accumulated fresh evidence against Oldcastle as one of the most influential supporters of the heretics. The archbishop, after describing him as their principal leader, wrote that

> especially in the dioceses of London, Rochester, and Hereford, he has sent Lollards to preach, not licensed by the bishops, and has been present at their wicked sermons, grievously punishing with threatenings, terrors, and power of the secular sword, such as withstood him.

He stood too high in the regard of the king, however, for the clergy to dare to proceed against him without first enlisting Henry on their side, and the archbishop waited on the king at court to lay his complaints before him. Henry desired him to deal leniently with Sir John, and in the meantime tried in a personal interview to reason with him. But his arguments led to his estrangement from his old comrade in arms, and he authorized the archbishop to proceed against him ; a summons was sent with a citation to Cowling, but Oldcastle refused to accept personal service, and another citation was affixed to the doors of Rochester Cathedral, 5 September, requiring him to appear before the archbishop at Leeds Castle, near Maidstone, on the 11th.[174] These citations were twice torn down by his friends, and, as he failed to appear, he was declared contumacious, and excommunicated. He submitted a written profession of belief to the king, who declined to accept it ; he was arrested in the Privy Chamber, and committed to the Tower,[175] when he was brought before the archbishop and the bishops of London and Winchester, and at last declared a heretic and handed over to the secular arm. His escape from the Tower was followed by Lollard conspiracies which are matter for general rather than local history, but it is probable that Kent furnished some of the hiding places in which he successfully concealed himself until he was finally captured and burnt as an outlaw, a heretic, and a traitor in 1418, and the sympathy won for him by those long years of pursuit, and by his terrible death, would do much to spread the doctrines for which he suffered. In 1416 a former chaplain of his, Robert Holbech, who, though excommunicated for heresy, had continued to celebrate mass and preach in the churches of Cobham, Cooling, and Shorne, was brought for a second time before Archbishop Chicheley, and asked pardon. In the end Bishop Young persuaded him to abjure, and absolved him on condition that he should not say mass

[171] *Gesta Henrici V* (Rolls Ser.), 2. [172] Wilkins, *Concilia*, iii, 329. [173] Ibid. 338.
[174] *Fasciculi Zizaniorum* (Rolls Ser.), 436 ; Walsingham, *Hist. Angl.* (Rolls Ser.), ii, 292.
[175] *Fasciculi Zizaniorum* (Rolls Ser.), 437.

without a dispensation from the pope, and that he should confess his errors at Paul's Cross. The manner in which Kentish heretics summoned before Archbishop Chicheley disappeared and successfully concealed themselves from diligent searching shows to what an extent the public feeling in his diocese was on their side.[176] One of the most active agents in the spread of the new doctrine was William White, a priest. Though his conviction and condemnation, which resulted in his being burnt at Norwich in 1428, followed on his administrations in Norfolk, where most of the heretics of his day were said by Foxe to have been his converts, Kent had been the scene of his earlier labours, and his success there had led to his being cited before Convocation in 1422, when, under urgent pressure, he renounced, and regained his freedom, but only to use it in such a fashion that in the end he suffered at the stake.[177]

In 1423 the archbishop proclaimed an indulgence to all who should in that year make a pilgrimage to Canterbury, and was sharply rebuked by the pope for his presumption.[178] This was among many direct affronts and rebukes directed by this pope against the archbishop ; and when the bestowal of a cardinalate on Archbishop Kemp of York, who claimed precedence in right of it over Canterbury, resulted in the dispute being referred to his successor, Pope Eugenius, it was decided in favour of Archbishop Kemp on the ground that cardinals were set by the pope over the universal church.

Chicheley had begged to be allowed to resign when he died 12 April, 1443. His name stands high above that of other primates of the fifteenth century, but the labours of diplomacy and statecraft in which he was involved made his connexion with his diocese one of which there is not much to be recorded.

For the same reason the primacy of John Stafford, his successor, was one which left no mark, though he did good service to the cause of peace in Kent during the rebellion under Jack Cade in 1450.[179] He was bishop of Bath and Wells and chancellor (the first styled lord) when he was promoted to Canterbury 13 May, 1443.

His successor, John Kemp, translated from the archbishopric of York by papal provision,[180] and prominent also in the diplomacy and statecraft of

---

[176] Foxe, *Acts and Monuments*, iii, 540–1. *Anno* 1417, on the 'affliction and trouble in Kent under Chicheley.' 'Many . . . for their faith and religion were greatly troubled and vexed, especially in the diocese of Kent, in the towns of Romney, Tenterden, Woodchurch, Cranbrook, Staplehurst, Benenden, Halden, Rolvenyden, and others ; where whole households, both man and wife, were driven to forsake their houses and towns for danger of persecution ; as sufficiently appeareth in the process of the archbishop Chicheley against the said persons, and in the certificate of Burbath, his official, wherein are named the following sixteen persons : W. White, priest ; Tho. Grenested, priest ; Bartho. Cornmonger, John Wadnon, Joan his wife, Tho. Everden, Wm. Everden, Stephen Robin, W. Chiveling, John Tame, John Fowlin, Wm. Somer, Marion his wife, John Abraham, Robert Munden, Laurence Coke. These being cited together by the bishop did not appear : whereupon great inquisition being made for them by his officers, they were constrained to fly their houses and towns and shift for themselves as covertly as they might. When Burbath and other officers had sent to the archbishop that they could not be found, then he directed down an order that citations should be set up for them on every church door. . . . But notwithstanding, when they could not be taken, neither would appear, the archbishop, sitting in his tribunal seat, proceeded to the sentence of excommunication against them. What afterwards happened to them in the register doth not appear.'

[177] Capes, *Hist. of Engl. Ch.* (ed. Stephens and Hunt), iii, 189.

[178] The jubilee of 1420 was a most successful celebration ; according to an entry in a contemporary record of the city, 100,000 pilgrims visited the shrine, and the oblations reached the sum of £600 (*Lit. Cant.* iii, p. xxxv). The festival of 1470 was the last, as it was extinguished in 1520, owing to the extravagant demands made then by the pope, Leo X, for participation in the profits of the impending festival.

[179] Fabyan, *Chron.* 623 ; Ramsay, *Lanc. and York.* ii, 132 ; *Lit. Cant.* (Rolls Ser.), iii, 205.

[180] Wharton, *Angl. Sac.* i, 379.

his times, seems to have utterly neglected the ecclesiastical duties of his high office during his short tenure of it. He was a native of Wye, in Kent, and showed his affection for his birthplace by the foundation of a college of priests there. He died 22 March, 1454, at Lambeth, and Cardinal Thomas Bourchier was translated to Canterbury from Ely 22 April, 1454.

At Rochester the record of Bishop John Kemp (1419–21) had been as uneventful as that of his subsequent rule at Canterbury. John Langdon, his successor, appointed by papal provision to Rochester, 17 November, 1421, was also engaged on numerous embassies and missions before he died at the Council of Basle, 30 September, 1434, and like his predecessors had also been appointed to inquire into the doctrines of Wycliffe. At Basle his place was taken by Thomas Brown, who succeeded him as bishop, but was translated to Norwich in 1436, after augmenting the vicarages of Wilmington and Kingsdown, and admonishing beneficed clergy to reside on their cures, as well as showing considerable zeal against 'heretics' and 'preachers.' William Wells seems also to have been active in visitation and the discharge of his duties. He died in 1444, and was succeeded by John Lowe, confessor to Henry VI, who held the bishopric for a somewhat longer period, dying in 1467.[181] He made an agreement with the citizens of Rochester respecting his jurisdiction in the town. Three short episcopates followed his; that of Thomas Scot or Rotherham, translated to Lincoln in 1471, who in his three years of office was employed on various embassies; and that of John Alcock, master of the Rolls when he was appointed to Rochester in 1472;[182] he was translated to Worcester in 1476, being succeeded at Rochester by John Russell, archdeacon of Berkshire, consecrated 22 September, 1476, and then keeper of the Privy Seal. Bishop Audley's connexion with Rochester was longer, and between his consecration in 1480 and his translation to Hereford in 1492, he united the churches of West Barming and Nettlestead, and augmented the vicarage of St. Margaret's, Rochester.

The study of church life in Kent in the fourteenth and fifteenth centuries brings the mind back to the open road and the pilgrims of Chaucer, who, year in year out, must have wended their way along the roads that led to Canterbury and the cathedral, though the groups were naturally larger and more frequent at the two great commemorations, those of the death of St. Thomas in 1170, and his translation in 1220.

In the cathedral itself, the chantries founded in 1363 by the Black Prince as the price of the dispensation allowing him to marry his cousin Joan, the Fair Maid of Kent, are an instance of a custom by which the resources of cathedral and parish church alike must, at this time, have received valuable augmentation. Mostly founded in the fourteenth and fifteenth centuries, chantries had already begun to exist in Kent in the thirteenth century. They were of every degree, from these chantries of the Black Prince or such sumptuous endowments as those which Archbishops Arundel, Chicheley, Bourchier, and later Warham, established in the cathedral for the performance of daily offices at an altar near the tomb of the founder, to the more

---

[181] Under him Kingsdown was constituted a rectory, and so, but for the patronage, dissociated from the monastery of Rochester; the vicarage of Speldhurst was also constituted a rectory, and its emoluments increased, and the rector of Murston was discharged from residence till there should be a conflux of people to the place.

[182] He also acted as chancellor in 1475.

humble chantry established in the parish church,[183] or in a side chapel, or in distant chapels which served the purpose of chapels of ease to the mother church, and which were endowed with an income sufficient for the support of one priest, bound to perform certain religious offices on behalf of the founder and his nominees.[184] The religious services were always carefully prescribed, and varied but little in the recitation of the daily offices, and the vespers and nocturns for the dead. In country churches the chantry priest was expected to act as assistant to the parish priest in the services of Sundays and festivals. Another kind of chantry is indicated in the indentures by which the chapter of Canterbury pledged themselves to provide commemorative services for Archbishop Courtenay, in gratitude for benefits already conferred on them, or in which the chapter requited the favour of Richard II, who had relieved them of burdensome corrodies, by annual celebrations, when the priests were monks of the monastery who were told off to officiate for a small payment.[185]

It can easily be imagined how the chantry priests would add to the dignity of church service by the number of ministrants assisting, in a town which, like Sandwich, contained many chantries. Another want was supplied by the chapels at each end of the bridge at Rochester, expressly built for the use of travellers.[186]

A similar institution was that of collegiate churches or colleges, which consisted of a number of secular clergy, living under the government of a dean, warden, provost, or master, and having for the more solemn performance of divine service chaplains, singing men, and choristers belonging to them.

Yet another way in which the resources of the church were supplemented was by the institution of gilds, which, though in the first place organized for industrial and commercial purposes, were often of a distinctly religious or charitable nature, and in most cases contributed to the support of a priest, an obit, or lights. Besides the church worship in common and the processions on the festival day of the patron saint enjoined in their regulations, these gilds frequently undertook the performance of religious plays in the different towns of Kent. The records of the corporations of Lydd and Romney show that performances by the players were frequent, among the plays acted being those of St. George, the Resurrection of our Lord, and the Interlude of Our Lord's Passion ;[187] these representations were not only given in the town to which the players belonged, but from the accounts of fees, which include payment for John Baptist's painted coat and for the cotton coat of Judas, it appears that the players went from town to town, and that quite small parishes

[183] Cf. the chantry for two priests in the church of Stoke founded by Nicholas de Carreu, sen., lord of the manor of Malmeynes, in 1388. Hasted, *Kent*, ii, 580.

[184] Cf. *Lit. Cant.* (Rolls Ser.), iii, 52, the foundation of Doreward's chantry in Bocking Church, 23 March, 1397, and the chantry in Ickham Church, endowed by John Denys in Aug. 1392 (ibid. 21) ; cf. also the foundation deed of a chantry in the chapel of the nunnery of St. Sepulchre, Canterbury, which makes provision for a daily mass in an obscure chapel which was selected because the nuns were too poor to maintain a chaplain, and were thus provided with a daily mass, while the founder received the spiritual benefit of the service (*Hist. MSS. Com. Rep.* v, App. 435).

[185] *Lit. Cant.* (Rolls Ser.), iii, p. li. At the end of the fourteenth century and for some time after it was held that a stipend of 10 marks with a dwelling-house free of rent was sufficient for the maintenance of a chantry priest. At Bocking the chaplain had £7 and a house standing in a rood of ground. The third chantry priest at Maidstone was endowed with exactly 10 marks. Though the priests of the Black Prince's chantry had between them an income of £20 and a dwelling in common, this sum was found insufficient for the chaplains of a royal foundation. Various foundation deeds of chantries are to be found in *Lit. Cant.* (Rolls Ser.) ; for chantries see also *Valor Eccl.* (Rec. Com.).

[186] Roff. Epis. Reg. Hen. Holbeche, fol. 42b.   [187] *Hist. MSS. Com. Rep.* v and vi.

vied with Romney, Lydd, and Folkestone in getting up popular representations of scriptural history. The procession and performances of the boy bishop were also the occasion for an entertainment of Lydd by the young parishioners of Romney on the festival of St. Nicholas.[188]

An entry among the Romney corporation accounts gives a picture of the customs obtaining in the church of St. Nicholas. Under the year 1407–8 appears the receipt of ' 3s. 4d., a free gift of John Hacche, vicar of Romene, that the jurats in future shall not hold their sessions in his church while divine service is being celebrated.'[189] The jurats are mentioned (6 Henry IV) as holding sessions in the church of St. Nicholas, and it is only at a recent date that their sitting in the church at other times than during divine service has been suspended. The yearly election of the mayor still takes place at the tomb of Richard Stuppeney in the church.

The vicar of Faversham, William Thornbury, resigned in order to become an anchorite, and ended his days in a cell in Faversham churchyard, his successor being admitted to the vicarage, 16 October, 1476.[190] His will, dated 7 December, 1480, and proved 19 March, 1483–4, describes him as vicar of Faversham, and in it he leaves directions for the repair and sustenance of his chapel and parvise in the corner of the churchyard, and among small payments to be made on the anniversary of his death appears one to the anchoress and another to her servant, which looks as though a succession of recluses followed each other there.[191] This inclusion of devout men or women in a solitary cell, never to be left henceforth in the life of its occupier, was practised at other places in Kent besides Faversham at this time. An anchorite (sex unknown) at Dartford was a legatee under the will of the third Lord Scrope, dated 1415. Robert, inclosed at Hartlip, is mentioned in *Registrum Roffense* as the donor of a silver cup,[192] and a female recluse Sungiva is also mentioned as a donor to the priory.[193] Hasted states that an anchoress had her cell at the east end of St. Mary's church in Sandwich as late as 20 Henry VIII, and in a letter of 1531 Sir Thomas Crakynthorpe, 'aunkyre' of Faversham, appeals to Cromwell to direct the abbot of St. Austin's to see that reparations are done in his 'ancrage' at Faversham.[194] Christopher, the anchorite with the Black Friars at Canterbury, is mentioned in letters to Cromwell of 1533.[194a] In an obituary of Davington Priory, believed to date as early as the reign of Richard II, are two entries, ' 16 Kal : Feb : Hic obiit Celestria monacha et anachorita,' and ' 10 Dec : Hic obiitt Adilda monacha et anachorita.'[194b]

One of the oldest sets of churchwardens' accounts now existing in England is that of St. Leonard's, Hythe, for the years 1412–13 ; this has been transcribed,[195] and the receipts and payments furnish most valuable evidence as to customs in this parish. The receipts are divided into arrears, rents, offertories, indulgences, and legacies, and amounted to £6 7s. 2d.

---

[188] *Hist. MSS. Com. Rep.* v, App. 517.   [189] Ibid. *Rep.* v, App. 537.

[190] Cant. Archiepis. Reg. Bourchier, fol. 114b.

[191] Reg. Archdeaconry of Cant. iii, Sec. 128. The will of Richard Wynston of Faversham (ibid. i, fol. 59a), dated 16 Mar. 1464–5, bequeaths a legacy of 2d. to the anchoress ; that of John Beverley, dated 12 Mar. 1470 (ibid. Sec. 16), directs that his grave shall be dug in the north part of Faversham churchyard, opposite the anchoress's cell.

[192] Op. cit. 124.   [193] Ibid.   [194] *L. and P. Hen. VIII*, v, 638.   [194a] Ibid. vi, 1333–6.

[194b] Cotton MSS. Faustina, B. vi, fol. 101b, quoted in *Arch. Cant.* xi, 25.

[195] By Mr. Mackeson, *Arch. Cant.* x, 242.

The offertories, amounting to £1 14s. 7½d., were collected upon twenty-six Sundays in the year. Twenty-five of the collections varied in amount from 6d. to 1s. 6d. each, and included those on Trinity Sunday, Relic Sunday, Advent Sunday, and Christmas Day. The twenty-sixth collection, made upon Easter Day, when all adults were expected to communicate, amounted to 10s. 6d. Under the head of indulgences only the meagre sum of 16d. is entered, and this is for ten days in the year. The main bulk of the receipts appear under the head of legacies, and are twenty-four in number, making a total of £3 6s. 1d., and varying in amount from 1d. to 13s. 4d. The payments, thirty-six in number, exceeded the receipts, and amounted to £8 6s. 11½d. Expenses were mainly for the purchase and repair of books. Some repairs to the clock cost 4d.

It was in Christchurch monastery that the movement which was to bring about a new order in the sixteenth century received a great impetus in the fifteenth, by the action of its prior, William Sellyng, the great scholar and statesman who re-introduced the study of Greek there. Some Greek manuscripts he brought back with him from a long stay in Italy he bestowed on his convent, together with the knowledge of the language, which he first taught to Thomas Linacre. Later, at Cambridge, it was by the great influence of John Fisher, subsequently bishop of Rochester, that the new learning gained a hold. Lectureships in Greek and Hebrew were founded by his fostering care, and Erasmus was induced by him to settle for a time in England, and give lessons in Greek.

John Morton, bishop of Ely when he was appointed to Canterbury in October, 1486, was made Lord Chancellor 6 March following by Henry VII, the final victory of the Lancastrians having already been attributed to his counsels. It was for his service in secular rather than in ecclesiastical affairs that the king in 1493 requested that he might be made a cardinal. He died in 1501, and Thomas Langton, bishop of Winchester, was elected to succeed him by the chapter, 22 January, but died suddenly of the plague in five days. In April Henry Dean, bishop of Salisbury, was made archbishop, and died in less than two years.

At Rochester Thomas Savage, who had been appointed by papal provision, 3 December, 1492, was much trusted and employed by Henry VII. Richard Fitz James, who succeeded him in 1497, a man of high character of a strongly conservative type, was almoner to Henry VII at his consecration, and much engaged in diplomatic affairs until his translation to Chichester in 1504; he was succeeded by John Fisher, the famous chancellor of the university of Cambridge.

Archbishop Warham's primacy was to be a memorable period of transition, and was inaugurated by an enthronement, the last under the old conditions, which was an occasion of even more than usual magnificence. He desired to avoid active participation in politics, but as chancellor he was continually called to the king's councils.

'A man of integrity and ability, celebrated for his eloquence, a sincere reformer of abuses, and an eminent friend of the humanists,'[196] in his extreme old age he was destined to watch the progress of a revolution which was intolerable in his eyes, and was to taste humiliation after humiliation, from the

[196] Canon Dixon, *Hist. of Ch. of Engl.* i, 26.

day when Wolsey, then archbishop of York, received his cardinal's hat at Westminster from his hands,[197] after which, when the new-made cardinal left the church, he took precedence of the archbishop of Canterbury, before whom the cross of Canterbury was no longer carried as heretofore. The subordination thus typified was no matter of empty form, and was still further emphasized at the bestowal of the legateship on Wolsey in 1518, after which Warham's jurisdiction as archbishop was encroached on by Wolsey as legate, and the state correspondence shows them engaged in disputes about testamentary jurisdiction and other matters of official procedure connected with the province and diocese of Canterbury.[198]

In his diocese Warham's first care was to deal with heresy, which was reaching a high degree of activity. In 1511, when a commission was appointed to try heretics in the diocese of Canterbury,[199] one of the judges appointed by him was Dean Colet, the mystical novelty of whose teaching was having a very stirring effect.

The archbishop showed that he shared Colet's belief in the necessity for reformation in the Church itself by the thoroughness of the visitation he carried out in his diocese in this year; but the proceedings against heretics were vigorously prosecuted there under his commissary, Cuthbert Tunstall. William Carder was condemned as a heretic by the archbishop, and delivered as an excommunicated person to the secular power. The sexagenarian Agnes Grebil was brought to the stake on the evidence of her own husband and of her two sons. Numbers who escaped death were compelled to abjure, and among these were Christopher Grebil and John Grebil, both of Benenden; William Rich of Benenden; William Olbert of Godmersham; Agnes Ive of Canterbury; Joan Colin, Stephen Castelin, William Olbert the younger, John Frank of Tenterden, and others. Instances of recantation occur also in the diocese of Rochester, where in 1507 Richard Gavell of Westerham recanted in Bromley Church, after maintaining that the curse of the Church is not to be feared, and that the use of holy water and of offering days is needless; and in 1514 an inhabitant of Snodland was punished for irreverent words concerning the elements in the Eucharist.

The details revealed by the visitation of 1511 have especial value on account of the testimony they afford, not only as to the condition of the parochial clergy, but as to the state of the religious houses in Kent at this time; for, since the visitation carried out in 1535, previous to the Dissolution, was undertaken with the purpose of procuring evidence which should justify that measure, its verdicts are apt to be regarded as suspect. But the picture presented in Kent in 1511 is black enough, perhaps the worst case being that of Higham Convent, which was dissolved before the general suppression, that is to say as early as 1521.

The parochial visitations show that the ruin and dilapidations of the chancels, which were a constant subject of complaint, were in many cases due to the neglect of the religious foundation to which the church was appropriated; the portion of the building which depended upon the parishioners for its support was generally in a satisfactory state. But at Ivychurch, where

---

[197] Nov. 1515. In the following month Warham resigned the great seal, and the king delivered it to Wolsey.

[198] *L. and P. Hen. VIII*, iii, 98 &c. [199] Gairdner, *Hist. of Engl. Ch.* (ed. Stephens and Hunt), iv, 61.

the parson was described as 'an outlandish man, who has never come among us sith his induction,' the churchwardens complained that 'the parish church is sorely decayed, and likely to fall down.'

Instances of non-residence occur, and of these many were where the churches were appropriated to religious houses. The religious houses also were guilty in several cases of serving their cures by one of their own members, instead of by appointing a vicar. In the case of the church of the Holy Cross, Westgate, it was returned that

> there is no secular priest that serveth the cure these three years, but the prior of St. Gregory's of Canterbury causeth one of his own canons to serve it, the which goeth to the priory every night, and when we should have him, oftentimes in the night season, we cannot have him.

A similar charge is made against the same prior in regard to the church of Thanington. At the church of Sibertswold, appropriated to the priory of St. Radegund, the archbishop had augmented the vicarage, and thereby much displeased the canons, one of whom came and

> spake many opprobrious and contumelious words openly, and said, 'Thou priest, what doest thou here in our church ? get thee hence or we shall pluck thee out by the head ; howbeit thou bearest thee bold, and wast instituted by my lord of Canterbury, he hath nought to do here, for we are exempt from him, and so tell him,' with many more words long to rehearse.

At Monk's Horton 'the parson had not been among the people for five years,' and having been called to residence by the archbishop, did not appear, and was therefore deprived.

In addition to the serious matters already exemplified, careful examination was made into such statements as that 'the vicar of Stodmarsh is sometimes malicious and looking on his neighbours with a glym and sower countenance where they think him, God knoweth, no hurt,' or that the 'Vicar of Bridge giveth no rights to them that will not content his mind, and when they do not agree with him after his pleasure'; at Herne one Valentine Cole was charged with troubling the church by reason of his evil disposition.

In some churches books and ornaments were wanting, in others surplices ; in the church of Milton the rood 'lacketh Mary and John.' At Seasalter a man was charged with 'laying violent hands upon his ghostly father for asking his tithes.' Masses and obits were again and again neglected. Other returns show that contributions had been withheld which should have been paid towards the salary of the parish clerk.[200]

[200] The duties of this functionary have been fully described in *Archaeologia Cantiana*, xx, 203, in a transcript by F. F. Giraud of rules for the parish clerks and sexton of Faversham, 1506–93. These direct that the clerks, of whom at Faversham there were two until in 1548 their number was reduced to one, should attend to much of the cleaning of the church, act as servers at the mass, as *rectores chori*, or cantors, help the sexton to ring bells, carry holy water to each house, and teach the children to read or sing in the choir. It was expected of both clerk and sexton that he 'or his sufficient depute every nyght from All Hallowtide unto the fest of the Annunciation of our Lady nyghtly shalbe in the said churche or stepill by vii at clok in the evyn and ther shall contynue abyde and lye from that howre until vii at clok on the next morowe and from the Annunciation of our Lady unto All Hallowtyde the same or his sufficient depute nyghtly shalbe in the churche or stepyll by viii at clok in the evyn and there shall contynue and ly from that howre unto v at clok in next mornyng. And every nyght the same sextayn or his sufficient depute at viii at clok shall ryng couvrefewe by the space of oon quarter of an hour with such a bell as of old tyme hath been accustomed. The said sextayne or his depute every day in the morning in somer shall open the Churche doores at v at clok, and in winter at vi at clok.' The sexton also has directions to light lamps, tapers, large candles, fill holy-water stoups, clean the church, and guard the churchyard from beasts, &c.

It is probable that few of the bishops of his day were as assiduous in the discharge of their duties as Bishop Fisher, and allowance must therefore be made for the sensitiveness of a tender conscience in what he says of himself at Wolsey's synod in 1517, when he declared that the bishops were conspicuously guilty of the worldliness they rebuked in others.

> No man do I blame more than myself, for several times when I have settled to visit my diocese, and to answer the enemies of Christ, suddenly has come to me a message from the Court that I must attend such a triumph, or public entry, or receive an ambassador, whereas what have bishops to do with princes' courts? What this vanity in temporal things may work on *you* I know not, but for myself I find it a great impediment to devotion.

In a letter to Wolsey of 13 August, 1525,[201] describing the difficulty of collecting the loan demanded by Henry, Warham gives an account of the condition of his clergy in Kent:

> I have assembled eleven deaneries adjoining to Canterbury, and I perceive they are very well minded to the loan, but their substance is not equal to their wishes. They are very poor. As the chief benefices are appropriated to religious houses, the vicars' portion is so small they can scarcely live. If there be any good vicarages the religious obtain faculties from the pope to have them served by the religious. In all the deaneries there are twenty-two benefices at the sum of 40 *li* (?) and six or seven are so decayed as to be nothing like that value. As I have no power over religious men, they must be left to your grace, and unless they contribute to the loan according to their benefices, the clergy will complain. Had the religious houses not been exempted, but appeared before me, the loan derived from my diocese would be much greater than now. The value of all the benefices in the diocese of Canterbury would then amount to a tax of £1,903 15*s.* 2*d.* The clergy will not declare the quantity of their corn, their plate, or their cattle, as they say they cannot estimate them, and are afraid of perjury.

Cranbrook was a place where seditious movements would naturally originate, as it was always an abode of heretics, of whom at this time it was furnishing its contingent. Richard Harman, a Kentishman whose apprehension as a heretic Wolsey's official, John Hacket, tried so hard to effect at Antwerp,[202] was born at Cranbrook, and correspondence of his seized by Hacket's agent, John Weste, included two letters from heretical sympathizers in Cranbrook; one from Thomas Davy of Cranbrook, in 1528, urged Harman, who is described by Hacket as 'a root of great mischief,' with a wife 'a mischeivous woman of her tongue, and as ill of deeds,' to have patience in the true faith of Christ, and told him that 'no man in England may speak of the New Testament on pain of bearing a faggot'; another from John Andrews[203] of Cranbrook, dated 20 February, 1527, about the New Testament, informed him that Andrews himself was in prison in the Fleet.

This activity was the result of a mandate of Archbishop Warham's of 3 November, 1526, ordering search to be made for Tyndal's New Testament and other heretical books in England. He himself contributed liberally to buy up the whole impression of the book, and other bishops did the same.

In the summer of 1528 the archbishop's household, like the rest of Kent, was visited by the sweating sickness, and the outbreak among his dependants

---

[201] *L. and P. Hen. VIII,* iv, 4631.

[202] Ibid. iv, 4511, 4569, 4693, 4694, 4714, 5078, 5275, 5462.

[203] This John Andrews, described as a clothier, was subsequently sent to Wolsey himself for examination by Sir Edward Guldeford, shortly before the date of the above depositions, 22 May, 1528. Ibid. 4287.

must have been of a terrible nature, as in one day eighteen members died in four hours. A letter of Sir Edward Guldeford's to Wolsey of 11 July, 1528, inclosing a bill of the lewd sayings of Sir John Crake, parish priest of Brenzett, says that he has committed the priest to Maidstone Gaol until Wolsey's pleasure be known, as it was not meet to trouble him with strangers at the time of the plague.[204]

Wolsey made the occasion of his passing through Kent[205] in 1527, on his way to France, an opportunity for visiting both Warham and Fisher, and bringing them into line with him in his schemes for the execution of the king's projects as to his divorce. Archbishop Warham wondered how the queen had come to hear of the proceedings, but said that however disagreeable to her, the law must prevail. Fisher he persuaded that the king's sole object was not to find objections against the marriage, but rather reasons, with the advice of skilful doctors and casuists, to prove it good and lawful. In October, 1528, Canterbury witnessed the opening movements of the divorce campaign in the arrival of Cardinal Campeggio.

> He was first greeted by the mayor and aldermen . . . the street from the gate where he entered unto the gate of the priory was set full . . . with the orders of the friars and all other priests and clerks. At the entry into the church there was another canopy and a little afore . . . cloths and cushions laid for him . . . downe. My lord of Caunterbury, with the p [rior of Christchurch], the Abbot of Awstynes, and a sufferygan, *in pontificalibus*, sens hym and so wan he to the high awter, where he sange himselfe and bless . . . his lodging into the priory.[206]

The day on which this entry occurred, Warham was writing[207] to Wolsey of Elizabeth [Barton], a religious woman, professed in St. Sepulchre's, Canterbury, 'whiche hadd all the visions at our Lady of Courtopstret,' a well-disposed and virtuous woman, as he hears from her sisters, who wishes to speak with Wolsey and who has asked Warham to write to him to that effect.

It is always difficult to decide how much of the element of imposture consciously enters into such a career as that of the Nun of Kent, or to what extent she herself believed in the inspiration of her utterances : it is impossible, however, to suppose that either the archbishop or Bishop Fisher ever had the smallest idea of making her a tool. Though at last it was for withholding information of her sayings that Sir Thomas More and Bishop Fisher were accused, this letter of the archbishop's shows that from the first there really was no attempt at concealment. More, whose connexion with the Ropers may have brought the Nun to his notice, lost no time in speaking of her to the king himself.

When the archbishop's official, Dr. Bocking, was appointed in 1525 to examine into the miracles and other marvels for which she had gained celebrity, he had been sufficiently impressed by her, or by the enormous concourse of people who thronged to hear and see her, to recommend her appointment to a vacant place in the convent of St. Sepulchre, Canterbury. An account of her career after she left Courthope Street survives in the reluctant testimony of the prior of Christchurch,[208] given in 1533

---

[204] *L. and P. Hen. VIII*, iv, 4501.

[205] At Canterbury on this occasion he ordered a special litany to be sung by the monks of Christchurch for Pope Clement VI, who had been compelled to take refuge in the castle of St. Angelo, after the sack of Rome by the emperor's troops.   [206] *L. and P. Hen. VIII*, iv, 4805 (1 Oct. 1528).

[207] Ibid. 4806 (1 Oct. 1528).   [208] Ibid. vi, 1470.

after the death of Warham, and after the accusation of collusion with her had been made against Fisher and More. The prior, whom Cranmer then describes as 'a man of great simplicity and void of malice,'[209] said of the nun's revelations :—

> At the beginning thereof, about seven or eight years ago, Archbishop Warham sent his controller, Thomas Walle, to Canterbury, and made me send two of my brethren, Dr. Bocking, the cellarer, and dompne M. Hadley, B.D., to Courthope Strete, to see this woman and her trances . . . Father Risby, now warden of the Observant Friars of Canterbury, was the cause of my being acquainted with her, for my mind was not to be familiarly acquainted with women. He said she was a person much in favour with God, and that I should have much comfort in her speaking.

When More had his interview with her, she spoke of herself in such terms of humility that he declared he found 'nothing indiscreet' in what she said. It seems extraordinary that the very fact of his having then written to her to beware of conversation on political subjects should have brought him under suspicion, as is shown in a long letter of his to Cromwell,[210] in which he thanks the latter for telling his son (Roper) that he wished to hear from More about his communications with the lewd nun of Canterbury. Possibly More's connexion with the Ropers was the most serious ground of suspicion against him in the first place.

Bishop Fisher, in his account of her introduction to him, says he

> sought not the woman's coming to him, nor thought in her any manner of deceit. He believed her to be honest and virtuous because of the bruit of the country which called her the Holy Maid ; because of her entrance into religion upon certain visions ; because of the good religion and holiness of her ghostly father and other priests who testified of her holiness ; and because the archbishop of Canterbury, who then was her ordinary and a man reputed of high wisdom and learning, told him that she had many great visions . . . is bound to believe the best of every person till the contrary be proved.[211]

But it was not till July of the year 1533 that the attention of the authorities was seriously directed to her rhapsodies and trances. Fisher's doom had been sealed ever since he had incurred the king's ill-will by his formal protest against his divorce in 1528. When the Commons began to formulate complaints against the clergy,[212] and in the House of Lords Fisher complained that ' Now with the Commons is nothing but *Down with the Church !* and all this, meseemeth, is for lack of faith only,' the king called the bishops before him, and compelled Bishop Fisher especially to explain the words he had used.

By every possible means the king was preparing the way for his marriage with Anne Boleyn, and his indirect encouragement of heresy was directed to this end. But the punishment for heresy was still enforced, and Kent provided its share of victims. Thomas Hitton, a Norfolk man, was burned at Maidstone as a heretic in 1530, after being brought before Archbishop Warham and Bishop Fisher. He was one of Tyndal's secret agents, and had been arrested at Gravesend, where letters he was to have delivered to heretics abroad were found on him. Warham died 22 August, 1532,[213] and Cranmer, who had

---

[209] *L. and P. Hen. VIII*, vi, 1519.   [210] Ibid. vii, 287.   [211] Ibid. 240.

[212] Mainly for excessive fees, non-residence, and pluralities. Sir Henry Guildford complained that he had paid 1,000 marks to the cardinal and Archbishop Warham for probate of Sir William Compton's will.

[213] He died incredibly poor, though his munificence to public objects and scholars had been great. Just before his death he is said to have called his steward to him and asked him how much money he had in hand, and when he was told £30, to have replied ' *Sat est viatici* ' (Erasmus, Preface to St. Jerome's works. Paris, 1534). He left barely sufficient to pay his debts and funeral expenses, and in his will said he thought his executors should be freed from charges for dilapidations as he had spent £30,000 in repairs and new building of houses belonging to the see.

been chaplain to the Boleyn family, and who had just married in Germany his second wife, was promoted to Canterbury. The year after his appointment, on 4 July, 1533, little more than a month after the coronation of Anne Boleyn, two Kentish heretics were burned together at Smithfield. These were John Frith, a scholar, and one Hewet, a tailor, apparently his disciple.[214] Frith had given evidence of heretical leanings at Oxford and escaped abroad, but returned, leaving a wife in Flanders. He had been engaged in the secret dissemination of heretical writings in manuscript, a course which he had adopted in consequence of the proclamation against printed heretical books. His writings were considered to be of such importance as to call for a reply from Sir Thomas More to one that he had written upon the subject of the Sacrament. At his examination he declared that he did not believe in purgatory or transubstantiation, and that he did not consider either an essential part of the Christian faith.

It was to stop the growing disaffection manifested after the coronation of Anne Boleyn that Elizabeth Barton was arrested. By this time, besides rebuking various heresies, she declared that God was displeased with the king's divorce, that if he married Anne Boleyn he would lose his kingdom in seven months, and further that she had seen the very place in hell prepared for him.

Cranmer allowed her to resort for a last time to Courthope Street in order that she might make further statements that would help to expose her imposture, and while he was considering the best method of proceeding with her she made a confession of having uttered feigned revelations to please her ghostly father, Dr. Bocking, who frequently railed against the king's marriage, and that before this she had feigned to have revelations from God ; she declared also the names of various persons who had seen her revelations or communicated with her.[215]

Chapuys, writing to Charles V, 24 November, 1533,[216] describes how, the day before, she and some of her 'accomplices' had been set on a high scaffold before St. Paul's Cathedral, while 'a monk lately made bishop in order to support the Lady's party '[217] narrated the whole story of her hypocrisy. These accomplices were Hugh Riche, late warden of the Franciscans or Friars Observants, Canterbury, Richard Risby, their present warden ; the two monks, Edward Bocking, D.D., and John Dering, both of Canterbury ; two secular priests,[218] Richard Master, parson of Aldington, Kent, and Henry Gold, parson of St. Mary Aldermary, London, and chaplain to the archbishop ; two laymen, Thomas Gold and Edward Thwaites ; and Thomas Lawrence, registrar to the archdeacon of Canterbury.[219]

Cranmer wrote to the king in December[220] that he had examined the prior and convent of his church, and found them as conformable as any, and

---

[214] Gairdner, *Hist. of Engl. Ch.* (ed. Stephens and Hunt), iv, 133–4.

[215] *L. and P. Hen. VIII*, vii, 72, 372 ; ibid. vi, 1468.

[216] Ibid. vi, 1460.

[217] i.e. the bishop of Bangor.

[218] The parson of Aldington, where Elizabeth Barton first had her trances, had brought the nun to the notice of Warham. Christopher Hales had written to Cromwell, 29 Sept. 1533 : 'Till now I could not conveniently get together the official and parson of Aldyngton, whom I now send to you. The parson is a man of good fame; and if the official have not offended in the manner presupposed, I can speak largely for his honesty. I can find no spot of matter in his house.' *L. and P. Hen. VIII*, vi, 1169.

[219] *L. and P. Hen. VIII*, vi, 1460, *note*.   [220] Ibid. 1519.

that only a few had consented to these revelations. The convent themselves wrote to the king [221] imploring his forgiveness, and interceding for Edward Bocking, who suffered death next year at Tyburn, with Richard Dering, Richard Master, Henry Gold, Richard Risby, and the nun herself.[222] Bishop Fisher, who was sentenced with Adyson, his chaplain, to be attainted of misprision and imprisoned at the king's will, and to forfeit all his goods, was ultimately permitted to compound for his offence by a payment of £300.

When summoned to Lambeth 13 April, 1534, to take the oath of compliance with the Act of Succession, both Fisher and More, though they declared their willingness to take that portion of the oath which fixed the succession in the offspring of the king and of Anne Boleyn, declined that part which declared the offspring of Catherine illegitimate, and forbade faith, truth, and obedience to any foreign authority or potentate. They were lodged in the Tower, an inventory of the bishop's goods at Rochester was taken, and his fate was considered sealed. In advanced age and feeble health he was subjected to a rigorous imprisonment.

Fisher and More were then declared attainted of misprision of treason, and the see of Rochester was pronounced vacant from 2 January, 1534-5. Just when he had been granted six weeks in which to swear to the new statute or suffer death for refusing, Fisher was made a cardinal. Cromwell and others of the council visited him in the Tower and read to him a copy of the Act making Henry supreme head of the Church, and of another making it treason to deny the supremacy. Ultimately he promised to obey and swear to the Act of Succession, but persisted in his inability to recognize in the preamble the king as head of the Church. He was brought to trial at Westminster, sentenced, and executed on Tower Hill, 22 June, 1535. He was succeeded by John Hilsey or Hildesleigh, D.D., who had been appointed provincial of the Dominicans by Cromwell in the preceding year, and commissioner with Dr. George Browne, provincial of the Augustinians, to visit the friaries throughout England. Bishop Hilsey was consecrated 18 September, 1535.

It was in Kent, that is to say by the Grey Friars of Greenwich, that the most determined resistance was offered to some of the articles declaring renunciation of papal authority, administered in the visitation of 1534 to monasteries and friaries. But on the whole the great changes had been quietly accepted in Kent. George, Lord Cobham, wrote to Cromwell, 31 May, 1534, 'The commission sent into Kent is very well received, except my Lady Mary, the King's daughter, her schoolmaster which hath a benefice by me, the which went into Wales three days before that I did sit upon this commission, and he is not yet sworn.' [223] An agent of Cromwell's, John Johnson *alias* Antony, wrote to him 7 June, 1534, 'Most part of Kent have taken the oath, except two of our Observants at Canterbury, named Father Mychelsen and Father Gam, and the Vicar of Sittingborne. I shall do with the said parties as you command me.' [224] Sir Christopher Hales wrote from Canterbury to Cromwell, 4 June, 1534, 'the people of this county are well contented with the

[221] *L. and P. Hen. VIII*, vi, 1409.   [222] 5 May, 1534.   [223] Ibid. vii, App. 21.

[224] Ibid. App. 27. This letter suggests that Cromwell's emissary met with great submissiveness on the part of the heads of religious houses. 'At my coming to Kent, I delivered your letter to the master of Nyewerke near Rochester, being admitted by your mastership receiver general of the bishop of Rochester's lands to the king's use. The master according to your letter was content that I should have the parsonage of Hawlyng, and the prior of Christ Church at your request is very good to me.'

oath.'[225]   The signatures of the clergy of Kent to their renunciation of the papal authority seem all to have been obtained in the first half of 1534.[226] It was not to be expected, however, that no murmuring would make itself heard, and probably many others had uttered sentiments similar to those for which Gervase Shelby, inhabitant of the parish of St. Peter, Thanet, was arrested at Ramsgate.[227]   He had said that

> his conscience grieved him sore to take the oath commanded to be taken of all the king's subjects in Kent, as the king had broken the sacrament of matrimony, and that when he went over the sea he went to Rome to the pope to have his favour to marry with Queen Anne, but the pope would give him no licence.

Private grudges may have counted for somewhat in the accusations of heresy or seditious words made at this time, but whatever the malice that prompted the deposition of one monk named Fell against William Wynchelsey, a monk of St. Augustine's, Canterbury, it seems likely enough that the accused had said [228]

> (1) that the archbishop commanded Twynne, the schoolmaster, to ride twice in one week to Sandwich to read a lecture of heresy, and promised a buck in summer and a doe in winter to the heretics of Sandwich ; (2) that he thanked God he had lived to see the cross of Canterbury carried to a bull-baiting ; (3) that the new learning would set men together by the ears, and that my lord of Canterbury was the maintainer of it ; (4) that the king had made a fool archbishop of Canterbury because he would take his pleasure of the church.

In March, 1535, it is recorded that

> on Passion Sunday last, Arthur, a Grey Friar of Canterbury, preached in the parish church of Herne, before a great audience, and blamed these new books and new preachers for misleading the people and discouraging fasts and prayers and pilgrimages.   He called them Judases. . . . Beside that, he prayed not for the King as Head of the Church, nor for the Queen either, but for the spirituality, the temporality, and the souls in purgatory.[229]

The vicar of the parish church of Herne, Sir William Cobbe, against whom a bill of detection was subsequently presented in 1536 by one Alexander Norwood at 'the king's visitation,' is also represented as having upheld the supremacy of the pope since the 'command for the abolition of the authority of the bishop of Rome,' and to have said, 'As for the taking away of his name it is no matter, for he never wrote himself *Papa*, but *summus pontifex*, and as for his authority he hath not lost an inch thereof I warrant you.'   Cobbe was for this committed to gaol at Canterbury.[230]

In the same month Thomas Lawney wrote to his friend, Master Marbere : 'It fortuned me to preach at Wingham before the archdeacon,[231] where I inveighed against the pope according to my duty.   Dr. Benger, LL.D., canon of Wingham, was so offended, that he came to the archdeacon's house, and began to invent a matter to me. . . .'   It appears that Dr. Benger, who 'affirmed the authority of the bishop of Rome,' after many arguments, said : 'These new laws may be suffered for a season, but in time they will cause broken heads and set men together by the ears.'[232]   Thomas Shellowe,

---

[225] *L. and P. Hen. VIII*, vii, 788.   [226] *Arch. Cant.* xxii, 293.

[227] *L. and P. Hen. VIII*, vi, 634 (12 June, 1533).

[228] In a paper endorsed 'Against a monk in Canterbury and a priest in Tenet, accused in Dr. Peters' circuit in the visitation.'   *L. and P. Hen. VIII*, vii, 1608 (1534).

[229] *L. and P. Hen. VIII*, viii, 480.   [230] Ibid. xi, 464 (18 Sept. 1536).

[231] Edmund Cranmer, brother of the archbishop, and provost of Wingham, archdeacon 1534-54.

[232] *L. and P. Hen. VIII*, viii, 386, 387.

curate of Wingham, deposed that Dr. Benger had said 'men might as well deny the authority of Paul and of all Scripture as the pope.' Other depositions then taken show that sermons had been preached at Wingham less satisfactory to the authorities than that of Thomas Lawney.

> Friar Brenchley after many railing words in his sermon said : 'Masters, take heed, we have nowadays many new laws. I trow ye shall have a new God shortly.' At the next preaching came a doctor of the monks of Canterbury, who prayed for the king, but did not name him head of the church, and introduced a story of a covetous king who reserved goods to himself that he took from certain transgressors, wherefore he lost his kingdom and never recovered it, and thus left it undeclared. By the which many gathered opinion that he meant it by the king, to move the commons to insurrection.

If these were the sermons preached at Wingham, it is probable that the tenor of many others preached in Kent at this time by the monks and their sympathizers was the same. That they did not succeed in 'moving the commons to insurrection' must have been due to their own previous history in the county, of which Wingham itself affords an example. A letter of one Raymond Harflete to Cromwell of the year 1535 says :[233]

> In the king's county of Kent is a village called Asshe, the benefice of which belongs to the canons of Wyngham where I am. It has a parsonage and a vicarage, of which the parsonage is in the hands of the canons, but there has always been a vicar there to serve the cure, till for the last twenty-two years the said canons have usurped the vicarage to their own use, and let it to farm to temporal men, who have put in such curates as are unable to serve, but were obtained by the farmer best cheap for his money. Within a quarter of a year we have had seven curates, which has caused much strife, as we are 500 residents. By our complaint to the archbishop of Canterbury, the canons were compelled to appoint us Sir Robert Ell . . . who has been resident among us for a year, but the canons, pretending displeasure to the vicar, keep from him the tithes of wool and lamb which his predecessors have always had, and without them he cannot maintain hospitality. So, with the consent of all the parish, I desire you to have compassion on us, and that the vicar may enjoy his rights.

The valuation of benefices went on through the summer. A royal visitation[234] for the present superseded the authority of the bishops, and even the obsequious Bishop Hilsey was taken sharply to task for visiting his see of Rochester without royal licence, although he had previously sued to Cromwell for leave to exercise his episcopal jurisdiction.[235] The returns from Kent were the first to come in,[236] and are to be found in the volume entitled *Valor Ecclesiasticus*. The value of the spiritualities and temporalities belonging to the bishopric of Rochester is given as £411 0s. 11½d. ; of the manors, lands, &c., of the archbishopric of Canterbury as £3,204 15s. 2½d. ; of Christchurch Priory as £2,289 0s. 8½d. ; of the monastery of St. Augustine as £1,274 0s. 10d. ; and of the suppressed priory of St. Gregory as £104 14s. 7d.

This valuation was preliminary to the visitation of the monasteries which began in October of the same year, Kent being the first county visited.[237] The visitors were Layton and Bedyl.

From a letter of Layton's to Cromwell dated 23 October, 1535,[238] we learn that when he went on to Christchurch he was very nearly burnt in his bed, the great dining chamber having caught fire 'by some firebrand or

---

[233] *L. and P. Hen. VIII*, ix, 1110.
[234] Conducted in Kent by Dr. William Peters. *L. and P. Hen. VIII*, xi, 476.
[235] *L. and P. Hen. VIII*, ix, 517, 693.
[236] Ibid. 354.
[237] Dixon, *Hist. of the Ch. of Engl.* i, 325.
[238] *L. and P. Hen. VIII*, ix, 669.

snuff of a candle setting the rushes on fire.' He describes the precautions he took to preserve the jewels :

> As soon as I had set men to quench the fire, I went into the church and set four monks with ban dogs to keep the shrine, and put the sexton in the vestry to keep the jewels, appointing monks in every quarter of the church with candles. Also I sent for the Abbot of St. Augustine's to be in readiness to take down the shrine, and send the jewels into St. Augustine's.

John Whalley, paymaster of the works at Dover, had previously written to Cromwell (4 October, 1535[239]) : ' The monks of Canterbury are afraid, and they of Christ Church will make their hands, as it is said. It is the richest house in jewels, plate, and money in England.' He also said that he knew a person who could show Cromwell's visitors where secret treasure was kept ; that is to say the said person, the town clerk, would show the places, if Whalley might accompany the visitors. The paymaster seems to have had a keen eye to the interests of those who would inherit the property of the monks, and wrote to Cromwell again, 5 April, 1536,[240] that the abbot of St. Radegund's was setting men to fell his woods a great pace, and if Cromwell did not stop him, would do much harm to the place, ' one of the properyst in Kent.' Altogether John Whalley appears to have been not the least energetic of Cromwell's numberless spies, for only three days previously (2 April, 1536) he had written to him[241] that he hears that the parson of Woodnesborough, who was sent to Cromwell accused of treason, had a book of prophecies ; that he was very familiar with the master of the Maison Dieu here and other parsons and vicars in Kent, and that if well handled he can declare a great number of papists in this county ; also that two chaplains of the archbishop of Canterbury have been here this Lent, having preached at Calais, so that the deputy and his wife ' are well brought home with divers others which were Pharisees there.'

This new word papist was used by Cranmer in a letter to Cromwell of 12 October, 1535,[242] concerning one of whose preaching complaints had been made.

> When I was at Court some complained to me of him, but as I had heard good reports of him before from honest men, I told them I could not tell to whom to give credence. Again since I came to Kent, I have had complaints of him from some who seem honest, but I rather think the latter are papistical, not friendly to the gospel.

Cranmer, in a letter to the king, has left a record[243] of the sermon he preached in Canterbury Cathedral in the presence of Dr. Layton. His sermon declared : (1) That the bishop of Rome was not God's vicar on earth ; (2) that though the see of Rome was called *Sancta sedes Romana*, and the bishop *sanctissimus Papa*, that was but a holiness in name, seeing the vices of Rome ; (3) that the bishop of Rome's laws were many of them contrary to God's laws. . . . The laws of the Church were originally intended, like the common law of the realm, for the observance of order, and as such only people ought to observe them. . . . This letter says that the people were glad they heard so much until the prior of the Black Friars at Canterbury preached a sermon clean contrary. For first, concerning the bishop of Rome's power, the prior spake generally : (1) That the Church of Christ never erred ; (2) as to vices,

---

[239] *L. and P. Hen. VIII*, ix, 534.
[241] Ibid. x, 614.
[240] Ibid. x, 624
[242] Ibid. ix, 592.
[243] Ibid. xi, 361.

he would not slander the bishop of Rome so, and that Cranmer preached uncharitably in saying he prayed to see the power of Rome destroyed; (3) he preached craftily the laws of the Church to be equal with God's laws.

So serious did Cranmer consider this matter to be that he wrote for redress to the king himself, telling his highness that if this man, who has preached against the archbishop in his own church, be not looked on, the king may 'expende' what an example it may be to others, and how Cranmer's credit will be affected.

Sermons such as these must have done their work, but even more the suppression of the smaller monasteries enacted by Parliament this year cannot have failed to rouse a certain degree of resentment among the people of a county where so many had existed to relieve, however faultily, the poor and indigent; and to the suspicion, which proved correct, that the larger ones were before long to follow, was also added another, that no Church property was safe. By the autumn of this year the names of various persons from Kent appear in the State Papers, appended to sayings of theirs which show sympathy with the rebels in the north.[244]

Cromwell's order to provide Bibles in churches first appeared in his injunctions of 1536, and was a fruitful cause of dissensions in parishes. An example may be seen in certain 'articles of injuries and wrongs done to us your beadsmen, for presenting of our parson to the Lord Archbishop of Canterbury.'[245] After the bill of presentment had been delivered one James Newynden fetched a forest bill and threatened and chased him that delivered it, and on the Sunday following reviled him before all the parish, in church, crying out, 'Drive these heretic knaves out of the parish!' A fellow parishioner declared he 'was weary of all together, and there would be no peace till five or six of these new fellows be killed': other parishioners 'go daily together with unlawful weapons, and we dare not go out of our houses to speak to each other for fear of our lives.'

In the same year Cranmer was engaged in a hot correspondence with a Kentish justice[246] who declared that the things which Cranmer imputed to him as having omitted to set forth in sessions are more pertinent to the office of a preacher than of a sitting justiciar in a temporal sessions. As the archbishop writes, on the one hand, 'It is everywhere said in Kent that the people dare not read God's word for fear of your threats at 'sizes and sessions,' and on the other, that, but for the favour he bears to him, he would proceed against some of his servants as heretics, it is a little difficult to be certain in what direction the offender had erred. The irritation displayed in Kent late in this and early in the following year reached a point which kept Cranmer and Lord Cobham and others busy there in taking depositions and committing offenders to prison.

Punishments are recorded at Canterbury and Sandwich, and of a priest at Ashford.[247] William Knell, a head yeoman of Brookland in Romney Marsh, spoke 'words concerning the bishop of Rome' which amounted to treason,[248] and was attainted in April following,[249] and executed.[250] Various

---

[244] *L. and P. Hen. VIII*, xi, 841 (22 Oct. 1536); and later in Dec. 1538, xiii, 996.

[245] Ibid. xii, 957, *anno* 1537.

[246] Thought to be Sir Thomas Cheyney, treasurer of the king's household, and Lord Warden of the Cinque Ports; *L. and P. Hen. VIII*, xii, 846 (Oct. 1537).

[247] *L. and P. Hen. VIII*, xiii, 6, 57, 141, 171. [248] Ibid. 12, 48, 79. [249] Ibid. 783. [250] Ibid. 877.

persons in Nonington, Eastry, Adisham, and Wingham were accused of spreading the report of the king's death ; and Cranmer related to Cromwell that it was deposed that Sir John Hartely, parish priest of Smeeth, and the parish priest of Brabourne, said shortly after the prince's birth that because the queen was not crowned there was like to be business in the years to come.[250a]

The Rood of Grace at Boxley seems to have been turned to valuable account as an object lesson to rouse the public mind to indignation against monkish impostures. John Chamber wrote to Cromwell, 7 February, 1538,

> Considering that the people of Kent had in time past a great devotion to the image and used continued pilgrimages there, I conveyed it to Maidstone this present Thursday being market day, and shewed it to the people ; who had the matter in wondrous detestation and hatred, so that if the monastery had to be defaced again, they would pluck it down or burn it.[251]

A few days after, the bishop of Rochester preached at London with the image opposite him, when it performed again.[252] Mr. Pollard,[253] an important officer of the Exchequer, was employed in carrying off the spoils of the magnificent shrine of St. Thomas, the wonder of all Christendom. According to Stowe the gold and precious stones filled two great chests, such that six or seven strong men could do no more than convey one at once out of the church.

The efforts of Cranmer to suppress sedition in his diocese were accompanied by appeals to those in authority not to set stumbling-blocks in the way of the weak and unlearned. He wrote to Cromwell in 1537, that since coming from London to Kent he has found the people very obstinate to observe their holidays lately abrogated,[254] and added : 'But, my lord, if in the court you do keep such holidays and fasting days as be abrogated, when shall we persuade the people to cease from keeping them ?' In April, 1538,[255] he addressed Cromwell in favour of certain men of Smarden and Pluckley, indicted for unlawful assemblies at the last sessions at Canterbury, as he alleged, only 'because they were accounted "fawters of the new doctrine" as they call it,' and told him that 'if the king's subjects who favour God's word are unjustly vexed at sessions, it will be no marvel if much sedition be daily engendered.' 'Seditious words' seem to have been frequently reported concerning the fifteenth and tenth levied at this time, called 'horn money' and 'poll money' in Kent,[256] and articles were alleged against Lancelot Pococke, curate at Hunton,[257] and Sir John Bromfyld, priest.[258] In June, 1539, a Frenchman got himself into trouble at Dover[259] for saying to some Picards come to buy fish in the town that 'the king of England hath pulled down all the abbeys in England, and he will pull down all the churches also,' and further that the king had caused twenty cart-loads of gold and silver to be carried from Canterbury to London. The Frenchman, when attached, confessed that he had said the words imputed to him, but that he had often heard it said within the realm. In March, two parish churches in Canterbury were robbed ;[260] such

---

[250a] *L. and P. Hen. VIII*, Introd. p. ii.   [251] Ibid. 231.
[252] Ibid. 348. It had been ordered earlier in the year that images should be taken down when they conduced to pilgrimages or offerings, and that lights should no longer be burnt before them.
[253] *L. and P. Hen. VIII*, xiii, 303 (8 Sept. 1538).
[254] Ibid. xii, 592. The same complaint had been made before by John Whalley, ibid. ix, 142.
[255] Ibid. xiii, 865.   [256] Ibid. 483.   [257] Ibid. 921.
[258] Ibid. 1074.   [259] Ibid. 1073.   [260] Ibid. xiv, 423.

robberies were sometimes the work of parishioners who thought they might as well be beforehand with the king's official robbers.

In 1541 the cathedral foundation of Canterbury was altered to the new establishment of a dean and chapter, by letters patent of 8 April. The prior and twenty-six of the monks were pensioned off; seven others were made prebendaries; a gospeller and an epistoler were appointed (probably reappointed); and the remainder provided for as petty canons or scholars. Five other persons not on the old establishment were also appointed prebendaries, thus making their number up to twelve. Among these must be mentioned Dr. Nicholas Ridley, vicar of Herne, and three who had been monks, Richard Thornden, warden of the manors, William Sandwich *alias* Gardiner, and John Warham *alias* Milles. It was also, no doubt, intended from the first to have six preachers attached to the cathedral, but they do not seem to have been named until a few months later.[261] It was at first proposed to convert the prior and convent of Rochester into a chapter of one dean and ten prebendaries besides the archdeacon, four canons, six choristers, one master of the choristers, one porter, two sextons, and one verger, 'with one learned man freely to teach a grammar school, and bring up poor men's children in learning'; one of the prebendaries to read continually a lecture of divinity, having for his prebend the hospital of Strood beside Rochester of the bishop's foundation, and another to preach continually within the town and diocese,[262] but the establishment created by the charter of 18 June, 33 Henry VIII, finally consisted of one dean, six prebendaries, six minor canons, one deacon and one sub-deacon, six lay clerks, one master of the choristers, eight choristers, one teacher of the boys in grammar, twenty scholars to be taught the same, and two sub-sacrists.[263] Both foundations maintained a certain number of almsmen.

The first dean appointed at Canterbury was Nicholas Wotton, the celebrated courtier and diplomatist, one of the ablest and most experienced of Tudor statesmen, unique in his simultaneous tenure of the deaneries of Canterbury and York. His religious opinions were catholic in tendency; his honesty was shown by his subsequent refusals of the episcopacy on the ground of unworthiness.

At Rochester the first dean appointed was Walter Phillips, a native of Maidstone, prior of Rochester at its surrender. Among the canons first appointed on the new foundation must be mentioned John Simkins, the last prior of St. Gregory's, Canterbury, who was deprived as a married man under Mary, but restored by Elizabeth.

Another great change carried out in 1541 was the execution of the king's order for the destruction of shrines.[264] The removal of the image of the patron saint of England in St. George's Church at Canterbury roused such strong feeling that it was apparently set up again for a time, in spite of the resolute proceedings of Cranmer's commissary, Nevinson, who had married Cranmer's niece,[265] and who by his zeal in requiring the abrogation of old and cherished customs roused much ill will against Cranmer in Kent. The injunctions had hitherto been only against images which were abused with pilgrimages or offerings,[266] but some of the canons maintained that four

---

[261] *L. and P. Hen. VIII*, xviii (2), p. xxxvi.   [262] Ibid. xv, 379.   [263] Hasted, *Kent*, ii, 25.
[264] *L. and P. Hen. VIII*, xvi, 1233, 1262.   [265] Ibid. xviii (2), 295, 309.   [266] Ibid. xiii (2), 281.

images taken down in Canterbury Cathedral had not been abused at all,[267] and there seems to have been a great deal of iconoclasm in the whole diocese.[268] The most glaring offender was Thomas Cawby or Dawby,[269] lately parson of Lenham, now of Wichling, who took down eight or more images in his own church 'that never were abused by any pilgrimage.' At Lenham, where he had tried in vain to persuade his parishioners to take down every one of the images, he persuaded his successor, Sir John Abbey, to steal the key of the church door from the sexton's keeping, and secretly take down and break in pieces the image of Our Lady of Pity, said to be the fairest image in the church, and one that had never been abused. At Sittingbourne, being told that images stood in the church there, he said, 'Your curate is more knave.' 'Why do they stand in Cranbrooke then?' he was asked, 'seeing that there dwelleth worshipful men, the king's justices, and, as I think, some of them be of the king's council. And, by that, they are now building a goodly rood loft.' 'They are pope-holy knaves,' was the reply, 'and I would that the rood loft were money in my purse.'

Cranmer and his commissary were accused of extending their protection to heresy by their handling at this time of Joan Bocher, burnt for strange opinions in the following reign, and Prebendary Milles wrote that it was the general opinion that heresies were increased in Kent by the fact that such cases as hers were allowed to go unpunished.[270] It was felt, moreover, that new-fangled preaching was tolerated, and that those who disliked it had better be on their guard. Bishop Gardiner, in a conversation he had with his namesake, the prebendary of Canterbury, in 1541,[271] advised him to write his sermon beforehand, and before going up into the pulpit to hand it to someone to read, who could swear then that he spoke that and nothing else, but that if the prebendary should himself hear another preach otherwise than well, it would be best to take no notice. While the preaching of Dr. Nicholas Ridley was much disliked, and that of his brother, Lancelot, who objected to prayers in an unknown tongue, was, with that of Mr. Scory (under Edward VI bishop of Rochester), equally resented, Robert Serles, one of the six preachers, maintained that reverence was due to images, and did not involve idolatry.

Even Cranmer's wonted mildness gave way to indignation at the unruliness of his subordinates ;[272] but for their divided minds he was really responsible, having appointed as preachers three of the old learning and three of the new 'to the intent that they might try out the doctrine.'[273] These are his own words, and when Gardiner had replied to him 'My lord, that is a mean to set us at variance,' he was silenced by the archbishop's reply, 'The king's pleasure is to have it so.'[274]

A conspiracy was formed against the archbishop 'by his secret enemies the papists,' including members of the council, justices of Kent, and some of

---

[267] L. and P. Hen. VIII, xviii (2), 349, 369.
[268] Ibid. xviii (2), 279, 309, 311, 315. [269] Ibid. 315, 316.
[270] She had been acquitted of heresy at Calais, but after half a year's detention was sent back to England for examination on heresies objected to her at Canterbury. L. and P. Hen. VIII, xvii, 829 (23 Sept. 1542). A sharp contest concerning her ensued between the commissary and Prebendary Milles, and when Nevinson was forced to pronounce her a heretic, he advised her how to save herself by appealing to a proclamation of pardon to those who had been seduced from the church and meant to return to it. Ibid. xviii (2), 314.
[271] Ibid. Introd. p. xl.
[272] L. and P. Hen. VIII, xviii (2), 378. [273] Ibid. 323, 353. [274] Ibid. 348.

the prebendaries of his own cathedral, who complained to the king ' of the doctrine by him and his chaplains taught in Kent.'[275] Prebendary Serles and Dr. Willoughby, vicar of Chilham, seem to have been actually responsible for the conveyance of articles against him to the council.[276] The archbishop presided over the commission appointed to inquire into the matter, which held its sittings in October, 1542.[277] Since August Cranmer had been busy with a visitation of his diocese ; and on 27 October he held a sessions of the Six Articles at Canterbury, when indictments were preferred against John Bland and Richard Turner, two preachers of Cranmer's own school, and Cranmer took down with his own hand depositions against Prebendaries Gardiner, Parkhurst, and Milles, and the preachers Serles, Shether, and Willoughby ; a record of the investigations survives and shows them to have been clearly one-sided, and against maintainers of the old learning.[278] All who had joined in drawing up or presenting the articles against him were imprisoned or brought to submission. It was thought advisable in the following year to send a ' generall commission into Kent with certeyne speciall articles, and generally all abuses and enormities of religion to be examined.'[279] In the same year various persons were reported to the privy council from Kent for ' lewd and seditious words.'[280] When, in the Parliament of 1545, Sir John Gostwick complained of Cranmer's preaching at Sandwich and Canterbury, the king only regarded this as further evidence of a confederacy against the archbishop.[281]

Although, after the death of Henry, Cranmer with characteristic prudence urged that the nonage of Edward VI was not the time for ritualistic changes and measures of reform, the action of Parliament necessitated the issue in 1548 of the new Prayer Book ; this, with certain ceremonial changes ordained in council in the same year, resulted in 1550 in commotions in Kent.[282] In April, 1549, under a commission issued in that month for the prosecution of Anabaptists, heretics, or contemners of the Book of Common Prayer, Joan Bocher, or Joan of Kent, who denied the human nature of Christ, was condemned and sentenced. She was not, however, burnt until 2 May, 1550, and in that interval Cranmer himself, and Bishop Ridley, who had been consecrated to Rochester[283] in September, 1547, did their best to convert her, but in vain.

In 1549 Cranmer held a visitation in his diocese, and among the ' articles to be inquired of ' is included ' Item, whether they have not monished their parishioners openly that they should not sell, give, nor otherwise alienate any of their churches' goods.'[284] A letter of the Protector Somerset, and of the Lords of the Council to Cranmer, dated 30 April, 1548, had directed him to

---

[275] Nichol, *Narratives of the Reformation* (Camd. Soc.), 251.

[276] *L. and P. Hen. VIII*, xviii (2), pp. 324–7, 331–2.   [277] Ibid. pp. 321, 323, 359.

[278] Ibid. pp. 291–378.   [279] *Acts of the P.C.* i, 126.   [280] Ibid. 124, 148.

[281] As time went on it began to be realized, however, that in preaching more latitude must be allowed. Sir Richard Blostoke, priest, late curate of Tenterden, who had preached against heresy, and was in 1546 before the council, described as ' by himself and a light prest which he mayntaind in his parsonage, having brought sondry of his parishioners to light opinions about religion ' was ' with a good lesson dismissed.' *Acts of the P.C.* i, 419, 421, 492.

[282] *Acts of the P.C.* iii, 53, 117, 198, 199 ; Gairdner, *Hist. of Engl. Ch.* (ed. Stephens and Hunt) iv, 266.

[283] Bishop Holbeche had succeeded Bishop Heath in 1544, and was translated to Lincoln in 1547. Nicholas Ridley had long been connected with Kent, having held the vicarage of Herne since 1538, as well as his prebendal stall since 1541.   [284] Cardwell, *Documentary Annals*, i, 48.

charge every parish in his diocese in no wise to sell, give, or otherwise alienate any bells or other ornament or jewels belonging to the parish church.[285] These instructions were preliminary to the issue of commissions for the seizure of church plate in 1552–3, and the inventories taken in 1552 in Kent show that in many cases, as for instance at Chilham, Crayford, and Godmersham, the parishioners had, in spite of them, with one consent turned to account their superfluous church goods, by selling them to meet the Edwardian requirements as to the provision of new books, communion tables, removal of altars, roods and images, and whitening of walls to obliterate frescoes. The inventories surviving for Kent[286] are peculiarly defective, more than half being lacking, those which are preserved belonging almost entirely to the lathes of Shepway and Sutton at Hone, together with the cities of Canterbury and Rochester. The surviving inventories have been transcribed *in extenso* in *Archaelogia Cantiana*,[287] and show an amazing wealth, multitude, and variety of church goods and ornaments, while none of the old service books appear, and nearly every church was possessed of the great Bible, and the Paraphrase of Erasmus, in obedience to the Injunctions of 1547. Certain churches, however, are described as 'broken up and robbed,' though in only five of these was any silver stolen, at Chislehurst, Cudham, Great and Little Chart, and Eltham. The method of procedure adopted in Kent at this date is fully described in a letter[288] written in the next reign to the commissioners of Queen Mary in 1556, by the Kentish commissioners who had acted under Edward's orders in 1553 ; the Marian commissioners being then concerned to get back vestments which had been sold, and deliver them to those churches to which they originally belonged, as the more costly vestments made of gold, and tissue, and jewels, and the plate considered superfluous had been sent up from Kent to the master of the jewel house in the last month of the king's life.[289]

The vice-dean and chapter of Canterbury were summoned before the council 23 October, 1547, in the person of John Poynet, priest,[290] a member of the chapter, to account for jewels they were said to have converted into money, i.e., a pyx of gold, 'garnisshed with perles and stones conntrefaicted and wayeng xxxvj oz *di*, yet remaining intier and wholl,' and a silver crucifix, already converted into money. Poynet was ordered to keep the pyx entire and whole, and neither it nor the money received for the crucifix was to be converted to any use, but to be kept in a safe manner in their house. In January the dean and prebendaries had orders to deliver the 'silver table that stoode upon the high aulter' to Sir Anthony Aucher.[291] It is possible that the reason for the incompleteness of the Edwardian inventories for Kent is that the commission had not really finished its work at Edward's death.

[285] Strype, *Mem. Cranmer*, ii, 8.

[286] Contained in MSS. Church Goods, Kent, Temp. Edw. VI, $\frac{3}{13}$–$\frac{3}{43}$, (P.R.O.).

[287] Beginning viii, 99–163, and completed in subsequent volumes.

[288] Land Revenue Rec., Church Goods, $\frac{6}{442}$, P.R.O.; *Arch. Cant.* xiv, 313.

[289] Ibid. ; and Land Revenue Rec., Church Goods, $\frac{6}{449}$, P.R.O.   [290] *Acts of the P.C.* ii, 139.

[291] *Acts of the P.C.* ii, 539. Another entry in this volume is suggestive, as showing a possible destination for some of the lead stripped off the suppressed religious houses in Kent. Warrant for lead 'to be sent to Bulloin, to be had at Canterbury and Dover.' Ibid. 216. How much church property must have disappeared in this and subsequent years in Kent may be gathered from a letter of Archbishop Parker's to Cecil, 12 Aug. 1567 (*Cal. S.P. Dom.* 1547–80, p. 297), in which he informs him 'The produce of the broken plate and bullion found in the cathedral has been applied to church uses only. Not a tenth of the plate and ornaments was left which was there at the time of Dr. Wotton's coming.'

JOHN SCORY,
BISHOP OF ROCHESTER.
(1551–1552.)

CANTERBURY
SEAL AD CAUSAS.
(14th Century.)

THOMAS CRANMER,
ARCHBISHOP OF CANTERBURY.
(1540.)

Strype says that the inquiry for which this commission was issued to the archbishop and other gentlemen of Kent 'being somewhat an odious work, he was not very forward to enter upon it.'[292]

Both Cranmer and his friend and former chaplain, Bishop Ridley, had gone far in the formulation of the doctrines of the Reformation before Ridley was translated to London in 1550, being succeeded at Rochester by John Poynet,[293] a strong divine of the reforming school, who had been proctor for the diocese of Canterbury, and chaplain to Cranmer. They were assisted by the eminent foreign reformers who responded to Cranmer's invitation to come over and help him. Peter Martyr and Bernardino Ochino, who had been driven out of Italy by the Inquisition, and Peter Alexander, a divine of the French Church, arrived in 1547, and Alexander and Ochino became canons of Canterbury. John a Lasco, a Polish nobleman, spent some months with Cranmer in Canterbury before he went to form a congregation at London. Most of the foreign divines and scholars who were the guests of Cranmer passed on to London or the universities : but John Utenhovius and Francois de la Rivière remained a longer time in the city, and in 1548–9, were engaged in the foundation of a refugee congregation there[294] among those who had been fleeing from persecution in France and Flanders since the latter half of the reign of Henry VIII. For some time before the close of Edward's life it must have been felt that the end could not be far off, and that Mary and persecution must follow. This period, according to Strype, was spent by Cranmer in retirement at his house near Canterbury, where in 1552 he received an order from the council to examine 'the sect newly sprung in Kent,' 'and to take such ordre in the same as these errours be not suffred thus to over spred the kinges faithful subjectes.'[295] This sect Strype considers to have been not the Anabaptists,[296] but the Family of Love.[297]

The reluctant signature by Cranmer of his name to the will of Edward VI had for its natural sequence in the next reign an order to appear in consistory at St. Paul's and bring with him an inventory of his goods, which he did on 27 August, 1552. About the same time Dr. Thornden, suffragan bishop of Dover,[298] ventured without his leave to restore the mass in Canterbury Cathedral, and he straightway drew up a declaration that it was not done by his authority, and contradicted a rumour that he was willing to say mass before Queen Mary.[299] He was committed to the Tower for disseminating seditious bills, and put on his trial for treason. His life was spared by the clemency of the queen, but he was cited to appear at Rome, and answer such matter as might be objected against him by the king and queen, 7 September, 1555. After watching the martyrdom of Ridley and

---

[292] *Mem. Cranmer* (ed. 1812) i, 419.

[293] The first bishop consecrated according to the new ordinal (Strype, *Mem. Cranmer*, i, 274, 363), and the last to hold his other preferments (these included the vicarage of Ashford and ninth stall at Canterbury), with his bishopric. The Order in Council gave as the reason for this indulgence that the bishop had no house to dwell in. He was twice married.

[294] Pyper, *Jan Utenhove*, App. Letter 3.   [295] *Acts of the P.C.* iii, 131, 26 Sept.

[296] Northumberland, writing to Sir Wm. Cecil, 28 Oct. 1552, wishes the king would appoint Mr. Knox to the bishopric of Rochester. 'He would be a whetstone to the archbishop of Canterbury, and a confounder of the Anabaptists lately sprung up in Kent.' *Cal. S.P. Dom.* 1547–80, p. 46.

[297] *Mem. Cranmer* (ed. 1812), i, 418.

[298] This bishopric was instituted under the Act of 26 Hen. VIII, cap. 14.

[299] It was a strongly-worded document, and was published with premature haste by Bishop Scory, who in 1551 had succeeded John Poynet, translated in that year from Rochester to Winchester.

Latimer, he was degraded by Bishops Bonner and Thirlby. His recantation was followed by abjuration before he was executed, showing much courage and patience in his torments.

There was but one man Mary would appoint to succeed him, her kinsman, Cardinal Pole, the protégé of Henry VIII until he incurred his royal benefactor's displeasure, when his opinion on the divorce question was asked, by giving an adverse one.[300] His attainder was reversed by Mary's third Parliament, and he was appointed by papal bull to succeed Cranmer. He crossed to Dover, 12 November, 1554, not as legate but as cardinal, and was received with salvoes of artillery. By Canterbury he travelled to Rochester, and there received a message requesting him to come to the queen in his legatine capacity, for the exercise of which a patent had been made.[301] Hitherto he had been in deacon's orders only, and he was not ordained priest until 20 March following, at the church of the Grey Friars, Greenwich ; before that date he had procured absolution for the realm and reunion with the Church of Rome.

Even before his arrival much had been done to accomplish the restoration of the old order, the whole of the Edwardine legislation concerning the sacraments, uniformity, and priests' marriages was repealed, an Act was passed against disturbing divine service, and much was done to restore to the parishes vestments and plate of which they had been denuded.

In Kent resentment was audible from the first. In August, 1553, a letter from the council to the mayor of Canterbury directed him to 'set on the Pillorye one Panton, vicare of St. Dunstanes besides Canterbury, and one John Burden, for uttering certayn unsemely woordes against the quenes heignes.'[302]

The clergy of the county suffered heavily in consequence of the queen's injunctions ordering deprivation of the married clergy.[303] The evidence as to these deprivations shows how large a number had availed themselves of the permission to marry, and also throws a light on the tacit recognition of clerical marriage long before it was publicly authorized. At Canterbury, where the record of the dean and chapter seems complete, fifty-nine cases of deprivation are recorded for February and March, 1553–4, and nine in the following year.[304] (This does not include London parishes.) At Rochester a return was made 12 January, 1554–5, which gives evidence of thirty-three cases.[305] In the Canterbury Institutions[306] marriage is given as the cause of deprivation in twenty-three cases, and in many other cases it is known that the deprived priest was married.

An inquiry was held at Rochester by the commissioners of the dean and chapter of Canterbury. The case of the canon, John Simkins, has been already alluded to. He was married five years before and had two children[307]

---

[300] He had probably taken up his residence abroad to avoid having to give one : and the prolonged exile as well as the greater disasters which followed it proved the wisdom of his course.

[301] On his way to London he was received by Lord Cobham at Cowling Castle. *Arch. Cant.* xii, 123.

[302] *Acts of the P.C.* iv, 330.

[303] Issued 4 Mar. 1553–4. The deprivations at Canterbury can be followed in the archiepiscopal registers at Lambeth and in the registers of the dean and chapter at Canterbury. (The dean and chapter administered the see during the long vacancy between Cranmer's attainder and Pole's accession.)

[304] W. H. Frere, *Marian Reaction in its Relation to the Engl. Clergy*, 47.   [305] Ibid. 48.
[306] Ibid. 57.   [307] Ibid. 67.

Nicholas Arnold was ordained priest as a Benedictine at Rochester, and became *lector evangelii*; he married Joane Perse, widow, six years before in his own house, but gave her up on All Saints' Day.[308] Thomas Bedlow was ordained priest twenty years before at Halling Church, Rochester diocese, and shortly after married Joan Rawlins at St. Nicholas Church, Rochester.[309] One Robert Vevian, clerk, parson of Hever, a priest for twenty-six years, was subsequently restored on reading, signing and delivering an act of recantation promising never to return to Agnes Stanton, the wife he had married.[310]

At Canterbury fourteen members of the chapter were summoned to appear 15 March, but only half of them did so, admitted their marriage, and defended it.[311] Sentence of suspension from priestly function, sequestration, deprivation, and prohibition to live with their wives was pronounced against all, present or absent; the absent, John Joseph, Peter Alexander, Bernard Ochino, prebendaries; and Lancelot Ridley, Richard Turner, Thomas Becon, and Richard Besely, preachers, being pronounced contumacious. Those who were present and signed a confession were the archbishop's brother, Archdeacon and Prebendary Cranmer, Prebendaries William Willoughby, William Devenish, and Robert Goldson; Thomas Brook and Thomas Stevens, preachers; and Sherland and Goodrick, petty canons.[312] The commissioners included Richard, bishop of Dover, sub-dean, and Prebendaries Richard Parkhurst and John Milles.[313]

The most interesting case was that of Rowland Taylor, parson of Hadleigh, where he was burnt on other charges 9 January, 1555–6, summoned at Rochester perhaps because of his Rochester canonry. He had been married twenty-nine years before in the presence of Benet a priest, and ordained priest eleven or twelve years previously by Yngworth, bishop of Dover.[314]

In March, 1554–5, one of the 'six bishops after the old sort' appointed by Mary was Maurice Griffin, made bishop of Rochester. Bishop Scory had been translated to Chichester, May, 1552, and the bishopric had thus been left vacant for nearly three years. Fuller describes Griffin as a great persecutor.[315] In the convocation that sat at Oxford in April, Walter Phillips, dean of Rochester,[316] a sympathizer hitherto with the opinions then condemned, made a retractation first before the Upper and then before the Lower House.

The rising of Sir Thomas Wyat in Kent in the preceding January, the only formidable movement of the sort in the country, belongs more properly to the domain of political history, but though its pretext was a political one, its motive was in truth heretical conspiracy.[317]

Pole refused to be consecrated until 22 March, 1556, the day after Cranmer's execution. He was consecrated at the church of the Grey Friars, Greenwich,[318] by Heath, archbishop of York, and six suffragans, and did not

---

[308] W. H. Frere, *Marian Reaction*, 69.   [309] Ibid.   [310] Ibid. 82.

[311] Reg. D. and C. fol. 155.   [312] Strype, *Mem. Cranmer*, iii, 471.   [313] Ibid.

[314] W. H. Frere, *Marian Reaction*, 67.   [315] *Church Hist.* bk. viii, 18.

[316] Gairdner, *Hist. of Engl. Ch.* (ed. Stephens and Hunt), iv, 337.

[317] The changes witnessed in the reigns of Edward and Mary are clearly shown by a comparison of the visitation articles for the diocese of Canterbury of 1549 and 1557. Cardwell, *Documentary Annals*, 41, &c.; and 170, &c.

[318] In pursuance of the attempt to restore the monastic system in England, a company of Grey Friars had been placed in April of the preceding year in their old house at Greenwich.

go to Canterbury until three days later ; he evidenced a desire to make the ceremonies which followed thus hard upon the tragic death of his predecessor as private as possible.[319]   On 27 March,[320] the new archbishop gave a commission to David Pole, LL.D., to be his vicar-general in spirituals, and bestowed on him other offices.

Before this date persecution had already begun in Kent,[321] and was claiming many victims.   Foxe says that Nicholas Harpsfield, who had succeeded Cranmer in the archdeaconry, was 'the sorest and of least compassion as a persecutor, only Dunning of Norwich excepted.'[322]   In a council held 30 June, 1555, letters had been dispatched to the noblemen and gentlemen of Kent

> to be present themselves upon warnyng given them by the shiriefe at the places of execution, and to assist him for that purpose ; viz. Rochestre, Dartford, and Tunbridge, where the sundrie persones condempned for heresie are appointed to suffre.[323]

Strype gives the numbers burnt for religion in Kent in this reign as fifty-four : eighteen in 1555, of whom fifteen suffered at Canterbury, one at Rochester, one at Dartford, and one at Tonbridge ; seven in 1556, of whom five suffered at Canterbury, and two at Rochester ; twenty-four in 1557, of whom two suffered at Wye, two at Ashford, seven at Maidstone, and thirteen at Canterbury ; and in 1558, five at Canterbury.[324]   A letter of sharp reprimand was addressed by the council, 28 July, 1557,[325] to the sheriff of Kent and mayor of Rochester, directing them to signify hither what hath moved them to 'staye such personnes as have byn condempned for heresy from execucion, who have been delivered unto them by thordinarye.'[326]

Queen Mary and her archbishop died on the same day, 17 November, 1557.   By this date persecution had been carried to such a point in the county as to make it one where, when the revulsion that followed on their deaths was succeeded by inevitable reaction, Popish recusancy had singularly few adherents.

At the accession of Elizabeth it was the estimate of Feria, the Spanish ambassador, that 'all the young men and most of the old are attacked with heresy, and that London, Kent, and the sea-ports are very heretical.'[327]

It was not until 1 August following that Matthew Parker, a married man,[328] and an ardent supporter of the reformed doctrines, who had been living in retirement since his deprivation of all his emoluments in Mary's reign, was elected to the archbishopric, in spite of his urgent petitions (based on his lameness, even his unworthiness), to be dispensed from the high

---

[319] Cal. S.P. Venetian, &c. vi, pt i, 377.

[320] Strype, Eccl. Mem. iii (1), 476.

[321] The Heresy Laws were revived in Dec. 1554.

[322] Foxe, Acts and Monuments, viii, 253.

[323] Acts of the P.C. v, 154.

[324] Eccl. Mem. iii (2) ; Catalogue of Originals, No. lxxxv.

[325] Acts of the P.C. vi, 135.

[326] Details as to the names and heresies of those who suffered at this time in Kent under Nicholas Harpsfield, and Thornden, bishop of Dover, and the localities to which they belonged, are to be found : Harl. MSS. 421, fol. 92 et seq.; ibid. 590, fol. 78 et seq. ; Stowe MSS. 743, fol. 116; Strype, Eccl. Mem. iii (2), 120; Foxe, Acts and Monuments, viii, 254, 300, 321, 326, 328, 504, 505, as well as in the archiepiscopal registers, and registers of the dean and chapter.   For other charges against persons holding heretical opinions, see the cardinal's visitation of his diocese, begun in 1556 ; Cant. Archiepis. Reg. Pole.   Examples from the register are quoted in Diocesan Hist. of Cant. 283–9.

[327] W. H. Frere, Hist. of Engl. Ch. (ed. Stephens and Hunt), v, 15.

[328] His love for his beautiful and refined wife was one of the most prominent features of his private life, and must have made the queen's order of 9 Aug. 1561, excluding women and children from residence in inclosures of colleges and cathedrals, particularly distasteful to him.

office, which the history of his primacy was to show no other man could have filled so well.

A commission was appointed to revise the Prayer Book, December, 1558, and by the end of April, 1559, the English service was already in use in Kent.[329] The passing of the Supremacy Act and of the Act of Uniformity was the first step towards the enforcement of reformed doctrines, and these were at once initiated by the royal visitation of 1559, carried out in Canterbury and Rochester dioceses by Thomas Becon, a returned exile, rewarded by a stall at Canterbury, and formerly Cranmer's chaplain, by an advocate named Weste, and by Robert Nowell.[330]

When Parker was elected, Dean Wotton professed his adherence to Elizabeth's measures in the chapter-house, with four canons. The rest he preconized, but neither Nicholas Harpsfield, the archdeacon, nor the canons Hugh Turnbull, Richard Fawcett, Ralf Jackson, Robert Collins, John Knight, and Thomas Wood[331] made their appearance, and they were pronounced contumacious. An order of council of 11 February, 1558, had directed an examination to be made into a report that the archdeacon 'hath used himself of late very dissorderly in steringe up the people as much as in him liethe to sedytion,' and that 'one man of the Colledge of Christ Church hath nere one hundred harnesses';[332] while others say that 'religion could not nor should not be altered.' After the archdeacon's refusal of obedience to the Prayer Book and the queen's injunctions in October, 1559, he was committed to the Tower, and remained a prisoner until his death in 1575.

He was succeeded by Edmund Gheast, formerly vice-provost of Cambridge, who had been in continual hiding in Mary's reign, and since then one of the revisers of the liturgy. His first official act was to instal Parker, to whom he was domestic chaplain,[333] as archbishop. He pleased the queen by remaining unmarried, and was consecrated bishop of Rochester by Parker, 24 January, 1559–60, when he was licensed to keep the rectory of Cliffe and his archdeaconry.

In 1560 a metropolitical visitation was undertaken by Parker, who started with his own diocese in September. The dean, Wotton, the prebendaries, minor canons, and preachers, among them Becon, Bale, Nowell, and Goodrick, assembled in the chapter-house and made mutual presentations: that the prebendaries came not to the daily services; that the ministers were negligent; that the minor canons were drunkards, railers, jesters, and disobedient; that of the minor canons there were but seven instead of twelve, men out of the town supplying the vacant rooms; Bale and Goodrick presented that the arms of Pole and his cardinal's hat were hung up in the church, which they thought not decent nor tolerable, but abominable.[334] Rochester was visited next after Canterbury by the same

---

[329] W. H. Frere, *Hist. of Engl. Ch.* (ed. Stephens and Hunt), v, 25.

[330] Lambeth MSS. 959, fol. 424. [331] Strype, *Parker*, i, 103.

[332] *Acts of the P.C.* vii, 53–4. In the same month (ibid. 62–3) William Baslenden, parson of St. George's Canterbury, was sent for by the council for his lewd words. The mayor had at the same time instructions to deal with Sir Loye, the curate of All Saints, after calling to him the two next justices of the peace, 'and to take ordre for suche his punishement as the qualitie of his offences shall seme to him and the sayd justices to have deserved,' and to deal with such offenders in the future without 'troublyng or molestinge the Counsell of any such matters.' In 1559, Wm. Baslenden was apprehended as he was endeavouring 'to pass the seas' at Dover; ibid. 100.

[333] Cole MSS. 5815, fol. 5. [334] Dixon, *Hist. of the Ch. of Engl.* v, 341.

visitors, before whom a returned exile, Richard Turner, now vicar of Dartford, preached a sermon.[335]

It is possible to make complete lists from the archbishop's and bishop's registers of the clergy deprived in Canterbury and Rochester for refusing to acquiesce in the settlement of religion.[336] These were : From Canterbury diocese, the archdeacon, Nicholas Harpsfield, Prebendaries Glazier, Wood, Colyns, and Fawcett, and ten incumbents,[337] and from Rochester diocese, where no dignitaries were deprived, two incumbents.[338] The breach grew wider, too, between the Anglican and the Genevan parties among the reformers, and ecclesiastical discipline was tightened up by Convocation and Parliament in 1563, when an inquiry was ordered into the state of each diocese.

The archbishop's certificate as to his own diocese[339] states the number of churches and chapels in the diocese as 276, the number of households 10,948. The bishop of Rochester's certificate[340] states that the diocese

> is no shyre but a parte of the shyre of Kent. . . The regyment of the diocesse of Rochester belongeth to the bysshop only, and the archdeacon hath no jurisdiction, but onely then when he visiteth. Ther is but one archdeacon in the diocesse of Rochester, and his name is John Bridgwater, and wateth ordinarely of my Ld Robert Dudley.

The number of parish churches is given by him as 91. Rochester was the smallest diocese in the kingdom.

The archdeacon's records from 1560 down to these returns of 1563 shew a great lack of clergy and number of vacant benefices, with many decayed churches, in the diocese of Canterbury.[341] The proportion of married to unmarried clergy in Canterbury and Rochester at this time was nearly equal. The metropolitical inquiry of 1561[342] showed that more than half the chapter at Rochester were pluralists, that five out of the eight members of the chapter there were preachers, and only thirteen out of sixty-four parochial clergy[343] were preachers.

Hatred of ceremonial and vestiarian troubles were beginning to show themselves, and in January, 1565, the queen sent to Parker a peremptory letter reproaching him with slackness and inaction. The archbishop within a week sent orders to his suffragans to certify to him what disorder and variety there might be in doctrine, in ceremonies, or in the behaviour of their clergy, by the last day of February at the latest.[344] Only two certificates survive, neither for a diocese, but one that of the chapter of Canterbury. The prebendaries declared[345] that no doctrine was taught in Christchurch other than that which was appointed by public authority ; that daily prayers were sung at the communion table standing north and south ; that it stood east and west once a month when Holy Communion was ministered ; that when there was no communion the minister used a surplice only ; that in communion the priest who ministered and the epistoler and gospeller wore copes ; that when the prebendaries preached it was with surplice and hood ; that they were all present once a day at least apparelled in the choir ; that the preachers (peculiar to Canter-

[335] Strype, *Parker*, i, 75. [336] Dr. Gee, *The Elizabethan Settlement*, 237.
[337] Ibid. 252. [338] Ibid. 283. [339] Harleian MSS. 594, fol. 63, etc. 4 July, 1563.
[340] Lansdowne MSS. vi. fol. 141, etc.; ibid. vii, fol. 22.
[341] W. H. Frere, *Hist. of Engl. Ch.* (ed. Stephens and Hunt.), v, 105. [342] Ibid. 106.
[343] Even this is a high proportion compared with other dioceses.
[344] Strype, *Parker*, bk. ii. App. No. xxvi. [345] Dixon, *Hist. of the Ch. of Engl.* vi, 47.

bury) wore surplices and hoods, and that all other members wore surplices; that as to the bread used in the Holy Communion they followed the queen's injunctions, and used cakes resembling those served formerly for private masses, and that none lived disorderly.[346]

The council on 6 November, 1569, directed a letter to Parker about the recovering of the discipline of the Church, with the object of suppressing papists and Puritans.[347]   The visitation [348] in his diocese in this year seems to have been the result of this letter.   Among the new inquiries are (art. 16) 'Whether there be in your quarters any that openly or privily use or frequent any kind of divine service or common prayer, other than is set forth by the laws of the realm,' and (art. 18) 'whether there be any that keep any secret conventicles, preachings, lectures, or readings, contrary to the laws.'   It was also inquired whether altars were plucked down and replaced by communion tables, whether the communion were administered in wafer bread or common bread, in 'prophane cuppes' heretofore used at mass, or in a decent communion cup, whether all monuments of idolatry were destroyed, and whether the Book of Common Prayer and the Bible in the largest edition were provided.

The foundation of English Catholic colleges abroad [349] was to result in an increase of recusancy in the southern counties, and the bull of 1570 excommunicating and deposing the queen was the signal for more plotting and the arrival of more missionaries from the continent, but in that year itself the archbishop was able to give a satisfactory account of his diocese.   In 274 parishes he reported only 113 persons as irregular churchgoers, with about the same number out of communion, 10 of them persons of quality and absentees these ten years.   The proportion of communicants was seven in every two households, and the number of persons confirmed in the year 2,000.[350]

Puritan discontent was increased by the publication of the Thirty-nine Articles 4 May, 1570, and by an order issued May, 1571, that the preachers were to have a new licence, and that no minister was to officate unlicensed or otherwise than according to the Prayer Book.   It was about this time that we notice the beginning of prophesyings.

In September of this year Bishop Gheast was translated to Salisbury; Edmund Freke, dean of Salisbury, succeeded him at Rochester, and was enthroned 22 March following.   He was then almoner to Queen Elizabeth, and held the archdeaconry of Canterbury *in commendam*.   Later, when the queen wished that the bishops should put down prophesyings,[351] which she considered a fruitful source of discord, but which their adherents believed to be likely to promote that capacity for preaching in which the returns show the Kentish clergy to have been very deficient, he did his best to maintain them.[352]

During the queen's progress through Kent this summer her interest in the foreigners settled in Sandwich is recorded, but no mention is made of the

---

[346] Strype, *Parker*, bk. ii. ch. xxvi. (i. 183)   [347] Cardwell, *Documentary Annals*, 315.
[348] Ibid. 320, &c., and Cant. Archiepis. Reg. Parker, i, fol. 302*a*, &c.
[349] Louvain was at first the great centre.   A more permanent stronghold was founded at Douai in 1568; this was removed to Rheims in 1578.
[350] W. H. Frere, *Hist. of Engl. Ch.* (ed. Stephens and Hunt), v, 155.   [351] Strype, *Grindal*, App. x.
[352] To Bishop Parkhurst of Norwich, their staunch supporter, he wrote 'I have taken such order that no man shall have anything to do with any matter of controversy.   By this means the exercise is continued without offence, to the comfort of God's church and increase of knowledge in the ministry.' Quoted *Diocesan Hist. of Rochester*, 272.

settlement in Canterbury.[353] After the accession of Mary, all foreign Protestants had been ordered to depart, and instructions were sent to the Kentish ports that they should be allowed to pass out of the kingdom. There is no certainty as to the date at which the church vaguely referred to in the letters of Peter Martyr and Jan Utenhove was re-established in Canterbury, but it must have been in existence again in 1575 when by order of the Privy Council, the general body of the Walloon congregation at Sandwich was removed to Canterbury.[354]

Parker's death in 1575 was a great loss, and his successor, the stern, puritanical Grindal, transferred from York to Canterbury 10 January, 1575, was an ineffective primate, in consequence of his rupture with the queen on the question of prophesyings. He was suspended from ecclesiastical but not spiritual functions, and his visitation carried out by officials. He refused to submit until, in 1583, blindness and sickness led him to accept the queen's suggestion that he should resign, but he died before doing so.

At the time of his death Rochester was in the hands of Bishop Young,[355] of whom Aylmer, bishop of London, wrote commending his ' quickness in government, and readiness in learning,' and ability ' to bridle innovators, not by authority only but by weight of arguments.'

Archbishop Whitgift was promoted from Worcester in succession to Grindal, 14 August, 1583.[356] His first action was to draw up a scheme of reform, and this was followed by a return of the clergy in each diocese with a report as to conformity and recusancy. The returns for Canterbury[357] give the names of 128 preachers who are conformable, and of twelve who are recusants. Of the 128 conformable preachers seven are doctors, fifteen bachelors of divinity, sixty masters of art, eleven bachelors of art, thirty-five no graduates. Of the twelve not conformable,

> 2, Mr. Calver and Mr. Case, curates, are masters of art; 4, Sirs Carslacke, Elvyn, Halden, and Nicolles, are beneficed and bachelors of art; 2, Sirs Goliford and Knight are bachelors of art, neither having nor serving cure; 3, Sirs Brimston, Evane, and Grimstone, are beneficed, but noe graduates; 1, Sir Wood, noe graduate, and deprived for sondrie Contempts.

[353] F. W. Cross, *Hist. of the Walloon and Huguenot Ch. at Cant.* (Huguenot Soc. Lond. xv), 17.

[354] By order under the great seal of 6 July, 1561, the mayor, jurats and commonalty of Sandwich were directed to receive twenty or twenty-five households of ten or twelve persons each ' belonging to the church of strangers in our said city of London,' the settlers to be chosen by the archbishop or bishop of London. Letters Patent of 1567 permitted a similar settlement at Maidstone. These settlements of French and Dutch refugees were essentially congregations, even their industrial organization being founded on an ecclesiastical basis. The hospitality shown by Kent to the foreign reforming divines, some of whom, both before this date and after it, were included in the chapter of Canterbury, did not fail these congregations, and an entry for 15 Nov. 1576, in the *Actes du Consistoire* shows them already in possession of the temple in the crypt of the cathedral where their descendants worship to-day. This, according to the eighteenth-century antiquary, Alderman Cyprian Bunce, was assigned to them by royal favour, and not by grant of the dean and chapter. (*Translation of the several Charters &c., granted to the Citizens of Canterbury.* By a Citizen, 1791). The dean and chapter had in the previous year licensed ' the Wallons Strangers to have their common prayer and sermons in the parish church of St. Elphies in Canterbury.' F. W. Cross, *Hist. of the Walloon and Huguenot Ch. at Cant.* 37–41.

The acts of the Privy Council show that considerable trouble was taken by the archbishop, the mayor of Canterbury, and Lord Cobham to arrange for the disposal of the ' overplus ' from Sandwich to be removed, according to the council's instructions ' to places more remote from the sea-side,' a reminder of the many sorts of attack and invasion to which Kentish shores were at this time liable. *Acts of the P.C.* viii, 306, 336, 345.

[355] Consecrated 15 March, 1578, in succession to John Piers, who filled the see for a year only, after the translation of Bishop Freke to Norwich.

[356] Unlike his three predecessors he was enthroned in person at Canterbury (23 Oct.)

[357] Add. MSS. 34729, fol. 50 *b*.

The evidence shows that Kent had not been unaffected by the recent immigration of seminary priests. The council directed the justices of assize in Kent, 23 February, 1577, to summon a jury to try one Thomas Wells, a priest.[358] On 8 June, 1578, the dean and mayor of Canterbury apprehended there an Irishman, Edward Burnell, 'that hath brought into this realme sundrie books and munimentes of superstition, contrary to the present state of religion established in this realme.'[359] On 15 May, 1579, the dean and archdeacon of Canterbury and William Cromer, esq., forwarded to the council their 'examination of John Donne by them stayed in Canterbury for certen lewd speeches by him uttered in defence of the Romishe religion, appearing further that he had an intent to have passed over the Seas.'[360] A letter to the archbishop of 28 June, 1580, bids him to 'have regarde to the daily corruption growne by scolemasters, both publicque and private, in teaching and instructing of youthe in his diocese.'[361] The examination of Thomas Clarke, a seminary priest, 7 January, 1593,[362] before Richard, bishop suffragan of Dover, William Redman, archdeacon of Canterbury, and others, elicited the information that he was then thirty-seven years of age; was born at Erith in Kent, brought up at Winchester School, then at Douai half a year, and returned to England in 1576, being then twenty years of age, and after service with Lady Pembroke and others went to Dunkirk, then to Rheims College, was made a priest by the bishop of Laon in France, and ordered by Mr. Barnet, president at Rheims, to come to England to reconcile the people to the Church of Rome, say mass, &c. But if his account of himself was correct, he had been but an ineffective missionary, as he pleaded that 'he had persuaded none to the Catholic religion, having consorted with none but Catholics.'

Among the Old Kentish families the most obstinately recusant were the Ropers, the Darrels, the Guildfords, the Finches, and the Culpepers. William Roper, the son-in-law of Sir Thomas More, was an ardent Catholic, and was summoned before the Privy Council 8 July, 1568, for having relieved with money certain persons who had fled the country and had printed books against the queen's government.[363] On 27 July, 1581, his son Thomas Roper of Eltham, late of Orpington, was required to send up to the council his servants, Thompson and Paine,[364] and on 30 July Frauncis Thompson, priest, steward to the said Thomas Roper, was committed to the Marshalsea for saying mass on Whit Sunday last.[365] On 2 August Thomas Roper himself was committed to the Fleet to be kept a close prisoner, save only that the bishop of Rochester, to whose diocese he belonged, should be allowed to resort to him, or cause him to be conveyed to himself under the guard of his keeper, 'to conferre with him for the reducing of him to conformitye.'[366] A letter to this bishop of 7 August informed him that the council had

> of late convented before them Thomas Roper of Orpington, Esquier, in whose house upon search made was found and apprehended a Masse Prieste with certen Popishe trashe for massing, and upon conference with the said Roper, they, finding him very obstinate in Religion, have (as well in respect thereof as of his offence otherwise,) committed him unto the prisonne of the Fleete,

and requested the bishop to confer with him himself, or appoint an efficient and learned preacher to do so, to reduce him to conformity.[367] Bishop Young's

---

[358] *Acts of the P.C.* x, 174. [359] Ibid. xi, 245-6. [360] Ibid. 124. [361] Ibid. xii, 130.
[362] *Cal. S.P. Dom.* 1591-4, p. 304. [363] Ibid. 1547-80, p. 311. [364] *Acts of the P.C.* xiii, 141.
[365] Ibid. 147. [366] Ibid. 148. [367] Ibid. 158, 159.

measures were so successful that on 5 September, 1581,[368] Thomas Roper entered into a bond of £500, ' to resorte unto the parishe churche of the place where he shalbe abidinge,' and 'not to consort with or employ recusants.' He was summoned again on 29 October ' to answer of certyn matters concerning Campion the Jesuit.' [369] Subsequently his name appears with other members of his family as recusants contributing for horse in Ireland.[370]

On 4 May, 1586, instructions were issued for domiciliary visits in Deptford, Greenwich, Lewisham, Eltham, Lye, Charlton, and Woolwich, in the county of Kent, in search for Jesuit emissaries and seminary priests.[371] But the most remarkable of the measures taken against recusants was an order

> for the restraint of such principall gentleweomen, wives, widows, and others as have ben founde to be obstinate Recusantes, in respect that besides other disorders given by their libertie, their children and familyes by their examples have ben corrupted in religion,

and understanding that there be divers gentlewomen of this sort, ' wives to sondrie gentlemen of good accompte,' in the county of Kent, the council in a letter of 7 January, 1592–3, directed the archbishop to take measures to keep them from ' furder infecting of others.' [372]

Other Kentish gentlemen whose names appear among recusant lists at this time are Samuel Love, esq.,[373] Thomas Wilford of Lingham, and Sir Alexander Culpeper,[374] Mr. Wyborne,[375] Richard Culpeper,[376] William Turwhit ; [377] and to these are added in the next reign Sir Henry James of Smarden.[378] Other prisoners at Canterbury are described as ' of small value.' [379] Considering the position the county had always held in pre-Reformation days as a centre of pilgrimage, and considering its proximity to the continent, the number and importance of the recusants furnished by Kent is much smaller than might have been expected.[380]

A letter of 22 September, 1589, requesting the archbishop to appoint a chaplain for the Kentish contingent sent to the aid of the French King, from among the clergy of his diocese, sets forth her Majesty's desire for the religious welfare of her subjects, and that the preacher selected shall be well paid, and directs that his expenses shall be levied from the clergy of the diocese.[381]

The publication of the Marprelate pamphlets had begun in 1588, and in 1589 the bishop of Rochester [382] was one of the commissioners appointed to examine such as were suspected of being implicated in their publication.

The hostility of the Puritans to the Prayer Book and the Act of Supremacy had been declared without delay in Kent under the leadership of Mr. Dudley Fenner, then curate at Cranbrook. Born in Kent, where he

---

[368] *Acts of the P.C.* xiii, 196.　　[369] Ibid. 249.　　[370] Ibid. xxix, 309.

[371] Ibid. xiv, 90.　　[372] Ibid. xxiv, 9.

[373] Ibid. xiii, 231 (12 Oct. 1581) ; ibid. xxix, 309 (11 May, 1600).

[374] Ibid. 118.　　　　　　　　　　　　　　　　[375] Ibid. 53.

[376] *Cal. S.P. Dom.* 1581–90, p. 460 (31 Jan. 1388).　　[377] Ibid. 461.

[378] Ibid. 1603–10, p. 621.　　　　　　　　　　[379] Ibid. 1581–90, p. 460.

[380] The passing of the Act decreeing the banishment of Jesuits, seminary priests, &c., from the country, unless they would take the oath of supremacy, in 1585, was considerably accelerated by the discovery of the plot to murder the queen sanctioned by the pope, in which Dr. Parry, member for Queenborough, who had made a strong speech against the Jesuit Bill, and who had become a Romanist, was implicated, and for his share in which plot he was executed 3 March, 1585.　　[381] *Acts of the P.C.* xviii, 127–8.

[382] Ibid. xviii, 227 (16 Nov. 1589). Among the most active of the clergy appointed to act in this matter was also Richard Bancroft, the future archbishop of Canterbury.

was heir to great possessions, he became a follower of Cartwright, and left Cambridge suddenly without taking his degree ; then, being dissatisfied with the episcopal ordination of the Church of England,[383] he went to Antwerp, and was ordained according to the reformed church there.[384] When Whitgift required of the clergy universal subscription to his articles, he and sixteen other Kentish ministers refused to subscribe, but in January, 1584, petitioned the archbishop to renew their licences.[385]

The archbishop suspended all the seventeen who declared themselves unable to subscribe, and they appealed to the council.[386] The council addressed an expostulation to Whitgift, and asked him to attend its meeting on the following Sunday. He expressed his surprise at this irregular way of dealing with the question, and refused, describing these ministers as ' most of them unlearned and young and such as he would be loath to admit into the ministry,' who had come to him unbidden and argued for three days. In May, Sir Thomas Scott of Scott's Hall, Ashford, and twenty-six gentlemen of Kent waited upon Whitgift and pleaded with him on their behalf.[387] But in spite of interference the commission went on with its work.[388]

The accession of James was followed by proclamations against Jesuits, seminary priests,[389] and recusants,[390] as the result of the discovery of fresh plots, including the Main Plot, engineered by Lord Cobham, who was convicted and executed. Though toleration then for a time marked the policy of James, a noticeable increase of severity again occurred in 1615, after the pope's commission to the English papists at the Spa authorizing them to choose a Catholic archbishop of Canterbury, when they chose Dr. Thomas Worthington.[391]

A return of the diocese of Canterbury in 1603 [392] gives parishes 252, whereof impropriations 140, preachers 201. Of these preachers, six are doctors in divinity, sixteen bachelors in divinity, ninety-three masters of art, thirty-five bachelors of art, fifty-two are described as no graduates. The number of communicants is given as 52,753 ; of recusants thirty-eight, of whom eighteen are men, and twenty women. Under peculiars belonging to Canterbury, fifty-four parishes are given, whereof impropriate fourteen, preachers thirty-eight, communicants 17,603, recusants eighteen, of whom thirteen are women, and five men. A similar return [392a] for the same date for Rochester gives parishes ninety-eight, whereof impropriations forty-two, and preachers seventy-six ; of these preachers, two being doctors in divinity, three bachelors in divinity, forty masters of art, eighteen bachelors of art, thirteen no graduates. The number of communicants in this diocese is given as 18,956, of recusants eighteen, of whom eleven are men, and seven women.

There is a memorandum that, besides the preachers here mentioned, there are many honest ministers ' well hable to catechize, and privately to

---

[383] Benjamin Brook, *Lives of the Puritans*, i, 392.   [384] Heylyn, *Hist. of the Presbyterians*, i, 252.

[385] Benjamin Brook, *Lives of the Puritans*, i, 392. The other signatories were Joseph Nichols, Joseph Minge, George Caslocke, William Evans, James Grove, George Ely, Richard Holden, Anthony Brimstone, Robert Golleford, John Elvin, Lever Wood, William Knight, Anthony Hilton, Theophilus Calver, John Mayor, John Grimestone.

[386] Fuller, *Church Hist.* v, 12–14.   [387] Strype, *Whitgift*, i, 272.

[388] The ecclesiastical commission had been renewed 9 Dec. 1583.

[389] Cardwell, *Documentary Annals*, ii, 50.   [390] Ibid. 113.

[391] *Cal. S.P. Dom.* 1611–16, pp. 285, 300.   [392] Harl. MSS. 280, fol. 157, 173.   [392a] Ibid.

exhorte, thoughe they have not ye gifte of utterance and audacitie to preach in ye pulpitt.'

One of the most creditable things known of James I, and one which shed the lustre of foreign learning on the chapter of Canterbury, was his genuine admiration for, and his patronage of, the great French scholar, Isaac Casaubon, the gifted son of a persecuted Huguenot family, who, by the independent study of the Fathers, had arrived at that *via media* between Puritanism and Romanism which is the essential position of the English Church. Though a layman, he was collated to a prebendal stall at Canterbury, and had a pension of £300 a year assigned to him from the Exchequer. When Sir Julius Caesar made a difficulty about payment, James sent him a note in his own hand, 'Chanceler of my excheker, I will have Mr. Casaubon paid before me, my wife, and my barnes.' [393] Early in the next reign another of the great scholars of the world, the Dutch Vossius, the life-long friend of Grotius, who had refused a professorship at Cambridge in 1624, came to Canterbury to be installed in a canonry there, being at the same time made LL.D. at Oxford. [394]

Other learned and distinguished foreign reformers included in the chapter in the first half of the seventeenth century were John Castilion, John Maximilian de Langle, the two Du Moulins, and Antoine le Chevalier.

Archbishop Whitgift lived only just long enough to be present at the Hampton Court Conference held 16 January, 1603–4. He died 29 February following, and was worthily succeeded by Archbishop Bancroft, who had been his chaplain. Though himself loath to proceed to extremities, the refusals of many to conform or subscribe had its inevitable result in deprivations and ejections, but of these his own diocese furnished but one. [395] He died 2 November, 1610, and was succeeded by Archbishop Abbot. On the promotion of Bishop Barlow [396] to Lincoln in 1608, he was succeeded at Rochester by Bishop Neile, 'a man,' wrote Heylyn later,

> who very well understood the constitution of the church in England, though otherwise not so eminent in all parts of learning as some other bishops of his time ; but what he wanted in himself he made good in the choice of his servants, having more able men about him from time to time than any other man of that age.

The most able of these was William Laud, whom he appointed his chaplain in 1608, and whom he presented in May, 1610, to the rectory of Cuxton and later in that year to that of Norton, near Faversham. To attend to his parochial duties, Laud gave up his fellowship at St. John's, Oxford, but was elected to the presidentship there 10 May, 1611, in succession to his former tutor, John Buckeridge, one of those who, during the closing years of the reign

[393] Among the first petitions presented at the Restoration is that of Meric Casaubon, D.D., prebendary of Christchurch, Canterbury, for the arrears of this pension granted to his father Isaac Casaubon, his wife, and the longest liver of his children. The petitioner states that he is old and crazy himself, and has his indigent brother James, King James's godson, to support, and has always tried to do what service he could for God and the Church by his pen. *Cal. S.P. Dom.* 1660–1, p. 446.

[394] *Ibid.* 1629–37, p. 107. After speaking of his arrival at Canterbury, admission into a canonry, and friendly reception there, and acknowledging the great honours paid to him in England, he says that he should have returned from London to Canterbury, but finding a ship of war about to sail with a fair wind, intended to take advantage of it to return to Flushing, and begs the secretary to excuse his sudden departure to the king.

[395] W. H. Frere, *Hist. of Engl. Ch.* (ed. Stephens and Hunt), v, 321.

[396] He succeeded Bishop Young at Rochester, 30 June, 1605.

of Elizabeth, headed at the two universities a reaction against the dominant Calvinism, and who, standing between Romanism on the one hand, and Puritanism on the other, laid stress on sacramental grace and the episcopal organization of the Church of England. He succeeded Neile at Rochester, and the friendship between Laud and himself that had begun when Laud came under his influence at Oxford never wavered; in their desire to restore to the Church of England a dignified simplicity of worship and loyal obedience to the formularies which had come to her from the past through the age of reformation, Neile, Buckeridge, and Laud were in perfect sympathy, and the death of Neile, then archbishop of York and one of the first to attract the attention of the Puritan Commons, was a great loss to Laud when it occurred in 1640. Bishop Buckeridge was translated to Ely 1628, and succeeded by Bishop Curll, who was translated after eighteen months from Rochester, and was succeeded by Dr. John Bowle in 1630; Bishop Bowle appears to have been 'very ill of a palsy,' during most of the seven years during which he held the see.

Before the death of James, a commission was summoned to decide whether Archbishop Abbot was capable of exercising ecclesiastical jurisdiction in consequence of an unfortunate accident by which he killed a man, when hunting in 1621. The commission was equally divided as to the extent of his disability, but the king granted him a formal pardon or dispensation, 24 December, 1621. After James's death it was not long before he fell into displeasure at court, and on 5 July, 1627, he was ordered to retire to Canterbury, no cause being assigned; and on 9 October a commission was issued to five bishops, including Laud, authorizing them to exercise all archiepiscopal powers and jurisdictions in the place of Abbot.[397] At the end of 1628 he was restored to favour, but his authority was practically at an end, and was exercised by Laud, then bishop of London, and constantly at the king's side. His last important act in his diocese, before he died 4 August, 1633, after a long period of broken health, had been his settlement at Crayford[398] of differences arising out of the question which was then dividing the two great religious parties, the position of the communion table. His decision, given after the evidence had been examined by Sir Nathaniel Brent, his vicar-general, is the more noteworthy because it would be considered adverse to the wishes of the Puritan party, to which he was supposed to belong. It decreed

that the parishioners and inhabitants of the said parish of Crayford, and others intending hereafter to receive the holy communion there, shall repair unto the two ascents, or foot paces in the chancel before the communion table, and then mats being laid upon the said two ascents, or foot paces, to kneel upon, and mats being also laid on either side above the said steps to kneel upon (if by reason of the number of communicants it seems requisite, the two ascents or foot paces being first filled), they shall in decent and reverend manner humbly kneeling upon their knees on the said two ascents or foot paces, receive the holy communion and sacrament of the body and blood of our Lord and Saviour Jesus Christ; and after the first company hath received the same, they to return to their seats and places in the said church, and to give way for a second company to receive in like manner, and the second, after they have received in like manner, to return and give way for a third company; and the third to the fourth, and so successively, until all the communicants there have received the Holy Communion in manner and form aforesaid.[399]

[397] Rushworth, *Coll.* i, 431–3.   [398] 21 May, 1633.
[399] Cant. Archiepis. Reg. Abbot, ii, fol. 135*b*; Cardwell, *Documentary Annals*, ii, 174.

Charles in 1634 required annual reports from the archbishop and from every diocesan bishop, and Laud determined at once to carry out a general visitation of his diocese and province. In his return for 1634 he stated : 'In all the dioceses, it is the general grievance of the poor vicars, that the stipends are scarce able to feed and clothe them.' He therefore set to work to procure details as to impropriations and decayed churches within the diocese of Canterbury served by curates, and what their several stipends were.[400] The question of the foreign churches in Kent also engaged his attention, as there seemed every possibility of the creation of a number of new sects through the existence of the French, Italian, and Dutch congregations, who already had been censured by previous archbishops for their objections to intermarriage with the English.[401] He thought that the second generation (the second born in England) should conform to the English Church, and set about procuring such conformity.

Of Rochester he reported to the king in 1633 :

> The bishop complained that the cathedral church suffered much from want of glass in the windows, and the churchyard lies very undecently, and the gates down, and that he hath no power to remedy these things, because the dean and chapter refuse to be visited by him, upon pretence that their statutes are not confirmed under the broad seal.[402]

The chapter denied that there was much wrong, declaring that beyond the annual repairs they had spent more than £1,000 on the fabric and organ, so that the building was in good condition ; the archbishop contented himself with enjoining that the windows shall be repaired without delay and the bells and frames put in order, that there shall be a new desk in the choir and new books ; that the communion table shall be placed at the east end, and a fair rail set to cross the choir, as in other cathedrals ; and ready obedience was promised.

In his own chapter he found a very unedifying condition existing of bickerings and divisions ; and such animadversions on his visitation reached his ears that he wrote sharply he hoped

> all reports are not true, but he hears that some of that body have been a little too bold with him. If he find it is true, he shall not forget that nine of the twelve prebends are in the king's gift. He cannot take it well to be ill used and undeservedly, especially at such a time as he was endeavouring their good.[403]

Frivolous squabbling and trivial complaining seem to have occupied the Canterbury chapter in the years immediately preceding the great Civil War, to judge from the correspondence he had at that time with the dean, Dr. Bargrave, the registrar, William Somner, and some of the prebendaries.[403a] Throughout his primacy he was rigorous in prosecuting recusants [404] in the county.

[400] A list of 14 April, 1634, enumerates eight impropriations among exempts of the diocese, four of them in the archbishop's hands. The decayed churches were ten. *Cal. S.P. Dom.* 1633–4, p. 551.
[401] F. W. Cross, *Hist. of the Walloon and Huguenot Ch. at Cant.* 31.
[402] Quoted Furley, *Weald of Kent*, ii, App. 848.
[403] *Cal. S.P. Dom.* 1633–4, p. 331.   [403a] Ibid. 1635, pp. 6, 7.
[404] The old names still occur in the Recusant Lists. As late as 1641 the names of recusants presented by the knights for the county are Sir Henry Guildeford, knt., and Edward Guildeford, esq., both of Rolvenden ; Clement Finch, esq. of Milton juxta Sittingbourne ; Richard Hawkins, esq. of Selling ; William Petit, esq. of Boughton under the Blean ; John Best, gent. of St. Lawrence juxta Cantuariam ; George Littleboy, gent.

Laud issued injunctions 19 December, 1634, to the foreign churches in Kent, at Sandwich, Canterbury, and Maidstone, that (1) all natives [i.e of the second descent] of the Dutch and Walloon congregations in his grace's diocese are to resort to their several parish churches to hear divine service and sermon, and to perform all duties required of parishioners ; (2) the ministers and all others of the Dutch and Walloon congregations who are not natives and born subjects to the king, or any other strangers that shall come over, while they remain strangers, may use their own discipline as formerly, yet it is thought fit the English liturgy should be translated into French and Dutch for the better fitting of their children to the English [Church] government.[405]   These were to be enforced by 13 April following.   On 14 April, William Somner writes that

> they have not called upon the Dutch church at Maidstone, because they are informed that they have broken up their congregation on the former monition, and all resort to the English church, having so long abode among the English that they are hardly to be known by face or language from them.

The writer thought that they were willing to entertain the order, for that their paucity would not maintain a minister.[406]   In May the mayor and commonalty of Canterbury petitioned the archbishop, setting forth 'the inconveniences which will fall upon the city by remitting the strangers to their parish churches . . . mainly in the great number of their poor which will fall upon the parishes ; '[407] and on 26 September it was ordered that all the aliens of those congregations and their descendants of the first generation might retain the privileges formerly granted to them, but that all others should frequent their parish churches with the rest of the king's subjects, so nevertheless that they remain liable to the support of the ministers and poor of the same congregations.[408]   The dean and chapter seem to have made no attempt to interfere with their services, and the parish officials also to have taken no action.   The congregations themselves appear to have been at first fairly quiescent, but to have finally joined forces with the party at work against Laud ; his action in the matter was made the ground of one of the articles against him presented in 1641.

The return for 1635 states that there were 'yet very many refractory persons to the government of the church of England about Maidstone and Ashford and some other parts' ; that for 1636 shows that the 'Brownists and other separatists' still continued about Ashford, but that 'the Walloons and other strangers' had conformed ; the return for 1637 still complains of the conventicles at Ashford, and it begins to appear that the strangers at Canterbury did not resort to their parish churches as formerly.   Of Rochester Laud wrote in 1634 that he had found 'no eminent thing amiss' ; in 1637

of Birling ; Ralph Loane, gent. of the same ; George Loane, esq. of Sevenoaks ; Henry Whetenhall, esq. of East Peckham ; Benjamin Wyborne, gent. of Pembury ; Anthony Roper, esq. of Eltham ; Sir Anthony Roper, gent. and Henry Roper esq. of Farningham, Thomas Turner, gent. of Linsted ; and —— Stiche, attorney-at-law, of Orpington : nine of these are from Rochester diocese and seven from Canterbury. *Proceedings in Kent*, edited by Rev. L. B. Larking (Camd. Soc.), 65.   In his Return for 1637, Laud stated that at Sittingbourne 'were more recusants than in any other part of his diocese, and the Lady Roper (Dowager) is thought to be a great means of the increase of them.' Quoted in Furley, *Weald of Kent*, ii, App. 850.

[405] *Cal. S.P. Dom.* 1640–1, p. 526.   [406] Ibid. 1635, p. 25.

[407] Ibid. p. 77.   It had been stated by the mayor and aldermen in 1629 that the Walloons were a third or fourth part of the city of Canterbury. Ibid. 1628–9, p. 117.   [408] Ibid. 1635, p. 399.

he had to inform King Charles that Dr. Bowle, who died 9 October, 1637, had been ill for the last three years, and forced to neglect his diocese.[409] Dr. Bowle was succeeded by John Warner, D.D., a devoted adherent of the Church and monarchy, whose indomitable spirit was not only to carry him through the humiliations and trials of the Commonwealth government, but to lead him, in spite of all the risks he incurred by such a course, to make in speech and writing a valiant defence of the Church and her property. He had been long connected with Kent, having been made made a prebendary and canon of Canterbury in 1616, rector of Bishopsbourne in 1619, and of Hollingbourne in 1624.

The storm was gathering strength, and charges of innovation were levelled at Laud and those who held with him ; the nature of these charges is best seen in the Kentish petitions, in the proceedings against the Kentish clergy of the years 1640–1, and in the articles of accusation against Laud himself. Article 9 of these was the testimony of Richard Culmer, heretofore minister of Goodnestone,[410] that the said Richard Culmer, Mr. John Player, minister of Kennington, Mr. Thomas Heiron, minister of Herne Hill, and Mr. Gardner of Sandwich, were called before the archbishop's commissioners at his metropolitical visitation. Mr. Gardner had farther day given him to publish the book for Sabbath dancing, but died before that day came ; but Culmer, Player, and Heiron, were then suspended for refusing to publish it, and so continued for above three and a half years. Immediately after their suspension they jointly petitioned the archbishop for absolution at Lambeth, but he having read the petition, said, ' If you know not how to obey, I know not how to grant,' and departed. . . . ' So the archbishop suffered me to continue suspended and deprived by the patron, who gave away my living immediately upon my suspension, so I had not one farthing profit of my ministry for three and a half years, having my wife and seven children to provide for.' Extraordinary bitterness marked the speech of Sir Edward Dering on 16 November, 1640, when he presented a petition from the Puritan rector of Otham, Mr. Wilson, to the House of Commons, and referred to Laud as ' the centre whence our miseries grow ' ;[411] but even he found it necessary to tone down the Kentish petition against episcopacy sent to him through Mr. Richard Robson of Cranbrook, 1 December, 1640, from the inhabitants of the Weald.[412] In his own words,

> if it were not the spawne of the London petition, yet finding it a parat taught to speak the syllables of that, and by roate calling for Root and Branch, I dealt with the presenters thereof, and with other parties thereunto, until (with their consent) I reduced it to lesse than a quarter of its former length, and taught it a new and more modest language.

In this ' more modest language ' the petitioners presented[413] that they

> doe daily finde the government in the church of England by archbishops, lord bishops, deans and archdeacons, with their courts, jurisdictions and administrations, by them and their inferior officers, to be very dangerous, both in the church and commonwealth, and to be the occasion of manifold grievances unto His Majesty's subjects, in their consciences, liberties, and estates.

[409] These returns are quoted from Furley, *Weald of Kent*, ii, App. 848, &c.
[410] *Cal. S.P. Dom.* 1644, p. 15 (15 Feb. 1643–4).   [411] Rushworth, *Coll.* iv, 39.
[412] *Proc. in Kent*, 1640 ; edited by the Rev. L. B. Larking, D.D. (Camd. Soc.), 26.
[413] The petition thus finally presented is given in the *Proceedings*, 28–32. 2,500 names were appended to
it. W. A. Shaw, Litt. D., *Hist. of Engl. Ch. during the Civil Wars*, 21.

ECCLESIASTICAL HISTORY

The original petition [414] contained a 'Perticuler of manyfold evills, pressures, and grievances, cawsed, practiced, or occasioned by the Prelacy, and their dependances,' among which they enumerate

> the great increase of idle, lewd, dissolute, ignorant, and erroneous men in the ministry, which swarme like locusts of Egypt over the whole kingdome; for, will they but weare a canonicall coate, a sirplus, a hood, bow at the name of Jesus, and be zealous for superstitious ceremonies, they may live as they list, confront whome they please, preach and vent what errors they will, and neglect preaching at their pleasure without controle. Whence proceeds . . .

A long list of evils which follows includes the following remarkable one :

> 8. The swarming of lascivious, idle, and unprofitable bookes, Pamphlettes, Playebookes and Ballades; as namely, Ovid's Art of Love, The Parliament of Women (come out at the Dissolution of the last Parliament), Carewes Poems, Parker's Ballades, in disgrace of Religion, etc., to the increase of vice, and withdrawing of the people from reading, studdying, and hearing the word of God, and other good Bookes.

A petition was presented from the gentlemen, ministers, freeholders, and subsidy men of Kent in 1641 to the House of Commons, for the reformation not abrogation of the Liturgy :[415] but when the Kentish grand jury at Maidstone, 28 March, 1642, after the bill excluding the bishops from the House of Lords had received the royal assent, petitioned Parliament for the preservation of episcopal government and of the solemn liturgy of the Church, the petitioners were imprisoned.[416] At this date another petition came up from Kent congratulating the lords upon the exclusion of the bishops, and praying them 'to go on to a thorough reformation, especially of the church according to the word of God.' [416a]

The sub-committee appointed to sit in the county, under the chairmanship of Sir Edward Dering, himself one of the bitterest Puritans in the House of Commons, by the Commons Grand Committee for Religion, was in existence from 23 November, 1640, to July, 1641, 'to discover the sufferings of ministers by ecclesiastical proceedings.' Petitions to it poured in from every quarter of Kent,[417] the Weald being especially distinguished by the number and animus displayed. Even more numerous than complaints of insufficiency of stipend, of non-residence, and of plurality, matters which Laud had done his best to remedy, were complaints of 'bowinge and cringeinge,' 'railing in the communion table,' 'going up to the communion table to read the Ten Commandments,' of being a 'common lyar, a notorious swearer, a foule obscene and bawdy speaker of ribaldrye,' of being 'contentious, and troublesome, a haunter of taverns, a gamester,' or 'very insolent, proud, and haughtie.' An accusation of popish practices was brought against William Gervis, the vicar of Sturry, on the ground of his having 'a large crucifix, painted, in a frame, in his parlour.'

At Snargate [418] the parishioners petitioned again to recall their petition against their curate, protesting that they had not wished to disgrace Mr. John Freeman, ' but onely he seemed to carry himselfe something too lofty, and to be hasty towards us, which we perswade ourselves will be much amended . . .

---

[414] *Proc. in Kent.* 30.　　　　　　　　　　　　　　　　[415] Ibid. 60.
[416] W. H Frere, *Hist. of Engl. Ch.* (ed. Stephens and Hunt), v, 97.
[416a] *Lords' Journ.* iv, 571.　　　　　　　[417] These are to be found in the *Proceedings in Kent.*
[418] *Proc. in Kent,* 198.

we all confesse his deserts are well known to us.' After a petition had been presented against Mr. Richard Tray by Lidsing and Bredhurst,[419] alleging that he was very contentious, a common railer and reviler of his neighbours, given to fighting, and did strike once heretofore the parish clerk of Bredhurst in the church of Lidsing, Mr. Richard Tray supported his declaration that these complaints were idle and frivolous, by pointing out his own advanced age, he having been in the ministry now forty years, by sending the confession of the man he was alleged to have struck, who owned that he had been drinking all the night before and consequently snored in chapel, 'when Mr. Tray gogged him with his hand to wake him, and did not strike him,' and by the fact that five out of the eight petitioners against him disclaimed their signatures, some of them declaring they had been obtained when they were too drunk to know what they were doing, and by producing petitions in his favour, in addition to the duly attested disclaimers.[420]

Such cases make it easy to understand the comment of Walker in his *Sufferings of the Clergy*, when, writing of Edward Ashburnham, vicar of Tonbridge, that he was sequestered for paying obedience to the canons of the Church, neglecting the Parliament fasts, and encouraging his parishioners to assist his Majesty, he drily adds 'and therefore there is no question to be made, but that he must have been an ale-house haunter and drunkard.' They also rouse a wonder whether in the case of Chislet, which petitioned against its vicar Edward Barbet,[421] and enumerated among his offences that he ' reads soe false, and with suche ill gesture and behaviour, laughing when some women come into the church, and soe careles in readinge, that sometimes he reads the Ten Commandments twice over, with many other slips,' the hackneyed charge of drinking and swearing might be similarly discounted.

By the time of the execution of Laud, on 10 January, 1645, the Church of England was no longer recognized by the state, its worship was illegal, and its ministry deposed. On 15 June, 1641, Parliament had resolved that all deans and chapters, archdeacons, prebendaries, chanters, canons and petty canons, and their officers, shall be abolished, and the opposition to the measure had been led by Dr. Isaac Bargrave, the dean of Canterbury : after the exclusion of the bishops, 13 February, 1642, from the House of Lords, Dr. Warner, who had defended their rights with much ability, when his lands and goods were, in addition, sequestrated with those of all other bishops in 1643, left his palace at Bromley in disguise, and led a wandering life in the west of England. The abolition of Christian festivals, including Christmas Day itself, the deprivation of 'scandalous' clergy,[422] and sequestrations of others,[423] and the provision of a very plentiful supply of lecturers,[424] should have produced great unanimity and contentment of mind in Kent by the year 1646, in which Parliament ordered the establishment of the Presbyterian system ; but the Kent certificate [425] shows that the county hesitated for some time before proceeding to institute the ' classes,' the system of organization

[419] *Proc. in Kent*, 160.   [420] Ibid. 163.   [421] Ibid. 176.
[422] For those in Kent see **W. A.** Shaw, *Hist. of the Engl. Ch. during the Civil Wars*, ii, 295, &c.
[423] Ibid. 306, &c.   [424] Ibid. ii, 300, &c.
[425] The House of Commons had ordered the division of the counties into distinct classical presbyteries, the divisions and persons named as belonging to each division to be certified to Parliament.

then ordained. The committee in Kent presented, 21 April, 1646, the following report to the Speaker :[426]

> S[r]. In obedience to yo[r] letter of the 16th of December last Requiring us with the advice of godly ministers and others to consider how the countie of Kent may be conveniently divided into distinct Classical Presbyteryes and what ministers and others are fitt to be of each classis. Wee have called together twentie ministers and twentie gentlemen for the severall divisions of the Countie, and doe finde the ministers in generall and the major part of the gentry to be desirous yet a while to wayte the further directions of the parliament. Therein having given you this accompt of our proceedings wee rest, your most humble servantes, [Sir] John Rivers, Antho' Weldon, John Oxindem, John Honywood, Rich[ard] Beale, Lambarde Godfrey, William Bothby, [Sir] Thomas Peirs, N. Godfrey, Robert Scott, John Browne, William Kenwicke, John Bex, Humfry Scott, John Dixwell. Maidstone, 21 Aprill 1646.

In this year appeared a 'Declaration' set forth by the Presbyterians within the county of Kent.[427]

> Whereas we understand that severall Petitions[428] are set on foot, and promoted by divers persons within this county, wherein they take to themselves a liberty of venting their own private thoughts and desires, in matters concerning the publike and great affaires of the Church and State, which can produce no other effect, then the raising and countenancing of contrary parties and factions within the county : We doe hereby declare & admonishe all sorts of persons whatsoever within the County, that they forbear to give any countenance or furtherance to any such Petitions, upon what Pretence soever ; and that they avoid all such occasions of new distractions in the county ; as they tender the welfare thereof. And we doe hereby require all Ministers of the severall Parish Churches openly to read this signification in the Parish Churches upon the next Lord's Day after the receipt hereof, before the end of the morning exercise.

The riots produced in Canterbury by the suppression of Christmas Day in 1648 were followed by a declaration from the loyalists of Kent. In 'Canterbury Christmas ; or, a True Relation of the Insurrection in Canterbury on Christmas Day last with the great hurt that befell divers persons thereby. Written by a Citizen there to his friend in London, 1648,'[429] we learn that

> Upon Wednesday, December 22, the Cryer of Canterbury, by the appointment of Master Major, openly proclaimed, that Christmas Day and all other Superstitious Festivals should be put downe, and that a Market should be kept upon Christmas Day.
>
> Which being not observed (but very ill taken by the Country), the towne was thereby unserved with provision and trading very much hindered, which occasioned great discontent among the people, and caused them to rise in a Rebellious way. . . .
>
> The Towne Rose againe and the Country came in, took possession of the gates. . . . setting open the prison doors and releasing those that were in hold. . . . Next they vowed revenge on the Major, pulling up his posts, breaking his windowes. . . .

Finally an agreement was come to by both parties that forty or fifty of the protesting party armed should keep the town that night. This was carried out, 'And upon faire composition the multitude have delivered their Armes into the handes of the city, upon engagements of the best of the city, that no man shall further question or trouble them.'

---

[426] Tanner MSS. Bodleian, lix, 77 ; W. A. Shaw, *Hist. of the Engl. Ch. during the Civil Wars*, i, 372.

[427] B.M., E.370 (25).

[428] Among others, the committee for the county had this year petitioned 'that a timely provision may be made for the peaceable and comfortable support of a pious and painfull Ministry in lieu of Tythes within this County.' B.M., E.365 (4). The House of Commons had replied thanking them 'for their former services' and taking notice of 'their goode affections to the publique,' but informing them that 'the great businesses of the kingdome are nowe instant and pressing upon them' had promised to 'take the Petition into consideration in due time, and in the meantime to take care that Tythes may be paid according to the law.' [429] B.M., E. 421 (22).

This victory was followed by the

> Declaration [430] of Many Thousands of the City of Canterbury or County of Kent. Concerning the late Tumult in the City of Canterbury, provokt by the Mayors violent proceedings against those who desired to continue the celebration of the Feast of Christs Nativity, 1500 years and upwards maintained in the Church. Together with their Resolutions for the restitution of His Majestie to his Crown and Dignitie, whereby Religion may be restored to its ancient splendour, and the known Laws of the Kingdome maintained. As also, Their Desires to all His Majesties loyall Subjects within his Dominions, for their concurrence and assistance in this so good and pious a work.

Twelve years later Kent welcomed King Charles to its shores, and received him with acclamation from the moment of his landing at Dover,[431] where he was presented with a Bible by the Mayor, and the corporation addressed to him a speech congratulating him on his restoration and the restoration of the ancient church of England, by the mouth of John Reading, formerly chaplain to King Charles I, and curate of the parish of St. Mary's, Dover.[432]

The Kentish clergy had suffered severely, in proportion to their numbers, during the days of the Commonwealth. In 1641 both Houses of Parliament had arbitrarily assumed jurisdiction over the clergy and their livings, and in 1654 the ordinance published for the ejection of scandalous, ignorant and insufficient ministers and schoolmasters had made it impossible for clergy obnoxious to the Commonwealth party to earn a living even by teaching or obtaining chaplaincies, as a result of which enactments Walker mentions in his *Sufferings of the Clergy* eighty-eight who suffered in the county; and even then does not consider his list exhaustive. The seventy-six enumerated by Calamy[433] as ejected to make way at the Restoration for the Episcopalian clergy they had replaced, or for non-conformity, seem in most cases to have continued preaching and to have even enjoyed the friendship of the established clergy.

As Canterbury, in the person of its archbishop, had borne the worst of the storm, so had it also suffered in the fabric of its metropolitan cathedral, and Rochester fared no better. An invaluable description of the condition of the cathedral at the Restoration survives in the handwriting of the antiquary Somner,[434] who was auditor of the cathedral from 1660 to 1669. 'An accompt' published of sums then disbursed[435] contains this description of the

> 'sad, forlorne and languishing condition of our church at our returne, which (in short) was such as made it look more like a ruined monastery than a church : so little had the fury of the late Reformers left remaining of it besides the bare walles and roofe, and these, partly through neglect, and partly by the assaultes and batteries of the disaffected, so shaken, ruinated and defaced, as it was not more unserviceable in the way of a cathedral, then justly scandalous to all who delight to serve God in the beauty of holiness. The windowes (famous both for strength and beauty,) so generally battered and broken downe, as it lay exposed to the injury of all weathers : the whole roofe with that of the steeples, the Chapterhowse, and Cloyster, extremely impaired and ruined, both in the timber work and lead : the water tables, pipes, and much other of the lead in almost all places cut off, and with the leaden cisterne of one of our conduities, purloyned : the quire stripped and robbed of her faire and goodly hangings, her Organ and Organ loft : the Communion table, of the best and chiefest of her

---

[430] B.M., E. 421 (23).

[431] The nobility, gentry, ministry, and commonalty of Kent, with Canterbury, and Rochester, and other parts of the county, had previously declared for a full and free Parliament. *Cal. S.P. Dom.* 1659–60, p. 340.   [432] *Proceedings in Kent*, 57.   [433] *The Nonconformists' Memorial* (ed. 1802), ii, 318–47.

[434] Quoted in *Arch. Cant.* x. 93, etc. by Canon J. C. Robertson.

[435] Mr. Peter du Moulin, canon of Canterbury, in a letter quoted by Hasted, says that the chapter spent £12,000 on the cathedral, and that exclusive of this, they divided out of their first fines £1,100 apiece, besides making a handsome present to the king.

furniture and ornaments, with the raile before it, and skreene of Tabernacle work, richly overlaid with gold, behind it : many of the goodly monuments of the dead shamefully ab-used, defaced, rifled and plundered of their brasses, iron-grates, and barres : the common Dortor (affording good housing for many members of our church) with the Deanes privat Chappell, and a faire and goodly Library over it, quite demolished, the Bookes and other furniture of it sold away : our Houses, with those of our six Preachers and Peti-canons, (many of them) much impaired, some by neglect of reparations . . . . . our very Common Seale, our Registers and other books, together with our Records and evidences of all sortes, seized and distracted : many of them irrecoverably lost, and the rest not retrived without much trouble and cost : . . . . . and in fine, a goodly brave Cathedral become no better (in respect of those who gott and kept possession of it) than a den of thieves : and to make the better way for such invaders to abuse it, the Churches Guardians, her faire and strong gates, betimes turned off the hookes and burned.'

This melancholy picture is borne out by an entry in the State Papers in September, 1653 [436] of the payment of the surgeon, Peter de la Rue, for attendance on ' twelve Dutch prisoners, sick in Canterbury church,' wording which leaves no doubt that the very cathedral itself was used as a hospital for foreign prisoners. A little later (7 October, 1657) [437] the Gov-ernors of the Chest at Chatham, in great need of money, writing of sick and wounded seamen, add ' We have begged for the ruinous cathedral of Roches-ter to help us, and had bills drawn up to have been presented to Parliament, but Providence, it seems, afforded not that opportunity of offering them, by which means hitherto the thing has not been effected.' A draft letter of the king's, of 11 December, 1663,[438] recommending the gentry of Kent to promote by personal subscriptions and other means the repair of Rochester Cathedral, declares that His Majesty had ' observed with compassion the ruin into which it was brought by the discords of the late times, that the dean and chapter have expended £7,000 on it, yet on Whit Sunday last, part fell, and more had to be pulled down for safety, that its restoration will cost £14,000, towards which the bishop will assist, and the gentry, always loyal, should be forward therein.'

The bishop referred to by the king was Dr. Warner, who at the age of eighty was restored to his see, where he was to continue until his death, 14 October, 1666. Possessed of a large private fortune, his charities were munificent, not only to his own cathedral, but to Canterbury, and, as well as giving £8,000 to the relief of sequestered clergy, he endowed with great liberality Bromley College for the relief of distressed widows of the clergy, whose numbers must have been greatly augmented at this time.

The same ready assistance had been rendered to the deprived clergy by Archbishop Juxon, bishop of London when he was elected on 3 September, 1660, to succeed Laud. He had visited Laud in the Tower, and attended Charles on the scaffold, and was held to be ' the closest link with memories which loyalists of the Revolution felt to be sacred.' In spite of the infirmities of old age, which rendered his death before many years were over already inevitable,[439] it was felt that he was the one man who must occupy the primacy and crown Charles II.

Even before his consecration the loyal clergy of Kent had presented an address [440] to the king in which they combined an assurance that they them-

---

[436] *Cal. S. P. Dom.* 1653-4, p. 179.
[438] Ibid. 1663-4, p. 370.
[440] B.M. 669, fol. 25, 16. *The Humble Addresse of your Majesties most loyall Subjects of the Clergy in the county of Kent.*

[437] Ibid. 1657-8, Pref. p. xiv.
[439] He died 4 June, 1663.

selves had given no assent to the acts of the late government, with an exposition of what they expected from their restored monarch.

The State Papers for the years 1661-2 contain various references to the 'scandalous divisions' then dividing the Walloons at Canterbury, which appear to have existed for the last twenty years,[441] but a settlement seems to have been obtained in perfectly equitable fashion. Perhaps there is in both dioceses on the whole less of actual infliction of penalty recorded than of sentiments of ill will on the part of a public impatient that so little punishment is carried into execution. Sir Edward Hales wrote to Secretary Nicholas, 5 October, 1661 :[442] 'The wild of Kent is a receptacle for distressed running parsons, who vent abundance of sedition on their new created lecture days.' Colonel Culpeper wrote to Secretary Bennet, 12 November, 1662,[443] that he had found Mr. Palmer, the preacher, at Egerton, in disguise, attempting to get through his men ; that he seized him and 200 of his men, but going to search the town, his soldiers let them all escape except thirty, who remained, and being ready to take the oath of allegiance, and promising to meet no more, were freed on bonds to appear ; that he had Mr. Palmer prisoner at Canterbury, though ordained, and another preacher from Ashford who refused to desist. He also stated that in the wilds of Kent the sectaries were wild and insolent. Anthony Cooley wrote to Henry Muddiman from Canterbury 15 October, 1665 :[444]

> In duty I am bound to say nothing was prosecuted at the last quarter sessions against the Quakers, nor the rest of that diabolical rabble, although several bills of indictment have been framed and presented at sessions against that viperous brood, yet by reason most of the grand jury are fanatics the bills were not found, and that they have several places of meeting will manifestly appear, as at the house of Mr. Taylor, a blind man, formerly a minister, (he liveth in St. George's parish, Canterbury); at Francis Germain's a tanner, in St. Paul's parish, Canterbury ; at one Hill's a tanner, in the parish of Holy Cross, Westgate, Canterbury ; at one Widow Clarembold's, at St. Stephen's, a mile distant ; at Henry Rogers, a desperate Quaker, in St. Mary Magdalen's, Canterbury ; at one Thomas Pollard's, a cordwinder, in the same parish, every Thursday ; at one Vidions, at North Gate, Canterbury ; at one Tritton's a miller, in the parish of Westgate, Canterbury, a fifth monarchy man ; at one Garard's, a bricklayer, at Ickham, three miles from Canterbury ; besides the many sturdy pieces of presbytery no less dangerous than the other ; all which are most bitter enemies of the laws ecclesiasticall and civil. God preserve his sacred Majesty. . . .

The stringent Act passed, 28 April, 1668, for suppressing conventicles, seems to have been more rigorously enforced in Kent, and was followed by the petition of Robert Beak, Nicholas Thoroughgood, and Francis Taylor, ordained ministers, prisoners in Canterbury gaol (who protest they are loyal and peaceable and forwarded the Restoration,) for their liberty, they having been sent to prison for six months, on the Act restraining Nonconformists from living in corporations.[445]

---

[441] *Cal. S.P. Dom.* 1661-2, pp. 55, 114, 478. An Order in Council 14 Nov. 1662 ordered them to unite in their worship, permit no one to do anything contrary to the Church of England, and to maintain their own poor without being burdensome to the city. On these conditions the king agreed to allow them their usual place of meeting near the Cathedral, to declare them part of the reformed churches in order to avoid the penalties of the Act of Uniformity, and not to allow them to be taxed to maintain other than their own poor. Ibid. 556.　　[442] Ibid. 107.　　[443] Ibid. 555.　　[444] Ibid. 1665-6, p. 15.

[445] Ibid. 1667-8, p. 416 (May (?) 1668); ibid. 514 (July (?) 1668). It must be remembered in estimating these sentences, which seem harsh enough 250 years after the Great Rebellion, what real cause there was at this date to fear that the object of these meetings might be to promote sedition and bring back once more ' the late discords ' which had caused so much suffering in Kent, where the rapidity with which licences for Nonconformist worship were applied for as soon as these were to be obtained shows that the adherents of the re-established monarchy might reasonably suspect they were not the strongest party in the county.

On 6 August, 1672, Major Nathaniel Darrell wrote :[446]

> Sir William Penn's son, a renowned quaker, and two or three brethren more, are very busy in the Wild of Kent, in planting their gospel and enlightening that dark country, which is the receptacle of all schism and rebellion.

There were evidently a considerable number of Anabaptist ministers in Kent,[447] but no sect of 'fanatics' seems to have aroused such animosity as the Quakers. The methods pursued by the earlier brethren were decidedly provocative, and it is hardly to be wondered at that their custom of going into the churches or 'steeple-houses,' as they chose to call them, and interrupting service to offer their own testimony, brought them into conflict with all the religious bodies of the day ; while their refusal to pay tithes again and again laid them open to legal prosecution. Already by 1658 an address to the Protector gave a list of Friends in the several gaols of this nation, including that of Canterbury, for conscience sake.[448] The same year other Kentish Quakers were in prison for tithes ;[449] and in 1659 several Quakers 'entered the Cathedral during service, and interrupted it by disturbing the minister in his preaching, and caused a tumult afterwards.'[450]

The journal of George Fox shows that he manifested the same interest in the soldiery quartered in the county that we find later in the memoirs of John Wesley. He seems to have met with the greatest opposition among the Baptists. According to the *Journal*, he first came to Kent in 1655.[451]

> When we came to Rochester, there was a guard kept to examine passengers, but we passed by and were not stopped. So I went to Cranbrook where there was a great meeting ; several soldiers were at it, and many were turned to the Lord that day. After the meeting, some of the soldiers were somewhat rude, but the Lord's power came over them. Thomas Housegoe, an Independent preacher, who lived near Cranbrook, was convinced, and became a faithful minister for the Lord Jesus. Some friends had travelled into Kent before, as John Stubbs and William Caton, and the priests and professors had stirred up the magistrates at Maidstone to whip them. . . . Captain Dunk was also convinced in Kent. He went with me to Rye. . . . From Rye I went to Romney, where, the people having had notice of my coming some time before, there was a very large meeting. Thither came Samuel Fisher, an eminent preacher among the Baptists, who had had a parsonage worth about £200 a year which for conscience' sake he had given up. There was also the power of the Baptists, and abundance of the people. The power of the Lord was so mightily over the meeting, that many were reached thereby . . . a great convincement there was that day. . . .
>
> From Romney I passed to Dover, and had a meeting, where several were convinced. Near Dover a governor and his wife were convinced, who had been Baptists ; and the Baptists thereabout were much offended, and grew very envious ; but the Lord's power came over all. Luke Howard of Dover was convinced some time before and became a faithful minister of Christ. . . .[452]
>
> Returning from Dover, I went to Canterbury, where a few honest-hearted people were turned to the Lord, who sat down under Christ's teaching. Thence I passed to Cranbrook again, where I had a great meeting.
>
> A friend went to the steeple-house and was cast into prison ; but the Lord's power was manifested, and his truth spread.

[446] *Cal. S.P. Dom.* 1672, p. 450.

[447] Ibid. pp. 100, 101. A register made in the year 1662–3, and preserved in Sancroft's correspondence, gives the number of dissenters in the lathe of St..Augustine as 393; of these, 116 are described as Independent, 181 as Anabaptists, and 96 as Quakers. Rev. C. E. Woodruff, *Arch. Cant.* xxi, 175. This register gives many details of Nonconformity in Kent at this time.

[448] *Cal. S.P. Dom.* 1658–9, p. 147.

[449] Ibid. 150.

[450] Ibid. 364 (1 June).

[451] *Journ.* (ed. 1901), i, 227.

[452] Luke Howard subsequently suffered various imprisonments for attending meetings.

The next year George Fox was again in Kent,[453] where he writes : 'I had great meetings ; and many times met with opposition from Baptists and other jangling professors ; but the Lord's power went over them.'

After the Restoration, Quakerism seems to have rapidly gained a hold in Kent ; of his first visit there after that event George Fox writes : [454]

> We went to Ashford, where we had a quiet and a very blessed meeting ; and on First Day we had a very good and peaceable one at Cranbrook. Then we went to Tenterden, and had a meeting there, to which many Friends came from several parts, and many other people came in, and were reached by the truth.

Meeting over, he was arrested by soldiers, taken to the jailer's house, examined by justices, and told there was a law against Quakers' meetings. 'They told us we should see they were civil to us, for it was the mayor's pleasure we should all be set at liberty. I told them their civility was noble and so we parted.'

Another visit to Kent in 1668, 'where, after we had been at several meetings, we had a general meeting for the men Friends of that county,'[455] seems to have been the occasion of the settlement of monthly meetings there. The last recorded by him is in 1670 : [456]

> I went into Kent, and had many glorious and precious meetings in several parts of that county. I went to a meeting near Deal, which was very large ; and returning from thence to Canterbury, visited Friends there. I then passed into the Isle of Sheppey, where I stayed two or three days ; and thither came Alexander Parker, George Whitehead, and John Rous to me. Next day to Rochester, but I was much spent, being so extremely laden and burdened under the world's spirits that my life was oppressed under them. . . . I was brought into the deep.

The Sufferings of the People called Quakers, by Joseph Besse, gives valuable supplementary evidence as to the methods of those early days, methods which, in fact, were not for a long time abandoned.[457]

Between the issue by Charles II of his Declaration of Indulgence 15 March, 1671–2, and its withdrawal 7 March in the following year owing to the action of Parliament, licences for Nonconformist worship had been granted in Kent to seventeen Presbyterian, twelve Congregational, and twenty-four Baptist congregations.[458]

A religious census for 1693 states that the compilers found 'these things observable' : [459]

> (3) That they are Walloons chiefly that make up the number of dissenters in Canterbury, Sandwich, and Dover. (7) At Ashford and other places we find a new sort of heretics, after the name of Muggleton, a London tailor, in number 30. (8) The rest of the dissenters are presbyterians, anabaptists, independents, and quakers, about equal numbers, only two or three called self-willers professedly. The heads and preachers of the several factions are such as had a great share in the late rebellion.

This return gives the Conformists in Canterbury diocese as 59,596, and in Rochester as 27,886; of Nonconformists in Canterbury as 6,287, and in Rochester as 17,520; of Papists in Canterbury as 143, and in Rochester as sixty-four.

[453] *Journ.* i, 357.   [454] Ibid. ii, 1, 2.

[455] Ibid. ii, 97. An interesting statement in view of the fact that it was a feature of Quakerism that women were admitted to an equality with men in their meetings, which they had a right to address, and were generally present.   [456] Ibid. 130.   [457] For instances connected with Kent see op. cit. (ed. 1753), i, 289–91.

[458] *Cal. S.P. Dom.* 1672–3, Pref. p. xxxvi. Four Congregationalist ministers in Canterbury are mentioned, ibid. 1672, p. 101, as also seven Kentish Anabaptist ministers in Kent. The indices to these calendars for the years 1671–3 give the geographical position of Nonconformist congregations in Kent applying for licences.

[459] Ibid. 1693, Pref. p. xxxvi ; and pp. 448–9.

ECCLESIASTICAL HISTORY

The strong religious feeling in Kent of which the multiplying of sects there may be taken to have been an expression, was not lacking even in the lax days following the Restoration among the clergy of the Established Church. In the latter end of the seventeenth century it was among the Kentish clergy that many of the Church's most brilliant examples of learning and devotion were to be found. At their head, in every sense, may be placed Archbishop Sheldon, who succeeded Juxon in 1663, and who did not hesitate to forfeit the high favour he at first enjoyed with Charles by his consistent attitude of reproval; and with him Bishop Dolben,[460] who had married Archbishop Sheldon's niece Catherine, and succeeded Dr. Warner at Rochester in 1666. The bishop was then allowed to hold the deanery of Westminster *in commendam* on account of the inadequate income of his see, and crowds flocked to hear him at Westminster. A year after his consecration he fell into temporary disgrace at court at the fall of Clarendon, but soon recovered his position and was promoted to York in 1683, being succeeded by Francis Turner, who only held the bishopric for a year, when he was translated to Ely, and replaced at Rochester by Bishop Spratt, the friend and imitator of Cowley, whose life he wrote. He was described by Evelyn as 'that great wit, Dr. Sprat,' and was recognized both as an attractive preacher and a bold upholder of high church doctrine and of the right of kings.

Archbishop Sancroft, memorable for his contest with King James (whose declaration of 4 May, 1688, he induced his clergy to disobey,[461] ' not from any want of tenderness towards dissenters, but because the declaration, being founded on such a dispensing power as may at pleasure set aside all laws ecclesiastical and civil, appears to me illegal '), for his subsequent trial and acquittal after presenting a petition against it with six other bishops,[462] for his refusal to take the oath of allegiance to William and Mary, and for his consequent suspension and then deprivation, did not fail to leave in his diocese the impress that would be expected from one of his character. He succeeded Archbishop Sheldon in 1677, but had already been connected with the diocese of Canterbury, where he held the archdeaconry from 1668–70.[463] He was assiduous in the ecclesiastical duties of his office, and ordered that there should be weekly communions, which resulted in their being re-introduced at Canterbury, and apparently at Rochester.[464] He resolved to revive the ancient office of rural dean, which seems to have fallen into disuse in Canterbury in the fifteenth century, and which was heard no more of from Archbishop Tillotson's succession to the see until its re-institution by Archbishop Howley in 1833.

The rural deans he appointed were Dr. George Thorpe to Canterbury, Dr. Giles Hinton to Charing, Dr. John Castilion to Westbere, Dr. Henry Ullock to Sandwich, Dr. William Wickens to Ospringe, and Dr. James Wilson to Sutton. The result of an inquiry into the condition of the parishes in their deaneries furnishes many interesting particulars. Out of

---

[460] An ardent Royalist who had volunteered when a student at Oxford for King Charles.
[461] Tanner MSS. 28, fol. 20.   [462] Ibid. fol. 34, 35, 36, 38.
[463] In the Sancroft correspondence among the Tanner MSS. in the Bodleian is an account of some Kentish parishes, with an amusingly frank description of incumbents, which it has been suggested was drawn up for his use when entering on his duties, the names indicating that it must have been written about 1668. Transcribed in *Arch. Cant.* xxi, 176, &c.
[464] Rev. W. H. Hutton, *Hist. of Engl. Ch.* (ed. Stephens and Hunt), vi, 327.

nineteen incumbents in the deanery of Sandwich, Dr. Ullock says, 4 April, 1683,[466] that ten were pluralists, but that their cures were for the most part small, contiguous, and modestly endowed ; even when extenuating circumstances might be pleaded the archbishop brought pressure to bear upon the incumbent in order to induce him to resign one of his benefices. Dr. Wilson wrote,[467] concerning Francis Green, minister of East Farleigh, a village in the diocese of Rochester, that he was never qualified for the office of priest, having been a common trooper in the late rebellion, and for several years past under pretence to grant licences hath married all comers of what diocese soever to the prejudice of neighbouring ministers in the deanery of Sutton : he returns also that it 'is the general report of all parishes in his deanery that many of the meaner sort of people besides dissenters absent themselves from public worship.' Of his own rectory at Biddenden [468] Dr. Giles Hinton wrote that the parsonage house had not been dwelt in by a rector for nigh four score years and had been

> tenemented out to vile and vicious people who made it so ragged and unclean that I never saw any building stand more in need of a lustration. However, I brought my family into it, and since I have had a title to it I have laid out neer two hundred pounds only to make it capable of a bed and a table, a stoole and a candlesticke. I was not borne in a pigstie, though I may die in a worse place, soe thicke have been upon me my charges in removing, in first fruits (£35) and necessary reparations.

This first letter, dated 1683, had a melancholy sequel, for another of 1685 informed the archbishop that in consequence of the necessary charges of faculties, first fruits, and reparation of dilapidated houses (amounting to above £300), which 'came soe fast on me that I could not by my best thrift and parsimony in this scantling of time satisfie my creditors,' he is about to go to the common place of confinement at Maidstone, and cannot, in consequence, perform the respective offices of his charge and his two livings.

A previous letter had given a description of this cure that might well have made its incumbent despair. There had been no rector resident for fifty-one years, and

> the parishioners (as elsewhere in the Weald of Kent) have among them all the vulgar sects about London and one more, for there are alsoe remaining some Brownists who boast that they have kept themselves unmingled with all other dissenters ever since the days of that notable seismatic from whom they have their denomination.

A letter from Thomas Paramore, vicar of Guston, to Dr. Robert Thompson, secretary to the archbishop,[469] gives an equally lamentable account of the parishes of Guston and West Langdon.

> As for Guston the parishioners being all (within two or three families) dissenters from our Church, as Anabaptists chiefly, and some Quakers, there is noe pulpit cushion, noe pulpit cloth, noe surplice, noe Common Prayer Book, the Bible out of the cover and imperfect, and I think noe table, neither have they any churchwarden or a clark. . . . the number of families in this parish is 16.

As for West Langdon

> the church of it is fallen down and noe use can be made of it, but the walls of it are standing both east and west, north and south, and may be serviceable again upon occasion. . . . The number of families in this parish is 18. . . . The people are conformable to our constitution.

---

[466] 'Letters relating to the condition of the church in Kent during the primacy of Archbishop Sancroft.' Transcribed from the Sancroft correspondence preserved among the Tanner MSS. in the Bodleian Library. *Arch. Cant.* xxi, 172–96.   [467] Ibid.   [468] Ibid.   [469] Ibid.

Good men, however, were to be found officiating even in remote and desolate Kentish villages. Sancroft surrounded himself with men of character and distinction, and a powerful attraction was exercised by the extraordinary piety and gentle simplicity of Archbishop Tillotson, qualities possessed in a high degree by Archbishop Tenison,[470] who succeeded him in 1694, a man of stronger mould, who like him was a warm advocate of comprehension throughout his primacy of twenty years.

The little village of Chartham had for its sincere and conscientious priest from 1689 to 1695 Henry Wharton, unique among his contemporaries for the greatness of his work, who 'died at the age of thirty, having done for the elucidation of English Church history more than any one before or since,'[471] and whose zeal and activity were never diminished, though he was forced to make the familiar complaint of the country parson, that he was employed in teaching a 'few plough joggers, who look upon what I say as concerning them but little.' This devoted student, shrewd controversialist, and keen antiquary, had been appointed by Sancroft to be his chaplain on 10 September, 1688,[472] and had won great fame by his works against the Romanists, but it is for that 'work of incredible pains,' the *Anglia Sacra*, that he is best known. His many friends included Henry Maurice, another chaplain of Archbishop Sancroft's, who like himself did not follow the archbishop in his refusal to take the oath of allegiance to William, and he was assisted by Maurice in the composition of his *Defence of Pluralities* published in 1692. Both Wood and Hearne praise highly Maurice's firm scholarship, solid judgement, ready wit, and blameless life. He held the rectory of Chevening in Kent from 1681–5.

It is to John Johnson of Cranbrook, not only a Kentish clergyman himself, but the son of Thomas Johnson, vicar of Frindsbury, and of Mary, daughter of Francis Drayton, rector of Little Chart, that we owe our best knowledge of the position of the clergy at the close of the seventeenth century. His best known work, *The Clergyman's Vade Mecum*, which ran through edition after edition, is full of interesting details as to the position, legal and to some extent social, of the clergy of his day. This very able writer was a diligent parish priest and always had daily service in his parish, his sympathies being with the Non-jurors, whose withdrawal from the Church was all the greater loss to her, in that the over sensitiveness which condemned them to an act of abnegation and consequent poverty was often the accompaniment of a saintly life and character.[473] He was intimate with Dr. George Hickes, and his correspondence includes interesting letters from

---

[470] A great supporter of the religious societies, especially the S.P.G. of which he was to some extent the founder.

[471] Rev. Wm. H. Hutton, *Hist. of Engl. Ch.* (ed. Stephens and Hunt), vi, 301.

[472] He had been ordained deacon 27 Feb. 1686–7, though under canonical age, on account of his extraordinary learning.

[473] Kent, as was to be expected, lost severely from their ejection, the Kentish non-jurors at this time including Henry Barrow, vicar of Horton Kirkby (Rochester), William Brooke, curate of Brookland (Cant.), Thomas Brett, rector of Betteshanger (Cant.), Thomas Brett, Jr., his son, Isaac Gosling, vicar of Sturry and curate of St. Mary Bredin (Cant.), —— Jones, curate of Lydd (Cant.), Simon Lowth, vicar of Harbledown, rector of Cosmus Blean, and dean elect of Rochester, —— Metcalfe, vicar of Voles (*sic*) Cray, Robert Orme, vicar of Wouldham (Roch.), Henry Paman, master of the Faculties to the archbishop of Canterbury, —— Schmid, preacher to the Walloon congregation at Sandwich, —— Symmes, vicar of Chislet (Cant.). —— Wingfield of Canterbury refused to take his M.A. degree. Canon J. H. Overton, D.D., *The Non-jurors*.

him and from Robert Nelson, as well as from Dr. Thomas Brett, whose life of him was published in 1748.

Dr. Thomas Brett, the son of Thomas Brett, of Spring Grove, Wye, became rector of Betteshanger on the death of his uncle Thomas Boys. Archbishop Tenison made him rector of Ruckinge 12 April, 1705, having previously allowed him to hold the small vicarage of Chislet in sequestration. Before Sacheverel's trial he had taken the oaths without scruple, but this induced him to resolve never to take them again, and on the accession of George I he declined to do so, resigned his living, and was received into communion by the non-juring bishop, Dr. Hickes. Afterwards he officiated in his own house, and in 1718 and 1729 complaints were made against him to Archbishop Wake for interfering with the duties of the parish clergyman, but he was let off with a reproof. He supported Collier in proposing to return to the use of the first liturgy of Edward VI, as nearer to the use of the primitive church, and joined with him in consecrating bishops; he consecrated his son Thomas Brett in 1727.

Dr. Francis Atterbury, who had been made bishop of Rochester and dean of Westminster (two posts then always held together) in 1713, had proved himself the able champion of the general mass of the clergy by his brilliant defence of the rights of Convocation against Dr. Wake, who subsequently succeeded Archbishop Tenison at Canterbury in 1716. He held a high rank as a debater and public speaker in Convocation and in the House of Lords, and was brought into great prominence by the Tory reaction at the end of Queen Anne's reign. He refused to sign the declaration of confidence in the government after the rebellion of 1715;[474] but how far he was really implicated in the Jacobite plots for which he suffered banishment in 1723, it is hard to determine. He was replaced at Rochester by Samuel Bradford, a very devoted adherent of the house of Hanover.

Archbishop Wake was eminently a man of his century, the century of common sense. He embodied its best characteristics, and was a sincere and devout churchman. But he had the same aversion from enthusiasm as his successors, Archbishops Potter and Herring, Hutton and Secker,[475] and the same devotion to reasonableness and moderation, which, excellent in itself, tended to produce the dead level of monotony that was to be disturbed by the preaching of John Wesley; and this characteristic was shared by Dr. Joseph Wilcocks, bishop of Rochester in 1731, and by Dr. Zachary Pearce, who succeeded him there in 1756, as it was a distinguishing mark of the most weighty work that survives out of the theological literature of this period, the *Analogy* of Butler, who was made prebendary of Rochester in 1736, the year of its publication.[476]

It was during the primacy of Archbishop Potter, who, as bishop of Oxford, ordained John Wesley deacon and priest, that the Methodist movement began. Potter, who after he became archbishop had several interviews with Wesley, always spoke kindly of his revival, which, in its founder's lifetime, endeavoured to secure punctual attendance at public worship within the

---

[474] The old Kentish recusant names reappear in the register of the estates taken under the Act of George I, cap. 55, entitled 'An Act to oblige Papists to register their names and real estates.' See E. C. Estcourt and J. O. Payne, *Engl. Catholic Non-jurors of* 1715, p. 84.

[475] Archbishop Potter, 1737-47; Abp. Herring, 1747-57; Abp. Hutton, 1757-8; Abp. Secker, 1758-68.

[476] His house, adjoining the deanery gateway, was pulled down by his successor.

Church itself. In spite of the opposition which Wesley met at the hands of the mob and some of the clergy on his coming to Canterbury in 1750,[477] when he preached for three days in the Butter Market and elsewhere, he always wrote with especial kindness of Kent, which he first visited on his return from Georgia in 1738, continuing to do so regularly ever afterwards, the county being part of his ' home circuit.'

A society had already been formed at Canterbury in 1750, and two of his most influential friends there were Edward Perronett, and his brother Vincent, vicar of Shoreham. Among the soldiers of this great depot Methodism had a great success, and large numbers of them were ' converted,' and became deeply attached to the few Canterbury Methodists who showed them kindness. It is said that on one occasion when certain regiments were on their way to Holland and had to pass through the city, the Methodists in them determined to avail themselves of the opportunity of meeting in class with their former leader, and did so in such numbers that the military class meeting lasted for nine successive hours.[478] On 26 January, 1756, and three following days John Wesley paid a visit to Canterbury, where he had a congregation containing ' abundance of soldiers and not a few of their officers.'[479] A month later he was there again,[480] when he dined with one of the colonels who said, ' No men fight like those who fear God ; I had rather command 500 such than any regiment in his Majesty's army.'

In 1758 he wrote of his visit to Canterbury that he found ' the little society there free from all divisions and offences ' ;[481] and in 1759 tells of his journey to Canterbury, where his congregation included 200 soldiers and a whole row of officers, after which he was at Dover, where he found a new chapel just finished, and opened it.[482] In November, 1761, he went to Canterbury, where he found ' many with a deeper work of God in their heart than they ever had before.'[483] In 1766 he made his usual Kentish tour,[484] and again in 1767,[485] when he wrote that he was at Sheerness on 16 December, when the governor of the fort gave him the use of the chapel, in which he preached to a large congregation.

Wesleyan Methodism took a firm hold in Kent, and the Report of the Wesleyan Centenary Fund in 1844 gives circuits at Canterbury, Rochester, Gravesend, Sheerness, Margate, Dover, Deal, Rye, Tenterden, Sandhurst, and Maidstone.

The years which had witnessed the vigorous growth and spread of the Methodist movement were not years of stagnation in the Church of England in Kent. Though amiability and affability seem to be the most striking characteristics of Archbishop Cornwallis, the twin brother of General Cornwallis,[486] who kept up a princely hospitality and was generally beloved in his diocese according to Hasted, as also of Archbishop Moore,[487] who succeeded him, the re-awakening of spiritual life which marked the beginning of the nineteenth century was testified to by their promotion of the Sunday School movement and of missionary enterprise ; while Archbishop Manners-Sutton[488] brought all his influence to support the small band of high churchmen then

[477] Rev. L. Tyerman, *Life of Wesley*, ii, 69.
[478] *Methodist Magazine*, 1837, p. 423.
[479] Rev. L. Tyerman, *Life of Wesley*, ii, 230.
[480] Ibid. 231. [481] Ibid. 309.
[482] Ibid. 339. [483] Ibid. 425.
[484] Ibid. 588. [485] Ibid. 615.
[486] 1768-83. Fourth son of Lord Cornwallis. His wife incurred the royal rebuke for the gaiety of her routs and parties at Lambeth.
[487] 1783-1805. [488] 1805-28.

promoting a revival within the Church, and chose for his chaplains men who were in the van of the movement. He presided over the meeting which issued in the foundation of the National Society, and did much to ensure the success of that society, as well as to revive the S.P.C.K.

At Rochester Bishop Thomas,[489] who repaired the deanery and rebuilt the bishop's palace at Bromley, but whose episcopate is not otherwise memorable, was succeeded by Bishop Samuel Horsley,[490] ' beyond all question the ablest and most eminent prelate still living at the commencement of the nineteenth century.'[491] A high churchman and one who gloried to proclaim himself one, he was described by the evangelical Isaac Milner as the light and glory of the Established Church,[492] and by Samuel Taylor Coleridge as ' the one red leaf, the last of its clan, with relation to the learned teachers of our Church.'[493] He defended Methodism, and won great renown by his vigorous refutations of Dr. Priestley ; the note of his work is to be found in his charge of 1800 to Rochester, which also gives a glimpse of the inertia he and his like were endeavouring to combat. He says :

> The festivals and fasts of the church are, I fear, not without some connivance of the clergy, gone too much into oblivion and neglect. There can be no excuse for the neglect of the feast of our Lord's Nativity, and the stated fasts of Ash Wednesday and Good Friday, even in the smallest country parishes, but in towns and the more populous villages the church ought certainly to be opened for worship on the forenoon at least of every day in the Passion Week, of the Mondays and Tuesdays of Easter Week and Whitsuntide, on the Epiphany, and on some, if not all, of the other festivals.

He was succeeded by Bishop Dampier,[494] who had been dean of Rochester since 1782, and who was instrumental in promoting the S.P.C.K. in Rochester, but who was translated to Ely six years later, when he was replaced by Bishop Walker King, followed in 1827 by the Hon. Hugh Percy, who in 1806 had married the eldest daughter of Archbishop Manners-Sutton, after which he had been collated to the benefices of Bishopsbourne and Ivychurch, and later to a prebendal stall at Canterbury, where he had been made archdeacon in 1822 and dean in 1825, his long connexion with the county suddenly ceasing by his translation to Carlisle a few months after he was made bishop of Rochester.

In the first year of the episcopate of his successor, Dr. George Murray,[495] a great meeting of Kentishmen, at which upwards of 20,000 persons are said to have been present, was held at Penenden Heath, 24 October, 1828, ' to petition Parliament to adopt such measures as are best calculated to support the Protestant establishment in church and state.'[496]

Archbishop Howley,[497] who in the following spring led the opposition[498] to the second reading of the Roman Catholic Relief Bill, in his place in the House of Lords continued in the same manner to oppose all change. But change and reform were to produce many alterations in the dioceses of Kent and Rochester in the ensuing years. Archbishop Howley himself lived to see the reinstitution of the office of rural dean in his diocese in 1833, the foundation and endowment of the new archdeaconry of

---

[489] 1774–93

[490] 1793–1802.

[491] J. H. Overton, *Engl. Ch. in the Nineteenth Century*, 26.

[492] *Life*, 212.

[493] Introduction to *Essay on Our Own Times*.

[494] 1802–8.

[495] 1827–60.

[496] B.M. 8138, fol. 34.

[497] 1828–48. His best memorial is the Howley-Harrison Library at Canterbury, of which his own collection forms part.

[498] *Parl. Debates* (New Ser.), xxi, 58–67.

Maidstone in 1841,[499] and a rearrangement in 1845[500] of the limits of the deaneries and archdeaconries in the dioceses of Canterbury and Rochester, with a scheme for providing a competent income and a fit house of residence for the bishops of Rochester. Archbishop Sumner,[501] who exercised the most active oversight over his diocese, whose sound theological views and ripe scholarship were held to reflect all that was best in the teaching of the evangelical party, presided over the opening of St. Augustine's College, the training college for missionary clergy which St. Augustine's monastery finally became, after its purchase and restoration by Alexander James Beresford Hope, in 1848. The abolition of peculiar jurisdictions in 1845 was accompanied by further territorial changes in the dioceses of Canterbury and Rochester.[502]

The diocesan society for church building, originated by Archbishop Longley,[503] and the activity shown in the building, restoration, and preservation of churches under him and his successors, Archbishops Tait[504] and Benson and Temple,[505] give valuable testimony to the vitality and energy of the churchmanship of Kent in their time ; a vitality further exhibited by the continual formation of new parishes both in the diocese of Canterbury[506] and in that of Rochester.[507] In the latter diocese a further impetus has recently been given to church life by the reconstitution of the Rochester Diocesan Conference. Rochester under Bishop Thorold,[508] who succeeded Bishop Claughton[509] in 1877, was practically reorganized after the constitution of the new archdeaconry of Southwark[510] (by Order of Council of 18 April, 1878) and the rearrangement of the deaneries of Rochester archdeaconry in consequence (by Order of Council of 30 December, 1878).[511] In 1879 a new archdeaconry of Kingston-on-Thames was endowed in Rochester diocese.[512] After the consecration of Dr. Talbot, the cathedral of St. Saviour's, Southwark, was opened in its renovated form, 16 February, 1897 ; the bishop of Rochester then acted as dean of the Collegiate Church, the suffragan bishop of Southwark (instituted 1891) as sub-dean, and four clergy, including the rector, as canons, with whom, for certain purposes, representative laymen had been associated. Under the Act of 1904, constituting the bishoprics of Southwark and Birmingham, it was decreed that the new bishopric of Southwark should include in its deaneries Greenwich, Lewisham, and Woolwich.[513]

The final rearrangement of the diocesan boundaries has left the metropolitan see (occupied by Archbishop Randall Thomas Davidson, translated from Winchester in 1903 with a population of 600,000 in 309 parishes, and the see of Rochester (occupied by Bishop John Reginald Harmer, translated from Adelaide in 1905) with a population of 500,000 in nearly two hundred parishes.

---

[499] *Orders in Council*, i, 204, No. 38. [500] Ibid. iii, 197, 263. [501] 1848–62.
[502] *Orders in Council*, General Index to 1854, i, 204 ; iii, 263, 462 ; viii, 394.
[503] 1862–8. [504] 1868–82. [505] 1882–96.
[506] *Rep. of Eccl. Com.* Nos. 19, 21, 27, 28, 30, 31, &c. [507] Ibid. Nos. 22, 28, &c.
[508] 1877–90. [509] 1867–77. [510] Ibid. Nos. 25, 71. [511] Ibid. No. 28.
[512] Ibid. No. 29. [513] Public General Acts, 1904, cap. 30, sched. 2.

APPENDIX I

SUFFRAGAN BISHOPS OF DOVER

Before the Conquest Kent seems to have possessed, besides the archbishopric and the bishopric of Rochester, a bishopric of St. Martin's, as mention is made of Eadsin, bishop of St. Martin's 1032–8, and of Godwin, appointed bishop in 1061,[1] after whose death no other bishop of St. Martin's was appointed. These bishops of St. Martin's seem to have acted as suffragan to the archbishop. After they ceased to exist his suffragan was known by the title of a foreign bishopric, until by the Act of 26 Hen. VIII, cap. 14, these foreign titles were abrogated, and the title of suffragan bishop of Dover was directed to be the future style of the suffragans of the archbishop of Canterbury. Richard Yngworth, prior of Langley Regis, was consecrated bishop of Dover 9 December, 1537, the archbishop in his commission declaring that his duty and the exercise of his office was confined within the diocese and city of Canterbury, and the jurisdiction of Calais, and the marches thereof.[1b] The Act of 26 Hen. VIII was repealed by Mary, and the suffragan bishops again assumed foreign titles, Thomas Chetham being consecrated suffragan to Archbishop Pole in 1558 as *Episcopus Sidoniensis*. This last Act was repealed by Elizabeth, who revived that of 26 Hen. VIII, when Richard Rogers, archdeacon of St. Asaph, was consecrated suffragan bishop in 1569, being suffragan to Parker, Grindal, and Whitgift successively. After his death in 1597 there was no further consecration of a suffragan bishop of Dover until the title was again revived by the consecration of Bishop Parry in 1870. At the present time there is also a suffragan bishop deriving his title from Croydon.

APPENDIX II

ECCLESIASTICAL DIVISIONS OF THE COUNTY

It was held by Kemble that the two bishoprics of Canterbury and Rochester corresponded to two kingdoms, into which the kingdom of Kent was at one time divided, East Kent and West Kent.[1c] Archdeaconries as territorial divisions had their origin soon after the Norman Conquest, but until 1841 there was only one archdeacon in each diocese.[2] Kentish rural deaneries had probably been in existence for some time before the *Taxatio* of 1291,[3] when the diocese of Canterbury contains eleven deaneries, i.e. Bridge, Canterbury, Charing, Dover, Elham, Lympne, Ospringe, Sandwich, Sittingbourne, Sutton, and Westbere ; and the diocese of Rochester four, i.e. Dartford, Malling, Rochester, and Shoreham. These divisions are given in the *Valor Ecclesiasticus*;[4] there were then 245 rectories, 172 vicarages, 52 chapels, and 41 chantries existing in the county. By Order in Council of 4 June, 1841, the archdeaconry of Maidstone was founded, and the deaneries of Sittingbourne, Charing, and Sutton transferred to it from the archdeaconry of Canterbury.[5] At this time the diocese of London had become unmanageably large, and accordingly, by Order in Council of 20 August, 1845,[6] it was directed that the diocese of Rochester should consist of the city and deanery of Rochester, and the counties of Hertford and Essex, pending the creation of a separate see for those counties ; the remainder of the county of Kent previously in the diocese and archdeaconry of Rochester to be included in, and form part of, the archdeaconry of Maidstone in the diocese of Canterbury, except the parishes of Charlton, Lee, Lewisham, Greenwich, Woolwich, Eltham, Plumstead, and St. Nicholas, in the county of Kent, and of St. Paul, Deptford, in the counties of Kent and Surrey, which were to be transferred to the bishopric of London ; these nine parishes were restored to Rochester, however, in 1867. By Order in Council of 30 December, 1845,[7] it was also decreed that henceforth the parishes of Eynsford, Farningham, Otford, Shoreham, and Stansted should be held to be not situate in the diocese of Rochester, but within the diocese of Canterbury and archdeaconry of Maidstone. At the census of 1871 the diocese of Canterbury consisted, in Kent, of the entire county (except the city and deanery of Rochester, the deaneries of Cobham, Gravesend, and Woolwich, part of the

---

[1] *Angl.-Sax. Chron.* ; Hasted, *Kent*, iv, 100 ; Lambarde, *Perambulations*, 233.
[1b] Strype, *Life of Cranmer*, App. No. xxii.   [1c] *The Saxons in England*, i, 148.
[2] With the exception of the appointment of three archdeacons in the place of the archdeacon of Canterbury by Archbishop Richard in 1175. Matt. Paris, *Chron. Maj.* ii, 297.
[3] Rec. Com.   [4] Ibid.   [5] *Orders in Council*, i, 204, No. 38.
[6] Ibid. iii, 263, No. 197.   [7] Ibid. iii, 462, No. 226.

deanery of Greenwich, and parts of the parishes of Frant and Hawkhurst).[8]   The diocese of Rochester then consisted, in Kent, of the city and deanery of Rochester, the deaneries of Cobham, Gravesend, and Woolwich, and of part of the deanery of Greenwich.   In 1877 the diocese of St. Albans came into being and relieved Rochester of the counties of Essex and Hertford, but East and Mid-Surrey were at the same time transferred from Winchester diocese to that of Rochester, pending the creation of a diocese of South London.[9]   At the foundation of the bishopric of Southwark in 1904,[10] the rural deaneries of Greenwich, Lewisham, and Woolwich were transferred to that bishopric, and the deaneries of Malling, Dartford, and Shoreham were restored from Canterbury to Rochester.   As a result of this last change Canterbury resumed its original boundaries, with the addition of Croydon and the loss of its peculiars in Shoreham ; Rochester also resumed its ancient boundaries, less that part of Kent which lies in the county of London and now belongs to the see of Southwark.   At the present time there are 476 ecclesiastical parishes in the county.

[8] Parts of these parishes were then included in the diocese of Chichester.
[9] Order in Council, 30 April, 1877.   [10] Public General Acts, 1904, cap. 30, sched. 2.

THE
RELIGIOUS HOUSES OF KENT

INTRODUCTION

Kent had the distinction of being the only English county with two mediaeval sees and cathedrals, and in St. Augustine's at Canterbury it possessed an abbey of the first rank ; but the remaining monasteries proper were hardly as numerous or as important as might have been expected in consideration of its size and the fact that it was practically the birthplace of Christianity in England. The Danish raids may have had something to do with this, and they are probably the principal cause of the fall of three abbeys, Reculver, Lyminge, and Minster in Thanet, before the Conquest.

These houses all belonged to the Benedictine order, as also did the abbey of Faversham, founded in 1147. Dover was founded in the seventh century as a house of secular canons, but was changed into a Benedictine priory after the Conquest. The nunnery of Minster in Sheppey, also founded in the seventh century, was of the same order ; and so were those of St. Sepulchre at Canterbury and Malling, founded about the end of the eleventh century, and Davington and Higham, half a century later.

The Cluniac and Cistercian orders, branches of the Benedictine, had each a single house in the county, dating from the middle of the twelfth century, at Horton and Boxley respectively. There were six houses of Austin canons; the priory of St. Gregory at Canterbury appearing first as a house of seculars at the end of the eleventh century, Leeds, Combwell, Lesnes, and Tonbridge belonging to the twelfth, while Bilsington was not founded until 1253. The Premonstratensian canons, a reformed branch of the Austins, corresponding to the Cistercians among monks, had abbeys at Langdon and St. Radegund's, founded towards the close of the twelfth century. Several foreign houses also owned possessions in the county, and though some of them appear merely as absentee landlords, others had dependent priories at Folkestone, Lewisham, Patrixbourne, Romney, and Throwley. Of these Folkestone obtained a grant of denization, but the other four came to an end early in the fifteenth century, and passed into the possession of religious houses in other counties.

The Knights Templars were settled at Ewell, and the Knights Hospitallers at West Peckham, Sutton at Hone, and Swingfield.

There were colleges of secular canons at Bredgar, Cobham, Maidstone, Wingham, and Wye.

The most noteworthy point about the religious houses of the county was certainly the great number of friaries and hospitals. The Grey Friars had

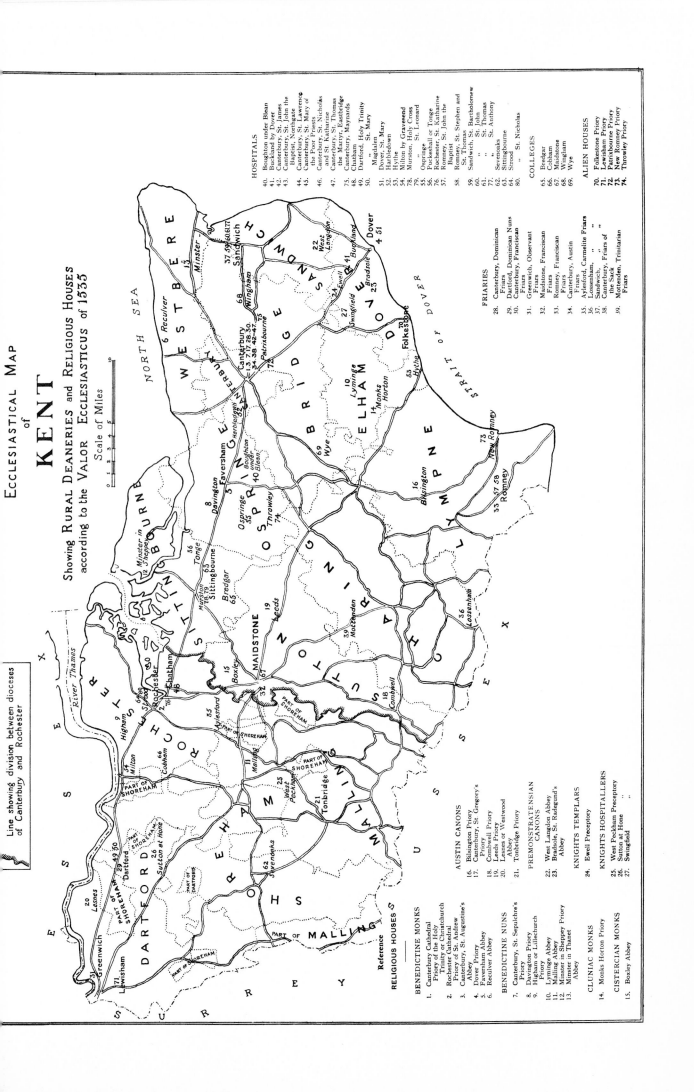

ECCLESIASTICAL MAP
of
KENT

Showing RURAL DEANERIES and RELIGIOUS HOUSES
according to the VALOR ECCLESIASTICUS of 1535

Scale of Miles
0 1 2 3 4 5 10

Reference

Line showing division between dioceses
of Canterbury and Rochester

RELIGIOUS HOUSES

BENEDICTINE MONKS

1. Canterbury Cathedral
   Priory of the Holy
   Trinity or Christchurch
2. Rochester Cathedral
   Priory of St. Andrew
3. Canterbury, St. Augustine's
   Abbey
4. Dover Priory
5. Faversham Abbey
6. Reculver Abbey

BENEDICTINE NUNS

7. Canterbury, St. Sepulchre's
   Priory
8. Davington Priory
9. Higham or Lillechurch
   Priory
10. Lyminge Abbey
11. Malling Abbey
12. Minster in Sheppey Priory
13. Minster in Thanet
    Abbey

CLUNIAC MONKS

14. Monks Horton Priory

CISTERCIAN MONKS

15. Boxley Abbey

AUSTIN CANONS

16. Bilsington Priory
17. Canterbury, St. Gregory's
    Priory
18. Combwell Priory
19. Leeds Priory
20. Lesnes or Westwood
    Abbey
21. Tonbridge Priory

PREMONSTRATENSIAN
CANONS

22. West Langdon Abbey
23. Bradsole, St. Radegund's
    Abbey

KNIGHTS TEMPLARS

24. Ewell Preceptory

KNIGHTS HOSPITALLERS

25. West Peckham Preceptory
26. Sutton at Hone   "
27. Swingfield   "

FRIARIES

28. Canterbury, Dominican
    Friars
29. Dartford, Dominican Nuns
30. Canterbury, Franciscan
    Friars
31. Greenwich, Observant
    Friars
32. Maidstone, Franciscan
    Friars
33. Romney, Franciscan
    Friars
34. Canterbury, Austin
    Friars
35. Aylesford, Carmelite Friars
36. Lossenham,   "   "
37. Sandwich,   "   "
38. Canterbury, Friars of
    the Sack
39. Mottenden, Trinitarian
    Friars

HOSPITALS

40. Boughton under Blean
41. Buckland by Dover
42. Canterbury, St. James
43. Canterbury, St. John the
    Baptist, Northgate
44. Canterbury, St. Lawrence
45. Canterbury, St. Mary of
    the Poor Priests
46. Canterbury, St. Nicholas
    and St. Katharine
47. Canterbury, St. Thomas
    the Martyr, Eastbridge
75. Canterbury, Maynards
48. Chatham
49. Dartford, Holy Trinity
50. Dover, St. Mary
    Magdalen
51. Dover, St. Mary
52. Harbledown
53. Hythe
54. Milton by Gravesend
78. Murston, Holy Cross
79. Ospringe, St. Leonard
55. Ospringe
56. Puckeshall or Tonge
76. Rochester, St. Katharine
57. Romney, St. John the
    Baptist
58. Romney, St. Stephen and
    St. Thomas
59. Sandwich, St. Bartholomew
60.   "   St. John
61.   "   St. Thomas
77.   "   St. Anthony
62. Sevenoaks
63. Sittingbourne
64. Strood
80.   "   St. Nicholas

COLLEGES

65. Bredgar
66. Cobham
67. Maidstone
68. Wingham
69. Wye

ALIEN HOUSES

70. Folkestone Priory
71. Lewisham Priory
72. Patrixbourne Priory
73. New Romney Priory
74. Throwley Priory

houses at Canterbury, Maidstone, and Romney ; the Carmelites at Aylesford, Lossenham, and Sandwich ; The Austin Friars, Black Friars, and Friars of the Sack at Canterbury ; the Observants at Greenwich ; the Trinitarian Friars at Mottenden ; and the Dominican Nuns at Dartford ; making a total of twelve in all. There were not less than twenty-five hospitals, several of which survive to the present day, though a few vanished before the general Dissolution.

The Kentish monasteries do not appear to advantage near their end. The reports on the two Premonstratensian abbeys made by visitors of their own order were distinctly unfavourable. Archbishop Warham's visitations in 1511 do not reveal any great immorality, but they certainly show that the early high monastic ideal had completely vanished ; and Warham was no enemy of monasticism, nor was Bishop Fisher, who suppressed Higham with good reason in 1522. No more glaring imposture was exposed at the Reformation than that of the Rood of Boxley ; and no worse instance of superstition and fraud than that of the Nun of Kent, backed by monks of Canterbury.

After Higham the next houses to fall were Lesnes and Tonbridge, suppressed by Wolsey in 1525, by authority from the king and pope, for the foundation of his college at Oxford. Davington came to a very uncommon end, being deserted in 1535. Not much is known of the visitation made by Layton and others in that year, but the reports appear to have been unfavourable, and it was probably on this account that Langdon, Folkestone, and Dover were surrendered in November. Bilsington was surrendered on 28 February, 1536, just before the Act of Dissolution came into effect ; and under this the remaining smaller monasteries fell.

St. Augustine's, Faversham, Malling, Boxley, and Leeds had net incomes of over £200, and so survived as 'greater monasteries,' but yielded to pressure and fell in the next two or three years ; and the two cathedrals were likewise surrendered, but were reconstituted as secular establishments. Under a later act, the colleges and most of the hospitals came to an end.

HOUSES OF BENEDICTINE MONKS

1. THE CATHEDRAL PRIORY OF THE HOLY TRINITY OR CHRIST-CHURCH, CANTERBURY

Bede[1] tells us that

'the bishop St. Augustine, as soon as he received the episcopal seat in the royal city, repaired and restored with the king's help the church, which he learned had been constructed long ago of old Roman work ; and he consecrated it in the name of our Lord and Saviour Christ ; and there he established a habitation for himself and all his successors.'

Thorne's version[2] is that in 598, the year after his arrival at Canterbury, the king granted to him his royal palace within the city, and he

restored it to a church and consecrated it in the name of the Saviour. The two accounts do not differ in any essential point, and may no doubt be considered reliable descriptions of the foundation.

The first point to be noted is that from the foundation to the Conquest the cathedral establishment, as on the Continent, consisted of secular clerks and not of monks. Gervase declares that monks were settled there originally,[3] and that it was only on account of a great mortality among them that clerks were introduced under Ceolnoth and tolerated by his successor Ethelred ;[4] being afterwards removed by Sigeric[5] and again tolerated by Ethelnoth.[6]

[1] *Hist. Eccl.* i, c. 33.
[2] Twysden, *Decem Scriptores*, 1760.

[3] Gervase of Cant. *Opera* (Rolls. Ser.) ii, 28.
[4] Ibid. 348–50.   [5] Ibid. 357.   [6] Ibid. 361.

But, apart from the fact that a monastic chapter was a comparatively late institution even in English cathedrals, there is the conclusive evidence that the head of Canterbury was always a dean before the Conquest and never a prior. The introduction of the monks was only brought about in the time of Lanfranc ;[7] Dunstan himself, the great supporter of monasticism, not having effected it.

Very little is known of the history of the cathedral before the Conquest. Archbishop Cuthbert[8] began the system of the burials of the archbishops there instead of at St. Augustine's, but the story belongs rather to the latter house. In September, 1011, Canterbury was sacked and the cathedral burnt by the Danes, who killed Archbishop Alphege because he refused to pay ransom.[9]

William the Conqueror treated the cathedral well, confirming its liberties and restoring many lands which had been taken away from it. Lanfranc made a division of these, retaining some himself, allotting others to the convent and surrendering some which properly belonged to Rochester.[10] After his death the see was vacant for four years, and William Rufus heavily oppressed the church, confiscating its lands and annulling its liberties.[11]

The cathedral church, which had been begun by Lanfranc and enlarged by Anselm, was dedicated by Archbishop William on 4 May, 1130, in the presence of the king and queen, David king of Scotland, and a large number of bishops, abbots and nobles.[12] Archbishop Theobald crowned Stephen and his queen there.[13] Archbishop Becket was murdered in the church on 29 December, 1170, and in consequence of the pollution it was closed for nearly a year, being reconciled by the bishops of Exeter and Chester on 21 December following.[14] On 12 July, 1174, the king made a solemn pilgrimage to Becket's tomb.[15] On 5 September in the same year, the church was destroyed by fire, and an elaborate account of the catastrophe and the rebuilding is given by Gervase, who was probably an eye-witness.[16] This was the third conflagration, the first having occurred at the time when Alfege was murdered and the second at the arrival of Lanfranc. Gervase quotes Eadmer's account of the old church, and himself describes Lanfranc's and the newest. There was a difference of opinion among architects as to the course to be adopted, but at last the work was entrusted to William of Sens, who carried it on until he was disabled by an accident in 1178, when he

was succeeded by another William, an Englishman ; and the choir was finally re-consecrated on 19 April, 1180.

Several large registers and a great number of miscellaneous documents relating to its history are still preserved in the cathedral. These have been described or partially calendared by the late Dr. J. Brigstocke Sheppard for the Historical Manuscripts Commission ;[17] and the possessions and liberties of the house will be found set out in great detail in them. Very many privileges were granted by various popes.[18] The prior and monks had almost complete self-government ; and the prior obtained from Honorius III the right of wearing the episcopal ring and mitre, in addition to other insignia. Alexander III exempted the lands of Christchurch from the payment of small tithes. Urban IV empowered the prior to absolve monks lying under ecclesiastical censures.

Many charters of grants and confirmations of liberties were also obtained from successive kings ;[19] and several of the liberties were successfully proved before justices and commissioners in eyre in 1279, 1286, 1293 and 1313.[20] Henry III on 27 February, 1264, granted to the prior and convent free warren in all their demesne lands in the counties of Kent, Surrey, Sussex, Essex, Norfolk, Suffolk, Buckingham, Oxford and Devon, but without specifying the towns in which they held lands ; and on account of this vagueness they obtained a fresh charter, in which the place-names are given, from Edward II in 1316.[21] Richard II on 2 October, 1383, granted to them four fairs yearly within the site of the priory.[22]

The possessions are recorded in detail in the registers, and lists of the names and dates of donors are given by Gervase and others.[23] Archbishop Theodore is said[24] to have made the division of the estates of the archbishop and the chapter, which was clearly recognized at the time of the Domesday Survey.[25] The prior and convent owned the manors of Meopham, Basser, Leysdown, Eylwarton, Copton, Ham, Selgrave, Boyton, Hollingbourne, Westwell, Orpington, East

[7] Gervase of Cant. *Opera* (Rolls Ser.), ii, 368.

[8] Ibid. 345.

[9] Ibid. 53, 359 ; *Anglo.-Sax. Chron.* (Rolls Ser.), ii, 117.

[10] Gervase, op. cit. ii, 64.   [11] Ibid. 370.

[12] Ibid. i, 96 ; ii, 383.

[13] Ibid. i, 123.   [14] Ibid. i, 226, 236 ; ii, 395.

[15] Ibid. i, 248.   [16] Ibid. i, 1–29.

[17] *Hist. MSS. Com. Rep.* v. App. pt. i, 426–62 ; ibid. viii, App. pt. i, 315–55 ; ibid. ix, App. pt. i, 72–129. Some selections from these have been printed in *Literae Cantuarienses* and *Epistolae Cantuarienses* (Rolls Ser.) and *Christchurch Letters* (Camden Soc.). One of the cathedral registers is now in the University Library at Cambridge (Ee. v, 31).

[18] *Hist. MSS. Com. Rep.* viii, App. pt. i, 317–18.

[19] Ibid. 318–19.

[20] *Plac. de Quo Warr.* (Rec. Com.), 86, 321, 325, 335, 341, 348, 352, 355, 357.

[21] *Chart. R.* 10 Edw. II, No. 60.

[22] Ibid. 7–8 Ric. II, No. 32.

[23] Gervase, op. cit. ii ; *Decem Scriptores* 2207–26 ; Dugdale, *Mon.* i, 89, 95–8.

[24] Gervase, op. cit. ii, 64, 341.

[25] V.C.H. Kent, iii, 'Domesday Survey.'

CHRISTCHURCH PRIORY,
CANTERBURY.
(12th Century.)

CHRISTCHURCH PRIORY,
CANTERBURY.
(1418.)

FAVERSHAM ABBEY.
(13th Century.)

CHRISTCHURCH PRIORY,
CANTERBURY.
(Reverse.)

and West Farleigh, Loose, Ebony, Appledore, Chartham, Godmersham, Brook, Little and Great Chart, Orgarswick, Ruckinge, Fairfield, Aghne Court, Seasalter, Shouart, Thornden, Ickham, Bramling, Adisham, Eastry, Monkton and Brooksend, and the churches of Farningham, Meopham, Halstow, Milton, Faversham, Sheldwich, Preston, East Peckham, Boughton under Blean, Cranbrook, Tenterden, Westwell, Godmersham, Willesborough, Fairfield, Brookland, Stone, Seasalter, Brook, Littlebourne, West Cliffe, Eastry, Monkton and Birchington in Kent ; the manors of Cheam, Merstham, Charlwood, Horsley, Vauxhall and Walworth in Surrey ; the manors of Bocking, Bocking in Mersea, Milton, Lalling,[26] Southchurch, Stisted, Panfield and Borley in Essex ; the manor of Wotton in Sussex ; the manor of Newington in Oxfordshire ; the manors of Risborough and Halton in Buckinghamshire ; the manors of Eleigh and Hadleigh in Suffolk ; [27] the manor of Deopham in Norfolk ; and the manor of Daccombe [28] in Devonshire. In the Taxation of 1291 the temporalities in the diocese of Canterbury were valued at £1,066 8s. 1d. yearly.[29] In the Valor of 1535 the gross value of the possessions was returned as £2,493 6s. 2¾d., with deductions of £143 17s. 9½d., leaving the net value £2,349 8s. 5¼d. yearly.[30]

The formal revenue as set out in the Taxation and Valor of course does not represent the whole income of the cathedral, which was swelled by offerings and other irregular receipts, and which can still be traced in the treasurer's accounts.[31] In 1207 the whole income amounted to over £1,460 and the expenditure to £1,425. Then the monks were exiled for seven years and an administrator was appointed by the king ; but in 1219 the total receipts were £1,527. In the next year the translation of the relics of St. Thomas took place and the ceremony attracted an enormous crowd of visitors, the receipts rising to £2,707 ; the average being £1,460 for the six years preceding 1220, and £2,340 for the next six. The offerings at the shrine of St. Thomas and other holy places formed a large proportion. It must be remembered that these sums must be multiplied about twenty-fold to represent the corresponding value at the present day.

[26] Granted by Brithnoth before the battle of Maldon in 991.
[27] These two manors were situated within hundreds belonging to the abbey of Bury St. Edmunds, and a keen dispute about rights and jurisdictions raged between the two houses for more than two centuries. It is mentioned by Jocelin of Brakelond, and was only finally settled by arbitration and compromise in 1408 (Pat. 10 Hen. IV, pt. i, m. 18).
[28] Granted by William de Tracy as atonement for the murder of Becket.
[29] Pope Nich. Tax. (Rec. Com.), 4.
[30] Valor Eccl. (Rec. Com.), i, 7–16.
[31] Lit. Cant. (Rolls Ser.), ii, Introduction.

Louis VII of France, who had offered his devotions at the shrine of St. Thomas for the recovery of his son from illness, made a grant to the chapter in 1179 of 100 muids (1,600 gallons) of wine yearly, which was confirmed by several of his successors. It came originally from Triel near Poissy, but when the vineyards there were ruined in the last part of the fifteenth century it was taken from Gascony and the Bordelais.[32]

The convent claimed the right of election of the archbishop as a reality and not merely a form, and came into collision with the king and pope on several occasions in consequence. In 1123, in spite of their protests, the election was made at Gloucester by an assembly of bishops, abbots, and nobles, and William, prior of St. Osyth's, an Austin canon, was chosen.[33] In 1184 the bishops again claimed to take part in the election, declaring authority from the pope, and a long dispute followed, in which the king and Ranulph Glanville intervened, until Baldwin, bishop of Worcester, the nominee of the bishops, was eventually chosen ; though the chapter secured the observance of their formalities.[33a] After the death of Hubert in July, 1205, the king persuaded the convent to postpone the election until after St. Andrew's Day, and in the meantime sent messengers to Rome, on hearing of which the convent sent the sub-prior and some other monks there to watch over their interests.[34] The king came to Canterbury in December, and the convent elected the bishop of Norwich, but the monks at Rome disputed this, and the election was quashed, and Stephen Langton chosen ; with the result that in July, 1207, all the monks were expelled from Canterbury by the angry king, and took refuge abroad at the abbey of St. Bertin, where they remained until peace was made by Pandulf in 1213. On the death of Langton in 1228 the chapter obtained licence for election from the king, and chose Walter of Eynesham by compromise, but the election was quashed by the pope, who appointed Richard le Grant, chancellor of Lincoln ; [35] and after his death in 1231 the chapter made no fewer than four elections, including their own prior, until the pope was satisfied.[36] Pope Innocent IV granted that the bishops of the province should not interfere in the election,[37] but the time of freedom of the chapter was already really past. In 1270 they again chose their own prior, Adam de Chillenden, but he was rejected by the pope and Robert Kilwardby appointed.[38] The new archbishop quarrelled about the expenses of the election,

[32] Hist. MSS. Com. Rep. v, App. pt. i, 460-1 ; ibid. viii, App. pt. i, 321, 350, 353.
[33] Gervase, op. cit. ii, 380.
[33a] Ibid. i, 318-25.   [34] Ibid. ii, 98-101.
[35] Ibid. ii, 115-27.
[36] Ibid. 129-30.
[37] Hist. MSS. Com. Rep. viii, App. pt. i, 318.
[38] Gervase, op. cit. ii, 252-73.

which amounted to the enormous sum of 3,000 marks, and eventually they were divided, the convent paying 1,300.

But though the convent claimed to elect the archbishop, who stood in the position of their abbot, and was the *persona* of the cathedral, they hardly recognized his authority when elected.[39] They were generously treated by Anselm, who gave them a large degree of independence, made many gifts, and settled on them the whole oblations of the high altar and the xenia or Christmas and Easter offerings : but Eadmer distinctly states that his object was not to exempt them from the authority of the archbishop, but to save the estates from the king during the vacancies of the see. Archbishops Thomas and Richard were also generous. William de Corbeuil, a canon archbishop, quarrelled with them about the church of Dover ; and Theobald with the prior Jeremiah, who was forced to resign. The real dispute began in 1150, when the conventual property was so much wasted by war and other expenses that the prior restored the administration of it to Theobald, asking him to provide for the convent until better times should come. Theobald exercised strict economy in every way, only allowing them the simplest food ; and this forced abstinence was so little to their liking that they charged him with self-aggrandisement at their expense, and appealed to Rome. He retorted vigorously, and after three years of quarrel a compromise was come to, by which the estates were restored ; but the prior resigned.

Archbishop Baldwin, who succeeded Richard in 1184, was a Cistercian monk and a scholar, and did not look favourably upon the luxury, independence, and ignorance of the chapter. Urged probably by the clerks around him, he planned a large collegiate church, to be maintained out of the property of the see ; and obtained from Lucius III permission to recover the estates alienated to the convent by his predecessor, of which the principal were the oblations, belonging canonically to the archbishop, and the churches of Monkton, Eastry, Meopham, and Eynsford ; and began proceedings by confiscating the xenia on 15 December, 1185, and taking possession of the churches of Monkton and Eastry on 25 January, 1186. The monks, besides resenting this loss, considered that the cathedral would be supplanted by the new church, among the canons of which were to be the bishops of the province, and appealed to the new pope, Urban III. Baldwin, however, secured bulls from him, and in November came down to found his church at Hackington, a suburb of Canterbury, where he instituted the

canons on 16 December. Alan, the prior, had been made abbot of Tewkesbury, but his successor Honorius was confirmed in fidelity to the convent by a vision which appeared opportunely to one of the monks, and went abroad to Verona to lay his case before the pope in person.

Everywhere sympathies were divided between the parties. The king favoured the archbishop, and the convent looked for support from the friends of Becket. St. Augustine's was equally hostile to both, but the other great Benedictine and Cluniac houses supported the convent, and the Cistercian houses the archbishop. The bishops were mostly on his side, but the king's ministers, the foreign princes, and the cardinals were divided. Henry II came to Canterbury to offer mediation on 11 February, 1187, but the monks refused, and they won an initial success by securing help from the pope. Baldwin changed the site of the college to the parish of St. Dunstan and built a wooden chapel there, which he proceeded with in spite of the pope's prohibition. Then followed many months of squabbling. Urban died ; his successor only reigned for a few weeks, but was favourable to the archbishop ; and the next pope, Clement III, was lukewarm. The monks were blockaded in their monastery from January, 1188, to August, 1189, and Honorius died abroad. After the death of Henry II Baldwin visited the convent and offered some concessions, but no agreement was come to, and he appointed as prior Roger Norreys, who was extremely distasteful to the monks and seems to have been quite unfit for the position. Finally Richard I, who was much firmer than his father in the matter, came to Canterbury in November, 1189, and an agreement was made by which their estates were restored to the convent, the prior was removed, and the proposed collegiate church was abandoned ; but, on the other hand, another was to be built on land at Lambeth obtained by the archbishop by exchange with the convent of Rochester, and he made the appointment of a new prior, Osbert de Bristo. Baldwin soon afterwards went to the Holy Land on the crusade and died ; and as soon as the news reached Canterbury Osbert was forced to resign.

The college at Lambeth was begun before Baldwin left England, but in May, 1192, Celestine III gave orders that the canons there should be released from their oath and the church closed. They probably appealed, for the same pope in January, 1193, took them under his protection ; and in 1197 the new archbishop, Hubert Walter, who in the mean time had acquired the manor of Lambeth and had by common law the right to build a religious house on it, proceeded with the scheme. In November he sent envoys to lay before the convent the proposals he had drawn up to secure their rights,

---

[39] The principal documents relating to this dispute are given in *Epistolae Cantuarienses* (Rolls Ser.), and the story is told admirably and in considerable detail by Bishop Stubbs in the Introduction.

but after some delay they definitely refused to agree to them ; and once more appeal was made to Rome, and a new pope, Innocent III, ordered the demolition of the college within thirty days. The king forbade the execution of the mandate, took the college under his protection, and seized the possessions of the convent for infringing the liberties of the realm. The old dispute went on, with the king on one side and the pope on the other ; Hubert agreed to demolish the chapel, but obtained a bull for the erection of another on a new site at Lambeth, and seemed to be winning ; but the death of the king turned the scales. Probably John's support could not be relied on in the same way ; and on 30 June, 1201, it was agreed that the archbishop might build a church on a new site at Lambeth, but it was to be of Premonstratensian canons, endowed from the archiepiscopal estates and only to the value of £100 yearly, and no consecrations or ordinations were to be celebrated in it. Practically Baldwin had won, and Hubert lost, all the important points.

Archbishop Edmund had a similar quarrel with the convent in 1238–9, in which he is said to have wished to erect a prebendal church, consecrate bishops elsewhere than in the cathedral, and expel the monks and institute seculars ; but nothing much happened beyond his excommunication and suspension of the convent, the chief points of interest being the acknowledgement by some monks of the forgery of a charter of St. Thomas and the burning of a papal bull.[40]

The chapter claimed to exercise almost all the spiritual rights of the archbishop during the vacancies of the see, and two large registers[41] are filled with their acts at the vacancies from 1343 to 1413, 1500 and 1502. Gervase notes that they exercised complete jurisdiction in the dioceses of Bath and Wells, St. Asaph, and St. Davids in 1293 without any opposition, these bishoprics being then vacant simultaneously with the archbishopric ;[42] and he also records several similar acts.[43] On the death of Archbishop Edmund in 1241 the archdeacon of Canterbury, an old enemy of theirs, took advantage of their quarrel with the archbishop to usurp their rights.[44] In 1243 they came into conflict with the bishop of Lincoln, who had deposed the abbot of Bardney.[45]

About 1275 there was a quarrel between Thomas Ringmer, then prior, and a faction of the monks, who charged him with mismanagement and oppression.[46] The truth of this is not likely ever to be known, but in 1284 this prior

resigned and joined the stricter Cistercian order at Beaulieu in Hampshire ;[47] and at the vacancy the priory was taken into the king's hands, which had never been done before. The sub-prior and convent protested, and the king eventually withdrew his claim, but nevertheless in 1297 again took possession of the monastery. In 1320 another quarrel broke out between Prior Henry of Eastry and some monks,[48] which appears to have lasted for some years ; for in 1325 the archbishop interfered about one of the mutinous monks, Robert de Aledone, whom he declared to have been punished with excessive severity.[49] A long list of offences attributed to Robert is set out, and he was believed by some to be mad ; but he rose in after years to eminence in the convent. Two years later there was still trouble with six monks ; and one of these, Thomas de Sandwico, fled from the monastery, but was eventually allowed to return, after making a complete subjection.[50] Prior Henry was at the head of the house for many years, and reached a great age ; and several letters are preserved between him and Archbishop Reynolds, who was a comparatively young man, and sought his advice on many occasions.[51] Archbishop Mepeham also sought advice from him and his successor, Richard Oxenden ; but John Stratford, the next archbishop, was more self-willed, and Oxenden soon lost all his influence, the friendly correspondence ceasing or turning to bickering.[52]

Several times in the fourteenth century attempts were made to compel the attendance of the prior at the provincial chapter ; but he invariably refused, as he considered himself the chief person of the order in England and did not wish to have to take a place below the president of the occasion ; and he was backed up by Edward III on the ground of his special position, and also by Urban V and Innocent VI.[53] In 1395, after the usual refusal, the chapter appointed the abbot of Battle to make a visitation of the priory in their name ; and the prior appealed to the archbishop, who forbade anyone to make any visitation of the cathedral except himself.[54] Urban VI granted a bull of exemption from attendance at the chapter,[55] and after this the prior does not seem to have been troubled further.

Edward the Black Prince, in consideration of a dispensation for his marriage with his cousin, the countess of Kent, founded a chantry of two priests in the cathedral in 1362, granting the manor of Vauxhall, in Surrey, to the chapter for

[40] Gervase, *Opera*, ii, 130–79 ; *Hist. MSS. Com. Rep.* v, App. pt. i, 439.
[41] *Hist. MSS. Com. Rep.* viii, App. pt. i, 331–40.
[42] Gervase, *Opera*, ii, 301.
[43] Ibid. 251–2. [44] Ibid. 180.
[45] Matt. Paris, *Chron. Maj.* (Rolls Ser.), iv, 245.
[46] *Hist. MSS. Com. Rep.* v, App. pt. i, 438.

[47] Ibid. 432 ; viii, App. pt. i, 345.
[48] Ibid. v, App. pt. i, 438.
[49] Ibid. ix, App. pt. i, 92, 94.
[50] Ibid. 96.
[51] *Lit. Cant.* i, *passim*.
[52] *Hist. MSS. Com. Rep.* ix, App. pt. i, 84.
[53] Ibid. v, App. pt. i, 461 ; ibid. viii, App. pt. i, 342 ; ibid. ix, App. pt. i, 74, 82, 83, 89.
[54] Ibid. viii, App. pt. i, 339. [55] Ibid. 318.

their maintenance.[56] In the middle of the next century a dispute between the priests was settled by arbitration,[57] and in 1472 the chapter complained that the income of the chantry was insufficient, and wished to be relieved of the charge.[58] The earl of Warwick offered the manor of Easole for a chantry in 1368, but it was refused.[59] Archbishop Courtenay founded a chantry in 1395,[60] which was augmented later by Archbishop Arundel.[61] Archbishop Bourchier granted the manor of Panfield, in Essex, for the foundation of a chantry in 1473 ; [62] and chantries were also founded by John Buckingham, bishop of Lincoln, in 1389, Joan Brenchley in 1458, Archbishop Warham in 1529, and others.[63] Anniversary services were maintained for Henry VII and his queen.

We read of three Canterbury monks staying at Oxford in 1331, living there in hired lodgings under the charge of the senior, and being supplied with necessaries from the convent's manor of Newington ; but they appear to have moved soon afterwards to the general Benedictine establishment known as Gloucester College. Archbishop Islip in 1361 obtained a royal licence to found a college of religious and seculars at Oxford, and to endow it with the church of Pagham in Sussex, his nephew adding the manor of Woodford in Northamptonshire ; and soon after he allowed the chapter of Canterbury to nominate three persons to it, one of whom was to be warden. Towards the end of his life the influence of the seculars prevailed, and one John Wyclif succeeded in ousting this warden ; but Archbishop Langham took up the cause of the monks. The seculars appealed to Rome, but were finally defeated in 1370, and from thence until the Dissolution the college seems to have been considered a daughter to Canterbury. Archbishop Courtenay remodelled the statutes in 1382, with considerable differences ; and in 1396–7 the building of the college was carried out, the details and expenses being still preserved.[64]

The cathedral and the city seem always to have been quarrelling.[65] Early in the thirteenth century the monks provided some timber for fortifying the city, but induced Hubert de Burgh, the justiciary, to certify that it was given out of goodwill and could not be taken as a precedent. In 1428 the city seized some fish which had been bought by the convent, on the ground that it was an act of forestalling, and the dispute was submitted to arbitrators. In 1492 a long agree-

ment was made to put a final stop to all the quarrels, and the city released to the cathedral a part of the town wall with some waste land. Nevertheless, eight years later the quarrel broke out again fiercely, the prior accusing the mayor of trespass, assault, and various other offences, and the mayor retorting with other charges, such as that of fouling the city ditch with sewage. Near the Dissolution the city presented another long list of wrongs done to them by the chapter.[66]

John Stone, a monk of the cathedral, wrote a chronicle [67] of the house from 1415–71. This is chiefly concerned with the deaths of his brethren, but he also mentions the enthronements of the archbishops, a few consecrations, the battles and other political events of the Wars of the Roses, epidemics of the plague, the worst of which were in 1420 and 1470, and the visits of many important people to Canterbury, generally on their way between London and the Continent. Henry VI and Edward IV each visited the cathedral several times. Fifty offices in the cathedral are mentioned, possibly with some repetitions.

Several unimportant letters from the prior to Cromwell are preserved,[68] but not much is known of what happened at the cathedral immediately before the Dissolution. Prior Thomas and sixty-nine others signed the acknowledgement of the royal supremacy on 10 December, 1534.[69] Richard Layton visited the cathedral in October, 1535, and was nearly burnt in his bed by an outbreak of fire, which did a great deal of damage ; and he gave several injunctions which the monks seem to have resented extremely.[70] Among other things, they were to remain within the walls of the monastery, to dine together, to keep three or four more of their number at Oxford besides the five whom they had been accustomed to maintain there ; the sextons and other church officers were to sleep in the dorter and not in the church ; the fairs at the abbey were prohibited ; and seculars were forbidden to keep shops within the monastery. The prior and a few others seem to have carried out Cromwell's orders, though some said that the prior was merely a hypocrite and really disobeyed. The principal murmuring was against 'young men coartyng them to use prescript meates, nother savery nor holsom,' a form of abstinence which was evidently highly unpopular. In January, 1537, when the number of the monks had sunk to fifty-eight, there was trouble[71] about

[56] *Lit. Cant.* ii, 422–31.

[57] Ibid. iii, 210.   [58] Ibid. 257.

[59] Ibid. ii, 484–8.   [60] Ibid. iii, 41.

[61] Ibid. 109, 123.   [62] Ibid. 258, 263, 316.

[63] *Hist. MSS. Com. Rep.* v, App. pt. i, 435–6.

[64] *Lit. Cant.* ; *Hist. MSS. Com. Rep.* v, App. pt. i, 444, 450–1.

[65] *Hist. MSS. Com. Rep.* v, App. pt. i, 433.

[66] *L. and P. Hen. VIII*, xv, 453.

[67] Printed in *Camb. Antiq. Soc. Publ.* 34. The same volume also contains full and detailed lists, with references, of all the known deans, priors, and other members of the house before the Dissolution.

[68] *L. and P. Hen. VIII, passim.*

[69] Ibid. vii, 1594 (1).

[70] Ibid. ix, 669, 707, 784, 832, 840, 879, 881.

[71] Ibid. xii (1), 256, 436–7.

seditious words used by some and the mention of the names of two bishops of Rome, but not much notice seems to have been taken.

Dissolution was already spoken of in 1538,[72] and in the next year some exchanges of lands were made with the king.[73] Canterbury was of course to be one of the new cathedrals; and the scheme for the establishment was in existence in November, when it was criticized by Cranmer in a letter to Cromwell.[74] A commission to the archbishop and others to take the surrender of the monastery was issued on 20 March, 1540;[75] and on 4 April pensions were allotted of £80 to the prior, and smaller sums to those monks who were not provided for on the new foundation.[76]

The new cathedral was reconstituted by letters patent on 8 April, 1540, with Nicholas Wotton as dean and twelve priests as prebendaries,[77] and endowed in May with numerous possessions, including most of those of the old monastery and also some from other houses,[78] and fresh statutes were given for it.[79]

A number of inventories of the cathedral of various dates, from 1294 to the eighteenth century, have been printed in *Inventories of Christchurch, Canterbury*, by Messrs. J. Wickham Legg and W. H. St. John Hope.

Archbishop Parker made a visitation of the cathedral on 3 July, 1570, and gave several injunctions concerning it, and in the same year put an end to some disputes between the prebendaries.[80] In September, 1573, he made another visitation, with fresh injunctions,[81] the most important of which related to the granting of leases and division of fines, by which the dean and prebendaries had enriched themselves at the expense of the common chest. Dispensation was granted for the non-observance of such statutes as were repugnant to the Word of God and the statutes of the realm, and a reader of divinity was to be appointed. In November commissioners were sent to Canterbury to see whether these injunctions had been properly observed, and replies were received from the dean and chapter, who do not appear to have been pleased.[82] Archbishop Whitgift appointed commissioners to visit the cathedral in 1597, and several faults were noted and orders for reform made by them.[83] Archbishop Laud made a visitation of the diocese in 1634,[84] and issued fresh statutes for the cathedral in 1635,[85] which

were confirmed by the king on 3 January, 1637.[86] On 9 May, 1637, the same archbishop made an order for the proper keeping of all muniments and records belonging to the church.[87]

DEANS OF CANTERBURY[88]

Cuba, occurs 798
Beornheard, occurs 805
Heahfrith, occurs 813
Ceolnoth, resigned 833[89]
Æthelwine, occurs c. 860
Eadmund, occurs c. 871
Æthelnoth, resigned 1020[89]
Godric, occurs 1020, 1023
Æthelric, resigned 1058[90]
Ælfric[91]
Ælfsige
Ælfwine
Ælfwine
Kynsige
Maurice

PRIORS OF CANTERBURY

Henry,[92] resigned 1096
Ernulf,[93] 1096–1107
Conrad,[94] 1108–26
Geoffrey,[95] 1126–8
Elmer, 1128–37
Jeremiah,[96] 1137–43
Walter Durdent,[97] 1143–9
Walter the Little,[98] 1149–50
Wibert,[99] 1150–67
Odo,[100] 1167–75
Benedict,[101] 1175–7
Herlewin,[102] 1177–9
Alan,[103] 1179–86

[72] *L. and P. Hen. VIII*, xiii (2), 139, 465.
[73] Ibid. xiv (1), 219, 252, 1286; (2), 281.
[74] Ibid. 601.   [75] Ibid. xv, 378.
[76] Ibid. 452; xvi, 718.   [77] Ibid. xvi, 779 (5).
[78] Ibid. 878 (59).   [79] Ibid. App. 4.
[80] Strype, *Life of Parker*, ii, 21–6.
[81] Ibid. iii, 309–316.
[82] Ibid. ii, 299–306, 308–13.
[83] Strype, *Life of Whitgift*, ii, 384; iii, 382.
[84] *Cal. S.P. Dom.* 1633–4, p. 401; 1634–5, p. 470.
[85] Ibid. 1635, p. 512.

[86] Rymer, *Foedera*, xx, 99.
[87] *Cal. S.P. Dom.* 1637, p. 87.
[88] The names of the early deans and of the priors are taken from lists in *Camb. Antiq. Soc. Publ.* 34, collected from various sources. Those of the later deans are taken from Le Neve's *Fasti*.
[89] Became archbishop.
[90] Became bishop of Selsey.
[91] Only the obituaries of these are known.
[92] He became abbot of Battle.
[93] He became abbot of Peterborough and bishop of Rochester.
[94] He was confessor of Henry I, and became abbot of St. Benet, Holme.
[95] He was sub-prior, and became abbot of Dunfermline.
[96] He resigned and became an inmate of St. Augustine's.
[97] He became bishop of Coventry and Lichfield.
[98] He was chaplain of Archbishop Theobald, and was deposed.
[99] He was sub-prior.
[100] He became abbot of Battle.
[101] He was chancellor of Archbishop Richard, and became abbot of Peterborough.
[102] He was chaplain of the same archbishop.
[103] He became abbot of Tewkesbury.

Honorius,[104] 1186–8
Roger Norreis,[105] 1189
Osbert de Bristo,[106] 1189–91
Geoffrey,[107] 1191–1213
Walter, 1213–22
John Sittingborne, 1222–32
John de Chetham,[108] 1232–8
Roger de la Lee,[109] 1239–44
Nicholas de Sandwyco,[109] 1244–58
Roger de Sancto Elphego, 1258–63
Adam de Chillenden, 1264–74
Thomas de Ringmere,[110] 1274–84
Henry de Eastria, 1285–1331
Richard de Oxenden, 1332–8
Robert Hathbrande, 1338–70
Richard Gillyngham, 1370–6
Stephen Mongeham, 1376–7
John Fynch, 1377–91
Thomas Chillenden, 1391–1411
John Woodnesbergh, 1411–28
William Molashe, 1428–38
John Salisbury, 1438-46
John Elham, 1446–9
Thomas Goldston, 1449–68
John Oxne, 1468–71
William Pettham, 1471–2
William Sellyng, 1472–94
Thomas Goldston, 1495–1517
Thomas Goldwell, 1517–40, the last prior

DEANS OF CANTERBURY

Nicholas Wotton, 1540
Thomas Godwin,[111] 1567
Richard Rogers, 1584
Thomas Neville, 1597
Charles Fetherby, 1615
John Boys, 1619
Isaac Bargrave, 1625
George Aglionby, 1643
Thomas Turner, 1644
John Tillotson,[112] 1672
John Sharpe,[113] 1689
George Hooper,[114] 1691
George Stanhope, 1704
Elias Sydall,[115] 1728

[104] He was cellarer and chaplain of Archbishop Baldwin.
[105] He was cellarer and treasurer.
[106] He was deposed.   [107] He was sub-prior.
[108] He resigned and became a Carthusian.
[109] These resigned.
[110] He resigned and became a Cistercian at Beaulieu, and afterwards a hermit at Brookwood in Windsor Forest.
[111] He became bishop of Bath and Wells.
[112] He became dean of St. Paul's, London.
[113] He became archbishop of York.
[114] He became bishop of St. Asaph, holding the deanery *in commendam*, and then bishop of Bath and Wells.
[115] He became bishop of St. David's, holding the deanery *in commendam*.

John Lynch, 1734
William Friend, 1760
John Potter, 1766
Brownlow North,[116] 1770
John Moore, 1771
James Cornwallis,[117] 1775
George Horne,[118] 1781
William Buller,[119] 1790
Ffolliot Herbert Walker Cornewall,[120] 1793
Thomas Powys, 1797
Gerrard Andrewes, 1809
Hugh Percy,[121] 1825
Richard Bagot,[122] 1827
William Rowe Lyall, 1845
Henry Alford, 1857
Robert Payne Smith, 1871
Frederic William Farrar, 1895
Henry Wace, 1903

The seal [123] (twelfth century) of the cathedral is of red wax, measuring $3\frac{3}{8}$ inches.

Obverse.—The cathedral from the south carefully detailed ; central tower with pent roof capped with a four-winged seraph, four turreted towers, and at the east end a towered apse. In the body of the church under the crossing is shown the figure of the Saviour full-length with nimbus and cross, lifting up the right hand in benediction. The two side towers nearest to view contain heads of saints in the lower stories. The two turrets on the left bear weathercocks, those on the right flags and crosses. In the field overhead two stars. Legend :—

S . . . LLUM ECCLE XPI CA . . . . . . EDIS
BRITTANIE

Reverse.—A pointed oval counterseal measuring $2\frac{1}{2}$ by $1\frac{3}{8}$ inches, representing the Saviour seated on a rainbow with nimbus, lifting up the right hand in benediction, and holding in the left hand a book. Legend :—

EGO SUM VIA VERITAS ET VITA

Another seal [124] (1418) is of red wax measuring $3\frac{3}{4}$ inches.

Obverse.—An elaborate elevation of the west front of the cathedral, showing the central and two side towers pinnacled. Over the portal is a triangular tympanum in which is the Saviour with the inscription IHC XC. On the corbel table below this figure the inscription EST DOMUS H' XPI, completed by MURI METROPOL' ISTI upon the

[116] He became bishop of Lichfield.
[117] He became bishop of Lichfield.
[118] He became bishop of Norwich.
[119] He became bishop of Exeter.
[120] He became bishop of Bristol.
[121] He became bishop of Rochester.
[122] He became bishop of Oxford, holding the deanery *in commendam*.
[123] B.M. Seals, xl, 2.
[124] B.M. Cott. Chart. xxi, 11.

embattled and turreted walls of the city of Canterbury in the foreground in the base. The side towers of the cathedral are pierced, each in two stories, the upper containing, within quatrefoils, two female heads, the lower, within niches, saints' heads with inscriptions, s DUNSTAN[9] on the right and s ELPHEGUS on the left. In the field over the roof line two angels descending from clouds and swinging censers towards the central tower, which is capped by a seraphic figure with four wings. Legend :—

SIGILLUM ECCLESIE XPISTI CANTUARIE PRIME
SEDIS BRITTANNIE

Reverse.—Becket's martyrdom in the cathedral, shown behind a shaft supporting two pointed arches. In the spandrel between is a small panel with a head in it : in the three windows of an arcade or clearstory the soul of the martyr in a cloth held up by two angels ; and in a trefoiled niche above them the Saviour, half-length, with nimbus and crown on breast between the letters A Ω. The side compartments contain two knights in armour ; above them in circular openings two angels issuing from clouds. In the sky above the roof two angels, each holding a crown. An arcading and wall with three faces run round the base of the building. Legend :—

EST HUIC VITA MORI PRO QUA DUM VIXIT
AMORI.

MORS ERAT ET MEMORI PER MORTEM VIVIT
HONORI.

On the rim of the seal the legend :—

SIT MICHI CAUSA MERA STILUS APTUS LITERA
VERA.

CIRCUMSPECTA SERA TENOR UTILIS INTEGRA
CERA.

2. THE CATHEDRAL PRIORY OF ST. ANDREW, ROCHESTER

Ethelbert, king of Kent, founded the church of St. Andrew the Apostle at Rochester, and granted to it a portion of land called 'Prestefeld,' and all the land on the Medway to the east gate of the city on the south, and other land without the wall of the city on the north ; and in 604 Augustine consecrated as the first bishop Justus, who had been sent to England with others in 601 by Pope Gregory, and ordained priests to serve God in the church.[1]

[1] Three registers of Rochester are preserved among the Cotton MSS. in the British Museum (Dom. A. x, 91–209 ; Faust. C. v. ; Vesp. A. xxii, 63–128) ; and additional information about its early history is given in the *Textus Roffensis*, compiled by Bishop Ernulf soon after the Conquest. Edmund de Hadenham, a monk of Rochester, compiled annals down to the year 1307 (Cott. MS. Nero, D. ii, printed by Wharton in *Anglia Sacra*, i, 341–55, and also in *Flores*

Beyond the succession of bishops and the records of grants of lands made to Rochester little is known of its history before the Conquest. When Ethelred, king of Mercia, wasted Kent in 676, the city and the cathedral shared in the general disaster, the bishop removing to another church ; and ravages of the Danes were frequent for three centuries. On the death of Bishop Siward in 1075 there were only four canons in the church, and many of its possessions had been lost. Archbishop Lanfranc recovered some of these from Odo, bishop of Bayeux, and others in a great assembly at Penenden and granted them back to Rochester, appointing Arnostus, a monk of Bec, as bishop, in 1076. Arnostus only survived for a few months and was succeeded by Gundulf, sacrist of Bec, who ruled for thirty-one years and with Lanfranc practically refounded the cathedral. He rebuilt the church, which was old and ruinous, and in 1080, in place of the five canons whom he found there, introduced twenty-two monks, the number rising to sixty at his death. The Domesday Survey makes no distinction between the possessions of the bishop and of the convent, but a division was made (apparently afterwards) by Gundulf, who granted to the monks a charter to that effect in the time of Henry I. He also built the castle of Rochester at his own expense for William Rufus, receiving in return the manor of Haddenham in Buckinghamshire, which he and Lanfranc granted to the monks. The next few bishops are said to have made many grants of vestments and ornaments, and Bishop Ernulf built a dormitory, chapter-house, and refectory.

Gervase records[2] that the cathedral church was consecrated by William, archbishop of Canterbury, in the presence of several bishops on 5 May, 1130, the day after the consecration of Canterbury. The Anglo-Saxon Chronicle mentions the consecration without the date, and adds that the king was at Rochester on 8 May and that the town was then almost burnt down.[3] The church and city were actually burnt in 1138 with all the offices of the monks, who were dispersed among various abbeys ; and another general conflagration occurred on 11 April, 1177. Rebuilding went on vigorously. Prior Silvester made a refectory, a dormitory, and three windows in the chapter-house towards the east ; Prior Ralph de Ros while sacrist, besides other things, covered the church and leaded most of it ; and

Historiarum (Rolls Ser.)) ; and William de Dene, a notary, wrote a history from 1315 to 1350 (Cott. MS. Faust. B. v., 1–100 ; *Anglia Sacra*, i, 356–77). The principal documents relating to its history preserved in the cathedral and elsewhere are printed by Thorpe in *Registrum Roffense*, and several are given in Dugdale, *Mon.* i, 154–83. Several books which formerly belonged to the cathedral are now among the Royal MSS. at the British Museum.

[2] Gervase of Canterbury, *Opera* (Rolls Ser.), ii, 383.
[3] *Angl.-Sax. Chron.* (Rolls Ser.), ii, 227.

Prior Elias finished the leading of the church and leaded the part of the cloister towards the dormitory. Prior William de Hoo while sacrist built the choirs, and the first formal entry into it was made in 1227. The church was dedicated on 5 November, 1240, by the bishops of Rochester and Bangor.

The relation between the cathedrals of Rochester and Canterbury was unique in England. The patronage of Rochester appears to have always pertained to the archbishop and not to the king, and after disputes in the twelfth century John, by a charter[4] on 22 November, 1214, recognized this and renounced all rights of interference at vacancies of the see. A long dispute between the bishop and archbishop was concluded by an agreement on 19 July, 1259, that the bishop should have return of writs and amercements and other liberties on his lands, paying a rent of 12 marks yearly to the archbishop as service in return.[5] The election of the bishop was made by the monks of Rochester, but in the chapter-house of Canterbury, and as far back as 1148, it is said that this was according to old custom.[6] The bishop elect took an oath on the Gospels of fealty to Christchurch, Canterbury, and the archbishop, and during the vacancy of the see of Canterbury or the absence of the archbishop he was to perform episcopal ministrations in the cathedral of Canterbury when summoned by the chapter. The chapter of Canterbury also claimed that on the death of the bishop his pastoral staff should be brought to the altar of Christchurch by the monks of Rochester, but the latter denied the usage and buried the staff on the death of Walter in 1182.[7] The question came up again at the election of Gilbert de Glanville and was settled by a compromise, the staff being given to the archbishop, who handed it to the prior of Canterbury.[8] The monks of Canterbury repeated their claim in 1227, but were defeated on arbitration. At the vacancy in 1235 Richard of Wendover or Wendene, rector of Bromley, was elected, but the archbishop refused confirmation, and the convent was forced to appeal to the pope, to whom they sent three sets of envoys before the case was decided in their favour in 1238.

Bishop John of Seez took advantage of the dispersal of the monks by the conflagration of 1138 to grant away some of their churches, but on their return they complained to Rome, and after litigation Ascelin, the next bishop, was made to restore some of them, granting back the church of Southfleet for his anniversary. There seem to have been frequent quarrels between the bishops and convent in these times, and the annalist says of Ascelin that the evil which he

did remained, but not the good, noting especially his presumption in granting offices and serjeanties in the church. The papal legate interfered with success on behalf of the monks, but the matter was not finally settled until 1250, when Innocent IV ordered that the bishop should be content with the same right of appointment of keepers of manors and serjeants for offices of the church which the archbishop had in the church of Canterbury.[9] The chief abuse of the monks was, however, reserved for Bishop Gilbert de Glanville (1184–1214), epigrammatically described as *inter fundatores confundator*, who is said to have broken the great chest of the monks, carried off the great seal and several charters, and seized some churches and the *exenium* or offering of St. Andrew, besides inflicting the crowning injury of the foundation of the hospital of Strood, until at last the monks were forced to sell silver and other goods to maintain their struggle against him. Bishops Walter de Merton and John Bradfield are not favourably spoken of, and Thomas Ingaldsthorpe is said to have renewed the old disputes with the monks, but to have been checked by the archbishop.

In 1201 a Scot named William of Perth was murdered outside the city and buried in the church; and in 1256 he was canonized, many offerings being made at his tomb and many miracles reported. Pope Boniface IX in 1398 granted indulgence to penitents visiting his altar at certain times.[10]

King John besieged and captured the castle of Rochester after Michaelmas in 1215, and in the disturbances the cathedral was plundered so thoroughly that not even the host was left on the altar. Rochester suffered again in the civil war in 1264, and once more the cathedral was robbed of gold and silver and other precious things, many charters were lost or torn, some of the monks were imprisoned, and horsemen rode round the altars and stabled their horses in the cathedral.

Archbishop Boniface made a visitation of Rochester with great pomp in 1250, and extorted from the house more than 30 marks; and another visitation by him is recorded in 1253.[11] Bishop Laurence made a strict inquiry into the claims of the monks to their manors and privileges in 1252, and the prior was struck dumb when trying to reply to him and died before evening.

Archbishop Peckham made a visitation of the cathedral by metropolitical authority in 1283, and sent injunctions in consequence in a letter to the bishop on 24 October.[12] The prior was accused of wasting the goods of the house and had no satisfactory answer to give; he was suspected of having interfered in an unlawful and simoniacal manner in the election of the last bishop; and he and others were believed to have laid up a secret

[4] *Rotuli Chartarum* (Rec. Com.), 202.
[5] *Reg. Roff.* 70–85; Gervase, *Opera*, ii, 208.
[6] Gervase, *Opera*, i, 132.
[7] Ibid. 312.   [8] Ibid. 327–31.

[9] *Cal. Papal Let.* i, 259.   [10] Ibid. v, 257.
[11] Matt. Paris, *Chron. Maj.* (Rolls Ser.), v, 120, 382.
[12] *Reg. Epist. J. Peckham* (Rolls Ser.), ii, 621–5.

hoard for themselves. The archbishop directed the bishop to inquire more fully into these three points and correct them, and he also removed the prior from office and ordered that three treasurers should be chosen by the chapter. A further point noticed was that the people of the city had no parish church except the cathedral, from which they were debarred at night by the closing of the gates of the priory ; and he ordered that either they should have access to it at all times, or a parish church, which had formerly been begun within the precincts of the monastery and had afterwards been destroyed, should be built again.

Reference is here made to the fact that the people of the parish of St. Nicholas had no church of their own, but heard mass at the altar of St. Nicholas in the cathedral, to which the chapel of St. Margaret was dependent. The patronage of this had been given to the monks by Bishop Gundulf, but after some uncertainty and dispute was resigned by them to Bishop Glanville.[13] The orders of the archbishop appear to have been neglected, although in 1312 an agreement was made with the people about the altar and services in the cathedral[14] ; and it was not until 1418 that Bishop Young ordered the building of the church to be proceeded with.[15] Even then little was done till Archbishop Chicheley interfered and brought about a fresh agreement in 1422[16] ; but at last in 1423 the new church was consecrated and the parishioners resigned their rights in the cathedral.[17]

Archbishop Winchelsey issued long injunctions, many of which were practically repetitions of Peckham's, after a visitation in 1299.[18] There was to be no absence from service and no eating with nuns, the gates were to be closed at the right times, proper care was to be taken of the possessions, and full accounts were to be given.

Stephen le Dane, constable of Rochester Castle, in 1304 incited the citizens to claim tallage from the close of Prestfelde, which had always been considered as a spirituality ; but the monks carried the case before the barons of the Exchequer and secured exemption.

William Dene's history deals almost entirely with the doings of Hamo de Hethe as prior and bishop. He was appointed prior by the bishop at the nomination of the brethren in May, 1314, but a rival faction appealed to the archbishop, who ordered three commissioners to make a visitation of the cathedral, and it was asserted before these that only five had nominated Hamo, while twenty had nominated another. Hamo, however, retained his position in spite of the efforts of the visitors, and Dene says that he did much for the house, which he found in a state of poverty and dissension. When the bishopric fell vacant in 1317 he was elected to it by

twenty-six votes out of thirty-five, but the pope had made a provision to John de Puteolis, confessor of the queen, and a long argument followed, in which Dene acted as one of the proctors of the bishop, before he was finally consecrated and enthroned in 1319.[19] His expenses appear to have been very heavy, and in addition he had a dispute with the archbishop about the revenues of the see during the vacancy. During his episcopate he made many repairs and buildings at his manors and at the cathedral, and gave large sums for this purpose to the monks ; but they do not seem to have relished his masterful manner, and in 1329 made several complaints against him to the archbishop, while in 1336 a monk preached an insulting sermon before him on the subject of visitation, to which, according to Dene, who always took his part, he made an effective reply. In 1344 he founded a chantry in the cathedral.[20] In 1349, weakened by old age and financial troubles, he wished to resign the bishopric in favour of John Sheppey, the prior, with whom he had always been on friendly terms, but actually held it until his death in 1352. John Sheppey then succeeded, but he had previously resigned the priorship. On his representation that during his sixteen years of office he had freed the priory from burdens laid on it by his predecessors, built the refectory, hospice and vestibule, repaired the dormitory, infirmary and cellars, added to the lands and rents of the church, and inclosed the whole with a strong wall,[21] the pope in 1350 granted licence for him to resign with a yearly pension of £40 and several other privileges ;[22] and the pension was confirmed to him by the king in 1351.[23]

The grants of lands and liberties to the cathedral are set out in detail in the registers, and general charters of confirmation were obtained from several kings.[24] Various liberties were proved by the monks before the justices in eyre in 1279, 1293, and 1313 ;[25] and in 1295 Edward I granted to them a market on Thursday and a fair on the vigil, the day and the morrow of the Assumption at Haddenham, and free warren on their demesne lands there and at Cuddington (Bucks.) and Frindsbury, Darenth, Southfleet, Wouldham, and Stoke.[26] At the second of these eyres the liberties of chattels of fugitives and of gallows were allowed to the

[19] *Cal. Papal Let.* ii, 189.
[20] Pat. 18 Edw III, pt. 2, m. 45.
[21] Ibid. pt. 1, m. 6 ; 19 Edw. III, pt. 2, m. 20.
[22] *Cal. Papal Pet.* i, 192, 217.
[23] Pat. 25 Edw. III, pt. 1, m. 32.
[24] Chart. 50 Hen. III, m. 1 ; Chart. 3 Edw. I, Nos. 1, 2 ; Chart. 9 Edw. III, No. 36 ; Chart. 10 Edw. III, No. 51 ; Pat. 2 Hen. VI, pt. 2, m. 27 ; Pat. 12 Edw. IV, pt. 2, m. 14.
[25] *Plac. de Quo Warr.* (Rec. Com.), 320, 351, 355, 361.
[26] Chart 23 Edw. I, No. 7.

[13] *Reg. Roff.* 54.   [14] Ibid. 545.   [15] Ibid. 560.
[16] Ibid. 563.   [17] Ibid. 568–71.
[18] Cant. Archiepis. Reg. Winchelsey, fol. 70.

bishop and not to the monks, and they ascribed this to the influence over the justices of Solomon, 'not of the Bible, but of Rochester,' who had desired the bishopric, but had been rejected by them, and gladly noted his death by poison not long afterwards. Pope Innocent IV in 1245 gave licence for the prior and convent to wear caps in choir, provided that due reverence be observed at the gospel and elevation.[27] Pope Martin V in 1424 granted an indult to Prior William and his successors to administer or cause to be administered as often as expedient any ecclesiastical sacraments to the members of their household and their servants.[28]

The priory of Felixstowe or Walton in Suffolk was a cell of Rochester, to which it was granted by Roger Bigod, and was under the jurisdiction of the bishop and prior and not of the ordinary ;[29] but its monks had no claim to be called to the election of the prior.[30] The manor of Lambeth was granted by the convent in 1195 to Hubert Walter, archbishop of Canterbury, in exchange for the manor and church of Darenth and the chapel of Helles.[31] The bishop and convent held the advowsons of the churches of Bexley and Stourmouth jointly. Henry I granted the church of Bexley to the prior and it was appropriated to him by authority of Archbishop William and the chapter of Canterbury, but Archbishop Theobald intruded secular clerks to it, and the prior thus lost the church for more than two centuries. Archbishop Simon at last restored it to the convent, confirmation being obtained from the king and pope in 1391, and the convent surrendered their moiety of the church of Stourmouth to the bishop.[32]

In the Taxation of 1291 the temporalities of the monks were valued at £95 7s. 4d. yearly in the diocese of Rochester, including the manors of Frindsbury, Stoke, Wouldham, Denton, Southfleet and Darenth ; £1 18s. 10d. in the diocese of Canterbury ; 14s. in London ; £34 12s. 4d. in Buckinghamshire ; and £2 in Southwark ; making a total of £134 12s. 6d. yearly. In the Valor[33] of 1535 the possessions allotted to the office of treasurer, occupied by Laurence Mereworth, prior, amounted to the yearly value of £455 10s. 3d. gross and £388 13s. 9½d. net, and included the manors and rectories of Haddenham and Cuddington and the rectory of Kingsey in Buckinghamshire, the manor and rectory of Darenth, the manors of Denton, Southfleet, Frindsbury, Wouldham, Stoke and Sharsted, and the rectories of Hartlip and Hoo ; those of the office of Walter Boxley, cellarer, to £39 13s. 7¾d.

gross and £32 13s. 9¼d. net ; those of the office of Antony London, sacrist, to £33 17s. 6d. gross and £24 9s. 10d. net, including the rectory of Sutton with the chapel of Wilmington ; those of the office of Thomas Nevylle, chamberlain, to £35 0s. 8d. gross and £33 1s. 2d. net, including the rectory of Allhallows ; those of the office of Robert Maydeston, precentor, to £1 11s. 8d. gross and £1 10s. 2d. net ; those of the office of John Rye, warden of the chapel of St. Mary, to £1 6s. 8¼d. ; and those of the office of Robert Rochester, almoner, to £5 0s. 8d. gross and £4 16s. net ; the whole net income of the convent being given as £486 11s. 5d.

Bishop John Sheppey founded a chantry of one secular priest at the altar of St. John the Baptist in the cathedral by licence of Edward III, and the prior and chapter bound themselves to its maintenance on 19 October, 1360. The priest was to be appointed by the founder during his life and afterwards by the chancellor of England ; his duties were prescribed in detail, and he was not to hold any other ecclesiastical benefice ; and he was to receive 16 marks yearly. The prior and chapter also bound themselves to distribute 10 marks yearly on the day of the bishop's obit or anniversary, viz. bread to the value of 13s. 4d. to the poor, 26s. 8d. for a pittance for the monks, 12d. to each monk in the priesthood, and 6d. to every other monk, any residue being applied to the fabric of the church. A curious point was that the chantry priest was to entertain the chancellor with three quarters of oats and the chief justice of the Common Bench and the keeper of the rolls of Chancery with two quarters each on All Saints' Day.[34]

Sir Robert Bealknap had licence in 1374 to grant to the convent the manor of Sharsted, a moiety of the manor of Lidsing, and land in Chatham and Wouldham at a rent of 22 marks, to find a monk to celebrate divine service daily in the cathedral according to his ordinance, and he afterwards released to them 2 marks of the rent. The remaining 20 marks were afterwards released to them by William Makenade, in consideration of services for himself, his parents and friends.[35] Thomas earl of Nottingham granted the church of Findon in Sussex, and it was appropriated to them in 1395, they undertaking to celebrate offices for him perpetually at the altar of Sts. Andrew and Ithamar on the east side of the high altar.[36]

Pope Boniface IX in 1390 granted licence for the early ordination of six monks of the cathedral as deacons and priests, as the number of monks of sufficient age had been much diminished by pestilence and other causes.[37]

[27] Cal. Papal Let. i, 211. [28] Ibid. vii, 367.
[29] Ibid. iv, 66, 79.
[30] Wharton, Angl. Sac. i, 371.
[31] Reg. Roff. 270 ; Chart. 1 John, pt. 1, m. 9.
[32] Pat. 14 Ric. II, pt. 2, m. 14 ; Cal. Papal Let. iv, 365 ; vi, 80.
[33] Valor Eccl. (Rec. Com.), i, 101–4.

[34] Pat. 26 Hen. VI, pt. 1, m. 3.
[35] Pat. 16 Ric. II, pt. 3, m. 7.
[36] Pat. 18 Ric. II, pt. 2, m. 7 ; Cal. Papal Let. iv, 520.
[37] Cal. Papal Let. iv, 366.

Bishop Wells issued injunctions after a visitation in 1439, the principal points of which were that silence was to be kept, the beds were to be open and uniform, the Benedictine statutes concerning eating were to be observed, the entry of women was to be guarded against, there was to be no mixing with seculars, private property was discouraged, and the administration was to be properly looked after.[38]

Little is known of the history of the cathedral for some time before the Dissolution. The oath of acknowledgement of the royal supremacy was taken on 10 June, 1534, by Laurence Mereworth, prior, Robert Rochester, sub-prior, and eighteen others[39]; and in 1535 the house was visited by Dr. Layton,[40] though no account of this has been preserved. The prior resigned in 1538, and the bishop wrote afterwards to Cromwell that since then many things had gone amiss with the house and he would like to have him back again.[41] Some exchanges of land were made in the following year.[42]

A commission to the archbishop of Canterbury, the chancellor of the Augmentations, the Master of the Rolls and others to receive the surrender of the priory was issued on 20 March, 1540;[43] and on 8 April pensions were allotted to those monks who were not fully provided for in the new secular establishment.[44] The original proposal[45] for this mentioned ten prebendaries besides the dean; but only six were included in the actual foundation by letters patent in June, 1541.[46] The endowment consisted of a large proportion of the possessions of the priory of Leeds and the hospital of Strood, besides those of the old cathedral.[47]

The later history of the cathedral does not present any features of special interest.

PRIORS OF ROCHESTER [48]

Ordouvin, occurs 1089, resigned
Ernulf, resigned 1096 [49]
Ralph, resigned 1107 [50]
Ordouvin, again
Letard [51]
Brian, occurs 1146
Reginald, occurs 1154
Ernulf [52]
William Borstalle

Silvester, occurs 1178
Richard, resigned 1182 [53]
Alfred [54]
Osbern de Scapeya [55]
Ralph de Ros,[56] occurs 1199
Elias
William, occurs 1222
Richard de Derente, elected 1225
William de Hoo, elected 1239 [56]
Alexander de Glanville, elected 1242, died 1252
Simon de Clyve,[56] succeeded 1252, resigned 1262
John de Renham or Rensham, elected 1262, deposed 1283
Thomas de Wouldham, elected 1283, resigned 1291 [57]
John de Renham, again, died 1294
Thomas de Shelford, succeeded 1294, resigned 1301
John de Greenstreet, elected 1301, resigned 1314
Hamo de Hethe, elected 1314, resigned 1319 [57]
John de Westerham, appointed 1320, died 1321
John de Speldherst, elected 1321,[58] resigned 1333
John de Scapeya, succeeded 1333, resigned 1351
Robert de Suthflete, succeeded 1352,[59] died 1361
John de Hertlepe, elected 1361,[59] resigned 1380
John de Sheppey, elected 1380, died 1419
William Tunbrygg, elected 1419 [60]
John Cardone, occurs 1449 [61]
Richard Pekham, occurs 1467 [61a]
William Wod, occurs 1468, 1475 [62]
Thomas Bourne, occurs 1480 [63]
William Bisshop, occurs 1496 [64]
William Frysell or Fresell, elected 1509, occurs 1519 [65]
Laurence Mereworth, occurs 1534,[66] resigned 1538 [67]
Walter Philips, the last prior [68]

[38] Roch. Epis. Reg. iii, fol. 150 d.
[39] L. and P. Hen. VIII, vii, 921.
[40] Ibid. ix, 691.   [41] Ibid. xiii (1), 1391.
[42] Ibid. xiv (1), 1056 (6), 1192 (41), 1354 (38).
[43] Ibid. xv, 378.   [44] Ibid. 474.   [45] Ibid. 379.
[46] Ibid. xvi, 947 (36).   [47] Ibid. 947 (42).
[48] The names of the priors are given in a list collected in Wharton's Anglia Sacra, i, 392-4.
[49] He became in succession prior of Canterbury, abbot of Peterborough, and bishop of Rochester.
[50] He became abbot of Battle.
[51] In the time of Bishop Ernulf.
[52] In the time of Bishop Walter.

[53] He became abbot of Burton.
[54] He became abbot of Abingdon.
[55] He was sacrist.   [56] He was sacrist.
[57] He became bishop of Rochester.
[58] He was cellarer.
[59] These two were wardens of the cell of Felixstowe.
[60] William occurs as prior in 1443.
[61] Reg. Roff. 580.
[61a] Exch. of Pleas, Plea R. 7 Edw. IV, 19 d.
[62] Reg. Roff. 583-4.
[63] Ibid. 138. Thomas occurs in 1489 (ibid. 585).
[64] Cant. Archiepis. Reg. Morton, 161. There were then eighteen others in the convent.
[65] L. and P. Hen. VIII, iii, 487. He had been prior of Binham in Norfolk (Pard. R. 1 Hen. VIII. pt. 3, m. 24). William occurs as prior in 1529 (L. and P. Hen. VIII, iv, 5353).   [66] Ibid. vii, 921.
[67] Ibid. xiii (1), 1391.   [68] Ibid. xv, 474.

The seal [83] of the cathedral (twelfth century), measuring 2¼ in., shows St. Andrew seated on a throne of ecclesiastical architecture representing the cathedral, holding in the right hand an orb and cross, in the left an open book. Legend :—

SIGILLU[M S]ANCTI ANDREE APLI ROFENSIS ECCLE

Another seal [84] (1371) is a pointed oval of red wax representing St. Andrew, with nimbus and saltire cross, and a bishop in two carved and canopied niches. In base a carved string-course and on the corbel a branch of three oak leaves.

Another seal [85] (1459) is of green wax measuring 2⅝ in.

Obverse.—Our Lord with nimbus, seated, holding a cross in right hand and a book in left hand, the feet resting on a footstool, held up by a man, half-length, in a niche of architectural details, probably intended to represent an elevation of the cathedral from the west. Legend :—

SIGILLUM SANCTI ANDREE APOSTOLI ROFFENSIS ECCLE

Reverse.—The martyrdom of St. Andrew ; two executioners tying him upon a saltire cross. Legend :—

EGO CRUCIS CHRISTI SERVUS SUM

On the rim of the seal the inscription—

. . . . AM DOMINUS I . . . . VAU VITAI

3. THE ABBEY OF ST. AUGUSTINE, CANTERBURY [1]

Augustine's following included both clerks and monks, and when the former were settled in the cathedral the latter were not neglected. Bede [2] tells us that

Augustine also erected a monastery to the east of the town, in which by his exhortation and direction King Æthelberht ordered a church to be erected of becoming splendour, dedicated to the blessed apostles Peter and Paul, and endowed it with a variety of gifts ; in which church the body of Augustine and also those of all bishops and kings of Canterbury might be laid.

There is little doubt, however, that the principal object of the foundation was the establishment of a residence for the monks, and not of a burial place.

[69] From Le Neve's Fasti.
[70] Became bishop of Rochester.
[71] Became bishop of Salisbury.
[72] Became bishop of St. Davids.
[73] Became bishop of Gloucester.
[74] Became bishop of Chichester.
[75] Became bishop of Peterborough.
[76] Became bishop of Bath and Wells.
[77] Became archbishop of York.
[78] Became bishop of St. Davids.
[79] Became bishop of Bangor and archbishop of York.   [80] Became bishop of Raphoe.
[81] Became bishop of Rochester.
[82] Became bishop of Carlisle.
[83] B.M. Seals, lvi, 45.
[84] B.M. Harl. Chart. 44, I, 4.
[85] B.M. Cott. Chart. iv, 53.
[1] Our knowledge of the early history of the abbey is derived for the most part from its own historians. The thirteenth-century chronicle of Thomas Sprott appears to be no longer extant, but probably everything of value in it was copied by his successors. That of William Thorne (Twysden, Decem Scriptores, cols. 1758–2202) extends from the foundation to the year 1397, and gives a large amount of valuable information, almost entirely about the abbey. Thomas of Elmham a few years later planned a more extensive account, but only part of it was finished (Historia Monasterii Sancti Augustini Cantuariensis, Rolls Ser.), and this, though fuller than Thorne's, treats of many matters only remotely connected with his subject. Both make use of Bede and other early writers, and in addition give the text of several charters and bulls. A short history was published in 1890 by the Rev. R. J. E. Boggis, B.D. The customary of the abbey has been edited for the Henry Bradshaw Society by Sir E. M. Thompson.
[2] Hist. Eccl. i, 33.

Thorne and Elmham both give 598 as the year of the foundation. They narrate[3] how Ethelbert with his queen Berta, their son Edbald, and Augustine and others celebrated the Christmas of 605 at Canterbury; and give the text of a charter by which a few days later he marked the boundaries of the land given by him for the monastery. But apart from the fact that Augustine died on 26 May, either in 604 or 605, it is plain from the style of the charter that it is a forgery of much later date, as are also several others belonging to the abbey. The Saxon place-names in it appear to be genuine, and the substance may perhaps be correct.

A monk named Peter was appointed as the first abbot, and soon afterwards was sent with Laurence the priest, afterwards archbishop, to Rome on a mission to Pope Gregory. He brought back, as a present from the pope, several books, vestments, vessels of gold and silver, and relics, all of which are catalogued[4] by Elmham, though most of them had disappeared before his time. This abbot was drowned on 30 December, 607, at Ambleteuse near Boulogne, when sent on a mission to France by Ethelbert, and a monk, John, was elected in his place.[5] In the first year of the abbey the monks used for worship an old heathen temple which had been consecrated and dedicated to St. Pancras; but in 613 Archbishop Laurence consecrated the conventual church in the presence of Ethelbert and many others.[6] The body of Augustine was removed from the cemetery and re-interred in the north porch, as were also those of Queen Berta and her chaplain Liuthard, bishop of Senlis, in the porch of St. Martin. In 978 the church was re-dedicated by Dunstan in honour of Sts. Peter and Paul and St. Augustine.[7]

Ethelbert himself, and several of his successors were buried in the church, as were also the first ten archbishops of Canterbury. This of course was of great importance to the abbey, on account partly of the prestige it thus gained, but principally of the burial fees and offerings of visitors, and the jealousy of the cathedral was aroused. Cuthbert, the eleventh archbishop, determined to make a change, and secured the consent of the king. In 758, when he found his death approaching, he gave strict orders that it was to be kept secret for three days; and when the abbot and monks came to bear away his body they found that it had already been buried. Bregowine, the next archbishop, played the same trick, and the monks were again defrauded; but Jaenberht, who was then abbot, appealed to Rome. The chapter of the cathedral elected him archbishop, probably thinking to win him over to their side, but he was faithful to St. Augustine's,

and was buried there. No more archbishops, however, were buried at the abbey; and the fact was bitterly resented by its historians,[8] and was probably one of the principal causes of the feud that always raged between the two houses.

Not much is known of the history of the abbey during these times, though several charters to it were preserved. Benedict Biscop, a celebrated figure in the north of England, appears to have been abbot for a short time in the seventh century. Thorne ignores him, and Elmham distinctly says that he was never abbot; but on the other hand Gervase says that he was appointed by Archbishop Theodore,[9] and Ranulph Higden that he was appointed by the king.[10] Probably the monks declined to recognize him, and this may have been the reason of his retirement. He was succeeded by Theodore's friend Adrian, perhaps the greatest of the whole line, who ruled for about forty years, and had under him at one time St. Aldhelm, afterwards bishop of Sherborne.[11] He in turn was succeeded by Albinus,[12] the friend of Bede, a celebrated scholar and the first English abbot of the house. For the next two or three centuries the abbots, with few exceptions, are mere shadows.

St. Augustine's seems not to have suffered as much as some other places in Kent from the frequent visits of the Danes. In 1011, when Canterbury, after three weeks of siege, was captured through the treachery of Ælfmaer the archdeacon, we are told[13] that his namesake the abbot 'was permitted to depart.' Thorne tells a story of a miracle which frightened the Danes away, but it seems more likely that they were bought off.

Egelsin, the last abbot of Saxon times, joined Stigand, then archbishop, in offering resistance to William the Conqueror. The latter promised well to them at first, but after his coronation began to lay hands on the possessions of the monasteries, and Egelsin fled to Denmark in 1070.[14] The king in consequence confiscated the abbey and appointed a Norman named Scotland as abbot, apparently against the wishes of the monks, who dared not object. Scotland, however, proved to be a most capable head, and recovered for the abbey Plumstead and Fordwich, which had been taken from it, besides obtaining grants from the king of the churches of Faversham, Milton and Newington, and various liberties. He also began the complete rebuilding of the abbey, which was carried on by his successors. At his death the monks succeeded in electing one of their number as the new abbot, in opposition to

[3] Thorne, *Chron.* 1761; Elmham, *Hist.* 110.
[4] Ibid. 98–102. [5] Ibid. 126–7.
[6] Thorne, *Chron.* 1767; Elmham, *Hist.* 131.
[7] Thorne, *Chron.* 1780.

[8] Ibid. 1772; Elmham, *Hist.* 317.
[9] Gervase of Cant. *Opera* (Rolls Ser.), i, 69; ii, 338.
[10] Ranulphi Higden, *Polychronicon* (Rolls Ser.), vi, 78.
[11] *Dict. Nat. Biog* i, 245. [12] Ibid. 234.
[13] Thorne, *Chron.* 1781; *Angl.-Sax. Chron.* (Rolls Ser.), ii, 117.
[14] Thorne, *Chron.* 1787.

the wishes of Lanfranc; but they were not so fortunate at the next vacancy, and William Rufus appointed a kinsman of his own named Hugh Flory, who had been a Norman warrior and was said to have been much impressed by a visit to the abbey. He added largely to the building at his own expense, obtained a grant of a five days' fair, and probably justified his appointment. The crown also made the appointment of the next abbot, Hugh de Trottesclive, a monk of Rochester, whose principal works were the assignment of definite estates to the officers of the abbey and the foundation of the hospital of St. Laurence. After him the monks elected their prior Silvester as abbot; but on the death of the latter Henry II appointed a secular priest named Clarembald, who pleased no one, and being opposed to the archbishop as well as to his own monks, is abused by both sets of historians. Gervase accuses him of having connived at the murder of Becket.[15] His rule was certainly unfortunate, for he lost the mint which the abbey had owned for centuries, alienated many of its possessions and loaded it with debt. The monks never allowed him to enter the chapter or celebrate mass in the church; and eventually Pope Alexander III ordered the bishops of Exeter and Worcester and the abbot of Faversham to inquire into the complaints against him, with the result that he was removed. The king was exceedingly angry, and took the abbey into his own hands for two years and a half.[16] During this abbacy, on the day of the Decollation of St. John the Baptist, 1168, the church was almost entirely burnt; and many old charters perished, and the shrine of Augustine suffered wofully.[17]

Everything in the history of St. Augustine's is overshadowed by the great question of its relations with the archbishop and the pope, the claim for privilege which was unsettled for centuries and cost far more than it gained. Augustine is said to have granted it absolute freedom from the jurisdiction of his successors; and this may have been the case, although the charter[18] attributed to him is certainly a forgery, as also are some of the early bulls. The abbey undoubtedly secured extensive privileges. Abbot Wlfric I went to a council at Rome in 1056, and Leo IX then granted that the abbots of St. Augustine's should have precedence over all others except those of Monte Cassino.[19] His successor Egelsin went to Rome on a mission seven years later, and Alexander II granted to him the right of wearing the mitre and other episcopal insignia;[20] this being the first instance of such a grant. The relations between the archbishops and abbots are said to have been very friendly before the Conquest,[21] but with the arrival of Lanfranc the quarrel soon began. He forbade the bells of the abbey to be rung for services before those of the cathedral, and as Scotland did not respond to the protests of the monks with sufficient energy, several years elapsed before they were specially allowed by papal bull to ring their bells whenever they pleased.[22] Lanfranc also endeavoured in vain to nominate the successor to Scotland.

Until the end of the eleventh century the new abbots appear to have been blessed by the archbishop in the cathedral; although Hugh Flory was blessed in the absence of Anselm by Maurice, bishop of London, at Westminster.[23] His successor, Hugh de Trottesclive, claimed to be blessed in the abbey church, and this the archbishop refused. The matter was referred to the king and the papal legate, who decided as a compromise that the abbot should be blessed by the bishop of Chichester.[24] The next quarrel occurred when Archbishop Theobald laid England under an interdict in 1148.[25] Abbot Hugh submitted, but his nephew William, whom the cathedral party called William the Devil, and Silvester, the prior, stirred up several of the monks to resist it and celebrate service as usual. The archbishop was eventually successful, and the abbey was condemned to a corresponding period of silence later on,[26] which unfortunately happened to coincide with the stay of the queen there, while her abbey of Faversham was being built,[27] with the result that monks from the cathedral were called in to celebrate service for her. Silvester himself was the next abbot, and it is not surprising to find that he pressed his claims vigorously. Thorne represents him as being completely victorious on all points, after fighting the matter before three popes;[28] but it is clear that although he was blessed in his own monastery,[29] he was at last, on 17 July, 1157, forced to make the profession of obedience to the archbishop which he had before refused.[30] Abbot Clarembald appears neither to have received benediction nor to have made profession, his own peculiar position and the strained relations between the king and Becket doubtless accounting for this. His successor, Roger, however, practically secured the victory. The archbishop rejected his claim to be blessed in the abbey with only a modified form of the oath of profession, and the matter was decided by Pope Alexander III, before whom Roger appeared in person. The forged *privilegium* of Augustine and other documents were produced and declared to be genuine by the pope, who ruled that the archbishops should give benediction in the abbey

[15] Gervase, *Opera*, i, 224.   [16] Thorne, *Chron.* 1819.
[17] Ibid. 1815.   [18] Elmham, *Hist.* 119.
[19] Thorne, *Chron.* 1784.   [20] Ibid. 1785.
[21] Gervase, *Opera*, i, 69.

[22] Thorne, *Chron.* 1792, 1797.   [23] Ibid. 1795.
[24] Ibid. 1798; Gervase, *Opera*, i, 73.
[25] Thorne, *Chron.* 1805.
[26] Gervase, *Opera*, i, 75-6.   [27] Ibid. 139.
[28] Thorne, *Chron.* 1811-14.
[29] Gervase, *Opera*, i, 76, 148.
[30] Ibid. 77, 164; Cathedral MS. A. 41.

without any profession of obedience, and that failing this the abbots should go to receive benediction from the pope. He himself blessed Roger in 1179, and moreover granted him permission to wear the mitre and other insignia, a right which the abbots since Egelsin had dropped on account of the opposition of the archbishops.[31] There is no doubt about the matter, for it is admitted by the cathedral party, Gervase bitterly lamenting that not even lavish expenditure of money had availed to prevent it.[32] A formal agreement was made between the abbot and the archbishop in 1182,[33] and in 1185 Archbishop Baldwin was amicably and respectfully received at the abbey.[34]

But the dispute was not yet finished. Archbishop Langton refused to give the required benediction to Alexander, the next abbot, who had to go to Rome to receive it from Innocent III.[35] Langton was abroad when Alexander died in 1220. We have a long and detailed account[36] of the election that followed; but though Pandulf, the papal legate, superintended it with great care, he was unable to give the benediction to the abbot elect, who had also to go to Rome. So too had Robert of Battle, elected in 1224; and there he found the opposition of the archbishop so powerful that to gain his case he had to give to the pope the church of Littlebourne for the support of the monastery of Monte Mirteto.[37] Archbishop Rich yielded on the points of benediction and profession in a general settlement with the abbot in 1237;[38] but fresh quarrels on other subjects kept this one alive, and it was not extinguished until Archbishop Arundel came to an agreement in 1397.[39]

Meanwhile, having gained its exemption, the abbey was paying the bill. The abbots were too proud to meet the archbishops half way, and so sought benediction from the popes. Abbot Poucyn's expenses in 1334 on his journey to Avignon amounted to £148.[40] He only ruled nine years and his successor three, and then came two years of dispute. The monks elected William de Kenyngton, but the pope granted the abbacy to John Devenish, a monk of Winchester, to whom he had promised preferment as consolation for a disappointment about the bishopric of Winchester.[41] The king and the monks obstinately resisted him, and he never entered the abbey; but after his death in 1348 the monks had to pay his debts, which amounted to £1,000. These frequent vacancies were a heavy charge on the abbey, and in consideration

of this the king in 1347 remitted two months' payment of the rent at which they held the temporalities,[42] with a further remission in 1349.[43] The next vacancy did not occur till 1375, and the pope then allowed the abbot to receive benediction in England from the bishop of Winchester instead of coming to Avignon; but the expenses of this, principally in bribes to the pope and cardinals, amounted to the enormous sum of £575.[44] When William Welde was elected abbot in 1387, Thorne, the chronicler, was sent to the pope to get confirmation of the election, and gives a graphic account of his experiences.[45] He reached the pope at Lucca on 11 June, and followed him to Perugia and Rome, but though he got smooth promises he was merely referred to a greedy cardinal, who procrastinated as long as possible. His bribes were insufficient, and a detailed explanation of the heavy charges on the abbey availed nothing. Meanwhile he made use of his delay to inquire about the monastery of Monte Mirteto, to which the abbey had granted the church of Littlebourne, and found that it was merely a cell to another monastery, and inhabited only by two disreputable monks; and part of the rent-charge was wrung out of them. The pope finally decided that the abbot must appear at Rome in person, which he did, and received the benediction on 13 December, 1388. But this delay and the long journey home occupied so much time that the temporalities were not restored until 5 April, 1389,[46] after having been in the king's hands for more than two years. In consequence of the great expenses incurred on this occasion, the king granted in 1392 that the convent should in future pay a yearly rent of 50 marks and have the custody of the temporalities at all vacancies.[47]

Besides enumerating a long list of grants of land and privileges, Thorne gives a considerable amount of miscellaneous information in the thirteenth and fourteenth centuries. The rebuilding of the abbey was commenced in 1260 and continued for many years, Adam de Kyngesnoth, the chamberlain, making large benefactions towards this and other purposes in 1267.[48] The abbey had frequent disputes with the cathedral about their respective rights at the adjoining ports of Stonar and Sandwich, and agreements were made about these in 1242, 1270, and 1283,[49] and about buildings at Fordwich in 1285.[50] In 1264 a chantry for Hamo Doge was founded in the church of St. Paul, Canterbury;[51] and the engagement of professional

[31] Thorne, *Chron.* 1824.
[32] Gervase, *Opera*, i, 78.
[33] Thorne, *Chron.* 1836; Elmham, *Hist.* 449.
[34] Gervase, *Opera*, i, 326.
[35] Thorne, *Chron.* 1864.　　[36] Ibid. 1872.
[37] Ibid. 1880; *Cal. Papal Let.* i, 164–6.
[38] Thorne, *Chron.* 1882.　　[39] Ibid. 2199.
[40] Ibid. 2067.　　[41] Ibid. 2082.

[42] Pat. 21 Edw. III, pt. 1, m. 7.
[43] Pat. 23 Edw. III, pt. 2, m. 27.
[44] Thorne, *Chron.* 2152.　　[45] Ibid. 2184–94.
[46] Pat. 13 Ric. II, pt. 2, m. 12.
[47] Pat. 15 Ric. II, pt. 2, m. 12.
[48] Thorne, *Chron.* 1915.
[49] Ibid. 1888, 1919, 1933.
[50] Ibid. 1939.　　[51] Ibid. 1913.

barbers is recorded in the same year.[52] In 1268 an agreement was made with the citizens of Canterbury about the punishment of thieves caught on the possessions of the abbey.[53] Some disputes with the cathedral about lands were settled in 1287;[54] and in the same year an agreement of confraternity was made with the monks of the cathedral,[55] as had also been done earlier with those of the cathedral of Winchester.[56] Abbot Nicholas is noted as having made arrangements for the shortening of the services and the distribution of moneys to the convent on various occasions.[57] He was appointed conservator of the privileges of the Premonstratensian order in 1277.[58]

Edward I was entertained at St. Augustine's on his return from France in 1279, and Archbishop Peckham visited him there with his cross borne before him, after solemnly declaring that this should not be to the prejudice of the abbey.[59] Ten years later the king was there again and invited the archbishop to dine with him; but on this occasion the abbot and monks objected to the bearing of the cross, and a long dispute followed. They yielded the point to please the king, but the quarrel continued about the wording of the archbishop's declaration that it should not prejudice the abbey, and here the king supported the monks against the archbishop, who withdrew in disgust, although afterwards friendship was restored.[60] In 1294 the king, when staying at the abbey, is said to have been frightened by a miraculous dream from depriving the monks of some possessions in Minster, as he had intended.[61] The archbishop of York was entertained in 1305, again after a formal renunciation of claim to authority.[62]

Archbishop Winchelsey summoned the abbot and monks to appear before him in his visitation in 1297 to show their claim to exemption and their title to appropriated benefices, but after a long dispute at Rome they were successful and obtained from the pope a new bull of privileges.[63] Relying apparently on this the abbot in 1300 ventured to form three new deaneries, under the names of Sturry, Minster, and Lenham, of the benefices belonging to the abbey, which were henceforward to be subject to the abbey alone.[64] Here, however, he sustained a humiliating defeat, for the archbishop appealed to Rome and gained every point; the pope deciding that the abbey had no special jurisdiction in this matter. The next two archbishops summoned the abbot and monks to visitations, but without success.[65] The relations between the abbey and the cathedral

were not always hostile, however, for in 1320 and 1370 the abbot assisted at the celebrations of the jubilees of Becket in the cathedral, and was received with great respect.[66]

The abbey was at the height of its prosperity at the beginning of the thirteenth century, although extravagance was evidently setting in. We are told on one hand of large benefactions made to it by John Peccham, one of the monks, and John of Pontoise, bishop of Winchester;[67] and on the other of an elaborate banquet given by Ralph de Bourn at his installation as abbot,[68] when the guests numbered over six thousand, and the cost amounted to £287 7s. This abbot did good service by clearing a waste and dangerous place and laying it out as a vineyard,[69] but found that the finances of the abbey were beginning to be insufficient for the building schemes.[70] In 1318 an insurrection of the tenants at Thanet caused great trouble and expense.[71]

Perhaps the most curious incident in the history of the abbey is the story of Peter de Dene.[72] He had been a distinguished ecclesiastical lawyer, and was at one time counsel to the abbey, to which he was a generous benefactor; but, getting into trouble in politics, in 1322 he sought admission there as a monk, and was received under a relaxed form of profession with many privileges, after bringing a present of silver and making his will in favour of the abbey. Eight years later he wished to leave it again, but the abbot refused to permit him; and he thereupon fled to Bishopsbourne, but a few days later was captured and brought back. He managed, however, to appeal to the pope, who in 1331 ordered the prior of the cathedral to inquire into the matter.[73] Great resistance was offered to the prior, and it was not till he had entered the abbey church with a powerful force that he was able to get any conversation with Peter at all; and then from a distance, surrounded by monks, Peter declared himself perfectly contented. It seems certain that Peter must have been forcibly detained and impersonated by someone else, but nothing more could be done for him; and the abbot and monks received pardon from the king for what they had done.[74] In 1334 Peter was one of the monks who elected the new abbot.[75]

Archbishop Segrave of Armagh consecrated some ornaments in the church of the abbey in 1322, and in 1325 a Hungarian bishop dedicated some altars under a commission from the arch-

[52] Thorne, *Chron.* 1915.
[53] Ibid. 1916.
[54] Ibid. 1944.
[55] Ibid. 1948.
[56] Ibid. 1904.
[57] Ibid. 1935.
[58] Ibid. 1925.
[59] Ibid. 1929.
[60] Ibid. 1951-6.
[61] Ibid. 1962.
[62] Ibid. 2005.
[63] Ibid. 1966.
[64] Ibid. 1976.
[65] Ibid. 2013, 2039.
[66] Ibid. 2036, 2145.
[67] Ibid. 2003.
[68] Ibid. 2009.
[69] Ibid. 2036.
[70] Ibid. 2038-9.
[71] Ibid. 2034.
[72] Ibid. 2036, 2054-66; *Lit. Cant.* (Rolls Ser), ii, 7, 17, 19, 40, 41, 43.
[73] *Cal. Papal Let.* ii, 369.
[74] Pat. 6 Edw. III, pt. 1, m. 31.
[75] *Cal. Papal Let.* ii, 405.

St. Andrew's Priory,
Rochester.
(1459.)

St. Augustine's Abbey,
Canterbury.
(1351.)

St. Augustine's Abbey,
Canterbury.
(Reverse.)

St. Andrew's Priory,
Rochester.
(Reverse.)

bishop of Canterbury.[76] The abbot of Cluni paid a visit in 1361.[77] Archbishops Courtenay and Arundel came unofficially in 1389 and 1397 ;[78] and the provincial chapter of the Friars Preachers were entertained in 1394.[79] Richard II visited the abbey twice, in 1393 and 1397 ;[80] and Henry VI in 1432, an account of the expenses on the occasion being still preserved.[81]

After the chronicles of Thorne and Elmham come to an end little is known about the history of the abbey. In 1412 the abbot had licence to go on pilgrimage to Jerusalem ;[82] and in 1468 a later abbot had licence to go on pilgrimage to any foreign parts for five years with one monk and four servants.[83] The finances of the abbey appear to have been in a bad state about this time, according to a letter from one of the monks in 1464.[84]

No details of any importance are known about the dissolution of the abbey; though a few letters from the abbot to Cromwell are preserved,[85] and some charges of sedition were brought against one of the monks in 1534.[86] It was of course rich enough to escape the first dissolution, but was finally surrendered[87] on 30 July, 1538, by the abbot and thirty monks, including a prior, infirmarer, treasurer, precentor, cellarer, sacrist, vestiary, sub-prior, third prior, fourth prior, and other minor officials. Pensions[88] were granted to these, the abbot receiving £61 yearly and the manor of Sturry.

A very large number of grants of lands and privileges are preserved in the registers[89] of the abbey ; and the more important of these are also to be found in the general charters of confirmation by various kings.[90] Several of the liberties were proved before Edward I and Edward II.[91] The possessions at the time of the Domesday Survey have already been set out.[92] In the Taxation of 1291 the spiritualities of the

abbey were valued at £424 13s. 4d. yearly and the temporalities at £808 1s. 0¼d. in the diocese of Canterbury and 22s. in St. Olave's, Southwark.[93] In the Valor[94] of 1535 the gross value of the possessions of the abbey is given as £1,729 9s. 11¼d., and the net value as £1,413 4s. 11d. Among them were the churches of Sturry, St. Paul in Canterbury, Chislet, Minster, Preston, Littlebourne, Tenterden, Lenham, Kennington, Milton, Faversham, Sellinge, Willesborough, Stone, Northbourne, Goodnestone, and Brookland ; and the manors of Minster, Chislet, Sturry, Northbourne, Stodmarsh, Littlebourne, Ripple, Deal, Goodneston, Langdon, Snave, Langport, Kennington, Burmarsh, Plumstead, Salmstone, Dean, Natingdon, Oare, Hull, and Swalecliffe.

The following list of seventy-two abbots is complete[95] :—

ABBOTS OF ST. AUGUSTINE'S, CANTERBURY

Peter, the first abbot, died 607
John, elected 608, died 618
Rufinian, elected 618, died 626
Gratiosus, elected 626, died 638
Petronius, blessed 640, died 654
Nathanael, elected 654, blessed 655, died 667
Benedict Biscop[96]
Adrian, appointed 669,[97] died 708
Albinus, elected 708,[98] died 732
Northbald, elected 732, died 748
Aldhun, elected 748, died 760
Jaenberht, elected 760, resigned 762[99]
Ethelnoth, elected 762, blessed 764, died 787
Guttard, elected 787, died 803
Cunred, elected 803, died 822
Wernod, elected 822, died 844
Diernod, elected 844, died 864
Wynher, elected 864, died 866
Bewmund, elected 866, died 874
Kynebert, elected 874, died 879
Etans, elected 879, died 883
Degmund, elected 883, died 886
Alfrid, elected 886, died 894
Ceolbert, elected 894, died 902
Beccan, elected 902, died 907
Ethelwold, elected 907, died 910
Tilbert, elected 910, died 917
Edred, elected 917, died 920
Alcherind, elected 920, died 928

[76] Thorne, *Chron.* 2038.
[77] Ibid. 2122.   [78] Ibid. 2194, 2198.
[79] Ibid. 2197.   [80] Ibid.
[81] Treasurer's return in Cathedral MSS.
[82] Pat. 13 Hen. IV, pt. 2, m. 17.
[83] *Lit. Cant.* (Rolls Ser.), iii, 243.
[84] *Paston Letters*, ii, 146.
[85] *L. and P. Hen. VIII, passim.*
[86] Ibid. vii, 1608.   [87] Ibid. xiii (1), 1503.
[88] Ibid. xiv (1), p. 597.
[89] Exch. K.R. Misc. Bks. 27 ; B.M. Cott. MSS. Claud. D. x, Faust. A. i. ; Canterbury Cathedral MS. E. 19. These last two collections contain several other documents relating to the abbey, and further references are given in Tanner's *Notitia Monastica.*
[90] Chart. R. 20 Edw. II, Nos. 3, 6 ; ibid. 36 Edw. III, Nos. 2, 3 ; ibid. 8 Hen. IV, No. 1 ; Pat. 2 Hen. VI, pt. 3, m. 5 ; ibid. 4 Edw. IV, pt. 4, m. 29 ; ibid. 14 Hen. VII, pt. 1, m. 7 (16).
[91] *Plac. de Quo Warr.* (Rec. Com.), 318, 341, 352, 353, 367.
[92] V.C.H. Kent, iii, 'Domesday Survey.'

[93] *Pope Nich. Tax.* (Rec. Com.), 4 ; Thorne, *Chron.* 2161.
[94] *Valor Eccl.* (Rec. Com.), i, 17–23.
[95] The names and dates of the earlier abbots are given by Thorne and Elmham, and the burial places and epitaphs of some are recorded.
[96] See above. Elmham does not recognize him, and declares that the abbey was vacant for two years.
[97] By Archbishop Theodore, by authority from the pope. Thorne says in 670.
[98] He was the first English abbot.
[99] He was made archbishop of Canterbury.

Guttulf, elected 928, died 935
Eadred, elected 935, died 937
Lulling, elected 937, died 939
Beornelm, elected 939, died 942
Sigeric, elected 942, died 956
Alfric, elected 956, died 971
Elfnoth, elected 971, died 980
Sigeric, elected 980, resigned 988 [100]
Wlfric, elected 989, died 1006
Ælfmaer, elected 1006, resigned 1022 [101]
Elstan, elected 1022, died 1047
Wlfric, elected 1047, died 1059
Egelsin, elected 1059, fled 1070
Scotland, appointed 1070, died 1087
Wide, elected 1087, died 1099
Hugh Flory, appointed 1099, died 1124
Hugh de Trottesclive, appointed 1126, died 1151
Silvester, elected 1151,[102] died 1161
Clarembald, appointed 1161, ejected 1176
Roger, elected 1176,[103] blessed 1179, died 1212
Alexander, elected 1212, died 1220
Hugh, elected 1221,[104] died 1224
Robert de Bello, elected 1224,[105] died 1253
Roger de Cicestria, elected 1253,[106] died 1273
Nicholas de Spina, elected 1273,[107] resigned 1283
Thomas de Fyndone, appointed 1283,[108] died 1310
Ralph de Burne, elected 1310, died 1334
Thomas Poucyn, elected 1334, died 1343
William de Thurlegh, elected 1343, died 1346
John Devenish, appointed 1346,[109] died 1348
Thomas Colwell, elected 1348,[110] died 1375
Michael Pecham, elected 1375,[111] died 1387
William Welde, elected 1387, died 1405 [112]
Thomas Hunden, elected 1405,[113] died 1420
Marcellus Daundelyon, elected 1420,[114] died 1426 [115]
John Hawkhurst, elected 1427,[116] died 1430[117]
George Pensherst, elected 1430,[118] died 1457

James Sevenoke, elected 1457,[119] died 1464 [120]
William Sellyng, elected 1464,[121] resigned 1482 [122]
John Dunster, elected 1482,[123] died 1496 [124]
John Dygon, elected 1497,[125] died 1510 [126]
Thomas Hampton, elected 1510,[127] died 1522 [128]
John Essex or Foche, elected 1522,[128] surrendered 1538,[129] the last abbot.

The seal [130] (twelfth century) of the abbey measures 2¾ inches.

Obverse.—St. Augustine seated on a carved throne with mitre, cusped nimbus and pall, lifting up the right hand in benediction and holding in the left a crozier. In the field on each side a quatrefoiled panel containing a head. Legend :—

SIGILL' E . . . USTINI CANTU RIE . . . APLI.

Reverse.—St. Paul, with sword in right hand, and St. Peter, with keys in left hand, each with nimbus, seated on a throne ornamented with two stories of arcaded panel work, holding up between them a circular panel. In the field round the inner edge near the two saints are the names [S PAUL]US S PETRUS. In base under a semicircular arch, between two smaller arches, a man crouching. The border of this arch is inscribed HER. . . . Legend :—

HOC SIGILL' FACTUM EST ANNO DECIMO RICA[RDI REGIS AN]GLOR.

Another seal [131] (1351) measures 3¾ inches.

Obverse.—An edifice representing a combined elevation and section of the conventual church, inclosed in the foreground at the base by an arcaded corbel table of three sides of an octagon with embattled parapet. The central subject is the baptism of Ethelbert by Augustine. Above this in a double niche, each with a cinquefoiled arch and crocketed canopy, seated on thrones, are St. Peter on the left holding book and keys and St. Paul on the right holding book and a sword by the blade. At each side in the transept, which has a double clearstory of small arcaded windows, two trefoiled arches with a full-length figure under each one, two monks on the left, and a king and a monk on the right. Over the

[100] He was made bishop of Ramsbury, and afterwards archbishop of Canterbury.
[101] He was made bishop of Sherborne.
[102] He was prior.
[103] He was a monk of Christchurch, Canterbury.
[104] He was chamberlain.
[105] He was treasurer.
[106] He was chamberlain.
[107] He was third prior.
[108] By the pope. He was third prior.
[109] By the pope. See above.
[110] He was sacrist.
[111] He was chamberlain.
[112] Pat. 6 Hen. IV, pt. 2, m. 3.
[113] Ibid. m. 2.
[114] Ibid. 8 Hen. V, m. 5.
[115] Ibid. 5 Hen. VI, pt. 1, m. 17.
[116] Ibid. m. 16.
[117] Ibid. 8 Hen. VI, pt. 2, m. 31.
[118] Ibid. pt. 1, m. 7. He was prior.

[119] Ibid. 36 Hen. VI, pt. 1, m. 11.
[120] Ibid. 3 Edw. IV, pt. 2, m. 2.
[121] Ibid. m. 1. He was prior.
[122] Ibid. 22 Edw. IV, pt. 1, m. 1.
[123] Ibid. m. 11. He was prior of Bath, and was charged afterwards by the latter house with dilapidation and waste. (*Select Cases in the Star Chamber* [Selden Soc.] 20–36.)
[124] Pat. 12 Hen. VII, pt. 1, m. 9 (15).
[125] Ibid. m. 5 (19).
[126] *L. and P. Hen. VIII*, i, 1056.
[127] Ibid. 1180.   [128] Ibid. iii, 1987.
[129] Ibid. xiii (1), 1503.
[130] B.M. Seals, lxvii, 63, 64.   [131] Ibid. 66, 67.

roof on each side an angel issuing from heaven holding a censer ; and on the left a star, on the right a crescent. Between these angels two shields of arms ; two keys in saltire. Legend:—

SIGILL' MON[ASTERI]I BEATOR APLOR PETRI ET PAULI SCIQ AUGUSTINI ANGLOR APLI C[ANT]UAR.

Reverse.—St. Augustine, seated on a throne in a carved niche under a canopy with mitre and pall, lifting up the right hand in benediction and holding in the left a crozier. In the field at the sides the inscription AU-G'-TI-N'. On his breast a reliquary with three half-length saints on it, the one in the centre crowned, those at the sides mitred. Over the arch on each side in a small niche an archbishop seated with an indistinct name on the plinth below. In the field over these niches a shield of arms : a cross. At each side of the principal figure a small niche, containing on the left Birinus with pastoral staff and book, and on the right Queen Berta, the plinth below bearing their names. Over these niches on each side a smaller arched niche containing an archbishop seated with the names [THE]ODOR and IUSTUS on the plinth below. Over these on each side of the field a star of six points. In base, under the corbel table of the inscribed plinth, a horned head between a sea-dragon and a wyvern. Legend :—

ANGLIA Q DOMINO FIDEI SOCIATUR AMORE
HOC AUGUSTINO DEBETUR PATRIS HONORE.

4. THE PRIORY OF DOVER

Two short accounts of the early history of this house are preserved,[1] from which it appears that Eadbald, king of Kent, who died in 640, ordained twenty-two secular canons to serve God in the chapel of St. Mary in the castle of Dover, subject to no one except the court of Rome and the king, and granted to them prebends with all liberties. Wihtred, king of Kent, in 696 removed them from the castle to the church of St. Martin in the town, but confirmed to them their prebends, possessions and liberties with a moiety of the toll of the port. The names and possessions of the canons are set out in the Domesday Survey,[2] which moreover tells us that in the time of Edward the Confessor the prebends were held in common and worth £61 yearly, but that they had since been divided up by the bishop of Bayeux.

Nothing more is known of the history of these secular canons, but they remained undisturbed until the latter part of the reign of Henry I. Archbishop de Corbeuil, who had himself been a canon regular of St. Osyth's in Essex, then procured their removal on the ground that they led evil lives, and proposed to replace them by canons regular. The king granted the

church to Christchurch, Canterbury, on the occasion of the dedication of the latter house in 1130 ; but in 1131 he complicated matters by a charter[3] in which he formally granted it to the archbishop and the cathedral for the construction of a monastery of canons regular which was to be under the archbishop alone. Having secured this charter, the archbishop proceeded to build a new monastery[4] with stone from Caen in Normandy and placed canons regular[5] in it, sending the bishops of Rochester and St. Davids to institute them ; but although he obtained the assent of the prior of Christchurch the chapter had been left in ignorance, and when the news was known the sub-prior, Jeremiah, defied the bishops and appealed to Rome. The death of Corbeuil in 1136 gave the victory to Christchurch and the canons were forced to withdraw; and during the vacancy of the see in the same year the convent of Christchurch sent a colony of twelve monks to Dover, appointing William de Longueville as prior.[6]

Theobald, a monk, succeeded to the vacant archbishopric in 1139 ; and though he seems not to have recognized the action of the convent he practically confirmed it, sending twelve monks to Dover in that year with Ascelin, sacrist of Christchurch, as prior.[7] He ordained by charter[8] that Dover should always be a cell to Canterbury, the prior was to be a professed monk of Canterbury, monks taking the habit at Dover should make their profession at Canterbury, and the appointment of the prior of Dover was to be reserved to the archbishop. Pope Innocent II confirmed Dover to him and the church of Canterbury by bull in 1139, and ordered that the Benedictine order should always be observed there ;[9] and Henry II granted a charter to the same effect.[10] Archbishop Richard, who had himself been prior of Dover, later granted a charter confirming the possessions of the priory in detail.[11] The subjection of Dover to Canterbury was also confirmed by John in 1199[12] and Henry III in 1237 ;[13] and general charters of confirmation were granted by Edward II in 1315,[14] Richard II in 1380,[15] Edward IV in 1461[16] and Henry VII in 1504.[17]

---

[1] B.M. Cott. Jul. D. v̄; Vesp. B. xi. *See* Dugdale, *Mon.* iv, 528.　　[2] V.C.H. Kent, iii.

[3] *Mon.* iv, 538.

[4] It is often afterwards called the priory of St. Martin of the new work.

[5] According to Gervase of Canterbury, *Opera* (Rolls Ser.), i, 96 ; ii, 287, 383, where the fullest account of the affair is given, they came from Merton in Surrey ; but according to Cott. MS. Vesp. B. xi, from St. Osyth's, which seems more probable.

[6] Gervase, *Opera*, i, 99.　　[7] Ibid. 109.

[8] Ibid. ii, 288 ; *Lit. Cant.* (Rolls Ser.), iii, 370.

[9] Ibid. 369.　　[10] Ibid. 371.　　[11] Ibid. 372.

[12] Ibid. 374.　　[13] Chart. 21 Hen. III, m. 5.

[14] Pat. 8 Edw. II, pt. 2, m. 12.

[15] Pat. 3 Ric. II, pt. 3, m. 14.

[16] Pat. 1 Edw. IV, pt. 6, m. 24.

[17] Pat. 20 Hen. VII, pt. 1, m. 30 (7).

The double grant of the priory by Henry I to the archbishop and the chapter of the cathedral produced complications between the four parties concerned which were not settled for two centuries.[18] The system of appointing priors from the monks of Christchurch was found to be injurious to Dover, and Edward I directed Ralph de Hengham, the chief justice, to find a way out of the difficulty.[19] Accordingly the king in 1286 claimed the advowson against the prior of Canterbury and, as the latter claimed nothing in the advowson except that the archbishop in time of vacancy assigned a monk out of his house as prior, judgement was given for the king. It had been intended to stop here and, by thus excluding the prior of Canterbury, to leave the archbishop in possession of the advowson ; but one of the justices issued a writ to the sheriff to take seisin of the advowson in the king's name, and by this 'fatuous and ill-conceived writ,' as the chief justice calls it in a letter to the chancellor, the archbishop was effectually barred. The suit was then reopened, and when the prior of Canterbury produced the ordinance of Theobald, the counsel for the king and the archbishop both argued that it was not binding because it had not been confirmed and because the royal charter declared that no one but the archbishop should meddle with the advowson. The ordinance was declared not to be binding, and the prior of Canterbury was excluded from any right in the advowson.[20] In the vacancy of the archbishopric following the death of Winchelsey in 1313 the cathedral chapter endeavoured to assert authority over Dover, excommunicated the monks on their refusal to submit, prevented them from electing a prior when a vacancy occurred, and appealed to the court of Rome ; but the king again in 1321 secured judgement against them,[21] and granted the advowson unconditionally to the archbishop.[22] The chapter did not, however, give up their claims against the priory ; and Archbishop Sudbury made an ordinance on 20 May, 1350, which the king confirmed on 26 May,[23] that at every vacancy of the archbishopric the prior of Dover, by reason of the parish churches of Hougham, Appledore, and Coldred with the chapel of Popeshall, appropriated to the priory, should render canonical obedience to the prior of Canterbury and should not prevent the vicars, chaplains, and ministers of these churches from rendering canonical obedience and from making procession in Christ-

church, Canterbury, on the third day in Whitsun week. The monastery of St. Martin, Dover, and the prior and convent as well as the prebendal church of St. Martin, Dover, and the churches and chapels in Dover annexed to or dependent from it, which the prior and convent had by royal grant before the foundation of the monastery and at all time since, were free from all ecclesiastical jurisdiction of the chapter except so far as related to the rendering of obedience as above ; but judgement was reserved in the case of the churches of Deal, Buckland, Guston, and St. Margaret's, as it was doubtful whether these were prebendal. In compensation, for the sake of peace and quiet, the chapter were to pay to the prior and convent a rent of 100s. out of the manor of Shepherdswell.

Pope Gregory IX in 1234 exempted the priory from liability to be vexed with ecclesiastical censures by papal legates and nuncii passing through Dover, and ordered that the prior should not be molested on account of his opposition to the election of the archbishop.[24] Urban V in 1369 granted relaxation of penance to visitors giving alms for the repair of the church on the principal feasts of the year.[25] John XXIII in 1412 granted that as the fruits of the old parish church of St. Martin, appropriated to the prior and convent and served by an archpriest, were insufficient for his maintenance, they might upon his resignation or death have it served by one of their monks.[26]

Geoffrey, archbishop of York, who landed in disguise at Dover on 14 September, 1191, was recognized and forced to take refuge in the priory ; but after five days' blockade the party of the chancellor, his rival, dragged him away from the altar by force on 18 September.[27]

The temporalities of the priory were valued at £188 10s. yearly in the Taxation of 1291.

Henry I granted to the prior and convent by charter a moiety of the issues of the port of Dover and a third of the toll of the market at Dover on Saturday. They had these without interruption until the end of the thirteenth century, when the allowance was refused in the Exchequer, and at their complaint the king in 1306 ordered the matter to be investigated. A certificate in support of their claim was found in the Red Book, but it was held not thus to be sufficiently established ; and an inquisition was taken, by which it was found that the charter had been granted to them and they had received the profits, but that lately the French had landed at Dover and plundered the priory, carrying off the charter among other things. Some of the jury testified to having seen the charter ; and judgement was given for the prior and convent,

---

[18] Many details in this elaborate case will be found in Gervase of Canterbury, *Opera ; Lit. Cant. ;* and *Reg. Epist. J. Peckham* (Rolls Ser.).
[19] *Lit. Cant.* (Rolls Ser.), iii, 378.
[20] Pat. 8 Edw. II, pt. 2, m. 12.
[21] Pat. 11 Edw. III, pt. 1, m. 20.
[22] Pat. 14 Edw. II, pt. 2, m. 9.
[23] Pat. 24 Edw. III, pt. 1, m. 7.

[24] *Lit. Cant.* (Rolls Ser.), iii, 374 ; *Cal. Papal Let.* i, 139.
[25] *Cal. Papal Let.* iv, 77.   [26] Ibid. vi, 281.
[27] Gervase of Canterbury, *Opera* (Rolls Ser.), i, 505.

who obtained an exemplification of it in 1338.[28] The income from the port was seriously diminished about this time on account of the French war.[29]

On the evening of Sunday before St. Vincent the Martyr, 1308, Edward II was in his chamber in the priory and there received the great seal from the chancellor and took it with him when he crossed the sea next morning; and delivered to the chancellor a new seal to be used in his absence.[30]

Edward III in 1327[31] sent John Pyk to the prior and convent to receive such maintenance in the priory as William de Kent had by order of Edward I; but in 1328 he gave the corrody to Richard de Dovorr, to whom they had previously granted it at the request of Queen Isabel.[32] John Pyk secured it in 1331 on the death of Richard;[33] but the king in 1333 promised that this grant of maintenance should not be taken as a precedent.[34]

In 1372 a register[35] of the priory was compiled by Robert de Welle and John Hwytefeld, monks, by the consent and at the expense of John Newenam, prior; and in this the possessions of the house are set out in full, charters of many kings, popes, bishops, and others being given.

Archbishop Warham issued ordinances in 1507, because he had found that the rule was very laxly observed in the priory. No monk was to absent himself from divine office by day or night or to go out of the cloister without licence, and silence was to be kept. Offenders were to be put on bread and water.[36]

The same archbishop made a visitation[37] of Dover in September, 1511, when John, bishop of Cyrene, was prior and Thomas Shrewsbury sub-prior, with ten other monks besides two apostates. The sub-prior said that the monastery was in ruins in many places for lack of repairs. Several monks said that the mayor and citizens of Dover deprived the monastery of the mortuaries of the church of St. Martin, belonging to it from its first foundation for the repair of the chancel of the church; and other complaints were made against the town. The cellarer and other officers had access to the town, so that the monastery was defamed there. There were three novices who were not taught grammar and had no teacher but the sub-prior;

he read the Gospel to them twice a week and nothing else. The sheets were of linen and not of wool. The archbishop ordered the prior not to let his brethren go into the town without the special licence of himself or the sub-prior, and they were on no account to eat or drink in any house there, lest dissension arise. They were to go to the dormitory immediately after leaving the refectory. The officers were to render accounts regularly. The prior was to provide an instructor to teach grammar, and the novices were to work in the grammar-school on three day in the week. The monks were to use woollen both for sheets and shirts. The prior and officers were to make a full account of the state of the monastery and an inventory of its goods, jewels, and ornaments before Easter.

A full balance-sheet of the monastery, drawn up by Thomas Lenham, prior, for the year ending at Michaelmas, 1531, is preserved.[38] In this £65 7s. 8d. were received from spiritualities, £100 19s. 8d. from farms of manors and lands, £75 2s. 8¾d. from rents of houses, £3 13s. 4d. from dues of the court of the monastery and £12 12s. 6d. from sale of wools and hides, and the stock, including 700 sheep and 120 quarters of wheat, was valued at £185 16s. 8d., making a total to the credit side of £443 12s. 6¾d. On the other hand rents, pensions, stipends, wages, repairs, presents, and general expenses of the household, implements, and cattle (including a large item of £65 14s. for expenses of the brewer) amounted to £557 11s. 4½d., so there was a considerable deficit.

The acknowledgement of the royal supremacy was signed in December, 1534, by John, prior, and twelve others.[39]

In the Valor[40] of 1535 the temporalities of the priory, including the manors of Farthinglowe, Frith, Guston, 'Ryche,' Barton, Dudmancombe, and Westcourt, amounted to £171 3s. 9½d. yearly, and the spiritualities, including the parsonages of St. Margaret's, Guston, Hougham, Appledore, Ebury, Coldred, and Buckland, to £60 17s. 8d. yearly, so that the gross income was £232 1s. 5½d. The deductions included 53s. 4d. each to the schoolmasters of the grammar-school and the song-school, £13 19s. 2d. distributed in alms on various days, and £6 9s. 6d. allowance for rents and pensions decayed and long unpaid, and amounted in all to £61 6s. 6d. yearly; the net income being thus £170 14s. 11½d.

Richard Layton visited Dover in the autumn of 1535 and reported that the prior and monks were immoral and as bad as others.[41] It was no doubt in consequence of this that the house was sequestrated on 31 October, and an inventory[42]

---

[28] Pat. 12 Edw. III, pt. 1, m. 31.

[29] Close, 12 Edw. III, pt. 1, m. 37; 15 Edw. III, pt. 3, m. 17 d; Pat. 21 Edw. III, pt. 2, m. 19.

[30] Close, 1 Edw. II, m. 11.

[31] Close, 1 Edw. III, pt. 2, m. 8 d.

[32] Ibid. 2 d.

[33] Close, 5 Edw. III, pt. 1, m. 7 d.

[34] Pat. 7 Edw. III, pt. 1, m. 26.

[35] Lambeth MS. 241. The same two monks in the next year compiled a register of the hospital of Buckland.   [36] Ibid. fol. 258b.

[37] Cant. Archiepis. Reg. Warham. fol. 38.

[38] L. and P. Hen. VIII, v, 446.

[39] Ibid. vii, 1594 (7).

[40] Valor Eccl. (Rec. Com.), i, 53; Dugdale, Mon. iv, 539.   [41] L. and P. Henry. VIII, ix, 669.

[42] Ibid. 717; Mon. iv, 541; Arch. Cant. vii, 281.

of its jewels, plate, ornaments, and other goods and chattels taken by Christopher Hales, general attorney to the king, and Sir John Tompson, master of the Maison Dieu. Three days later the prior wrote an appealing letter to Cromwell, perceiving that complaints had been made to the king of his negligence and evil governance.[43] He was thirty-one years old and had been in possession of the house only three years, 'the foresaid house being but of the yearly stent of £200 by the year £12 13s. 4d. was seven score pounds in debt' at his predecessor's departure. He was at great expense in repairing the church; the glass in the windows which was rusty and dark was taken down and scoured, and new glass added where necessary at his expense; he paved the church, bought new vestments for £16, and spent other sums, and mended the bakehouse and dorter. He had procured new brass and pewter at his own cost,

and no marvel though it be simple and scarceness thereof, for the strangers resorting be such wasteful streyars that it is not possible to keep any good stuff long in good order, and many times and specially strangers ambassadors have such noyous and hurtful fellows that have packed up table cloths, napkins, sheets, coverpanes, with such other things as they could get.

He had been at great cost with English and foreign ambassadors; and asks Cromwell to consider deeds more than words which may not be true. From the negligence and destroying of hired servants he had been at great charges in buying and renewing oxen, horses, carts, ploughs, &c, and through their untrustworthiness was compelled to let his husbandry to farm and give his brethren 20 nobles each a year to go to commons together, that he might get the house out of debt.

The appeal was useless, and on 16 November the priory was surrendered by John Lambert or Folkeston, prior, and eight others;[43a] but it seems probable that the prior's letter was correct, especially in that part relating to the visitors, for Thomas Bodyll, Henry Polsted, and John Antony, who took the surrender, reported[43b] to Cromwell that the house was well repaired and the prior had reduced the debt from £180 to £100, 'of whose new case divers of the honest inhabitants of Dover show themselves very sorry.' The monks were dispersed after the surrender, two of them being sent to Christchurch, Canterbury.[43c] They evidently left early, for in January, 1536, the master of the Maison Dieu went to the priory to see in what order it was and found that it had been ransacked.[44] The prior received a pension of £20 yearly.[45]

The site of the priory was granted on 31 July, 1538, to the archbishop of Canterbury.[46]

[43] L. and P. Hen. VIII, ix, 756.
[43a] Ibid. 816.   [43b] Ibid. 829.
[43c] Ibid. x, 13.   [44] Ibid. x, 146.
[45] Ibid. xiii (1), p. 575.   [46] Ibid. 1519 (68).

PRIORS OF DOVER

William de Longueville, appointed 1136[47]
Ascelin, appointed 1139,[48] resigned 1142[49]
William, resigned 1149[50]
Hugh de Cadomo, succeeded 1149[51]
Richard, appointed 1157,[52] resigned 1173[53]
Warin, appointed 1174,[54] died 1180[55]
John, succeeded 1180[56]
William, appointed 1187[57]
Osbern, succeeded 1189, died 1193[58]
Robert, resigned 1197[59]
Felix de Rosa,[60] succeeded 1197,[61] died 1212[62]
Reginald de Schepeya,[63] succeeded 1212,[64] died 1228[65]
William de Staunford,[63] elected 1229[65]
Robert de Olecumbe, elected 1235,[63] died 1248[65]
Eustace de Faversham[63]
John de Northflet,[63] resigned 1251[66]
Guy de Walda,[67] succeeded 1253,[68] resigned 1260[69]
William de Bucwelle, succeeded 1260,[69] died 1268[70]
Richard de Wencheape, succeeded 1268,[71] resigned 1273[72]
Anselm de Eastria, appointed 1275[73]
Robert de Whetekre, appointed 1289[74]
John de Scholdone[75]

[47] Gervase of Cant. Opera (Rolls Ser.), i, 99.
[48] Ibid. 109. He was sacrist of Christchurch.
[49] Wharton, Anglia Sacra, i, 343. He was made bishop of Rochester.
[50] Gervase, i, 141. He became abbot of Evesham.
[51] Ibid.
[52] Cott. MS. Jul. D. V. 23. He was chaplain of the archbishop.
[53] Gervase, i, 244. He became archbishop of Canterbury.
[54] Ibid. 251. He was cellarer of Christchurch.
[55] Ibid. 295.
[56] Ibid. He was cellarer of Christchurch.
[57] Ibid. 365.   [58] Cott. MS. Jul. D. V. 24.
[59] Gervase, Opera, i, 543. He was elected abbot of Eynsham.
[60] Lit. Cant. (Rolls Ser.), iii, 376.
[61] Gervase, Opera, i, 544. He was sacrist of Christchurch.
[62] Cott. MS. Jul. D. V. 24b.
[63] Lit. Cant. (Rolls Ser.), iii, 376.
[64] Cott. MS. Jul. D. V. 24b.   [65] Ibid. 25.
[66] Gervase, Opera, ii, 203.
[67] Lit. Cant. (Rolls Ser.), iii, 377.
[68] Gervase, Opera, ii, 204. He was sacrist of Christchurch.
[69] Ibid. 211.   [70] Ibid. 247.
[71] Ibid. He was sacrist of Christchurch.
[72] Ibid. 275.
[73] Ibid. 282. He was sub-prior of Christchurch.
[74] Ibid. 295. He was the first monk of Dover to become prior. Robert occurs as prior in 1317 (Pat. 2 Edw. II. pt. 1, m. 19) and died in 1319 (Close, 13 Edw. II. m. 3).
[75] Lit. Cant. (Rolls Ser.), iii, 377. He was deposed by Archbishop Simon (1328–33).

Robert de Hathbrand [76]

Richard de Hugham, appointed 1350,[77] resigned 1351[78]

William de Peryton, appointed 1351,[79] resigned 1351[80]

Thomas Beanys, appointed 1351[80]

William de Chartham, appointed 1356,[81] died 1366[82]

James de Stone, appointed 1366,[82] died 1371[83]

John Newenham, appointed 1371,[83] occurs 1380[84]

William Dover, occurs 1392[85]

Walter Causton, appointed 1392,[86] removed 1416[87]

John Wotton, appointed 1416[88]

John Combe, elected 1435[89]

John Asheford, succeeded 1446,[90] resigned 1453[91]

Thomas Dover, elected 1453[91]

Humphrey Tutbury, occurs 1468[92]

Robert Norborne, occurs 1504[93]

John Thornton, bishop of Cyrene, occurs 1509,[94] resigned 1513[95]

William, occurs 1529[96]

Thomas Lenham, occurs 1530-1[97]

John Lambert or Folkeston, surrendered 1535, the last prior [98]

The seal [99] (thirteenth century) of the priory measures 3 in.

Obverse.—St. Martin with nimbus seated on a horse pacing to the left and dividing his cloak with his sword. On the right a beggar receiving the gift of the cloak. Legend :—

SIGILLUM ECCLESIE SCĪ MARTINI DE [DOV]ORIA

Reverse.—St. Martin lying on a bed with arcaded plinth ; overhead our Lord, half-length,

issuing from clouds, with nimbus, holding the cloak in his right hand and in the left a book. Legend :—

[MAR]TIN[I] VES[T]E S[UM T]ECTUS PAUPERE TES[TE]

5. THE ABBEY OF FAVERSHAM [1]

King Stephen and his queen Maud founded the abbey of St. Saviour, Faversham ; perhaps with the definite idea of making it their burial place. The king in a charter [2] dated at Bermondsey states that he has granted the manor of Faversham for making a Cluniac monastery with full liberties, and in exchange for this manor he has granted to William of Ypres the queen's manor of Lillechurch and part of his own manor of Milton. The new abbey was colonized from Bermondsey, and for this permission had to be obtained from the abbot of Cluni and the prior of La Charité sur Loire, as superiors of Bermondsey, who gave licence [3] for Prior Clarembald to leave his house and take twelve monks with him to the abbey, which was to be as free and independent as the abbey of Reading, made from monks of their order. These letters were read on 11 November, 1147, when Archbishop Theobald blessed Clarembald as abbot at the altar of Canterbury Cathedral in the presence of the bishops of Worcester, Bath, Exeter, and Chichester.[4] The annals of Bermondsey say that Clarembald and his twelve monks left Bermondsey for Faversham in 1148.[5]

Queen Maud appears to have taken a great interest in the building of the abbey, staying at St. Augustine's, Canterbury, while it was in progress in 1148 ; and it is recorded that as silence was imposed on the monks of St. Augustine's she summoned monks of Christchurch there to celebrate divine service for her.[6] She was buried at Faversham in 1152, as were also the king in 1154 and their son Eustace in 1153.[7]

The manor of Tring in Hertfordshire was granted to the abbey by the queen and confirmed by the king and their son William, count of Boulogne, who also granted his manor of Bendish (in Radwinter) in Essex.[8] Henry II confirmed all these grants and others, and granted a fair of eight days beginning on the feast of

---

[76] *Lit. Cant.* (Rolls Ser.), iii, 377. He was appointed by the same archbishop.

[77] Cant. Archiepis. Reg. Islip, fol. 253*b*.

[78] Ibid. 50*b*.

[79] Ibid. He was a monk of Battle.

[80] Ibid. 51.   [81] Ibid. 272*b*.

[82] Cant. Archiepis. Reg. Langham, fol. 96*b*.

[83] Cant. Archiepis. Reg. Whittlesey, fol. 85*b*.

[84] Pat. 3 Ric. II. pt. 3, m. 14.

[85] Hasted, *Hist. and Topog. Surv. of Kent.*

[86] Ibid.

[87] Cant. Archiepis. Reg. Chicheley,fol. 79. Through old age.

[88] Ibid.   [89] Ibid. 211*b*.

[90] Cant. Archiepis. Reg. Stafford, fol. 23*b*.

[91] Cant. Archiepis. Reg. Kemp, fol. 325*b*.

[92] B.M. Add. Chart 16437. Humphrey occurs in 1490. (*Materials for History of Henry VII* [Rolls Ser.], ii, 546.)

[93] Pat. 20 Hen. VII, pt. 1, m. 30 (7).

[94] Aug. Off. Conv. Leases, Kent, 50.

[95] Cant. Archiepis. Reg. Warham, fol. 353. He became prior of Folkestone.

[96] *L. and P. Hen. VIII,* iv (3), 6047.

[97] Ibid. v, 446.   [98] Ibid. ix, 816.

[99] B. M. Seals, lxv, 47, 48, and 49, 50.

[1] Besides the accounts of Faversham in Dugdale, *Mon.* iv, 568, and Hasted, *Hist. and Topog. Surv. of Kent,* ii, 698, detailed information has been given by Thomas Southouse in *Monasticon Favershamiense* (1671) and John Lewis in *History of the Abbey of Faversham* (1727).

[2] Dugdale, *Mon.* iv, 573.   [3] Ibid. 575.

[4] Gervase of Canterbury, *Opera* (Rolls Ser.), i, 138.

[5] *Annales Mon.* (Rolls Ser.), iii, 438.

[6] Gervase of Canterbury, *Opera* (Rolls Ser.), i, 139.

[7] Ibid. 151, 155, 159.

[8] Dugdale, *Mon.* ii, 574.

St. Peter ad Vincula;[9] and by other charters he granted that the men of the manor of Faversham should be quit of toll throughout the realm, and that the monks might take royal fishes in the fisheries of Seasalter for a rent of 20s. yearly to the king.[10] John on 19 May, 1205, made another grant to them of the fisheries,[11] and on 7 March, 1215, he confirmed their possessions and liberties generally.[12] Edward I on 20 August, 1297, granted free warren at the manors of Faversham, Bendish, and Tring;[13] and Edward II on 1 September, 1315, granted a market on Tuesday at Tring and a fair there on the vigil, the feast, and the morrow of Sts. Peter and Paul and the seven days following.[14] General charters of confirmation were also granted by Henry III in 1227,[15] Edward II in 1315,[16] and Edward IV in 1465.[17] Pope Gregory IX in 1230 confirmed to the abbot and convent the church of Luddenham and all possessions and liberties granted to them by kings, bishops, and others; and this was confirmed by Pope Boniface IX in 1401.[18]

In the Taxation of 1291 the manor of Faversham was valued at £133 6s. 8d. yearly, and the abbey also owned temporalities worth £21 19s. 7d. in Luddenham, Goodnestone, Graveney, Harty, Hawkridge, and Boughton Malherbe, £1 2s. 7d. in London, £24 7s. 10d. in Radwinter, and £80 18s. 5d. in Tring. The manor of Tring was granted by the abbey to the archbishop of Canterbury in 1340 in exchange for the advowsons of the churches of Boughton under Blean and Preston; and these churches were appropriated in the same year, rents of 5 marks and 33s. 4d. from them being paid to the prior and convent of Christchurch, Canterbury, and 26s. 8d. from the church of Preston to the archdeacon of Canterbury in recompense for this.[19]

Faversham was still described as Cluniac in the charter of Henry III, but it appears to have joined the main Benedictine order; probably because its liberties and status as an abbey were inconsistent with the discipline required from Cluniac houses. In 1288 Abbot Oswald was cited to attend the Benedictine chapter to be held at Oxford, but refused, and the archbishop wrote a strong letter to the presiding abbots, upholding his action on the ground that by his charters he was under the authority of the archbishop alone.[20]

Abbot Peter de Rodmersham was formally deposed by the archbishop in public consistory on 9 September, 1275, because in the visitation of the preceding year many faults had been found, both in things spiritual and temporal.[21] The abbey had fallen into debt to merchants and others, and on 17 August the king had sequestrated it, appointing Fulk Peyforer and Master Hamo Doges to its custody.[22] One of the monks, writing for help to the sacrist of St. Augustine's, Canterbury, says that for three weeks past they had not had a grain of barley to support their household, nor could they make any malt nor sow their lands, for none of the neighbours would let them have any corn on the credit of their words or bonds; and—what was still worse and disgraceful to men of their profession—they were forced to procure drink in ale-houses or such as was to be bought in the town, and even that was in a manner taken by stealth.[23] This was no doubt a considerable exaggeration of the bad condition of the house, but in view of its trouble at this time and the amount of its income at the Dissolution it seems probable that the large income attributed to it in 1291 was somehow miscalculated. Peter appealed to the pope against his deposition, and his case was still proceeding in 1283;[24] but though he made a good show at Rome, there is no sign that his successor was ever seriously troubled in England. A similar state of things occurred in 1325. Abbot John le Orefreiser was found guilty of dilapidation and simony by the archbishop and forced to resign;[25] and the king on 28 August appointed Stephen de la Dane to the custody of the abbey, with orders to apply its surplus revenues to its relief with the advice of its more discreet members.[26] The ex-abbot eventually complained to the pope, who in 1328 simply referred the matter back to the new archbishop, with orders to settle it on the spot.[27]

A long dispute with the men of Faversham, which appears to have been raging in 1293,[28] was settled by an agreement dated 13 December, 1310.[29] The abbot and convent gave up their right to the custom of 'gavelsestre' or 1½d. for every brewing exposed for sale, the custom

[9] Dugdale, *Mon.* ii, 573.

[10] Chart. R. 11 Edw. III, No. 23.

[11] *Rotuli Chartarum* (Rec. Com.), 150. In 1413 the abbey had long lawsuits with the corporation of London and others about their fisheries of Oare, Luddenham, Faversham, and Harty. [Coram Rege R. Mich. 1 Hen. V, 90; Early Chan. Proc. bdle. 6, 241.] [12] Dugdale, *Mon.* iv, 573.

[13] Chart. R. 25 Edw. I, No. 4.

[14] Ibid. 9 Edw. II, No. 53.

[15] Ibid. 11 Hen. III, pt. 1, m. 14.

[16] Ibid. 9 Edw. II, No. 48.

[17] Pat. 4 Edw. IV, pt. 3, m. 6.

[18] *Cal. Papal Let.* v, 361.

[19] *Bodleian Charters* (ed. Turner and Coxe), 136; *Lit. Cant.* (Rolls Ser.), ii, 219; Pat. 14 Edw. III, pt. 2, m. 11.

[20] *Reg. Epist. J. Peckham* (Rolls Ser.), iii, 959.

[21] Gervase of Canterbury, *Opera* (Rolls Ser.), ii, 280.

[22] Pat. 3 Edw. I, m. 13.

[23] Dugdale, *Mon.* iv, 569.

[24] *Cal. Papal Let.* i, 470.

[25] Cant. Archiepis. Reg. Reynolds, fol. 136, 139b.

[26] Pat. 19 Edw. II, pt. 1, m. 29.

[27] *Cal. Papal Let.* ii, 279.

[28] Pat. 21 Edw. I, m. 8 d.

[29] Pat. 4 Edw. II, pt. 2, m. 25.

called 'fenstrage' or $\frac{1}{4}d.$ for each window in which wares were exposed for sale on Saturday, and toll payable by merchants and residents of the town and their kinsmen ; and in return the men of Faversham granted to the abbot and convent a rent of £10 yearly until land to that value in Kent should be bought by them for the abbey. The right of making any stranger coming to the town with wares free from toll was reserved to the abbot ; disputes about any person's freedom from such payment were to be inquired into in the abbot's court by a jury of the town ; and disputes about the interpretation of the clauses were to be decided in the king's courts, notwithstanding any liberty of the Cinque Ports. It may be noted here that the mayor of Faversham was appointed by the abbot and convent from three persons elected by the mayor, jurates, and commonalty on the morrow of Michaelmas, and the mayor took an oath to do true service to the king and the monastery.[30]

Corrodies were claimed by the crown in the abbey. Edward I in 1293 sent Reginald de Staneweye there, requesting the abbot and convent to provide him with the necessaries of life in their house.[31] Edward II in 1325 claimed a pension for one of his clerks by reason of the new creation of an abbot.[32]

Pope Boniface IX in 1400 granted indulgence[33] to penitents visiting the abbey from the first to the second vespers of the Invention of the Cross in May and the Exaltation of the Cross in September ; and in 1401 he exempted the abbot and convent from all payment of tithes on their possessions for which from time immemorial they had not paid tithes.[34] Pope Innocent VII in 1405 granted relaxation of penance to penitents visiting the abbey church at various specified times.[35]

Theobalde Evias of Faversham, widow, by her will in 1479 ordered her body to be buried within this monastery, and among other bequests devised 20s. to the new making of a window in the chapter-house there, her great cloth of tapestry work to do worship to God in the presbytery and on the sepulchre next the high altar there on high days, and her vestment of green velvet and a chalice, two cruets, a bell and a paxbrede, all of silver, to be used only in her chapel there, the vestment to be embroidered with the words *Orate pro anima Theobalde Evias.* Richard Goore, gentleman, of Faversham, by his will in 1504 ordered his body to be buried here in the chapel of St. Anne. Robert Browne by his will in 1509 ordered his body to be buried in the abbey before the rood of pity in the overhand of the church.[36]

Archbishop Langham gave injunctions after a visitation on 20 April, 1368, in which he referred to the eating of flesh and the failure to observe the rule of silence. The elder monks had 20s. yearly where the younger ones had only necessaries ; none showed the abbot what they had ; and one monk was quarrelsome and a producer of discord. Moreover the management had been extravagant, wood had been sold, and the house was £12 in debt. The porter was to be removed because he was the cause of access of dishonourable women.[37]

Archbishop Warham made a visitation of Faversham in the autumn of 1511, when there were thirteen monks besides the abbot. Robert Faversham, prior, said that the alms of victuals and drink were no longer given bountifully to the poor, but distributed at one time or another among friends of the monks ; and that women had ingress to the cloister and refectory. William Bidenden, sub-prior, and others complained that the old stipend was no longer paid in money, according to old custom, but in clothes ; and he said that some avoided entering religion in the monastery because of this ; though it was admitted that this payment exceeded in value the sum of money paid of old. Moreover, there was nobody deputed to give out clothes ; so if they lacked shoes or anything they must go to the abbot, to whom they thought they ought not to go, but rather to an inferior person. One monk, ten years professed, said that he had been punished for an offence according to rule, but besides this the abbot had deprived him of all his money. Several other monks complained that fees and other moneys due to them had been taken away. One complained of insufficient clothing in winter. Two said that the butler, who was not a monk, was hostile and conducted himself rather as a master than a servant, often making complaints against the monks without cause, and once giving to the abbot a letter entrusted to him by a monk. Evidence was given that the number of professed monks had been sixteen and seventeen within memory. The last examined said that the cellarer did not provide good food for the refectory, and the meat there was only half roasted ; also that another monk was a fool and illiterate and exempted from returning an account of his rents. The archbishop ordered alms to be distributed in food and drink ; women were not to be allowed in the cloister, and no monk was to speak with any woman in the nave of the church ; the abbot was to appoint a chamberlain, who should provide the convent with the necessary clothes ; proper food and drink and clothes were to be provided ; none were to be exempted from rendering accounts ; the abbot was to distribute to each monk his share of the money gained from the burials or obits of the dead ; a quarrelsome monk was

[30] *L. and P. Hen. VIII,* xiii (2), 274, 290.
[31] Close, 21 Edw. I, m. 10.
[32] Ibid. 19 Edw. II, m. 20 d.
[33] *Cal. Papal Let.* v, 284.
[34] Ibid. 358. [35] Ibid. vi, 29. [36] Hasted, loc. cit.
[37] Cant. Archiepis. Reg. Langham, fol. 77b.

ordered to conduct himself charitably towards the brethren in future; the abbot was to make the butler behave himself better towards the monks; and he was to give an account of the state of his house before Easter next.[38]

The oath of acknowledgement of the royal supremacy was taken on 10 December, 1534, by John, abbot, Robert Faversham, prior, John Harte, sacrist, Thomas Sellyng, cellarer, John Lynstyd, precentor, Dunstan, sub-prior, and eight other monks.[39]

In the Valor of 1535 the gross value of the temporalities of the abbey in Kent amounted [40] to £261 5s. 2d. and the net value to £200 5s. 6¾d. yearly, besides a quarter and a half of barley, the deductions including £10 ordained by the founders to be expended in alms yearly for their souls. The net value of the spiritualities, including the parsonages of Boughton, Hernhill, and Preston, and pensions in the churches of Luddenham and Newenham, was £58 3s. 4d. yearly, and that of the manor of Bendish Hall in Essex £28 3s. 8d. The whole net income of the abbey thus amounted to £286 12s. 6¾d. besides the barley, and it was rich enough to escape the first dissolution.

Some letters from the abbot to Cromwell are preserved. On 20 February, 1532, he complains[41] that he is marvellously annoyed with rooks, crows, choughs, and buzzards, which not only destroy his doves, but the fruit of his orchard, and asks licence for his servants to have handguns and crossbows to destroy 'the said ravenous fowls.' He had lately sent the king a goshawk and two spaniels; there were few better in England for pheasant and partridge. Cromwell wrote to him on 8 March, 1536, suggesting his resignation of the house of which he had so long had the rule, because of his age and debility; and on 16 March he writes a polite refusal in a long and interesting letter.[42] He trusts he is not yet so far enfeebled but he can govern as well as ever, though he cannot so well perchance ride and journey abroad; even if an abbot's peculiar office were to survey the possessions of his house, he took such pains in his younger days that he need do less now, and his servants, whom he has brought up from their youth, have such experience in these worldly matters that they can supply this part. He thinks, however, the chief office and profession of an abbot is to live chaste and solitary, to be separate from the intermeddling of worldly things, to serve God quietly, to distribute his faculties in the refreshing of poor indigent persons, and to have a vigilant eye to the good order and rule of his house and the flock committed to him by God. Doubtless

it would be, as Cromwell says, more to his ease to resign for a reasonable pension, and he has no doubt of Cromwell's conscience therein, considering the benevolence he has always found in him. For his own part he should be contented, not being ambitious; but, considering the miserable state in which the house would be left, God forbid that he should think his office irkful or tedious. The house is much impoverished, partly by the debts left by his predecessor, who was but a right slender husband to the house, partly by the necessary repairs of the church and other buildings and the 'innyng' of marshes which the sea had won, by lawsuits for the recovery of their rights, and by dismes and subsidies to the king, amounting to more than £2,000. The house was now more than £400 in debt, which he might see repaid if he continued in office six or seven years; but if he should resign, the charges of first-fruits and tenths due to the king, added to the debt, would ruin the house. God forbid that he should so heinously offend against God and the king as to further the ruin of so godly and ancient a foundation, dedicated to St. Saviour by one of the king's progenitors, whose body with those of his queen and son lies buried in honourable sepulture, and are had all three in perpetual memory with continual suffrages and commendations of prayers. Cromwell, no doubt, considered that in view of the abbot's age there was no need to hurry the matter, and on 6 April the abbot wrote to thank him for his loving letters, and sent him a token in consideration of his goodness to the monastery.[43]

After the dissolution of the smaller monasteries the pressure on Faversham was renewed, and the end came in 1538. The abbot was summoned to appear before the king on 1 July, but wrote [44] two days later to Cromwell to say that this was impossible, for he was too lame to go or ride and could scarcely get to the church with two staves. If he came before his majesty he was so weak that he could neither kneel nor stand but for a very little space. He asked Cromwell to obtain leave for him to stay at Faversham, or else it would shorten his time. He would accomplish the king's pleasure cheerfully, as well as if he were present. This of course meant the surrender, which was formally made by the abbot and convent on 8 July.[45] The officers of the abbey were the same as in 1534, but the number of monks was five less; the younger ones having probably been released from their vows in the meantime by the royal visitors. Pensions were given to all, the abbot receiving 100 marks yearly.

The site of the monastery was leased to John Wheler on 10 May, 1539; and the reversion was granted on 16 March, 1540, to Sir Thomas Cheyne, warden of the Cinque Ports and treasurer of the household.[46]

[38] Cant. Archiepis. Reg. Warham, fol. 40b.
[39] L. and P. Hen. VIII, vii, 1594 (2).
[40] Valor Eccl. (Rec. Com.), i, 82.
[41] L. and P. Hen. VIII, v, 812.
[42] Ibid. x, 484.
[43] Ibid. 627.
[44] Ibid. xiii (1), 1322.
[45] Ibid. 1339-40.
[46] Ibid. xv, 436 (44).

The following list of abbots is probably complete. The great length of rule of the later ones will be noticed.

ABBOTS OF FAVERSHAM

Clarembald, the first abbot, appointed 1147 [47]
Guerric, elected 1178 [48]
Ailgar, elected 1189,[49] occurs 1206 [50]
Nicholas, elected 1215,[51] resigned 1234 [52]
Peter, elected 1234,[53] resigned 1267 [54]
John de Horeapeldore, elected 1268,[55] died 1271 [56]
Peter de Herdeslos, elected 1271,[57] died 1272 [58]
Peter de Rodmersham, elected 1272,[59] deposed 1275 [60]
Oswald de Estri, appointed 1275,[61] died 1292 [62]
Geoffrey de Bocton, elected 1292,[63] died 1308 [64]
Clement de Lodenne, elected 1308,[65] died 1318 [66]
Thomas de Wyngeham, elected [67] and resigned [68] 1318
John le Orefreiser, elected 1318,[69] deposed 1325 [70]
John Ive, elected 1325,[71] died 1356 [72]
William de Maydenstan, elected 1356,[73] died 1370 [74]

Robert de Faversham, elected 1370,[75] died 1409 [76]
Robert Elham, elected 1409,[77] died 1426 [78]
John Chartham, elected 1426,[79] died 1458 [80]
Walter Gore, elected 1458,[81] resigned 1498 [82]
John Sheppey or Casteloke, elected 1499,[83] surrendered 1538 [84]

The seal [85] (thirteenth century) of the abbey measures 2⅝ inches.

Obverse.—Our Lord seated on a throne with nimbus, in a niche with carved and trefoiled arch, lifting up the right hand in benediction and holding in the left a book. On each side a smaller niche, containing on the left St. Peter seated on a throne with nimbus, holding in the right hand two keys and in the left a book, and on the right St. Paul with nimbus, holding in the right hand a sword and in the left a book. Outside these niches, on each side a narrow buttress with three stories of arcaded work, supported on a bracket. Over the roof of the central niche, on the left a star, on the right a crescent. In base, two circular panels, each containing a king's head, with arcades at the sides. Legend :—

[S C]OMMUNE MONASTERII SCI SALVATORIS DE FFAVER . . . .

Reverse.—The abbey church with Our Lord standing on a mount under a trefoiled arch below the central tower ; under smaller arches, on the left Moses and on the right Elias, the whole thus representing the Transfiguration. In each of the side towers two small openings, the upper quatrefoiled, the lower sixfoiled. Each contains the head of one of the emblems of the four evangelists ; on the left an eagle and a lion, on the right a man and a calf. Over the roof of the church between the spires two angels with outspread wings issuing from the heavens and each swinging a censer. In base beneath the plinth of the building three crouching figures. Legend :—

TRANSFIGURATUR VELUT ET SOL CLARIFICATUR.

6. THE ABBEY OF RECULVER

The Anglo-Saxon Chronicle tells us that in 669 King Ecgbriht gave 'Reculf' to Bass, the mass-priest, to build a monastery on.[1] The

---

[47] Gervase of Canterbury, *Opera* (Rolls Ser.), i, 138. He was prior of Bermondsey.
[48] Ibid. 277. He too was prior of Bermondsey.
[49] Ibid. i, 458 ; ii, 405.
[50] Feet of Fines, Kent.
[51] Gervase of Canterbury, *Opera*, ii, 109.
[52] Pat. 19 Hen. III, m. 7.
[53] Ibid. He was cellarer.
[54] Pat. 52 Hen. III, m. 34.
[55] Ibid. m. 29. He was cellarer.
[56] Pat. 55 Hen. III, m. 23.   [57] Ibid. m. 20.
[58] Ibid. 1 Edw. I, m. 20. The convent paid 100 marks for the temporalities on this occasion.
[59] Ibid. m. 19.
[60] Gervase of Canterbury, *Opera*, ii, 280.
[61] Ibid. 282 ; Pat. 3 Edw. I, m. 4 ; Close, 3 Edw. I, m. 2 d. The monks elected John de Romenhale, one of themselves, but the archbishop quashed the election and appointed Oswald, a monk of Christchurch, Canterbury.
[62] Gervase of Canterbury, *Opera*, ii, 300 ; Pat. 20 Edw. I, m. 12.
[63] Pat. 20 Edw. I, m. 9. He was sub-prior.
[64] Ibid. 2 Edw. II, pt. 2, m. 22.
[65] Ibid. He was prior.
[66] Ibid. 12 Edw. II, pt. 1, m. 20.
[67] Ibid. m. 19. The king gave his assent to the election on 19 November.   [68] Ibid. m. 7.
[69] Ibid. The king gave his assent to the election on 28 December.
[70] Cant. Archiepis. Reg. Reynolds, fol. 139b.
[71] Ibid. 143b. He was sub-prior (Pat. 19 Edw. II, pt. 1, m. 22.)
[72] Cant. Archiepis. Reg. Islip, fol. 113.
[73] Ibid.   [74] Pat. 44 Edw. III, pt. 2, m. 5.

[75] Ibid. m. 2.
[76] Cant. Archiepis. Reg. Arundel, fol. 123.
[77] Pat. 11 Hen. IV, pt. 1, m. 11. He was sub-prior.
[78] Cant. Archiepis. Reg. Chicheley, fol. 45.
[79] Pat. 5 Hen. VI, pt. 1, m. 21.
[80] Pat. 37 Hen. VI, pt. 1, m. 18.   [81] Ibid.
[82] Pat. 14 Hen. VII, pt. 1, m. 11 (12) ; pt. 3. m. 10 (11).   [83] Ibid.
[84] *L. and P. Hen. VIII*, xiii (1), 1339.
[85] B. M. Seals, lxv, 59, 60.
[1] *Angl.-Sax. Chron.* (Rolls Ser.), i, 56-7 ; ii, 30.

foundation of this appears to have followed shortly afterwards; for Lothair, king of Kent, by a charter[2] in 679 granted land in Thanet and Sturry to Brihtwald, abbot of the monastery of 'Raculf.' On 1 July, 692, Brihtwald, described as 'abbot in the monastery called Raculf situated by the north mouth of the stream Genlade,' was made archbishop of Canterbury.[3]

Some other charters to this monastery are preserved.[4] Eardulf, king of Kent, granted a plough-land called Perhamstede to Heahbert, abbot. Eadbert, king of Kent, who was buried at Reculver on his death in 761,[5] in 747 granted the toll of one ship in the port of Fordwich to Denehaeh, abbot; and Ealhmund, king of Kent, in 784 granted twelve plough-lands in Sheldwich to Hwitrede, abbot. The exact end of the monastery is not known; but King Edred by a charter in 949 granted it with its possessions to the archbishopric of Canterbury, and it was held by the archbishop at the time of the Domesday Survey.[6]

ABBOTS OF RECULVER

Brihtwald, occurs 679, resigned 692
Heahbert
Denehaeh, occurs 747
Hwitrede, occurs 784

HOUSES OF BENEDICTINE NUNS

7. THE PRIORY OF ST. SEPULCHRE, CANTERBURY

In the chronicle of William Thorne this house is said to have been founded by Anselm, archbishop of Canterbury (1093–1109), in the parish church of St. Sepulchre, of his patronage.[1] William Calwell is called the founder in the Valor; and probably the bulk of the endowment came from him, the archbishop merely sharing in the foundation. The priory was situated within the limits of the fee of St. Augustine, and in 1244 the prioress and nuns bound themselves not to enter on or appropriate any lands belonging to the abbey without licence from it.[2] In 1184 the abbot and convent gave the church of St. Edmund, Redingate, Canterbury, to them in frankalmoign for a rent of 12d. yearly.[3] The prior and convent of Christchurch granted to them as much wood in the wood of Blean as one horse, going twice each week-day, could bring thence; but in 1270 in lieu of this they granted a definite portion of the wood.[4]

Henry III on 19 March, 1247, granted to the prioress and nuns a charter confirming in detail gifts of land by various donors;[5] and in 1255, at the instance of Lauretta, recluse of Hackington, he granted that they should be quit for five years of suit of court for certain land.[6]

Archbishop Peckham in 1285 gave 10 marks to the nuns for roofing their dormitory.[7] On 20 April, 1284, he issued injunctions[8] to them, in consequence of a visitation. The prioress was to be strictly impartial, and strife was to cease in the monastery. Quarrelsome nuns were to be put in solitary confinement in a dark house under the dormitory, where no secular was ever to enter, whether a nun be there or not. The new house where religious and even secular men used to come for talk with the nuns and other women was interdicted. Any nun talking with any man, except in the case of confession, was to go with two of her fellows to the common parlour. Seculars were not to frequent the refectory or cloister. No man was to enter the precinct after sunset unless life be in peril, and then only in suitable society. No nun was to enter the town without a companion or go to any place for confession unless she had no other confessor; and she was not to take food or drink or prolong her stay. All suspected women and servants were to be removed, and no woman was to stay in the nunnery in future without the archbishop's special licence. This ordinance was to be read in chapter on the first day of each month. The archbishop at the same time ordered[9] his commissary to take the ordinance to the priory and appoint two coadjutors for the prioress, as the goods of the house had been much wasted by her negligence; Sarah was to be one of these, but Benedicta was not to be one, as she had offended the whole college by her abuse. The vicar of Wickham was to take care of the goods of the house. The commissary was also to receive the purgation of Isabel de Scorue, who had been guilty of a scandal with the cellarer of Christchurch, and to forbid her and other nuns to go to that church or the cellarer to come to the nunnery or have access to any nun.

---

[2] Printed in Dugdale, *Mon.* i, 455, from Bodleian MS. Tanner, 222.

[3] *Hist. Mon. St. Aug.* (Rolls Ser.), 287; Bede, *Eccl. Hist.* v, 8.

[4] Dugdale, *Mon.* ut supra; Twysden, *Decem Scriptores*, 2211, 2220.

[5] *Hist. Mon. St. Aug.* 324.   [6] V.C.H. Kent, iii.

[1] Twysden, *Decem Scriptores*, 1893.

[2] Ibid.   [3] Ibid. 1838.

[4] Harl. Chart. 75. F. 46.

[5] Chart. 31 Hen. III, m. 7.

[6] Pat. 40 Hen. III, m. 2.

[7] *Reg. Epist. J. Peckham* (Rolls Ser.), iii, 894.

[8] Ibid. ii, 706.   [9] Ibid. 708.

DOVER PRIORY.
(13th Century.)

DOVER PRIORY.
(Reverse.)

ST. BARTHOLOMEW'S
HOSPITAL, SANDWICH.
(12th Century.)

THOMAS ARUNDEL,
ARCHBISHOP OF CANTERBURY.
(1397–1414.)

ST. SEPULCHRE'S PRIORY,
CANTERBURY.
(12th Century.)

Archbishop Langham found at a visitation on 3 March, 1368, that Joan Chiriton, prioress, did not govern well. Among other faults she permitted the rector of Dover and other suspected persons to have access to Marjory Child and Joan Aldelose, and these alone among the nuns were allowed to visit the town. The prioress was removed on account of the scandal, and Agnes Broman appointed in her place.[9a]

In 1369 a chantry was founded [10] in the priory church for the soul of Robert Vyntier of Maidstone and his parents and brothers, and his executors granted the manor of 'Scheforde by Maidstone called La Mote' to the chaplain. The patronage of the chantry was to belong to the archbishop, and the prioress and nuns were to have all profits from the manor in times of vacancy for the use of a chaplain to be found by them. Archbishop Morton by his will in 1500 granted the manor to the convent to find a priest to serve the chantry.[11]

Archbishop Warham ordered proper accounts to be given after a visitation in 1511.[12] At this visitation Mildred Hale, prioress, said that the nuns did not rise for mattins in the middle of the night, but at dawn, because the doors of the cloister were being mended and the roof covered, and there was so much noise outside the church. There were then five other nuns in the priory.

St. Sepulchre's came into unenviable notoriety towards the end of its career through Elizabeth Barton, the Nun of Kent.[13] She was originally a domestic servant at Aldington, and was attacked by disease and in consequence developed religious mania about the year 1525. The parson of the parish reported the case to Archbishop Warham, and the latter ordered the prior of Christchurch to inquire into it. Two monks were sent for this purpose, and one of these, Edward Bockyng, conceived the idea of making use of her for the Catholic party; he carefully educated her in the legends of the saints and theological arguments, gave as much publicity as possible to her utterances, and in 1527 procured her admission to St. Sepulchre's, where for several years she continued to grow in importance, Bockyng's information enabling her to avoid serious error in her prophecies. She became one of the chief opponents of the divorce of Queen Katharine, and declared that if it came to pass the king would die a villain's death, although Katharine refused to have anything to do with her, and it is clear from the letters [14] of Eustace Chapuys, the Imperial ambassador, that he was under no

illusions whatever about her. So far she had been allowed to talk unchecked. But when the marriage of Henry VIII with Anne Boleyn had come to pass and he still lived, it was necessary to explain her prophecies, and she did so by saying that he was no longer king. Cromwell then took the matter up; Cranmer, who had succeeded Warham as archbishop, examined her carefully and secured her confession; an act of attainder [15] was passed against her and her accomplices; and she was executed on 20 April, 1534. St. Sepulchre's cannot, however, be considered principally responsible for the affair.

In the Valor of 1535 the possessions of the priory, including the parsonage of St. Mary Bredne, Canterbury, and the manor of the Mote by Maidstone, were valued [16] at £38 19s. 7½d. yearly. The deductions amounted to £9 7s. 2d. and included one quarter of wheat to be given yearly for the soul of William Calwell, the founder, on Thursday before Easter; and so the net income remaining 'to the seid prioresse and vii nonnes for their mete, drynk, apparell and other chargs' was £29 12s. 5½d. The house consequently came under the operation of the Act of 1536 and was dissolved, the prioress receiving a pension [17] of 100s. yearly.

The site and possessions of the monastery were leased [18] to Robert Darkenall of Canterbury on 21 May, 1537, for twenty-one years at a rent of £39 9s. 3d.; and on 31 July, 1538, the reversion was granted to the archbishop of Canterbury.[19]

PRIORESSES OF CANTERBURY

Juliana, occurs 1227,[20] 1236, 1244,[21] died 1258 [22]

Lettice, succeeded 1258 [22]

Benedicta, occurs *circa* 1300 [23]

Sarah de Peckham, elected 1324 [23a]

Margaret Terry appointed 1349 [23b]

Margery, occurs 1356 [20]

Cecily de Tonford, appointed 1356,[24] resigned 1366 [25]

Joan de Chiriton, elected 1366,[26] resigned 1368 [27]

[15] Stat. 25 Hen. VIII, cap. 12.
[16] *Valor Eccl.* (Rec. Com.), i, 29 ; *Mon.* iv, 415.
[17] *L. and P. Hen. VIII*, xiii (1), p. 583.
[18] Ibid. p. 585.
[19] Ibid. 1519 (68).
[20] Dugdale, *Mon.* iv, 413.
[21] Feet of F. Kent, 20, 28 Hen. III.
[22] Gervase of Canterbury, *Opera* (Rolls Ser.), ii, 208.
[23] Harl. Chart. 76. G. 34.
[23a] Cant. Archiepis. Reg. Reynolds, 131b.
[23b] *Hist. MSS. Com. Rep.* viii, App. 337.
[24] Cant. Archiepis. Reg. Islip, fol. 130b.
[25] *Lit. Cant.* (Rolls Ser.), ii, 467.
[26] Ibid. 468.
[27] Cant. Archiepis. Reg. Langham, fol 77.

[9a] Cant. Archiepis. Reg. Langham, fol. 76b.
[10] *Lit. Cant.* (Rolls Ser.), ii, 493.
[11] Dugdale, *Mon.* iv, 413.
[12] Cant. Archiepis. Reg. Warham, fol. 36.
[13] For a fuller account of her, see *Dict. Nat. Biog.* iii, 343; *Trans. Royal Hist. Soc.* xviii, 107.
[14] *Cal. of S.P. Spanish*, 1531-3, ii.

Agnes Broman or Bourghman, elected 1368,[28] died 1369 [29]

    Alice Guston, elected 1369,[29] removed 1376 [30]

    Margery Child, succeeded 1376 [30]

    Joan Whitfelde, died 1427 [31]

    Lettice Hamon, elected 1427 [32]

    Mildred Hale, occurs 1511 [33]

    Philippa Jonys [34] or John,[35] the last prioress

The seal [36] (twelfth century) measures 2½ inches and represents the Holy Sepulchre in the form of a rectangular case with mosaic front; on it an angel seated; over it four columns supporting a dome-shaped tent or baldachin. Legend :—

SIGILLUM ECLE · SEPULCHRI CANTUARIE.

8. THE PRIORY OF DAVINGTON

This priory was founded, according to Tanner, by Fulk de Newenham in 1153. It is said that he gave the church to it, but the abbey of Faversham claimed it under another grant, and the dispute was referred to Hubert, archbishop of Canterbury, who gave the church to the nuns subject to the payment by them of a rent of 2 marks yearly to the abbot and convent.[1]

Henry III by a charter [2] dated 22 April, 1255, confirmed the possessions of the nuns and granted liberties to them, which they claimed successfully in 1279.[3] The priory is not mentioned in the Taxation of 1291, but a return [4] in 1385 shows that it then owned the churches of Harty, Newnham, and Davington, worth £12, the church of Bardfield, worth 13s. 4d., and temporalities worth £14 6s. 5d. yearly. Lands were acquired in mortmain in 1341 [5] and 1392.[6]

Archbishop Peckham on 10 October, 1279, committed the custody of the priory to the vicar of Faversham, ordering him to be careful of its possessions, and to see that the provisions made by himself and his predecessor at their visitations should be observed.[7]

In 1343 the king remitted [8] to the prioress and nuns the demand made upon them for wool, sheaves, and lambs, granted by the commons, and the tenth granted by the clergy. They had complained of their poverty, and a return [9] of their possessions had been made; and it was found that these hardly sufficed for their maintenance and the support of alms and other works of piety ordained.

Archbishop Langham briefly reported all things well after a visitation on 20 April, 1368.[10]

Archbishop Warham made a visitation of Davington in the autumn of 1511, when Maud Awdeley was prioress. The convent had rents to the value of £31 14s. besides demesne lands which they held and cultivated to the value of £10 yearly. The house had to pay 20s. to the archbishop for board at the time of his visitation. Elizabeth Awdeley, professed at Cambridge, had been there twenty years, and Elizabeth Bath, professed at Malling, ten years; and they said that all was well except that the revenues of the house decreased. There were also two other inmates, not professed, who had been there for fifteen and ten years respectively.[11]

Davington eventually succumbed to poverty, as happened also to a few other small priories in England.[12] It was found by inquisition on 26 October, 1535, that there had been there a priory of Benedictine nuns dedicated to St. Mary Magdalen, where one Maud Dynmarke was prioress, Elizabeth Audle a nun, and Sybil Moonyngs a novice. Elizabeth had died on 12 June, 1526, and no more nuns had been professed there, and the prioress died on 11 March, 1535, and after her death Sybil left the priory, so that it was forsaken and extinct. The prioress and convent owned the manor of Fishbourne, two parts of the manor of Monkton, the advowsons and rectories of Davington and 'Stanger,' the rectory and advowson of the vicarage of Newnham, and lands in Davington, Fishbourne, Faversham, 'Overperston,' Newnham, the Isle of Harty, 'Durdevile,' Minster in Sheppey, Harbledown, Norton, Luddenham, Sittingbourne, Sandwich, Thanet, Ash by Sandwich, Sellinge, Linsted, and Stanstead at Ospringe; and they also had once the advowson of Bradfield, and two parts of the advowson of Monkton, but John, archbishop of Canterbury, in 1522 united these churches to Otterden with the consent of Joan, then prioress. The priory and all its possessions thus came into the hands of the king, who on 8 September, 1546, sold them to Sir Thomas Cheyne, treasurer of the household.[13]

---

[28] Cant. Archiepis. Reg. Langham, fol. 77.

[29] Ibid. Whittlesey, fol. 15.

[30] Ibid. Sudbury, fol. 13.

[31] Ibid. Chicheley, i, fol. 47.

[32] Ibid.; Lettice occurs as prioress in 1439 (Early Chan. Proc. bdle. 9, No. 105 ; bdle. 16, No. 625).

[33] See above.

[34] Valor Eccl. (Rec. Com.), i, 29.

[35] L. and P. Hen. VIII, xiii (1), p. 583.

[36] B.M. Seals, lxv, 17.

[1] Lewis, Hist. of Faversham, 36.

[2] Chart. 39 Hen. III, m. 7 ; Dugdale, Mon. iv, 289.

[3] Plac. de Quo Warr. (Rec. Com.), 347.

[4] Twysden, Decem Scriptores, 2168.

[5] Pat. 14 Edw. III, pt. 3, m. 3.

[6] Pat. 16 Ric. II, pt. 1, m. 26.

[7] Reg. Epist. J. Peckham (Rolls Ser.), i, 72.

[8] Close, 17 Edw. III, pt. 1, m. 3.

[9] Mon. iv, 290, from Dodsworth MS. cxv, fol. 158.

[10] Cant. Archiepis. Reg. Langham, fol. 78.

[11] Ibid. Warham, fol. 40.

[12] For the similar cases of Bicknacre and Latton in Essex see V.C.H. Essex, ii, 'Religious Houses.'

[13] Pat. 38 Hen. VIII, pt. 5 ; Chan. Inq. (Ser. 2), vol. 81, No. 257 ; Exch. Inq. (Ser. 2), file 489, No. 1.

9. THE PRIORY OF HIGHAM OR LILLECHURCH

Mary daughter of King Stephen appears to have settled in the nunnery of St. Leonard, Stratford at Bow, accompanied by some nuns of the abbey of St. Sulpice, at Rennes in Brittany, of which she was abbess,[1] and bringing with her as endowment the manor of Lillechurch. But quarrels with the English nuns resulted, and a writing[2] of Theobald, archbishop of Canterbury, records that in the presence of himself, Queen Maud, Hilary, bishop of Chichester, and Clarembald, abbot of Faversham, an agreement was made that Mary and the nuns of St. Sulpice should leave Stratford and dwell at Lillechurch, and the nuns of Stratford should release all claim to that manor.

Abbot Hugh and the convent of Colchester granted the church of Lillechurch to the nuns,[3] and it was appropriated to them by Walter, bishop of Rochester.[4] Queen Maud had granted land in Colchester in compensation, but the exchange does not appear to have been completely settled until an agreement was made a few years later, when Walter was abbot and Juliana prioress.[5]

Consideration of the various persons concerned indicates 1148 as the probable year of the foundation of the priory. It seems originally to have been considered a cell to St. Sulpice. William son of Stephen by charter[6] confirmed to his sister Mary and the nuns of St. Sulpice the grant of Lillechurch by his father, mother, and brother. Henry II granted to the abbess and nuns of St. Sulpice the church of Hoo, and the grant was confirmed by Henry III in 1232,[7] but a few years later the church passed by exchange to the cathedral of Rochester.[8] Henry III on 6 July, 1227, confirmed to the prioress and nuns of Lillechurch several gifts of lands,[9] and on the same day he granted[10] to the abbey of St. Mary and St. Sulpice and the prioress and nuns of Lillechurch the manor of Lillechurch in frankalmoign with a yearly fair on Michaelmas and the two days following, pursuant to charters of John. Edward I granted the same fair to the nuns on 4 September, 1289, but it was to be one day earlier.[11] The house is not mentioned in the Taxation of 1291.

The bishop made a visitation of the priory in 1343.[11a]

The prioress and nuns had licence in 1346 to make a conduit to their priory,[12] and to acquire land in Higham;[13] and in 1392 to acquire land.[14]

Higham came to an end before the general dissolution. Margaret, countess of Richmond, had begun the foundation of the college of St. John the Evangelist at Cambridge, but died while it was in progress, leaving the completion of the work to her executors, of whom John Fisher, bishop of Rochester, was one; and as the priory was now in a very bad state he procured its suppression and appropriation to the college. The process[15] of dissolution was begun in 1521. Inquiry showed that there had been originally sixteen nuns at the priory, but for many years past only three or four, and there were now only three, Agnes Swayne, Elizabeth Penney, and Godliff Laurence; and the last two were convicted of gross immorality by several witnesses. The three nuns formally resigned all claim to the priory at the end of the year; and on 21 October, 1522, the king made a grant[16] to the college of the priory, and all its possessions in Higham, Lillechurch, Shorne, Elmley, Dartford, Yalding, Brenchley, Pympe, Lamberhurst, Cliffe, Hoo, Horndon on the Hill, and 'Hylbrondeslands' in the counties of Kent and Essex. The commissary of the bishop carried

---

[14] Feet of F. Kent, 16 Hen. III.
[15] Ibid. 43, 47 Hen. III.
[16] Cant. Archiepis. Reg. Islip, 30b.
[17] Ibid. 36b.   [18] Ibid. Courtenay, 255.
[19] Ibid. Arundel, i, 465b.
[20] Ibid. Chicheley, 50b. Lora, probably the same, occurs in 1416 (Assize R. 1528, m. 32 d.).
[21] Cant. Archiepis. Reg. Chicheley, 50b. Alice occurs as prioress circa 1465 (Early Chan. Proc. 30 (45)).
[22] Cant. Archiepis. Reg. Warham, 326.
[23] See above.   [1] Gallia Christ. xiv, 787.
[2] Dugdale, Mon. iv, 381.   [3] Ibid. 382.
[4] Reg. Roff. 476.
[5] Ibid. 475 ; Chartul. of St. John's, Colchester (Roxburghe Club), 525.

[6] Dugdale, Mon. iv, 382.
[7] Chart. 17 Hen. III, m. 15.
[8] Pat. 12 Edw. IV, pt. 2, m. 14.
[9] Chart. 11 Hen. III, pt. 2, m. 17.
[10] Ibid. The nuns paid £100 for the charter of John for the manor (Fine Roll, 3 John, m. 6).
[11] Chart. 17 Edw. I, No. 8.
[11a] Wharton, Angl. Sac. i, 375.
[12] Pat. 20 Edw. III, pt. 1, m. 31.
[13] Pat. m. 30.
[14] Pat. 16 Ric. II, pt. 1, m. 32.
[15] Printed in Mon. iv, 379.
[16] L. and P. Hen. VIII, iii (2), 2630.

out the appropriation on 19 May, 1523,[17] and it was confirmed by the bishop and the dean and chapter in March, 1524, and by the archdeacon of Rochester on 1 May, 1525. Pope Clement VII confirmed it by a bull dated 28 September, 1524.[18]

PRIORESSES OF HIGHAM

Mary daughter of Stephen, the first prioress [19]
Juliana,[20] occurs *circa* 1170
Alice [21]
Joan de Merliston, elected 1247 [22]
Acelina, occurs 1266,[23] resigned 1275 [24]
Amfelisia de Dunlegh, elected 1275,[24] died 1295 [25]
Maud de London, elected 1295,[26] died 1301 [27]
Joan de Handlo, elected 1301,[28] died 1329 [29]
Maud de Grenestede, or Colcestre,[29a] elected 1329,[30] died 1340 [31]
Elizabeth de Delham, elected 1340,[32] died 1361 [33]
Cecily Leyham, elected 1361 [34]
Olive, died 1388 [35]
Joan de Haleghesto, elected 1388 [36]
Joan Cobham, elected 1390,[37] died 1394 [38]
Joan Sone, elected 1394 [39]
Alice Pecham, elected 1418,[40] died 1419 [41]
Isabel Wade, elected 1419,[42] died 1462 [43]
Margaret Boteler, elected 1462,[44] died 1475 [45]

Christina, died 1486 [45a]
Elizabeth Bradforth, or Bradfeld, occurs 1494,[46] 1496,[47] resigned 1501 [48]
Agnes Swayne, elected 1501 [49]
Marjory Hilgerden, occurs 1509 [50]
Anchoreta Ungothorpe, appointed 1514,[51] died 1521 [52]

10. THE ABBEY OF LYMINGE

Ethelburga daughter of Ethelbert, king of Kent, married Edwin, king of Northumbria, in 625; and after his death in 633 she returned with Paulinus, the bishop, to Kent, and founded a monastery at 'Limninge' which her brother Eadbald, king of Kent, had granted to her; taking the veil herself with other nuns, and being buried there at her death.[1]

The monastery appears to have been double, for men and women, as was often the case in early times; for Cuthbert, archbishop of Canterbury, is said in a charter[2] granted to it by Ethelbert, king of Kent, in 741 to have been abbot there; while a charter of Cynewulf, king of Mercia, and Cuthred, king of Kent, in 804 is addressed to Selethrytha, abbess. Charters were also granted by Wihtred, king of Kent, in 694, and Ethelstan in 964; but little is known of the history of the monastery, which eventually came into the possession of Christchurch, Canterbury.

11. THE ABBEY OF MALLING

Gundulf, bishop of Rochester (1077–1108), towards the end of the twelfth century founded this monastery in the manor of Malling, which had been in the possession of the bishopric before the Conquest. William II confirmed the grant by a charter which is witnessed by R. bishop of Durham, and must therefore belong to the years 1099 or 1100; and it seems probable that the foundation was not much earlier. Henry I confirmed the grant of the manor to the nuns by charter early in his reign; and by another charter, witnessed by Anselm, archbishop of Canterbury (1093–1109), he confirmed to them the manor of Cornard in Suffolk, which Robert son of Hamo had granted to them. These three

[17] *Reg. Roff.* 418.
[18] *L. and P. Hen. VIII*, iv (1), 686.
[19] See above. According to Matthew Paris (*Chron. Maj.* [Rolls Ser.], ii, 216) she was afterwards abbess of Romsey in Hampshire and then married Matthew, son of the count of Flanders, in 1160; but according to *Gallia Christiana*, xiv, 787, she was abbess of St. Sulpice and died in 1159.
[20] *Chartul. of St. John, Colchester* (Roxburghe Club), 525.
[21] Dugdale, *Mon.* iv, 378.
[22] Pat. 32 Hen. III, m. 13.
[23] Pat. 50 Hen. III, m. 25.
[24] Pat. 3 Edw. I, m. 29.
[25] Pat. 23 Edw. I, m. 13.
[26] Pat. m. 12. [27] Pat. 29 Edw. I, m. 31.
[28] Pat. m. 27.
[29] Pat. 2 Edw. III, pt. 2, m. 1.
[29a] Wharton, *Angl. Sac.* i, 369.
[30] Roch. Epis. Reg. i, fol. 87 *d.* 149 *d.*
[31] Ibid. 181.
[32] Ibid. She was sub-prioress. There were then thirteen nuns.
[33] Ibid. 308.
[34] Ibid; Pat. 35 Edw. III, pt. 3, m. 38. Cecily died in 1386 (Pat. 10 Ric. II, pt. 1, m. 27).
[35] Escheators' Inq. Ser. I, file 1001.
[36] Ibid. Joan died in 1390 (Pat. 14 Ric. II, pt. 1, m. 10).
[37] Ibid. m. 4. [38] Pat. 17 Ric. II, pt. 1, m. 1.
[39] Ibid. pt. 2, m. 37. Joan died in 1418 (Pat. 6 Hen. V, m. 11).
[40] Ibid. m. 10. [41] Pat. 7 Hen. V, m. 8.
[42] Ibid. m. 6. [43] Pat. 2 Edw. IV, pt. 1, m. 13.
[44] Ibid. m. 7. [45] Pat. 15 Edw. IV, pt. 3, m. 9.

[45a] Pat. 1 Hen. VII, pt. 2, m. 14 (12).
[46] Roch. Epis. Reg. iv, fol. 14 *d.*
[47] Cant. Archiepis. Reg. Morton, fol. 160 *d.* There were then five other nuns.
[48] Roch. Epis. Reg. iv, fol. 30. [49] Ibid. 30 *d.*
[50] Ibid. 51. She appears as a nun of Malling in 1524 (ibid. 112).
[51] Ibid. 72. By the bishop.
[52] *L. and P. Hen. VIII*, iii (1), 1173. Licence for election was granted on 20 February, but appears never to have been made use of.
[1] *Hist. Mon. St. Aug.* (Rolls Ser.), 176, 177, 227.
[2] For these charters see Dugdale, *Mon.* i, 452; Twysden, *Decem Scriptores*, 2208–9, 2213, 2223.

charters were confirmed by Edward III in 1347.[3] John on 12 April, 1206, confirmed the church of East Malling to the abbey ;[4] and a vicarage was ordained there in 1339.[5] The possessions and rights of the abbey, which was dedicated to St. Mary, were also confirmed by several bishops of Rochester ;[6] and the abbess paid ten pounds of wax and a boar yearly to them.[7]

On 27 July, 1190, the monastery and nearly all the town were consumed by fire.[8]

The Taxation of 1291 mentions temporalities of the abbey valued at £45 yearly in the diocese of Rochester, £3 0s. 10d. at Westwell, £33 19s. 11d. at Cornard in Suffolk, and £1 2s. 6d. at Wimbish and 6s. 8d. at Sible Hedingham in Essex, making a total of £83 9s. 11d. ; besides spiritualities of £5 6s. 8d. in Wouldham[9] and 10s. in Wimbish. In 1318 the abbess and convent had licence[10] to make an exchange of lands in Suffolk with Thomas Grey, but the transaction does not appear to have been finally settled until 1446.[11]

The abbess successfully claimed view of frank-pledge and various other liberties at East Malling and Malling in 1293[12] and 1313 ;[13] and on the latter occasion she also claimed and was allowed to have markets at Malling on Wednesdays and Saturdays, and three fairs there yearly, viz. on the vigils and the days of St. Peter, St. Martin, and St. Leonard.

Archbishop Winchelsey issued long injunctions after a visitation of the abbey in 1299, in which he expressed his approval of the statutes made by Thomas, bishop of Rochester. In addition he ordered the profession of nuns after probation, regular attendance at divine service, the frequent presence of the abbess in the cloister, and the exclusion of seculars from thence, and forbade the sale of bread and ale. Two of the seniors were appointed to the office of treasurer, and four incontinent nuns were punished.[14]

William de Dene mentions Malling several times in his history of the church of Rochester. In 1321 he narrates[15] how the king directed the bishop to go to Malling, which according to the complaints of all the nuns had been ruined by the abbess, a sister of the rebel Bartholomew de Badlesmere, and to correct the defects and depose her. The bishop made a visitation[16] in Novem-ber and heard many complaints. All the officials were made to give up their keys, and the abbess was called upon to render an account, but could not do so and was removed from administration. The office of cellarer, which she had held, was given to Alice de Gaunt, and the abbey was committed to the custody of the prioress and sacrist, the rector of Offham and a layman. Agnes de Leyburne was elected abbess, though rather informally, according to Dene ; and he says that on her death in 1324, about the time of the feast of the Exaltation of the Cross, at the unanimous desire of the nuns the bishop unwillingly appointed Lora de Retlyng abbess, though knowing her to be unfit and ignorant, but forbade her to give a corrody to her maid according to the bad old custom and sequestrated the common seal.[17]

In 1336 the bishop inhibited the nuns from receiving seculars in the abbey and from going out of it themselves.[18] In 1349, the year of the plague, two abbesses were appointed, both of whom died, and there only remained four professed nuns, and four not professed ; and the bishop committed the temporalities to one, and the spiritualities to another, as none was fit to be abbess.[19] In the next year the monastery was found at his visitation to be so ruined by bad management, that it seemed unlikely that it could be repaired by the Day of Judgement.[20]

Pope Boniface IX on 5 December, 1400, ordered the abbess and convent to assign a room within the precincts of the monastery to Cecily Batesford, one of the nuns, and a nun chosen by her to be her companion for life ; as a certain infirmity prevented her from being present at the canonical hours in choir and chapter without great affliction.[21] Cecily appears to have recovered, for she died abbess in 1439 ; and in the next year her sister Joan Brincheslee made grants to the convent, who agreed in return that on 14 July, the day of Cecily's death, there should be celebration for Cecily and Joan with a distribution of three flagons of wine, one to the abbess if present and two to the convent.[22]

The bishop gave notice of visitation of the abbey in August, 1441,[23] but the result is not recorded.

In the Valor[24] of 1535 the possessions of the abbey were valued at £245 10s. 2½d. yearly, from which rents, pensions, and fees amounting to £27 6s. had to be deducted, leaving the net income £218 4s. 2½d. ; and it was thus rich enough to escape the first dissolution. Elizabeth

[3] Chart. 21 Edw. III, No. 22 ; Dugdale, *Mon.* iii, 383 ; Thorpe, *Reg. Roff.* 486.
[4] Chart. 7 John, m. 2 ; *Reg. Roff.* 480.
[5] *Reg. Roff.* 484. [6] Ibid. 480. [7] Ibid. 62.
[8] Gervase of Canterbury, *Opera* (Rolls Ser.), i, 485.
[9] A detailed account of the tithes in Wouldham is printed in *Reg. Roff.* 694.
[10] Pat. 11 Edw. II, pt. 2, m. 28.
[11] Close, 24 Hen. VI, pt. 2, m. 11d.
[12] *Plac. de Quo Warr.* (Rec. Com.), 356, 363.
[13] Ibid. 312.
[14] Cant. Archiepis. Reg. Winchelsey, fol. 70.
[15] Wharton, *Angl. Sac.* 1, 362.
[16] Roch. Epis. Reg. 1, fol. 84d.

[17] Wharton, *Angl. Sac.* 1, 364.
[18] Roch. Epis. Reg. 1, fol. 212.
[19] *Angl. Sac.* 1, 375.   [20] Ibid. 377.
[21] *Cal. Papal Let.* iii, 355.
[22] Roch. Epis. Reg. iii, fol. 157d. [23] Ibid. 162d.
[24] *Valor Eccl.* (Rec. Com.), i, 106. The abbey owed £80 to Bishop Fisher at the time of his death (*L. and P. Hen. VIII,* viii, 888, (2)).

Rede was then abbess, and had trouble in the early part of the year in connexion with the stewardship of the abbey, which she had promised to her brother-in-law Sir Thomas Willoughby for his son,[25] and then granted to Sir Edward Wotton, another brother-in-law.[26] Cromwell wished it to be given to his nephew Richard,[27] and Sir Thomas Neville was another applicant,[28] but the king promised it to Thomas Wyatt. Wotton wrote to Cromwell on 27 February to protest against being deprived of it,[29] but soon recognized the uselessness of this, and a week later[30] wrote to say that he had returned his patent to the abbess, who was not at all pleased. This affair was probably one of the reasons that brought about her resignation in the following year. The details are not known; but on 24 September she made application[31] through Sir Thomas Willoughby to Cromwell that she might have the lodging in the monastery which her predecessors 'that have likewise resigned' had had, and also the plate which her father had given her for her chamber. The new abbess was Margaret Vernon, who had shown herself to be a capable administrator when prioress of the recently dissolved nunnery of Little Marlow,[32] but whose principal recommendation was the fact that she was an old personal friend of Cromwell.[33]

When the abbey was seen to be doomed, attempts to secure possession of it were made by Sir Thomas Neville and Sir Thomas Wyatt and others,[34] but we know no more of its history until it was formally surrendered[35] on 29 October, 1538. The abbess asked leave to sell the manor of Cornard to make provision for the nuns instead of pensions, pay off her servants and buy herself a living with such of her friends as would take her;[36] but this was not granted. In the next year pensions were given,[37] of £40 yearly to herself and smaller sums to eleven other nuns, Felex Cockes, Arminal Gere, Margaret Gyles, Joan Randall, Lettice Bucke, Beatrice Wylliams, Juliana Wheatnall, Joan Hull, Elizabeth Pympe, Agnes West, and Rose Morton.

The site of the monastery and most of its possessions, including the manors of West Malling, Ewell, East Malling, Parrock, Leyton, and Great Cornard and the rectories of West Malling, East Malling, and Great Cornard were granted on 28 April, 1540, to the archbishop of Canterbury.[38]

ABBESSES OF MALLING

Avice,[39] the first abbess

Elizabeth de Badlesmere, deposed 1321 [40]

Agnes de Leyburne, elected 1321,[41] died 1324 [42]

Lora de Retlyng, elected 1324,[43] died 1345 [44]

Isabel de Pecham, elected 1345,[44] died 1349 [45]

Benedicta de Grey, elected and died 1349 [46]

Alice de Tendring, elected 1349 [47]

Marjory de Pateshull, died 1369 [48]

Isabel Ruton, occurs 1414 [48a]

Joan, occurs 1420 [49]

Cecily Batesford, died 1439 [50]

Katharine Weston, elected 1439,[51] occurs 1469 [51a]

Joan Mone or Moone, occurs circa 1484,[52] died 1495 [53]

Elizabeth Hulle, elected 1495,[54] died 1524 [55]

Elizabeth Danyell, elected and died 1524 [56]

Elizabeth Rede, elected 1524,[57] resigned 1536 [58]

Margaret Vernon, appointed 1536,[59] the last abbess [60]

The seal[61] of the abbey (fifteenth century) is a pointed oval measuring $2\frac{5}{8}$ by $1\frac{1}{4}$ inches, representing the Virgin, with crown and nimbus, seated in a canopied niche with tabernacle work at the sides, holding the Child on the right knee and a sceptre in the left hand. In base, under a round-headed arch, an abbess with pastoral staff. The inner border engrailed. Legend :—

SIGILLŪ COMMUNE MONA . . . . BEATE MARIE DE MALLING.

[39] Dugdale, *Mon.* iii, 384.
[40] Roch. Epis. Reg. i, fol. 84 *d.*   [41] See above.
[42] Roch. Epis. Reg. i, fol. 64.
[43] Ibid. 65. She was prioress, and fifteen nuns voted for her and twelve for Joan de Chellesfeld, one being absent and one ill. But another version is given above.
[44] Ibid. 220 *d.*   [45] Ibid. 245.
[46] Ibid. 245 *d.*   [47] Ibid. 246.
[48] Ibid. 339. Marjory was abbess in 1355 (ibid. 263).
[48a] Exch. K.R. Acct. bdle. 214, No. 5.
[49] *Cal. Pap. Let.* vii, 337.
[50] Roch. Reg. Epis. iii, fol. 144.
[51] Ibid. 144 *d.* Katharine occurs as abbess in 1480 (*Reg. Roff.* 695).
[51a] Pardon R. 8–9 Edw. IV, m. 4.
[52] Early Chan. Proc. 59 (66).
[53] Roch. Epis. Reg. iv, fol. 10.
[54] Ibid. She was prioress.   [55] Ibid. 111 *d.*
[56] Ibid. 112, 120 She was elected in March, seventeen nuns voting, and died in October.
[57] Ibid. 120 *d.* Fourteen nuns voted. She was a daughter of Sir Robert Rede, chief justice of the Common Pleas (*Dict. Nat. Biog.* xlvii, 374).
[58] *L. and P. Hen. VIII,* xi, 490.
[59] Ibid. She had been prioress of Marlow in Buckinghamshire.
[60] Ibid. xiv (1), p. 599.   [61] B.M. Seals, lxv, 87.

[25] *L. and P. Hen. VIII,* viii, 230.
[26] Ibid. 249.   [27] Ibid. 230.
[28] Ibid. 249.   [29] Ibid. 275.
[30] Ibid. 349.   [31] Ibid. xi, 490.
[32] *V.C.H. Bucks.* i, 359.
[33] Many letters from her are preserved in the *L. and P. Hen. VIII.*
[34] *L. and P. Hen. VIII,* xiii (1), 808, 1228, 1251.
[35] Ibid. xiii (2), 717.   [36] Ibid. 716.
[37] Ibid. xiv (1), p. 599.
[38] Ibid. xv, 613 (32).

12. THE PRIORY OF MINSTER IN SHEPPEY

Sexburga, a daughter of Anna, king of the East Angles, married Ercombert, king of Kent. After his death in 664 she ruled the kingdom until their son Egbert was grown, and then, probably about 670, founded a nunnery at Sheppey, endowed it, and settled there with seventy-seven disciples. About 675, in consequence of a dream, she departed from Sheppey, leaving her daughter Ermenilda in her place, and went to Ely, where she succeeded her sister Etheldreda as abbess in 679. Ermenilda married Wulfhere, king of the Mercians, and succeeded her mother at Ely in 699. Sexburga was afterwards canonized, and eventually shared the dedication of Sheppey with St. Mary.[1]

Very little is known of the intermediate history of the monastery; but Sheppey was a favourite landing-place of the Danes, and it probably suffered severely from them. About the end of the eleventh century, it is said, there were certain nuns at the manor of Newington, whose prioress was strangled in bed at night by her cook, and in consequence the king took the manor into his own hands and removed them to Sheppey.[2] Nothing else is known of this monastery of Newington, and it seems likely that it may have been merely a refuge of some of the nuns from Sheppey. In 1186, Roger, abbot of St. Augustine's, Canterbury, gave to Agnes, prioress of Sheppey, certain tithes in the parish of Bobbing for a rent of 10s. yearly, and in 1188 he gave the tithes of 'Westlonde' for a rent of 14s. yearly.[3]

Henry III in 1225 gave three marks to the prioress in aid of the repair of her houses burnt,[3a] and on 7 April, 1234, granted to the nuns a charter[4] confirming their possessions and liberties in detail, pursuant to a charter of Richard I. Edward III confirmed this in 1329, and at the same time confirmed the tenor of a similar but longer charter of Henry III, which had been carried off when the castle of Leeds was besieged by Edward II, and granted additional liberties.[5] He granted confirmation again in 1343,[6] as the nuns complained that they had been hindered in holding their yearly fair at Minster, and exercising other liberties; and further confirmations were obtained from Richard II in 1381,[7] Henry IV in 1400,[8] Henry V in 1414, Henry VI in 1429,[9]

and Henry VII in 1504.[10] The prioress had complained in 1332 that her pillory in Minster had been cut down,[11] and in 1339 that she had been besieged for more than five days in the priory.[12]

Sir Roger de Northwode, who died in 1286, did much to relieve the poverty of the house, which had fallen into ruin, and was buried before the altar there.[13] In 1303 licence was granted to the prioress and nuns to acquire land from Henry de Northwode to find a chaplain to celebrate divine service daily in their church for the souls of Roger and Bona his wife for ever.[14]

Archbishop Peckham wrote to the prioress and convent on 11 May, 1286, forbidding them to receive secular women, young or old, without his special licence, as the priory had been much troubled before by the long stay of these.[15] Archbishop Winchelsey made a visitation in April, 1296, and ordered that silence should be observed in the choir, cloister, refectory, and dormitory, and that the nuns should not be garrulous or quarrelsome, hold secret conventicles, or acquire money without express licence from the prioress. These faults were to be punished by solitary confinement, and, if necessary, by more severe measures.[16] He gave further orders in 1299 that the nuns were not to leave the monastery, noting that the rule had become very lax on this point.[17] In 1322 the church and cemetery were polluted by bloodshed and required re-consecration.[18] Archbishop Reynolds in 1326 gave orders that disputes with the parishioners of Minster were to cease.[19]

Archbishop John de Stratford in 1340 confirmed the appropriation to the priory of the churches belonging to it; the convent producing as evidence for the church of Minster letters of John de Peckham, archbishop, mentioning that he had inspected letters and muniments of William and Theobald, archbishops, for the church of Bobbing grants of Richard and John, kings of England, and for the church of Gillingham with the chapel of Grain the grant of Richard, archbishop elect of Canterbury. Archbishop William confirmed the same in 1396; and added that as he had found from documents that by the foundation of the priory there should be a prioress and a certain number of canonesses professing the order of St. Augustine, but the prioress and sisters lived under the habit and rule of St. Benedict without professing that order, he restored them to the habit and rule of St. Augustine and

[1] This early history of the house is taken from Wharton, *Anglia Sacra*, i, 595–6, and *Historia Monasterii Sancti Augustini* (Rolls Ser.), 176, 191.
[2] Twysden, *Decem Scriptores*, 1931.
[3] Ibid. 1839.   [3a] Close, 9 Hen. III, m. 14.
[4] Printed in Dugdale, *Mon.* ii, 50.
[5] Chart. 3 Edw. III, No. 38.
[6] Ibid. 17 Edw. III, No. 17.
[7] Pat. 4 Ric. II, pt. 3, m. 19.
[8] Ibid. 1 Hen. IV, pt. 8, m. 8.
[9] Ibid. 8 Hen. VI, pt. 2, m. 37.

[10] Ibid. 20 Hen. VII, pt. 2, m. 12 (18).
[11] Ibid. 6 Edw. III, pt. 2, m. 3 d.
[12] Ibid. 13 Edw. III, pt. 2, m. 17 d.
[13] *Arch. Cant.* ii, 11–12.
[14] Pat. 31 Edw. I, m. 32.
[15] *Reg. Epist. J. Peckham* (Rolls Ser.), iii, 924.
[16] Cant. Archiepis. Reg. Winchelsey, fol. 63, 188b.
[17] Ibid. 75.
[18] Ibid. Reynolds, fol. 128b.
[19] Ibid. fol. 273b.

received the profession of the order from them. His letters were confirmed by Henry IV in 1400.[20] This statement about the order is difficult to understand, as the original monastery could not have belonged to the Augustinian order. Perhaps it may refer to some re-foundation by Archbishop William de Corbeuil, who had himself been an Augustinian canon.

Licence was granted in 1344 for the prioress and convent to appropriate the church of Wichling, but this appears never to have taken effect.[21]

Peter Cleve, who died in 1479, left money for the repair of the chapel of St. John the Baptist, and for the belfry on the priory side and that on the side of the parish church.[22]

Archbishop Warham made a visitation of the priory on 2 October, 1511.[23] Agnes Revers, prioress, said that everything was in good order, except that she doubted whether Avice Tanfeld, chantress, behaved well to the nuns and provided properly for the observances in the choir. She had heard that there had been seventeen nuns, and knew of fourteen, and wished to increase the number to this if she could find any wishing to enter religion. Evidence was also given by Agnes Norton, sub-prioress, Avice Tanfeld, Elizabeth Chatok, Elizabeth Stradlyng, Mildred Wigmor, Dorothy Darell, Agnes Bolney, Anne Petitt, and Ursula Gosborn. These said that they had no maid called the convent servant to serve them with food and drink and other necessaries, but the house was served by an outsider, a woman from the town; there was no infirmary, but those who were ill died in the dormitory; the gate of the cloister was closed too strictly, not only after supper, but at the time of vespers; and the prioress never gave any accounts. One said that the menservants of the prioress spoke contemptuously and dishonestly of the convent. The prioress was ordered to render accounts and to make an inventory, to provide an honest woman servant, to make up the number of the nuns to fourteen as soon as possible, and to build an infirmary at her earliest convenience. The chancel of Bobbing was to be repaired before Midsummer.

The priory is not mentioned in the Taxation of 1291, but in 1385 it owned temporalities worth £66 8s. yearly.[24] In the Valor of 1535 the gross value of its possessions, including the manors of Minster, 'Upberye' in Gillingham, and Pitstock in Rodmersham, the parsonages of Gillingham, Grain, Bobbing and Minster, and the chapel of Queenborough, was £173 9s. 3½d., and the net value £129 7s. 10½d. yearly, besides £10 from a marsh then in dispute

between the priory and Sir Thomas Cheyne.[25] It was accordingly dissolved with the rest of the lesser monasteries, the prioress receiving a pension of £14 yearly.[26] On 27 March, 1536, an inventory[27] was taken of the goods in the church and various chambers of the priory, and of the corn and cattle belonging to it, with a list of the servants of the house and their wages; and eight nuns are mentioned besides the prioress, viz. Agnes Bownes, Marg . . . ocks, Dorothy Toplyve, Anne Loveden, Elizabeth Stradlyng, Anne Clifford, Margaret Ryvers, and Ursula Gosbore, sub-prioress.

The site of the monastery and part of its possessions were granted to Sir Thomas Cheyne in fee on 12 December, 1539.[28]

ABBESSES OF MINSTER IN SHEPPEY

St. Sexburga, circa 670–5[29]
Ermenilda, circa 675–99[29]

PRIORESSES OF MINSTER IN SHEPPEY

Agnes, occurs 1186 [29]
— de Burgherssh, occurs 1343 [30]
Joan de Cobham, died 1368 [31]
Isabel de Honyngton, elected 1368 [32]
Joan Cobham, occurs 1446 [32a]
Agnes Ryvers or Revers, occurs 1504,[33] 1511 [29]
Alice Cranmer [34] or Crane,[35] the last prioress

The names of the following prioresses are given in an obituary list [36]:—
Joan de Badlesmere, died 2 Id. March
Eustachia, died 12 Kal. May
Agnes, died 4 Non. October
Christina, died 13 Kal. October
Gunnora, died 11 Kal. December

The seal [37] (early twelfth century) is a pointed oval measuring 2¾ by 1¾ inches, representing St. Sexburga full-length with mantle and crown, holding in the right hand a sceptre and in the left a book. Legend :—

SIGILLU . . . ANCTE SEXBURGE DE SCAPEIA.

[25] *Valor Eccl.* (Rec. Com.), i, 77.
[26] *L. and P. Hen. VIII*, xiii, (1), p. 576.
[27] Ibid. x, 562, printed in *Arch. Cant.* vii, 290–306.
[28] Ibid. xii (2), 1311 (16).
[29] See above.
[30] Chart. 17 Edw. III, No. 17 ; she was a sister of Bartholomew de Burgherssh.
[31] Cant. Archiepis. Reg. Langham, fol. 64.
[32] Ibid. 65.
[32a] Pardon R. 24–5 Hen. VI, m. 11. Joan occurs in 1437 (ibid. 15 Hen. VI, m. 17).
[33] Pat. 20 Hen. VII, pt. 1, m. 8 (29).
[34] *L. and P. Hen. VIII*, xii (2), 1311 (16).
[35] Ibid. xiii (1), p. 576.
[36] Cott. MS. Faust. B. vi.
[37] B.M. Seals, lxvi, 13.

[20] Pat. 1 Hen. IV, pt. 8, m. 7.
[21] Pat. 18 Edw. III, pt. 1, m. 10.
[22] *Arch. Cant.* xxii, 154.
[23] Cant. Archiepis. Reg. Warham, fol. 42b.
[24] Twysden, *Decem Scriptores*, 2168.

13. THE ABBEY OF MINSTER IN THANET

The story of this house is told by William Thorne[1] and Thomas de Elmham,[2] the latter of whom gives the text of several doubtful charters[3] granted to it by early Kentish kings. Egbert, king of Kent, is said in expiation of the murder of his kinsmen Ethelred and Ethelbert at Eastry with his consent by his servant Thunor to have given land in Thanet to their sister Domneva for the foundation of a monastery. The boundaries were determined by the course taken by a tame doe belonging to her, and Domneva, who is also called Ermenburga and Eabba, built the monastery on the south side of the island near the water and was consecrated abbess by Theodore, archbishop of Canterbury (669–90). She was succeeded on her death by her daughter Mildred,[4] who had earlier been a nun at Chelles near Paris, and who afterwards became the principal Kentish saint with the exception of St. Augustine.

Edburga[5] became abbess on the death of Mildred, and finding the monastery too small she built another near by, which she caused to be dedicated in honour of St. Peter and St. Paul by Cuthbert, archbishop of Canterbury (741–58), and removed the body of Mildred there, the translation producing many miracles. In or before her time Ermengitha, sister of Domneva, built another monastery a mile to the east, but all traces of this had disappeared before Elmham wrote his chronicle.

Edburga died in 751, and in her place Sigeburga was ordained abbess by Cuthbert. The first raid of the Danes took place in her time, and thenceforward little by little the monastery began to decline. She died in 797, and was succeeded by Siledritha, who worked hard at restoration, but was eventually burnt with all her nuns in the monastery by the Danes.

The monastery was again burnt by the Danes in 980,[6] and in 1011 Leofruna, the abbess, was taken captive by Sweyn.[7] After this it was deserted by the nuns and inhabited only by a few clerks; and in 1027 Cnut granted the body of Mildred and all her land to the abbey of St. Augustine, the body being translated to Canterbury on 18 May, 1030.[8]

ABBESSES OF THANET

Domneva
St. Mildred
St. Edburga, died 751 [9]
St. Sigeburga, died 797 [10]
Siledritha
Leofruna, occurs 1011

HOUSE OF CLUNIAC MONKS

14. THE PRIORY OF MONK'S HORTON [1]

The priory of St. John the Evangelist, Horton, was founded as a cell to the priory of Lewes in Sussex, probably early in the reign of Stephen, by Robert de Vere, son of Bernard de Vere and constable of England, and his wife Adelina the daughter of Hugh de Montfort. The founders granted to the priory the manors of Horton and Tinton[2] and the churches of Brabourne in Kent, Purleigh in Essex, and Stanstead in Suffolk, with various lands and liberties ; and decreed that the prior should pay a mark of silver yearly to Lewes as recognition of the authority of the latter house, but might receive whom he chose as novices. Their heir Henry of Essex, constable of England, confirmed the grants and made others. Pope Lucius II granted a bull of confirmation on 11 May, 1144 ; and Stephen and Henry II confirmed the lands and liberties of the priory by charters. The latter mentions a long list of benefactors by name.

The temporalities of the priory in the diocese of Canterbury were valued at £65 10s. yearly in the Taxation of 1291. Licence for the appropriation of the church of Purleigh was granted in 1337[3] and confirmed in 1401,[4] but seems never to have taken effect. The priory seems to have parted with its right in the church of Stanstead at an early date.

[1] Twysden, *Decem Scriptores*, 1906–12.
[2] *Hist. Mon. St. Aug.* (Rolls Ser.), 215–25.
[3] Ibid. 288, 305, 310, 314.
[4] For an account of her life see *Dict. Nat. Biog.* xxxvii, 376.
[5] Ibid. xvi, 305.
[6] *Decem Scriptores*, 1780.
[7] Ibid. 1908.   [8] Ibid. 1783.
[9] *Hist. Mon. St. Aug.* (Rolls Ser.), 220.
[10] Ibid. 221.
[1] Hasted in his account of Horton (*Hist. and Topog. Surv. of Kent*, iii, 318) refers to a register or chartulary of the priory to which he had access, and which is now in the British Museum (Stowe MS. 935). Some of the charters in it are printed in *Arch. Cant.* x, 269–81 from copies in B.M. Harl. MS. 2044 and Add. MS. 5516.

[2] In connexion with this manor the priory had to contribute to the repair of the sea-walls of Romney Marsh (Pat. 18 Edw. II, pt. 2, m. 7).
[3] Pat. 11 Edw. III, pt. 2, m. 2.
[4] Pat. 2 Hen. IV, pt. 2, m. 41.

Horton is mentioned several times in the Cluniac records. In the visitation of England in 1275–6 the visitors were at Horton on Thursday before the feast of St. Lucy.[5] They found eleven monks there, or two below the proper number, and they proposed to make the deficiency good. The mass of St. Mary was not celebrated, and this was ordered to be done daily. The Gospel was to be read by a deacon daily at high mass, as the house was conventual, and there was to be regular reading at dinner in the refectory. The seal of the convent was to be kept by three, and not by two as it had been. They appointed a third for hearing confessions in addition to the prior and sub-prior. Regulations as to boots were made; and the prior and convent were ordered not to eat meat before seculars. The house owed 80½ marks, but everything else was in order.

In 1279 the visitors found thirteen monks at Horton, and the house was in an excellent state. The prior, who was English, had newly roofed the church and extended the cloister.[6]

In 1314 the visitors complained that they were irreverently received and their expenses not paid. The prior disobeyed their command to send a monk to Prittlewell, and when cited to the general chapter to answer for this did not come. The prior of Lewes was ordered to send him to Cluni before Michaelmas to receive punishment. The sacrist had not rents enough properly to supply lights and other ornaments for the church or provide for the sick, and the prior of Lewes was ordered to go to Horton and see that this was amended.[7]

In an enumeration of the Cluniac houses of England (about 1450) it is said that there should be at Horton according to some eight monks, and according to others thirteen. There should be there three masses, the greater and second of St. Mary and the third for the dead.[8]

Horton, being a Cluniac house, was treated as alien and frequently taken into the king's hands during the war with France. In 1295 the prior was allowed to remain in his priory, notwithstanding the order that aliens should be removed from the coast, as it was testified that he was not French.[9] In the account[10] of the keeper of the priory for the time when it was taken into the king's hands in 1325 its stock and expenses are set out in detail. Wages of 3s. weekly were allowed to the prior, and 1s. 6d. to each of seven monks. In 1338[11] the prior paid 40 marks yearly to the king for the custody of the priory during the war; but in

1339[12] he was permitted to hold it without rendering any farm as an alien, as he had shown that he was an Englishman, and neither he nor his predecessors had been bound to pay any tax to any religious house beyond the seas. This favour was probably merely due to the fact that this particular prior was the son of the earl of Surrey, for in 1341 the priory was again treated as alien.[13] In 1373, however, Lewes and its cells were finally made denizen.[14]

In the Valor of 1535 the possessions of the priory, including the parsonage of Brabourne and the manors of Horton and Tinton, were valued[15] at £111 16s. 7d. yearly; but deductions of £16 4s. 5d. in fees and rents brought the net income down to £95 12s. 2d. The priory was accordingly dissolved under the Act of 1536, the prior receiving a pension of £15 yearly.[16]

The site of the priory was leased[17] to Richard Tate of Stockbury on 22 May, 1537; and on 25 April, 1538, it was granted to him in fee.[18]

PRIORS OF HORTON

William,[19] occurs 1144
Adam,[20] occurs 1227
Peter de Aldinge,[21] occurs 1258, 1264
William,[22] occurs 1272, 1278
Geoffrey [22a]
Hugh,[22b] occurs 1282
James, occurs 1297,[23] 1302[24]
Conon, resigned 1320[25]
John, occurs 1324[26]
James, occurs 1310,[26a] 1327[27]
John, occurs 1331[28]
William de Warenna,[29] occurs 1336, 1339

[5] Duckett, *Rec. of Cluni*, i, 124.
[6] Ibid. ii, 144.
[7] Duckett, *Visitations of Cluni*, 301.
[8] *Rec. of Cluni*, ii, 211.
[9] Close, 23 Edw. I, m. 4 d.
[10] Mins. Accts. bdle. 1125, Nos. 18, 20.
[11] Close, 12 Edw. III, pt. 1, m. 20.

[12] Close, 13 Edw. III, pt. 1, m. 2.
[13] Ibid. 15 Edw. III, pt. 3, m. 6 d.
[14] Pat. 47 Edw. III, pt. 1, m. 10.
[15] *Valor Eccl.* (Rec. Com.), i, 41.
[16] *L. and P. Hen. VIII*, xiii (1), p. 577.
[17] Ibid. p. 585.   [18] Ibid. p. 889 (3).
[19] *Arch. Cant.* x, 272.
[20] Feet of F. 11 Hen. III.
[21] Hasted, loc. cit.; Peter occurs in Feet of F. 47 Hen. III.
[22] Hasted, loc. cit.
[22a] Chartul. fol. 44 d.
[22b] Ibid. fol. 45.
[23] Pat. 25 Edw. I, pt. 1, m. 12 d.
[24] Ibid. 30 Edw. I, m. 19.
[25] Ibid. 13 Edw. II, pt. 2, m. 16; he was made prior of Northampton.
[26] Ibid. 18 Edw. II, pt. 2, m. 7.
[26a] Chartul. fol. 30.
[27] Close, 1 Edw. III, pt. 1, m. 9 d.
[28] Ibid. 5 Edw. III, pt. 1, m. 18 d.
[29] Ibid. 10 Edw. III, m. 39 d.; 13 Edw. III, pt. 1, m. 2. He was son of John de Warenna, earl of Surrey, and was soon afterwards made prior of Castleacre by Iterius, abbot of Cluni, with a dispensation from Pope Benedict XII (*Cal. Papal Let.* i, 12, 124, 139).

Hugh Falouns,[30] occurs 1345, 1348
Peter de Tenoleo, occurs 1363 [31]
Peter de Whitsand [32] or Huissant,[33] occurs 1370,[34] 1384, 1401
John Pepynbury, occurs 1416 [34a]

James Holbech, occurs 1438 [35]
William Wynchelse, occurs 1445 [36]
Richard Keter, occurs 1477 [37]
Richard Brysleve [38] or Gloucester,[39] the last prior

HOUSE OF CISTERCIAN MONKS

15. THE ABBEY OF BOXLEY

The abbey of St. Mary, Boxley, was founded, according to Manrique,[1] on 28 October, 1146, by William of Ypres, son of the count of Flanders, and colonized from Clairvaux in France, one of the four principal daughter-houses of Cîteaux. The founder was the ruler of practically the whole of Kent under Stephen, and a man of evil reputation ; and it is said that the Cistercians promised him absolution from his sins if he would give them the manor of Boxley, which the king had given him, for the foundation of a monastery.[2]

The abbey is mentioned occasionally in the early chronicles. In 1171 the abbot was one of those who hastily buried Thomas Becket, the murdered archbishop of Canterbury.[3] In 1175 he attended the council held at Westminster on 18 May.[4] In 1193 the abbots of Boxley and Robertsbridge were sent abroad to search for Richard I, whom they found in Bavaria on Palm Sunday.[5] In 1233 the abbot was appointed with two colleagues by the pope to make a visitation of some exempt Benedictine monasteries ; but this was strongly resented, especially by St. Augustine's, Canterbury, and in consequence the commission was superseded.[6]

In the general Cistercian chapter in 1198 the abbot was sentenced to three days' punishment, one of them on bread and water, for having received gifts from houses where he had made visitations.[6a]

The abbot was summoned to Parliament several times under Edward I, but not afterwards.[7]

Richard I on 7 December, 1189, granted to the monks a charter confirming their possessions, which was renewed by him on 10 November, 1198, and confirmed by Henry III on 24 April, 1253.[8] The latter king also in the same year granted to them free warren in their demesne lands in the counties of Kent and Sussex.[9] These charters were also confirmed by Edward I in 1290,[10] and Edward IV in 1473.[11] In 1279, before the justices in eyre at Canterbury, the abbot claimed [12] various liberties, some of which were allowed, citing the charters of Richard I and Henry III. The jury found, however, that he had no user of free warren except in the manor of Boxley. Edward III on 24 September, 1359, at the request of Richard de Cherteseye, a lay-brother of the abbey, granted to the abbot and convent free warren in certain of their demesne lands.[13]

In the Taxation of 1291 the temporalities of the abbey in the diocese of Canterbury, including the manor of Boxley, were valued at £62 14s. 7d. yearly ; and it also owned temporalities worth £9 4s. 10d. in Hoo, £1 18s. 8d. in London, £1 4s. in Chessington in Surrey, and 13s. 4d. in Yarmouth, making a total of £75 15s. 5d. The church of Stoke was appropriated to it by Richard, bishop of Rochester, in 1244, and confirmed by Pope Clement IV and Boniface, archbishop of Canterbury.[14] The abbot and convent had licence in 1314 to acquire from the Cistercian abbey of Dunes in Flanders land and the advowson of the church of Eastchurch in Sheppey, and to appropriate the

[30] Close, 19 Edw. III, pt. 2, m. 22 d. ; 22 Edw. III, pt. 1, m. 36 d.
[31] Cal. Papal Pet. i, 400. He prayed the pope to make him prior of Prittlewell in Essex, and at the same time Denys de Hopton, sub-prior and almoner of Prittlewell, prayed to be made prior of Horton. Both petitions were granted, but it is not known whether they took effect.
[32] Pat. 8 Ric. II, pt. 1, m. 9.
[33] Rec. of Cluni, i, 184.
[34] Exch. K.R. Alien Priories, 10 (10).
[34a] Stowe MS. 935, fol. 43 d.
[35] Pat. 16 Hen. VI, pt. 2, m. 32 ; Stowe MS. 935, fol. 1. He transcribed the register about the time of Henry VI.
[36] Stowe MS. 935, fol. 77.   [37] Ibid. 77b.
[38] L. and P. Hen. VIII, xiii (1), 577. Richard was prior in 1529 (ibid. iv, 6047).
[39] Valor Eccl. (Rec. Com.), i, 141.
[1] Annales Cistercienses, ii, 48. Lists in Cott. MS. Faust. B. vii, and Vesp. A. vi, and the Louth Park Chron. give the same date. Some annals give the year 1144.

[2] Giraldus Cambrensis, Opera (Rolls Ser.), iv, 201.
[3] Matt. Paris, Hist. Angl. (Rolls Ser.), i, 369.
[4] Walter of Coventry, Memoriale (Rolls Ser.), i, 239.
[5] Ibid. ii, 25.
[6] Matt. Paris, Chron. Maj. (Rolls Ser.), iii, 239 ; Ann. Mon. (Rolls Ser.), iii, 133 ; Cal. Papal Let. i, 132–3.
[6a] Martene, Thesaurus Novus Anecdotorum, iv, 1292.
[7] Report on the Dignity of a Peer, App. 1.
[8] Chart. R. 37 Hen. III, m. 6.
[9] Ibid. m. 14.   [10] Ibid. 18 Edw. I, No. 48.
[11] Pat. 12 Edw. IV, pt. 2, m. 2.
[12] Plac. de Quo Warr. (Rec. Com.), 344.
[13] Chart. R. 33 Edw. III, No. 4.
[14] Thorpe, Reg. Roff. 620-1.

church.[15] They were also pardoned for acquiring lands in mortmain without licence in Boxley, Hoo, and Chingley in 1309,[16] and in Upchurch, Hoo, Chessington, Ticehurst, Goudhurst, Staplehurst, Wrotham, Maidstone, and Eastchurch in 1329.[17] The parish church of Boxley belonged to the cathedral priory of Rochester before the foundation of the abbey. The Cistercians claimed exemption from payment of tithes, but Pope Alexander III ordered the monks to pay the tithes due to the church,[18] and an agreement between the two houses was made in 1180, and confirmed by Richard, archbishop of Canterbury.[19]

A number of accounts[19a] are preserved of obedientiaries of the abbey in the fourteenth and fifteenth centuries, including the bursar, cellarer, sub-cellarer, sacristan and keepers of the bakery, granary, infirmary, and mills; and in these the expenses are set out in considerable detail.

The crown claimed corrodies in the abbey. In 1331, when summoned before the King's Bench to answer for their refusal to admit John Maunsel to a corrody in their house, such as Andrew Trayour, deceased, had, the abbot and convent produced charters of the king's progenitors proving that they held their lands in frankalmoign discharged of all secular charges and demands.[20] But, nevertheless, in 1432 Thomas Barton was sent to the abbey for such maintenance as Richard Durant, deceased, had.[21]

In 1395 the abbots of Stratford, Boxley, and St. Mary Graces held a chapter of the order at London, and visited the other houses in England, Wales, and Ireland by authority of Pope Boniface IX, the abbot of Cîteaux being a schismatic.[22]

In 1411 a chantry was founded at the altar of St. Stephen in the abbey for the souls of John Freningham, Alice his wife, Ralph his father, and Katharine his mother, buried there.[22a]

In 1422 a commission was appointed to inquire whether the abbot and convent had been ejected from any lands belonging to them.[23]

There appear to have been dissensions in the abbey in 1512–13, for Abbot John appealed then to the crown for the arrest of four monks, William Milton, William Sandwich, Robert Blechenden, and John Farham, as rebellious and apostate.[24]

Boxley is best known through its celebrated

Rood of Grace, a cross with an image supposed to be miraculously gifted with movement and speech. More than a century before the Dissolution the abbey is spoken[25] of as 'called the abbey of the Holy Cross of Grace.' Archbishop Warham, writing[26] to Wolsey in connexion with claims against the abbey, says that it was much sought after by visitors to the Rood from all parts of the realm, and so he would be sorry to put it under an interdict. He calls it 'so holy a place where so many miracles be showed.' But the image proved to be a gross imposture. Geoffrey Chamber, employed in defacing the monastery and plucking it down, wrote[27] to Cromwell on 7 February, 1538, that he found in it certain engines and old wire, with old rotten sticks in the back, which caused the eyes to move and stir in the head thereof, 'like unto a lively thing,' and also the nether lip likewise to move as though it should speak, 'which was not a little strange to him and others present.' He examined the abbot and old monks, who declared themselves ignorant of it; and considering that the people of Kent had in time past a great devotion to the image and used continual pilgrimages there, he conveyed it to Maidstone that day, a market day, and showed it to the people, 'who had the matter in wondrous detestation and hatred so that if the monastery had to be defaced again they would pluck it down or burn it.' The image was afterwards taken to London and exhibited during a sermon by the bishop of Rochester at St. Paul's Cross, and then cut to pieces and burnt.[28] The news of the exposure appears to have been widely spread, and probably nothing was more damaging to the case for the monasteries.

Cardinal Campeggio passed the night of Monday, 26 July, 1518, at the abbey on his way to London.[29] Three years later we hear of a priest sent to prison at Maidstone for pulling down writings and seals set up at the abbey against the ill opinions of Martin Luther.[30]

Thomas, abbot of Ford, was commissioned[31] to visit Boxley among other Cistercian houses in 1535, but nothing is known of the result of his visitation. In the Valor[32] of that year the gross value of all the possessions of the abbey, including the manors of Hoo, Ham in Upchurch, Chingley in Goudhurst, and Friern in Chessington, and the parsonages of Eastchurch and Stoke, amounted to £218 19s. 10d. yearly, besides 25 quarters of barley; from which deductions of £14 14s. 11d. were made for rents and fees, leaving the net value £208 4s. 11d. besides the barley. The abbey thus just passed the limit of wealth drawn

[15] Pat. 7 Edw. II, pt. 2, m. 18.
[16] Ibid. 2 Edw. II, pt. 2, m. 12.
[17] Ibid. 3 Edw. III, pt. 1, m. 32.
[18] Materials for Hist. of Becket (Rolls Ser.), v, 129.
[19] Thorpe, Reg. Roff. 178–9.
[19a] Mins. Accts. bdles. 1251–6.
[20] Pat. 5 Edw. III, pt. 2, m. 5.
[21] Close, 10 Hen. VI, m. 5 d.
[22] Pat. 18 Ric. II, pt. 2, m. 21.
[22a] B.M. Add. Chart. 16464; Hist. MSS. Com. Rep. viii, App. 329.
[23] Pat. 1 Hen. VI, pt. 1, m. 28 d.
[24] Chan. Warrants, 1761.

[25] Close, 10 Hen. VI, m. 5 d.
[26] L. and P. Hen. VIII, iv, 299.
[27] Ibid. xiii (1), 231.
[28] Ibid. 339, 348, 754.
[29] Ibid. iv (2), 4333.
[30] Ibid. (3), 1353.
[31] Ibid. viii, 74 (2).
[32] Valor Eccl. (Rec. Com.), i, 79.

for the first dissolution. But it did not survive long; on 29 January, 1538, it was formally surrendered [33] by John Dobbes, abbot, and the convent. A pension of £50 yearly was assigned [34] to the abbot on 12 February and smaller sums to nine others. The site of the monastery and other possessions, including the manors of Boxley, Hoo and Newnham Court, were granted [35] to Sir Thomas Wyatt on 10 July, 1540.

ABBOTS OF BOXLEY

Lambert [36]
Thomas,[37] elected 1152–3
Walter [38]
John [39]
Denis [40]
Robert, occurs 1197,[41] died 1214 [42]
John, elected 1216,[43] resigned 1236 [44]
Simon, occurs 1243 [45]
Alexander, occurs 1248 [45a]
Henry, occurs 1279 [46]
Gilbert, elected 1289 [46a]
Robert, occurs 1303 [47]
William de Romenee, occurs 1345 [48]
John de Heriettisham, occurs 1368 [49]
Richard Shepey, elected 1415 [50]

John, occurs 1446 [51]
John Wormsell, occurs 1474, 1481 [52]
Thomas Essex, occurs 1489 [52a]
Robert Rayfelde or Reyfeld, occurs 1494,[53] 1498 [54]
John, occurs 1513,[55] 1516, 1527 [55a]
John Dobbes, occurs 1533,[56] the last abbot [57]

The seal [58] of the abbey (1336) is of red wax measuring 2½ in.

Obverse.—The Virgin, crowned; in the right hand a cinquefoiled rose, in the left the Child, wearing nimbus and lifting up his right hand in benediction, in his left hand an orb. She is seated on a carved throne under a canopy or arcade of three pointed arches, trefoiled, pinnacled, and crocketed, supported with a column of tabernacle work on either side, in each arch a small quatrefoiled opening containing a saint's head. In base, under a trefoiled arch, with arcading in the spandrels, three monks half-length, in profile to the right in prayer. In the field at the side two box trees. Above the crocketings of the canopy two small birds. Legend in two rings :—

Outer :—SIGILLŪ [COMM]UNE ECC̄E B[E MARIE DE BOXEL]E.

Inner :—SIT BUXUS . . . TIBI [CORDI VIRGO BEATA].

Reverse.—Two abbots standing in two niches with trefoiled arches, each holding a book in the outer and a pastoral staff in the inner hand. Over them a church-like canopy, supported by a slender column in the centre, and at the sides by carved buttresses, pinnacled and crocketed. In the field at the sides two box trees. Legend in two rings :—

Outer :—[QUI LAVDANT HIC TE] DEFENDE [TUOS B]ENEḎCE.

Inner :— . . . . [P̄P̄ICIA FACITO] B[ERNARDE] MARIAM.

Illegible legend on the rim.

[33] L. and P. Hen. VIII, xiii (1), 173.
[34] Ibid. p. 583. [35] Ibid. xv, 942 (49).
[36] Gervase of Cant. Opera (Rolls Ser.), ii, 385. He was blessed abbot by Archbishop Theobald (1139–61).
[37] Ibid. i, 151. He was blessed by the archbishop in Christchurch, Canterbury, on 3 March, 1153.
[38] Ibid. ii, 385. Blessed by Archbishop Theobald.
[39] Ibid. Blessed by Archbishop Richard (1174–84).
[40] Ibid. Blessed by Archbishop Baldwin (1184–90).
[41] Feet of F. Kent, 8 Ric. I.
[42] Ann. Mon. ii, 282.
[43] Harl. MS. 247, fol. 47. He was prior of Robertsbridge.
[44] Ann. Mon. ii, 316. He was made twentieth abbot of Cîteaux, the second Englishman to occupy the position.
[45] Feet of F. Kent, 27 Hen. III.
[45a] Ibid. 32 Hen. III.
[46] Ibid. 7 Edw. I.
[46a] Gervase, op. cit. ii, 294.
[47] Thorpe, Reg. Roff. 622.
[48] Cal. Papal Pet. i, 93.
[49] Carte Misc. (Aug. Off.), vol. i, No. 155. Abbot John was one of the visitors of Meaux Abbey in 1362 (Chronica Monasterii de Melsa [Rolls Ser.], iii, 150), and occurs in 1379 (Anct. Deeds, D. 923), and 1397 (Pat. 20 Ric. II, pt. 3, m. 13).
[50] Cant. Archiepis. Reg. Chicheley, pt. 1, fol. 9b. Richard occurs in 1427 (Pat. 5 Hen. VI, pt. 1, m. 6).

[51] Pardon, R. 24–5 Hen. VI, m. 29.
[52] Brit. Arch. Assoc. Journ. xlvii, 320.
[52a] Harl. R. cc. 16.
[53] Hasted, Hist. and Topog. Surv. of Kent, ii, 124.
[54] Pat. 14 Hen. VII, pt. 3, m. 18 (3). He received a grant of the deanery of the college of Shrewsbury. Robert occurs in 1509 (Pardon R. 1 Hen. VIII, pt. 3, m. 32).
[55] See above.
[55a] Aug. Off. Misc. Bks. xcii, fol. 31 d. 37 d.
[56] L. and P. Hen. VIII, xiii (1), 888 (5).
[57] Ibid. 173.
[58] B.M. Add. Chart. 20008 ; Seals, lxv, 2, 3.

HOUSES OF AUSTIN CANONS

16. THE PRIORY OF BILSINGTON

John Mansel, provost of Beverley, by a charter[1] dated in June, 1253,[2] with a long list of witnesses, states that with the consent of Henry III and the authority of Boniface, archbishop of Canterbury, he has founded a monastery of canons regular professing the rule of St. Augustine, in honour of St. Mary, for the good estate of the king and Queen Eleanor, and has granted in frankalmoign to William, prior, and the canons, as endowment, that part of the manor of Bilsington which he had of the grant of the heirs of Hugh, earl of Arundel, and all his land of Polre, Gozehale, and Ecche. The priory was to be free and subject to no other house, and at times of vacancy the sub-prior and convent might elect a new prior without asking licence from anyone. This and several other charters and documents relating to the priory are to be found in a small chartulary preserved at the British Museum.[3]

The foundation charter was confirmed by a charter of Henry III, dated 12 June, 1253, which was confirmed afterwards by Henry VI in 1444[4] and Edward IV in 1466.[5] Edward I in 1276 confirmed to the convent their rights at vacancies, provided that when they elected a prior they should present him for the royal assent and the confirmation of the archbishop of Canterbury, and that after the prior had been confirmed he should come to the king with letters testimonial.[6]

Henry III on 9 March, 1266, reciting that the priory was vacant and the patronage of it pertained to him by the grant of the founder, committed it to the custody of Simon de Daunteseye, one of the executors of the will of the founder, during pleasure.[7] On 7 June, 1272, he granted the manor and priory of Bilsington to the abbot and canons of St. Mary, Boulogne;[8] though this grant seems not to have taken effect.

Archbishop Peckham wrote to the prior and convent on 26 April, 1284, forbidding them to waste their woods and other possessions without his permission, and adding that if they did not fear canonical censure he would denounce them to the king, their patron.[9]

In the Taxation of 1291 the temporalities of the priory, in Bilsington, Woodnesborough, Newchurch, Brookland, Lydd, Ruckinge, Hinxhill, Eastbridge, Othe, and Woldene, were valued at £33 16s. 5d. yearly. In 1328 the prior and canons had licence to acquire the advowson of the church of Bilsington from the prior and convent of Boxgrave, and to appropriate it.[10] In 1327 they had licence to drain, inclose, and bring into cultivation a salt marsh of 60 acres in Lydd;[11] but the expense was too great for them, and in 1337 they had another licence to lease 40 acres of it in perpetuity to tenants who might drain it.[12]

The priors of Tonbridge and St. Gregory's, Canterbury, gave notice of intended visitation of the priory of Bilsington in 1353, by authority of the Augustinian chapter.[13]

By an inquisition[14] taken in 1372 it was found that the priory was of the king's foundation to find seven canons to celebrate for the king and his progenitors, and that for four years past there had been no priests there except the prior and one canon, and the canon celebrated in the parish church, which was appropriated to the priory. The prior was bound to find a canon to celebrate for the souls of Thomas de Meyne and his ancestors for certain lands in Lede given by him for that cause, but the prior was a common merchant and went to all fairs to trade, and no mass was celebrated for the souls. It does not appear whether the prior was properly called to account for his shortcomings.

Archbishop Arundel issued injunctions after a visitation in 1402, in which he forbade the entry of women, as observed by him, and sales of wood without the consent of the archbishop. The prior was further ordered to show the state of the house.[15]

In 1510 the archbishop held an inquiry by request, when it was found that William Tilman, the prior, had run the house into debt and neglected his spiritual duties. The prior of Leeds, who had been induced to endorse the bills of the prior of Bilsington, begged that the goods of the monastery might be sequestrated with a view to the speedy clearing off of the debt. The archbishop thereupon granted a decree of sequestration against Bilsington.[16]

The oath of acknowledgement of the royal supremacy was taken on 26 December, 1534,

---

[1] Printed in Dugdale, *Mon.* vi, 492.
[2] Matthew Paris (*Chron. Maj.* v, 691) mentions the foundation, but assigns it to the year 1258.
[3] Add. MS. 37018.
[4] Pat. 23 Hen. VI, pt. 2, m. 13.
[5] Pat. 5 Edw. IV, pt. 3, m. 23.
[6] Pat. 4 Edw. I, m. 20.
[7] Pat. 50 Hen. III, m. 24.
[8] Pat. 56 Hen. III, m. 10.
[9] *Reg. Epist. J. Peckham* (Rolls Ser.), ii, 709.

[10] Pat. 2 Edw. III, pt. 2, m. 21.
[11] Pat. 1 Edw. III, pt. 1, m. 32.
[12] Pat. 11 Edw. III, pt. 3, m. 13.
[13] *Cal. Bodleian Chart.* 135.
[14] Inq. a.q.d. 51 Edw. III, No. 28.
[15] Cant. Archiepis. Reg. Arundel, i, fol. 409b.
[16] *Hist. MSS. Com. Rep.* ix, App. pt 1, 120a.

by John, prior, and six others.[17] In the Valor of 1535 the gross value of the possessions of the priory, including the manors of Belgar in Lydd and Over Bilsington, is given as £122 0s. 8d. yearly, and the deductions amounted to £40 19s. 1¾d., leaving the net value £81 1s. 6d. (sic) yearly.[18] The house would thus have come under the operation of the Act of Dissolution of the next year; but, as happened in a few other cases, this was anticipated, and the prior and convent surrendered on 28 February, 1536.[19] A pension of £10 yearly was afterwards given to the prior.[20]

The site of the priory was leased on 29 July, 1537, to Anthony Seyntleger;[21] and on 31 July, 1538, the reversion of this and most of its possessions were granted to the archbishop of Canterbury.[22]

PRIORS OF BILSINGTON

William, occurs 1253 [23]
Walter, occurs 1255 [24]
John de Romenale, elected 1276 [25]
Hamo de Clopton, elected 1279 [26]
John de Sandwyco, elected 1293,[27] died 1317 [28]
Simon de Hauekeshell, elected 1317,[28] resigned 1320 [29]
John de Wy, elected 1320 [29]
John de Romene, elected 1342,[30] died 1349 [31]
Edmund de Cantuaria, elected 1349,[31] resigned 1361 [32]
John de Aldham, elected 1361,[33] resigned 1363 [34]
John de Romene, elected 1363 [34]
Thomas Brenchesle, elected 1390 [35]
John Broke, elected 1411,[36] resigned 1426 [37]
William Peers or Pyers, elected 1426 [38]
Roger Erle, elected 1435 [39]

William Mungeham, elected 1439 [40]
Hamo Betrysden, elected 1441 [41]
Laurence Wattes, elected 1442 [42]
Paul Pyre, elected 1457 [43]
Robert Carpenter, elected 1460,[44] occurs 1470 [45]
Thomas Andrewe, elected 1491,[45a] occurs 1501 [46]
William Tilman, occurs 1510 [46a]
William Tiseherste, resigned 1513 [47]
Richard Cotyndone, elected 1513 [48]
Arthur Sentleger, resigned 1528 [49]
John Tenterden or Moyse, appointed 1528,[50] the last prior [51]

The seal [52] of the priory (fourteenth century) is a pointed oval measuring 2¾ by 1¾ inches. In a carved niche with three trefoiled canopies, pinnacled and crocketed, the coronation of the Virgin; an angel issuing from above and placing the crown on her head. The background diapered. In the base, under an arcaded corbel, the founder turning to the right, holding a model of the church, and a group of kneeling canons. Legend:—

SIGILLŪ CŌMUNE ECCLIE B̄E MARIE DE BILSINGTONE

17. THE PRIORY OF ST. GREGORY, CANTERBURY

The foundation of this house is by common consent attributed to Lanfranc, archbishop of Canterbury (1070–89), but different accounts of its original status are given. Eadmer says that he built the church on the opposite side of the road to St. John's Hospital, and placed canons in it to minister to the infirm there.[1] Gervase speaks of it as having been originally a hospital.[2] William of Malmesbury says that Lanfranc placed canons regular in it;[3] but there is good evidence that the order was unknown in

---

[17] L. and P. Hen. VIII, vii, 1594 (6).
[18] Valor Eccl. (Rec. Com.), i, 50.
[19] L. and P. Hen. VIII, ix, 816 (5).
[20] Ibid. xiii (1), p. 577.   [21] Ibid. p. 586.
[22] Ibid. 1519 (68).   [23] See above.
[24] Close, 4 Edw. III, m. 17.
[25] Pat. 4 Edw. I, m. 6. He was a canon of Leeds.
[26] Pat. 7 Edw. I, m. 6.
[27] Pat. 21 Edw. I, m. 18.
[28] Pat. 10 Edw. II, pt. 1, m. 30.
[29] Pat. 14 Edw. II, pt. 1, m. 13.
[30] Pat. 16 Edw. III, pt. 2, m. 26; he was sacrist.
[31] Pat. 23 Edw. III, pt. 3, m. 24.
[32] Pat. 35 Edw. III, pt. 2, m. 24.
[33] Ibid. He was a canon of Leeds and was appointed by the archbishop, to whom the convent resigned their right of election.
[34] Pat. 37 Edw. III, pt. 1, m. 27.
[35] Pat. 13 Ric. II, pt. 2, m. 8.
[36] Pat. 13 Hen. IV, pt. 1, m. 21. He was sub-prior.
[37] Cant. Archiepis. Reg. Chicheley, i, fol. 46b.
[38] Ibid.; Pat. 5 Hen. VI, pt. 1, m. 19, 17.
[39] Pat. 13 Hen. VI, m. 8, 1.

[40] Pat. 17 Hen. VI, pt. 2, m. 13.
[41] Pat. 19 Hen. VI, pt. 2, m. 23.
[42] Pat. 20 Hen. VI, pt. 3, m. 21. He was a canon of Combwell.
[43] Pat. 36 Hen. VI, pt. 1, m. 7.
[44] Pat. 38 Hen. VI, pt. 2, m. 3. Robert occurs as prior in 1466 (Pat. 5 Edw. IV, pt. 3, m. 23) and 1479 (Pat. 19 Edw. IV, m. 22 d.).
[45] Hist. MSS. Com. Rep. vi, App. 543.
[45a] Pat. 7 Hen. VII, m. 33 (4).
[46] Dugdale, Mon. vi, 492.   [46a] See above.
[47] Thorpe, Reg. Roff. 331. He became abbot of Lesnes.
[48] Cant. Archiepis. Reg. Warham, fol. 349b.
[49] L. and P. Hen. VIII, iv, 4557. He appears to have become prior of Leeds.
[50] Ibid.   [51] Ibid. ix, 816 (5).
[52] B.M. Seals, lxv, 1.
[1] Eadmeri Historia (Rolls Ser.), 16.
[2] Gervase of Canterbury, Opera (Rolls Ser.), ii, 368.
[3] Gesta Pontificum (Rolls Ser.), 72.

England until the settlement at the priory of St. Botolph at Colchester in the time of Anselm, Lanfranc's successor ; and the version of Leland [4] that Lanfranc placed secular canons there, and William,[5] archbishop of Canterbury (1123–36), replaced them by canons regular, is probably correct. The possessions of the clerks of St. Gregory's are mentioned in the Domesday Survey.[6] Lanfranc's foundation charter and others are given in a chartulary preserved in the University Library at Cambridge.[6a]

Gervase records that the church was burnt on 2 July, 1145,[7] and in 1241 it suffered from the violence of the party of the archdeacon of Canterbury in his dispute with the chapter of Christchurch.[8]

Archbishop Hubert (1193–1205) granted to the convent a charter [9] confirming its possessions, including a long list of churches, Northgate, Westgate, and St. Dunstan's, Canterbury ; Thanington, Waltham, Bethersden, 'Lyvyngsborne' (Beakesbourne), Nackington, Stalisfield, Oare, and Elmsted, and various tithes. In the Taxation of 1291 the priory is said to own temporalities worth £25 15s. yearly in the diocese of Canterbury and £2 in Northfleet. Henry de Clyf had licence [10] in 1326 to grant land in Nackington to the prior and convent in aid of the maintenance of a chaplain to celebrate divine service daily in their church for the souls of himself and his ancestors ; and John Mot had licence [11] in 1392 to grant land in Chartham, Harbledown, and Thanington to them to find a lamp burning daily before the altar at high mass.

William de Brichull was sent by the king in 1309 to the prior and convent to have the necessaries of life in food and clothing during his life.[12]

On 31 May, 1329, the great seal of England was given into the custody of Henry de Clyf, who sealed writs with it in the priory ; [13] and on 13 June he gave it back again in the hall in the priory, where the chancellor was lodged.[14] John Knyvet, chancellor, sealed charters, letters patent, and writs with the great seal on 1 September, 1372, in the priory.[15]

Archbishop Reynolds found many defects at his visitation in March, 1326, and suspended the prior.[15a] There were further disturbances in the

priory in 1330, and the prior of Christchurch and others, appointed by the archbishop to correct matters, ordered the removal of three canons, sending Robert de Wenchepe to the priory of Combwell, and John de Hagh and Adam de Wenchepe to Bentley in Middlesex, where the priory had property, under the charge of J. de Merston, one of the canons.[16] John and Adam were not to go out except to look after the property of the house,[17] but nevertheless were afterwards reproved for breaking bounds.[18] Richard atte Notebeame, another canon, was imprisoned about the same time, probably in connexion with the same affair, and appealed to the archbishop, who ordered his case to be inquired into ; but it was found in January, 1331, that he had broken the treasury at night and carried off goods of the priory and then fled in secular habit, but was taken and brought back and imprisoned in consequence.[19] Robert de Wenchepe was afterwards in 1340 ordered by the archbishop to be sent to the priory of Leeds, but the chapter of Christchurch interceded for him on the ground that when he was treasurer he had done well in his office.[20]

The prior of St. Gregory's was appointed visitor of the Augustinian houses in the dioceses of Canterbury and Rochester with the prior of Tonbridge in 1353,[21] and with the prior of Leeds in 1356.[22]

Archbishop Langham at a visitation in February, 1368, found that the rule of silence was not observed and that women had access to the priory, and ordered both these points to be corrected.[23]

Archbishop Warham made a visitation [24] of the priory in 1511 ; when Thomas Well or Wellys had been prior for six years and Walter Canterbury was sub-prior, Edmund Faversham sacrist, and William Tailor precentor, with six other canons, including a student of Cambridge. The sub-prior said that the precentor was fond of quarrelling with the brethren, and feared that if he were allowed to remain in office much contention would arise ; in the absence of the prior and sub-prior he acted as president of the chapter, but there were others better fitted for this office. The prior only gave a general account to the brethren, not the items, so they could not know the state of the priory. Others corroborated his evidence. One said that the prior did not give his account in writing, but only verbally, and also that the butler gave the brethren very bad beer ; another that the precentor was unfit for office, as he did not know how to sing ; and a third that

---

[4] *Collectanea*, i, 84.
[5] He had himself been an Augustinian canon at St. Osyth's.   [6] V.C.H. Kent, iii.
[6a] Ll. ii, 15. An abstract is given in the *Catalogue of the library* (1861), iv, 28–43.
[7] Op. cit. i, 130.   [8] Ibid. ii, 182.
[9] Printed in Dugdale, *Mon.* vi, 615.
[10] Pat. 20 Edw. II, m. 15.
[11] Pat. 16 Ric. II, pt. 1, m. 32.
[12] Close, 2 Edw. II, m. 6 d.
[13] Ibid. 3 Edw. III, m. 20 d.   [14] Ibid. 19 d.
[15] Ibid. 46 Edw. III, m. 12 d.
[15a] Cant. Archiepis. Reg. Reynolds, fol. 147b.

[16] *Lit. Cant.* (Rolls Ser.), i, 336–9.
[17] Ibid. 344.   [18] Ibid. 346.
[19] Ibid. 343.   [20] Ibid. ii, 218.
[21] *Cal. Bodleian Charters* (ed. Turner and Coxe), 134–5.   [22] Ibid. 139.
[23] Cant. Archiepis. Reg. Langham, fol. 76b.
[24] Ibid. Warham, fol. 35 b.

they had no bell-ringer, so that the brethren did not know the time of divine service. The prior and other officers were ordered to show their accounts annually in writing, and also to show them to the bishop on 1 April with an inventory of the goods of the priory at the time of the prior's accession to office. Tailor was forbidden to quarrel, under pain of removal from office.

The prior resigned in 1533, and Cromwell endeavoured to secure the succession of a nominee of his own. Cranmer wrote to him in answer on 6 May that he was resolved to prefer to the office a member of the same house if fit, or if not fit, the fittest he could find ; and asked for further details, trusting that Cromwell would oppose the unseasonable ambition of men of the church and consider how unreasonable a thing it was for any man to labour for his own promotion.[25] The abbot of Waltham pressed the candidature of John Symkyns, cellarer of St. Bartholomew's, Smithfield[26] ; and the latter got the post, writing to thank Cromwell on 3 December.[27]

The oath of acknowledgement of the royal supremacy was taken on 9 January, 1535, by John, prior, and six other canons, Thomas Wellys, Christopher Cherche, Gregory Botolfe, Nicholas Champyon, Thomas Cawntterbury, and William Hamond.[28]

In the Valor of that year the possessions of the priory, including the manor of Howfield in Chartham, the manors and rectories of Bethersden, Waltham, and Nackington, and the rectories of Stalisfield, Elmsted, and Beakesbourne, amounted[29] to the value of £166 4s. 5½d. yearly ; and deductions of £44 9s. 4½d. for rents, alms, pensions and fees brought the net income down to £121 15s. 1d. The priory was accordingly dissolved under the Act of 1536, the prior receiving a pension of 20 marks yearly.[30]

PRIORS OF ST. GREGORY'S, CANTERBURY

Richard, occurs c. 1183,[31] resigned 1187[31a]
Dunstan, occurs 1198[32]
Robert de Oseneye, elected 1213[33]
Peter, occurs 1223[34]
Elias de Dierham, occurs 1225[35]
Thomas, occurs 1227[36]

Nicholas de Shotindon, elected 1241[37]
Robert, occurs 1253[38]
Hugh, occurs 1263[38a]
William Pig, occurs 1271[39]
Henry, occurs 1275, 1278[33a]
Guy, died 1294[40]
Elias de Sandwyco, elected 1294[41]
William de Lyndstede, elected 1301[42]
John, occurs 1325[43]
Thomas, occurs 1340[44]
Robert de Wenchepe, died 1349[38a]
William atte Thorne, elected 1349,[38a] died 1378[45]
Thomas Rauf, elected 1378[45]
John de Bedynden, died 1409[46]
William Cauntirbury, elected 1409[46]
William Surrenden, resigned 1426[47]
Thomas Kenyngton, elected 1426,[57] occurs 1460[48]
William Egyrton, occurs c. 1470[49]
Edward Gyldford[38a]
Clement Harding[38a]
Edward, occurs 1486[49a]
Thomas Welles, elected 1505,[50] occurs 1151[50]
William Braborne, occurs 1528[38a]
John Symkyns, elected 1535,[51] the last prior[52]

The seal[53] (thirteenth century) of the priory measures 2⅞ in.

Obverse.—In a niche with trefoiled arch topped with a small cross and supported on slender columns Lanfranc seated on a throne with mitre and pall, lifting up the right hand in benediction and holding in the left a crosier, between two saints seated on thrones in smaller niches at the sides, that on the right being Edburga. Legend :—

SIGILLUM CONVENTUS ECCLESIE S . . . . .
NTUARIE.

Reverse.—A geometrical design of circles inclosing quatrefoiled flowers.

[25] L. and P. Hen. VIII, vi, 447.
[26] Ibid. 449.   [27] Ibid. 1495.
[28] Ibid. viii, 31.
[29] Valor Eccl. (Rec. Com.), i, 24.
[30] L. and P. Hen. VIII, xiii (1), p. 576.
[31] Thorpe, Reg. Roff. 170.
[31a] Hasted, op. cit. He became abbot of Cirencester.
[32] Feet of F. Kent, 10 Ric. I.
[33] Ann. Mon. (Rolls Ser.), iii, 41. After a few years he resigned and became a monk of Clairvaux.
[34] Feet of F. Kent, 7 Hen. III.
[35] Arch. Cant. vi, 211.
[36] Feet of F. Kent, 11 Hen. III.

[37] Pat. 25 Hen. III, m. 6. Nicholas occurs as prior in 1248 (Feet of F. Kent, 32 Hen. III).
[38] Feet of F. Kent, 37 Hen. III.
[38a] Hasted, op. cit.
[39] Feet of F. Kent, 55 Hen. III.
[40] Pat. 22 Edw. I, m. 19   [41] Ibid. m. 14.
[42] Cant. Archiepis. Reg. Winchelsey, fol. 284b.
[43] Close, 18 Edw. II, m. 19 d.
[44] Ibid. 14 Edw. III, pt. 2, m. 30 d.
[45] Cant. Archiepis. Reg. Sudbury, fol. 47.
[46] Ibid. Arundel, ii, fol. 122.
[47] Ibid. Chicheley, i, fol. 43.
[48] De Banco R. Easter, 38 Hen. VI, 314.
[49] Early Chan. Proc. bdle. 46, No. 399 ; bdle. 57, No. 64.
[49a] De Banco R. Mich. 2 Hen. VII, 62.
[50] See above. He had previously been prior of Bicknacre in Essex for rather less than a year (V.C.H. Essex, ii, 146), and before that a canon of St. Gregory's. For a short account of him see Arch. Cant. xiv, 164.
[51] See above.
[52] L. and P. Hen. VIII, xiii (1), p. 576.
[53] B.M. Seals, lxv, 14, 15.

18. THE PRIORY OF COMBWELL [1]

The monastery of St. Mary Magdalen, Combwell, was founded as an abbey by Robert de Turneham in the reign of Henry II.[2] His son Stephen de Turneham by a charter [3] which was confirmed by Henry III in 1227,[4] and by Richard II in 1381,[5] confirmed the grant by his father of 'Henle,' the site of the abbey, the churches of Thornham and Brickhill (Bucks.) and various lands; and added further lands and tithes. The grants of the founder were confirmed by a charter [6] of Walkelin de Maminot, his over-lord; and several grants by Stephen and his daughter Mabel de Gatton are preserved. Richard, archbishop of Canterbury (1174–84), at the petition of Stephen granted the church of Thornham to the monastery after the death of the incumbent and settled a dispute between the latter and Stephen.[7]

The same archbishop confirmed the gift of the advowson of the church of Biausfeld (Whitfield near Dover) by Denise [8]; and about the same time William son of Helto granted the church of Aldington.[9] Richard de Lunguil granted the church of Little Woolstone (Bucks.) [10]; and William son of Walter de Hevre the church of Hever,[11] his grant being confirmed by Archbishop Stephen in 1225.[12] The monastery also owned the church of Benenden [13]; and in the Taxation of 1291 its temporalities were valued at £20 15s. 10d. yearly in the diocese of Canterbury and £3 3s. in the diocese of Rochester.

About 1220 the possessions of Combwell were found to be too small properly to maintain its estate as an abbey. Abbot William was induced to resign, being in bad health, and with the consent of Mabel de Gatton, the patroness, and Stephen, archbishop of Canterbury, the house was reduced to a priory, the rights of the patroness and archbishop being reserved.[14] The advowson descended later to the family of Say, and in 1432 it came into the possession of Sir John Fenys.[15]

Henry III on 6 July, 1227, granted to the prior and convent a fair yearly at Combwell on the feast and the morrow of St. Mary Magdalen [16];

and on 5 February, 1232, he granted to them a market there on Fridays,[17] but on 27 February, 1233, altered the day to Tuesday.[18]

The abbot of Bayham charged the prior and convent with having deserted the Premonstratensian order; and Clement, abbot of Prémontré, in 1229 referred the matter to the archbishop of Canterbury, who decided in 1230 after a visitation that they followed the rule of St. Augustine as practised at Waltham.[19]

In 1317 Robert Henry, a servant of the king and his father, was sent to the priory to receive maintenance in food and clothing according to the requirements of his estate.[20]

The prior of Combwell was visitor with the prior of Leeds of the Augustinian houses in the dioceses of Canterbury and Rochester in 1311 and 1317 [21]; and in 1353 the priory of Combwell was visited by the priors of Leeds and Tonbridge.[22]

Archbishop Langham made a visitation of the priory on 3 July, 1368, when many charges were brought against the prior. He had gone to Rome without leave, had sold corrodies and wood improvidently, led an immoral life, followed the advice not of his brethren but of secular officials, and wasted the stock of the priory. He was ordered to render an account, and was admonished.[23] A similar state of things was found by Archbishop Courtenay at another visitation on 16 September, 1387.[24] Roger Tyshurst, prior, was absent, having gone away on Tuesday before St. Laurence and taken goods of the priory with him. He was charged with having cut down trees and made dilapidations, and with being adulterous and apostate; and was removed from office, but received back into the priory as canon. Simon Mudiston succeeded him as prior; but after a long suit at Rome Roger obtained a definitive sentence by which Simon was condemned and he himself restored. Simon was excommunicated for obstinacy, but at last in 1395 was received back into the church.[25]

Archbishop Warham made a visitation of the priory in 1512. Thomas Patenden had been prior for thirty-two years, and there were six other canons, who stated in their evidence that the infirmary was in great need of repairs and nobody attended to the sick, who had to lie in the dormitory. They had not enough food and drink or clothing, the prior never rendered any accounts, and there was no teacher of grammar. The manors of Benenden and Thornham needed

---

[1] In the parish of Goudhurst.
[2] A large number of early charters relating to this monastery are preserved at the College of Arms, and the more important of these have been printed in *Arch. Cant.* v, 194–222; vi, 190–222; viii, 271–293. Several are to be found in the Harleian collection.
[3] Printed in Dugdale, *Mon.* vi, 413.
[4] Chart. 11 Hen. III, pt. 2, m. 9.
[5] Pat. 4 Ric. II, pt. 2, m. 30.
[6] *Arch. Cant.* v, 196.   [7] Ibid. 201.
[8] Ibid. vi, 192.   [9] Ibid. 190.
[10] Ibid. 201.   [11] Ibid. 209.
[12] Ibid. 211.
[13] Ibid. 196; Feet of F. Kent, 11 Hen. III.
[14] *Arch. Cant.* v, 213, 214.
[15] Close, 11 Hen. VI, m. 20 d.
[16] Chart. R. 11 Hen. III, pt. 2, m. 9.

[17] Ibid. 16 Hen. III, m. 14.
[18] Ibid. 17 Hen. III, m. 11.
[19] *Arch. Cant.* viii. 283–5.
[20] Close, 10 Edw. II, m. 10 d.
[21] *Cal. Bodleian Charters* (ed. Turner and Coxe), 125, 128.
[22] Ibid. 135.
[23] Cant. Archiepis. Reg. Langham, fol. 79b.
[24] Ibid. Courtenay, fol. 168b.
[25] *Cal. Papal Let.* iv, 522.

ST. GREGORY'S PRIORY,
CANTERBURY.
(12th Century.)

BILSINGTON PRIORY.
(14th Century.)

ROGER DE LA LEE,
PRIOR OF CHRISTCHURCH,
CANTERBURY.
(1239-44.)

LEEDS PRIORY.
(12th Century.)

COMBWELL PRIORY.
(13th Century.)

great repairs. John Lanny said that the prior and convent laid him under a debt of £40 in an obligation without any condition to two outsiders, now remaining in the hands of the minister of Mottenden, and arranged that the house should not be indebted by this. The prior said that the obligation was cancelled, and was ordered to show it to the archbishop ; and he was also ordered to make a proper account and inventory, to make sufficient repairs to the infirmary before All Saints and to correct the other points mentioned.[26]

The oath of acknowledgement of the royal supremacy was taken on 23 December, 1534, by Thomas Vyncent, prior, and five other canons.[27] In the Valor of the next year the net value of the possessions of the priory, including the manors of Lofeherst in Staplehurst, Hoke in Thornham and Coldred, was only £80 17s. 5¼d. yearly ;[28] and it was consequently suppressed in 1536, the prior receiving a pension of £10 yearly.[29]

The site and possessions of the priory were granted on 20 November, 1537, to Thomas Culpeper in tail male ;[30] and, after his attainder, on 2 April, 1542, to Sir John Gage in tail male.[31]

ABBOTS OF COMBWELL

Hurso, the first abbot [32]
Andrew [33]
John [34]
William, resigned c. 1220 [35]

PRIORS OF COMBWELL

Hugh, occurs 1227 [36]
Henry, occurs 1236 [37]
Robert, occurs 1249 [38]
Walter, occurs 1271 [39]
John de Meredenn, occurs 1275 [39a]
John de Lose, elected 1315 [40]
Stephen, died 1324 [41]
John de Hawe or Hagh, appointed 1324,[42] died 1363 [43]

William de Chert, elected 1363 [44]
Roger Tyshurst, occurs 1387,[45] 1395,[46] 1399 [47]
Simon Mudiston [47a]
William Bourgeys, died 1420 [48]
Henry Talo, elected 1420 [49]
Henry Cranebroke, occurs 1460 [49]
Thomas Chester, occurs 1476 [49a]
Thomas Patenden, c. 1480, occurs 1512,[50] died 1513 [51]
Thomas Vincent, elected 1513,[51] the last prior [52]

The seal [53] (late twelfth century) is a pointed oval measuring 2¼ by 1¾ in., representing the head of St. Mary Magdalen with nimbus and long hair under a round-headed arch of a church, having a central tower topped with a cross, and two smaller side towers. Legend :—

SIC' SATE MARIE MAGDAL' D CUMBWELL.

Another seal [54] (1133 for 1233).

Obverse.—The church of the monastery with a large trefoiled arch having in the pediment a circular panel and two small trefoiled panels, each containing a head, and two narrow windows, with a circular tower, at each side. Under the arch St. Mary Magdalen at the feet of our Lord, who is seated at a banqueting table between two disciples, each with nimbus. On the front edge of the table the inscription

MARIA FIDES TUA TE SALVAM FECIT.

Below the table on the right are the demons who have been cast out of the saint, and in the centre a small box of precious ointment. In the field over the roof on the left a crescent inclosing a star, on the right a wavy star. Legend :—

SIGILL' ECCLESIE SANCTE MARIE MAGDALENE DE CUMBWELL.

Reverse.—Our Lord appearing after His resurrection to St. Mary Magdalen in the garden, holding in His right hand a long cross with banner, the saint prostrating herself before Him under two trees. Over the group a carved, round-headed arch, supported by two clustered shafts with pinnacles. In the field on each side a small round panel containing a head. Legend:—

FACTUM ANNO GRATIE Mº Cº XXX TERCIO MENSE NOVEMBRI.

[26] Cant. Archiepis. Reg. Warham, fol. 44.
[27] L. and P. Hen. VIII, vii, 1594 (5).
[28] Valor Eccl. (Rec. Com.), i, 87.
[29] L. and P. Hen. VIII, xiii, (1), p. 577.
[30] Ibid. xii (2), 1150 (31).
[31] Ibid. xvii, 285 (11).
[32] Arch. Cant. v, 197.
[33] Chart. R. 13 Edw. I, No. 72.
[34] Gervase of Canterbury, Opera (Rolls Ser.), ii, 405. He was blessed abbot by Archbishop Baldwin (1184–90).
[35] Arch. Cant. v, 214.
[36] Feet of F. Kent, 11 Hen. III.
[37] Ibid. 20 Hen. III.
[38] Ibid. 33 Hen. III.   [39] Ibid. 55 Hen. III.
[39a] Harl. Chart. 78. A. 19.
[40] Cant. Archiepis. Reg. Reynolds, fol. 52.
[41] Ibid. 253b.
[42] Ibid. Guy de Natyngton was elected, but renounced the election.   [43] Ibid. Islip, fol. 190b.
[44] Ibid.   [45] See above.
[46] Cal. Papal Let. iv, 522.
[47] Ibid. v, 193. Roger occurs in 1409 (Harl. Chart. 75. G. 1).   [47a] See above.
[48] Cant. Archepis. Reg. Chicheley, ii, fol. 349.
[49] De Banco, R. Hil. 38 Hen. VI, 212.
[49a] Harl. Chart. 76. F. 13.   [50] See above.
[51] Cant. Archepis. Reg. Warham, fol. 349.
[52] L. and P. Hen. VIII, xiii (1), p. 577.
[53] B.M. Seals, lxv, 35.   [54] Ibid. 36, 37.

19. THE PRIORY OF LEEDS

The priory of St. Mary and St. Nicholas, Leeds, was founded by Robert de Crepido Corde or Crevequer in 1119.[1] By one charter[2] he made a grant of the site for the foundation, and by another he granted to the canons the advowsons of all the churches of his land, viz. Leeds, Goudhurst, Lamberhurst, Farleigh, Teston, Chatham, and Rainham; and charters were also granted by Daniel his son, Robert his grandson and several others of the family. Among the liberties included in the grants were a fair at Chatham (afterwards surrendered to Edward I), the right to take hares, rabbits, partridges and the like in the demesne lands, full power to dispose of the possessions in times of the vacancy of the priorship, and the right to elect a prior without asking licence. The advowson of the priory passed from the Crevequer family to the crown in the latter part of the thirteenth century.[3] It was granted to Bartholomew de Badlesmere in 1318,[4] but afterwards came back to the crown.

The charters mentioned above and several others are set out in full in long charters of confirmation by Edward I in 1285[5] and Edward III in 1367.[6] In addition to lands and rents, Leeds received a large number of churches, some of which it secured full possession of, while it had ultimately to be content with pensions from others. Henry I granted the church of Chart, which was appropriated to the priory in 1320.[7] Edward I granted the church of Little Peckham, appropriated in 1387.[8] Daniel de Crevequer granted a moiety of the church of Hallaton (Leicestershire), which the convent afterwards parted with.[9] Elias de Crevequer granted the churches of Thanet (Sarre) and Etchingham; William son of Hamo the church of Ditton; John de Bouton, son of Basilia de Bendevill, the church of (East) Barming; Henry de Bockton the churches of Boughton Monchelsea, and South Hanningfield (Essex); William de Morestun the church of Emley; William de Cusington the church of Acrise; Simon son of Peter de Borden the church of Borden, confirmed by John in 1205;[10] Ascelina de Wodenesbergh the church of Woodnesborough; Hugh, lord of Bergested, the church of Bearsted; and William son of Helto the church of Stockbury, which the

convent had licence to appropriate in 1340.[11] Hamo son of Richard de Ottringbery granted the church of Wateringbury;[12] Eugenia Picot the churches of Ham and Chillenden;[13] and the priory also owned a pension from the church of Mereworth.[14] The temporalities were valued in the Taxation of 1291 at £37 18s. yearly, lying in Leeds, Rainham, Borden, Orpington, Tonge, Sheppey, Cranbrook, Woodnesborough, Boxley, Chart, Langley, Goudhurst, and Lamberhurst.[15]

Confirmations of early grants were also made by Edward III in 1328[16] and 1335.[17] Richard II in 1395 granted to the prior and convent the advowson of the church of Harrietsham, with licence for its appropriation; and in 1397 he granted to them the reversion of the advowson of the church of Sutton Valence on the death of Philippa the wife of Richard, earl of Arundel, with licence for its appropriation for the support of two canons to celebrate divine service in the priory for the king.[18]

Edward I on 24 May, 1293, made a grant to the prior and convent of 28 marks yearly from the issues of the manor of Leeds for the maintenance of four canons in the priory, with one clerk to serve them, celebrating divine service daily in the chapel of the castle of Leeds for the soul of Eleanor, the late queen consort;[19] and in 1301 he transferred the charge to the manor of Bockingfold.[20] Edward II in 1326 granted to them the church of Old Romney, an escheat by the forfeiture of the rebel Bartholomew de Badlesmere, with licence for its appropriation, instead of the 28 marks yearly, for the maintenance of the said canons and clerk and an additional canon to celebrate divine service in the priory for the soul of Peter de Gavaston;[21] but this grant was afterwards cancelled, the prior and convent receiving licence instead to acquire lands to the value of £10 yearly.[22] The chantry was finally established by Edward III, who in 1341, in consideration of their losses at the siege of Leeds Castle, granted to them the advowson of the church of Leatherhead in Surrey with licence for its appropriation, for the maintenance of six canons and a clerk to celebrate divine service daily in the chapel of the castle for the good estate of the king and his mother Queen

[1] *Flores Hist.* (Rolls Ser.), ii, 48.
[2] Printed with some others in Dugdale, *Mon.* vi, 215.   [3] Pat. 27 Edw. I, m. 34.
[4] Pat. 11 Edw. II, pt. 2, m. 21; Close, 11 Edw. II, m. 7 d.
[5] Chart. R. 13 Edw. I, Nos. 71, 72.
[6] Ibid. 41 Edw. III, Nos. 14–19.
[7] Pat. 13 Edw. II, m. 13; *Cal. Bodleian Charters* (ed. Turner and Coxe), 131, 133; Thorpe, *Reg. Roff.* 207–9.   [8] Ibid. 514.
[9] Pat. 10 Ric. II, pt. 2, m. 19.
[10] Chart. R. 7 John, m. 6.

[11] Pat. 14 Edw. III, pt. 2, m. 31; *Cal. Papal Let.* iii, 467.   [12] *Reg. Roff.* 213, 676.
[13] Ibid. 410.   [14] Ibid. 496–7.
[15] Pat. 16 Edw. III, pt. 2, m. 38; Close, 14 Edw. III, pt. 1, m. 11 d.
[16] Pat. 2 Edw. III, pt. 2, m. 25.
[17] Pat. 9 Edw. III, pt. 2, m. 25.
[18] Pat. 19 Ric. II, pt. 1, m. 26; Pat. 20 Ric. II, pt. 2, m. 11; Pat. 18 Hen. VI. pt. 2, m. 12; *Cal. Papal Let.* v, 576; vi, 103.
[19] Pat. 21 Edw. I, m. 15.
[20] Pat. 29 Edw. I, m. 8.
[21] Pat. 19 Edw. II, pt. 2, m. 2.
[22] Pat. 5 Edw. III, pt. 1, m. 37.

Isabel and for their souls after death and the souls of his brother John de Eltham, earl of Cornwall, and Queen Eleanor.[23] The church was accordingly appropriated to the priory.[24] In 1439, in consideration of the chantry, the prior, who was aged and infirm, received an exemption for life from being made collector of tenths and subsidies granted by the clergy of the province of Canterbury.[25]

A dispute between the priories of Leeds and Christchurch, Canterbury, about common of pasture in Harbledown and Blean was settled by a partition in 1278.[26] In 1299 a special commission of oyer and terminer was appointed to settle a complaint by the prior that his servants had been assaulted and imprisoned at Woodnesborough;[27] and another in the same year to settle a complaint by the abbot of St. Albans that the prior of Leeds and others had assaulted John de Stopeslee, a monk of St. Albans, at Leeds.[28] In 1312 the prior complained that his trees in his wood of Frittenden had been felled, and obtained the appointment of another commission.[29]

Corrodies were claimed by the crown in the priory, William de la Spyneye being sent there by Edward II in 1317 to receive maintenance for life.[30] Edward III in 1329 promised the prior and convent that the grant of maintenance for life which they had made at his request to William de Balsham, cook of Queen Isabel, should not be taken as a precedent;[31] but nevertheless on the death of William he sent Joan de Bureford there for maintenance,[32] and on her death William de Scanderwyk.[33]

In 1318 and 1356 the prior was one of the visitors of the Augustinian houses in the dioceses of Canterbury and Rochester;[34] and in 1353 the priory was visited by the priors of Tonbridge and St. Gregory, Canterbury.[35]

Pope Boniface IX, on 29 November, 1398, granted relaxation of penance to penitents who at certain times of the year should visit and give alms to the altar of St. Mary in the priory.[36] Pope Martin V, on 25 March, 1425, granted that the prior and twenty-four canons, to be named by him, might choose a confessor who should hear their confessions and grant them absolution.[37]

Edward IV in 1483, in recompense of 20 acres of land in Leeds and Bromfield which the prior and convent granted to him for the enlargement of his park of Leeds, granted that they should be quit of tenths and subsidies granted by the clergy.[38]

James Goldwell, bishop of Norwich, finding the convent deep in debt, relieved them; and in return, on 12 June, 1487, they granted that one of their canons should celebrate divine service daily for the soul of the bishop and his parents at the altar of St. Mary in the south part of their church.[39]

Archbishop Winchelsey issued injunctions after a visitation of the priory on 31 July, 1299, in which he had found that the ordinances previously made were negligently observed. These related principally to the proper assembly in choir, the prohibition of playing with bows without licence, and the exclusion of women. J. de Brabourn, a student of medicine, was not to practise outside the priory or in it without licence. No corrody was to be granted without special licence.[40]

Archbishop Langham made a long visitation of Leeds on 25 April, 1368, in which several charges were brought against the prior, Thomas de Roffa. It was said that he neglected the house, did not stop the excesses of the cellarer, made extravagant sales of wood and corrodies, and intended to resign, and in the meantime to secure what he could. Other details are given, but they seem to be of not much importance, as he was fully excused. Detailed charges were brought at the same time against the sacrist and cellarer of drunkenness, playing dice till midnight, &c.; and these were evidently considered more serious, being adjourned for further consideration.[41]

Archbishop Warham made a visitation[42] of the priory in 1511. Richard Chetham, prior, said that all was well; John Bredgar, formerly prior, was now vicar of Marden, and rarely came to the monastery, but thought that all things were well; and Thomas Vincent, sub-prior, said that much had been reformed, but much still remained to be reformed by the prior and sub-prior. John Goldstone, professed thirty years, said that he performed the divine offices in the parish church of Bilsington, appropriated to the priory of Bilsington. Thomas Langley said that the prior had taken away five of the ten wax lights which used to burn before the image of St. Mary in her chapel. The prior admitted William Parys, a Frenchman, to the priory without the consent of the brethren, sent a scholar to study at the university, and presented chaplains to benefices without their consent, and did not distribute among them what ought to be given for the souls of the founders. Others gave evidence that the prior did not punish the

---

[23] Pat. 15 Edw. III, pt. 3, m. 14, 7, 3.
[24] *Cal. Papal Let.* iii, 213; *Bodl. Chart.* 133, 138, 139.   [25] Pat. 18 Hen. VI, pt. 1, m. 20.
[26] Ibid. 6 Edw. I, m. 16.
[27] Ibid. 27 Edw. I, m. 13 *d.*   [28] Ibid. m. 5 *d.*
[29] Ibid. 5 Edw. II, pt. 1, m. 3 *d.*
[30] Close, 11 Edw. II, m. 7 *d.*
[31] Pat. 3 Edw. III, pt. 1, m. 10.
[32] Close, 5 Edw. III, m. 5 *d.*
[33] Ibid. 6 Edw. III, m. 26 *d.*
[34] *Bodl. Chart.* 125, 128, 139.   [35] Ibid. 135.
[36] *Cal. Papal Let.* v, 253.   [37] Ibid. vii, 420.

[38] Pat. 22 Edw. IV, pt. 2, m. 6.
[39] Hasted, *Hist. and Topog. Surv. of Kent,* ii, 479, 480.
[40] Cant. Archiepis. Reg. Winchelsey, fol. 74*b.*
[41] Ibid. Langham, fol. 78.
[42] Ibid. Warham, fol. 41*b.*

brethren according to rule, but too rigorously and in an arbitrary manner ; did not give his accounts yearly ; did not pay the weekly fees of 12d., 4d., and 4d. to the brother celebrating high mass according to the wills of Nicholas Potyn, William Clerke, and Stephen Norton ; sealed with the common seal without the consent of the seniors ; and did not allow the brethren to have access to the archbishop for the purpose of securing reforms as Archbishop Bourchier had ordered. William Parys complained of having been assaulted by the prior. John Fortte, professed of the priory of Launceston, in the diocese of Exeter, had been here three years, and asked to be sent back to Launceston. Thomas Broke, a canon of Launceston, had been here one year. John London was vicar of Stockbury. The archbishop ordered the correction of all the points mentioned, and also directed the prior to pay a teacher to instruct the younger brethren. Besides the eight canons already named there were twelve others, making a total of twenty in addition to the prior.

The oath of acknowledgement of the royal supremacy was taken on 22 December, 1534, by Arthur Sentleger, prior, Thomas Egerton, sub-prior, and eleven other canons.[43] In the next year the priory was visited by Dr. Layton, but no details of the visitation are known, except that he ordered the canons not to go out of the precincts. Anthony Sentleger mentioned this when writing to Cromwell to ask that his brother, the prior, might take recreation with his hounds, as he had been accustomed for a certain infirmity with which he was troubled.[44]

The net value of the possessions of the priory mentioned in the Valor of 1535 was £362 7s. 7d. yearly,[45] and it thus escaped the first dissolution. It appears, however, to have been in a very bad state, for Thomas, the last prior, writing to Cromwell on 8 April, 1537, says that his predecessor, Arthur Sentleger, left debts due to the king of £951 19s. 8¾d., and to his brothers Anthony and Robert Sentleger and others of £447 18s. 4½d. ; and asks whether pensions are to be paid to the last two priors, suggesting that they should be stayed until the debts be paid.[46] The exact end of the house is not known, but it was surrendered some time in the next two or three years, and on 18 March, 1540, pensions were allotted, the prior receiving £60 (afterwards raised to £80) yearly, and fourteen other canons benefices or smaller amounts.[47]

The bulk of the possessions of the priory, including the manors of Ulcombe, Chart Sutton, Lamberhurst, Marden, Brisshing, Horsmonden, Maidstone, Chatham, Rodmersham, and Bearsted,

and the rectories and advowsons of the vicarages of East Sutton, Sutton Valence, Chart Sutton, Lamberhurst, Goudhurst, Wateringbury, West Farleigh, Chatham, Stockbury, Woodnesborough, Bearsted, Boughton Monchelsea, Ashford, Little Peckham, and Leatherhead, were granted in June, 1541, to the dean and chapter of Rochester.[48] The site of the priory was granted on 13 August, 1550, to Anthony Sentleger in fee.[49]

PRIORS OF LEEDS

Alexander [50]
Robert,[51] occurs c. 1175
Fulk, occurs 1205,[52] 1228 [53]
Roger, occurs 1231 [54]
William, occurs 1237 [55]
Nicholas [56]
Stephen, occurs 1267, 1271 [57]
John, occurs 1283 [58]
Adam de Maydenstan, resigned 1299 [59]
William de Bordenne, elected 1299 [59]
Robert de Maidenstan, died 1338 [60]
Thomas, occurs 1347,[61] 1351 [62]
Thomas de Roffa, occurs 1368,[63] died 1380 [64]
Aymar Odenhelle, elected 1380 [65]
William de Verdun, occurs 1397 [65a]
Thomas Sidyngbourne, died 1409 [66]
John Surynden, elected 1409,[66] died 1447
John Wittisham, elected 1447,[67] died 1453 [68]
Robert Goudeherst, elected 1453 [69]
John Bredgar, occurs 1487 [70]
Richard Chetham, occurs 1511,[63] resigned 1524 [71]
Thomas Chetham, elected 1524 [71]
Arthur Sentleger, elected 1528,[72] resigned 1536 [73]
Thomas Dey, or Daye, elected 1536,[73] the last prior [74]

[48] Ibid. xvi, 947 (42).   [49] Pat. 4 Edw. VI, pt. 8.
[50] Chart. R. 13 Edw. I, No. 72.
[51] Arch. Cant. vi, 190.
[52] Feet of F. Kent, 7 John.   [53] Ibid. 12 Hen. III.
[54] Ibid. 16 Hen. III.   [55] Ibid. 21 Hen. III.
[56] Close, 13 Edw. III, pt. 3, m. 25.
[57] Feet of F. Kent, 51 & 55 Hen. III.
[58] Reg. Epist. J. Peckham (Rolls Ser.), ii, 579.
[59] Pat. 27 Edw. I, m. 34.
[60] Close, 12 Edw. III, pt. 1, m. 40.
[61] Ibid. 21 Edw. III, pt. 2, m. 36 d.
[62] Cal. Papal Let. iii, 377.   [63] See above.
[64] Pat. 3 Ric. II, pt. 3, m. 11.
[65] Ibid. He was sub-prior. Aymar occurs in 1395 (Pat. 19 Ric. II, pt. 1, m. 26).
[65a] Harl. Chart. 43. A. 49.
[66] Cant. Archiepis. Reg. Arundel, ii, fol. 125.
[67] Pat. 25 Hen. VI, pt. 2, m. 30.
[68] Eccl. Pet. 47 (43).
[69] Ibid. Robert was prior in 1461 (Pat. 12 Edw. IV, pt. 2, m. 6).   [70] B.M. Add. Chart. 8586.
[71] L. and P. Hen. VIII, iv, 1147.
[72] Ibid. 4993 (16). He appears to have been prior of Bilsington.
[73] Ibid. xi, 519 (20).   [74] Ibid. xv, 359, p. 55

[43] L. and P. Hen. VIII, vii, 1594 (4).
[44] Ibid. ix, 713.
[45] Valor Eccl. (Rec. Com), i, 72.
[46] L. and P. Hen. VIII, xii, 867.
[47] Ibid. xv, 359, p. 551.

The seal[75] of the priory (1293) measures 2¾ inches.

Obverse—The Virgin seated crowned on a throne in a niche with canopy of three arches, pinnacled and crocketed, with carved sides of four orders of arched niches, holding on the left knee the Child between two angels, each with one wing elevated. In base, under a trefoiled arch with an arcade at each side, the prior between two monks half-length in prayer to the right. In the field on the right a triple-towered castle with a cinquefoiled rose over it, and a drooping lily flower below it. Legend :—

IGILLUM COMMUNE EC . . . . S.

Reverse—A niche containing St. Nicholas seated, lifting up the right hand in benediction and holding in the left a pastoral staff, between two clerks standing and each holding a book. In base, under a trefoiled arcade, three children in a tub (restored to life by the saint) between two angels. In the field on the left a wavy sprig of foliage, with the inscription NICHOLAUS. Legend :—

. . . E A[NNO] DÑI M CC NONOG' TERCIO.

20. THE ABBEY OF LESNES OR WESTWOOD [1]

Richard de Luci, justiciary of England, on 11 June, 1178, laid the foundations of a conventual church in honour of St. Thomas the Martyr in a place called 'Westwode.'[2] The first abbot was blessed by Walter, bishop of Rochester, in 1179 ;[3] and in the same year after Easter the founder became a canon there, dying soon afterwards.[4]

Besides the site the founder granted to the abbey the churches of Newington and Marden. Robert de Luci granted the church of Elmdon in Essex ; Roger son of Reinfrid the church of Ramsden Bellhouse in Essex ; Jordan the chamberlain the church of 'Coldreia'; and Fulk Painel and Henry II the church of Rainham in Essex. The same king also granted a charter of confirmation,[5] as also did Richard I on 3 July, 1190, and John on 4 April, 1206 ;[6] and these charters were afterwards confirmed by Edward II in 1317,[7] and Edward III in 1331.[8] Various

liberties are specified in the charter of John ; and in addition Edward I on 5 December, 1280, granted to the abbot free warren in his demesne lands of Lesnes, Tonge, and Acol.[9]

Several accounts, court rolls, &c., of the abbey are preserved, in which its possessions are set out in considerable detail.[10] In the Taxation of 1291 it is returned as owning temporalities worth £7 6s. 8d. in the diocese of Canterbury, £22 18s. 8d. in the diocese of Rochester, £1 in London, £2 3s. 4d. in Essex, and £1 4s. 6d. in Cambridgeshire, making a total of £34 13s. 2d. yearly. The church of Wenden Lofts[11] in Essex, and a moiety of the church of Godstone in Surrey, belonged to it from an early period ; and the church of Aveley in Essex was acquired from John de Brianzoun and appropriated by licence of Edward II.[12] The abbot and convent had licence in 1344 to grant a rent of 6 marks (6s. 8d.) yearly from the manors of Lesnes and Acol to the prior and convent of Rochester to find a chaplain to celebrate divine service daily in the cathedral for Hamo, bishop of Rochester, and for his soul after death, the bishop having paid them £106 13s. for this purpose.[13] In 1345 John de Whatton had licence to grant to them the reversion of the manor of Nethewode on the death of Joan, late the wife of William Faunt, to find a secular chaplain to celebrate divine service daily in their church for John and Joan, and for their souls after death, and the soul of William.[14] In 1432 they had licence[15] to exchange the manor of Tonge for land in Plumstead called 'Fulhammes Place.'

Archbishop Peckham wrote on 24 October, 1283, to Thomas, bishop of Rochester, that when lately passing by the monastery of Lesnes on his metropolitical visitation, he had found the abbot notorious for injuring the property of the house, and the latter when questioned had given unsatisfactory answers. He ordered, therefore, that three brethren of the house should be chosen by the convent, and all the property of the house, except that assigned of old to certain offices, should come into their hands, the abbot and other officials receiving the necessary expenses from them and giving accounts in return. Further, he had found that the canons did not eat flesh in the common refectory, but in chambers and other places ; and he ordered that they should eat flesh in the refectory on three days in the week, as he had observed to be done in other places of the order, unless this conflicted with the

[75] B.M. Seals, lxv, 76, 77.

[1] In the parish of Erith.

[2] Roger of Wendover, *Flor. Hist.* (Rolls Ser.), i, 108; Matt. Paris, *Chron. Maj.* (Rolls Ser.), ii, 301 ; Ralph de Diceto, *Opera Hist.* (Rolls Ser.), i, 425.

[3] Gervase of Canterbury, *Opera* (Rolls Ser.), i, 292.

[4] Ibid. 293 ; *Gesta Henrici Secundi* (Rolls Ser.), i, 238 ; Roger de Hoveden, *Chron.* (Rolls Ser.), ii, 190 ; Ralph of Coggeshall, *Chron.* (Rolls Ser.), 19.

[5] Printed in Dugdale, *Mon.* vi, 457.

[6] Chart. R. 7 John, m. 2.

[7] Ibid. 10 Edw. II, No. 11.

[8] Ibid. 5 Edw. III, No. 61.

[9] Chart. R. 9 Edw. I, No. 85.

[10] *L. and P. Hen. VIII*, iv, 3537 ; Rentals and Surv. ; Court Rolls.

[11] Newcourt, *Repert.* ii, 648.

[12] Ibid. 21 ; Pat. 7 Edw. II, pt. 2, m. 4.

[13] Pat. 18 Edw. III, pt. 2, m. 45 ; Wharton, *Anglia Sacra*, i, 375 ; Thorpe, *Reg. Roff.* 324, 329.

[14] Pat. 19 Edw. III, pt. 2, m. 15.

[15] Ibid. 11 Hen. VI, pt. 1, m. 13.

custom of the house, in which case not more than a third of the convent might leave the refectory. Nuns were on no account to pass the night within the cloister. In other matters the abbot was to be allowed full exercise of his office.[16]

Archbishop Winchelsey also issued injunctions after a visitation of Lesnes in 1299. The principal points were that all were to eat in the refectory, no money was to be given for vestments, alms were to be properly distributed, only professed canons were to be appointed to offices, the statutes were to be read regularly, and women were to be excluded.[17]

Abbot John was accused of immorality before the bishop in 1336, and, acknowledging his fault, was condemned to penance.[18] The bishop made visitations of the abbey in 1340, when the abbot was convicted of gross misgovernment and deprived in consequence, and again in 1349, when it was ·found to be so destroyed that it seemed as though it could hardly be repaired by the Day of Judgement.[19] Discipline was probably very slack about this time, for on three occasions the aid of the crown was asked for the arrest of vagabond and apostate canons,[20] John de Hoddesdon (perhaps the late abbot) in 1341, Edmund Baudri in 1344, and John de Garton in 1349.

Pope Gregory XI in 1371 granted relaxation of penance to penitents who at certain times of the year should visit and give alms towards the repair and decoration of the chapel of St. Mary in the abbey.[21] Pope John XXIII in 1412 granted licence for Roger Palmeri, a canon of Lesnes, to return to the priory of Christchurch, London, in which he had originally been professed and from which he had come to Lesnes, notwithstanding that he had taken an oath never to return.[22] The abbey is here spoken of as Arrouasian.

At the beginning of the fifteenth century the abbey had fallen into a bad state of impoverishment and debt through the misgovernance of the abbots, many pensions and corrodies having been charged on it, and many of its possessions having been indiscreetly demised at farm and otherwise alienated;[22a] and the king, on 1 February, 1402, sequestrated it, appointing the prior of Christchurch, Canterbury, and others to its custody, with orders that all issues beyond the necessary maintenance of the abbot and canons and their servants should be applied to its relief.[23] The resignation of the abbot in the next year[24] was doubtless connected with this. The Commons complained in Parliament that the abbot of Lesnes and others sold annuities and corrodies under the common seal of their houses, and then purchased protections from the king in order to defraud the buyers.[25]

Lesnes was one of the monasteries suppressed by Wolsey in accordance with the bull of Clement VII, dated 11 September, 1524, and the assent of Henry VIII on 1 October.[26] It was dissolved by his agent, William Burbank, on 13 February, 1525,[27] and granted to Cardinal's College, Oxford, on 10 February, 1526.[28] Its spiritualities were valued at £75, and its temporalities at £111 5s. 8d. yearly;[29] and by an inquisition[30] taken on 28 July, 1525, it was found that there were at the monastery five canons under the abbot, and that these had been transferred to other places, and that it owned the manors of Lesnes, 'Fantz,' 'Baudewyns' and Acol in Kent.

After Wolsey's attainder the site of the monastery was granted, on 5 March, 1534, to William Brereton in tail.[31]

ABBOTS OF LESNES

Fulk, occurs 1197[32]
Hugh, occurs 1237[33]
Richard, occurs 1266[34]
Robert, occurs 1279[35]
Thomas de Sandwico, occurs 1315[36]
Adam de Hanifeld, elected 1319,[37] died 1321[38]
Roger de Derteford, elected 1321,[39] died 1327[40]
John de Hodisdon, elected 1327[41]
Robert de Clyve, occurs 1345,[42] died 1347[43]
Richard de Gaytone, elected 1347,[44] died 1362[45]
William de Hethe, elected 1362[45]

---

[16] *Reg. Epist. J. Peckham* (Rolls Ser.), ii, 625.
[17] Cant. Archiepis. Reg. Winchelsey, fol. 73b.
[18] Roch. Epis. Reg. i, fol. 186.
[19] Wharton, *Anglia Sacra*, i, 374, 377.
[20] Chan. Warrants, 1762.
[21] *Cal. Papal Let.* iv, 163, 165.
[22] Ibid. vi, 282.
[22a] An account of Henry Holcote, abbot, for the year 1386-7 gives the total receipts as £564 1s. 9d. and the expenses as £614 7s. 6¾d. (*Hist. MSS. Com. Rep.* ix, App. pt. i, 352).

[23] Pat. 3 Hen. IV, pt. i, m. 15.
[24] Ibid. 4 Hen. IV, pt. 2, m. 17.
[25] *Rolls of Parliament* (Rec. Com.), iii, 520.
[26] *L. and P. Hen. VIII*, iv, 697.
[27] Ibid. 1137 (8).   [28] Ibid. 1964.
[29] Ibid. 3538.
[30] Exch. Inq. (Ser. ii), file 480 (15).
[31] *L. and P. Hen. VIII*, vii, 419 (6).
[32] Feet of F. Kent, 9 Ric. I.
[33] Ibid. 21 Hen. III.   [34] Ibid. 50 Hen. III.
[35] Ibid. 7 Edw. I.
[36] B.M. Cott. MS. Nero, E. vi, 202 d.
[37] Roch. Epis. Reg. i, fol. 54.   [38] Ibid. 79 d.
[39] Ibid. 53 d. 79.   [40] Ibid. 149.
[41] Ibid. 87, 149. John was abbot in 1336 (see above). The abbot was deprived by the bishop for misgovernment in 1340 (Wharton, *Angl. Sac.* i, 374).
[42] Close, 18 Edw. III, pt. 2, m. 8 d.
[43] Roch. Epis. Reg. i, fol. 227b.
[44] Ibid. 226b. He was prior.   [45] Ibid. 309 d.

John Haunsard, died 1386 [46]

Henry Heliere, or Holcote, elected 1386,[47] resigned 1403 [48]

William Sampson, appointed 1403,[49] died 1405 [50]

John Brokhole, elected 1405,[50] died 1423 [51]

John Elmedon, elected 1423,[52] died 1426 [53]

Thomas Plymton, appointed 1426 [54]

Adam Say, occurs 1455 [55]

John Colman, occurs 1472 [55]

William, occurs 1474 [56]

Thomas, occurs 1483 [57]

William Bright, occurs 1496 [58]

Robert Marten, appointed and died 1502 [59]

Henry Blakmore, elected 1502,[60] resigned 1513 [61]

William Tisehurste, elected 1513,[62] the last abbot [63]

The seal [64] of the abbey (thirteenth-century) is a pointed oval measuring 2¾ in. by 1¾ in.

Obverse—St. Thomas Becket full-length with mitre and pall, lifting up the right hand in benediction and holding in the left a crosier. In the field on each side a luce or pike haurient palewise (in allusion to the arms of the founder), and on the right also a pierced mullet of eight points. Legend :—

SIGILL' ECL'IE S . . . . MARTIRIS DE LIESNES.

Reverse—A small round counterseal measuring ⅜ in. representing St. Thomas half - length. Legend :—

SIGILL' SANCTI TOME MARTIRIS.

21. THE PRIORY OF TONBRIDGE

It was found by an inquisition taken in 1326 that Richard de Clare, earl of Hertford, founded a priory in his manor of Tonbridge and granted

to the canons regular there 10 marks yearly from the manor, and 51s. 5d. yearly from his corn lands of ' Dennemannesbroke,' and also granted that they should have one hundred and twenty swine pastured in his forest at Tonbridge, two wagon-loads of dead wood daily from the forest, and a buck yearly at the hands of his men at the feast of St. Mary Magdalen. They duly received these benefits until the manor and forest came to the crown by the forfeiture of Hugh de Audeley the younger; and Edward II then ordered that they should be allowed to continue to do so.[1] The number of swine appears, however, to have been afterwards reduced to sixty.[2]

The date of the foundation of the priory, which was dedicated to St. Mary Magdalen, can therefore be assigned to the last quarter of the twelfth century. Pope Celestine III, by a bull [3] dated 2 January, 1192, confirmed the foundation and the grants made by the founder, including the church of Yalding with the chapel of Brenchley, the church of Stradishall (Suffolk), and the church of Mereworth.

A number of early deeds and other documents relating to the priory are preserved in the Bodleian Library,[4] and the substance of the more important of these has been given by Mr. J. F. Wadmore in an article in *Archaeologia Cantiana*.[5] Among the possessions of the priory were a moiety of the manor of Bottisham in Cambridgeshire, granted by the founder,[6] and the church of Tudeley, where a vicarage was ordained.[7] In the Taxation of 1291 the temporalities were valued at £21 8s. yearly in the diocese of Rochester, £20 3s. 4d. in Bottisham, £8 in Norfolk, £1 11s. 8d. in Surrey, 15s. in Sussex, and 6d. in Suffolk, making a total of £51 18s. 6d. In 1353 a payment of one halfpenny for each mark from the goods of the Augustinian houses according to their taxation for the support of the order produced 6s. 2½d. from Tonbridge,[8] corresponding to a total of about £99 6s. 8d.

On 11 July, 1337, the church, chapter-house, dormitory, refectory, library, vestry, and other buildings of the monastery, and the books, vestments, ornaments, and relics, were destroyed by fire. John, archbishop of Canterbury, granted indulgence of forty days to all who should assist in rebuilding the priory,[9] and further indulgences, amounting in all to 8 years and 230 days, were obtained from the pope and bishops.[10] The

---

[46] Pat. 10 Ric. II, pt. 1, m. 33. John was abbot in 1378 (Anct. D. A. 7372).

[47] Pat. 10 Ric. II, pt. 1, m. 31. He was prior.

[48] Ibid. 4 Hen. IV, pt. 2, m. 18.

[49] Roch. Epis. Reg. iii, fol 38 d. He was a canon of Tonbridge, and was appointed by the bishop, to whom the convent submitted.

[50] Ibid. ii, fol. 189. [51] Ibid. iii, fol. 54 d.

[52] Ibid. 55. He was sub-prior. John Stebbyng was elected, but renounced. [53] Ibid. 75 d.

[54] Ibid. 75. The convent submitted to the bishop to save expense.

[55] Rentals and Surv. R. 357 ; Pardon R. 33-4 Hen. VI, m. 30.

[56] Pat. 14 Edw. IV, pt. 1, m. 20 d.

[57] Ibid. 1 Ric. III, pt. 5, m. 4 d.

[58] Cant. Archiepis. Reg. Morton, fol. 160. William occurs in 1500 (Pat. 16 Hen. VII, pt. 1, m. 5 (22)).

[59] Roch. Epis. Reg. iv, fol. 32 d. 33 d. The convent submitted to the bishop.

[60] Ibid. 35. [61] Ibid. 61 d.

[62] Ibid. 62 d. He was prior of Bilsington.

[63] Ibid. 129 d. [64] B.M. Seals, L.F.C. xiv, 23.

[1] Close, 19 Edw. II, m. 20.

[2] *Cal. Bodl. Chart.* 140.

[3] Printed by Thorpe in *Reg. Roff.* 666.

[4] For details see the *Cal. of Chart. and Rolls in the Bodl. Lib.* ed. Turner and Coxe.

[5] Vol. xiv, pp. 326–43.

[6] *Cal. Bodl. Chart.* 135.

[7] Ibid. 136 ; Roch. Epis. Reg. ii, fol. 120 ; *Reg. Roff.* 664.

[8] *Cal. Bodl. Chart.* 135.

[9] Ibid. 132. [10] Ibid. 134.

convent also made petition[11] to the king, the bishop, and the pope to be allowed to appropriate the church of Leigh, which was of their own advowson, in consideration of their losses; and licence was obtained from the king in 1348,[12] but the appropriation was not actually carried out until 1354.[13] Licence was also obtained in 1352[14] for Ralph, earl of Stafford, to grant the advowson of the church of High Hardres and the chapel of Stelling to the prior and canons for the maintenance of certain chantries in the priory, and for them to appropriate the church and chapel; but disputes arose afterwards, and the licence appears never to have taken effect.[15]

The priory was visited by the priors of Leeds and Combwell in 1312[16] and 1317,[17] and by the priors of Leeds and St. Gregory, Canterbury, in 1356,[18] as visitors of the houses of the Augustinian order in the dioceses of Canterbury and Rochester; and the prior of Tonbridge was himself one of such visitors in 1322, 1334, 1339, and 1353.[19]

The founder was buried in the priory,[20] as was also Ralph, earl of Stafford, in the fourteenth century.[21] Clarice and Alice, the daughters and heirs of Sir Roland de Hokstede, presented their clerk Robert Quyntyn for admission to the priory as a canon in 1319;[22] and in 1329 the prior received Laurence de la Wealde at the instance of Sir Hugh Audeley and his consort Margaret, countess of Cornwall.[23] Among other miscellaneous information we have small grants by the prior and convent of corrodies and pensions,[24] though they pleaded poverty when applied to by a nominee of the archbishop of Canterbury,[25] details of the dress and equipment of a novice[26] and of the weekly consumption of food in the priory,[27] stipends of servants, payments, allowances, &c.[28]

Application was made to the crown by the prior for the arrest of Robert, an apostate canon, in 1280,[29] and of Thomas Starky, another apostate, in 1502.[30]

In 1393 it was found by inquisition that John Osprengg, William Frendesbery, and William Mallyng, former priors, had acquired messuages, shops, gardens, and lands in Tonbridge, Brenchley, Bidborough, Leigh, and Shipborne, under a general licence by letters patent of the late king and entered thereon without proper formalities; and the prior had to pay 100s. for pardon.[31]

Tonbridge was one of the monasteries suppressed by Wolsey for the foundation of his colleges. It was dissolved by his agent William Burbank on 8 February, 1525,[32] and granted by him to Cardinal's College, Oxford, on 10 February, 1526.[33] By an inquisition[34] taken on 28 July, 1525, it was found that there were at the priory seven canons under the prior, Richard Tomlyn, and these were transferred to other places, and that its possessions in Kent included the manors of Tonbridge, Langport, Shipborne, 'Nysells,' Leigh, 'Hallond' in Speldhurst, Brenchley, and 'Lomwod,' and the rectories of Tudeley, Brenchley, Leigh, and Yalding. The whole of the spiritualities of the priory were valued at £48 13s. 4d., and the temporalities at £120 16s. 11d. yearly;[35] although a detailed valuation,[36] perhaps incomplete, amounts to rather less.

Wolsey proposed to found a grammar school at Tonbridge for forty scholars, with exhibitions to his college at Oxford; but it appears from some letters of Archbishop Warham that a section of the townspeople wished for the restoration of the priory instead.[37] Warham called a meeting at Tonbridge in June, 1525, to explain the scheme to them; but they appear to have been very apathetic, only sixteen appearing before him, of whom thirteen were in favour of the priory, but desired a few days' notice to discuss the matter with their neighbours. A lukewarm resolution in favour of the restoration of the canons was reported to Wolsey, but nothing was done, and with his fall Tonbridge lost both priory and grammar school.

After Wolsey's attainder the priory came into the possession of the crown, and was granted with most of its possessions to the dean and chapter of Windsor on 27 September, 1532.[38]

PRIORS OF TONBRIDGE

John, occurs 1248[39]
Peter, occurs 1272[40]
David, occurs 1273, 1274[41]
John, occurs 1286, 1305[42]
Roger, occurs 1311[43]

---

[11] *Cal. Bodl. Chart.* 137.
[12] Pat. 22 Edw. III, pt. 2, m. 4.
[13] *Reg. Roff.* 464.
[14] Pat. 26 Edw. III, pt. 1, m. 5.
[15] *Cal. Bodl. Chart.* 136, 138.
[16] Ibid. 125.
[17] Ibid. 128.
[18] Ibid. 139.
[19] Ibid. 127, 130, 131, 135.
[20] Ibid. 127.
[21] Ibid. 136.
[22] Ibid. 126.
[23] Ibid. 129.
[24] Ibid. 126, 129, 130.
[25] Ibid. 140.
[26] Ibid. Preface.
[27] Ibid.
[28] Ibid. 141.
[29] Pat. 8 Edw. I, m. 1.
[30] Chan. Warrants, 1762.
[31] Pat. 16 Ric. II, pt. 2, m. 2.
[32] *L. and P. Hen. VIII*, iv, 1137 (16).
[33] Ibid. 1964.
[34] Exch. Inq. (Ser. 2), file 480, No. 14.
[35] *L. and P. Hen. VIII*, iv, 3538.
[36] Ibid. 1672.
[37] Ibid. 1459, 1470–1.
[38] Ibid. v, 1351.
[39] Feet of F. Kent, 32 Hen. III.
[40] Ibid. Camb. 56 Hen. III.
[41] *Cal. Bodl. Chart.* 117, 136.
[42] Ibid. 118, 114.
[43] Ibid. 125.

John Osprengg [44]
William Frendesbery [45]
William de Mallyng, occurs 1352 [46]
John de Pecham, appointed 1361 [47]
Robert Mallyng, resigned 1379 [48]
Robert de Maidenstan, elected 1379 [49]

John London, occurs 1455 [49a]
Thomas Burton, occurs 1463 [50]
Ralph Langton, occurs 1482, 1485 [50a]
Edmund, occurs 1493 [51]
Richard Thomlyn or Tomlyn, occurs 1509, [52]
the last prior [53]

HOUSES OF PREMONSTRATENSIAN CANONS

22. THE ABBEY OF WEST LANGDON

The abbey of St. Mary and St. Thomas the Martyr, Langdon, was founded by William de Aubervilla and colonized from the abbey of Leiston in Suffolk. The founder, by a charter which is witnessed by Hubert, bishop-elect of Salisbury, and must therefore belong to the year 1189, with the assent of Maud his wife and his heirs, granted all his town of Langdon for the making of a Premonstratensian abbey by Robert, abbot of Leiston, and gave to it the churches of Langdon, Walmer, Oxney, and Lydden, for the soul of Henry II and the souls of William his son, Emma his daughter, Hugh his father, and Wymarc his mother, and Ranulph de Glanvilla and Berta his wife. The phrasing seems to indicate that Henry II was then dead, and in that case the date of the foundation must lie between 6 July and 22 October, when Bishop Hubert was consecrated.

A chartulary [1] of the abbey is preserved, in which the foundation charter and others are set out. The grants of the founder were confirmed by his over-lord Simon de Abrincis, and also by his son Hugh de Aubervilla, his grandson William de Aubervilla, and his great-grandson Nicholas de Cryoll; and Archbishops Baldwin (1184–90), Hubert (1193–1205), and Stephen granted charters of confirmation. Gunnora de Soneldon and Denise de Newesole granted the chapel of St. Katharine, Newsole, in the parish of Coldred.

At the Taxation of 1291 the temporalities of

the abbey were valued at £25 17s. 10d. yearly, and besides its churches it owned tithes of £1 10s. in Coldred. Edward II on 28 August, 1325, 'out of affection for Abbot William and the canons' granted to them the advowson of the church of Tonge, which had belonged to the rebel Bartholomew de Badlesmere; with licence for appropriation. [2] The king was then staying at Langdon, and it is possible that his affection for the abbot may have been more than a phrase; for the latter was afterwards mixed up with the disastrous attempt of the earl of Kent to restore Edward, supposed to be still alive. [3] The church of Waldershare came into the possession of the abbey in a somewhat similar way. The king on 21 July, 1322, granted [4] to the abbot the body and forfeited lands of Sir John Malmeins, a rebel; and though the abbot apparently was not able to enjoy this grant to the full, he secured from Sir John all his land of Apelton in Waldershare and the advowson of the church of Waldershare in exchange for 66 acres of land in Lydden, [5] releasing all claims against him on 4 April, 1323. [6] The king granted licence [7] for the appropriation of the church on 28 September, 1322, and it was effected on 20 March following; but in 1336 the abbot and convent had to pay heavily for a final settlement with the Malmeins family. [8]

In 1331 protection was granted [9] to the abbot while going beyond the seas on the king's service; and in 1316, [10] 1325, [11] and 1329 [12] he had licence to cross at Dover to attend the chapter general at Prémontré, taking 20 marks with him for his expenses on the last occasion.

[44] See above. John occurs as prior from 1320 to 1336 (*Cal. Bodl. Chart.* 118, 133).
[45] See above. William occurs as prior in 1337 and 1348 (ibid. 131, 121).
[46] Ibid. 139. William occurs as prior in 1358 (Anct. D., A. 7971).
[47] Cant. Archiepis. Reg. Islip. fol. 226. John occurs as prior in 1372 (*Cal. Bodl. Chart.* 110).
[48] Cant. Archiepis. Reg. Sudbury, fol. 57b.
[49] Ibid. Robert occurs as prior in 1386, 1396 (*Cal. Bodl. Chart.* 111), 1404 (Assize R. 1512), and 1408 (Assize R. 1521).
[49a] Pardon R. 33–4 Hen. VI, m. 21. John occurs in 1430 (De Banco R. Mich. 9 Hen. VI, 170).
[50] Pardon R. 1–6 Edw. IV, m. 10.
[50a] Exch. of Pleas, Plea. R. 1 Hen. VII, m. 7.
[51] Roch. Epis. Reg. iv, 4.
[52] *Cal. Bodl. Chart.* 123. Richard was prior in 1502 (Chan. Warrants, file 1762).

[53] See above. In the surrender the prior is called William.
[1] Misc. Books, Exch. K.R. 29. The foundation charter and a few others are printed in Dugdale, *Mon.* vii, 898.
[2] Pat. 19 Edw. II, pt. 1, m. 28.
[3] Close, 5 Edw. III, pt. 1, m. 27 d.
[4] Pat. 16 Edw. II, pt. 1, m. 30.
[5] Ibid. 3 Edw. III, pt. 1, m. 12.
[6] Ibid. 17 Edw. II, pt. 1, m. 11.
[7] Ibid. 16 Edw. II, pt. 1, m. 20.
[8] Close, 10 Edw. III, m. 26 d.
[9] Pat. 5 Edw. III, pt. 2, m. 24; Close, 10 Edw. III, m. 43.
[10] Close, 10 Edw. II, m. 28 d.
[11] Ibid. 18 Edw. II, m. 1 d.
[12] Ibid. 3 Edw. III, m. 9.

The Premonstratensian abbey of Egglestone in Yorkshire was destroyed by the Scots in 1323, and its eight canons temporarily dispersed among other houses of the order. One of these, Bernard de Langeton, was sent by the king to Langdon on 20 September with a request that the abbot and convent should receive him as one of themselves until his own house be relieved.[13]

Edward III on 20 August, 1347, made a grant to the abbot of free warren in his demesne lands of Holyrood (in Stelling), Enbrook (in Cheriton), Lydden, Newsole, Southwood (in Waldershare), and Langdon Wood;[14] and on 10 March, 1348, he gave licence for the crenellation of the gatehouse of the abbey.[15] Pope Boniface IX in 1400 granted indulgence to penitents visiting the abbey from the first to the second vespers of Easter Tuesday and the following day.[16]

Langdon is often mentioned in the Premonstratensian records.[17] Abbot William was the principal intermediary in the dispute between the abbot of Prémontré and the English houses of the order in 1310; and Abbot W. appears as vicegerent of the abbot of Prémontré in 1345. A list of the community on 6 June, 1475, gives the names of John Kentwell, late abbot, John Lyon, sub-prior, and six other canons, one of whom was not professed. A similar list in 1478 mentions John Brondysch, abbot, and eleven other canons; and in answer to a set form of questions it was stated[18] that Sir Thomas Keryell was patron, the abbot of Leiston was father abbot, the abbey was founded in honour of St. Thomas the Martyr in 1212, and it had six churches, served by canons who were not perpetual.

Richard Redman, bishop of St. Asaph, abbot of Shap and vicar of the abbot of Prémontré in England, made several visitations of Langdon. On 29 August, 1482, he found an excellent abbot, who had inclosed and cultivated many fields, and whom he exhorted to pay equal attention to internal discipline. The canons were to remember that the rule enjoined work, to rise to mattins, to keep to the traditional chant in singing, and not to go out of the monastery without leave. The debt at the creation of the abbot had been £100, but this was more than cleared off, and the house was excellently supplied with provisions. Robert Waynflett was abbot and John Lyon sub-prior, and the names of nine other canons are given.

In 1488 there were thirteen priests and four novices besides the abbot. The bishop visited on 12 July and directed the abbot to send a canon who did not get on with the rest to some cure of souls. John Kentwell was appointed prior and ordered to punish with a day's bread and water anyone absent from mattins, leaving the cloister without permission, or breaking the rule of silence. Incorrigible offenders were to be sent to the bishop. The hours of St. Mary were to be sung. More attention was to be paid to the tonsure, and two canons were reproved for appearing in choir without cloaks. The house was free from debt and well provisioned.

At the visitation on 7 October, 1491, Robert Waynflett was still abbot and John Kentwell prior, but only five other canons are mentioned. One who had been convicted of incontinence with a married woman was to receive 40 days' severe punishment and then to be sent to the monastery of Wendling for three years. The canons were again reminded of the form of the tonsure, and ordered to rise to mattins under pain of a day on bread and water. The abbot had repaired the big bell and the walls of the cloister, and done many other things; and the house was prosperous.

In 1494 the bishop visited on 30 June, when Richard Coley was abbot and John Kentwell prior with six other canons, including one apostate. The administration of the abbot was excellent, but he was directed not to receive canons of other monasteries except by order of the visitor; and the tonsure was once more referred to. The house was still prosperous.

The number of the canons was the same at the visitation on 11 October, 1497, and again there was one apostate. The bishop perceived that the church was ruined, and ordered the abbot to repair it and also to pay the stipends of the canons more regularly. One was punished with bread and water till Christmas for not rising to mattins, and others offending in this way were to receive the same punishment on the morrow. The house had a debt of £10, but was well provided with corn and animals.

Redman made his last recorded visitation on 5 October, 1500. Richard Coley was still abbot, and there were eight other canons, including John Kentwell, John Lyon, sub-prior, and two novices. The abbot was ordered not to receive any canon of another monastery, but to increase the number of his own as soon as possible. The law of silence was to be observed. The debts of the house amounted to £60, but more was owing to it, and it was sufficiently provided with corn and animals.

Thomas Wilkinson, abbot of Welbeck, arranged to visit Langdon on 4 October, 1506, but no record of his visitation is preserved.

The gross income of the abbey amounted[19] in 1535 to £91 3s. 4d., and the net income to £56 6s. 9d. yearly, the deductions including a

[13] Close, 17 Edw. II, m. 37 d.

[14] Pat. 21 Edw. III, pt. 4, m. 21.

[15] Ibid. 22 Edw. III, pt. 1, m. 17.

[16] Cal. Papal Let. v, 375.

[17] B.M. Add. MSS. 4934–5 and Ashmolean MS. 1519. Printed in Collectanea Anglo-Praemonstratensia (Camd. Soc.).

[18] Two slightly different versions are given.

[19] Valor Eccl. (Rec. Com.), i, 43.

pension of £9 to John Yorke, late abbot, and £3 18s. 9d. in rents to the castle of Dover for castle-ward for the manors of West Langdon, Enbrook, Lydden, Apelton, and Southwood.

Langdon was visited on Friday, 22 October, in the same year by Richard Layton, who gave a most unfavourable and curiously circumstantial report [20] to Cromwell. Probably he had heard of it beforehand, for he writes that he sent Cromwell's servant, Bartlett, and his own servants to circumcept the abbey and keep all starting holes. He himself went alone to the abbot's lodging 'joining upon the fields and wood even like a cony clapper full of starting holes,' and was a good space knocking at the door. He found a short poleaxe and dashed the door in pieces, and went about the house with the pole-axe, for the abbot was 'a dangerous desperate knave and hardy.' Finally the abbot's 'gentle-woman bestirred her stumps towards her starting holes,' where Bartlett took 'the tender damoisel.' Her apparel was found in the abbot's coffer. After examination he sent her to Dover to the mayor to set in some cage or prison for eight days, and brought the abbot to Canterbury, where he would leave him in prison in Christchurch. He gives further details about the abbot and canons, and says that the house is in utter decay and will shortly tumble down.

It was no doubt in direct consequence of this that the abbey was formally surrendered [21] on 13 November by William Dayer, abbot, William Feyld, sub-prior, and nine other canons, before the Act of Dissolution ; and Thomas Bedyll, who took the surrender, bears Layton out, declaring the house in decay, the abbot unthrifty, and the convent ignorant.[22] The abbot was, however, well treated, receiving a pension [23] of £7.

The site and possessions of the abbey were granted on 31 July, 1538, to the archbishop of Canterbury.[24]

ABBOTS OF LANGDON

Bartholomew [25]
William [26]
Richard,[27] occurs 1206 [28]
Peter, occurs 1227 [29]
Robert, occurs 1236 [30]
John, occurs 1248 [31]
Nicholas, occurs 1276 [32]

W., occurs 1284 [33]
Roger, blessed 1289 [34]
William de Digepet, occurs 1305 [34a]
William, occurs 1310,[35] 1316,[36] 1323,[37] 1331,[38] 1338 [39]
W., occurs 1345 [40]
John de Hakynton, elected 1369 [41]
Robert de Estry, elected 1381 [42]
John, elected 1392,[43] occurs 1415[43a]
Philip [44]
Thomas, occurs 1446,[44a] 1459 [45]
John Kentwell,[46] resigned (1475)
John Brondysch,[40] occurs 1478
Robert Waynflett [40] or Wanflete, occurs 1482, 1491
Richard Coley,[40] occurs 1494, 1500
John Yorke [47]
William Dayer [48] or Dare,[49] resigned 1535, the last abbot

The seal [50] of the abbey (late thirteenth century) measures $2\frac{5}{16}$ inches.

Obverse.—the Virgin seated, crowned, on a throne, in the left hand the Child, in a canopied niche, on a corbel ornamented with sunk quatre-foiled panels. The arch of the canopy with five cusps, the canopy crocketed, the sides ornamented with four stories of double niches ; outside these tabernacle work of corresponding character. Legend :—

SIGILL' COMMUNE MONASTERII E͡CCE B͡E MARIE DE LANGEDON.

Reverse.—Becket's martyrdom in the interior of Canterbury Cathedral. Legend :—

CAUSA DOMUS XP͞I MORTEM SIC INTULIT ISTI.

Another seal [51] (thirteenth century) is a pointed oval measuring $2\frac{1}{4}$ by $1\frac{1}{4}$ inches, representing the

[33] Ibid. 125 d.
[34] Gervase of Canterbury, Opera, ii, 295.
[34a] Exch. K.R. Eccl. 6 (18). [35] See above.
[36] Close, 10 Edw. II, m. 28 d.
[37] Ibid. 16 Edw. II, m. 11 d.
[38] Ibid. 5 Edw. III, pt. 1, m. 27 d.
[39] Chartulary, fol. 19 d. ; it appears from Close, 10 Edw. III, m. 43, that he was a brother of Robert de Canterbury.
[40] See above.
[41] Cant. Archiepis. Reg. Whittlesey, fol. 70b.
[42] Ibid. Courtenay, fol. 5.
[43] Ibid. Morton-Courtenay, fol. 206b.
[43a] Pardon R. 2–5 Hen. V, m. 40.
[44] Chartulary, fol. 182.
[44a] De Banco, Hil. 24 Hen. VI, 58. [45] Ibid. 49.
[46] See above ; his successor had not been elected by 6 June.
[47] See above. He was a novice at the visitation in 1500.
[48] L. and P. Hen. VIII, ix, 816.
[49] Ibid. xiii (1), p. 577. William was abbot in 1529 (ibid. iv, 6047).
[50] B.M. Seals, DC. E. 147.*
[51] Ibid. lxv, 73.

[20] L. and P. Hen. VIII, ix, 668–9.
[21] Ibid. 816. [22] Ibid. 829.
[23] Ibid. xiii (1), p. 577. [24] Ibid. 1519 (68).
[25] Addy, Beauchief, 51.
[26] Gervase of Canterbury, Opera (Rolls Ser.), ii, 410. He was blessed abbot by Archbishop Hubert [1193–1205].
[27] Ibid.; he was blessed later by the same.
[28] Feet of F. Kent, 7 John.
[29] Ibid. 11 Hen. III.
[30] Ibid. 20 Hen. III. [31] Ibid. 32 Hen. III.
[32] Chartulary, fol. 41 d.

Virgin seated, crowned, on a throne, on the left hand the Child, in the right hand a sceptre. The Child, with nimbus, lifts up the right hand in benediction, holding in the left hand a book. The Virgin's feet on a carved corbel. Legend :—

S' ECCLE BE MARIE DE LANGEDONNE.

23. THE ABBEY OF BRADSOLE OR ST. RADEGUND

This abbey, situated at Bradsole in the parish of Poulton and dedicated in honour of St. Radegund, was one of the two English houses colonized directly from the chief house of the order at Prémontré, Bayham in Sussex being the other. Tanner mentions two chartularies belonging to it, one of which is now preserved in the Bodleian Library[1]; and some extracts from them have been printed in the *Monasticon*.[1a]

The return of 1478[2] gives the date of the foundation as 1192 or 1193, which agrees well with the scanty evidence of the early deeds; and describes the abbot as being patron in himself, which is consistent with the statement of Leland,[3] that the founder was a canon named Hugh, who was the first abbot. It may be that Hugh was the moving spirit in the establishment of the house and procured grants from various charitable donors, none of whom was sufficiently predominant to claim the patronage. Walter Haket and Emma his wife, with the assent of William de Poltone and Stephen his heir, granted land at Bradsole, and this was confirmed by their over-lord Geoffrey, count of Perche, and later, with other grants, by his son Thomas, count of Perche. Robert de Poltone granted the manor of Poulton. Hamo de Crevequer and Maud de Abrincis his wife granted the advowson of the church of Alkham and the chapel of Mauregge, now Capel. The church of Leysdown in Sheppey was granted by Robert Arsiche and confirmed by Archbishop Stephen. Philip de Columbariis granted the church of Postling; Bertram de Criol the manor of Combe; Hubert de Burgh the churches of Portslade and Aldrington in Sussex; and Henry de Wengham, dean of St. Martin le Grand, London, the church of Shepherdswell.

In addition Richard I granted to the canons 100 acres of land adjoining their land of Bradsole. John, on 24 August, 1199, confirmed to them their place of Bradsole[4]; and on 12 May, 1204, he granted to them 100 acres of land in the manor of River.[5] On 26 March, 1208, he granted the church of River with the intention

that the abbey should be rebuilt there[6]; but this idea was soon abandoned, and on 26 July, 1215, he made another grant of the church for the maintenance of the canons and of pilgrims there, saving to John de Riveria his possession during his life.[7] Henry III on 16 March, 1227, granted a charter of confirmation;[8] and on the same day he gave to the abbot and convent a rent of 20s. which he used to receive from the mill in the court of River, which they had of the grant of Alan Corbell, and also gave them the site of the mill of 'Crabbehole.'[9] Edward II granted a charter of confirmation in 1315.[10]

There was at one time a small Premonstratensian monastery at Blackwose[11] in Newington in Kent, subject to the abbey of Lavendon in Buckinghamshire, where there were five canons and one lay-brother; but the place could not maintain them, and they were forced to wander about the country to the great scandal of the order. The Premonstratensian chapter put them under the obedience of the abbot of St. Radegund's, on account of his proximity, and he repaired their house and paid their debts; but the place was again destroyed on the recurrence of war, and at the request of the barons of Hythe was finally united with St. Radegund's.[12] It appears from the Valor of 1535 that 2s. yearly was paid to the abbot of Lavendon as compensation.

The temporalities of the abbey were valued at £27 19s. 8d. yearly in the Taxation of 1291. In the reign of Edward II the abbot complained that some of his lands had been wrongly charged for the sixteenth granted by the laity, and the matter was brought before the barons of the Exchequer. It was found by inquisition that he had temporalities taxed at 50s. at Paddlesworth and 'Clavertegh', 11 marks at Pising and Shepherdswell, 1 mark at River, 10 marks 2s. 8d. at St. Radegund's, Foxhole, Hawkinge, Combe, and Blackwose, 50s. 8d. at 'Stottemere' and in the port of Dover, 5s. at Leysdown, 5s. at Westbere, 40s. at Marshborough and in the port of Sandwich, 22s. at Canterbury and 'Shierch,' and 6 marks at Sutton, and that he paid a tenth on these with the other clergy. He consequently was discharged of the sixteenth in 1324, and his successor obtained an exemplification of the judgement in 1341.[13]

Early in the fourteenth century St. Radegund's was involved in a lawsuit with Bayham, apparently in connexion with a dispute about the abbacy of the latter house.[14] Abbot William and others were charged with having on Sunday, the Translation of St. Thomas the Martyr, 1303, in the

---

[1] Rawlinson MS. B. 336.
[1a] Dugdale, *Mon.* vii, 941.
[2] See below.   [3] *Collectanea*, i, 88.
[4] Chart. R. 1 John, m. 22.
[5] Ibid. 5 John, m. 3.

[6] Chart. R. 9 John, m. 2.
[7] Ibid. 17 John, m. 6.
[8] Ibid. 11 Hen. III, pt. 1, m. 18.   [9] Ibid.
[10] Ibid. 8 Edw. II, No. 33.
[11] Gervase of Canterbury, *Opera* (Rolls Ser.), ii, 418.
[12] Dugdale, *Mon.* vii, 942.
[13] Pat. 15 Edw. III, pt. 2, m. 30.
[14] *Suss. Arch. Coll.* xi, 124.

king's highway at Ash near Wingham, seized certain goods and chattels belonging to the abbot of Bayham in the custody of one John de Arundel, his fellow canon, viz. a horse with saddle and bridle, a prayer-book, a girdle and a purse, of the value of £10, and also a papal bull concerning the removal of Solomon de Wengham, canon of St. Radegund's, out of the abbey of Bayham and letters executory of the said bull, and 48s. in money. The defendants pleaded that they were acting in pursuance of a mandate from the abbot of Prémontré, and took the canon as rebellious to his superiors, that he might be punished ; the purse contained only 4s. 9d. and they offered everything to the abbot of Bayham, who refused to receive them, but did afterwards accept the horse.

The saddle and bridle had rotted by age, and the prayer-book had been given back to the canon, but the girdle and purse and 4s. 9d. they handed into court. The jury found for the defendants.

The abbot was summoned to Parliament under Edward I, but not afterwards.[15]

The king claimed the right of corrody in the abbey, and in 1316 sent Richard Trallock to the abbot and convent to receive maintenance in food, clothing, shoe-leather, and other necessaries of life and a chamber within the inclosure of the abbey for his residence.[16]

In 1327 the abbot was allowed to cross at Dover to the chapter general at Prémontré with £15 for his expenses.[17]

Pope Boniface IX in 1401 granted indulgence to penitents visiting the abbey on Palm Sunday and the feast of St. James the Apostle, with power for the abbot and seven other priests deputed by him to hear their confessions.[18]

Discipline does not appear to have been well kept at St. Radegund's ; for we hear of several apostate canons, and successive abbots appealed to the crown for the arrest of William de Sandwico as such in 1305, John Strete in 1388, Thomas Watsone in 1464, and John Newynton in 1473.[19]

Protection was granted in 1453 to the abbots of Bayham and St. Radegund's, making a visitation of the houses of the order in England.[20]

The Premonstratensian records[21] throw considerable light on the history of the abbey. The abbot was one of the intermediaries in the dispute between the abbot of Prémontré and the English houses of the order in 1311. On the resignation of Abbot Henry de S. in 1345 the election of John R. as his successor, which was conducted by the abbots of Dale and Bayham on 4 October and was by way of compromise, is described in detail.

Provision was made on the following day for the retiring abbot ; he was to have a manor belonging to the monastery, with all stock and utensils, and an allowance of 10 marks yearly ; he might have a canon of the house to stay with him for a week ; if he went to the monastery a competent chamber was to be assigned to him ; and he was to have all the furniture which he had before. In 1475 Ingram Fraunce was abbot, and there were ten other canons, of whom two are described as apostate. In 1478, in answer to the set form of questions, it was stated that the abbot was patron himself, the abbot of Prémontré was father abbot, the abbey had six churches, some served by canons and some by seculars, and it was founded in 1192 or 1193.[22] The names of Abbot Ingram, Thomas Howlett, sub-prior, and five other canons are given.

Richard Redman, bishop of St. Asaph, abbot of Shap, and vicar of the abbot of Prémontré in England, visited St. Radegund's several times. On 30 August, 1482, he ordered the abbot not to allow the canons to celebrate outside the monastery except in churches belonging to it, and not to receive canons professed in other houses. The monastery was in urgent need of repair, which should be undertaken at once. The canons were to work in the gardens or wherever else they might be required ; they were to wear amices, and their number was to be increased. An apostate canon of Shap appeared before him and asked for pardon, and he was put in charge of the abbot until his case should be considered at the next provincial chapter. The debt of the house, which was £70 at the preceding visitation, was now reduced to £40, and the house was sufficiently supplied with corn and other necessaries. Ingram was abbot and Thomas Reypost sub-prior, and there were four other canons.

In 1488 Redman visited on 14 July, when John Hey was abbot and Thomas Raypose prior, with ten other canons, including ex-abbot Ingram. He formally excommunicated John Newton as an apostate and a sower of discord. The abbot was ordered to provide properly for the canons, not to correct them before seculars, and to observe certain rules in their admission to the monastery. The canons were not to go out of the monastery without leave of the abbot, nor to play games for money, dice and cards being especially forbidden. The house was in moderately good state considering the ruin and waste made by the late abbot, whose debt of £212 had been diminished by £60.

In 1491 he visited on 9 October and found agreement between the abbot and convent and no complaints. The monastery needed great repairs, but the new abbot had already set about them and the debt was now reduced to 28 marks. John Newynton, the late apostate, was now abbot and William Kyrkby sub-prior, with the ex-abbot Ingram Francys and five other canons.

---

[15] *Report on the Dignity of a Peer*, App. i.
[16] Close, 9 Edw. II, m. 13 d.
[17] Ibid. 1 Edw. III, pt. 2, m. 12 d.
[18] *Cal. Papal Let.* v, 478.
[19] Chan. Warr. file 1763.
[20] Pat. 31 Hen. VI, pt. 1, m. 8.
[21] B.M. Add. MSS. 4934-5 and Ashmolean MS. 1519. Printed in *Collectanea Anglo-Praemonstratensia*.

[22] Two versions are given.

At the next visitation on 28 June, 1494, one of the canons who had been detected in apostasy and, what was worse, in wearing secular dress, submitted himself, and after explanations and at the intercession of the abbot his punishment was left over till the provincial chapter. The abbot and convent were charged to observe the customs of the order properly, and Thomas Haut was appointed sub-prior. The debt was now £20, but the supply of corn and animals was sufficient. John Newynton was still abbot, with nine other canons, of whom two were novices.

The number of the canons was the same in 1497, but three are described as apostate. The bishop visited on 14 October, and found great dissensions between the abbot and convent—so great that he could not discuss them, and adjourned the settlement until the provincial chapter. In the meantime he charged all to live in harmony and the abbot to increase the number of the canons and make repairs to the monastery. The debt amounted to £10, and the provision of corn and animals was sufficient.

Matters had only grown worse when Redman made his next (and last recorded) visitation on 3 October, 1500. John Newton was still abbot, with Edmund Norwich as sub-prior, and nine other canons, three of them novices. The convent charged the abbot with frequenting taverns on Sundays and feast-days, and with bad language and incontinence; and the visitor ordered him to repair the whole monastery, which was visibly ruinous, to cease frequenting taverns and other assemblies of laymen except at proper times, and to apply himself to his office. He admitted a debt of £30, but the supply of corn and animals was sufficient. It is significant that the next abbot appears to have come from Bayham.

St. Radegund's was marked for visitation by Thomas Wilkinson, abbot of Welbeck, on 2 October, 1506, but the result is not preserved.

The possessions of the abbey in 1535,[23] including the parsonages of Shepherdswell, River, Portslade, Postling, Leysdown, and Alkham, and the manors of River, Shepherdswell, Hawkinge, and Pising, amounted to the value of £142 8s. 9d. yearly; but deductions for rents, fees, pensions, and obits brought the net income down to £98 9s. 2½d. It was consequently dissolved under the Act of 1536. The canons appear to have tried to make the most of their last days, for a correspondent writes[24] to Cromwell that 'the abbot of St. Radegund's is setting men to fell his woods at a great pace, and, if Cromwell does not stop him, will do much harm to the place, one of the properest in Kent.' Thomas Dale, prior, received a pension of 20 marks,[25]

and it is probable that he is identical with Thomas, who was abbot in 1532.[25a]

The site of the monastery was leased[26] to Richard Kays on 10 May, 1537, for twenty-one years at a rent of £13 10s. 8d. and on 31 July, 1538, the reversion was granted to the archbishop of Canterbury.[27]

Leland, writing about the time of the Dissolution, says[28] of St. Radegund's: 'The Quier of the Chyrche is large and fayr. The Monastery ys at this tyme metely mayntayned, but yt appereth that yn tymes past the Buildinges have bene ther more ample then they be now.'

ABBOTS OF ST. RADEGUND'S

Hugh[29]
Richard,[30] occurs 1222
Henry,[31] occurs 1241, 1258, 1265
John,[32] occurs 1273
William, occurs 1303,[33] 1312[34]
Robert de Monyngeham, elected 1325[35]
Gilbert, occurs 1328[36]
Richard de Offynton[37]
Henry de S., resigned 1345[38]
John R., elected 1345[38]
Warisius de Cant', elected 1362[39]
Richard Brygge, deposed[40] 1386-7
Clement, elected 1387,[41] occurs 1391[41a]
John Strete, died 1396-7[41b]

[25a] Aug. Off. Misc. Bks. xci, fol. 53 d.
[26] L. and P. Hen. VIII, xiii (i), p. 584.
[27] Ibid. 1519 (68).   [28] Itin. vii, 128.
[29] Gervase of Canterbury, Opera (Rolls Ser.), ii, 410. He was blessed abbot by Archbishop Hubert [1193–1205].   [30] Feet of F. Kent, 6 Hen. III.
[31] Ibid. 25, 42, 49 Hen. III. Henry, prior (probably abbot) of St. Radegund's, was treasurer of the Exchequer in 49 Hen. III (Madox, Hist. of the Exchequer, 748).
[32] Feet of F. Kent, 1 Edw. I.   [33] See above.
[34] Collectanea Anglo-Premonstratensia, i, 42.
[35] Cant. Archiepis. Reg. Reynolds, fol. 255b.
[36] Dugdale, Mon. vii, 940.
[37] Cant. Archiepis. Reg. Reynolds, fol. 198. Richard occurs in 1338 (Langdon Chart. fol. 19 d.).
[38] See above.
[39] Cant. Archiepis. Reg. Islip, fol. 298.
[40] Langdon Chart. fol. 174.
[41] Ibid. The election was conducted by the abbot of Barlings, visitor of the order in England, and the abbot of Langdon. He was afterwards forced to resign by the abbot of Welbeck, who intruded John Strete, a canon of St. Radegund's. The abbot appealed to the crown for the arrest of John Strete (see above), but the matter was in dispute for some years. Pope Boniface IX in 1393 ordered Clement to be restored (Cal. Papal Let. iv, 463), but apparently this was not done.
[41a] Assize R. 1503, m. 83.
[41b] Pat. 20 Ric. II, pt. 1, m. 2. Licence to elect on his death was granted on 10 Jan. by the king, the abbey being said to be of the patronage of Richard son and heir of Richard de Ponynges. Such a licence is very unusual in the case of a Premonstratensian house.

[23] Valor Eccl. (Rec. Com.), i, 57.
[24] L. and P. Hen. VIII, x, 624.
[25] Ibid. xiii (1), p. 577.

John, occurs 1415,[41c] 1421 [41d]

William,[42] occurs 1446 [42a]

John Petre, died 1454 [43]

John Chilton, elected 1454 [43]

Thomas, occurs 1464 [44]

Ingram Fraunce or Francys,[45] occurs 1475, 1482

Henry [46]

John Hey,[47] occurs 1488

John Newynton or Newton,[47] occurs 1491, 1500

Thomas Willouse, occurs 1509 [47a]

William, occurs 1523,[47b] 1529 [48]

William Bukler, resigned c. 1530 [48a]

John Wylmerton, occurs 1531 [48b]

Thomas, occurs 1532 [48c]

The seal [49] (thirteenth-century) of the abbey is a pointed oval measuring $1\frac{5}{8}$ by $1\frac{1}{4}$ inches, representing St. Radegund seated on a throne, turned to the left, giving a pastoral staff to a kneeling abbot. Legend :—

SIGILL' ABBATIS ET CONVENTUS SANCTE
RADEGUNDIS

A later seal [50] (fifteenth-century) measures $2\frac{5}{8}$ by $1\frac{7}{8}$ inches, and represents St. Radegund crowned, standing in a canopied niche with carved towers at the sides, in the right hand a pastoral staff obliquely, in the left a book. The corbel of the niche in masonry. Legend :—

SIGILLŪ ABBATIS ET CONVENTUS SCR
RADEGUNDIS

HOUSE OF KNIGHTS TEMPLARS

24. THE PRECEPTORY OF EWELL

In the inquisition [1] taken in 1185 on the lands of the Templars William the king's brother and William de Peverelle are said to have granted to them lands in Ewell, and Henry of Essex the new mills of Ewell. A preceptory was certainly established here, although nothing is known of its history; for in 1309, when the inquiry was made into the charges brought against the Templars, Ralph de Malton was described as preceptor at Ewell, and Robert de Sautre as brother at Ewell.[2] After their suppression the manor of Ewell was granted to the Hospitallers, and in 1338 appears as demised to Hamo Godchep and his wife for life.[3] At the Dissolution it formed part of the preceptory of Swingfield.

The manors of Dartford and Strood also belonged to the Templars, but it is doubtful whether preceptories were ever established there.

HOUSES OF KNIGHTS HOSPITALLERS [4]

25. THE PRECEPTORY OF WEST PECKHAM

In the Valor of 1535 this preceptory, including the manors of West Peckham and Stalisfield, the rectories of Rodmersham, Hadlow, and Tonbridge, and the chapels of Shipborne and Capel, was valued [5] at £63 6s. 8d. yearly. Nothing is known of its history.

26. THE PRECEPTORY OF SUTTON AT HONE

Geoffrey Fitz Peter, earl of Essex, made a grant to William de Wrotham, archdeacon of Taunton, of all his land of 'Sutton de la Hane' to make a hospital for the maintenance of thirteen poor men and three chaplains in honour of the Holy Trinity, St. Mary, and All Saints.[6] King John confirmed the grant on 29 October, 1199,[7] and on 9 February, 1214, he granted that the brethren of the hospital should have that

[41c] Pardon R. 2–5 Hen. V, m. 39.

[41d] Assize R. 1532, m. 9.

[42] Early Chan. Proc. 15, 169 ; he appears here as visitor of the order in England.

[42a] Pardon R. 24–5 Hen. VI, m. 16.

[43] Hist. MSS. Com. Rep. ix, App. pt. i, 105.

[44] Chan. Warr. file 1763.

[45] See above. Ingram was elected in 1464 (Cant. Archiepis. Reg. Bourchier, fol. 96), and occurs as abbot in 1471 (Early Chan. Proc. 52, 278) ; and in 1472 a warrant was issued for his arrest (Pat. 12 Edw. IV, pt. 1. m. 18 d.). He was probably removed from office, for the abbot of Prémontré speaks of him in 1488 as a man of dissolute life (Collectanea, i, 84).

[46] Ibid. 107 ; Bishop Redman appointed a commission for the election after his death.

[47] See above.

[47a] Pardon R. 1 Hen. VIII, pt. 3, m. 9. He had been a canon of Bayham.

[47b] Aug. Off. Misc. Bks. civ, fol. 129.

[48] L. and P. Hen. VIII, iv, 6047.

[48a] Aug. Off. Misc. Bks. xci, fol. 89. Grant of a pension to him on 8 April, 1530.

[48b] Ibid. fol. 59. [48c] See above.

[49] B.M. Seals, lxv, 5.   [50] Ibid. xlvii, 460.

[1] Misc. Bks. Exch. K.R. 16 ; partly printed in Dugdale, Mon. vii, 821.

[2] Wilkins, Concilia, ii, 346.

[3] Larking, The Knights Hospitallers in Engl. (Camd. Soc.), 173.

[4] A detailed account of the possessions of the Hospitallers in Kent is given in Arch. Cant. xxii, 232.

[5] Valor Eccl. (Rec. Com.), i, 113.

[6] Cart. Antiq. m. 8.

[7] Chart. R. 1 John, m. 2.

land and whatever they might acquire afterwards with all liberties and customs such as the brethren of the hospital of St. John of Jerusalem had.[8] We do not hear more of the hospital, and it would seem to have passed to the Hospitallers, for in a list of their possessions Robert Basinge is said[9] to have given to them the manors of 'Sutton at Hoone,' Dartford and Hawley, and his son John de Basynges granted to them all the land which he held of their fee in those manors.[10] A large number of small grants in Sutton and Dartford are transcribed in the chartulary of the hospital,[11] and several of these are said to be made to the Hospitallers dwelling at Sutton at Hone, thus showing that a preceptory was established there. It was, however, broken up before 1338, when the manor of Sutton, with three carucates of land, was demised at farm to Sir John de Pulteneye for 40 marks yearly, the *fraria* or voluntary contribution, which was estimated at 20 marks yearly, being reserved to the Hospital.[12] After the Dissolution the manor and chapel of Sutton were granted in fee to Maurice Dennys on 22 March, 1544.[13]

MASTERS OF SUTTON

Walter [14]
Richard de Bramford, occurs 1251 [15]

27. THE PRECEPTORY OF SWINGFIELD

Swingfield was occupied by some of the sisters of the order of St. John of Jerusalem before these were collected together and removed to Buckland, in Somerset, in 1180.[1] After their departure the knights of the order appear to have taken possession, and a preceptory was established here at some time; perhaps when they secured the neighbouring manor of Ewell after the suppression of the Templars.

A full account of the *bajulia* of Swingfield is given in the report of the possessions of the hospital in England made by Prior Philip de Thame to the Grand Master in 1338.[2] The manor house, with a garden, was valued at 6s. 8d. yearly, the church at £10, a moiety of the church of Tilmanstone at £8, the *confraria* or voluntary contribution at £20; and rents and lands at Swingfield, Cocklescombe, and Bonnington brought the total receipts up to £82 4s. 4d. The expenses included £11 6s. for bread, £10 for beer, £11 for flesh, fish, and other necessaries for the kitchen, 69s. 4d. for robes and other necessaries for the preceptor and brother, 20s. for repair of houses, 40s. for the visit of the prior for two days, rents and suits of court, and stipends of three chaplains, an esquire and two clerks collecting the *fraria*, a chamberlain, a cook, a baker, a porter, a bailiff, a mower, two grooms and a page; and amounted to £52 18s. 4d., leaving 43 marks 12s. 8d. to be paid into the treasury. Ralph Basset, knight, was preceptor, and Alan Mounceux brother.

Pope Urban V in 1364 requested the master of the Hospital to make provision of the priory of Venice to Daniel de Carreto, preceptor of Swingfield and Buckland,[3] and on learning that it had already been filled he similarly recommended him for the priories of Rome or Pisa.[4]

In the Valor of 1535 the gross value of the preceptory of Swingfield, including the rectories of Swingfield, Ewell, and Tilmanstone, was £104 0s. 2½d. yearly, and the net value £85 3s. 3½d., the deductions including a pension of 40s. to the prioress of Buckland in Somerset.[5]

The preceptory and the rectories of Swingfield and Tilmanstone were leased on 16 March, 1541, to John Thorgood and Thomas Horseley for twenty-one years,[6] and on 20 July the reversion was granted to Anthony Awcher.[7]

PRECEPTORS OF SWINGFIELD

Ralph Basset, occurs 1338 [8]
Daniel de Carreto, occurs 1364 [8]
Edward Browne, occurs 1534 [9]

[8] *Cart. Antiq.* M. 7; Y. 6.
[9] Dugdale, *Mon.* vii, 833.
[10] B M. Cott. MS. Nero E. vi, fol. 240.
[11] Ibid. fol. 222–61.
[12] Larking, *The Knights Hospitallers in Engl.* (Camd. Soc.), 93.
[13] *L. and P. Hen. VIII*, xix (1), 278 (62).
[14] Cott. MS. Nero E. vi, 248 *d*.
[15] Ibid. 239.   [1] Dugdale, *Mon.* vii, 837.

[2] Larking, *The Knights Hospitallers in Engl.* (Camd. Soc.), 91.
[3] *Cal. Papal Let.* iv, 7.   [4] Ibid. 13.
[5] *Valor Eccl.* (Rec. Com.), i, 86.
[6] *L. and P. Hen. VIII*, xvi, p. 724.
[7] Ibid. 1056 (73).
[8] See above.
[9] *L. and P. Hen. VIII*, vii, 1675.

FRIARIES

28. THE DOMINICAN FRIARS OF CANTERBURY [1]

In 1221 a band of thirteen Dominican friars arrived in England, in the train of Peter des Roches bishop of Winchester, and passed through Canterbury on their way to London, which they reached on 10 August. At Canterbury they presented themselves to Archbishop Stephen Langton, who ordered their prior, Gilbert de Fresnoy, to preach before him, and was so much impressed with his sermon that he became henceforth a warm friend of the order.[2] It was, however, under Archbishop Edmund Rich that the Friars Preachers first made a permanent settlement in Canterbury.[3] It is probable that they came by the invitation of the archbishop, who made them a regular allowance of fuel from his woods,[4] with the consent of the monks of Christchurch,[5] but their chief founder and benefactor was the king.

On 10 March, 1236–7, Henry III granted them an island in the Stour,

between the land late of Master Richard de Meopham and the land late of Eleanor daughter of Iodwin on the east, and the land late of William de Bury and the stone house late of John Slupe on the west,[6]

and during the next twenty-three years the friars received of the royal bounty sums of money amounting in all to nearly £500.[7] Among the gifts were 30 marks for the fabric of the church from Queen Eleanor (17 June, 1237);[8] in 1242, £20 for their works, 20 marks and 30 marks for their church; in 1243, £20 for completing the church; in 1244, £10 for making two spiral staircases in the church;[9] in 1246, 20 marks for the fabric of the church; in 1253, 40 marks to pay debts; in 1256, 100s. for the glass windows in the church; in 1259, £20 for building the kitchen and the wall next it. The stonework of the church was probably finished in 1243;[10] and it seems to have been dedicated in honour of the king's patron saint, Edward the Confessor.[11] Henry on several occasions gave the friars timber from the royal forests,[12] the last grant being one of ten oaks for some repairs to their buildings in 1271;[13] and he continued Archbishop Edmund's gifts of fuel after his withdrawal from the country in 1237.[14] Further, the king permitted the friars to stop up a street leading to the mill of the abbot of St. Augustine in 1247, 'so that they made another road beyond a certain plot which the king had caused Stephen parson of Hadlinges to purchase with the royal money.'[15]

Another early benefactor of the Friars Preachers was John of Stockwell, citizen, who gave them a plot to enlarge their area. This plot was subject to a yearly rent of 4d. to the monastery of St. Augustine; Henry III requested the monks to remit this rent, but on 25 June, 1253, he ordered the sheriff of Kent, in case the monks refused, to find an equal rent for them in another part of the city, so that the friars might be quit of the charge.[16] To requite their benefactor the friars obtained from the king in 1256 that John of Stockwell should be free from all tallage of the city for three years.[17]

When the inquisitions were taken under the great commission of inquiry appointed by Edward I in 1274, it was found (1275) that these friars had enlarged their island and made a 'purpresture' on the bank, to the injury of and hindrance to the king's mills, blocked up and changed the common way by which people were accustomed to go to the water, and inclosed some land on the river bank 10 perches long and nearly six feet broad.[18] No proceedings were taken against the friars, who probably had legal justification for their actions.

On his return from Gascony in 1289 Edward I granted the Friars Preachers of Canterbury 50s.

---

[1] The Rev. C. F. R. Palmer, O.P., has given a detailed account of this friary in *Arch. Cant.* xiii, 81–96.

[2] Nic. Trivet, *Ann.* 209.

[3] Lib. R. 22 Hen. III, m. 2. Palmer erroneously states that there were twenty-two friars, having misread this entry.

[4] Close, 25 Hen. III, m. 10; *Arch. Cant. ut supra.*

[5] The armorial bearings of this priory were azure on a plain cross argent with the letters ᴵₓ in old English characters (being the arms of the priory of Christchurch) between four mitres labelled or; Hasted, *Kent*, iv, 448.

[6] Chart. R. 21 Hen. III, m. 6.

[7] See Lib. R. of the following years of Hen. III: 21, m. 7; 22, m. 10, 2; 23, m. 10, 14, 21; 24, m. 8, 11, 22; 26, m. 4, 5, 11; 28, m. 11, 16, 18; 30, m. 10; 31, m. 10; 32, m. 13; 33, m. 4; 35, m. 18; 37, m. 6; 40, m. 3; 42, m. 2; 43, m. 8; 44, m. 6, 10; Pat. 42. Hen. III, m. 2.

[8] Lib. R. 21 Hen. III, m. 7.

[9] Ibid. 28 Hen. III, m. 16, 'ad duas vermas faciendas.'

[10] Ibid. m. 18.

[11] Pat. 42 Hen. III, m. 2; Lib. R. 43 Hen. III, m. 8; acknowledgement and payment of a debt by the king of £32, 'which by our order they spent on buildings at Canterbury in honour of St. Edward the king our patron.'

[12] Lib. R. 25 Hen. III, m. 12; Close, 25 Hen. III, m. 16, 11; ibid. 28 Hen. III, m. 7.

[13] Close, 55 Hen. III, m. 5.

[14] Ibid. 25 Hen. III. m. 10.

[15] Ibid. 31 Hen. III, m. 11.

[16] Lib. R. 37 Hen. III, m. 21.

[17] Pat. 40 Hen. III, m. 2.

[18] *Hund.* R. (Rec. Com.), i, 203.

for three days' food;[19] in 1293, during the vacancy of the see, he supplied them with fuel from the archiepiscopal woods, and with twelve oaks for piles in order to make a quay.[20] Between 1297 and 1302 the king gave them several money grants for food, from which it would appear that the number of friars residing in the house at this time was about thirty.[21]

In 1294 Nicholas de Honyngton proposed to confer on these friars a messuage in Canterbury, held immediately of the heirs of Letitia, daughter of James de Porta, by an annual service of 8s. 9d. and two hens, and valued at 13s. 4d. a year.[22] An inquiry was held and a favourable return made, but no licence for the grant is on record.

In July of the same year the friars settled some disputes with the monks of Christchurch with regard to the rents due to the latter.[23] They were still paying an annual rent of 6s. 8d. to Christchurch in 1535.[24]

In 1300 Archbishop Winchelsey licensed six Friars Preachers to hear confessions in the diocese of Canterbury, namely, Edmund de Amory, John de Swanton, Walter de Cruce, Richard de Overlonde, Richard de Maydestan, Walter de Moningsham.[25]

Isabel of France, queen of Edward II, made an offering of a cloth of gold at the high altar of this church on 23 February, 1313–14.[26] Edward II, when at Canterbury on 5 March, 1319–20, gave 10s. to the friars for one day's food,[27] and made a similar grant on 29 May, 1326.[28] The number of friars at this time was probably thirty.

When in 1328 a subsidy was demanded of the city of Canterbury for the Scottish war, the convent of Christchurch was called upon to pay its share, and upon a refusal being given, William of Chilham, the bailiff, called a meeting of the citizens in the Black Friars' churchyard and organized a furious riot against the monks.[29]

In his journeys made between 23 February, 1334–5 and 26 March following, Edward III gave alms to many communities of friars for food, and amongst them 16s. 4d. to the Friars Preachers of Canterbury. On 18 June, 1336–7, he gave a groat to each of the thirty-four friars of this house.[30]

The friars continued to add to their area. In 1299 Thomas, parson of Chartham, gave them a plot of land 150 ft. by 120 ft., valued at 12d. a year, for the enlargement of their churchyard.[31] On 1 January, 1318–19, they obtained two small plots adjacent to their dwelling-place, one from Edward II, the other from Simon Bertelot of Canterbury; the former plot according to the jurors was never of any value; the latter brought in 1d. a year to the crown.[32] In 1338 a messuage held of the archbishop at a rent of 15s. a year and worth 6s. 8d. over and above the rent, was given them by William le Frenshe and John atte Brome of Canterbury.[33] Shortly after this they acquired from Isabel widow of Thomas Poldre and the heirs of Simon de Bertelot a plot of land, built on, containing 1 acre, 1 pole, for the enlargement of their dwelling-place, without the royal licence. In 1355, however, Edward III made them a free grant of it, on condition that the friars should be the more strongly bound to pray for the souls of his progenitors and himself.[34]

In 1356 the Black Friars by deed handed over to the hospital of Eastbridge a place, shops and garden, lying between 'our new gate and the entrance to our church,' i.e. between Friars' Way and 'Brekyepotes Lane.'[35] The new gate stood at the end of Friars' Way in St. Peter's Street; it was beautifully built of squared flint, ornamented with carved stone works, and over the middle was a niche, in which stood the image of their patron saint.

It was pulled down in 1787.[36]

Some time in the latter half of the fourteenth century these friars complained of injuries done to their houses, walls, and gardens by the abbot of St. Augustine's, who had raised his mill-pond, ' by

[19] Exch. Accts. (P.R.O.), bdle. 352, No. 18.
[20] Close, 21 Edw. I, m. 5.
[21] B.M. Add. MS. 7965, fol. 7 b; Exch. Accts. (P.R.O.), bdle. 356, No. 8, m. 12; cf. bdle. 362, No. 14; Liber Quotid. &c., 28 Edw. I (ed. Topham), 30. Other references are given by Palmer, Arch. Cant. xiii.
[22] Inq. a.q.d. file 22, No. 14; Palmer, Arch. Cant. xiii, 85, gives the jurors' names.
[23] Camb. Univ. Lib. MS. Eᵉ v, 3, fol. 62.
[24] Valor Eccl. (Rec. Com.), i, 7.
[25] Wilkins, Concilia, ii, 264; cf. Ann. Mon. (Rolls Ser.), iv, 546 (the Worcester annalist speaks of eight Friars Preachers and eight Friars Minors obtaining licence to preach and hear confessions). In 1349–50 Friars Anselm de Valoyns, S.T.P., and John Valoyns were licensed to hear confessions in the diocese. Cant. Archiepis. Reg. Islip, fol. 12, 18.
[26] Lib. Expens. Reg. 7 Edw. II (quoted by Palmer, Arch. Cant.).
[27] B.M. Add. MS. 17362, fol. 4.
[28] Palmer in Arch. Cant. ut supra; the entry in Exch. Accts. (P.R.O.), 381 (14), has now perished.
[29] Hist. MSS. Com. Rep. ix, App. pt. i, 96, 98. Palmer, following Somner, supposes this to have happened in 1277; Arch. Cant. xiii, 88–9.
[30] Cott. MS. Nero, C. viii, fol. 202, 205.
[31] Inq. a.q.d. file 28, No. 14; Pat. 27 Edw. I, m. 22.
[32] Inq. a.q.d. file 131, No. 4; Pat. 12 Edw. II, pt. i, m. 15; for names of the jurors see Palmer, Arch. Cant. xiii, 86.
[33] Inq. a.q.d. file 247, No. 12; Pat. 12 Edw. III, pt. i, m. 15; Palmer, Arch. Cant. xiii, 86, gives the names of the jurors.
[34] Pat. 29 Edw. III, pt. 2, m. 21.
[35] Somner, Antiq. of Cant. 56.
[36] Hasted, Hist. and Topog. Surv. of Kent, iv, 448; Palmer, Arch. Cant. xiii; ibid. xv, 340–1.

which their herbage is destroyed and they deprived of their disports and other profits'; the friars petitioned the king for redress.[37]

Friar Richard Bourne of this convent had concession from the master general of the order, 5 June, 1392, that he should not be removed hence, except in the case of crime or grave scandal, and that he should be relieved of the common services of the community; and every concession made to him by his convent was ratified.[38]

On Saturday, 15 August, 1394, and the following days, the provincial chapter was held at Canterbury. The friars went in procession to the abbey of St. Augustine, then to the cathedral, where a sermon was preached in the vulgar tongue. Mass was celebrated according to custom by the prior of Christchurch at the Black Friars, and on three successive days banquets were held in tents, torn and tattered by the rains and the fury of the winds. On the first day the archbishop, who was not present, furnished the feast; on the second, the abbot of St. Augustine's and the prior of Christchurch acted as hosts, the expenses of the abbot being £10; on the third the friars enjoyed the hospitality of the lords of the county. In return for these great benefits and honours the friars granted spiritual blessings to the two churches, undertaking that every priest of the order in England should say six masses of every monk of both the churches.[39]

Friar William Boscombe, S.T.M., prior of the Friars Preachers, Canterbury, on 30 December, 1395, was commissioned by the master general to hold inquiry into complaints made against John de Ping or Deping, prior of the Friars Preachers, London, for some breaches of the rule, and to remove him from office if the testimony of six trustworthy friars of the London convent went against him. John Deping was not deposed, and became bishop of Waterford and Lismore in 1397.[40]

In 1412 the friars obtained from Henry IV a confirmation of the grant of the island originally made by Henry III in 1237.[41] In 1447 the master general of the order admitted the prior of Christchurch to the privileges of confraternity.[42]

In a list of priests living at Canterbury who were licensed to hear confessions at some time when penitents appeared in greater number than usual, probably at the jubilee of St. Thomas in 1470, are four monks of Christchurch, five

Dominicans including the prior, and two Franciscans, of whom one was the warden.[43]

The mayor and commonalty made a grant of 6s. 8d. for pavage to these friars and to the Grey Friars in 1481-2.[44]

The following persons were buried in the church or cemetery or cloisters of the Black Friars:

Sir Edmund Hawte, kt., and his wife Bennet, daughter of John Shelving, afterwards the wife of Sir William Wendall, kt., temp. Edward III;[45] Robert and Bennet Browne, esquires;[46] Johanna, daughter and heir of Henry Knowghte, 1450;[47] Agnes Baker of St. Alphege, 1464; Thomas Baker of the same, 1473; John Whittill, 1479 (buried in the cemetery); Roger Breggeland, clerk, 1479; Thomas Peny of St. Alphege, 1481 (buried in the cloisters near his son William); John Sloden, brother of the hospital of St. John Baptist, 1481; John Nash of St. Alphege, 1486; Nicholas Boys, 1487; Thomas Goldsmith of St. Mary Bredman, 1498 (buried between the images of St. James and St. Nicholas); Alice Elleryngton, 1512; John Walker of St. Andrew, 1513, desired to be buried before the image of our Lady on the north side of the church, and left 8 marks for making his tomb, 13s. 4d. to the prior, and £4 to Friar John Rows to sing at our Lady altar for his soul.[48]

Others of their benefactors were; Richard de la Wych, bishop of Colchester in 1253, who bequeathed to these friars a copy of the book of Hosea with gloss, and 20s.;[49] Roger de Northwood, who gave them 12 marks in 1342 for the soul of his wife Elizabeth;[50] William de Clinton, earl of Huntingdon, 1354;[51] Elizabeth de Burgh, Lady Clare, third daughter of Gilbert de Clare, earl of Gloucester, and Joan of Acres, daughter of Edward I, 1360;[52] John Tyece of Canterbury, 1361;[53] Richard atte Lease, kt., 1393;[54] Richard Fitz Alan, earl of Arundel and Surrey, 1393;[55] John Roper of St. Dunstan's Church, Canterbury, 1401;[56] Sir Stephen le Scrope of

[43] Ibid. 101-2 (D. and C. Mun. Reg. N. pt. ii, fly leaf).

[44] Cant. City Accts. (MS.).

[45] Weever, Fun. Monum. 238 (Weever calls these friars 'The blacke Friers Minorites').   [46] Ibid.

[47] Nicolas, Test. Vet. 291; Test. Cant. ii, 66.

[48] Hasted, op. cit. iv, 448, from Wills in P.C.C. Test. Cant. ii, 66-7. These friars received a fee in 1521 for burying John Maister a surgeon, who had drowned himself in a well, Hist. MSS. Com. Rep. ix, App. pt. i, 151.

[49] Nicolas, Test. Vet. 761.

[50] Arch. Cant. ii, 17-18.

[51] Ibid. xiii, 90, from Plac. Coram Baron. de Scacc. Mich. 33 Edw. III, rot. 20.

[52] Nichols, Royal Wills, 23.

[53] Cant. City Arch. Wills and D. fol. 3.

[54] P.C.C. Rous, fol. 22.

[55] Nichols, Royal Wills, 135; he was beheaded 1397.

[56] Nicolas, Test. Vet. i, 155.

[37] Anct. Pet. (P.R.O.), 11318 (no date).

[38] Palmer, Arch. Cant. xiii, 'ex registro Mag. Gen. Ordinis Romae asservato.'

[39] Thorne, in Twysden, Decem Scriptores, col. 2197. His account is not without difficulties. The feast of the Assumption fell this year on a Saturday, not a Sunday, as Thorne says.

[40] Arch. Cant. xiii, 91-2, ex reg. Mag. Gen. Ord.

[41] Pat. 13 Hen. IV, pt. 2, m. 2.

[42] Hist. MSS. Com. Rep. ix, App. pt. i, 104.

Bentley, 1406 ; [57] Richard Fawkener, of Warehorn, 1442 ; [58] John Chamberlayn, who in 1464 left instructions that a fit chaplain of the order of Friars Preachers, Canterbury, should receive 100s. a year for seven years for celebrating divine service for his soul in the church of St. Paul without the walls of Canterbury ; [59] Richard Tylle or Tilley of Selling, 1485 ; [60] John Halden of Fordwich, who in 1493 left £2 13s. 4d. for the reparation of the house ; [60a] John Bakke of Canterbury, 1500 ; [61] Joan Hougham, 1504 ; [61a] Elizabeth, wife of John Hale, alderman, 1506 ; [62] John Roper of Eltham, 1524 ; [63] Henry Hatche of Faversham, 1533. [64]

The fraternity of the gild of St. Nicholas kept by the parish clerks of Canterbury in the house of the Friars Preachers is mentioned in some wills at the end of the fifteenth and beginning of the sixteenth centuries. [65]

Friar Robert Shroggs of this convent made a pilgrimage to Rome in 1505, and was received into the hospital of the English there *in forma nobilium*, or as one paying his own expenses. [66]

When in 1535 Cranmer preached in the cathedral against the authority of the pope and in favour of the royal supremacy, the prior of the Black Friars preached against him, and was summoned to appear before the archbishop. Cranmer, on 26 August, 1536, wrote to the king detailing the matter and complaining that he was ' marvellously slandered in these parts ' owing to the words of the friar. Being a party to the case he did not wish to have the judgement of the cause, but insisted it would be a bad example if this man were not ' looked upon.' The prior's name and fate are unknown ; he probably escaped over sea. [67]

The Black Friars surrendered on 14 or 15 December, 1538, to the bishop of Dover, who reported that though in debt they were able with their implements to pay their debts, the visitor's costs and a little more. [68]

Immediately after the suppression the houses and lands were let to tenants ; the site of the priory with churchyard, gardens and orchards, to John Batehurst, or Batherst, for 40s. a year ; a garden to James Thomson for 2s. ; another garden to Thomas Lawrence for 2s. 8d. The friars had already demised a garden to Robert Hunt for 20s. a year ; and a chamber near the river late held by Friar Richard Mede, a fuel house near the door of the chamber, and a chamber or cell in the dormitory, to Robert Collens, LL.B. for 13s. 4d. a year ; and both leases were continued. The total rent to the crown was thus 78s. [69]

Hunt's garden was demised 6 February, 1543–4, to Richard Burchard for twenty-one years at 13s. 4d., 20d. being added in 1549 for a house built in the garden wall. [70] Batehurst or Batherst secured a similar lease for what he, Thomson, and Lawrence, held at the old rents. [71] He was a clothier whom the king wished to settle in Canterbury for the erection of clothmaking, and the Black Friars' house seems to have been used for this purpose. [72] In 1560 the whole property was purchased by John Harrington and George Burden, gentlemen, at thirty years' purchase, or £109 10s., to be held as of the manor of East Greenwich, in socage and by fealty only. [73] They soon sold it, and it passed to William Hovenden of Christchurch, Canterbury, who died in 1587. Peter de la Pierre or Peters bought it in 1658 and divided it among his five children on his death in 1668. [74]

The principal house of the Black Friars was taken down in 1800. In William Smith's plan of the city of Canterbury in 1588 the church is represented as having a tower surmounted by a high spire. [75] In the more detailed and accurate drawing by Thomas Langdon, [76] made 30 September, 1595, the church has no tower or transepts and the cloister lies on the north side of the church.

PRIORS

Lawrence of Sandwich, 1326 [77]
John Ryngemere, 1342 [78]
William Boscumbe, S.T.M., 1395 [79]

[57] *Test. Ebor.* (Surtees Soc.), iii, 39.
[58] *Arch. Cant.* xi, 370 et seq.
[59] Cant. City Arch. Wills and D. fols. 23–4.
[60] Nicolas, *Test. Vet.* i, 384.
[60a] *Test. Cant.* ii, 67.
[61] Cant. City Arch. Wills and D. fol. 18.
[61a] *Test. Cant.* ii, 67.
[62] Cant. City Arch. Wills and D. fol. 21.
[63] *Arch. Cant.* ii, 169.
[64] Nicolas, *Test. Vet.* 662.
[65] Wills of Ric. Cram of Cant. 1490 (Somner, i, 58) ; James Burmond, 1491 ; John Russhelyn, 1501 (*Test. Cant.* ii, 67) ; and John Whytlock of St. Alphege, Cant. in 1503 (Hasted, *Hist. and Topog. Surv. of Kent*, iv, 448).
[66] *Arch. Cant.* xiii, 92 ; cf. *Coll. Topog. et Geneal.* i, 62 et seq.
[67] *L. and P. Hen. VIII*, xi, 361 ; xii (2), 600 ; *Arch. Cant.* xiii, 93–4 ; Cott. MS. Cleop. E. vi, fol. 232.
[68] *L. and P. Hen. VIII*, xiii (2), 600, 1058.

[69] Mins. Accts. 30–1 Hen. VIII, No. 105 (Kent), m. 72b, 73.
[70] Ibid. 2–3 Edw. VI, No. 24.
[71] Enrolment of Leases ; Misc. Bks. Ct. of Augment. vol. 218, fol. 161.
[72] *L. and P. Hen. VIII*, xiv (1), 423.
[73] Partic. for Grants 1 Eliz. (Herrington grantee) Pat. 2 Eliz. pt. 14, m. 17.
[74] Hasted, op. cit. iv, 448–9, where the later history of the site will be found.
[75] *Arch. Cant.* xv, 346–7.
[76] Reproduced in *Arch. Cant.* xiii. Orig. in B.M. (*Cat. of printed Maps, Plans and Charts*, K. 16, 38 dd.)
[77] *Lit. Cant.* (Rolls Ser.), i, 183.
[78] *Arch. Cant.* ii, 17–18.
[79] Ibid. xiii, 91–2.

29. THE DOMINICAN NUNS OF DARTFORD

The priory of Dartford was the only house of Dominican nuns, or 'Sisters of the Order of St. Augustine according to the institutes and under the care of the Friars Preachers,' in England. The foundation of such a house was contemplated by Queen Eleanor of Castile,[1] and her son Edward II took the matter up. He proposed that the Friars Preachers of Guildford should surrender their house to a sisterhood, that the monastery of nuns should be made subject to the friary of King's Langley and should hold endowments for the maintenance of the brethren, who were forbidden by their constitutions to receive endowments for themselves. He petitioned the pope 22 April, 1318, to sanction this scheme, and addressed several Dominican cardinals and the master general on the subject.[2] These efforts failing, he tried to make over the priory of King's Langley to the sisters, but again failed to secure the papal licence.[3] At length Pope John XXII, 1 November, 1321, gave full sanction for a new foundation of a monastery of nuns, who should have the same privileges as those of Belmont in Valenciennes.[4] Edward II requested the master general, 9 March, 1322–3, to choose four devout sisters from one of the houses in France, who should instruct the women to be placed in the new monastery in the observance of regular discipline,[5] but he was dethroned before he had done anything more in the matter.

Edward III seems to have taken no steps to carry out his father's intention until after Thomas Lord Wake of Liddell, 20 August, 1344, had licence to bring over four or six nuns of the Order of St. Dominic from Brabant and found a house in England.[6] The king now took measures to establish the monastery projected by Edward II, and Thomas Wake seems to have retired in favour of his royal kinsman. Edward III sought the permission of the bishop of Rochester, 8 October, 1345, to found a house of sisters of the Order of Preachers at Dartford, and the request was supported by the archbishop of Canterbury. The bishop referred the matter (3 November) to the chapter of his cathedral and to the vicar of the church of Dartford, directing special attention to the probable effects of the foundation on the position of the church of Dartford ; this was appropriated to the bishop,

while a pension was due from the vicar to the chapter. The chapter (13 November) approved the king's plan, but demanded that security should be given against any future diminution of the vicar's portion or of the pension due thence to the chapter. The bishop, having probably applied meantime to the pope, gave the king a favourable answer, 3 February, 1345–6, subject to the indemnification of the parish church against all detriment and to the preservation of episcopal rights.[7]

The choice of Dartford was probably due to the generosity of William Clapitus, vintner and afterwards sheriff of London, who had before 27 April, 1346, laid out large sums in founding the new monastery at Dartford ; to enable him better to bear these charges the king exempted him from certain taxes and other public burdens,[8] and gave him in December, 1348, the custody of the lands late of Robert le Reyny during the nonage of the heir.[9] He further granted William Clapitus licence, 29 June, 1349, to assign two messuages and ten acres of land in Dartford to the sisters.[10] This was probably the site on which the house and church were built, at the west end of the town. In November of the same year the king applied to the pope for confirmation of the new foundation.[11] The sisters had licence to acquire lands and rents, not held in chief of the crown, to the value of 100 marks a year.[12] The house with all its goods was committed, 6 January, 1350–1, to the custody of William de Carleton to administer and dispose for its benefit,[13] and he and William de Thorpe were appointed, March, 1351–2, to superintend the house and to inquire what lands and goods had been left to it for the weal of their souls by some who had died of the late plague, but had escheated to the crown and had passed thence to others contrary to the will and intentions of the donors.[14] Carleton was summoned to give in his accounts as receiver into the Exchequer, in Hilary term 1352–3, but as he did not then appear the sheriff of London was ordered to distrain him to attend on 1 April.[15]

[1] *Cal. Papal Let.* ii, 217. On the history of the house, see Father Palmer's articles in *Arch. Journ.* xxxvi and xxxix.

[2] R. *Rom. et Franc.* 11–14 Edw. II, m. 13, 13 *d.*

[3] Ibid. m. 9 *d.*

[4] *Cal. Papal Let.* ii, 217 ; R. *Rom. et Franc.* 15–18 Edw. II, m. 13 *d. Bull Ord. Praed.* (ed. Ripoll Rome, 1730).

[5] Close, 16 Edw. II, m. 12 *d.* ; Rymer, *Foedera* (Rec. Com.), ii, 510.

[6] Pat. 18 Edw. III, pt. 2, m. 26.

[7] Documents printed in Thorpe, *Reg. Roff.* 312–14.

[8] Pat. 20 Edw. III, pt. 1, m. 11. He was sheriff of London 1347.

[9] Pat. 22 Edw. III, pt. 3, m. 12. The king also supplied Clapitus, who is described as ' warden and overseer' of the house, with wood from the manors of Chiddingly and Oldcourt, Sussex, 12 March, 1348–9 ; Pat. 23 Edw. III, pt. 1, m. 20.

[10] Pat. 23 Edw. III, pt. 2, m. 22. A tenement and various gardens in Hithe Street, Dartford, most of them held in 1507 by Christopher Todde, and several plots in the north of Dartford, had been granted by William Clapitus. B.M. MS. Arundel, 61, fol. 24, 26, 34*b.*

[11] *Cal. Papal Pet.* i, 187.

[12] Pat. 24 Edw. III, pt. 3, m. 13.

[13] R. Fin. 24 Edw. III, m. 5.

[14] Pat. 26 Edw. III, pt. 1, m. 16 *d.*

[15] *Arch. Journ.* xxxvi, 244, from L.T.R. Memo. R. 27 Edw. III.

The sisterhood was placed under the care of the Friars Preachers of King's Langley, six of whom resided at Dartford. Edward III granted them in 1351 a pension of £20 (5 marks each), and in 1352 paid £192 13s. 4d. towards making them a dwelling-house.[16] Friar John Woderowe, the king's confessor, was for some time superintendent of the works,[17] and was succeeded in this office by Friar John of Northampton, who in March, 1353-4 had a tally for £100 on the prior of Spalding in aid of the works.[18] The king further (1355) caused the profits of all the lands which had escheated to the crown on the death of Roger Bavent to be used for the building of the nuns' houses;[19] and the profits of some property in London formerly belonging to Augustine and Matilda Waleys were applied to the same purpose in 1356.[20]

The buildings were so far advanced in 1356 that a community of sisters could now take possession and commence religious observance under the friars already there. Four sisters were brought over from France, for whose expenses £20 was paid from the Exchequer (7 October), and one of them, Matilda, became the first prioress.[21] Ten more sisters were added, and the king gave them a yearly pension of £100, till a royal endowment of the same amount was made for their maintenance.[22] On 19 November he made the formal grant of the 'monastery of St. Mary and St. Margaret' for the weal of his soul, the souls of Queen Eleanor and Edward II, of all his ancestors and successors and all the faithful departed.[23] The pension was increased in 1358 to 200 marks 'out of the issues of our customs and subsidies in the port of London' for the fourteen sisters and six brethren,[24] with an additional 5 marks a year for each of the four French sisters.[25] Of the king's bounty they also received four casks of wine a year from the port of London.[26] The original intention of the founder

was to establish a convent of forty nuns, which with the sixty friars of King's Langley would make up the hundred religious contemplated by Edward II when he founded the friary of King's Langley.[27] It is doubtful whether this number was ever reached.

A series of royal grants and orders shows the progress of the building. The king, 2 March, 1357-8, empowered John Onle to take as many workmen as were necessary for finishing the work, and also such as were needed for carrying timber and stone.[28] On 24 September, 1358, he gave 200 marks for the construction of the church, and 100 marks for lead to cover the church and other buildings.[29]

In the spring of 1361 the masons' work seems to have been approaching completion. Simon Kegworth and others were appointed to gather as many carpenters, cementers and others as were necessary for the royal works at the priory, and also for carrying stone, timber, tiles, &c., and a writ of 12 April required all sheriffs, mayors, bailiffs and others to aid in the matter.[30]

The permanent endowments of the house were also growing rapidly. William de Nessefeld and Richard Caumbray were appointed 20 February, 1356-7,[31] auditors of the issues and profits which the sisters received from their manors, and John de Berland was made seneschal and supervisor of their lands in 1358.[32] The king authorized the sisters to acquire £300 a year in lands, tenements, advowsons, &c., and receive the letters patent and writs in chancery on account of the same, free of fines and fees.[33] He also in 1357 made over to them 850 marks out of the 1,000 marks paid by Sir Peter de Braose for certain manors formerly in the tenure of Roger Bavent,[34] and Queen Philippa gave them the advowson of the church of Witley in Surrey.[35] In 1367 the king gave them 1,000 marks for

---

[16] Pat. 25 Edw. III, pt. 2, m. 26. Exch. Issue R. (Pells), Mich. 26 Edw. III, pt. 1 and pt. 2, m. 19, etc. On the position of the friars' quarters see Dunkin, *Hist. and Antiq. of Dartford*, 168-9, and Arundel MS. 61, fol. 47.

[17] *Arch. Journ.* xxxvi, 244-5.

[18] Exch. Issue R. Mich. 28 Edw. III, m. 26; *Arch. Journ.* xxxvi, 244-5; Cf. Pat. 32 Edw. III, pt. 1, m. 22; 36 Edw. III, pt. 2, m. 10.

[19] Pat. 29 Edw. III, pt. 2, m. 22; Fine R. 30 Edw. III, m. 10; *Arch. Journ.* xxxvi, 245-6; Orig. R. 30 Edw. III, m. 14.

[20] Close, 30 Edw. III, No. 9, m. 6 d.; Orig. R. 30 Edw. III, m. 15.

[21] Exch. Issue R. (Pells), Mich. 31 Edw. III, pt. 1, m. 2.

[22] Chart. R. 30 Edw. III, m. 2.

[23] Ibid. In the *Valor Eccl.* (Rec. Com.), i, 119, it is called 'the monastery of St. Mary and St. Katherine.'

[24] Pat. 32 Edw. III, pt. 2, m. 31.

[25] Ibid. m. 34.

[26] Ibid. 31 Edw. III, pt. 2, m. 2.

[27] *Cal. Papal Pet.* i, 187; Chart. R. 30 Edw. III, m. 2; Pat. 30 Edw. III, pt. 3, m. 4. A case reported in the Year Book 38 Edw. III, which probably refers to Dartford, speaks of thirty sisters being contemplated in the foundation charter; *Les Reports de Cases en Ley* (1679), Mich. 38 Edw. III, p. 28.

[28] Pat. 32 Edw. III, pt. 1, m. 26.

[29] Ibid. pt. 2, m. 27. This sum was a fine paid by Ralph de Middelneye, kt. In the same year the king gave the sisters a 'crayer' with its equipment, which John Godman of Dartford had forfeited to the crown; Pat. 32 Edw. III, pt. 1, m. 3.

[30] Pat. 35 Edw. III, pt. 1, m. 8.

[31] Orig. R. 31 Edw. III, m. 18; cf. Pat. 31 Edw. III, pt. 2, m. 22.

[32] Pat. 32 Edw. III, pt. 2, m. 13.

[33] Pat. 30 Edw. III, pt. 3, m. 5; 31 Edw. III, pt. 1, m. 24.

[34] Pat. 31 Edw. III, pt. 3, m. 1; Cf. *Coll. Topog. et Geneal.* vi, 76.

[35] Pat. 31 Edw. III, pt. 2, m. 12; Witley in diocese of Winchester. Cf. *Cal. Papal Pet.* i, 244; Winton Epis. Reg. Will. de Edendon, vol. 1, fol. 98; vol. 2, fol. 38; *Cal. Papal Let.* iv, 517.

buying lands and tenements for the endowment of their house.[36]

We give a list of their endowments on 20 July, 1372, when Edward made a formal grant of the priory and its possessions to the community, to hold in free alms.[37] In or near Dartford, besides the site, the sisters had the lands and tenements granted by John Brond, chaplain, formerly belonging to William Clapitus and Jane his wife, in Dartford, Stone, Wilmington, and South-fleet; a messuage given by John of Chertsey;[38] three messuages once belonging to Roger Folkes; 2 acres given by Simon Kegworth; one messuage, one dovecote, 30 acres of land, 3 acres of meadow, 15 acres of pasture and 20s. rent, formerly of Robert Mount; 34 acres of land, 5 acres of meadow, and 6s. rent in Dartford and Wilming-ton, formerly of William of Wilmington; seven messuages, two tofts, four gardens, 128½ acres of land, 4 acres of meadow, 30 acres of pasture, 12 acres of marsh and 20s. rent and reversion of a messuage and 8½ acres, formerly of William Newport, citizen and fishmonger of London; a messuage and 7s. rent formerly Nicholas Crofton's; two messuages and a garden, formerly Alexander Folks'; a messuage formerly John Lambyn's; 3 rods of meadow and pasture for two oxen, formerly John Michel's; 16 acres of land, given by John Chipstede and John Walworth, citizens of London, in 1369;[39] 30 acres of land in Wilmington formerly John Pikman's; two mes-suages, lands, rents, tenements, and services in Dartford, Wilmington, Stone, Southfleet, and 'Mersch,'[40] of the yearly value of £40, which Alice Perers formerly held and which she gave up 10 December, 1371, for the priory, receiving from the king in exchange the manor of Wen-dover;[41] a plot of land called 'le castelplace' in Dartford, and 5s. 3d. rent formerly William Moraunt's. In London the sisters had certain property which came to them from Augustine and Matilda Waleys in 1356 and 1358, namely a tenement with six shops in Aldgate, one in Thames Street,[42] and a messuage and four shops in Fleet Street;[43] two messuages and three shops in Cordwainer Street,[44] paying a rent of £10 16s. 8d., acquired in 1358 of Margery de Weston, widow of Robert de Upton; a tene-ment acquired from the executors of Robert de Hauwode, late citizen and merchant of London; certain annual quit-rents in the parish of St. Martin Orgar, bequeathed to the Friars Preachers of Dartford by Peter Fyge, fishmonger, 1361;[45] and 66s. 8d. rent in Tannerfield and Westcheap, belonging to the manor of Portbridge, once Robert Bikenore's. The lands and rights granted to the priory on the death of Roger Bavent con-sisted of the manors of Shipborne in Kent with rents and services in Malling; the manors of Norton and Fifhide or Fyfield Bavant in Wilt-shire, with certain members and appurtenances of the same in Billegh, Ernewell, Traw, West-withyhull, Warminster, Bourton at Nash, Burton at More, Ditchampton, Foulestone, Wilton, Gerardston, Rollestone, Parva Durnford, Mad-dington and Purbeck, in Wiltshire and Dorset; the manors of Hatcham and Pitfold or Putford in Surrey; those of Brandeston and Combs in Suffolk; the manor of Colwinston in Glamorgan, with lands and tenements in Moldeston, Here-fordshire.[46] Further they had the manor of Portbridge, Kent, given to the king by John de Bikenore of Clavering, 1366, and the manor of Magna Belstead in Suffolk.[47] The advowson of the chapel of St. Edmund in Dartford belonged to them,[48] together with the advowsons of the churches of Witley, with the chapel of Thursley (Surrey), Washbrook, with the annexed chapel of Velechurch, and Appleton (Suffolk), Norton, Fyfield, and St. Michael in West Street, Wilton, (Wiltshire).[49]

For the tranquillity and quiet of the prioress and convent, the king, 12 August, 1372, ex-empted them from all royal taxes, gave them all manorial rights, freed the monastery from enforced hospitality towards any magnates or servants of the crown contrary to the will of the prioress, received it and all its goods into the royal pro-tection against the king's purveyors, freed it from all corrodies, and granted the sisters free warren in all their lands.[50] A royal licence of 18 April,

---

[36] *Arch. Journ.* from Exch. Issue R. Mich. 41 Edw. III, Easter, m. 1.

[37] Pat. 46 Edw. III, m. 28; cf. Anct. D. (P.R.O.), A. 5280. A translation is given in Dunkin's *Hist. and Antiq. of Dartford*, 115, and the charter is printed in Dugdale, *Mon.* vi, 538.

[38] A chaplain was maintained to celebrate for John of Chertsey and his family till the Dissolution; *Valor Eccl.* (Rec. Com.), i, 119–20. [39] Close, 43 Edw. III, m. 16 d.

[40] The saltmarsh of Dartford; B.M. MS. Arundel, 61, fol. 37.

[41] Orig. R. 45 Edw. III, m. 30, 34; Pat. 45 Edw. III, pt. 2, m. 7.

[42] Probably the dyehouse bought by John Lambard in 1544; *L. and P. Hen. VIII*, xix (1), 1035 (47).

[43] One tenement here called 'le Bell' paid a rent of 9s. to the prior of St. John of Jerusalem in England; *Valor Eccl.* (Rec. Com.), i, 120.

[44] Cf. *Cal. of Wills Proved in Ct. of Husting, Lond.* ii, 166; Close, 49 Edw. III, m. 32 d. 34; Pat. 49 Edw. III, pt. 1, m. 3; Pat. 19 Ric. II, pt. 1, m. 3. The sisters had some difficulty about this property in 1384, as their tenant, John of Northampton, draper, was convicted of high treason. Close, 8 Ric. II, m. 38.

[45] *Cal. of Wills proved in Ct. of Husting*, Lond. ii, 331.

[46] Feet of F. Suff. file 94, No. 5; cf. Close, 36 Edw. III, m. 43.

[47] Pat. 40 Edw. III, pt. 1, m. 26. For the manor of Bignors or Portbridge they paid a quit-rent of 10s. to the Knights Hospitallers; Dunkin, *Hist. and Antiq. of Dartford*, 286.

[48] Many presentations to this chapel are noted in Dunkin, *Hist. and Antiq. of Dartford*.

[49] Cf. *Cal. Papal Let.* iv, 517.

[50] Chart. R. 46 Edw. III, m. 2.

1373, enabled the community to lease for life or in fee-simple all the manors and lands which they had received of the royal gift.[51] In July they had the king's grant of the advowson of the church of King's Langley and licence to appropriate it.[52] A papal brief of Gregory XI had already been granted sanctioning this appropriation on the plea that the means of the sisters were so slender that they could not fitly maintain themselves and support the burdens incumbent on them.[53] They also had permission to appropriate the church of Norton Scudamore or Norton Bavant and to accept from William of Huntingfield the advowson of the church of Boxworth (co. Camb.).[54]

Sir John Daunteseye, kt., 11 November, 1373, acknowledged in Chancery his debt of 1,000 marks to the prioress of Dartford and bound himself to pay half at next Michaelmas and half at the Michaelmas following. He released to the prior and friars of Dartford his inheritance of Baventre (?), for which they gave him 300 marks. This sum was restored to the prior of King's Langley and the prioress of Dartford by the king in 1374 and 1376.[55]

Friar Thomas Walsh being at this time prior of King's Langley and of the house of the sisters at Dartford had a yearly pension of 10 marks granted to him out of the sisters' revenues as long as he remained in office.[56] The prioress and convent in 1386 granted to William of Gainsborough, clerk, parson of Norton Bavant, a yearly rent of £18 for his life.[57]

Richard II was reckoned the second founder of the house.[58] In 1380 he confirmed many of the grants of his grandfather,[59] and gave the sisters, 3 September, 1384, the manor of Massingham and the reversion of the manor of West Wrotham (Norfolk) to find a chaplain to celebrate mass daily in the chapel lately built in the infirmary, for the relief and maintenance of the sick sisters and friars there, and for continual prayers for the soul of the king and other bene-

factors.[60] Richard also granted to the convent in 1392 four messuages, one toft, four gardens, 48 acres of land, 2 acres of pasture, and 12s. 3½d. rent in Dartford, and a tenement built at 'le Haywharf' in London, all which he acquired of Walter atte Water of Dartford.[61]

In this reign the plan of endowing the priory of King's Langley through the medium of the sisters of Dartford was at length carried out; the advowson of the churches of 'Wylye' near Baldock and Great Gaddesden (Hertfordshire), the manors of Preston, Elmstone, Overland, Woodling, King's Ham, Westgate, Goodnestone, Wadeslade, Harrietsham, Beaurepaire, and Packmanstone, all in Kent, being granted to the sisters for the use and benefit of the friars of King's Langley.[62]

Henry IV confirmed the various grants of his predecessor,[63] and ordered the chief butler to deliver to the sisters all the arrears of the four casks of wine yearly which Edward III had granted in 1357.[64] In 1404–5 William Makenade and William Cave paid a fine of 5 marks for licence to confer on the priory three messuages with some land and wood in Bexley and Dartford, the whole being worth 13s. 4d. a year besides reprises.[65] By common recovery the prioress received in 1405 from William Baret of Dickleburgh and Jane his wife three tofts, a dovecote, 104 acres of land, 1 acre of meadow, 15d. rent, and the liberty of three folds in East Wrotham, West Wrotham, and Elryngton; for this she paid 20 marks of silver.[66] In 1406 Makenade and Cave had licence to assign to the sisters two tofts, 66 acres of land, 12 acres of 'bruery,' 22d. rent, and the liberty of three folds in West Wrotham; these were held of the countess of Warenne, and were worth 4 marks a year.[67] In 1407 the same benefactors, with John Martyn and others, had licence to assign to the sisters a messuage called Gyldenhill and another called Fyndares tenement, three tofts, 166 acres of land, pasture and wood, and 3½d. of rent in Sutton at Hone, and 20s. rent from a tenement called Crowchefeld in Dartford.[68] William

---

[51] Pat. 47 Edw. III, pt. 1, m. 7.

[52] Ibid. pt. 2, m. 34. From the church of King's Langley a pension of 2 marks a year was due to the priory of St. Oswald Nostell till 1390 when various persons granted the prior and convent lands in exchange for the pension; Pat. 13 Ric. II, pt. 3, m. 28.

[53] Linc. Epis. Reg. Buckingham, vol. 1, fol. 305; Clutterbuck, *County of Hertford*, i, 435.

[54] Pat. 47 Edw. III, pt. 2, m. 32, 30.

[55] Close, 47 Edw. III, m. 12 d.; Exch. Issue R. Mich. 49 Edw. III, m. 8; 50 Edw. III, m. 4; 51 Edw. III, m. 18.

[56] Pat. 48 Edw. III, pt. 1, m. 21.

[57] Close, 9 Ric. II, m. 21 d.; Pat. 9 Ric. II, pt. 2, m. 22.

[58] Weever, *Fun. Monum.* 335.

[59] Chart. R. 3 Ric. II, No. 1; Pat. 4 Ric. II, pt. 2, m. 29. A fine of 5 marks was paid for the confirmation.

[60] Pat. 8 Ric. II, pt. 2, m. 25, printed in Dugdale, *Mon.* vi, 539; translation in Dunkin, *Hist. and Antiq. of Dartford*, 121. These manors were held by several tenants during the life of Catherine de Breous or Braose, who became a nun at Dartford in 1378. See below. [61] Pat. 16 Ric. II, pt. 2, m. 31.

[62] Pat. 17 Ric. II, pt. 2, m. 35; cf. *Rot. Parl.* iii, 61; Pat. 22 Ric. II, pt. 3, m. 15.

[63] Pat. 1 Hen. IV, pt. 2, m. 24; pt. 5, m. 2; Chart. R. 1 Hen. IV, pt. 2, m. 14.

[64] Close, 1 Hen. IV, pt. 1, m. 29.

[65] Inq. a.q.d. fol. 436, No. 10; Pat. 6 Hen. IV, pt. 1, m. 15. [66] Feet of F. Norf. 7 Hen. IV, No. 61.

[67] Inq. a.q.d. file 437, No. 2; Pat. 8 Hen. IV, pt. 1, m. 29.

[68] Inq. a.q.d. file 438, No. 16; Pat. 8 Hen. IV, pt. 2, m. 14. Some of these were subject to quit-rents to the Knights Hospitallers; Dunkin, op. cit. 286.

Makenade was for many years one of the attorneys of the prioress; in this office he was for some years associated with Friar Walter Durant.[69]

Confirmations of several earlier grants were obtained from Henry V and Henry VI.[70]

Early in the fifteenth century the sisters tried to free themselves from subjection to the prior of King's Langley. In 1415 the provincial visited the priory 'for the increase of religion and reformation of due obedience,' and for this purpose sought the help of the king, who commissioned Master John Aylmere and Master Richard Alkyrton to assist his inquiry and to chastise offenders. The question was referred to the pope, and Martin V, 16 July, 1418, decided wholly in favour of King's Langley, to whose obedience the sisters were enforced by ecclesiastical censures.[71]

In 1436 the convent received a messuage and $17\frac{1}{2}$ acres of wood and land in Dartford from John Martyn, sometime justice of the Common Pleas, William Rotheley[72] and Walter Greneherst, and 7 acres of wood in Bexley from Martyn, the whole being valued at 10s. 4d. a year.[73] At the same time licence was given to Thomas Osborn, mercer, and John Selby, citizens of London, to assign to the priory two messuages in St. Alban's parish, Cripplegate Ward, worth 16s. 8d. a year; and the moiety of twenty messuages, part in Cripplegate, part in Broad Street Ward, valued at 58s. 4d. a year. A fine of 26 marks was paid for the mortmain licence.[74]

In 1446 Edmund Langford, esq., assigned to the prioress and convent all his property in Wood Street and Broad Street near to Austin Friars, consisting of lands, tenements, and rents worth £3 a year.[75] At this time Margaret Beaumont, daughter of Henry Lord Beaumont, was prioress. Having obtained royal licence 20 November, 1458, she sold with the consent of her chapter a messuage adjoining the churchyard of St. Mary de Arcubus, heavy expenses rendering this necessary.[76] About this time the bishop of Lincoln compelled the prioress of Dartford to increase

the portion of the vicar of Great Gaddesden by 5 marks, and to distribute 4s. yearly to the poor of the parish.[77]

Of the next prioress, Alice Branthwait, an interesting memorial is still preserved in the British Museum.[78] It is a manuscript containing 'The Treetis that is kallid Prickynge of Love made bi a frere menour Bonaventure that was Cardynal of the Court of Rome.' On the fly-leaf are the notes :—

Thys boyk longyth to Dame Alys braintwath the worchypfull prioras of Dartford. 'Orate pro anima Domina (sic) Elizabith Rede huius loci . . .[79] Orate pro anima Joanne Newmarche.'[80]

In 1471–2 Joan, daughter of Lord Scrope of Bolton, the prioress, obtained further grants of property : namely, from Sir Thomas Ursewyk, Chief Baron of the Exchequer, Henry Spelman, Richard Nedeham, and John Colard, the manor of Crokenhill in the parish of Eynsford, Kent, valued at 5 marks a year, some lands and tenements in Eynsford, Lullingstone, and Frindsbury, and elsewhere (valued at £4 5s. 5d. a year in all), and the rent of 20s. out of an inn called 'le Hole Bole,' of old called 'Whalesbone,' in Dartford; further, from the same donors, the manor of Pettescourt in the parishes of Bapchild and Linsted in Kent, with 1 acre of land and a croft, worth in all 100s. 6d. a year.[81]

An inquisition taken at Penn in Buckinghamshire 28 January, 1479–80, found that John Hunden, late bishop of Llandaff and formerly prior of King's Langley, and Sir Thomas Montgomery, kt., might assign to the prioress and convent £5 yearly rent at Chenies (Bucks.)[82]; and an inquisition held at Dartford, 1481, found that Sir Thomas Bryan, kt., might assign to them seven messuages in Dartford, 300 acres of land, 36 of pasture and meadow, 200 of wood, and 13s. rent in Dartford, North Cray, and Wilmington, valued altogether at £13 6s. 8d. a year.[83] The obits of other donors of lands were celebrated in the monastery, but the dates and circumstances of their grants are not known: their names are William or John Millett, who gave lands in Dartford; John Exmewe, who

<hr/>

[69] e.g. Pat. 11 Ric. II, pt. 1, m. 4 ; 14 Ric. II, pt. 2, m. 36 ; Pat. 5–6 Hen. IV, pt. 1, m. 29.

[70] Chart. R. 1 Hen. V, pt. 1, m. 8 ; Pat. 1 Hen. VI, pt. 5, m. 32 ; 3 Hen. VI, pt. 1, m. 13.

[71] Pat. 3 Hen. V, pt. 2, m. 36 ; *Bull. Ord. Praed.; Arch. Journ.* xxxvi, 256–7.

[72] Five cottages in Dartford were given to the priory by Roger Rotheley (*L. and P. Hen. VIII,* xix (2), 690 (15)), who died in 1468, leaving 10 marks to the convent ; Dunkin, op. cit. 129.

[73] Inq. a.q.d. file 448, No. 8 ; Pat. 16 Hen. VI, pt. 2, m. 30.

[74] Inq. a.q.d. file 448, No. 7 ; Pat. 16 Hen. VI, pt. 2, m. 30.

[75] Inq. a.q.d. file 450, No. 29. In 1460 30s. rent was still payable by the prioress for messuages in Wood Street near the church of St. Mary Staining ; Anct. D. (P.R.O.), B. 2082.

[76] Pat. 37 Hen. VI, pt. 1, m. 18.

[77] Linc. Epis. Reg. Chadworth, fol. 8b.

[78] Harl. MS. 2254.

[79] Possibly prioress.

[80] Another volume belonging to the house is in Bodl. MS. Douce 322, a fifteenth-century collection of religious poems by Lydgate, devotional treatises by Richard of Hampole and others, given to the nunnery by William Baron, esq., 'specially to the use of Dame Pernelle Wrattisley, sister of the same place,' his niece.

[81] Inq. a.q.d. file 453, No. 13. Two obits were celebrated yearly for John Reynauds for lands given by him in Pettescourt and 'Belstede Parva' ; *Valor Eccl.* (Rec. Com.), i, 120.

[82] Inq. a.q.d. file 454, No. 19.

[83] Ibid.

probably gave a tenement in London ; William Sedley and John Nedmers.[84]

Many citizens of London and residents in or near Dartford left legacies to the sisters, and several were buried in the church or cemetery. Among these benefactors were Thomas Chayner, mercer· of London, 1361 ; Peter Fyge, fishmonger of London, 1361 ; Henry Vanner, 1394 ;[85] Agnes, wife of Richard Fagg of Dartford, 1452, who was buried in ' the cemetery of the Blessed Mary and Margaret, virgins, of Bellomont'; Richard Bolton of Dartford, 1457 ; John Millman of Dartford, 1462.[86]

Roger Rotheley of Dartford in 1468 left the nuns 10 marks. Roos Pitt, sister of John Groverste in 1470 left 1 mark to the convent, 20d. to Joan Stokton, and 20d. and a candlestick to Joan Mores, both apparently nuns. The Groverste family, the principal inhabitants of Dartford at this period, were doubtless benefactors of the priory ; there was a room in their mansion hung with tapestry, which, according to tradition, was worked by the nuns.[87]

Catherine, widow of Sir Maurice Berkeley, late governor of Calais, desired, 1526, to be buried in the chapel of our Lady in this monastery, and ordered that a tomb should be constructed there to her memory at the cost of £13 6s. 8d. : she gave to the monastery a suit of vestments, price £20, and left £8 a year for four years that a priest should sing mass for her soul.[88] Hugh le Serle of Dartford left by will, 1523, to the convent, after the decease of his wife, half the rents of two tenements in Overy Street, Dartford, the other half to be applied to the repair of St. Edmund's Chapel.[89] Sir John Rudstone, kt., citizen and alderman of London, bequeathed, 1530, £20 towards the amendment of the walls about the monastery, and white habits to the prioress and four nuns. Three of these had been gentlewomen to the countess of Salisbury.[90] John Roper of Eltham, Kent, esq., 1524, left to his daughter Agnes, the nun of Dartford, £13 6s. 8d. ; for the prioress and convent £3 6s. 8d.; to the lady Fyneux, sub-prioress, 40s.[91]

The property of the sisters was managed by a staff of officers. At the head was the high steward or seneschal : John de Berland was seneschal and supervisor of the lands in 1358 ;[92]

the office was held by William de Nessefeld in 1366.[93] About 1534, when Thomas Cromwell recommended the appointment of his servant Mr. Palmer as steward, the prioress replied that the office had never been occupied save by one of the King's Council, as Sir Reginald Bray, Sir John Shaw, Mr. Hugh Denys, Sir John Heron, and Sir Robert Dymmock, who had just resigned ; she begged Cromwell to accept the post with the usual fee.[94] The usual fee seems to have been £6 13s. 4d.[95] Cromwell took the office, and in 1537 received 10 marks as a half-year's fee.[96] The office of overseer of all the lands or receiver-general was held in 1437 by John Martyn,[97] in 1535 by Martin Sedley, with a fee of £8,[98] and at the time of the Dissolution by William Sydenham, with an annuity of 10 marks, potherbs for himself and his servant, and the usual overseer's chamber within the precincts of the monastery.[99] Other officers were the auditor and the under-steward. William Roper, esq., in 1529 received an annuity of 40s. for acting as steward of the manorial court of Colwinston.[100] Much of the nuns' land was let on lease ; thus in 1437 the sisters were receiving rents from the prior of St. Peter's, Ipswich, for some of their Suffolk property ;[101] in 1533 the sisters leased to Robert Dove of Dartford, husbandman, their principal house in Stoneham or Stanham, with many pieces of land, for thirteen years, at a rent of £20 14s. a year ; in 1534 to George Tusser of Dartford their manor of ' Bignours' (Portbridge), their two water-mills called the Wheat Mill and the Malt Mill and other premises for twenty-one years at £12 a year ;[102] in 1538 their property at Bavent Combs (Suffolk) to Sir Richard Gresham for eighty years, for £4 a year ;[103] and other leases were granted on the eve of the Dissolution. They rented from the bishop of Rochester the ' manor and domain' of the rectory of Dartford.[104]

The friars who served the spiritual needs of the sisters were six in number in the fourteenth

---

[84] *Valor Eccl.* (Rec. Com.), i, 119–20. Elizabeth Exmewe was a nun at the time of the Dissolution.

[85] *Cal. of Wills proved in the Ct. of Husting, Lond.* ii, 37, 76, 331.

[86] Dunkin, op. cit. 126–8.

[87] Ibid. 129–30 ; cf. ibid. 13 and 286 ; the nuns held land in Soceden (?) formerly belonging to John Groverste.

[88] P.C.C. Porch, 10 ; Weever, *Fun. Monum.* 335.

[89] Dunkin, op. cit. 145.

[90] Harl. MS. 1231, fol. 1.

[91] *Arch. Cant.* ii, 169.

[92] Pat. 32 Edw. III, pt. 2, m. 12.

[93] Pat. 40 Edw. III, pt. 1, m. 37.

[94] *L. and P. Hen. VIII*, vii, 1634. Dymmock was high steward in 1535 ; *Valor Eccl.* (Rec. Com.), i, 120.

[95] *Valor Eccl.* (Rec. Com.), i, 120 ; *L. and P. Hen. VIII*, xiv (2), 782.

[96] *L. and P. Hen. VIII*, xiv (2), 782 (p. 318).

[97] Anct. D. (P.R.O.), A. 3739.

[98] *Valor Eccl.* (Rec. Com.), i, 120. In Jan. 1536–7 Thomas Maykyn, overseer, was granted 5 marks annually from a ' selda' in West Cheap ; *Arch. Journ.* xxxvi, 265.

[99] *Arch. Journ.* xxxvi, 266.

[100] Ibid. 263. On a claim suit for arrears of rent here 1518, see *Ducatus Lanc. Cal.* ii, 15.

[101] Anct. D. (P.R.O.), A. 3739.

[102] *Arch. Journ.* xxxvi, 263.

[103] *L. and P. Hen. VIII*, xvi, 723.

[104] Dunkin, op. cit. 125.

century, but in 1535 only three are mentioned, each having an annuity of £5 a year.[104a] John Sill was head of the friars' house in 1396.[104b] The chief of the friars had the title of president; and the close connexion with Langley Regis seems in course of time to have been lost; for in 1481 the provincial had the right of appointing a president with the consent of the sisters, and the prioress had the right of choosing a confessor for the convent.[105]

Strict discipline and plain living were characteristic of the monastery throughout its existence. Sister Beatrice, the prioress in 1474, obtained a special licence to use linen owing to weakness and old age. Sister Jane Tyrcllis (sic) was permitted by the Master-General of the Dominican Order in 1481 to speak in the common parlour with friends of honourable fame even without a companion. Another sister in 1500 was permitted by the same authority ' to speak at the grill with relatives and friends being persons of no blame.'[106]

The nunnery was noted as a place of education. Sister Jane Fitzh'er (sic) in 1481 was allowed by the Master-General to have a preceptor in grammar and Latin who might enter the common parlour, where she and other gentlewomen received instruction.[107] Among these were not only nuns and novices, but also the daughters of nobles and gentlefolks sent to Dartford for their education, and there is some evidence that even boys were taught in the nunnery.[108] The practice of admitting secular women was not always approved by the authorities, and was forbidden by the Master-General in 1503.[109] But about 1520 Elizabeth Cressener, the prioress, was authorized to receive any well-born matrons, widows of good repute, to live perpetually in the monastery, with or without the habit, and also receive young ladies and give them a suitable training according to the mode heretofore pursued.[110]

The monastery formed a retreat for many well-born women. Catherine de Breous, daughter of Sir Thomas of Norwich, resigned the lordship of Sculthorpe on entering this house in 1378.[111] Elizabeth Botraus, illegitimate daughter of noble parents, was a nun here in 1412.[112] Bridget, fourth daughter of Edward IV, was placed in this house at the age of ten years, when her mother retired to the monastery of Bermondsey, in 1490; here she took the veil, and here she died, and was buried about 1517.[113] Lady Fyneux was sub-prioress in 1524,[114] and several of the prioresses whose names are recorded belonged to noble houses.

Elizabeth Cressener was prioress for nearly fifty years. In her time, between 20 November, 1507, and 1 November, 1508, was drawn up the rental of the priory, of which an incomplete manuscript still exists; it gives with great minuteness the situation, extent, and tenancy of the convent's lands in Kent and some of those in Norfolk, with the rents and services due, and shows the prioress to have been a careful administrator.[115] She obtained several privileges from Henry VIII,[116] and exchanged the four casks of wine granted by Edward III (which she had great difficulty in collecting) for an annuity of £16 out of the customs of London.[117] The few remaining buildings of the monastery probably date from her time; but the last years of her rule[118] were full of troubles, great and small. An attempt was made to compel her under the statute of farms (21 Henry VIII) to give up the lease of the lordship, manor, and parsonage of Dartford which she held from the bishop of Rochester. This resulted in a long and costly action, in course of which she had to sue for Cromwell's favour.[119] A full and formal acknowledgement of the royal supremacy was made by the nuns assembled in their chapter-house 14 May, 1534, in the presence of the commissioners, Friars George Browne and John Hilsey, and the seal of the convent affixed to the deed, though none of the nuns signed it.[120]

In 1535 the valuation of church property was taken to ascertain the amount of the first-fruits

---

[104a] Valor Eccl. (Rec. Com.), i, 120.

[104b] Dunkin, op. cit. 122.

[105] See extracts from the registers of the Masters-General of the Dominican Order in Arch. Journ. xxxix, 177–8; cf. L. and P. Hen. VIII, xi, 1322.

[106] Reg. of the Masters-General, Arch. Journ. xxxix, 177.

[107] Ibid.

[108] Thus Friar John George of Cambridge seems to have received his early education from the nuns of Dartford; L. and P. Hen. VIII, vii, 939; Gasquet, Hen. VIII and the Engl. Mon. i, 183.

[109] Arch. Journ. xxxix, 178.

[110] Ibid. Cf. L. and P. Hen. VIII, vii, 1634; the prioress petitions Cromwell that none be received into the house ' except they be of the same profession and habit as themselves.'

[111] Blomefield, Norf. (1807), vii, 173.

[112] Cal. Pap. Let. vi, 392.

[113] Some details about her will be found in Arch. Journ. xxxvi, 261. She had a pension of 20 marks a year from her sister Elizabeth of York; her grandmother bequeathed to her in 1495 the Legenda aurea, a life of St. Catherine of Siena and a life of St. Hilda.

[114] Arch. Cant. ii, 169. See also Plumpton Corresp. (Camd. Soc.), 14–15.

[115] B.M. MS. Arundel 61. Of the 15 tenements which the priory owned in the main street of Dartford, four or five were inns or hostels.

[116] L. and P. Hen. VIII, i, 825, 3527.

[117] Ibid. ii, 2021, 2101 (A.D. 1516).

[118] She was at her own request absolved from her office by the General Master in 1527, but was soon reinstated; Arch. Journ. xxxix, 178.

[119] L. and P. Hen. VIII, vii, 666, 1264; App. 34; ix, 1104.

[120] Ibid. vii, 665, given in full in Dunkin, op. cit. 148–50.

and tenths appropriated to the king under the Act of 26 Henry VIII, cap. 3. The *Valor Ecclesiasticus* gives the net annual revenues of the monastery as £380 9s. 0½d. The totals do not, however, always correspond with the detailed figures in the *Valor*. According to these the gross revenue works out at £495 15s. 5d., the charges allowed amounted to £134 9s. 11½d. and so the net annual value is £361 5s. 5½d. The property in Dartford itself was worth yearly £49 9s. 11½d.; that in the rest of Kent £142 8s. 8d.; that in London (including the £16 for wine), £66 11s. 10d.; and that in the rest of England and Wales, £237 4s. 11½d. The manors held by the sisters for the use of the friars of Langley are not included in these estimates.

The deductions allowed by the king's commissioners were chiefly for rents, expenses of management, and the celebration of obits. The alms given by the sisters consisted of £5 12s. 8d. a year, given twice a week, for the support of thirteen poor by the ancient custom of the monastery; and £6 10s. a year, paid weekly, to five poor out of lands in Swanscombe and Bexley granted for this purpose by William Millet.[121]

Cromwell shortly after this gave the stewardship of the house to Mr. Palmer, one of his servants, and the prioress could only escape this indignity by begging Cromwell to accept the post himself.[122] Her relations with the president of the friars at Dartford was another cause of worry; John Hilsey, provincial of the Black Friars, finding that he could not live quietly with Dr. Robert Strowdel, prior of the London house, unkindly sent him to Dartford;[123] Strowdel assumed the office of president, for which he claimed the royal authority, and subsequently purchased from Cromwell letters under the founder's seal making him president for life.[124] In the midst of these and other troubles, Elizabeth Cressener died, probably in December, 1537.[125] Hilsey recommended to Cromwell the election of Joan Fane or Vane, as prioress; she was good and virtuous and over thirty years of age; there were many older but none more discreet.[126] She showed her discretion by sending to Cromwell a gift of £100 on her election,[127] besides a fee of £20 a year as steward,[128] and by granting to her brother, Sir

Ralph Fane, a lease of the manor of Shipborne for ninety-nine years at £5 a year, and stabling for six horses within the monastery, hay, litter, and provender for the horses, board and lodging for two men for his life, with forfeiture of 3s. a day for every day that any part of the grant was not fulfilled.[129] She also provided for a number of other friends and dependants.[130]

The dissolution of the priory took place some time after 1 April, 1539, when the bishop of Dover begged Cromwell to let him 'have the receiving' of Dartford.[131] Pensions were granted to the nuns; the prioress had a pension of 100 marks; Elizabeth Cressener, perhaps a niece of the late prioress, 106s. 8d.; Agnes Roper, £6; fifteen of the sisters received pensions of 100s. each; one 53s. 4d.; five lay sisters 40s. each, and two others £4 a year each.[132] Of these twenty-six sisters, twenty were still alive and in receipt of their pensions in 1556.[133] Dr. Strowdel obtained an annuity of £5.[134] Fees and annuities varying from £4 to 20s. were paid to the clerk, the auditor, the overseer, the physician, some servants and others.[135] The grant of stabling, &c. to Sir Ralph Fane was in 1540 commuted for an annuity of £20, which was still being paid to his widow in 1556.[136]

Henry VIII kept the site and buildings of the priory in his own hands as a house for the residence of himself and his successors, and in 1540 made Sir Richard Long, kt., keeper of the same, with wages of 8d. a day. On his decease this office was conferred by Edward VI (1547) on Sir Thomas Seymour, Baron Seymour of Sudeley, the Protector's brother. In 1548 the king, in consideration of the compulsory surrender of certain lands in Surrey, granted to Anne of Cleves the priory and manor of Dartford.[137] After her death in 1557 the priory was restored to the Dominican sisters. Seven of the nuns who were inmates of the priory at the Dissolution in 1539 had already been permitted by Queen Mary to re-establish the conventual observance at King's Langley, with Elizabeth Cressener as prioress, and they were now (8 September, 1558) removed to their ancient habitation at Dartford.[138] Mary died on 17 November, and in 1559 three visitors chosen from the Privy Council came to Dartford and tendered the oaths of supremacy and uni-

---

[121] *Valor Eccl.* (Rec. Com.), i, 119–20. No account is taken of offerings, and there are a few other omissions, e.g. the manor of Billegh in Tisbury, Wilts. valued at £4 a year in the Ministers' Accounts, 34 Hen. VIII, is omitted; Dugdale, *Mon.* vi, 539.

[122] *L. and P. Hen. VIII*, vii, 1634.

[123] Ibid. xi, 1322, 1323.

[124] Ibid. xiv (2), 782. He gave Cromwell £4 for his confirmation.

[125] Ibid. xi, 1324, 1325, 1326. *Arch. Journ.* xxxvi, 265.

[126] *L. and P. Hen. VIII*, xi, 1324–6.

[127] Ibid. xiv (2), 782.

[128] *Arch. Journ.* xxxvi, 662; 1 Jan. 1538–9.

[129] Ibid.

[130] Ibid.

[131] *L. and P. Hen. VIII*, xiv (1), 661.

[132] Ibid. 650. The pensions seem to have been paid, though irregularly. See *Arch. Journ.* xxxvi, 269.

[133] 'Cardinal Pole's Pension Book'; *Arch. Cant.* ii, 49 et seq.

[134] Ibid. 56.

[135] Ibid.; *Arch. Journ.* xxxvi, 266–7.

[136] Ibid.

[137] *L. and P. Hen. VIII*, xvi, 713, 722; *Arch. Journ.* xxxvi, 269; Hasted, *Hist. and Topog. Surv. of Kent*, i, 220.

[138] Pat. 5 & 6 Phil. and Mary, pt. 3, m. 20; *Arch. Journ.* xxxvi, 270; *Reliq.* xix, 218.

formity first to Richard Hargrave,[139] provincial prior, and then to each of the nuns separately. All refused to take it, whereupon the visitors sold the goods of the convent at a very low rate, paid the debts of the house, divided what little remained among the sisters, and ordered them to leave within twenty-four hours. The band of Dominican exiles, consisting of two priests, the prioress, four choir-nuns, and four lay sisters, and a young girl not yet professed, joined the nuns of Syon House, and crossed to the Netherlands. They went first to Antwerp and were then sent to Leliendael, where they suffered great hardships; after two months they returned to Antwerp and lived on casual alms till the iconoclastic outbreak in 1566 drove them from that city. At length in January 1573-5 the Master-General ordered the sisters of Engelendael near Bruges to receive charitably into their monastery the three surviving nuns from England.[140]

The priory, site and buildings again reverted to the crown, and Elizabeth kept them in her own hands and rested at her own house here on her return from progression into Kent in 1559 and 1573.[141] James I granted the premises to Sir Robert Cecil in exchange for Theobalds, Hertfordshire, and Robert Cecil and his son William conveyed them to Sir Robert Darcy, kt.[142]

Soon after the Dissolution in 1539, the property of the monastery in Dartford was granted to several persons.[143] Many tenements in Dartford, including messuages and a wharf[144] in 'le Hithstrete,' besides lands in Wilmington, were granted to John Beer and Henry Laurence in 1544;[145] a messuage called 'le Bulhedde' and a forge in the tenure of Thomas Yarde, farrier, were granted to John Cokke;[146] a tenement called the Crown or King's Inn was let to John Thompson.[147] Martin Bowes, alderman of London, purchased some of the property in Bexley, Welling, and Crayford in 1540;[148] Henry Cooke, of London, merchant tailor, bought a house called 'le Tylekyll' in Bexley, and various woods, &c. in the neighbouring parishes;[149] Sir

Ralph Fane the manor of Shipborne.[150] The group of manors in East Kent which the nuns held for the use of the friars of King's Langley was granted to the bishop of Dover for his life, and the reversion purchased in 1544 by Sir Thomas Moyle, one of the general surveyors, for £962 0s. 9½d.[151] Other purchasers of the priory lands in Kent were Walter Hendle, Sir Percival Harte, John Wrothe, Thomas Babington, and Cyriac Petytte of Canterbury.[152]

PRIORESSES

Matilda, 1356, 1372 [153]
Jane Barwe, c. 1377, 1400 [154]
Maud, 1413 [154a]
Rose, 1421, 1428,[154b] 1432 [155]
Margaret Beaumont, 1446, 1460[156]
Alice Branthwait, 1461, 1465,[156a] 1467 [157]
Joan, daughter of Lord Scrope of Bolton, c. 1470 [158]
Beatrice, 1474 [159]
Alice Branthwayt, 1475,[159a] 1479[159b]
Anne Barn, 1481 [160]
Alice, 1487, 1488 [161]
Elizabeth Cressener, 1488 or 1489–1537 [162]
Joan Fane, 1537 [163]
Elizabeth Cressener, 1557 [164]

[139] His letter to the Master-General, dated Antwerp, 1 Oct. 1559, is the chief authority for these events; printed in Pio, *Delle Vite Degli Huomini de S. Dominico* (1607), 337.
[140] *Arch. Journ.* xxxvi, 271; xxxix, 179; B.M. Add. MS. 32446.
[141] Nichols, *Progresses of Queen Eliz.* i, 73, 350.
[142] Hasted, *Hist. and Topog. Surv. of Kent*, i, 220; Dunkin, op. cit. 184.
[143] The accounts of the property in Mins. Accts. 30–1 Hen. VIII (Kent), No. 105 et seq. are incomplete, some of the membranes being lost.
[144] The priory or 'le Hegge wharf'; see Dunkin, op. cit. 327–8.
[145] *L. and P. Hen. VIII*, xix (2), 690 (15).
[146] Ibid. 166 (25). [147] Ibid. (1), 648.
[148] Ibid. xv, 611 (25).
[149] Ibid. xix (2), 166 (71).

[150] Pat. 36 Hen. VIII, pt. 23, m. 26.
[151] *L. and P. Hen. VIII*, xix (2), 610 (67); cf. ibid. 981 (36).
[152] Ibid. xiv (2), 113 (15); xix (2), 34 (36), 36 (60), 527 (15), 340 (2).
[153] Exch. Issue R. Mich. 31 Edw. III, pt. 1, m. 2; Anct. D. (P.R.O.), A. 5280; Pat. 46 Edw. III, m. 28.
[154] L.T.R. Memo. R. Mich. 9 Hen. V, m. 9 (in reference to 22 Ric. II); Pat. 7 Ric. II, pt. 2, m. 30; 9 Ric. II, pt. 2, m. 22; 11 Ric. II, pt. 1, m. 4; 14 Ric. II, pt. 2, m. 36; *Rot. Parl.* (Rec. Com.), iii, 258; Pat. 2 Hen. IV, pt. 1, m. 9; cf. Dunkin, op. cit. 123 (confused with Joan, daughter of Lord Scrope). [154a] Exch. K.R. Accts. bdle. 81, No. 9.
[154b] Ibid. No. 13.
[155] L.T.R. Memo. R. Mich. 9 Hen. V, m. 9; Dunkin, op. cit. 124.
[156] Inq. a.q.d. 25 Hen. VI, No. 12; Pat. 37 Hen. VI, pt. 1, m. 18; Close, 37 Hen. VI, m. 7 d. Weever, *Fun. Monum.* 335; Anct. D. (P.R.O.), B, 2082; Dunkin, op. cit. 125.
[156a] Exch. K.R. Accts. bdle. 84, No. 10.
[157] Dunkin, op. cit. 127; Cart. 5, 6, 7 Edw. IV, m. 5; B.M. Harl. MS. 2254; Roch. Epis. Reg. vol. 3, fol. 235 d.
[158] Weever, *Fun. Monum.* 335; Inq. a.q.d. file 453, No. 133.
[159] *Arch. Journ.* xxxix, 177 (from the Reg. of the Masters Gen. of the Dominican Order).
[159a] Exch. K.R. Accts. bdle. 82, No. 15.
[159b] Ibid. No. 16.
[160] *Arch. Journ.* xxxix, 177 as above. [161] Ibid.
[162] Ibid.; *L. and P. Hen. VIII*, xi, 1322, 1324, 1325.
[163] *L. and P. Hen. VIII*, xi, 1324, 1325; xiii (2), App. 38; xiv (1), 650.
[164] *Arch. Journ.* xxxix, 179.

Impressions of several seals of the priory remain. A pointed oval seal of the fourteenth century, in which the legend has been destroyed, represents the coronation of the Virgin, under a canopied niche; on the right, in a smaller niche, a saint with a long staff, perhaps St. Margaret.[165] The seal affixed to the acknowledgement of the royal supremacy has a full-length figure of St. Margaret, crowned, under a Gothic niche with canopy and buttresses; in her left hand a book, in her right a long cross with which she is piercing the head of a dragon; below, a king (Edward III) crowned, kneeling, holding a small model church; on either side of the chief figure, a shield pendent on a tree with the arms of England and France. Legend :—

SIGILLU COE SORORŪ ORDINIS PREDICATORŪ
DE DERTEFORDIA [166]

A rough drawing of another seal attached to a deed of 1446 is given by Cole : [167] this represents two female saints (St. Mary and St. Margaret) seated under a double canopy, both crowned, one having a globe on her knee, the other praying; in niches on either side of them a crowned figure holding a cross with left, and a book with right hand, and a bishop holding a crozier; below, under an arch, a man in armour (the founder) kneeling and holding a model church; on the ground a crown. Legend :—

S. CAUSARU' PRIORISSE ET CONVENTUS
MONASTERII DE DERTFORD [168]

30. THE FRANCISCAN FRIARS OF CANTERBURY

On 10 September, 1224, nine Franciscan friars, with Agnellus of Pisa as the provincial minister of the new province of England at their head, landed at Dover, and proceeding to Canterbury stayed two days at the priory of the Holy Trinity, i.e. at Christchurch. Four of them then set out for London, while the remaining five lodged at the hospital of Poor Priests in Stour Street. Soon a small room was granted to them in the schoolhouse : here they remained shut up in the daytime, but in the evening, after the scholars had gone home, they used to sit in the schoolroom and make a fire; and sometimes they would put on the fire a little pot in which were the dregs of beer, often diluted with water, and dip a cup in the pot and pass it round, each, as his turn came, saying some word of edification.[1] The friars won the favour of Archbishop Stephen Langton, who when promoting the first novice in England to the Order of Acolytes called him 'Brother Solomon of the Order of the Apostles.'[2] Alexander the master of the hospital of Poor Priests gave them a plot of ground and built them a chapel : as the friars could own no property, this was made over to the commonalty of the city, and the brethren had the use of it at the will of the citizens. Their other chief benefactors in these early years were Simon Langton, archdeacon of Canterbury and brother of the archbishop, Henry of Sandwich, and Loretta, countess of Leicester,

the lady ankeress of Hackington who cared for them in all things as a mother cares for her sons and obtained for them in wonderful manner the favour of princes and prelates by her wisdom.[3]

As early as 1236 or 1237 Henry of Coventry was appointed lector in this house by Albert of Pisa, the second provincial minister.[4] The friary was in the custody of London.[5]

Henry III, who lavished gifts on the Black Friars of Canterbury, seems to have done little for the Grey Friars. Fifteen cart-loads of fuel in 1241, 50s. to buy wood in 1246, and six beech trees in 1272 seem to be the only grants by this king recorded in the Public Records.[6]

In or about 1268 John Dygg or Diggs, alderman and afterwards bailiff of Canterbury, bought the island called Binnewiht, situated between two branches of the Stour and 'the place of the gate on Stour Street,' for the use of the Friars Minors, and in time transferred them thither.[7]

Licence to inclose a road which formed the western boundary of their land was granted them in 1279.[8]

---

[1] Thomas of Eccleston's chronicle in *Mon. Francisc.* (Rolls Ser.), i, 1, 7.

[2] Ibid. 11.

[3] Ibid. 16 ; Weever, *Fun. Monum.* 260. She was the daughter of William de Braose : her husband, Robert de Beaumont called Fitz Parnel, died 1204 ; Loretta was still living as a recluse at Hackington in Dec. 1235 ; Pat. 20 Hen. III, m. 13 ; cf. Close, 17 Hen. III, m. 12.

[4] *Mon. Francisc.* i, 38.

[5] Eubel, *Provinciale Vetustissimum.*

[6] Lib. R. 25 Hen. III, m. 5 ; 30 Hen. III, m. 9 ; Close, 56 Hen. III, m. 7.

[7] *Hist. MSS. Com. Rep.* ix, App. pt. i, 108 ; Somner, *Antiq. of Cant.* ; Hasted, *Hist. and Topog. Surv. of Kent,* iv, 446. Perhaps the place 'qui dicitur Binnanea, circiter xxx iugera, inter duos rivos gremiales fluminis quod dicitur Stur' granted to Archbishop Wulfred by King Cenwulph in 814. Kemble, *Cod. Dipl.* i, No. 205.

[8] Inq. a.q.d. file 5, No. 1 (printed in *Mon. Francisc.* ii, 286) ; Close, 7 Edw. I, m. 3. This is probably the highway 10 p. long by 11 ft. wide which the friars had appropriated in 1275 'to the serious injury of the city and country' ; *Hund. R.* (Rec. Com.), i, 203.

---

[165] B.M. Seals, lxv, 40.

[166] Cf. B.M. Seals, xlv, 36.

[167] Add. MS. 5846, fol. 389. 'Inter chartas societatis de Leathersellers Lond. dat. 1446, 25 Hen. 6.'

[168] In the British Museum are also impressions of the seals of Joan Fane, prioress ; and of William Spencer, *servus* of the prioress in 1416.

From an agreement dated 24 June, 1294, between these friars and the monks of Christchurch it appears that the former had inclosed in their precincts several tenements belonging to the fee of the prior and convent of Christchurch; namely, the tenement once held by Samuel the Dyer (from which was due 7¾d. a year), that once held by Berengar in With (12d.), that once held by Seron de Bocton (6d.), the rent of Wilbert formerly prior of Christchurch [1167] near Ottewel (12d.), and the tenement of Stephen son of Lewen Samuel (18d.). The monks agreed to remit all arrears due to them 'for charity,' on condition that the friars should pay them a yearly rent of 3s. in lieu of all services.[9]

Gregory de Rokesley, mayor of London, left the residue of his estate in the dioceses and cities of London, Canterbury, and Rochester, to the poor in 1291, and instructed his executors to consult the warden of the Friars Minors in London and the warden of the Friars Minors in Canterbury about the disposal of his property.[10]

About this time, while Peckham was archbishop, the monks of Christchurch were employing a Franciscan as lecturer to their convent. In 1285 the prior wrote to the provincial chapter of the Friars Minors assembled at Cambridge, asking that Friar Ralph de Wydeheye, who had already for long been their lector, might be confirmed in his office; and every year a similar letter was addressed to the provincial chapter till 1298.[11] Ralph was succeeded by Friar Robert de Fulham, who continued to lecture till 1314, when the monks wrote that

his teaching has so sweet an odour in the city of Canterbury and has so fructified many of our congregation, his sedulous hearers, with the waters of Holy Scripture, that we regard them as fit to undertake the office of lector in our schools.[12]

Edward I granted these friars firewood in 1278,[13] and in 1293 fuel from the archbishop's woods during the vacancy of the see.[14] In 1289 he gave them 60s. for three days' food, in 1297 39s. for three days' food, and in February 1299–1300, 34s. for three days' food, and 40s. for four days' food.[15] The number of friars was probably about thirty-five.

William de Gerberg, kt., indicted of procuring some persons to commit a murder in Norfolk, took sanctuary in the Minorites' church of Can-

terbury and remained there full half a year (1305).[16]

In 1309 they acquired from James or John de Bowme a roadway leading from the highway to the water of the Stour, and obtained royal licence to build a bridge across the Stour extending from the said roadway to their dwelling-house, for the benefit of persons wishing to attend service in their church: the bridge was to be so built as to allow a clear passage for boats underneath it.[17]

Their new church and cemetery were consecrated by Archbishop Reynolds in 1325.[18] From royal grants it appears there were thirty-five friars in this house in 1320,[19] and thirty-seven in 1336.[20] Friar Simon de Husshebourne, O.M., when visiting his convent at Canterbury in 1328, had 10 marks of the king's gift for his expenses.[21]

The friars at Canterbury seem to have had the usual troubles with the parish priests. In a letter to the archdeacon of Canterbury, dated 2 December, 1287, Peckham maintained their right to hear confessions against the assertions of some rectors and vicars, and claimed that they were more learned and holy than the secular priests.[22] Archbishop Winchelsey licensed eight Friars Minors to hear confessions in his diocese in 1300.[23] Archbishop Reynolds licensed Robert of St. Albans, the warden, Nicholas de Clive and Alan de Bourne and William Venable in 1323, in place of four other friars who had been transferred elsewhere, and this brought up the number of Friars Minors thus licensed living at Canterbury to twelve.[24]

Two friars of this house, John atte Noke of Newington and John of Bromesdon, received the royal pardon in 1338 for rescuing two felons adjudged to death at Canterbury, while on their way to execution.[25]

A further addition to their precinct was made in 1336, when they acquired from Master John of Romney, Hugh le Woder and William, parson of St. Mildred's, Canterbury, a messuage and garden 10 perches square.[26]

The friars neglected to pay the rent due to Christchurch, and the monks in consequence withdrew the annual grant which they were accustomed to make to the friars; the queen dowager, Isabella, begged them to renew the alms in 1343, but the prior refused to comply.[27]

[9] Somner, *Antiq. of Cant.* App.; *Coll. Anglo-Min.* ii, 10.

[10] *Cal. of Wills Ct. of Husting, Lond.* i, 99.

[11] Camb. Univ. Lib. MS. Ee, v, 31, fol. 21b, 24b, 28, 29, 34, 48b.

[12] Ibid. fol. 156b; *Grey Friars in Oxf.* (Oxf. Hist. Soc.), 66.   [13] Close, 6 Edw. I, m. 3.

[14] Ibid. 21 Edw. I, m. 5.

[15] Exch. Accts. (P.R.O.), bdle. 352, No. 18; bdle. 356, No. 8; cf. bdle. 362, No. 14; B.M. Add. MS. 7965, fol. 7b; *Liber Quotid.* &c., 28 Edw. I (ed. Topham), 30.

[16] *Year Books of Edw. I* (Rolls Ser.), 33 Edw. I, p. 55.

[17] Pat. 3 Edw. II, m. 42; Inq. a.q.d. file 73, No. 8.

[18] Cant. Archiepis. Reg. Reynolds, fol. 146b.

[19] B.M. Add. MS. 17362, fol. 4.

[20] Cott. MS. Nero, C. viii, fol. 205b; cf. fol. 202.

[21] Exch. Accts. (P.R.O.), bdle. 383, No. 14.

[22] *Reg. Epist. Peckham* (Rolls Ser.), 952.

[23] *Ann. Mon.* (Rolls Ser.), iv, 546.

[24] Cant. Archiepis. Reg. Reynolds, fol. 249b.

[25] Pat. 12 Edw. III, pt. 1, m. 29.

[26] Pat. 10 Edw. III, pt. 1, m. 26; Inq. a.q.d. file 235, No. 7.

[27] *Hist. MSS. Com. Rep.* ix, App. pt. i, 87; *Lit. Cant.* (Rolls Ser.), ii, 263.

In 1358 Archbishop Islip, perhaps in consequence of the ravages of the Black Death, authorized five Franciscans of the convent of Oxford and three of that of Cambridge to preach in the diocese of Canterbury.[28]

The Grey Friars received numerous bequests, and their church was the burial-place of many people of rank and many citizens of Canterbury. Among those buried here were William Balliol le Scot, sixth son of John Balliol and Devorguila, 1313;[29] Bartholomew lord Badlesmere, who was hanged at Canterbury in April, 1322;[30] Sir Giles Badlesmere, kt., his son, 1337;[31] Elizabeth, lady of Chilham;[32] Sir William Manston, kt., and Sir Roger Manston, kt., his brother;[33] Sir John Brockhill, kt., 1382, and several others of this family;[34] Sir Falcon Payfarer, kt.; Sir Thomas Dayner, kt.; Lady Alice of Maryms; Lady Candlin; 'Sir Alan Pennington of . . . in Lancashire, kt., who coming from the wars beyond seas died in this city'; Lady Ladrie of Valence; Sir William Trussell, kt.; Sir Bartholomew Ashburnham, kt.; Sir John Montenden, kt., a friar of this house;[35] Thomas Barton of Northgate, Canterbury, 1476;[36] Margaret Cherche of St. Alphege, 1486;[37] John Forde of the parish of St. George, who desired to be buried 'in the north part of the church near the altar of St. Clement,' 1487;[38] Milo Denne of Canterbury, barber, 1490-1;[39] Hamon Beale, twice mayor of Canterbury, 1492, and Isabel his wife;[40] Richard Martin, suffragan to the archbishop and sometime warden of the house, 1502, who bequeathed to the friars his chrismatory of silver and parcel gilt with its case, and mentions in his will the chapel of St. Saviour in this church;[41] Elizabeth Master, 1522;[42] Alexander Elyothe,[42a] priest, 1524; Anne Culpeper, widow of Harry Agar, esq., 1532.[43]

Other benefactors were Elizabeth de Burgh, lady of Clare, 1360;[44] Sir Richard atte Lease, kt. 1393;[45] William Woodland of Holy Cross,

Canterbury, who left £5 for the repair of the church and 5 marks for the repair of the dormitory, 1450;[46] Richard Tilley, 1485, John Bakke, 1500, and Elizabeth, wife of John Hales, alderman, 1506, all of Canterbury;[47] John Roper of Eltham, esq., 1523-4;[48] Sir John Rudstone, kt. and alderman of London, who bequeathed to the Observant Friars here 'one long gray woollen cloth for their habits,' price 5 marks, 1530;[49] H. Hatche, who bequeathed 15s. a year to the Observant Friars of Canterbury, and 5 marks to every house of Observant Friars in England, 1533.[50] From Lord Darcy they received 5 marks in 1526.[51] Lord Lisle in 1534 authorized the collection of money at Calais for 'the Grey Friars of Canterbury who have no lands or rents.'[52]

The friars seem to have had a valuable library. Friar Ralph of Maidstone, who was bishop of Hereford, 1234-9, gave them a New Testament with gloss, now in the British Museum.[53] Richard Wych, bishop of Chichester, bequeathed them a copy of the book of Isaiah with gloss in 1253.[54] Five other volumes now in the British Museum also belonged to them; namely a thirteenth-century copy of the Gospels of St. Mark and St. Matthew;[55] a volume also of the thirteenth century containing Geoffrey of Monmouth's *Historia Britonum*, the *Historia Hierosolimitana* of James of Vitry, *Gesta Alexandri* and *Historia Romanorum*, and the Chronicle of Martin of Troppau;[56] a fourteenth-century manuscript of Genesis and Exodus,[57] and another containing the books of Isaiah, Jeremiah, and Daniel, the gift of Master Adam of Richmond,[58] and another of St. Paul's Epistles, the gift of Friar Henry of Rye.[59] A collection of treatises by Aristotle, Albertus Magnus and others on natural science, now in the Bodleian Library, belonged to John Bruyl, a friar of this house,[60] who in 1397-8 was warden of London.[61] And in the fifteenth century the convent possessed a volume entitled 'Notabilia super ecclesiasticam historiam et tripartitam cum extractionibus Willelmi Malmesburiensis,' having on the back of the binding the letters ƿ ı ƀ.[62]

In 1498 the house was included by Henry VII among the convents of the Observant Friars or

---

[28] Cant. Archiepis. Reg. Islip, fol. 144*b*.

[29] Weever, *Fun. Monum.* 238; *Arch. Cant.* x, 260.

[30] Weever, loc. cit. (Weever calls these friars 'The White Friars Observants.')

[31] Weever, loc. cit.; *Early Linc. Wills* (ed. Gibbon), 6.

[32] Weever, loc. cit.; Chilham castle and manor passed on the death of Giles de Badlesmere, through his sister, to Lord Ros of Hamlake. [33] Weever, loc. cit.

[34] Weever, loc. cit.; Nicolas, *Test. Vet.* 115.

[35] These names are taken from Weever.

[36] Hasted, *Hist. and Topog. Surv. of Kent*, iv, 447.

[37] Ibid.; *Test. Cant.* ii, 67. [38] Ibid.

[39] Cant. City Arch. Wills and D. fol. 12*b*.

[40] Somner, *Antiq. of Cant.* 82; *Coll. Anglo-Min.* ii, 11; Hasted, op. cit. iv, 447; *Test. Cant.* ii, 67.

[41] Nicolas, *Test. Vet.* 456; Hasted, op. cit. iv, 447.

[42] Hasted, loc. cit. iv, 447.

[42a] *Test. Cant.* ii, 67.

[43] Nicolas, *Test. Vet.* 661.

[44] Cant. Archiepis. Reg. Islip, fol. 164; Nichols, *Royal Wills*, 23.

[45] P.C.C. Rous, fol. 22.

[46] Somner, *Antiq. of Cant.*; Hasted, op. cit. iv, 447.

[47] Cant. City Arch. Wills and D. fol. 18, 21.

[48] *Arch. Cant.* ii, 169.

[49] Harl. MS. 1231, fol. 2*b*.

[50] Nicolas, *Test. Vet.* 662.

[51] *L. and P. Hen. VIII*, iv, 2527.

[52] Ibid. vii, 1620; cf. 765, 836.

[53] MS. Royal, 3 C, xi.

[54] Nicolas, *Test. Vet.* 761.

[55] MS. Royal, 2 D, xxiv.

[56] Cott. MS. Galba, E. xi.

[57] MS. Royal, 3 E, ix. [58] Ibid. 3 D, ii.

[59] Ibid. 3 D, iv. [60] Digby MS. 153.

[61] *Mon. Francisc.* (Rolls Ser.), i, 523.

[62] *Hist. MSS. Com. Rep.* ix, App. pt. i, 108.

reformed branch of the Franciscans.[63] The Act of the king was confirmed by Pope Alexander VI in 1499, and the English Observants, who had since 1484 been under the government of the commissary of the vicar-general, were formed into a province.[64] In his will Henry VII left 100 marks to the Observant Friars of Canterbury and entrusted £200 for their use to the prior of Christchurch.[65] They received £13 6s. 8d. from Henry VIII for saying daily masses for the late king in 1509.[66] They seem to have been active preachers in the neighbourhood ; they are found, for instance, preaching at Romney and receiving alms from that town in 1506 and 1517-18.[67] Alexander Barclay, the translator of the *Ship of Fools*, appears to have been for a time a member of this community.[68] A provincial chapter was held here in 1532, which William Peto attended.[69] Two friars of this house, Hugh Rich, warden of Richmond, and Richard Risby, warden of Canterbury, were among the chief supporters of the Holy Maid of Kent. They stood with her on the scaffold at Paul's Cross, 23 November, 1533, when Dr. Capon denounced the two friars in particular, for having ' suborned and seduced their companions to maintain the false opinion and wicked quarrel of the queen against the king.' They were then taken to Canterbury and made to do public penance, and were hanged and beheaded at Tyburn with the Maid and others 20 April, 1534. The bodies of the two Observants and the Maid were buried at the Grey Friars, London.[70]

Other Observant Friars who died at Canterbury about this time were Judocus of Amsterdam and Lewis Wilkinson ; another, Christopher Burrell, remained at Canterbury, mad. Some were sent away for safe custody, others fled abroad.[71] Only two—Father Mychelsen and Father John Gam—are mentioned as having

refused to take the oath of allegiance and supremacy exacted from the friars in the spring of 1534.[72]

The king did not suppress the Grey Friars of Canterbury at this time, but forbade them to go out of their house and appointed John Arthur as warden, against the wishes of the provincial. Arthur, who had left a bad reputation behind him at Oxford,[73] treated the Observants of Canterbury with severity, imprisoning some ' because they rebelled against the king and held so stiffly to the bishop of Rome, for which he daily reproved them.' He and his opponents accused each other of theft and immoral intercourse with women. His special enemy was Friar Henry Bocher, who succeeded in turning the tables on the warden by accusing him of speaking against the king. The charge seems to have been founded on a sermon which Arthur preached in the church of Herne on Passion Sunday, 1535, in which he blamed these new books and new preachers for discouraging pilgrimages, especially to the shrine of St. Thomas :

and he said, if so be that St. Thomas were a devil in hell, if the church had canonized him, we ought to worship him, for you ought to believe us prelates though we preach false.

The result was that Bocher was set free, and Arthur imprisoned at Cromwell's command. The provincial appointed an Observant, Arthur's ' mortal enemy,' as warden. Arthur, fearing starvation, succeeded in escaping to France.[74]

The bishop of Dover came to Canterbury on 13 December, 1538, to dissolve the friaries ; he found them all in debt, but the Black and Grey Friars were able with their implements to pay all their debts, the visitor's costs, and a little more.[75] The documents relating to the surrender have disappeared.

Cranmer had already, 5 October, 1538, written to Cromwell that ' as the Grey Friars, Canterbury, is very commodious for my servant, Thomas Cobham, brother to Lord Cobham, I beg you will help him to the said house.'[76]

In the following February the site was let to Thomas Spilman, one of the receivers of the augmentations, for 40s. a year.[77] A clothier named John Batherst asserted that the king wished him to have the house for the erection of

---

[63] *Chron. of the Grey Friars, Lond.* (Camd. Soc.), 25.

[64] Cf. Wadding, *Ann.* xv, 187–91 ; *Analecta Franciscana*, ii, 489.

[65] Astle, *The Will of King Hen. VII*, 30.

[66] *L. and P. Hen. VIII*, ii, 1445.

[67] *Hist. MSS. Com. Rep.* v, 550–52 ; cf. *L. and P. Hen. VIII*, ix, 789.

[68] Jamieson, *Notice of the Life and Writings of A. Barclay*, 16.

[69] Fr. à St. Clara (Chr. Davenport), *Hist. Min.* 51.

[70] *Chron. of the Grey Friars, Lond.* (Camd. Soc.), 37 ; Wright, *Suppression*, 19 ; 'The Holy Maid of Kent,' A. Denton Cheyney in *Trans. Roy. Hist. Soc.* (New Ser.), xviii, 114 ; *L. and P. Hen. VIII*, vii, 70, 72, 522 ; Thomas Bourchier, *Hist. Eccl. de Martyrio Fratrum* (A.D. 1582), p. 6 et seq. The belief that Rich was not executed (Burnet, *Reformation* (ed. Pocock), 252 ; Cheyney, *Trans. Roy. Hist. Soc.* ut supra) seems erroneous ; see letter of John Husee, written on the day of the execution (*L. and P. Hen. VIII*, vii, 522).

[71] *L. and P. Hen. VIII*, vii, 1607 ; vi, 726 ; ix, 789.

[72] Ibid. vii, App. 27 (7 June, 1534) ; Gam or Game was sent to London ; ibid. vii, 1607. Nothing further appears about Mychelsen.

[73] *Grey Friars in Oxf.* (Oxf. Hist. Soc.), 95, 96, 284–5.

[74] *L. and P. Hen. VIII*, viii, 480 ; ix, 789 (i, ii) ; cf. x, 571.

[75] Ibid. xiii (1), 1058 ; Ellis, *Orig. Let.* (Ser. 3), iii, 181.

[76] *L. and P. Hen. VIII*, xiii (2), 537.

[77] Ibid. xiv (1), p. 609 ; Mins. Accts. 30–31 Hen. VIII (Kent), No. 105, fol. 72.

clothmaking, but he failed to eject Spilman,[78] who, in July, 1539, bought the premises, including the church and bell-tower, for £100, and sold them in 1544 to Thomas Rolf or Roffe.[79] The lands consisted of the site of the house and two messuages, two orchards, two gardens, 3 acres of land, 5 acres of meadow, and 4 acres of pasture in the parishes of St. Peter, St. Mildred, and St. Margaret, held in chief of the crown.[80] Rolf in 1549, with the permission of the commonalty, narrowed the principal entrance (in the High Street, opposite the Black Friars entry) to a passage.[81] William Lovelace died seised of the house in 1576, and the property remained in this family for many years.[82]

WARDENS

G. c. 1250 [83]
Robert of St. Albans, 1323 [84]
John, 1479 [85]
Richard Martin, c. 1490 (?) [86]
Richard Risby, 1532–3 [87]
Gabriel Pecock, 1532 [88]
John Arthur, 1533–5 [89]
Bernardine Covert, 1534 [90]

The seal [91] of this house in the fourteenth century represented Becket's martyrdom, under a carved gothic canopy. In base under a pointed arch between two half arches, a friar praying to the right. Legend:—

S FRATRVM MINORVM CANTVARIE

31. THE OBSERVANT FRIARS OF GREENWICH [1]

The Observant Friars or reformed branch of the Franciscan Order obtained formal recognition and a more or less independent organization in 1415, but though Edward IV interposed to protect their threatened independence in 1471,[2] they seem to have had no separate house in England till ten years later. In 1480 Edward IV negotiated with William Bertholdi, vicar-general cismontane of the order for the establishment of a house in England, and 4 January, 1480–1, obtained the approval of Pope Sixtus IV for the foundation of a friary at Greenwich. The land assigned for the purpose adjoined the royal palace, measured 12 'virgates' by 63 'virgates,' and comprised a level piece of ground surrounded by walls, 'where the game of ball used to be played,' together with some old buildings which the king bought. On 2 July, 1482, the bishop of Norwich in the king's name formally handed over the site in honour of God, the Blessed Virgin and St. Francis, to Friars Bernard de L . . . , Vincent of Ostend, and others who had been sent over from the Continent by John Philippi, now vicar-general. On the same day the bishop laid the first stone with due solemnity, whereupon the friars as a sign of true and genuine possession chanted the *Te Deum* and the mass.[3] They now began to build at their own cost and labour, with the assistance of some of the faithful, several poor little houses in honour of the Virgin Mary, St. Francis, and All Saints.[4] In the meantime they appear to have used a chantry chapel of the Holy Cross which they obtained by the means of Sir William Corbridge, and which was still to be seen in Lambarde's time.[5] Henry VII, 14 December, 1485, confirmed this grant and founded a convent of Observant Friars to consist of the warden and twelve brethren at least.[6] The elaborate instructions for a stained glass window in the friars' church were probably drawn up under Henry's supervision and before the death of his queen in

---

[78] L. and P. Hen. VIII, xiv (1), 423. Batherst obtained a lease of part of the Black Friars.

[79] Ibid. xiv (1), 1354 (40) ; xix (1), 443 (10) ; Pat. 31 Hen. VIII, pt. 1, m. 26 ; Hasted, op. cit. iv, 447–8 ; Mins. Accts. ut supra.

[80] Hasted, op. cit. iv, 448.

[81] Bunce, Minutes of the City of Cant. (reprinted from the Kentish Gaz. c. 1800).

[82] Arch. Cant. x, 201, 205 ; Hasted, op. cit. iv, 448, where the later history of the site will be found.

[83] Mon. Francisc. (Rolls Ser.), i, 211.

[84] Cant. Archiepis Reg. Reynolds, fol. 249b.

[85] Bodl. Chart. 153, a blank form for the admission of persons to the privileges of the Order of St. Francis, written 1479, by John, warden of the Friars of Cant. in accordance with a grant of Sixtus IV.

[86] Nicolas, Test. Vet. 456.

[87] Wright, Suppression, 19.

[88] L. and P. Hen. VIII, v, 1312.

[89] Ibid. ix, 789.   [90] Ibid. vii, 765, 836, 1607.

[91] B.M. Seals, lxv, 19 (Cat. No. 2862).

[1] Speed's erroneous statement that a Franciscan friary was founded here in 1376 is discussed and explained in Hasted, Kent : Hund. of Blackheath (ed. Drake), 54.

[2] Wadding, Ann. Min. xiv, 2–3 ; Fr. à St. Clara, Hist. Min. 35 ; Coll. Anglo-Min. 206. Edward was perhaps acting in conjunction with his sister Margaret of Burgundy, who appears to have given an illuminated gradual to the friars of Greenwich. B.M. Arundel MS. 71, fol. 9.

[3] These facts are derived from notarial copies of (a) the letter of Sixtus IV to the archbishop of Canterbury and the bishops of Lincoln and Rochester, dated pridie Non. Jan. A° x. reciting letter to Edw. IV of the same date ; (b) the official account of the foundation on 2 July, 1482 ; (c) the public instrument issued by Edmund, bishop of Rochester, concerning the same ; all contained in C.C.C. Camb. MS. 170, pp. 72–4 ; cf. Wadding, Ann. Min. xiv, 252. Also from the charter of Hen. VII printed in Arch. Journ. xxiii, 57 ; cf. Materials for Life of Hen. VII (Rolls Ser.), i, 216–17. Bertholdi was elected vicar-general 1478 ; on his death, 6 Feb. 1480–1, John Philippi was re-elected to the office. Wadding, Ann. Min. xiv, 194, 281.

[4] Arch. Journ. xxiii, 57.

[5] Lambarde, Perambulation of Kent, 389 ; cf. J. Rous, Hist. Reg. Angl. (ed. Hearne), 211.

[6] Foundation charter in Arch. Journ. ut supra.

February, 1502–3.[7] In his will he left them £200 to inclose their garden[8] and orchard with a brick-wall, and bequeathed £200 to the prior of the Charterhouse in trust for the use of the friars at Greenwich, as he 'knew they had been many times in peril of ruin for lack of food.'[9] He also left 100 marks to each of the five houses of Observant Friars.[10]

In 1502 the Grey Friars of England changed their habits from London russet into white grey 'as the sheep doth dye it.' The change was largely due to the Greenwich friars, who insisted on the cheaper material being used.[11]

Henry VIII, in 1513, wrote from his palace of Greenwich to Leo X that he

could not sufficiently commend the Observant Friars' strict adherence to poverty, their sincerity, charity and devotion. No Order battled more assiduously against vice, and none were more active in keeping Christ's fold.[12]

He made, moreover, frequent grants of money to the Greenwich house. He gave them £8 6s. 8d. for 500 masses in April, 1510, and £13 6s. 8d. for two masses daily for a year for his father's soul; in 1511, 58s.; in 1512, 48s. for 100 lb. of wax which he had given them; in 1514, 20s. for the repair of their wharf, and in 1519 he paid again for the repair of their wharf.[13] In October, 1516, a grant of £40 was made 'to a friar that gave the king an instrument.'[14] The Observant Friars seem to have carried out the mandates of the rule with regard to manual labour, and some of them were skilled workmen.[15]

The friars' church was used for royal baptisms and marriages. Henry VIII was christened probably in this church (1491), and certainly his brother Edmund (1498). The marriage of Henry and Catherine took place at Greenwich, probably in the friars' church (1509). The Princess Mary was christened here 20 February,

1515–16, and the Princess Elizabeth 8 September, 1533.[16] Muriel, daughter of Thomas Howard, duke of Norfolk, relict of John Grey, Viscount Lisle, was buried here in 1512;[17] John Hent, esq., in 1521;[18] Edith, wife of Thomas, Lord Darcy, in 1529.[19] Lord Darcy, who was a benefactor of the friars,[20] desired before his execution, 30 June, 1537, to be buried near his wife, but this request was refused.[21]

Bequests to the friars are numerous. The earliest recorded one seems to be that of Richard Tilley, who left them 100s. for building in 1485.[22] Thomas Ustwayte of East Greenwich, esquire, in 1496 left 6s. 8d. to 'the blessed house of St. Francis' and 3s. 4d. for repairs of All Hallows chapel in the same church[23]; Michael Walis of Woolwich left money for the repair of the friars' church about 1500.[24] Thomazine Sheby left the friars in 1506 'a diaper cloth 12 yards long' for the frontal of masses.[25] Richard Carpenter, yeoman of the pantry (1515), John Stile, armourer to the king (1524), William Derlington, vicar of Greenwich (1525), several London merchants, and a large proportion of women, left them legacies.[26]

The brilliant William Roy was a friar of this house for a short time about 1520, when he seems to have written the Montfort Codex of the Greek text of the New Testament, probably at the instigation of Friar Henry Standish, bishop of St. Asaph, and to help him in his controversy with Erasmus.[27]

In January, 1524–5, Wolsey attempted to carry out a visitation of the convent of Greenwich by his legatine authority; the friars resisted, many of them leaving the house: 'Friar John Forest was commanded to preach at Paul's Cross the Sunday after and there pronounced all accurst that went out of the place.' They at length submitted to the legate, some being imprisoned for their contumacy.[28]

---

[7] They are printed in full in Hasted, *Kent: Hund. of Blackheath* (ed. Drake), 86–7.

[8] He seems to have taken a personal interest in the garden; thus in 1509 he granted 'to him that laboureth in the friars garden of Greenwich in reward, 20s.' Hasted, *Kent: Hund. of Blackheath* (ed. Drake), 57, *n.* 2.

[9] T. Astle, *Will of King Hen. VII*, 30–1.

[10] *L. and P. Hen. VIII*, i, 5737, 5738; Hasted, *Kent: Hund. of Blackheath* (ed. Drake), 57, *n.* 2.

[11] Fabyan, *Chron.* (ed. Ellis), 687; Holinshed, *Chron.* (ed. Hooker), iii, 789; *Grey Friars Chron.* (Camd. Soc.), 27–8. Cf. bequest of Sir John Rudstone, kt. and alderman of London, 1530; to each of the five Observant houses, 'one long gray-woollen cloth for their habits of the price of 5 marks sterling every cloth as it shall cost me in Blackwell hall of London over and beside the charges of the workmanship of the same cloths.' Harl. MS. 1231, fol. 2b.

[12] *L. and P. Hen. VIII*, i, 4871.

[13] Ibid. ii, 1445, 1451, 1458, 1464; iii, 1535.

[14] Ibid. ii, 1473.   [15] Cf. ibid. vii, 837.

[16] Hasted, *Hist. of Kent: Hund. of Blackheath* (ed. Drake), 58, 88; *L. and P. Hen. VIII*, vi, 1111.

[17] Hasted, *Kent: Hund. of Blackheath* (ed. Drake), 88.   [18] Ibid. 278.

[19] Ibid. 88; *L. and P. Hen. VIII*, xii (2), 1; *Dict. Nat. Biog.* xiv, 53.

[20] *L. and P. Hen. VIII*, iii, 1261; iv, 2527.

[21] Hasted, *Kent: Hund. of Blackheath*, 88; *L. and P. Hen. VIII*, xii (2), 1.

[22] Nicolas, *Test. Vet.* 384; Hasted, *Kent: Hund. of Blackheath*, 169.

[23] Hasted, ibid. 110.   [24] Ibid. 169.

[25] Ibid. 110.

[26] Ibid. 110, 111, 278. See also *Hist. MSS. Com. Rep.* ix, App. pt. i, 48. P.C.C. Fetiplace, qu. 8, 10, 13, 14, 15, 21; P.C.C. Maynwaryng, qu. 24. *L. and P. Hen. VIII*, iv, 336, 952; Nicolas, *Test. Vet.* 609, 662, 740, 751; Harl. MS. 1231, fol. 2b.

[27] Rendel Harris, *Origin of the Leic. Codex.*

[28] *Grey Friars Chron.* (Camd. Soc.), 31–2; Hall, *Chron.* 691 (ed. 1809), followed by Grafton, *Chron.* ii, 371, says the recalcitrant friars numbered nineteen.

Catherine of Aragon is said to have belonged to the Third Order of St. Francis; she used

to rise at midnight to the Divine office and be present in the Franciscan church at Greenwich during the time that the friars were reading or singing their Matins and Lauds.[29]

John Forest was her confessor.[30]

The question of the nullity of the marriage of Henry VIII with Catherine brought the friars into direct conflict with the king. In December, 1528, a discontented friar asserted that many of his brethren were guilty of Lutheranism and spoke ill of the king and of Wolsey.[31] On Easter Sunday (31 March), 1532, William Peto, provincial of the friars, preached at Greenwich before the king, and warned him that he was endangering his crown, for both great and little were murmuring at the marriage. The king dissembled his ill-will, but on the provincial's departure for a chapter, he caused one of his chaplains, Dr. Curwen, to preach in the friars' church, contrary to the custom of the convent and the will of the warden. The chaplain's sermon roused the warden, Henry Elston, to expostulate; in the king's presence he gave the chaplain the lie. Henry was very angry, and bade the provincial on his return depose the warden. This he refused to do, and the king had them both arrested[32] Elston was confined at the Grey Friars of Bedford,[33] but some months later he and Peto were at Antwerp carrying on the campaign against the king.[34]

Meanwhile the general feeling in the Greenwich convent was strongly in favour of Catherine. Friar William Robinson, a former warden, offered to dispute and preach at Paul's Cross on the queen's behalf, and was strongly supported by William Curson, vicar of the house.[35] A young friar, Thomas Pereson, reproved the king's chaplain for speaking against the queen.[36] John Forest organized the opposition to the king in the provincial chapter (1532).[37] Cromwell was kept fully informed of the state of affairs by some friars[38] who acted as his agents and spies. The

chief of these were friars John Lawrence and Richard Lyst,[39] a lay brother who had been an apothecary in Wolsey's service, and who, on the death in prison of another lay brother named Ravenscroft, suggested that a charge of murder against his fellow friars would be an effective method of keeping them quiet.[40] Both these friars found life in the cloister intolerable and escaped.[41] The king tried to induce the general commissary of the province to deprive his enemies of their offices, but without much success.[42] Peto, however, was not re-elected provincial, and a more amenable brother was made warden of Greenwich;[43] but Forest

rejoiced to have put the king beside his purpose at our last chapter, saying that if he had not been there the king would have destroyed our whole religion.[44]

Two Observant Friars were caught by Cromwell's spies holding secret communications with the princess dowager in July, 1533: 'it is undoubted,' wrote Cromwell to his master, 23 July, 1533,

that they have intended and would confess some great matter if they might be examined as they ought to be, that is to say by pains.

The warden of Greenwich was anxious to have the punishing of them,[45] perhaps to save them from a worse fate. One of them, Hugh Payne, was soon at large again, preaching obedience to the pope and denouncing the king's marriage, in the west of England.[46]

Henry probably hoped to bend the friars to his will at this time. He gave them an alms of 10 marks;[47] the Princess Elizabeth was christened in the church with great pomp 10 September,[48] and the minister, warden, and friars of Greenwich begged for the king's pardon 21 December.[49] But on 13 April, 1534, a royal commission was issued to the provincial priors of the Austin and Black Friars to visit all the friars' houses and bind every friar by oath to acknowledge the king as supreme head of the church and repudiate the pope's authority.[50] On 14 June Roland Lee and Thomas Bedyll, acting on instructions from the commissioners, visited Richmond, and induced the friars there to entrust their case to four 'discreets' or representatives, who should attend the visitors the next day at Greenwich. On 15 June the visitors tried to induce the Greenwich friars to adopt

---

[29] Fr. a St. Clara, *Hist. Min.* 41; *Coll. Anglo-Min.* i, 218.

[30] See the correspondence between him and the queen in Bourchier, *Hist. Eccl. de Martyrio fratrum* (Paris, 1582), 53 et seq. *L. and P. Hen. VIII*, vii, 129–32.   [31] *L. and P. Hen. VIII*, iv, 5043.

[32] Ibid. v, 941; Stow, *Ann.* 559 (ed. 1615).

[33] *L. and P. Hen. VIII*, v, 1043.

[34] Ibid. vi, 705, 726.

[35] Strype, *Eccl. Mem.* i (2), 193.

[36] *L. and P. Hen. VIII*, vi, 168; Ellis, *Orig. Let.* (Ser. 3), ii, 257.

[37] *L. and P. Hen. VIII*, v, 1259, 1313; the lists in Cromwell's hand, ibid. 1312, evidently refer to this matter.

[38] James Beck also, to whose house 'at the Cross Keys in St. Magnus Parish' the friars sent their letters, was one of Cromwell's spies. *L. and P. Hen. VIII*, v, 1313; vi, 705, 1570; vii, 143, 1307–8.

[39] See their letters in *L. and P. Hen. VIII*, v, vi, vii.   [40] Ibid. vi, 168.

[41] Ibid. vi, 1264; vii, 139, 580.

[42] Ibid. v, 1358.   [43] Ibid. vi, 705, 887.

[44] Ibid. v, 1591.   [45] Ibid. vi, 887.

[46] Ibid. vii, 939, 1652.

[47] Ibid. vi, 1057; by the hands of James Beck.

[48] Ibid. vi, 1111; Hasted, *Kent: Hund. of Blackheath* (ed. Drake), 88.

[49] *L. and P. Hen. VIII*, vi, 1549.

[50] Ibid. vii, 587 (18), 590.

the same procedure, 'specially to the intent that if the discreets should refuse to consent, it were better after our minds to strain a few than a multitude.' The friars, however, 'stiffly affirmed that where the matter concerned particularly every one of their souls, they would answer particularly every man for himself.' After further discussion, the visitors were compelled to examine each friar separately, and each refused to accept the articles, especially that which denied the papal authority. In answer to all the arguments of the visitors they declared that 'they had professed St. Francis' religion, and in the observance thereof they would live and die.'[51]

On 17 June two cart-loads of friars drove through London to the Tower,[52] and it is possible that some of the Greenwich Observants were among them. On or before 11 August the friars were expelled from their convent[53] (though they seem to have made some kind of submission[54]) and distributed in different places, generally in houses of the Grey Friars, where, wrote Chapuys to Charles V, 'they were locked up in chains and treated worse than they could be in prison.'[55] Some, such as John Forest, were actually in prison in London.[56] Two of them, inclosed in a poor lodging at the Grey Friars, Stamford, and treated as prisoners, were 'in meetly good case as the world at this time requireth,' and sent to London for their little belongings, including a new Psalter, a pair of socks, a penner and inkhorn.[57] But the severity of their treatment is shown by the fact that out of 140 Observant Friars thirty-one soon died,[58] and this does not account for all the deaths. Thomas Bourchier, who was a member of the Greenwich friary in the reign of Mary, gives details of several martyrdoms which probably belong to this time, though the writer assigns them to 1537.[59] On 19 July Anthony Brorbe, formerly of Magdalen College, Oxford, a distinguished scholar, who had been imprisoned and tortured to such an extent that 'for twenty-five days he could not turn in bed or lift his hands to his mouth,' was strangled with his own cord.[60] On 27 July Thomas Cortt, who had been im-

prisoned for a sermon against the king in the church of St. Lawrence, London, died in Newgate.[61] On 3 August Thomas Belchiam, a young priest, who had composed a book against the king, one copy of which he left in the hands of his brethren at Greenwich, died of starvation in Newgate.[62] No mention of these three friars occurs in extant contemporary authorities, but Bourchier's account representing the tradition of the Order is probably substantially correct, though the names may be misspelt.

Some of the friars fled abroad, to Scotland or over sea.[63] Others obtained permission through Wriothesley's influence to leave the country.[64] Among Cromwell's 'remembrances' of this time is the entry: 'Item to remember the friars of Greenwich to have licence to go to Ireland.'[65]

It is clear that not a few made formal submission[66] and were set free, but they could not refrain from teaching what they believed, and after the rebellions of 1536 the king renewed his attack on them. Thus Friar Hugh Payne wrote from the prison into which he had been cast in July, 1534, promising to submit entirely to the king and begging for deliverance;[67] in 1536 he was acting as curate of Hadleigh, Suffolk, and then as priest of Stoke by Nayland.[68] Being denounced by Cranmer for his preaching, he was thrown into the Marshalsea, whence he wrote (1537) to the duke of Norfolk urging that his trial should be hastened, as he was like to die of sickness and the weight of his irons.[69] He died soon afterwards in prison, but not before a patron had presented him to the living of Sutton Magna in Essex, which another ex-Observant then tried to obtain.[70] The king, on 17 March, 1536–7, declaring that the Friars Observants were 'disciples of the bishop of Rome and sowers of sedition,' ordered that they should be arrested 'and placed in other houses of friars as prisoners, without liberty to speak to any man till we decide our pleasure concerning them.'[71]

Forest was the most famous victim of the new persecution. From his prison he had written to Catherine of Aragon in expectation of immediate death, probably in 1534; he was then sixty-four years of age, and had spent forty-three of these in religion.[72] He was, however, transferred to the Grey Friars, London, in consequence probably

[51] Wright, *Suppression*, 42–4.
[52] *L. and P. Hen. VIII*, vii, 856.
[53] Ibid. vii, 1057; Stow, *Ann.* (ed. 1615), 570; Holinshed, *Chron.* (ed. Hooker), iii, 789.
[54] *L. and P. Hen. VIII*, xiii (2), App. 28. Cf. ibid. vii, 1063.
[55] Ibid. vii, 1095. [56] Ibid. vii, 1607.
[57] Ibid. vii, 1307.
[58] Ibid. vii, 1607; cf. the statement in Bourchier, *Hist. Eccl. de Martyrio Fratrum* (ed. 1582), 26.
[59] Bourchier, *Hist. Eccl. de Martyrio Fratrum*. (He puts the deaths of Rich and Risby in 1537, p. 6); cf. Angelus a St. Francisco (R. Mason), *Certamen Seraphicum*, 5–7.
[60] Bourchier, op. cit. 11. Wood, *Fasti*, 106, calls him Anthony Brockby. Is he the same as Anthony Browne? (See below.)

[61] Bourchier, op. cit. 13–17. [62] Ibid. 17 et seq.
[63] *L. and P. Hen. VIII*, vii, 1607.
[64] Bourchier, op. cit. 24, 26.
[65] *L. and P. Hen. VIII*, vii, 49, 108, 850; cf. 957.
[66] Father Robinson, writing 4 July, 1538, says that he and all the brethren of the order promised four years ago to obey the statutes of the realm; *L. and P. Hen. VIII*, xiii (2), App. 28.
[67] Ibid. vii, 1652. [68] Ibid. xii (1), 256, 257.
[69] Ibid. xii (1), 257. [70] Ibid. xiv (1), 244.
[71] Ibid. xii (1), 666.
[72] Bourchier, *Hist. Eccl. de Martyrio Fratrum*, 53 et seq.

of having made his submission.[73] At the Grey Friars he enjoyed considerable liberty; from well-wishers he received small sums of money for fuel and other necessaries, and was allowed to celebrate mass and hear confessions.[74] Suspicion arising, Forest was cast into Newgate, and in examination admitted that he induced men in confession 'to hold and stick to the old fashion of belief.'[75] On 22 May, 1538, he was roasted alive as a traitor and heretic.[76] Another Greenwich friar, Anthony Browne, who on the break-up of the convent became a hermit, was brought before the justices at Norwich in July, 1538, confessed,[77] and received judgement accordingly; the execution was postponed for ten days, partly because the judges thought it well that a sermon should be made by the bishop of Norwich, as was done by the bishop of Worcester at Friar Forest's execution, partly in case Cromwell wished to have him brought to the Tower and tortured.[78]

Meanwhile the king instituted a convent of Grey Friars at Greenwich, to which in March, 1537, he assigned an annuity of £100;[79] and on 25 March, 1538, a payment of £25 was made to the warden of the Grey Friars of Greenwich for their relief;[80] this is the latest grant recorded.

The friary was revived by Mary, who repaired the buildings and had the Observant Friars reinstated on 7 April, 1555, by Maurice Griffin, bishop of Rochester.[81] Peto, now nominally bishop of Salisbury and soon to be cardinal,[82] and Elston returned to their old monastery.

They complained to the queen in July, 1555, of having been 'beaten with stones which were flung at them by divers lewd persons as they passed from London to Greenwich on Sunday last.' Among the inmates of the house were

Thomas Bourchier, author of the *Historia de Martyrio Fratrum Ordinis Divi Francisci*, &c., and several Spaniards.[83] Cardinal Pole was consecrated archbishop of Canterbury in the friars' church 23 March, 1555–6,[84] two days after the burning of Cranmer. The friars were again expelled by Elizabeth, 12 July, 1559;[85] most of them seem to have taken refuge in the Netherlands; they are found at Liège and Antwerp, Lisbon, and the convent of Ara Coeli in Rome.[86]

WARDENS [87]

William Robinson,[88] 1528
Henry Elston,[89] 1532
William Sydenham,[90] 1533
Henry Elston,[91] 1555
Stephen Fox,[92] *custos* of Greenwich, *c.* 1558

The seal of the warden in the time of Queen Mary was pointed oval, and represented the Assumption of the Virgin Mary, who is seen supported by four angels; a radiant nimbus round her head; beneath is an escutcheon of the arms of France and England, quarterly, ensigned with the head of a cherub. Legend :—

SIGILLVM GARDIANI GRVWVCESIS [93]

32. THE FRANCISCAN FRIARS OF MAIDSTONE

On 13 May, 1331, John atte Water obtained licence to alienate in mortmain to the minister and Friars Minors of England two messuages and six acres of land in Maidstone, to build an oratory and dwelling-place there.[94] The house was never founded.

[73] Hall, *Chron.* (ed. 1809), 825; *L. and P. Hen. VIII*, xiii (1), 1043; he told one Wafferer in confession 'that he had denied the bishop of Rome by an oath given by his outward man, but not in the inward man.'

[74] *L. and P. Hen. VIII*, xiii (1), 880, 1043.

[75] Froude, *Hist. of Engl.* (1870), iii, 106; *L. and P. Hen. VIII*, xiii (1), 1043.

[76] Hall, *Chron.* (ed. 1809), 825; Bourchier's account is detailed but not quite accurate; *Hist. Eccl. de Martyrio Fratrum*, 44 et seq.

[77] He was 'so handled that he would not stick on the authority of the bishop of Rome but denied that a temporal prince could be head of the church'; *L. and P. Hen. VIII*, xiii (2), 34; cf. ibid. vii, 1607.

[78] *L. and P. Hen. VIII*, xiii (2), 34.

[79] Ibid. xii (1), 795 (44); Stow, *Ann.* 570, says Austin Friars were placed in this convent for a time.

[80] *L. and P. Hen. VIII*, xiii (2), 1280.

[81] Wriothesley, *Chron.* (Camd. Soc.), ii, 128; *Grey Friars Chron.* (Camd. Soc.), 95; *Coll. Anglo-Min.* 251. The queen gave them an acre of wood for fuel 1557; Cott. MS. Titus, B. ii, fol. 106.

[82] *Dict. Nat. Biog.* xlv, 88.

[83] Fr. a St. Clara (Davenport), *Hist. Min.* 54; Wriothesley, *Chron.* (Camd. Soc.), ii, 128.

[84] Machyn, *Diary* (Camd. Soc.), 102; Wriothesley, *Chron.* (Camd. Soc.), ii, 134.

[85] Machyn, *Diary* (Camd. Soc.), 204.

[86] Fr. a St. Clara (Davenport), *Hist. Min.* 55–6; *Coll. Anglo-Min.* 254, &c. Some of those mentioned by these writers as Observants of Greenwich do not seem to have been friars, e.g. John Standish.

[87] There seems to be no evidence that Forest was ever warden.

[88] *L. and P. Hen. VIII*, iv, 5040.

[89] Ibid. v, 1312.

[90] Ibid. vi, 705.

[91] Burnet, *Hist. of the Reform.* (ed. Pocock), iii, 424 *n.*

[92] Angelus a St. Francisco (R. Mason), *Certamen Seraphicum*, 12; *Coll. Anglo-Min.* 257.

[93] B.M. Seals, xlvii, 552; *Arch. Journ.* xxiii, 57. The author of *Coll. Anglo-Min.* pt. ii, p. viii, says the seal of the friary was 'The Holy Name of Jesus.'

[94] Pat. 5 Edw. III, pt. 1, m. 8; Inq. a.q.d. file 216, No. 2. Fr. a St. Clara (Chr. Davenport), *Hist. Min.* (Douai, 1665), 7, says the house was founded by Edw. III and his brother John earl of Cornwall (who died 1336).

33. THE FRANCISCAN FRIARS OF ROMNEY

Henry III granted to the Friars Minors of Romney, 100s. out of the revenues of the arch-bishopric of Canterbury to buy clothes, on 5 December, 1241.[95] Friar Richard of Devon, one of the companions of Agnellus, after travelling through many provinces, lived here the last fifteen years of his life, worn out by quartan fevers.[96] The house existed only for a short time.

34. THE AUSTIN FRIARS OF CANTERBURY

Archbishop Walter Reynolds obtained, 4 July, 1318, licence to alienate in mortmain to the Austin Friars two acres of land in the parish of Westgate, Canterbury, on which they might build their houses.[1] The land was worth 13s. 4d. a year. In March, 1319–20, the friars seem to have numbered eight.[2] Some years later however the friars obtained leave to alienate their original site, provided they did not alienate it in mortmain, in order to acquire a more convenient place.[3]

They had already in 1324 obtained a place in St. George's parish, on or near the site of the old gaol, by purchasing from Thomas de Bonnington of Goodnestone a messuage, held of Elias Lambyn, and worth 13s. 4d. a year. The chief lord was the priory of Christchurch, and the monks, in spite of the prayers of Hugh Despenser, earl of Winchester, tried to prevent the settlement of the friars in this parish on the ground of the poverty of the church of St. George, of which they held the advowson. The friars however persisted. Their oratory was already founded in 1325 without the permission of the archbishop, who now intervened and ordered an inquiry into the circumstances. In 1326 they agreed to pay the parson of St. George's 9s.[4] a year in lieu of all tithes due to him from their land, and 20d. annual rent to the monks of Christchurch. The monks now withdrew their opposition.[5] The

number of friars had in 1336 increased to eighteen.[6]

In November, 1329, they obtained two additional plots adjacent to their area, one a vacant piece of land 82 ft. by 55 ft. to the west of their house, from the king, the other a messuage granted to them by Henry son of Robert atte Gayole, the jurors having declared that no loss would ensue except that the citizens, who held the city in fee-farm of the king, would in future lose the tallage of the tenants of the said mes-suage.[7] The two next additions to their area were made by Richard Fraunceys or le Frenshebaker, parson of the church of Monkton in the Isle of Thanet, who granted them two messuages in 1335, and a messuage and garden in 1344, for the enlargement of their dwelling-place.[8] They afterwards bought from John Chich, who was bailiff of Canterbury, 1351–2, a plot of ground in St. George's parish lying on the highway at the Cloth Market, upon part of which they built their outward gate on the north-east of the con-vent.[9] In 1354 John, parson of the church of St. Andrew, Canterbury, gave them a messuage adjacent to their place, worth 12d. a year.[10]

In 1356 they agreed to pay the prior and convent of Christchurch 2s. 4d. a year, appa-rently for these later acquisitions.[11]

John Chertesey gave them a messuage and garden, adjacent to their area and held of the crown in burgage, in 1394; the friars paying a fine of four marks for the licence.

In 1408 the friars obtained from Henry IV royal licence to reconstruct their houses and buildings which faced the highway, to let these houses and buildings as well as a messuage and garden in St. George's parish, and to apply the proceeds to the support of their church and other buildings and to the payment of their dues.[12] To carry out their improvements they found it neces-sary to inclose two winding lanes which sur-rounded a great part of their area. These lanes, they asserted, had fallen into disuse and were so full of dung and other filth that the stench was dangerous to the health of the inhabitants and 'disgusted the hearts of those celebrating and hearing divine service in the friars' church.' In 1429 John Sturreye, the prior, leased from the city for ninety years, at an annual rent of 4s., a

[95] Lib. R. 26 Hen. III, m. 15.

[96] Mon. Francisc. (Rolls Ser.), i, 6.

[1] Pat. 11 Edw. II, pt. 2, m. 3; Inq. a.q.d. file 133, No. 1. Part of the land was held by the archbishop of Adam Hurel; see account of Friars of the Sack.

[2] B.M. Add. MS. 17362, a royal grant of 2s. 8d. for one day's food.

[3] Pat. 2 Edw. III, pt. 1, m. 33.

[4] This is returned as 11s. in 1535; Valor Eccl. (Rec. Com.), i, 27.

[5] Lit. Cant. (Rolls Ser.), i, 100, 160; Camb. Univ. Lib. MS. Ee, v, 31, fol. 237b, 254b; Pat. 17 Edw. II, pt. 2, m. 18; Inq. a.q.d. file 169, No. 12; Hist. MSS. Com. Rep. ix, App. pt. i, 73; Bunce, 'Extracts from City Records,' fol. 173, 180 (MS. Canterbury); Somner, Hist. and Antiq. of Cant. (ed. Battely), i, 68; Dugdale, Mon. vi, 1592; on Th. of Bonnington, see Wilkins, Concilia, ii, 490.

[6] Cott. MS. Nero, C. viii, fol. 205; cf. fol. 202.

[7] Pat. 3 Edw. III, pt. 2, m. 13; Inq. a.q.d. file 207, Nos. 23, 24.

[8] Pat. 8 Edw. III, pt. 2, m. 2; Inq. a.q.d. file 226, No. 24; Pat. 18 Edw. III, pt. 1, m. 44; Inq. a.q.d. file 268, No. 24.

[9] Somner, Antiq. of Cant. (ed. Battely), i, 68.

[10] Pat. 28 Edw. III, pt. 1, m. 4. The inquest was for William Alayn de Mers and John, parson of the church of St. Andrew, to grant a messuage; Inq. a.q.d. file 307, No. 19.

[11] Bunce, MS. Extracts, fol. 180; Dugdale, Mon. vi, 592; Somner, Antiq. of Cant. i, 68.

[12] Pat. 9 Hen. IV, pt. 2, m. 25.

'crooked lane'[13] leading from the Cloth Market near the eastern or cemetery gate of the friars to the church of St. Mary Bredin ; and two years later the friars leased from the city for 12*d.* a year[14] and inclosed another lane

opposite to that church and extending from the new stone wall with the porch in it as far as the east part of the garden of the convent opening into Sheepshank Lane by a wooden door.

In the same year (1431) they obtained licence from the king and council to hold the two lanes and also a messuage and garden conferred on them by William Benet and Thomas Langdon. Their right to these various plots being called in question, the property was seized by the king's escheator ; the prior appeared by his attorney, Robert Shamell, before the Court of Exchequer in 1438, and obtained judgement in his favour.[15]

The friars received from the city 2*s.* a year in the latter part of the fifteenth century 'for the rent of the Boordehouse.'[16] Occasionally some of the commissioners appointed to arbitrate in the frequent disputes between the commonalty and the abbey of St. Augustine were lodged at the Austin Friars, at the city's expense.[17] The municipality granted these friars £1 6*s.* 8*d.* towards the cost of their pavage in 1481-2.[18]

The Austin Friars of Canterbury are often called the White Friars,[19] an error which has led to some confusion. The famous John Capgrave has been erroneously claimed as an inmate of this house.[20] It is said that several of the Hauts were buried here, especially William Haut of Bishopsbourne, esq., who was buried in the choir before the image of St. Katharine between his wives in 1462, and left 20 marks for the repair of the church.[21] Others buried here were Amabilia Gobion, who gave 10 marks for the repair of the church, 1405 ; John Brempe of St. Andrew's, 1462 ; William Bonyngton of St. George's, 1464, and Christina his wife ; William Benet, 1464, and his wife ; William

Catbery, carver, 1479, and his friend Christian Hamer ; William Walpole, chaplain of Lord Thomas Arundel, 1483 ; Simon Flegard, clerk, Thomas Linsey, corvesir, and Richard Dyne in 1484 ; William Faunt of St. Mary Bredin, 1485, and his father and mother ; William Colsor, 1485 ; William Aylard, smith, 1497 ; John Courteman, 1501, and Joan his widow, 1511 ; Richard Stephinson, 1510, and Margaret his wife, near the image of our Lady ; Nicholas Barry, 1513, 'in the churchyard next the chapel of the parson of St. Andrew' ; Isabel Walker, 1516, and William Courthope, 1530, 'before the image of our Lady of Pity' ; William Corall, 1532. William Geyre, 1539, and Lucas Gibbes, whose will was made 8 October, 1539, and proved 12 April, 1543, also desired to be buried at the Austin Friars.[22]

Legacies were left to these friars by Elizabeth de Burgh, lady of Clare, 1360 ;[23] John Tyece of Canterbury, who by his will, dated 1381 and proved in 1400, ordered that his grange at 'Redyngate' and all his other arable lands in Canterbury should be sold and the proceeds divided among the mendicant friars, nuns, and other poor religious[24] ; Sir Richard atte Lease, kt., 1393[25] ; Richard Pargate, citizen of Canterbury, who in 1457 bequeathed 40*s.* towards making their new gate[26] ; Cecilia Lady Kirriell, 1472[27] ; Richard Tilley, 1485[28] ; John Bakke of Canterbury, 1500[29] ; Didier Bargier, rector of St. Andrew's, who left to the altar of St. Didier in the Austin Friars 'my little brevet mass-book covered with red leather,' in 1504[29a] ; Elizabeth, wife of John Hale, alderman, who left them 3*s.* 4*d.* a year for ten years to celebrate her obit, 1506[30] ; John Roper of Eltham, esq., 1524 ;[31] and Richard Sandisbury of Sittingbourne, 1521, Margerie, widow of John Baylie of St. George's, 1522, and Sir Nicholas Hewys of Monkton in Thanet, 1530, provided for masses at the altar of Scala Celi in this church.[31a]

Sir John Fineux, Chief Justice of Common Pleas, having expended more than £40 in repairing the church, refectory, dormitory and walls of the friary, the brethren bound themselves by indenture in 1522 to provide one chaplain to celebrate mass daily in the chapel of the Visitation of the Blessed Virgin for the souls of Sir John, Elizabeth his wife, and others.[32]

[13] This appears to be the lane called 'Frerenlane,' described as near the inn called 'le twelve-mennes-hows' ; L.T.R. Memo. R. East. 16 Hen. VI, rot. 9 (P.R.O.).

[14] This rent ceased to be paid in 1447 ; the 4*s.* rent was paid by the friars till the Dissolution and continued by their successors ; Bunce, MS. Extracts, fol. 181 ; *Hist. MSS. Com. Rep.* ix, App. pt. i, 132.

[15] Cant. City Arch. Accts. of the City, *sub annis :* Bunce, MS. Extracts, fol. 61, 181, and printed *Minutes,* No. 1 ; Inq. a.q.d. file 448, No. 33 ; Pat. 10 Hen. VI, pt. 1, m. 3 ; L.T.R. Memo. R. East. 16 Hen. VI, rot. 9 (P.R.O.) ; Hasted, *Cant.* (2nd ed.), ii, 616.

[16] *Hist. MSS. Comp. Rep.* ix, App. pt. i, 133.

[17] Ibid. 136, 143.　　[18] Cant. City Arch. Accts.

[19] Hasted, *Hist. and Topog. Surv. of Kent,* iv, 622.

[20] *Dict. Nat. Biog.*

[21] Hasted, op. cit. iv, 623 ; cf. iii, 736, 747 ; *Test. Cant.* ii, 66.

[22] Hasted, op. cit. iv, 623 ; *Test. Cant.* ii, 65.

[23] Cant. Archiepis. Reg. Islip, fol. 164-6 ; Nichols, *Royal Wills,* 23 et seq.

[24] Cant. City Arch. Wills and D. 1290-1556, fol. 3.

[25] P.C.C. Rous, fol. 22.

[26] Hasted, op. cit. iv, 623 ; *Test. Cant.* ii, 66.

[27] Nicolas, *Test. Vet.* 327.　　[28] Ibid. 384.

[29] Cant. City Arch. Wills and D. fol. 18.

[29a] *Test. Cant.* ii, 66.

[30] Ibid. fol. 21.

[31] *Arch. Cant.* ii, 169.　　[31a] *Test. Cant.* ii, 66.

[32] Hasted, op. cit. iv, 623 ; Somner, *Antiq. of Cant.* (ed. Battely), App. 18, No. 22.

The religious observances of the 'Gild of the Assumption of our Lady of the Crafts and Misteries of the shoemakers, curriers, and cobblers of the city of Canterbury' were held in the church of the Austin Friars. The gild ordinances of 1518 provide that every brother shall solemnly attend high mass here at ten in the morning on the feasts of the Assumption, St. Cyprian, and St. Crispin, and shall offer at the mass 1*d*. Masses were to be said at this church for the souls of deceased brethren.[33] In 1524 William Fiernour left tapers to 'the Brotherhood of St. Erasmus in the Austin Friars.'[33a]

The bishop of Dover, who came to Canterbury on 13 December, 1538, to negotiate the surrender of the friaries, found the Austin Friars specially in great poverty.[34] Their debts were £40, and their implements not worth £6, except a little plate weighing 126 oz. He reports to Cromwell that at the Austin Friars on 14 December, 'one friar very rudely and traitorously used himself,' and declared he was ready to die for it that the king might not be the head of the Church, but it must be a spiritual father appointed by God. This was probably Friar Stone, and the sequel is thus noted in the City Accounts (1538–9) :—Paid for half a ton of timber to make a pair of gallows to hang Friar Stone, 2*s*. 6*d*.; to a labourer that digged the holes, 3*d*.; to four men that helped set up the gallows for drink to them, for carriage of the timber from Stablegate to Dongeon (i.e. Dane John), 1*s*.; for a hurdle, 6*d*.; for a load of wood and for a horse to draw him to the Dongeon, 2*s*. 3*d*.; paid two men that set the kettle and parboiled him, 1*s*.; to two men that carried his quarters to the gates and set them up, 1*s*.; for halters to hang him and Sandwich cord and for straw, 1*s*.; to a woman that scoured the kettle, 2*d*.; to him that did the execution, 3*s*. 8*d*.[35]

The priory of the Austin Friars was put under the charge of Sir Anthony St. Leger,[36] then sheriff of Kent, and in 1542 granted by the king, in exchange for other lands, to George Harper. The property, consisting of the site (1½ acres), a garden in the tenure of the rector of St. Andrew's, a tenement called 'le Welhouse,' and seven other tenements or gardens let to tenants at will, was valued at £5 10*s*. 4*d*. a year. Harper sold it in June, 1542, to Thomas Culpeper of

Beakesbourne, who had licence, February, 1543–4, to alienate it to Robert Brome.[37]

PRIORS

John Sturreye, 1429 [38]
John Godewyn, 1462 [39]
William Mallahan, 1522 [40]

The fourteenth-century seal of the house contained three niches with ogee arched canopies, under them a bishop with pastoral staff between two archbishops with crosiers ; over the canopies the Almighty, half-length, lifting up the right hand in benediction, in the left hand an orb. The background is diapered lozengy. In base, under a depressed square-headed arch the prior reading at a lectern, behind him two friars praying. Legend :—

S. COMMVNITATIS FRATRVM EREMIITARV
ORDINIS SCI AVGVSTINI CANTVARIE [41]

35. THE CARMELITE FRIARS OF AYLESFORD

Richard de Grey, lord of Cudnor, brought some Carmelites to England on his return from the Holy Land with Richard earl of Cornwall in January, 1241–2, and founded a house for them on his manor of Aylesford, with the consent of the bishop of Rochester.[1] As the founder's means were insufficient to complete the building of the church, the bishop, Richard of Wendover, on 25 January, 1246–7, granted a relaxation of thirty days of injoined penance to

---

[33] Bunce, printed *Mins. of the City*, No. xx.

[33a] *Test. Cant.* ii, 66.

[34] *L. and P. Hen. VIII*, xiii (2), 1058 ; Bunce, MS. Abridgement, i, fol. 484, refers to a petition of these friars to the city for relief ; it is probably still among the city records. An Austin Friar received 2*d*. for bringing a dish of medlars to a city banquet in 1500–1 ; *Hist. MSS. Com. Rep.* ix, App. pt. i, 147*a*.

[35] *Hist. MSS. Com. Rep.* ix, App. pt. i, 153 ; Bunce, MS. Extracts from the Accts. fol. 49.

[36] Mins. Accts. 30–31 Hen. VIII, Kent, No. 105, m. 73 ; Partic. for Grants, 545, m. 7.

[37] Partic. for Grants, 545 ; *L. and P. Hen. VIII*, xvii, 283 (48), 443 (48) ; xix (1), 141 (77) ; Mins. Accts. 30–1 Hen. VIII (Kent), No. 105, m. 12. For the later history, see Hasted, *Hist. and Topog. Surv. of Kent*, iv, 624 ; a fee-farm or tenth of 11*s*. 1*d*. is yearly paid to the crown for this estate ; ibid. The precinct of the 'White Friars' is extra-parochial ; disputes between the city and the owners led to a trial at the Maidstone Assizes in Lent, 1790, when it was determined that this precinct was wholly exempt from the liberty and jurisdiction of the city. The bounds of it are : towards the east, part of Sheepshank Lane ; towards the south, the gravel walk or alley leading from St. Mary Bredin's church towards the city wall eastwards. To Rose Lane toward the west ; and to the gardens behind the houses on the south side of St. George's Street toward the north ; Hasted, op. cit. iv, 622.

[38] Bunce, MS. Extracts, fol. 61.

[39] Hasted, op. cit. iv, 624.

[40] Somner, *Antiq. of Cant.* App. xxii.

[41] B.M. Seals, lxv, 18.

[1] *Mon. Francisc.* (Rolls Ser.), i, 71 ; cf. *Cal. Papal Let.* iii, 67 ; B.M. Stowe MS. 938, fol. 76 ; Harl. MS. 539, fol. 143 ; Aylesford and Hulne near Alnwick were the first Carmelite houses in England. Bale calls 'Lucia Greye' (wife of Richard) the first foundress. Harl. MS. 1819, fol. 198.

all who should contribute to the work.[2] When dedicating the church on 31 August, 1248, in honour of the Assumption of the Virgin, the bishop granted an indulgence of forty days to all who visited the church on the day of the dedication and the following week, and who contributed to the support of the house.[3]

St. Simon or Simeon Stock, a native of Kent, is said to have been received into this friary by the first prior, Ivo of Brittany.[4]

A general chapter was held here in 1245 according to the tradition of the order, at which Alan of Brittany resigned and Simon Stock was elected prior general.[5] A chapter, perhaps the general chapter above mentioned or a provincial chapter, was held here soon after 21 January, 1247-8, to which the king gave two marks as a pittance.[6] Edward I granted the friars of this house 6s. 8d. in 1289.[7] Edward II, when at Maidstone, 26 May, 1326, gave 4d. to each of the twenty Carmelites of Maidstone, by the hand of Friar John of Malmesbury. This probably is a mistake for the Carmelites of Aylesford.[8]

Richard de Grey, great-grandson of the original founder, gave them three acres of meadow, held in chief, adjacent to their dwelling-place in 1318.[9] On 13 September, 1348, the year of the Black Death, their cemetery and 'the place where the new church was to be built' were dedicated by John Pascall, a Carmelite friar and bishop of Llandaff.[10] John de Grey, Baron Cudnor, the son of Richard, and 'companion of the duke of Lancaster,' petitioned the pope in 1355 for relaxation of one year and forty days of injoined penance to those who should on certain festivals visit the Carmelites' church at Aylesford, where he had chosen his tomb. The indulgence was granted both to penitents visiting the church and to those who assisted in the building of the same, and was to hold good for ten years.[11]

In 1369 the executors of the will of John de Rynger of Aylesford carried out the testator's intention of founding a chantry where one of the brethren of this house should celebrate daily for the souls of the grantor, Alice his wife, his children, and friends. The executors having made sufficient provision for the support of the

chaplain, the Provincial of the Friars, the prior and convent of Aylesford, in order to ensure the proper fulfilment of the obligation, submitted their house in this respect to the jurisdiction and supervision of the archbishop of Canterbury.[12]

On 16 February, 1393-4, Robert Twyner of Aylesford granted the friars a piece of land 12 ft. square in the parish of Burham, within a garden called 'Haukysgardyn,' containing a number of springs; they also had licence to make a subterranean aqueduct from this spot to their house.[13]

The new church was dedicated by Richard Young, bishop of Rochester, 4 May, 1417, and an indulgence of forty days granted to all true penitents who came to the church on the day of the dedication and the following week, and who contributed to the support of the house. The bishop also consecrated various altars in the church—one in honour of St. John the Baptist, another in honour of St. Thomas the Martyr, a third, next the choir, in honour of the apostles St. Peter and St. Paul.[14] A provincial chapter was held here in 1489.[15] Friar Richard of Maidstone, D.D. of Oxford, confessor of John of Gaunt, and a writer of some distinction, was a brother of this house, where he died in 1396, and was buried under a marble stone in the cloister.[16]

Bequests, sometimes in the form of malt or corn, were left these friars by Sir Richard atte Lease, kt., 1393;[17] John Hodsoll, 1424;[18] William Wrenne of Southflete, 1443;[18a] Richard Brown or Cordon, archdeacon of Rochester, 1452;[19] Johanna Harrendon, 1516;[20] William Hunt, of Cobham, 1527.[20a]

Small sums were left 'for the new work of the cloister' by Sir William Redesdale, clerk, in 1451, and 'for the reparation of the cloister' by Robert Pirry, of Gillingham, yeoman, in 1513.[20b] Richard Grey of Codnore (1416) and his widow Elizabeth (1444) were buried here:[21] the latter left 10 marks to Friar Thomas Grey.[22] Thomas Palmer was buried in the church in 1452.[22a] Henry Lord Grey was buried 'in the chancel of our Lady in the Friars of Aylesford' in

---

[2] Stowe MS. 938, fol. 76b (extracts from a chartulary of the house).
[3] Ibid. fol. 76.
[4] Harl. MS. 3838, fol. 14.
[5] Ibid. fol. 15b; Dict. Nat. Biog. lii, 255.
[6] Lib. R. 32 Hen. III, m. 12. The traditional date for the coming of the Carmelites to England is 1240; the general chapter at Aylesford may also be similarly antedated.
[7] Exch. Accts. (P.R.O.), bdle. 352, No. 18.
[8] Ibid. 381, No. 14 (P.R.O.).
[9] Pat. 11 Edw. II, pt. 2, m. 16; Inq. a.q.d. file 132, No. 6; the latter is partly illegible.
[10] Stowe MS. 938, fol. 76.
[11] Cal. Pap. Pet. i, 286; Cal. Pap. Let. iii, 573.

[12] Thorpe, Reg. Roff. 154-5.
[13] Pat. 17 Ric. II, pt. 2, m. 36.
[14] Stowe MS. 938, fol. 76a-b.
[15] Tanner, Bibl. 634.
[16] Harl. MS. 3838, fol. 84, 191; the poem on the reconciliation of Richard II with the city of London, 1393, ascribed to him, is printed in Polit. Poems and Songs (Rolls Ser.), i, 282.
[17] P.C.C. Rous, fol. 22.
[18] Arch. Cant. xiv, 223.   [18a] Test. Cant. i, 3.
[19] Lambeth Palace, Reg. Kemp, fol. 263-5.
[20] P.C.C. Holder, qu. 6.
[20a] Test. Cant. i, 4.   [20b] Ibid. i, 3, 4.
[21] Dugdale, Baronage, i, 711; Gibbons, Early Linc. Wills, 168.
[22] Bury, Wills and Invent. (Camden Soc.), 90.
[22a] Test. Cant. i, 42.

1492.[23] Giles Ranchawe, gent., who appears to have been living in the house at the time of his last illness, desired to be buried in the choir, 'beside the old prior Arenolde,' in 1534.[23a]

In 1535 the royal commissioners reported that the friars held 18 acres of land with their house situated at St. Mary's Gate, of the annual value of 42s. 8d. (probably a low estimate); they paid a yearly contribution of 26s. 8d. to the provincial prior, and 2s. rent to Master de Strode.[24]

Richard of Ingworth, bishop of Dover, visited the White Friars of Aylesford in July, 1538, and found that they had sold much of their necessaries. The friars told him that two men came to the prior, saying that the house was given away, and that they had commission to put them out at their pleasure; so they sold what they had and paid their debts. The house was in a 'meet state.'[25] Before 13 December, 1538, the house was surrendered to the bishop of Dover.[26]

The property was put under the charge of Sir Thomas Wyatt, and was in 1542 granted to him by the king in exchange for other estates. Wyatt leased it to John Morse for forty years at an annual rent of 102s. in 1542.[27] The land consisted of nine acres of arable and eleven of pasture, besides the churchyard, gardens, orchard, ponds, &c. Some of the houses and gardens had been leased shortly before the Dissolution to William Tilgeman and his wife, and to John Clyffe.[28]

On the rebellion of Sir Thomas Wyatt, son of the above, the property was forfeited to the crown. It was rated for Thomas Morse in 1557 at twenty-six years' purchase, at £132 12s.,[29] but does not seem to have been purchased by him. Elizabeth granted the priory and lands to John Sedley, son of John Sedley of Southfleet. The subsequent history of the site is given by Hasted.[30]

The seal of the house in the fifteenth century represents the Virgin, crowned, seated in a canopied niche with tabernacle work at the sides; the Child in the right hand, in the left a sceptre fleur-de-lizé. In base, a shield of arms of the founder; three bars, Richard Lord Grey of Codnor, A.D. 1240. Legend :—

SIGILLŪ : PRIORATUS : OFFICII : ALYSFORDIE [31]

[23] Nicolas, *Test. Vet.* 411.   [23a] *Test. Cant.* i, 4.
[24] *Valor Eccl.* (Rec. Com.), i, 113.
[25] *L. and P. Hen. VIII*, xiii (1), 1456.
[26] Ibid. (2), 1058.
[27] Mins. Accts. 30 & 31 Hen. VIII (Kent), No. 105, m. 73b; Partic. for Grants (P.R.O.), file 1264; *L. and P. Hen. VIII*, xiv (1), 281; Cromwell 'has reserved for you the house of the friars at Aylesford'; xvii, 220 (98).
[28] Partic. for Grants (P.R.O.), file 1264; Mins. Accts. 30 & 31 Hen. VIII (Kent), No. 105, m. 73b. One of the arable fields was called the 'Sanctuary Field,' another the 'Novice Field.'
[29] Harl. MS. 606, fol. 36b.
[30] Hasted, *Kent*, ii, 169–70.
[31] B.M. *Cat. of Seals*, No. 2577.

36. THE CARMELITE FRIARS OF LOSSENHAM

A house of Carmelite Friars, the third established in England, was founded at Lossenham in the parish of Newenden in 1242 or soon afterwards, by Sir Thomas Alcher or Aucher, knt., whose body was buried in the choir of the church.[1] It remained under the patronage of the Alcher family, whose residence was close by, until the Dissolution.[2]

Henry III supplied these friars with oak for timber in 1271 and 1272.[3] Their church and houses were burnt in 1275 by persons unknown.[4]

Thomas of Dover, prior of Newenden, and Thomas of Thanet were licensed by Archbishop Islip to hear confessions in the diocese in 1350.[5]

Friar William Stranfield or Strenfeld, S.T.P., is said by Bale to have been prior of this house, and to have written, among other things, a history of the order; he died and was buried here in 1390.[6]

Among the benefactors of the house were Sir Richard atte Lease, knt., c. 1393,[7] and Anne Culpeper, 1532.[8]

The surrender took place on 25 July, 1538. The bishop of Dover, who came here from Aylesford, seems to have had no difficulty with these friars, whom he describes as 'honest men.' The stuff was priced at £6 10s., including bell and chalice. The house was poor in building, had no lead but only tile, and much of it was ready to fall. The lands had been let on lease to a farmer for 40s. a year, but the visitor obtained the surrender of the lease and proposed to let the friary, with orchard, garden, and land, for 5 marks a year.[9] Among the goods of the house valued by Sir John Welles, parson of Newenden, John Twysden, farmer there, and others, were three vestments, the most valuable being worth 6s. 8d.; a chalice of 14 oz., worth 49s.; a bell in the steeple, 10s.; a cross, hangings in the hall, two old feather-beds with a bolster, 'a book of Catholycon', 4d.; a number of cushions and kitchen utensils. For hay sold 16d. was obtained, and for a tree of timber 16d.[10]

The site, with two pieces of arable land containing 7 acres, and a marsh, called the Friars' Marsh, containing 9 acres, was leased, 10 March, 1538–9, for 46s. 8d. to William Culpeper of Hunton, Kent, who bought the buildings. It

[1] B.M. Harl. MS. 539, fol. 143; Harl. MS. 3838, fol. 16.
[2] Dugdale, *Mon.* vi, 1571; Hasted, *Hist. and Topog. Surv. of Kent*, iii, 79.
[3] Close, 55 Hen. III, m. 4; 56 Hen. III, m. 11.
[4] Pat. 4 Edw. I, m. 35d.
[5] Cant. Archiepis. Reg. Islip, fol. 19a.
[6] Stevens, *Add. to Mon.* ii, 167.
[7] P.C.C. Rous, fol. 22.   [8] Nicolas, *Test. Vet.* 661.
[9] *L. and P. Hen. VIII*, xiii (1), 1456–7.
[10] Ibid. xiii (2), App. 29; *Arch. Cant.* xiv, 311.

was rated in 1558 for Richard Lake (at twenty-two years' purchase) and granted in the same year to Edmund and Henry Gilberd. It afterwards passed to the Culpeper family.[11]

37. THE CARMELITE FRIARS OF SANDWICH

This friary, situated in the south-west of the town, is said by Richard Hely, prior of Maldon, to have been founded by Henry Cowfield, an 'Almain,' in 1272;[1] but his endowment of the house was so small, according to other accounts, that Raynold, or more properly William Lord Clinton, who was a much larger benefactor to it in 20 Edward I, was afterwards reputed its sole founder.[2] It is also said that Thomas de Crauthorne, who lived about the time of Edward I, was a principal benefactor towards re-edifying the priory of the Carmelite Friars of Sandwich.[3]

However this may be, it is certain that the friars were settled here before 1280 when John of Sandwich gave them a plot of ground adjoining their place.[4] In 1300 Edward I gave them 5s. for one day's food;[5] there were probably fifteen friars in the convent at this time. From Thomas Shelving of Sandwich they obtained a spring of water in Woodnesborough in 1306, with leave to make an underground conduit through his lands to their house.[6] In 1336 John de Welles, Raymond de Sparre, John de Thaxstede, Thomas Gilet, John Botoun, and William de Mounty gave them 2 acres of land.[7]

A friar of this house, Thomas Tulyet, gave evidence against the Knights Templars in 1311.[8] Two Carmelites were arrested in the port of Sandwich in 1344, with papal bulls and letters prejudicial to the king.[9]

In 1370, Thomas Brentingham, bishop of Exeter, granted forty days' indulgence to those of his diocese who should devoutly visit the church of the Carmelites at Sandwich, 'in which, as we have heard, a fair image of the blessed virgin and martyr Katherine is held in great veneration.'[10]

Thomas Walden, provincial prior, conferred on Friar Lawrence Clerke, who had long been a member of this community, a special dwelling-place in the priory for life, with the consent of the prior and friars of the house; the grant was confirmed by Pope Martin V in 1421.[11]

The epitaphs of several friars buried here in the fifteenth century have been preserved,[12] namely, those of John Sandwich, prior, 1403; Thomas Legatt, S.T.P., 1409; Thomas Hadlow, prior, 1417; William Beckley, prior, S.T.P. of Cambridge, 1438;[13] Denys Plumcooper, 1481. A provincial chapter was held here in 1482, to the expenses of which the town contributed 5 marks.[14] In 1487 Bernard Manny, who confessed to a murder in 1483, took sanctuary in the friars' church and forswore the realm.[15]

Henry Lunys of St. Peter's parish in 1477 desired to be buried before the image of Our Lord in the north side of the choir. John Drye, rector of Hame, 1486, desired to be buried before the altar of St. Ninian in this church, and left 6d. or 4d. to each friar, bedding for the infirmary, robes to Friars Richard Alkham, John Bradgate, Thomas Baker, and William Sexten; 12d. to Friar William Coly, and 3s. 4d. to Friar William Ash, lector. Richard Swinderly in 1510 desired to be buried before the image of St. Anne, Joan Frevill in 1526 before the crucifix in the church (for the reparation of which church she left 53s. 4d.), Agnes Hilton in 1529 before the image of St. Anne.[15a]

Bequests to the house were made by Sir Richard atte Lease, kt. (1393),[16] Thomas Walter of Birchington (1414), John Sackett of St. Peter's, Thanet (1444), John Malyn of Monkton (1464),[17] William Mountford, cordiner (1479), who left 6 lb. of wax to the light of St. Crispin and St. Crispianus in the church;[17a] Richard Tilley (1485),[18] William Harrison (1489) and William Tanner (1493), who each left wax to the light of St. Cosmus and St. Damian; Robert Saunder (1499), who gave 8d. for prayers for the soul of Constance at St. Trunian's altar;[18a] Benett Webbys (1508);[19] Jane Aschowe of St. Bartholomew's Hospital left her great kettle to St. Anne in the Friars in 1524, and 20 marks to the master prior, Sir John Kete, who was to sing two years for her soul—one in Eastrey church and the other in the White Friars; Alice Simpson, widow, 1526, wished to be buried

[11] L. and P. Hen. VIII, xiv (1), 609; (2), 72; Hasted, op. cit. iii, 79; Harl. MS. 608, fol. 80b; Mins. Accts. 30 & 31 Hen. VIII (Kent), No. 105, m. 74.

[1] Harl. MS. 539, fol. 143; the author adds that the second founder was Thomas Balsford, earl of Worcester (?).

[2] Dugdale, Mon. vi, 1571; Hasted, op. cit. iv, 267 and note (s); Boys, Hist. of Sandwich, 175 (William is perhaps a mistake for John de Clinton)

[3] Hasted, op. cit. iii, 506; iv, 267.

[4] Pat. 8 Edw. I, m. 1.

[5] Liber Quotid. etc. 28 Edw. I. (ed. Topham), 30.

[6] Pat. 34 Edw. I, m. 20.

[7] Ibid. 10 Edw. III, pt. 1, m. 37.

[8] Wilkins, Concilia, ii, 361.

[9] Close, 18 Edw. III, pt. 2, m. 27d.; Rymer, Foed. (Rec. Com.), iii (1), 11.

[10] Exeter Epis. Reg. Brantyngham, i, 223.

[11] Cal. Pap. Let. vii, 182.

[12] Weever, Fun. Monum. 263–4.

[13] See Stevens, Add. to Mon. ii, 171.

[14] Boys, Hist. of Sandwich, 178. [15] Ibid. 176.

[15a] Test. Cant. ii, 293–4.

[16] P. C. C. Rous, fol. 22.

[17] Boys, Hist. of Sandwich, 178.

[17a] Test. Cant. ii, 293.

[18] Nicolas, Test. Vet. 384.

[18a] Test. Cant. ii, 293–4. [19] Ibid. 492.

'before Our Lady in St. Barbary's Chapel,' and bequeathed some legacies to the friars.[19a] Sir John Peniel, kt., and William Eve were also among their benefactors.[20] John Trapham, prior, in 1508–9 granted two gardens in the parish of St. Peter to John Goldestone of Sandwich for ever at a rent of 12d. a year.[21]

The house was surrendered to the bishop of Dover in December, 1538.[22] The property was worth to the crown 51s. 7d. a year; much of it was already let out in small holdings; thus Elizabeth Ingeham and Thomas Gilbert held a barn, stable, and 1 acre of pasture for 10s.; among the other tenants were John Goldestone and John Trapham. The site, with its appurtenances, was purchased by Thomas Arderne of Faversham in 1540.[23]

The seal is an interesting one; it is oval in form, and consists of a patriarchal cross sable with a key on either side of the shaft of the cross, a crescent to the right, a star of six points to the left. The legend, in letters of ancient form, which has been misunderstood or carelessly copied by the engraver, runs :—

SI IHOANNIS PATEIAACNP IHEBVSALEM.[24]

38. THE FRIARS OF THE SACK OF CANTERBURY

The Friars of the Penance of Jesus Christ or Friars of the Sack must have settled here before 1274, when the order was suppressed by the Council of Lyons. Edward I gave them 3s. for three days' food in 1289,[25] and a similar sum in 1297; there were thus probably only three friars remaining at that time. The friary came to an end some time before 1314, when there was a dispute whether the land should escheat to the crown or to Adam Hurice or Hurel.[26] The king recovered it as an escheat, and the city paid the crown a yearly rent of 10s. for it till 1402.[27] The tenement continued to be known as 'the house of the friars of the Sac,' and was held by lease under the corporation of Canterbury in the fourteenth century. In 1544 it was granted to

Thomas Babington of Dethick, Derbyshire, being at that time in the tenure of John Welett.[28] It afterwards came into the hands of Sir James Hales, kt., who granted it in 1551, in exchange for other lands in Canterbury, to the mayor and commonalty; the latter soon sold it to a Mr. Bingham. The house was situated in St. Peter's Street to the west of the Grey Friars.[29]

39. THE TRINITARIAN FRIARS OF MOTTENDEN IN THE PARISH OF HEADCORN

The earliest reference to this priory is a royal writ issued 18 January, 1235–6, to inquire if the prior of Mottenden was seised of certain rents of the gift of Robert de Rokel or Rokeslay. The jurors returned that the prior was in seisin of 14s. 6d. and eight hens rent of the gift of Robert, out of a tenement which he held at Ospringe for two years before his death; also of 11 seams of barley from his tenement in Plumworth.

But of the entire domain which Robert had in Plumworth, they say the prior had no service therefrom before the death of Robert as they believe; but the prior had seisin of the rents homages and other pertinencies to the said domain two years before the death of the said Robert as above.[1]

By grant of Sir Robert de Rokeslay the friars were entitled to receive 60s. a year from the abbot of Boxley for a marsh and mill outside Sandwich. The sum was reduced to 50s. with the consent of Sir Robert's son and heir Richard, and subsequently to 40s. The friars are found asserting their rights in the court of the mayor of Sandwich as late as 1474.[2] Sir Robert de Rokeslay, seneschal of the archbishop of Canterbury, who died between 1230 and 1235, is called by Leland the original founder of the house,[3] though this title was afterwards given to Sir Michael de Ponynges, knt.[4] The friars of this house are sometimes described as of the 'Order of the Holy Cross,' or Cruciferi;[5] the confusion arose from the Trinitarian or Maturine friars wearing a blue and red cross on their habits. The friars of this house are first expressly mentioned as Trinitarians March, 1253–4, when Henry III granted them

---

[19a] *Test. Cant.* ii, 293.

[20] Hasted, *Hist. and Topog. Surv. of Kent*, iv, 267; Boys, *Hist. of Sandwich*, 842.

[21] Boys, *Hist. of Sandwich*, 180.

[22] *L. and P. Hen. VIII*, xiii (2), 1058.

[23] Mins. Accts. 30 & 31 Hen. VIII (Kent), No. 105, m 73; Partic. for Grants, file 33; *L. and P. Hen. VIII*, xv, 831 (17); Boys, *Hist. of Sandwich*, 176; Hasted, op. cit. iv, 267–8.

[24] Reproduced in Boys, *Hist. of Sandwich*, 177; the matrix is still among the seals of the corporation.

[25] P.R.O. Exch. Accts. 352 (18); B.M. Add. MS. 7965, fol. 7b; the entry in Pat. 52 Hen. III, m. 12, refers to the Friars of the Sack at Cambridge.

[26] *Abbrev. Plac.* (Rec. Com.), 319; *Arch.* iii, 130; Close, 8 Edw. II, m. 27.

[27] Pat. 3 Hen. IV, pt. 2, m. 21.

[28] *L. and P. Hen. VIII*, xix (2), 527 (15).

[29] Bunce, Minutes of the City of Cant. No. i, xxviii; Hasted, *Cant.* ii, 613 (ed. ii); Accts. of the City *sub annis* 1367, 1393 (in the City archives); *Arch.* iii, 130–1; *Hist. MSS. Com. Rep.* ix, App. pt. i, 146b.

[1] *Arch. Cant.* ii, 292; from Exch. No. 13, 20 Hen. III (P.R.O.). (Plumworth or Plumford is in Ospringe and Preston.)

[2] Boys, *Hist. of Sandwich*, 195; *Valor Eccl.* (Rec. Com.), i, 80, 81.

[3] Leland, *Coll.* i, 88; Pat. 9 Hen. III, m. 3.

[4] Tanner, *Notit. Mon.* Kent, xlii.

[5] Leland, *ut supra*; *L. and P. Hen. VIII*, xv, 1027 (25).

the right to hold a fair every year on the vigil and feast of the Holy Trinity and six following days.[6] The jurors in the great inquest of 1275 said that the friars of Mottenden had appropriated 40 acres or more, whereby the king lost 5s. a year.[7] In 1276 William de Welles and three other brethren of the house obtained a writ of protection for five years, probably while soliciting alms.[8] The minister and brethren having fallen into 'great mischief and poverty,' owing to the siege of Leeds Castle (1321) and the bad years and murrain of their beasts, petitioned the king for licence to acquire 10 librates of lands and rents.[9] Licence to acquire lands and rents to the value of 40s. a year was granted in 1337.[10] The house received several additions to its property in the fourteenth century. Robert Golde in 1325 granted to John le Bray, the warden, 5 acres of land in Aylesford, to celebrate divine service daily for the souls of Richard and John de Rokele, their ancestors and successors.[11] In July, 1338, Robert de Stangrave and Joan his wife granted to the ministers and friars 80 acres of land and 10 acres of meadow in Staplehurst and Frittenden, of the yearly value of 26s. 9d.[12] In 1347, at the request of Sir Michael de Ponynges, the king granted the friars licence to acquire in mortmain 30 librates of land and rent not held in chief.[13]

In 1362 Sir Michael de Ponynges, knt., Richard de Cressevill, parson of Rolvenden, and Robert Botillere, gave the friars half an acre of land in Lancing and the advowson of the church of Lancing, for finding two chaplains to celebrate divine service daily in their house of Mottenden, for the good estate of the king and the souls of the grantors and others. The grant was confirmed by John de Mowbray, lord of Bramber.[14]

In 1374, in part satisfaction of the grant of 30 librates, the king authorized the following gifts to the friars :—[15] John Wilde, parson of the church of Buckland, 100 acres of land, 250 acres of wood, and 11d. of rent in Cranbrook and Benenden ; [16] John Parmenter, John Mascal, and

William Waterman, 1 messuage, 104 acres of land, 10 acres of pasture, 2½ acres of wood, 9¼d. of rent, the rent of 1 quarter of barley, and 'the rent of one hen and three parts of a hen,' in Ospringe and Preston near Faversham ; William Benge, 1 messuage and 1 acre in Ospringe and Faversham ; William Waterman and William Bishop, 16 acres in Sutton Valence ; John Parmenter, 2s. 10d. of rent in Staplehurst ; the value of the whole being £7 18s. 11¼d. a year. In further satisfaction of the grant of 30 librates, Richard II, in January, 1393–4, permitted Stephen Norton of Chart, by Sutton Valence, and Stephen his son, John Herberfield, and John Blecche, to confer on the minister and friars of Mottenden

two messuages, 91 acres of land and 9 acres of meadow, rents to the value of 34s. 4d. and the rent of one cock and four hens, with their appurtenances, in Staplehurst and Headcorn and Boughton Monchelsea.

The annual value of the whole is certified by the jurors to be only 34s. 2d.[17]

About 1384 the temporalities of the ministry of Mottenden were reckoned at 100s. a year.[18]

In 1387 the prior and chapter of Christchurch, Canterbury, as lord of Hollingbourne, permitted certain tenants to alienate lands in the manor to these friars ; [19] and in 1394 an agreement was made between the prior and the minister as to some questions in dispute between them.[20]

Each house of Trinitarian friars had originally as a rule seven inmates—the minister, three clerks, and three lay brethren—but the number was afterwards increased. A third part of the income of the house from all sources had to be devoted to the redemption of captives imprisoned by the pagans for the faith of Christ.[21] The friars sometimes served chapels in different parts of the country ; thus the office of warden of the chapel of St. Laurence, Crediton, generally held by a Trinitarian friar of Hounslow, was in 1332 conferred by Bishop Grandison on William de Allertone in Shirwood, priest and friar of Mottenden.[22] Generally the friars of Mottenden seem to have been drawn from the immediate neighbourhood, or from the estates of the house.[23] In 1372 the minister of Mottenden was appointed

---

[6] *Roles Gascons* (ed. Michel), i, 323.

[7] *Hund. R.* (Rec. Com.), i, 223.

[8] Pat. 4 Edw. I, m. 6.

[9] Anct. Pet. (P.R.O.), 6344.

[10] Pat. 11 Edw. III, pt. 3, m. 22.

[11] Ibid. 18 Edw. II, pt. 2, m. 12. 'Totynton' is probably a mistake for 'Motynton.' This is perhaps the land in Maidstone in the *Valor Eccl.* (Rec. Com.), i, 81.

[12] Pat. 12 Edw. III, pt. 2, m. 9 ; Inq. a.q.d. file 246, No. 8.

[13] Pat. 21 Edw. III, pt. 4, m. 19 ; Inq. a.q.d. file 338, No. 18. An inquest had been held on this proposed grant as early as 1349, Inq. a.q.d. file 292, No. 19.

[14] Pat. 36 Edw. III, pt. 2, m. 16 ; 13 Ric. II, pt. 2, m. 21 ; Close, 38 Edw. III, m. 31 d.

[15] Pat. 48 Edw. III, pt. 2, m. 22.

[16] i.e. in the manor of Delmynden ; *Valor Eccl.* (Rec. Com.), i, 81.

[17] Pat. 17 Ric. II, pt. 2, m. 42.

[18] *Chron. W. Thorne*, in Twysden's *Decem Scriptores*, 2168.

[19] *Hist. MSS. Com. Rep.* viii, App. pt. i, 329. The friars did not hold land in Hollingbourne in 1535.

[20] Ibid. ix, App. pt. i, 110.

[21] See bulls of Innoc. III (17 Dec. 1198) and Clement IV (7 Dec. 1267) ; Cherubini, *Bullar. Rom.* i, 71, 135 ; Dugdale, *Mon.* vi, 1558.

[22] *Exeter Epis. Reg. Grandison*, 1291 ; Oliver, *Mon. Dioc. Exon.* 78.

[23] Thus in 1485 Richard of Lancing, the minister and provincial, appointed Jacob Ospring and Richard Sutton proctors in the ensuing provincial chapter. Eccl. Doc. (P.R.O.), 3 (1).

provincial of England in a general chapter of the order 'for the correction of abuses'; on his claiming jurisdiction over the house at Easton, Wiltshire, and summoning the minister of Easton to appear at a chapter of the order to be held in London on 3 May, 1382, Henry Sturmy, the patron of the house at Easton, denied his right, and caused him to be attached in the common pleas, 'and he is under mainprize to appear from day to day.' He petitioned the king to set him free.[24] Richard Lyming, a friar of this house, having unlawfully left his order, was admitted to the Cistercian monastery of Boxley, but subsequently returned to Mottenden.[25] In 1404 Richard de Berham brought an action against the minister to compel him to carry out an agreement made between Geoffrey of Sissinghurst and William de Bottune, late minister, whereby the latter engaged to supply two friars to celebrate in the chapel at Sissinghurst.[25a] Several letters of fraternity issued by the minister of this house are extant; thus in 1477, John Prince, lord of the manors of Theydon Gernon and Theydon Bois, and Lucy wife of William Margyte, having aided in an expedition against the Turks, were admitted as brother and sister of the order by Richard of Lancing, minister of Mottenden.[26]

This Richard of Lancing added to the library one of the two volumes[27] known to have belonged to Mottenden, namely MS. Bodley 643, which contains works on logic and grammar by Burley, Duns Scotus, Albertus Magnus, and John Esteby, with the note: 'Bought by Friar Richard de Lancing 1467, price 26s. 8d., but it is worth more.'[28] Richard was provincial and minister of Mottenden in 1488, when he induced the mayor and commonalty of Oxford to restore to the Order the chapel and tenements of the Trinitarian friars without the east gate of that city;[29] this land was at the Dissolution reckoned among the possessions of the friars of Mottenden.[30] Richard held the same offices in 1494, when he received John Davy and Elinor his wife, and John Dering of Surrenden Dering, esq., benefactors of the Order, to the privileges of confraternity.[31] One of the chief privileges of these *confratres* was the right to choose their own confessor.

Peter Husey, archdeacon of Northampton, by will made 31 December, 1499, left his body to be buried in the choir of this church; he seems to have died in this priory.[32]

On Trinity Sunday the friars were accustomed to hold a solemn procession and pageant, the chief feature of which was an attack on the holy company by some one arrayed like a devil, and his repulse by the use of holy water. Of this pageant, 'some lately alive in this shire have been eyewitnesses,' wrote Lambarde in 1570.[33]

The minister returned the net annual value of the property in 1535 as £60 13s. 0½d. According to the figures given in the *Valor Ecclesiasticus* however, the correct total, allowing for all deductions and adding 8d. received from the chantry of Headcorn, would be £58 1s. Among the deductions were charges for the obits of Robert Stangrave and Joan his wife, Richard Lyle, and William Appledorefield. The oblations in the church were wont to be worth yearly 40s., but were 'now scant worth 5s.'[34]

Early in 1538 Cromwell was warned that Sir Edward Neville was endeavouring to persuade the minister of Mottenden secretly to surrender his house.[35] But Cromwell, who was now, after the death of the earl of Northumberland in 1537,[36] honoured with the title of founder of the priory, had marked its property for his own. In November, 1538, Neville was sent to the Tower for complicity in the conspiracy of the Poles, and a patent was issued to Cromwell confirming his estate, possession and interest in the site of the late priory of Mottenden, and the manors of Mottenden, Plushenden, Plomford, and Delmynden in Kent; the rectory of Lancing, Sussex, and all tithes thereto belonging; the advowson of the parish church of Lancing and the vicarage of the same church; a saltmarsh in Canwynden (? Canewdon) *alias* Derwishop, Essex; and all lands, &c., in the counties of Kent, Sussex, and Essex, late of John Gregory *alias* John Harietsham, late minister of the Trinitarian priory of Mottenden.[37]

After Cromwell's attainder much of the property, comprising 361 acres with some woods, was leased in 1540 to Sir Anthony Aucher of Swingfield, Kent, esq., for twenty-one years at a rent of £25 a year, and in June, 1544, the site and

---

[24] *Hist. MSS. Com. Rep.* iv, 198–9.
[25] *Cal. Papal Let.* v, 276 (A.D. 1400).
[25a] De Banco R. Hil. 5 Hen. IV, rot. 103.
[26] *Hist. MSS. Com. Rep.* iii, 274; cf. 310. Tanner says that copies of several pardons and indulgences granted by several popes to benefactors of this house are preserved in the register of Hadrian de Castello, bishop of Bath and Wells.
[27] The other volume is MS. Bodl. Auct. D. ii, 20, bought by John Armorer, vicar of Sutton Valence and Headcorn, from Buckhurst, once friar of Mottenden, probably after the Dissolution.
[28] Richard of Lancing was proctor of the house in 1470, minister in 1474. Boys, *Hist. of Sandwich*, 195.
[29] Bridgwater Corp. Mun. Oxf. D. No. 35, 180; cf. Wood, *City of Oxf.* (Oxf. Hist. Soc.), i, 600.
[30] *L. and P. Hen. VIII*, xvi, 722; *Hist. MSS. Com. Rep.* iii, 310.

[31] Hasted, *Hist. and Topog. Surv. of Kent*, ii, 391.
[32] Ibid. 392.
[33] *Perambulation of Kent* (ed. 1826), 300.
[34] *Valor Eccl.* (Rec. Com.), i, 81, 63; Cranmer returned the annual value of the friary as £58 0s. 3½d.; ibid. 98. [35] *L. and P. Hen. VIII*, xiii (1), 229.
[36] Leland, *Collect.* i, 88, calls the earl of Northumberland the 'modern' founder. Henry Percy, third earl of Northumberland, had married Eleanor, granddaughter and heiress of Robert lord Poynings.
[37] *L. and P. Hen. VIII*, xiii (2), 967 (54).

the greater part of the Kentish possessions of the house, valued at £39 5s. 0¾d. a year, were purchased by him for £806 12s. 3½d.[38]

At the time of the Dissolution the priory held a messuage in Hertford called ' le Trinytie ' and lands in the fields of Hertford, and in the parishes of Digswell, Hatfield, and Amwell, Hertfordshire ; these were in the tenure of John Andrewe and Anne his wife, and were sold in August, 1540, to Anthony Denny.[39]

In February, 1555–6, four friars of this house were still in receipt of pensions : John Hendyman, £4 ; William Barker, Richard Broklehurst, and Andrew Pyttenden, 53s. 4d. each.[40]

MINISTERS

William, 1289 [41]
John le Bray, 1325
William de Bottune, c. 1400[42]

Thomas, 1404 [43]
Richard Lancing, 1477, 1494
Richard Sutton, *alias* Baker [44]
John Gregory *alias* John Harietsham, 1532, 1538 [45]

The seal of the priory, engraved in Hasted's *Kent*, represents the Almighty with nimbus, seated, holding in front of Him the crucified Saviour ; below a cross patée. Another seal of the priory has the Almighty with nimbus, seated, in a niche with triple canopy, with both arms upraised ; on each side a saint or attendant holding up one of the divine hands ; in base, a prior, half length, in prayer, to the left. Legend :—

S COMMVNE DOMVS ORDINIS SANCTE TRINITATIS
D . . . . YNDENNE . . . . CIA [46]

HOSPITALS

40. THE HOSPITAL OF BOUGHTON UNDER BLEAN

Richard II on 1 August, 1384, at the supplication of the earl of Arundel, pardoned the trespasses committed by Thomas atte Herst of ' Bocton atte Blee' in having without licence founded and built in honour of the Holy Trinity a chapel 150 ft. long by 50 ft. broad, and a house of the same dimensions for lepers and other infirm persons thither resorting, in the king's highway called ' Chyniot in Bocton under le Blee,' and in his having ordained a certain number of lay brethren and sisters to dwell in the said house to pray for the king, his progenitors and heirs and the whole realm ; pardoned the forfeitures incurred ; and granted to the said Thomas that he by the name of master or warden of the said chapel and house should with the said brethren and sisters hold the same in perpetuity by the king's gift, and the chapel should be the king's free chapel, the king the founder and the chancellor the patron, visitor and protector.[1]

Nothing more is known of this hospital.

41. THE HOSPITAL OF BUCKLAND BY DOVER

Almost all the knowledge which we possess of this hospital is derived from the register,[1a] unusually interesting and complete for so small a house, which was compiled in 1373 by Robert de Welle and John Hwytefeld, monks of Dover,[2] at the special instance of Thomas de Cant', sub-prior, warden of the hospital. It is there stated that in 1141 brothers Osbern and Godwyn, monks of Dover, from the goods of their parents by authority of Archbishop Theobald, and with the consent of the prior and convent of Dover, constructed the hospital of poor people of St. Bartholomew by Dover, appointing the prior of Dover disposer and ordainer of it internally and externally, and the prior and convent granted to the poor people all the ' teghe ' before the hospital ; and that Prior Hugh, not being able to attend to its business, appointed his sub-prior as their warden, reserving important business to himself, and this has been observed ' to this day.'

Regulations for the brothers and sisters were laid down in great detail. Each candidate must be examined by the warden, must be of free condition, either unmarried, or with the consent of the husband or wife remaining in secular life, and must pay 100s. for admission, or more, according to arrangement, 6s. 8d. to the warden for his fee, and 3d. or a *jentaculum* to each brother and sister. He (or she) will be brought by the master to the

---

[38] *L. and P. Hen. VIII*, xvi, p. 720 ; xix (1), 812 (48). P.R.O. Part. for Grants, 55 ; Hasted, op. cit. ii, 392. Neither the property in Kent lying to the south of Headcorn, namely at Staplehurst, Frittenden, Cranbrook, and Benenden, nor the property outside Kent, was included in this grant. The later history of the property will be found in Hasted.

[39] *L. and P. Hen. VIII*, xv, 1027 (25) ; cf. Tanner, *Notit. Mon. sub* Hertford.

[40] *Arch. Cant.* ii, 59.

[41] *Reg. Epist. J. Peckham* (Rolls Ser.), iii, 1010.

[42] De Banco R. Hil. 5 Hen. IV, rot. 103.

[43] Ibid.   [44] Pat. R. Supplem. 57.

[45] He was B. Can. L. of Oxf. ; *Reg. Univ. Oxon.* (Oxf. Hist. Soc.), i, 38 ; Wood, *Fasti*, 47 ; Bloxam, *Magd. Coll. Reg.* ii, 2.

[46] Hasted, op. cit. ii, 392 ; B.M. Seals, lxv, 88 ; Magd. Coll. Oxf. Mun. Ashurst, 8 ; cf. *Arch. Cant.* x, Abstract of Proc. 13 March, 1874.

[1] Pat. 8 Ric. II, pt. 1, m. 31.

[1a] Bodleian, Rawlinson MS. B. 335.

[2] These same two monks compiled the register of the priory of Dover in the preceding year.

door of the church, and will then take an oath before the warden, one of the articles of this being that at death he will leave half his goods to the hospital. The number of brothers and sisters was twenty in olden times, but 'now' sixteen at most is sufficient, and of these the master, who should be a leper, is appointed by the warden, and takes an oath that he will administer the property faithfully, and render an account when required. The allowances made to the brothers and sisters are specified. No brother may go outside the house except with the leave of the master, and no sister except with the leave of the prioress; they are to frequent no taverns; to say 200 paternosters and aves by day, and the same number in the middle of the night; none are to sleep outside the house for more than three nights without leave from the warden; they are to have a round tonsure, and wear a black or russet dress; the leprous are not to live with the hale; and though they may have private property, they may not indulge in usury. They are to have two proctors, one for Dover and the neighbourhood, the other for England in general. A priest is to be maintained at the cost of the house, to celebrate daily for the founders and to minister in the church; he is to hear the confessions of the brothers and sisters, and without the leave of the warden they may not have another confessor. Each brother and sister is to labour in the offices of the house rather than elsewhere, and at half the pay, except in autumn, when they may take four pence, two for dinner, and two for stipend.

Pope Adrian IV in 1158 confirmed to Godewyn, rector of the house, all its possessions, including 100s. of land given by Gilbert de Gant. Pope Clement urged the faithful to be liberal to it, and Archbishop Theobald promised indulgence to benefactors, as also did Richard, bishop of Chichester, in 1252. Edward III in 1369 granted protection for the master, brethren, and sisters, begging alms.[3] An early grant by Henry de Arcell' was made for a house to receive poor and infirm coming from ships. The lepers are mentioned down to about the end of the thirteenth century, but in 1346 the hospital is said to be a place where the poor are maintained for life and the sick are nursed until they are well, and leprosy is not spoken of.[4]

In the Chantry Certificates the gross value of the possessions of the hospital, lying in Dover, Buckland, Ewell, Leeds, Bobbing and Deal, is given as £10 7s. 6d., and the net value as £8 3s. 6d. yearly, after deductions of £2 to the manor of River, and 4s. to the priory.[5] After the Dissolution the hospital was granted to Sir Thomas Palmer in 6 Edward VI.

[3] Pat. 43 Edw. III, pt. 2, m. 37.
[4] Register, fol. 97.
[5] Chant. Cert. 29, No. 112.

MASTERS OF BUCKLAND

Henry, occurs 1267[6]
John de Macstone, occurs 1295[7]
Arnold ate Regge, occurs 1309,[8] 1312[9]
John, occurs 1323[10]
William Ricceghe, occurs 1327[11]
Peter Norreis[12] or Norman, occurs 1351,[13] 1357[14]
Thomas de Lymene, occurs 1381[15]

42. THE HOSPITAL OF ST. JAMES BY CANTERBURY

This hospital, which is also described as being situated at Thanington or Wincheap in the suburbs of Canterbury, appears to have been founded some time in the twelfth century, probably by the prior and convent of the cathedral; for it is mentioned as being under their rule and care in a bull of Pope Alexander III, dated 22 June, 1164, in which he forbids them to admit to the foundation any but the leprous women for whom it was intended.[1] The church of Bredgar was granted or confirmed to it by Henry II.[2] Towards the end of the century the prior and convent, by the will of Archbishop Hubert, and at the petition of Master Firmin, warden of the hospital, took it into their custody and protection, and bound themselves to maintain there three priests, one of whom was to celebrate daily a mass of the Virgin Mary, another a requiem for its benefactors, and the third the common service, and one clerk and twenty-five leprous women.[3]

A small chartulary compiled in 1474 by William Hadlegh, sub-prior of the cathedral and warden of the hospital, is preserved at the British Museum.[3a]

In 1329 the prior of Christchurch complained of the oppression of his hospital of St. James by the master of the hospital of St. Thomas, Eastbridge.[4] Prioress Christina and the convent of the hospital in 1342, with the assent of the prior, 'their warden,' granted to Alice de Hertlepe for life a chamber in the hospital with reversion to her sister Joan;[5] but Queen Philippa asked the prior in vain for a nomination to a corrody there, receiving the answer that it was not in his power to grant it.[6] The prior on one occasion certified that the prioress and sisters were not bound to religion;[7] and on another that they were too poor to pay a subsidy;[8] and exemption from this was several times granted to

[6] Register, fol. 36.   [7] Ibid. 25.   [8] Ibid. 9.
[9] Ibid. 14.   [10] Ibid. 47.   [11] Ibid. 20.
[12] Ibid. 12.   [13] Ibid. 17.   [14] Ibid. 40.
[15] Ibid. 85. Thomas occurs as *magister sive custos* in 1386 (ibid. 86).   [1] *Lit. Cant.* (Rolls Ser.), iii, 75.
[2] Ibid. 76.   [3] Ibid. 77.   [3a] Add. MS. 32098.
[4] *Lit. Cant.* (Rolls Ser.), i, 297.   [5] Ibid. ii, 262.
[6] Ibid. 282.   [7] Ibid. 300.   [8] Ibid. 285.

them by the king.[9] An inquisition was taken in this connexion in 1343, and it was found that their possessions, which were described in detail and included the church of Bredgar, appropriated to them and valued at £14 yearly, were worth nothing beyond their maintenance and charges. There were then in the hospital a prioress and twenty-three sisters, and they had to find two priests, to each of whom they paid £4 yearly, and one clerk.[10]

Archbishop Langham made a visitation of the hospital on Tuesday, 7 March, 1368.[11] The exact foundation could not be shown, but the prior of Christchurch was said to be the founder, and details were given concerning the prayers and food. There were then only ten sisters and one brother and one secular sister, and the house was £10 in debt to the prior of Christchurch.

Licences for further acquisitions of lands to a considerable amount were granted to the prioress and sisters in 1401 and 1403.[12] The manor of Capel was held of them by the service of 5 marks, 4s. rent, and 5 marks 4s. relief on the death of each tenant, and in 1421 they complained that William Kerby, tenant for life, had not paid this. A commission was appointed on 28 February to inquire into the matter;[13] and it was found that Clemencia Newe, late prioress, had the rent at the hands of William atte Capell, tenant, in the time of Richard II and Susan Wynchepe, late prioress, had the relief at the hands of William the son and heir of Thomas atte Capell; and that the manor came into the hands of Henry IV by the forfeiture of Thomas Shelley, and Henry V in his second year granted it for life to William Kerby, who had withdrawn the service.[14] Order was made accordingly on 26 November that he should pay.[15]

John, prior of Christchurch, issued fresh statutes after a visitation on 18 February, 1415. All the brethren and sisters were to attend the oratory daily at the accustomed time, and abstain from conversation when there; the number of chaplains was to be maintained; no brother, sister, or chaplain was to be admitted without the consent of the prior; the hospital chest was to have three different locks, of which the prioress, cellaress, and another were each to have one key; the prioress was only to receive moneys with the knowledge of the brethren and sisters, and was to render an account four times yearly; the church of Bredgar and other possessions were not to be let at farm or sold; the prioress was to appoint a deputy if absent for as much as a day; the allowance of 10s. yearly to

each brother and sister for clothing and other things was to be increased by 3s. 4d. on account of the late increase of the possessions; no sister or other woman was to assist in the celebration of divine service; the prioress was not to go to any great expense without the consent of the brethren and sisters; and these and earlier statutes were to be observed and read publicly six times yearly.[16]

Archbishop Warham made a visitation [17] of the hospital by Tunstall in 1511. The prioress and sisters did not have bread and wood as they ought to have, through the fault of the sub-prior of Christchurch; and they said this before in the last visitation of the house in the presence of the said commissioner. Dame Agnes Yuys, prioress, seventy-four years old, complained that Richard Welles stayed to talk in the precincts of the house, and his wife sold beer there; they were quarrelsome people, and there was also a crowd at Richard's house. Joan Chambers was eighty-four years old and had been a sister for forty years; and Alice Bromfield, Edith Keme, and Joan Croche were respectively eighty, thirty-six, and fifty years old, and of eighteen, fourteen, and three years' standing. These declared that the prioress defamed the sisters, saying publicly in the neighbourhood that they were incontinent, to the great scandal of the house. The prioress was ordered not to use abusive words to the sisters, either publicly or privately; and they were to be obedient to her.

In the Valor of 1535 the gross income of the hospital was returned as £53 16s. 11¼d. and the net income as £32 2s. 1¾d. yearly;[18] but in the certificates of colleges and chantries these values are given as £58 6s. 10½d. and £43 6s. 10d. respectively.[19] On 28 February, 1551, the hospital was surrendered [20] to the crown with all its possessions, including the manor of Fylther (in Egerton), the rectory and advowson of the vicarage of Bredgar and lands in Thanington, St. Martin's at Canterbury, Wincheap, Elham, Shadoxhurst, Egerton, Mersham, Aldington, Brabourne, Bredgar, and Hackington.

PRIORESSES OF ST. JAMES'S, CANTERBURY

Christina, occurs 1342 [21]
Susan Wynchepe [21]
Agnes Congesett, died 1396 [22]
Clemencia Newe,[21] succeeded 1396,[22] occurs 1417 [22]
Joan, occurs 1493 [23]
Agnes Yuys, occurs 1511 [21]

[9] e.g. Close, 16 Edw. III, pt. 2, m. 26 d.; 17 Edw. III, pt. 1, m. 3.
[10] Inq. p.m. 17 Edw. III (1st Nos.), No. 70.
[11] Cant. Archiepis. Reg. Langham, fol. 77b.
[12] Pat. 2 Hen. IV, pt. 3, m. 16; 4 Hen. IV, pt. 2, m. 7.   [13] Pat. 8 Hen. V, m. 2 d.
[14] Inq. a.q.d. 9 Hen. V, No. 13.
[15] Close, 9 Hen. V, m. 10.

[16] Hist. MSS. Com. Rep. ix, App. pt. i, 112. Printed in Bibl. Topog. Brit. i, 431–4.
[17] Cant. Archiepis. Reg. Warham, fol. 36b.
[18] Valor Eccl. (Rec. Com.), i, 32.
[19] Chant. Cert. 29, No. 23.
[20] Close, 5 Edw. VI, pt. 7, No. 14.
[21] See above.   [22] Inq. p.m. 5 Hen. V, No. 66.
[23] Bibl. Topog. Brit. ii.

43. THE HOSPITAL OF ST. JOHN THE BAPTIST, NORTHGATE, CANTERBURY

Eadmer[1] tells us that Lanfranc, archbishop of Canterbury (1070–89), built a decent and ample house of stone outside the north gate of the city of Canterbury for the benefit of poor and infirm persons, dividing it into two parts for men and women, made ordinances for their clothing and living, and appointed ministers for them ; and on the other side of the way built a church in honour of St. Gregory, in which he placed canons to minister spiritually to them. The same archbishop also made a hospital of lepers at the church of St. Nicholas at the west of the city, with wooden houses, instituted clerks to minister to them, and assigned victuals and rents to them.[2] The two hospitals appear always to have been considered as twin foundations, and much of their history is the same ; although they were distinct, and lepers were received only at that of St. Nicholas, or Harbledown, as it was afterwards called.[3]

The two hospitals were endowed with £140 out of the revenues of the see of Canterbury, to which Archbishop Richard in the latter part of the twelfth century added £20 ; and they received this £160 yearly until Archbishop Kilwardby granted the church of Reculver to them instead in 1276.[4] The parishioners, however, objected to being put under lepers, and mutual recriminations followed, one side declaring that the customary services and cure of souls were neglected, and the other that the parishioners did not pay their proper charges ; until Archbishop Peckham revoked the grant in 1290 with the consent of the king and pope.[5] They then had £140 yearly from the exchequer of the see and 1d. daily from the issues of the manor of Lyminge, belonging to the see, but had considerable trouble in getting this at vacancies,[6] until Edward III in 1335 definitely confirmed the same to them ; at the same time granting in consideration of their poverty that they should be quit of tallages, aids, and contributions,[7] which was confirmed by later kings.[8]

In 1348 the last £20 were paid by the rector of Reculver, and the king granted licence[9] for Archbishop Stratford to appropriate the church to himself on condition that the whole £160 should in future be paid by the archbishop or by the prior and convent of Christchurch at vacancies. The appropriation was carried out by Archbishop Islip, Stratford's successor, in 1356.[10]

Archbishop Winchelsey made ordinances for the hospitals after a visitation on 24 February, 1299. The brethren and sisters were to wear a prescribed dress, and were not to be admitted until after proper examination, to go out of the hospital without leave, or to be quarrelsome ; offences were to be properly punished ; and the possessions of the hospitals were not to be alienated or pledged, nor corrodies granted.[11] Archbishop Parker made fresh statutes on 15 September, 1560, in which he ordained that there should be in each thirty brethren and thirty sisters, none of whom should live out without licence from the archbishop, and then not more than ten brethren and ten sisters at any time ; and he made further additions on 20 August, 1565, and 20 May, 1574.[12] Archbishop Whitgift in 1591 ordered that no children should be admitted.[13] Further regulations were also added by Archbishops Abbot in 1618,[14] Sheldon in 1663,[15] and Sancroft in 1686.[15] The latest injunctions as to the management of the hospitals were given by Archbishop Benson on 2 April, 1895.

Edward III granted licence in 1328 for the brethren and sisters of the hospital of Northgate to acquire lands and rents in mortmain to the value of 100s. yearly ;[16] and they made several acquisitions accordingly.[17] In 1348 they had a grant of protection while collecting alms in churches.[18]

In 1500 a felon fled to the hospital for sanctuary, and a watch was set by the city authorities lest he should escape by night.[19] In 1542 Gregory Pers, a blind brother of the hospital, was accidentally drowned in the well there.[20]

In the Valor of 1535 the gross income of the hospital, including the £80 received from the archbishopric, amounted to £93 15s. and the net income to £91 16s. 8½d. yearly ;[21] but in

---

[1] Eadmeri Hist. (Rolls Ser.), 15.

[2] Ibid. 16 ; Gervase of Canterbury, Opera (Rolls Ser.), ii, 368.

[3] Pat. 19 Edw. I, m. 25. The Lamb. MSS. 1131 and 1132 contain transcripts of charters, deeds, statutes, &c., relating to the two hospitals ; and from these and the originals a long account of both foundations is given by Duncombe and Battely in Bibl. Topog. Brit. i, 173–296 ; where several documents are printed and abstracts given of many others.

[4] Gervase, Opera, ii, 284.

[5] Pat. 18 Edw. I, m. 26 ; 19 Edw. I, m. 25 ; Cal. Papal Let. i, 511.   [6] Close, 8 Edw. III, m. 37.

[7] Pat. 9 Edw. III, pt. 2, m. 10.

[8] Pat. 1 Ric. II, pt. 3, m. 36 ; 1 Hen. IV, pt. 4, m. 7 ; 1 Hen. V, pt. 3, m. 39 ; 8 Hen. VI, pt. 1, m 7 ; 4 Edw. IV, pt. 2, m. 11.

[9] Pat. 22 Edw. III, pt. 1, m. 14, 1.

[10] Lit. Cant. (Rolls Ser.), ii, 337–42 ; Cant. Archiepis. Reg. Islip, fol. 111–12 ; Bibl. Topog. Brit. i, 148–50.

[11] Cant. Archiepis. Reg. Winchelsey, fol. 69 ; Bibl. Topog. Brit. i, 211–13.

[12] Strype, Life of Parker, iii, 32–41 ; Bibl. Topog. Brit. i, 214–20.

[13] Strype, Life of Whitgift, ii, 118.

[14] Bibl. Topog. Brit. i, 221.   [15] Ibid. 223.

[16] Pat. 1 Edw. III, pt. 3, m. 1.

[17] Pat. 3 Edw. III, pt. 1, m. 13 ; 38 Edw. III, pt. 2, m. 43 ; 39 Edw. III, pt. 2, m. 10.

[18] Pat. 22 Edw. III, pt. 1, m. 18.

[19] Hist. MSS. Com. Rep. ix, App. pt. i, 146.

[20] L. and P. Hen. VIII, xvii, 133.

[21] Valor Eccl. (Rec. Com.), i, 30.

the certificates of colleges and chantries these values are returned as £117 12s. 5½d. and £105 1s. 8½d. respectively.[22]

The commissioners appointed to inquire into charities gave a long account [23] in 1837 of the arrangements then in force at the hospital, and of its rental and benefactions made to it.

The seal [24] of the hospital (sixteenth or seventeenth century) is an oval measuring 1⅝ in. by 1⅜ in., and represents the baptism of Our Lord by St. John the Baptist with a shell on a mount with trees and foliage; on the right the Agnus Dei; overhead the Holy Spirit as a dove, descending.

Legend incorrectly cut :—

✠ SIGILLUM SANGD ✠ IOHANNES BADISTUS

44. THE HOSPITAL OF ST. LAURENCE, CANTERBURY

A register[1] of this hospital is preserved among the muniments of the cathedral at Canterbury; from which it appears that it was founded [2] by Hugh, abbot, and the convent of St. Augustine's in 1137 for sixteen brothers and sisters, one chaplain, and one clerk. The founders granted 9 acres of land on the right side of the way leading from Canterbury to Dover, and tithes from certain lands; and Roger de Marci granted tithes of his land of Dodyngdale.[3] The hospital appears always to have been considered as appropriated to the abbey;[4] and in 1263 the abbot is called warden of it.[5]

Exemption from taxation was granted to the hospital in 1340 on the ground of its poverty.[6] A commission was appointed in the following year to inquire into the matter;[7] and it was found that the hospital was founded by Hugh, abbot of St. Augustine's, who granted to it 21 acres of land in Canterbury, 68 acres in Chislet, and 32 acres in Sturry, beside rents and tithes worth £18 18s. yearly; and that other donors gave lands in Bridge, Nackington, Canterbury, and Stodmarsh; it had one mill, but no church appropriated to it. There were then and should be in it five brethren and eleven sisters, each of whom had 1¼d. daily; the chaplain received £4, and the clerk 40s. yearly, and repairs cost 40s. yearly.[8]

The Valor of 1535 gave the gross income of the hospital as £39 8s. 6d. and the net income

as £31 7s. 10d. yearly;[9] but in the chantry certificates these are returned as £25 19s. and £25 14s. 2d. respectively.[10]

The hospital survived the general dissolution; but in a visitation made under Cardinal Pole in 1557 the sisters said that Christopher Hales had a lease of their land, and after his death it passed from one to another until it came to one Tipsal. There should be seven sisters, a prioress, and a priest, but there were then only Joan Francis, prioress, Elizabeth Oliver, and Florence Young, not yet admitted sister.[11] The hospital appears to have been then suppressed; and on 26 May, 1557, the site was granted to Sir John Parrott in fee.[12]

45. THE HOSPITAL OF ST. MARY OF THE POOR PRIESTS, CANTERBURY

The abbot of St. Augustine's granted the church of Stodmarsh to this hospital in 1243 at the instance of Simon Langton, archdeacon of Canterbury;[1] and the latter was believed in Thorne's time to have founded it by the alms of divers persons; but it appears to have been earlier, for Alexander, master of the hospital of the priests, is mentioned as a benefactor to the Grey Friars in Canterbury in 1225.[2] The hospital was situated in the parish of St. Margaret, and in 1249 an agreement [3] about their rights was made between the rector of the parish and the master of the hospital, who is also sometimes called the syndic or proctor. In 1271 the church was granted to the hospital by the abbot.[4]

Richard de Hoo, master of the hospital, failed to render an account when called upon in 1315, and the archbishop appointed a commission to inquire into the affairs of the house.[5]

Grants of protection were made to the hospital in 1317 and 1327.[6] In 1330 Henry de Cantuaria had licence[7] to grant four messuages in Canterbury to the master and brethren to find a chaplain to celebrate divine service daily in the oratory of the Holy Trinity adjoining the church of St. Dunstan without Westgate for the souls of Henry and his parents and benefactors.

Pope Boniface IX on 23 January, 1393, granted indulgence to penitents who at certain times should visit and give alms to the chapel of the hospital.[8]

---

[22] Chant. Cert. 29, Nos. 39–45.
[23] *Char. Com. Rep.* xxx, 226–41.
[24] B.M. Seals, lxv, 24.   [1] Cathedral MS. C, 20.
[2] See also Thorne, in Twysden, *Decem Scriptores,* 1810.
[3] Somner, *Antiq. of Cant.* (ed. Battely), i, 39; App. 9.   [4] *Cal. Papal Let.* i, 585; ii, 401.
[5] Feet of F. Kent, 47 Hen. III.
[6] Close, 14 Edw. III, pt. 2, m. 27.
[7] Pat. 15 Edw. III, pt. 3, m. 5 d.
[8] Inq. p.m. 15 Edw. III (2nd Nos.), 79.

[9] *Valor Eccl.* (Rec. Com.), i, 23.
[10] Chant. Cert. 29, Nos. 49, 50.
[11] Battely, op. cit. i, 40; ii, 173.
[12] Pat. 3 & 4 Phil. and Mary, pt. 3, m. 25.
[1] Thorne, *Chron.* in Twysden, *Decem Scriptores,* 1892.
[2] *Mon. Franc.* (Rolls Ser.), ii, 17.
[3] Thorne, op. cit. 1897.   [4] Ibid. 1920.
[5] Cant. Archiepis. Reg. Reynolds, fol. 112b.
[6] Pat. 11 Edw. II, pt. 1, m. 12; 1 Edw. III, pt. 1, m. 9.
[7] Pat. 4 Edw. III, pt. 2, m. 34.
[8] *Cal. Papal Let.* iv, 456.

Edward III on several occasions granted to the master and brethren exemption from payment of a subsidy on the ground of their poverty.[9] An inquiry was made into this on 25 April, 1343, and it was found [10] that there were at the hospital a master and three priests as of old, and that they owned the churches of Stodmarsh and St. Margaret, Canterbury, worth £10 and £6 yearly respectively, and lands in Ickham, Wingham, St. Dunstan and Harbledown by Canterbury, Thanington, Westgate and 'le Hamme' and Canterbury and the suburbs. Their whole income was £36 8s. 7d., and out of it they had to find two priests to serve the churches, each of whom received £4 yearly, and a chaplain celebrating daily in the chapel of Holy Trinity in the cemetery of St. Dunstan, Canterbury, who had £4 also. They spent half a mark on ornaments, &c., of the chapel, £6 on the repairs of the churches and hospital (and £10 would be really required because the buildings of the hospital were ruinous), 100s. in hospitality (for which the house was originally founded), 5 marks in a pension to Master Henry de Cantuaria, £4 12s. to two corrodaries, 40s. to attorneys, 6s. to a clerk serving in the chapel and at their table, and 6 quarters 4 bushels of wheat, worth 29s. 3d., to a servant employed to keep their lands and collect rents, making a total of £35 0s. 7d.; so that their claim to exemption was just.

In the Valor [11] of 1535 the gross income of the hospital is given as £28 16s. 1d., and the net income as £10 13s. 8½d. yearly, the deductions including £12 paid to the priests serving the churches of St. Margaret and Stodmarsh; but in the certificates of colleges taken later these values are £32 3s. 11d. and £13 9s. 5d. respectively.[12]

Archbishop Parker reported [13] of the hospital in 1562 that—

it is of the foundation and patronage of the archdeacon of Canterbury. It was ordained for the relief of poor and indigente prestes, and to be releved of the revenues of the house. Ther is a master of the said hospitals, videlicet one Mr. Bacon, a temporal man, who is not resident nether maketh any dystribution. The hospitall house is marveylouslye in ruyn and decaye. It is taxed to the perpetual tenth and payeth 22s. 10½d.

The hospital was surrendered to the crown on 14 May, 1575, by Blase Winter, master, Edmund Freake, archdeacon of Canterbury and patron, and Matthew Parker, archbishop and ordinary; and granted with all its lands to the city on 5 July.[14]

[9] e.g. Close, 14 Edw. III, pt. 2, m. 54.
[10] Chan. Misc. bdle. 20, No. 1.
[11] *Valor Eccl.* (Rec. Com.), i, 31.
[12] Chant. Cert. 29, Nos. 31–8.
[13] Cant. Archiepis. Reg. Parker, fol. 237b.
[14] Pat. 7 Eliz. pt. 12; Somner, *Antiq. of Cant.* (ed. Battely), i, 73, App. 19.

MASTERS OF THE POOR PRIESTS, CANTERBURY

Alexander, occurs 1225 [15]
William, occurs 1263 [16]
Richard de Hoo, occurs 1315 [15]
Henry de Cantuaria, occurs 1317 [17]
John de Dogworth, occurs 1356 [18]
John Duwyt, died 1368 [19]
Robert, occurs 1411 [20]
Henry Harvy, appointed 1490,[21] resigned 1497 [22]
Thomas Water, appointed 1497,[22] resigned 1511 [23]
Philip Taylour, appointed 1511,[23] died 1528 [24]
Nicholas Langdon, appointed 1528,[24] died 1554 [24]
Hugh Barret, appointed 1554 [25]
Robert Bacon, appointed 1560 [26]
Blase Winter, appointed 1575,[26] the last master

The seal [27] of the hospital (fourteenth century) is a pointed oval measuring 1⅜ in. by ⅞ in., representing Becket's martyrdom under a trefoiled arch with a pinnacled tower over it. In base under a trefoiled arch the bust of a priest in prayer to the left. Legend :—

P TE PASTOR AVE MICHI SIT PC͠'OR EXIT' A VE

Another seal [28] (fourteenth century) is a pointed oval measuring 1½ in. by 1 in., representing in a four-lobed panel Becket's martyrdom, divided by a line from the second subject overhead, the coronation of the Virgin. In base under a round-headed arch a priest, half-length, in prayer to the right. Legend :—

MARTIRIS ET MR̃IS PRECE ME REGE DEXTERA PR̃IS

46. THE HOSPITAL OF ST. NICHOLAS AND ST. KATHARINE, CANTERBURY

William Cokyn, citizen of Canterbury, founded this hospital in the parish of St. Peter in or before the time of Archbishop Hubert, but afterwards caused it to be united with the hospital of St. Thomas, Eastbridge, the union being confirmed by a bull of Innocent III dated 1203. Edward II in 1314 confirmed to the united hospitals the grants made to them by Cokyn.[1]

[15] See above. [16] Feet of F. Kent, 47 Hen. III.
[17] Pat. 11 Edw. II, pt. 1, m. 12. He had a grant of protection while going on the king's service to Gascony. [18] Cant. Archiepis. Reg. Islip, fol. 130b.
[19] Cant. Archiepis. Reg. Langham, fol. 77.
[20] Pat. 13 Hen. IV, pt. 1, m. 36.
[21] Cant. Archiepis. Reg. Morton-Courtenay, fol. 156b. [22] Ibid. 162b.
[23] Cant. Archiepis. Reg. Warham, fol. 343b.
[24] Ibid. 395. [25] Battely, op. cit. i, 73.
[26] Ibid. ii, 172.
[27] B.M. Seals, lxv, 30. [28] Ibid. 29.
[1] *Bibl. Topog. Brit.* i, 304–7; Somner, *Antiq. of Cant.* (ed. Battely), i, 60; ii, 170; Pat. 7 Edw. II, pt. 2, m. 21.

47. THE HOSPITAL OF ST. THOMAS THE MARTYR, EASTBRIDGE, CANTERBURY

Archbishop Stratford drew up fresh statutes[1] for the hospital of Eastbridge on 23 September, 1342, and in these he declares it to have been founded by Thomas Becket himself for the relief of poor pilgrims coming to Canterbury. It had suffered much from the neglect of masters and come to so great a condition of debt and dilapidation as no longer to be able to maintain its burdens, and accordingly he united to it the parish church of Harbledown, the patronage of which belonged to it.[2] The master of the hospital, who was to be in priest's orders and to be appointed by the archbishop, was to make a full inventory of the goods of the hospital within one month of his appointment and give a copy to the prior of Christchurch, and also to render a full account of his administration yearly. He was to have with him in the hospital a secular chaplain, and these were to celebrate services as prescribed. Twelve beds were to be maintained in the hospital for the use of poor pilgrims, and an honest woman of more than forty years of age was to minister to them. The masters were to take an oath to observe these articles and not to alienate the possessions of the house.

Archbishop Peckham in 1284 appointed commissioners to audit the account of Hamo, late warden;[3] and in 1367 the account of Thomas de Woltone, master, was duly audited by the prior of Christchurch.[4]

The hospital of St. Nicholas and St. Katharine at Canterbury was united by its founder William Cokyn to the hospital of Eastbridge about the beginning of the thirteenth century, and he made the united hospitals heirs of all his possessions. Edward II in 1314 confirmed this and some grants in Blean.[5] The church of Blean was granted to the hospital by Hamo Crevequer and confirmed by Archbishop Langton;[6] and in 1375 Archbishop Sudbury ordained a vicarage there.[7] The manor of Blean and Hothcourt was granted by Thomas de Roos of Hamelak in 1359.[8]

In 1313 it was found before the justices in eyre at Canterbury that the master and brethren were bound to maintain the East Bridge (from which the hospital took its name), because they held rents for that purpose.[9]

The master and brethren of the hospital received frequent grants of protection from the crown,[10] and on several occasions invoked its aid against persons who fraudulently represented themselves to be their proctors and appropriated alms thus collected.[11] Exemption from taxation on the ground of poverty was sometimes granted by Edward III.[12]

Thomas de Wolton, master, in 1356 sold corrodies in the hospital to Richard de Medeborne and Adam le Eyr in return for grants of rent of 4 marks and £10 in perpetuity;[13] and in 1358 another[14] to Robert de Dentone for a cash payment of £75. John Montagu, master, granted a corrody to Thomas atte Court in 1396.[15]

Archbishop Islip on 25 February, 1363, at the request of Bartholomew de Bourne transferred to the hospital a chantry which James de Bourne, his progenitor, had founded in the parish church of 'Livingsbourne'; and Archbishop Sudbury in 1375 amended the foundation by adding part of the income from a messuage in Canterbury called 'le Chaunge,' which Edward III had granted to the hospital.[16] Archbishop Islip in 1350 promised indulgence to visitors to the hospital;[17] as also did Popes Honorius III in 1220,[18] Innocent VI in 1360,[19] Urban V in 1363,[20] and Boniface IX in 1402.[21]

The priors of Christchurch, Canterbury, made visitations of the hospital in 1413[22] and 1454.[23]

In the Valor[24] of 1535 the gross value of the possessions of the hospital was given as £43 12s. 3¾d. yearly and the net value as £23 18s. 9¾d.; but in the certificates of colleges and chantries the gross and net incomes were returned as £43 12s. 5¼d. and £27 17s. 7¼d. respectively.[25]

The hospital survived the Dissolution. Nicholas Harpsfield, archdeacon of Canterbury, made a visitation of it on 14 August, 1557, when William Sworder was master, and reported[26]—

They are bound to receive wayfaring and hurt men and to have viii beds for men and four for women, to remain for a night or more, if they be not able to depart; and the master of the hospital is charged

[1] *Lit. Cant.* (Rolls Ser.), ii, 251–7. The dedication to Becket must have been after his death. A long account of the hospital and its possessions, collected from the records and other writings belonging to it, is given by Duncombe and Battely in *Bibl. Topog. Brit.* i, 297–419.
[2] The royal licence for this is given in Pat. 16 Edw. III, pt. 2, m. 25.
[3] *Reg. Epist. J. Peckham* (Rolls Ser.), iii, 1060.
[4] *Lit. Cant.* (Rolls Ser.), ii, 483.
[5] Pat. 7 Edw. II, pt. 2, m. 21.
[6] Somner, *Antiq. of Cant.* (ed. Battely), i, 61.
[7] Ibid. App. 15.   [8] *Bibl. Topog. Brit.* i, 332.
[9] Pat. 12 Ric. II, pt. 1, m. 12.
[10] e.g. Pat. 14 Edw. I, m. 9.
[11] e.g. Pat. 6 Edw. II, pt. 1, m. 15.
[12] e.g. Close, 15 Edw. III, pt. 2, m. 14.
[13] *Lit. Cant.* (Rolls Ser.), ii, 343.   [14] Ibid. 372.
[15] *Hist. MSS. Com. Rep.* ix, App. pt. i, 111.
[16] *Lit. Cant.* (Rolls Ser.), iii, 58–68.
[17] Cant. Archiepis. Reg. Islip, fol. 18b.
[18] *Cal. Papal Let.* i, 77.   [19] *Cal. Papal Pet.* i, 351.
[20] *Cal. Papal Let.* iv, 36.   [21] Ibid. v, 472.
[22] *Hist. MSS. Com. Rep.* ix, App. pt. i, 105.
[23] *Bibl. Topog. Brit.* i, 386.
[24] *Valor Eccl.* (Rec. Com.), i, 31.
[25] Chant. Cert. 29, Nos. 21–2.
[26] *Bibl. Topog. Brit.* i, 371.

with the burial, and they have xx loads of wood yearly allowed, and xxvis. for drink. There was 10l. land a year with a mansion, which the priest always had to serve the chapel, taken away by the king; and it is the head church to Cosmus Blene; but they have no ornaments but organs.

Archbishop Parker visited the hospital in 1569 and drew up fresh statutes on 20 May in consequence of what he had observed.[27] The master was to give a true account yearly of the state of the house, to reside either at the hospital or at the manor of Blean and Hothcourt, and to receive yearly £6 13s. 4d. and twelve cartloads of wood. Every Friday he was to distribute thirty pence to thirty poor people, but in war time he was instead to distribute four pence daily to soldiers passing through the city. Twelve beds were to be maintained for poor persons, and an honest woman of more than forty years of age was to attend to them. Two books of accounts of the lodgers were to be kept. A free school for boys, not exceeding twenty, was to be kept; and two scholars were to be maintained at Corpus Christi College, Cambridge.[28] The archbishop returned a certificate to the Exchequer to this effect after another visitation in 1573.[29]

Queen Elizabeth in 1576 directed a commission to Sir James Hales and others to inquire into the state of the hospital; and they certified that it was ruinous, let out into tenements for yearly rent, and without master or brethren. She granted it to John Farneham at fee-farm by letters patent on 20 June;[30] but Archbishop Whitgift afterwards recovered it, made fresh ordinances for it,[31] and obtained an Act of Parliament in confirmation in 1586.[32]

In 1690 the yearly income of the hospital amounted to £80 6s. 4d., besides twenty-four loads of wood and the master's house, valued at £6. The expenses included £28 to ten in-brothers and sisters, £13 6s. 8d. to ten out-brothers and sisters, £6 2s. to the schoolmaster, and about £2 for books, and amounted in all to £72 15s. 6½d., leaving about £8 yearly for repairs and other expenses.[33]

The Charity Commissioners reported in 1837[34] that there were then at the hospital a master,

five in-brothers, five out-brothers, five in-sisters, and five out-sisters; and that when a vacancy occurred the mayor sent to the master the names of two persons qualified according to the statutes, and the master made his selection. The hospital exists thus to the present day, each of the twenty brothers and sisters receiving a pension of £25 yearly and four more non-residents receiving £10 each.

MASTERS OF EASTBRIDGE

Ralph, occurs 1219[35]
Peter, occurs 1236, 1240[36]
John de Suff', appointed 1242[37]
Geoffrey, occurs 1261[36]
Walter, occurs 1264[36]
Hamo, resigned 1284[38]
William de Burghiss or Burgeys, appointed 1299,[39] resigned 1321[40]
John Kenting, appointed 1321[40]
John de Thingden, appointed 1323[41]
Richard de Ivyngho, occurs 1337[42]
Roger de Rondes, occurs 1342[43]
Matthew de Assheton, appointed 1349[44]
William de Braddele, appointed 1351[45]
Thomas Niewe de Wolton, appointed 1352,[46] occurs 1373[47]
Robert de Bradegar, appointed 1379[48]
John Ovyng, appointed 1380[49]
John Ludham, appointed 1382[50]
John Whitteclyff, appointed 1383[51]
Walter Cranston, appointed 1383[52]
John Mountagu, occurs 1396,[53] resigned 1399[54]
Thomas Pellycan, appointed 1399,[54] resigned 1405[55]
Thomas Burton, appointed 1405,[55] died 1430[56]
Thomas Chichele, appointed 1430[56]
John Stopyndon, appointed 1430,[57] occurs 1442[58]
Thomas Kemp, resigned 1445[59]

[27] Strype, *Life of Parker*, i, 565–7; iii, 169–76; Battely, op. cit. ii, App. 63–5; *Bibl. Topog. Brit.* i, 387–91.
[28] The indenture of William Morphet, master, for this is printed in Battely, op. cit. ii, App. 65; *Bibl. Topog. Brit.* i, 418–19.
[29] Strype, *Parker*, ii, 306.
[30] Pat. 18 Eliz. pt. 8.
[31] Strype, *Life of Whitgift*, i, 393–5; ii, 352–4; iii, 352–7; Battely, op. cit. ii, App. 66–9; *Bibl. Topog. Brit.* i, 404–8.
[32] 27 Eliz. cap. 43. Printed in Battely, op. cit. ii, App. 69–70; *Bibl. Topog. Brit.* i, 410–12.
[33] Strype, *Whitgift*, iii, 358.
[34] *Char. Com. Rep.* i, 88, App. p. 133; xxx, 226.

[35] Feet of F. Kent, 3 Hen. III.
[36] Battely, op. cit. ii, App. 62.
[37] Pat. 26 Hen. III, pt. 1, m. 8.
[38] *Reg. Epist. J. Peckham* (Rolls Ser.), iii, 1060.
[39] Cant. Archiepis. Reg. Winchelsey, fol. 272b.
[40] Ibid. Reynolds, fol. 27b.   [41] Ibid. fol. 250b.
[42] Close, 11 Edw. III, pt. 1, m. 18. He was imprisoned in the castle of Canterbury for theft.
[43] *Lit. Cant.* (Rolls Ser.), ii, 251.
[44] Pat. 23 Edw. III, pt. 1, m. 6. By reason of the vacancy of the see.
[45] Cant. Archiepis. Reg. Islip, fol. 258b.
[46] Ibid. fol. 259.   [47] Ibid. Whittlesey, fol. 65b.
[48] Ibid. Sudbury, fol. 130b.   [49] Ibid. fol. 61.
[50] Ibid. Courtenay, fol. 245b.
[51] Ibid. fol. 249b.   [52] Ibid. fol. 252b.
[53] *Hist. MSS. Com. Rep.* ix, App. pt. i, 111.
[54] Cant. Archiepis. Reg. Arundel, i, fol. 266.
[55] Ibid. fol. 303.
[56] Ibid. Chicheley, i, fol. 180b.
[57] Ibid. fol 181b.
[58] *Hist. MSS. Com. Rep.* ix, App. pt. i, 139.
[59] Cant. Archiepis. Reg. Stafford, fol. 84b.

Thomas Chichele, appointed 1445,[59] died 1467[60]

John Bourchier, appointed 1467,[60] resigned 1490[61]

Thomas Halywell, appointed 1490,[61] resigned 1512[62]

Robert Woodward, appointed 1512[62]

Peter Lygham, occurs 1535[63]

William Sworder, appointed 1538,[64] occurs 1557[65]

William Morphet, appointed 1562[66]

Thomas Lawse, appointed 1569,[67] died 1594

Richard Rogers, 1594-6

Isaac Colf, 1596-7

John Boise, 1597-1625

Robert Say, 1625-8

John Sackette, 1628-64

Edward Aldy, 1664-73

Samuel Parker, 1673-87

John Battely, 1688

John Paris, 1708

John Bradock, 1709-19

John Lewis, 1719-46

John Sackette, 1746

Henry Heaton, 1753-77

William Backhouse, 1777

The seal [68] of the hospital (twelfth century) is a pointed oval measuring 3 in. by 2 in., representing St. Thomas of Canterbury with mitre and pall, lifting up the right hand in benediction and holding in the left a pastoral staff, with which he is piercing the head of a knight in armour under foot, who is lying on his back with a sword in his left hand. Legend :—

SIGILLUM HOSPITALIS Ŝ TOME CANTUARIE DE EASTBREGE

Another seal [69] (fifteenth century) is a pointed oval measuring 2⅜ in. by 1½ in., representing the Virgin seated on a throne in a canopied niche, crowned, holding on the left knee the Child, also crowned. In base, in a small niche, St. Thomas with mitre and crosier, kneeling in prayer to the right. In the field on each side a sprig of foliage. Legend :—

S' CŌE HOSPITAL' SĈI THŌE MART SUP ESTB'GGE CANT.

[59] Cant. Archiepis. Reg. Stafford, fol. 84b.
[60] Ibid. Bourchier, fol. 96.
[61] Ibid. Morton-Courtenay, fol. 156b.
[62] Ibid. Warham, fol. 346.
[63] Valor Eccl. (Rec. Com.), i, 31.
[64] Battely, op. cit. ii, App. 63.
[65] See above.
[66] Lists of the later masters are given in Battely, op. cit. ii, 171, and Bibl. Topog. Brit. i, 373.
[67] Strype, Parker, i, 567.
[68] B.M. Seals, lxv, 201.
[69] Ibid. D.C. G. 46.

48. THE HOSPITAL OF CHATHAM

The hospital of St. Bartholomew, Chatham, by Rochester, is said [1] to have been founded by Gundulf, bishop of Rochester (1077–1108); and it was found by an inquisition [2] taken in 1444 that it belonged to the prior and convent of Rochester and that the king had no right in it.

Henry I by charter granted to the infirm of the hospital a livery of 1d. daily, and 10s. yearly which Alfer the falconer used to receive from the farm of Milton at the hands of the sheriff of Kent, and this grant was confirmed by Henry III.[3] This latter king also in 1246 granted to them livery of the 40s. yearly which Roger son of Stephen de Northwude used to render to them out of a land called Northwude within the hundred of Milton, and also a messuage by the market of Milton, pasture for one horse and two cows, and quittance from toll and team and lastage.[4]

In 1346 an inquisition [5] was taken concerning the hospital, and the net value of its possessions, described in detail, was found to be only £6 8s. yearly. There were in it nine brethren and seven sisters ; and some of these were blind, one sister was epileptic, and the prior was a leper. The income of the hospital was evidently insufficient for their maintenance ; and Edward III in 1342, 1344, and 1347 exempted them from payment of the wool tax.[6] In 1348 he granted to them exemption from taxation for ever ; [7] and this was confirmed by later kings.[8]

Ademere Baldocke, late prior of the hospital, brought a suit in Chancery about 1473 against Edmond Saynt, late a brother of the hospital, for the restoration of evidences of the house.[9]

The possessions of the hospital are not given in the Valor of 1535, but there is mention of a payment of 6s. yearly made by the almoner of the cathedral to the brethren and sisters for the soul of Gundulf, bishop of Rochester.[10] In 1546 the gross income was said to be £3 10s. 1d. and the net income £2 9s. 11d. yearly ; but it was noted that 40s. yearly, the price of certain corn accustomed to be paid at the hands of the farmer of the parsonage of Stoke, had been unpaid for nine years, and that 9d. for the farm of certain lands in Frindsbury likewise remained unpaid.[11]

[1] Leland, Collectanea, i, 115.
[2] Printed in Thorpe, Reg. Roff. 137.
[3] Chart. 17 Hen. III, m. 10 ; Pat. 30 Hen. III, m. 4.
[4] Pat. 15 Edw. IV, pt. 3, m. 12.
[5] Inq. p.m. 16 Edw. III, 62 (1st Nos.).
[6] Close, 16 Edw. III, pt. 1, m. 28 ; 18 Edw. III, pt. 1, m. 12 ; 21 Edw. III, pt. 2, m. 6.
[7] Pat. 22 Edw. III, pt. 1, m. 11.
[8] Pat. 3 Ric. II, pt. 2, m. 8 ; 15 Edw. IV, pt. 3, m. 12.
[9] Early Chan. Proc. bdle. 47, No. 107.
[10] Valor Eccl. (Rec. Com.), i, 104.
[11] Chant. Cert. 29, No. 73.

King James I on 13 July, 1619, made a grant of the hospital to nominees of James, Viscount Doncaster; but the dean of Rochester, as patron of the hospital, objected that the crown had no right in it; and after a long fight the hospital was saved, though at a heavy expense.[12]

In 1837 the Charity Commissioners reported that the institution consisted of five persons, viz. the patron or master, the office being held by the dean of Rochester for the time being without any specific appointment, and four brethren, two clerical and two laymen, who were appointed by the dean as vacancies occurred. Each brother received £27 yearly, and the dean the residue, and the property consisted of the old hospital, which was used as a chapel, and several premises mentioned in the rental, described in detail.[13]

49. THE HOSPITAL OF THE HOLY TRINITY, DARTFORD

Henry VI on 20 June, 1453, granted licence for John Bamburgh, William Rothele, Roger Jouet, and Thomas Boost, to found an alms-house of divers dwellings of the vicar and church-wardens of the parish church of Holy Trinity, Dartford, and five poor persons to be maintained in it by them, to pray for the good estate of the king and queen, and for their souls after death, and for the support of other works of charity. The vicar and churchwardens were to be masters of the house, and they might acquire lands and rents to the value of £20 yearly.[14]

50. THE HOSPITAL OF ST. MARY MAGDALEN, DARTFORD

Here also was a hospital in 1256,[15] which is mentioned in the will of William Quoyf in 1491.[16] In a rental of the manor of Temples in 1509 it is called the 'Spytell House.'

51. THE HOSPITAL OF ST. MARY, DOVER

Hubert de Burgh, earl of Kent, justiciary of England, founded the hospital of St. Mary or the Maison Dieu, Dover, for the maintenance of the poor and infirm and pilgrims; and by charter[1] in 1227 or 1228 he granted to it the manor of Eastbridge. We first hear of it in 1221, when a grant of protection was made to the brethren;[2]

and in the following year they had a presentation to the church of Sellinge,[3] which was confirmed to them in 1248.[4] In 1228 some treasure trove was given[5] to the brethren of 'the new hospital of Dover.'

The founder at an early date transferred the patronage of the hospital to Henry III, who granted on 11 October, 1229, that at every vacancy the brethren might elect a master, either from the hospital or otherwise, and should have the custody of the hospital without interference.[6] A large number of charters were made to the hospital by this king. On 6 July, 1227, he granted to it the tithe of the issues of the passage of the port of Dover;[7] in 1229 £10 yearly at Michaelmas out of the issues of the port;[8] in 1230 50s. yearly from the issues of the port for the support of a chaplain celebrating divine service daily in the hospital for the soul of Reymund de Burge;[9] and on 12 December, 1231, £10 yearly at Easter from the same as a dowry for the church of the hospital, which was dedicated in his presence.[10] On 14 February, 1229, he granted that the master and brethren should be quit of suit of shires and various other charges.[11] On 11 July, 1228, he granted to them a yearly fair at Bewsbury by their manor of Whitfield on the feast of Sts. Philip and James, and the two days following;[12] on 14 July in the same year the manor of River;[13] and on 24 October, 1231, the church of Warden in Sheppey.[14] In 1228 he confirmed the grant by the founder of the manor of Eastbridge with the advowson of the church;[15] in 1231 the grant by the same of land in Milk Street, London, and the advowson of the church of Ospringe;[16] in 1247 the grant by the same of the manor of Honeychild;[17] in 1228 the grant by Simon de Warden of possessions in Warden;[18] and in 1231 grants of land in Sheppey, 100s. from the manor of Dersyngham, and the manor of Coldred.[19] In 1235 several grants were repeated.[20] On 5 September, 1229, he granted to the brethren a porch which they had built in the highway before the hospital,[21] and which they afterwards, in 1278, had licence

[12] *Reg. Roff.* 224–6.
[13] *Char. Com. Rep.* xxx, 325.
[14] Pat. 31 Hen. VI, pt. 2, m. 4.
[15] Pat. 40 Hen. III, m. 2.
[16] Tanner, *Notitia Mon.* Kent, xx, 3.
[1] B.M. Campb. ii, 12. This and other charters are printed in Dugdale, *Mon.* vii, 655.
[2] Pat. 6 Hen. III, m. 5.

[3] Ibid. m. 2.
[4] Pat. 32 Hen. III, m. 4.
[5] *Annales Mon.* (Rolls Ser.), iii, 108.
[6] Chart. R. 13 Hen. III, pt. 1, m. 2.
[7] Ibid. 11 Hen. III, pt. 2, m. 9.
[8] Ibid. 13 Hen. III, pt. 1, m. 4.
[9] Ibid. 15 Hen. III, m. 13.
[10] Ibid. 16 Hen. III, m. 19.
[11] Ibid. 13 Hen. III, pt. 1, m. 12.
[12] Ibid. 12 Hen. III, m. 4.   [13] Ibid. m. 3.
[14] Ibid. 15 Hen. III, m. 3.
[15] Ibid. 12 Hen. III, m. 3.
[16] Ibid. 15 Hen. III, m. 1.
[17] Ibid. 31 Hen. III, m. 9.
[18] Ibid. 12 Hen. III, m. 3.
[19] Ibid. 15 Hen. III, m. 10.
[20] Ibid. 19 Hen. III, m. 17, 16, 9.
[21] Ibid. 13 Hen. III, pt. 1, m. 4.

to lengthen.[22] Edward I on 10 May, 1286, granted to them free warren in their demesne lands of Coldred, 'Kingesdune' by Middleton, and Whitfield;[23] and charters of confirmation were obtained from several later kings.[24] The master successfully proved his claim to liberties under Edward I and Edward II.[25]

Nicholas Haute had licence in 1410 to grant a rent in Dover to the master and brethren to find a lamp burning daily in the hospital before the high altar;[26] and Richard III in 1484 granted to them in frankalmoign lands in Birchington, Monkton, and River.[27]

Pope Gregory IX in 1236 made a grant of protection and confirmation of possessions and liberties to the master and brethren,[28] and in 1239 he granted that they and their successors should observe the rule of St. Augustine.[29]

The master had grants of protection in 1276, 1277, and 1280, when going beyond the seas on business of the house.[30] In 1290 the question of repair of dykes led to a dispute between him and the tenants of his manors of Honeychild and Eastbridge in Romney Marsh.[31]

The crown claimed corrodies in the hospital; Henry de Oldington being sent there in 1315 to receive such maintenance as Henry le Blessid, deceased, had by order of the late king;[32] Richard Waytewell in 1327,[33] and John Monyn in 1330.[34] The chancellor had livery for himself and the clerks of the chancery in the hospital by ancient custom at all times when the chancery was at Dover; and when the earl of Chester was lodged there in 1325 he formally promised that it should not be to the prejudice of the chancellor.[35] These charges may have formed part of the reasons why in 1325 and on several later occasions the hospital secured exemption from taxation on the alleged ground of poverty.[36]

In 1352 application was made to the crown for the arrest of Richard de Sellyngg, a vagabond brother of the hospital.[37] In 1359 Thomas Wodelonde was retained by a formal deed[38] to

keep the watergate, serve in the bakery when required, and do other odd jobs about the hospital, receiving in return a corrody and 6s. 8d. yearly.

Archbishop Warham made a visitation[39] of the hospital on 20 September, 1511, when John Clerke was master and there were five brethren or priests. Simon Tempilman, who had been instituted to the benefice of Leigh in the diocese of Rochester, begged to be re-admitted to the brotherhood of the house, so that he might reside there or in his benefice, as he pleased; but this was refused, as the master and brethren gave evidence that when he had before been a brother in the house he had been so quarrelsome, brawling, and litigious, that religion could not be properly observed. The brethren gave evidence that the master held no annual meeting to announce the amount of their pensions, and only told them the state of the house verbally and without any details; and these points were ordered to be rectified.

In August, 1533,[40] the master was ill and, thinking he would not recover, by the advice of friends he told the brethren that he intended to resign for the safety of the house, as it was likely none of them would have the mastership on his death. They proceeded to election, and after choosing two candidates whom he refused, they finally elected John Burnell, with whom he was satisfied, but from whom he insisted on having surety that he should be allowed to have his chamber, his keeper, and his kitchen for life. The lawyer who was sent for to make the obligation, however, advised them first to obtain the favour of some great man in the matter, lest the king should refuse to admit Burnell; and acting on this suggestion the master withdrew his resignation, telling the brethren to say that there was none, but that one was chosen to govern the house under him, 'and thus ye shall stop their speech.'

This master was apparently John Clerke, who must have reached a great age, as he was elected in 1484, and signed the oath of acknowledgement of the royal supremacy in December, 1534, with Henry Wood, William Coorte, John Burnell, William Nowlde, and John Enyver, brethren.[41] He probably died soon afterwards, for reference is made to the late master in an inventory[42] of the goods of the house, taken on 23 January, 1535, and signed by the above five brethren. It included £24 7s. 6d. in ready money, silver weighing 527½ oz., masers and nuts weighing 159 oz., 1,600 sheep, 119 bullocks and kine, 15 mares and colts, and 14 horses and geldings.

John Tompson succeeded to the mastership. Christopher Hales gave him a bad character in a

[22] Pat. 6 Edw. I, m. 21.

[23] Chart. R. 14 Edw. I, m. 1.

[24] Ibid. 12 Edw. III, Nos. 5, 33; ibid. 21 Edw. III, No. 16; Pat. 1 Ric. II, pt. 5, m. 31; Pat. 1 Hen. V, pt. 4, m. 21; Pat. 2 Hen. VI, pt. 1, m. 9; Pat. 4 Edw. IV. pt. 3, m. 15.

[25] *Plac. de Quo Warr.* (Rec. Com.), 330, 344, 353, 360.

[26] Pat. 11 Hen. IV, pt. 2, m. 8.

[27] Ibid. 1 Ric. III, pt. 2, m. 24.

[28] *Cal. Pap. Let.* i, 154.   [29] Ibid. 181.

[30] Pat. 4 Edw. I, m. 16; 5 Edw. I, m. 15; 8 Edw. I, m. 19.

[31] Ibid. 18 Edw. I, m. 6d.

[32] Close, 8 Edw. II, m. 11d; 9 Edw. II, m. 20d.

[33] Ibid. 1 Edw. III, pt. 2, m. 8d.

[34] Ibid. 3 Edw. III, m. 1d.

[35] Ibid. 19 Edw. II, m. 29d.

[36] Ibid. m. 23.   [37] Chan. Warrants, 1769.

[38] *Lit. Cant.* (Rolls Ser.), ii, 384.

[39] Cant. Archiepis. Reg. Warham, fol. 39.

[40] *L. and P. Hen. VIII*, vi, 952.

[41] Ibid. vii, 1594 (8).

[42] Ibid. viii, 96. Printed in *Arch. Cant.* vii, 274–80.

letter to Cromwell,[43] but he probably owed his appointment to business ability, for he is frequently mentioned during the next few years as superintendent of the new harbour works at Dover. He was master at the time of the Valor of 1535, in which the whole possessions of the house, including the manors of Dudmanswyk, Eastbridge, Great and Little Pokton, 'Northmersshe,' River, Whitfield, Coldred, Pising, Kingsdown, and Charlton, were valued[44] at £231 16s. 7¼d. yearly, the net value being £159 18s. 6¾d., after deductions of £71 18d. 0½d. for rents, pensions, fees, in dispute and 'charges by the foundation.' These last apparently were the only benefit that the poor now got from the hospital, as the brothers were of the nature of fellows or canons.

In 1544 the Maison Dieu was reported as suitable for a victualling yard,[45] and it was surrendered on 11 December by Henry Wood, John Burnell, William Noole, and John Tompson.[46]

MASTERS OF ST. MARY'S, DOVER

John de Hertford, resigned 1248[47]
Michael de Kenebalton, elected 1248[48]
Edmund, occurs 1271,[49] 1278[50]
Ralph de Marisco, elected 1280[51]
Thomas de Dovor, elected 1281[52]
Henry de Herefeld, elected 1305[53]
John de Dovorre, elected 1316[54]
Walter de Rydelyngweld or Hedebrand,[54a] elected 1338,[55] resigned 1358[56]
Simon de Brusele, elected 1359,[57] died 1368[58]
Alexander Wayte, elected 1368,[59] died 1378[60]
Valentine de Bere, elected 1378,[60] died 1407[61]
Roger Kympton, elected 1407,[61] died 1420[62]

James Brandred, elected 1420,[62] resigned 1439[63]
Giles Crouche, elected 1439[63]
John Wellys, elected 1442,[64] died 1446[65]
Thomas Moys, elected 1446[66]
John Barboure, elected 1467,[67] died 1478[68]
William Baker, elected 1478[69]
John Clerk, elected 1484,[70] occurs 1511,[71] 1534[71]
John Tompson, occurs 1535,[71] the last master[71]

The seal[72] of the hospital (twelfth century) is a pointed oval measuring 2½ in. by 1⅝ in., representing the Virgin seated on a carved throne under a trefoiled canopy, with the Child on her right knee. In the field on each side a countersunk quatrefoiled panel containing a head. Over these on the left a crescent and a star, on the right a demi-angel with a censer. In base under a trefoiled arch the master half-length in prayer, to the left. Legend :—

SIGIL' ꝯMUNE DOMꝰ HOSPITAL' B͞E MARIE DOVOR'

52. THE HOSPITAL OF HARBLEDOWN

The hospital of St. Nicholas, Harbledown, was founded by Lanfranc, archbishop of Canterbury (1070–89), who also founded the hospital of St. John, Northgate, Canterbury ; and much of its history is identical with that of its twin foundation, and has already been told.[1]

Henry I made a grant of wood to the hospital of Harbledown. Henry II granted to it 20 marks yearly from the farm of the city of Canterbury, and the grant was confirmed by Henry III and several later kings.[2] In 1412 the brethren and sisters were pardoned for having acquired various lands and rents in Reculver, Herne, Harbledown, Goodnestone, the suburbs of Canterbury, Westgate by Canterbury, and the Isle of Harty without licence since the publication of the statute of mortmain.[3]

Pope Clement VI in 1344 gave orders that John de Redeni, layman, should be received into the hospital of Harbledown, in which the inmates wore a distinct habit, heard mass daily and said the Lord's Prayer and Hail Mary and the

[43] L. and P. Hen. VIII, vi, 1148.
[44] Valor Eccl. (Rec. Com.), i, 55.
[45] L. and P. Hen. VIII, xix (1), 724.
[46] Ibid. (2), 728.
[47] Chart. R. 32 Hen. III, m. 5. The king on 25 April confirmed the grant made to him for life by his successor of all the holding of the hospital in the hundred of Milton. John was master in 1231 (Chart. R. 15 Hen. III, m. 11).
[48] Ibid. ; Pat. 32 Hen. III, m. 10. Michael occurs as master in 1260 (Feet of F. Kent, 44 Hen. III).
[49] Feet of F. Kent, 55 Hen. III.
[50] Pat. 6 Edward I, m. 22.
[51] Pat. 8 Edw. I, m. 11.
[52] Pat. 9 Edw. I, m. 23. Thomas was master in 1299 (Pat. 27 Edw. I, m. 22).
[53] Pat. 33 Edw. I, pt. 1, m. 2. Henry died in 1316 (Pat. 10 Edw. II, pt. 1, m. 13).
[54] Ibid.   [54a] Close, 32 Edw. III, m. 7.
[55] Pat. 12 Edw. III, pt. 1, m. 27.
[56] Eccl. Pet. 27, No. 42.
[57] Ibid. ; Pat. 32 Edw. III, pt. 2, m. 7.
[58] Eccl. Pet. 29, No. 42.
[59] Ibid.; Pat. 42 Edw. III, pt. 2, m. 17.
[60] Pat. 1 Ric. II, pt. 5, m. 26.
[61] Pat. 8 Hen. IV, pt. 1, m. 4.
[62] Cant. Archepis. Reg. Chicheley, i, fol. 120b.

[63] Eccl. Pet. 45, No. 44.
[64] Pat. 20 Hen. VI, pt. 2, m. 23.
[65] Cant. Archiepis. Reg. Stafford, fol. 20b.
[66] Pat. 24 Hen. VI, pt. 1, m. 16.
[67] Pat. 7 Edw. IV, pt. 1, m. 12.
[68] Cant. Archiepis. Reg. Bourchier, fol. 118.
[69] Pat. 18 Edw. IV, pt. 1, m. 17.
[70] Pat. 2 Ric. III, pt. 3, m. 9.   [71] See above.
[72] B.M. Seals, lxv, 53.   [1] See p. 211.
[2] Pat. 1 Hen. IV, pt. 6, m. 36 ; 1 Hen. V, pt. 1, m. 21 ; 12 Hen. VI, pt. 2, m. 30 ; 1 Edw. IV, pt. 2, m. 15.
[3] Pat. 13 Hen. IV, pt. 2, m. 18.

canonical hours, and had a common dormitory and ate separately, living on certain rents provided by the archbishop of Canterbury.[4]

In the Valor of 1535 the gross income of the hospital, including the £80 from the archbishopric and £13 6s. 8d. from the city, amounted to £112 15s. 7d., and the net income to £109 6s. 2d. yearly,[5] but in the certificates of colleges and chantries these values are given as £106 15s. 4½d. and £102 0s. 0½d. respectively.[6]

Archbishop Parker reported[7] in 1562 of this hospital that

it is of the foundation of the lord archbyshop of Cant. and there be placed sixty poor people, men and women, and they have three corrodyes by the lord archbushop for the tyme being of perpetuall almes. Item, they be not charged with the taxation of the tenthes.

Archbishop Whitgift interfered in 1595 to protect the brethren and sisters against oppression by one Norton who had carried away wood belonging to them.[8]

The commissioners appointed to inquire into charities gave a long account in 1837 of the arrangements then in force at the hospital, and of its rental and benefactions made to it.[9]

MASTERS OF HARBLEDOWN [10]

Martin Fotherby, 1612
Richard Clarke, 1620
Thomas Jackson, 1635
William Somner, 1660
George Thorpe, 1702
John Paris, 1708
John Bradock, 1709
Elias Sydall, 1711
John Lynch, 1731
Thomas Lamprey, 1744
Sir John Head, 1761
John Duncombe, 1770
John Lynch, 1786
Houston Radcliffe, 1803
Hugh Percy, 1822
James Croft, 1829
Edward Parry, 1869

The seal[11] of the hospital (fifteenth century) is a pointed oval measuring 3 in. by 1¾ in. representing St. Nicholas standing on a platform with mitre, lifting up the right hand in benediction and holding in the left a pastoral staff. The

field diapered lozengy, in each space a pierced cinquefoil. In base a six-foiled rose. Legend :—

SIGILL' INFIRMORIUM HOSPITALIS SCI NICHOLAI DE HERBALDOUNE

53. THE HOSPITALS OF HYTHE

Several deeds belonging to the hospital of St. Bartholomew, Hythe, have been calendared by the Historical Manuscripts Commission,[1] and from these it appears to have been in existence in 1276, although its foundation is unknown. A hospital of St. Andrew, Hythe, is mentioned in 1334.[1a]

Edward III on 11 May, 1336, granted licence for Hamo bishop of Rochester to acquire in mortmain land and rent to the value of £10 yearly to found a hospital for poor persons in the town of Hythe.[2] In the same year the bishop and the commonalty of the port of Hythe founded a hospital, to be called the hospital of St. Andrew, on the spot where the bishop and his parents had their origin in the parish of St. Leonard, Hythe, for ten poor persons of either sex, one of whom was to be master. The master and poor persons were to be appointed by three wardens, who were to be nominated by the commonalty ; and no leper was to be received into the house, as there was already another hospital in the town.[2a] But we hear no more of the hospital of St. Andrew, except in connexion with a loan by the prior and chapter of Christchurch, Canterbury, a few years later.[3] On 10 May, 1342, the bishop had another licence to found a hospital for thirteen poor persons on his own soil in the town of Hythe.[4]

The intermediate history of the hospitals is not known ; but there were two at the time of the Reformation, both of which survived the Dissolution. In the Valor[5] of 1535 the hospital of St. Bartholomew, Saltwood, is said to own possessions of the gross value of £4 6s. yearly, the net value being £3 12s. 4d. ; and in 1546 the gross income is given[6] as £8 16s. 4d., and the net income as £7 14s. 1d. Matthew Parker, archbishop of Canterbury, in a return of the hospitals in his diocese in 1562 calls it the hospital of St. Bartholomew near Hythe[7] and says :

It is of the foundation of Hamond, bishop of Rochester, in the time of Edward the third. Ther ar according to the foundation thirteen poor people, who are releaved by almes and by the revenues of the

---

[4] Cal. Papal Let. iii, 108 ; Cal. Papal Pet. i, 39.
[5] Valor Eccl. (Rec. Com.), i, 30.
[6] Chant. Cert. 29, Nos. 46–8.
[7] Cant. Archiepis. Reg. Parker, fol. 237b.
[8] Strype, Life of Whitgift, ii, 328.
[9] Char. Com. Rep. xxx, 241–6.
[10] From a list in Lambeth MS. 1131. The master is also master of the hospital of Northgate.
[11] B.M. Seals, lxv, 68.

[1] Hist. MSS. Com. Rep. vi, App. 511–19.
[1a] Ibid. 512–13.
[2] Pat. 10 Edw. III, pt. 1, m. 14.
[2a] Thorpe, Reg. Roff. 413.
[3] Lit. Cant. (Rolls Ser.), ii, 250.
[4] Pat. 16 Edw. III, pt. 1, m. 8.
[5] Valor Eccl. (Rec. Com.), i, 40, 42.
[6] Chant. Cert. 29, No. 82.
[7] Cant. Archiepis. Reg. Parker, fol. 237b.

said hospital, amounting to the summe of 8*l.* by yere, with the charges. The said hospitall is taxed to the tenth, and payeth 7*s.* 2*d.*

The almshouse of St. John, Hythe, was found in 1546[8] to have a gross income of £5 19*s.* 8½*d.* and a net income of £4 10*s.* 10½*d.* Archbishop Parker in 1562 calls it the hospital of St. John of Hythe, and says :

It is only founded, ordered and charitablie maynteyned by the jurates and commonaltye of the said town, and their are kept and dayly maynteyned eight beds for the needy poor people and such as ar meymed in the wars. The said hospital is endued with so much landes as do amount to 6*l.* by the yere. It is not taxed to the tenth.

The Charity Commissioners reported[9] in 1837 that the hospital of St. Bartholomew was under the control of three wardens appointed as vacancies occurred by the mayor, jurats and commonalty in common assembly ; the custom having been always to appoint the senior jurat resident in Hythe or the immediate neighbourhood. There were four in-brothers and eight in-sisters, besides one out-brother called the woodreeve, and appointed by the lord of the manor of Postling according to an old custom dating back as far as 1581, because a previous lord of Postling gave a wood to the hospital ; and each alms-person received £5 quarterly. The hospital of St. John consisted of a common kitchen and apartments for nine alms-people, who were appointed by the trustees and paid £4 quarterly each. The rentals of the two hospitals are given in detail.

MASTERS OR PRIORS OF ST. BARTHOLOMEW'S, HYTHE[10]

William Archer, occurs 1310
Walter de Ryadessole, occurs 1356
Philip Allom, occurs 1364
William Pedlynge, occurs 1406
Simon atte Stone, occurs 1414
William Pedlyng, occurs 1415
John Cowlese, occurs 1418
Richard Petham or Pecham, occurs 1428
Thomas Chesman, occurs 1456
John a Brege, occurs 1463
John Barbour, occurs 1464
John Martyne, occurs 1467
Thomas Norman, occurs 1471
William a Tighe, occurs 1477
John Rabere, occurs 1478
William Houlde, occurs 1480
Richard Prowde, occurs 1484
John Gararde, occurs 1493
John Brigge, occurs 1494
John Chillenden, occurs 1504
Edmund Copyn, occurs 1514

[8] Chant. Cert. 29, No. 75.
[9] Char. Com. Rep. xxx, 422–8.
[10] Hist. MSS. Com. Rep. vi, App. 512–19.

William Olyfant, occurs 1555
Richard Brachey, occurs 1575
John Miller, occurs 1583
Paul Brett, occurs 1616
John Adams, occurs 1646
John Hobday, occurs 1671, 1674

THE HOSPITAL OF MAIDSTONE

For an account of this house see the College of Maidstone, No. 67.

54. THE HOSPITAL OF MILTON BY GRAVESEND

The origin of this house is unknown, although lands in Essex granted to the hospital of Gravesend are mentioned in the Pipe Roll as far back as 2 Henry II. It appears to have been re-founded by Aymer de Valence, earl of Pembroke, who on 7 December, 1321, made a grant[1] to Roger de Stowe, master of the chapel or chantry, and the brethren of the site and lands of the chapel and all lands pertaining to it in the hundreds of Barstable and Rochford in Essex, these last apparently forming the principal part of its endowment. On 10 December he granted[2] to them the advowson of the church of Milton, and directed that there should be in the chapel a master priest and two chaplains, and that at each vacancy the chaplains might elect a master. Hamo, bishop of Rochester, at his instance on 15 April, 1322, ordained that the priests should be regular and should celebrate divine service for the earl and his wife and the souls of Warin, William and Denise de Monte Caniso his ancestors ; and this ordinance was confirmed by the earl on 11 May.[3] Edward II on 22 June, 1326, at the instance of Mary de Sancto Paulo, countess of Pembroke, granted licence[4] for the master and brethren of the chapel of St. Mary the Virgin, Milton, to appropriate the church ; and this was apparently done accordingly, though the date of the appropriation is given elsewhere as 1322.[5] The masters held the parish church with the hospital.

John Wynd, master or warden, was ordered by the bishop in 1402 to re-assume the habit of his order, which he had put off, and to appear to answer for the crime of apostasy.[6]

On the death of John Markettstede, the master, in 1416, William Clifforde, the patron, claimed the right of presentation, and a long dispute followed. The bishop upheld the right of election, but eventually an agreement was come to by which the patron was allowed to present for this turn, recognizing the right of election in

[1] Thorpe, Reg. Roff. 493.　　[2] Ibid. 492.
[3] Ibid. 491.　　[4] Pat. 19 Edw. II, pt. 2, m. 5.
[5] Reg. Roff. 495.
[6] Roch. Epis. Reg. vol. 2, fol. 179.

future.[7] Elizabeth Clyfford, late the wife of Reginald Cobham, knight, brought an unsuccessful suit against the bishop for the advowson of the church in 1438.[8]

In 1422 John Standulf, master, was cited to appear before the bishop to answer for dilapidations ; and the fruits of the church were sequestrated.[9] He exchanged shortly afterwards with the rector of West Wickham.[10]

An inquisition[11] was taken in Essex on 18 March, 1524, by which it was found that John Dygon, master, and the brethren regular of the hospital, chapel or chantry of Milton by Gravesend, were seised on 6 May, 16 Richard II, of certain lands in Nevendon, Basildon, Fange and South Benfleet in Essex, and that John Dygon died on that day, and after him all the brethren died without any other master being elected or appointed, and so the hospital was dissolved, and divers rectors of Milton received the issues of the lands until Michaelmas, 1522, and Sir Henry Wyatt since then. In consequence of this (erroneous) finding, the hospital came into the possession of the king, who on 1 April granted licence[12] for Sir Henry Wyatt to found a chantry of two chaplains in the old chapel of St. Mary in the church of Milton, which with other buildings occupied the site of a mansion formerly belonging to the master and three brethren of a hospital of regular priests, and to grant to them the said site and lands in Kent and Essex to the value of £20 yearly, formerly belonging to the hospital. On 1 August he granted to him the Essex possessions with all issues from 6 May, 16 Richard II.[13]

MASTERS OF MILTON

Roger de Stowe, occurs 1321,[14] resigned 1325[15]
Roger de Ocle, elected 1325,[16] died 1333[17]
John de Esscheby, elected 1333[17]
Warin de Wyleby, admitted 1353[18]
John Dygon, resigned 1397[19]
John Wynd, appointed 1397,[19] occurs 1402[14]
John Cryps, appointed 1405[20]
John Markettstede, died 1416[1i]
John Standulf, resigned 1422[21]
William Tabbard, appointed 1422[21]
William Sprener, resigned 1437[22]
William Midelton, appointed 1437,[22] resigned 1440[23]

John Boner, appointed 1440[24]
Richard Chestre, appointed 1442[25]
William Sprener, died 1461[26]
Thomas Candour, appointed 1461[26]
John Marten, died 1504[27]
Edmund Cholderton, appointed 1504,[27] resigned 1507[28]
Thomas Hedd, appointed 1507[28]

55. THE HOSPITAL OF OSPRINGE

In several grants of relief from taxation made to this hospital in the fourteenth century, on account of its alleged poverty,[1] it is said to have been founded by Henry III. It was dedicated to St. Mary, and references to the hospital of St. Nicholas without Ospringe,[2] and the hospital of St. John, Ospringe,[3] are probably merely wrong descriptions of it. We first hear of it in 1234, when the king granted to the warden the surplus corn on the manor of Ospringe.[4] The patronage always belonged to the crown, the earlier masters being appointed during pleasure only ; and in 1316 the archdeacon of Canterbury was forbidden to exact a procuration from the master and brethren, as the hospital, which was of the alms of the king's progenitors and founded upon a lay fee, had always been free and exempt from ordinary jurisdiction and from all contributions and procurations.[5]

Henry III made grants to the hospital in 1239 of a house in the parish of St. Mary Colechurch, London,[6] and in 1240 of land called 'La Denne' in the parish of Headcorn with the advowson of the church of Headcorn and land in Twithan, Staple, Adisham, Wingham, and 'Hammewolde' ;[7] and in 1252 he granted land in Trienstone in Romney Marsh for the finding of a chaplain to celebrate daily in the hospital the mass of Edward the Confessor.[8] In 1246 he granted to the brethren numerous liberties,[9] and in 1251 a weekly market at their manor of Headcorn and a yearly fair there on the vigil, the feast, and the morrow of Sts. Peter and Paul.[10] A number of grants by private donors were confirmed to them in 1247[11] and 1315.[12]

In 1245 Robert abbot of St. Augustine's, Canterbury, granted to them the right of burial

---

[24] Ibid. He was bishop of Annaghdown in Ireland.
[25] Ibid. 175. [26] Ibid. 234.
[27] Ibid. vol. 4, fol. 41. [28] Ibid. 46.
[1] e.g. Close, 19 Edw. II, m. 23.
[2] Pat. 31 Hen. III, m. 6.
[3] Close, 17 Edw. III, pt. 2, m. 27 d.
[4] Ibid. 18 Hen. III, m. 13, 12.
[5] Ibid. 10 Edw. II, m. 24 d.
[6] Chart. R. 23 Hen. III, m. 7.
[7] Ibid. 24 Hen. III, m. 1.
[8] Ibid. 26 Hen. III, m. 11.
[9] Ibid. 30 Hen. III, m. 6.
[10] Ibid. 35 Hen. III, m. 6.
[11] Ibid. 31 Hen. III, m. 8.
[12] Pat. 8 Edw. II, pt. 2, m. 20.

[7] *Reg. Roff.* 493.
[8] De Banco, Mich. 17 Hen. VI, 123 d.
[9] Roch. Epis. Reg. vol. 3, fol. 9. [10] Ibid. 20.
[11] Chan. Inq. (Ser. 2), vol. 80, No. 184.
[12] *L. and P. Hen. VIII*, iv, 297 (1).
[13] Ibid. 612 (1). [14] See above.
[15] Roch. Epis. Reg. vol. 1, fol. 69b. He became master of Strood.
[16] Ibid. 70b. [17] Ibid. 154. [18] Ibid. 261.
[19] Ibid. vol. 2, fol. 99b. [20] Ibid. 188.
[21] Ibid. vol. 3, fol. 20.
[22] Ibid. 133 d. [23] Ibid. 153 d.

of brethren wearing the habit and of infirm who might die in the hospital, and also granted that the priests ministering in the hospital might hear the confessions of and otherwise minister to the brethren and the poor there, but all emoluments were reserved to the mother church of Faversham and all its rights reserved. In return for these concessions the brethren were to pay to the abbey 12d. and two pounds of wax yearly.[13]

In 1384 the temporalities of the house were taxed at £51 5s. and the church of Headcorn at £13 6s. 8d. yearly.[14]

Edward I in 1278 granted two beeches for her fuel to Juliana, sometime damsel of his mother Eleanor, dwelling in the hospital.[15] In 1292 he sent Ralph le Bedel, who had also been in the service of the same queen, to receive maintenance in the hospital for life;[16] and the appointments of several other inmates by him and later kings are recorded. Edward III in 1330 granted to the master and brethren that they should be free from providing sustenance out of their house such as at the request of the late king they had granted to Robert le Messager;[17] but nevertheless sent Gilbert de Sheffeld there in 1335.[18] Richard II in 1382 granted to John Lovyn the reversion of the next vacant chaplaincy in the hospital.[19] In 1397 the master and brethren granted to Philip Wen, rector of Crundale, a chamber in the hospital and a corrody for life with various detailed provisions, which were confirmed by Henry IV in 1401.[20]

Nicholas de Staple, the master, was removed from the hospital in 1314 on account of dissensions between himself and the brethren, and sent to be received as a brother in the hospital of St. John, Oxford;[21] one of the brethren of this house being sent to Ospringe in his place;[22] but in 1334 he was allowed to return as one of the brethren to Ospringe.[23] Thomas Urre and Robert de Chilham were similarly removed from Ospringe in 1332, the former being sent to St. John's, Oxford.[24]

In 1331 Master Robert de Cantuaria and John de Wyndesore were ordered to make a visitation to the hospital, reported to be greatly decayed for lack of good rule, and to remedy any abuses which they might find.[25] Probably there was not much fault, for in 1333 John de Lenham, the master, who had been appointed during pleasure, received a grant of his office during good behaviour, on proof that he had ruled the house well and greatly relieved it by his industry.[26] Another visitation was directed in 1422,[27] but on this occasion the hospital was found to have fallen into decay through bad governance, and was sequestrated and committed to the custody of the bishop of London and the two visitors, the abbot of Faversham and John Martyn.[28] In 1458 the abbot of Faversham, the archdeacon of Canterbury and others were appointed to inquire into dilapidations and alienations committed by John Bacheler, warden;[29] with the result that the latter resigned shortly afterwards.[30]

In 1387 Thomas, the master, made application to the crown for the arrest of Richard Evesham, a vagabond brother.[31]

Archbishop Warham made a visitation[32] of the house on 28 September, 1511. Master Woodruff, professor of theology, the warden, said that he believed that in the first foundation the warden and fellows were priests professed of the order of the Holy Cross and used to wear the cross on their shoulders. When Master Darell, the brother of John Darell, kt., was warden, he and his three fellow priests were professed and used to wear the cross. One of the present fellows had obtained a benefice by papal permission.

Henry VIII on 10 March, 1516, granted[33] the advowson of the house in mortmain to the college of St. John the Evangelist, Cambridge, founded by Margaret, countess of Richmond; and it was appropriated to the college by her executors.[34] Its possessions, including the manors of Trianstone, Headcorn, Downe, Tangerton, Borstall, and Elverland, are set out in detail in an inquisition[34a] taken in November, 1518, where it is said that there were in it originally a master and three brethren, professed of the order of the Holy Cross, and two secular clerks, but that on the death of Robert Darell, master, no brethren remained, and so the hospital became secular.

Masters or Wardens of Ospringe

Geoffrey, occurs 1234[35]
Henry de Cobeham, occurs 1235[36]
William Gracien, occurs 1242,[37] 1247[38]
Roger, occurs 1258[38a]
Walter, occurs 1274[39]

---

[13] Twysden, *Decem Scriptores*, 1893.
[14] Ibid. 2168.   [15] Close, 6 Edw. I, m. 12.
[16] Ibid. 20 Edw. I, m. 11 d.
[17] Pat. 4 Edw. III, pt. 1, m. 41.
[18] Close, 9 Edw. III, m. 18 d.
[19] Pat. 6 Ric. II, pt. 1, m. 30.
[20] Pat. 3 Hen. IV, pt. 1, m. 32.
[21] Close, 7 Edw. II, m. 5.
[22] Ibid. 1 Edw. III, pt. 1, m. 10.
[23] Ibid. 8 Edw. III, m. 9 d.
[24] Ibid. 6 Edw. III, m. 29 d.
[25] Pat. 5 Edw. III, pt. 2, m. 1 d.
[26] Ibid. 7 Edw. III, pt. 1, m. 10.
[27] Ibid. 1 Hen. VI, pt. 1, m. 25 d.
[28] Ibid. 2 Hen. VI, pt. 2, m. 34.
[29] Ibid. 37 Hen. VI, pt. 1, m. 16 d.
[30] Ibid. m. 13.   [31] Chan. Warrants, 1769.
[32] Cant. Archiepis. Reg. Warham, fol. 40 b.
[33] *L. and P. Hen. VIII*, ii, 1647.   [34] Ibid. 4183.
[34a] Chan. Inq. (Ser. 2), vol. 79, No. 258.
[35] Close, 18 Hen. III, m. 13, 12.
[36] Feet of F. Kent, 19 Hen. III.
[37] Ibid. 26 Hen. III.
[38] Pat. 31 Hen. III, m. 8.
[38a] *Hist. MSS. Com. Rep.* vi, App. 487.
[39] Feet of F. Kent, 2 Edw. I.

Peter, occurs 1287,[40] 1294 [41]

Alexander de Staple, appointed 1295 [42]

Nicholas de Staple, appointed 1310,[43] removed 1314 [44]

Henry de Tenham, appointed 1314,[45] died 1319 [46]

Adam de Esshe, appointed 1319,[47] died 1330 [48]

John de Lenham, appointed 1330,[48] died 1349 [49]

William de Newenham, appointed 1349 [49]

Thomas de Newenham, appointed 1349 [50]

Paul de Dunton, resigned [51]

Thomas Honyngham, occurs 1378 [52]

John Carleton, appointed 1396,[53] resigned 1401 [54]

John Cranebourne, appointed 1401,[54] resigned 1411 [55]

John atte See, appointed 1411,[55] resigned 1412 [55a]

William Gamyn, appointed 1412 [55b]

John Fakenham, occurs 1416 [55]

William Palmer, occurs 1422 [56]

James Jerkevile, appointed 1428 [57]

Andrew Bircheford, occurs 1434 [58]

James Jerkevyle, occurs 1445 [58a]

John Bacheler, occurs 1452,[58b] resigned 1458 [59]

Robert Darell, appointed 1458,[59] died 1470 [60]

John Pemberton, appointed 1470,[66] resigned 1472 [61]

Stephen Close, appointed 1472,[61] resigned 1473 [62]

Thomas Asshby, appointed 1473,[62] resigned 1490 [63]

Robert Woderove, appointed 1490,[63] died 1515 [64]

John Underhill, appointed 1515,[64] the last master [65]

The seal [66] of the hospital (thirteenth century) is a pointed oval measuring about 2 in. by 1½ in., and represents a seeded fleur-de-lis. Legend :—

S . . . . ALIS BEATE MARIE DE OSPRENGE

Another seal [67] (thirteenth century) is a pointed oval measuring about 2 in. by 1¼ in. representing a patriarchal cross, between four circular panels, the upper two containing each a saint's head, the lower each an ox's head. Legend :—

[S' FRA]TRUM HOSPITALI . . . . RIE DE OSPREN . . .

56. THE HOSPITAL OF PUCKESHALL OR TONGE

We first hear of the hospital of St. James, 'Pokeleshal,' in the parish of Tonge, in 1252, in connexion with a tenement in Sheldwich.[1] The advowson passed on the death of Giles de Badelesmere in 1339 to his sister Elizabeth, countess of Northampton,[2] and later belonged to the Mortimers, earls of March.[3]

In 1546 the possessions of the fraternity or hospital in Tonge called St. James *alias* Pickeshall were valued at £7 13s. 4d. yearly, with deductions of £1 9s. 4d., the net income thus being £6 4s. The certificate [4] also mentions a chalice of silver and gilt, a vestment and all things belonging to it, and two bells, valued at 30s.

The site of the hospital and lands belonging to it in Tonge and Bapchild were granted on 26 May, 1557, to Sir John Parrott in fee.[5]

MASTERS OR WARDENS OF TONGE

Robert, occurs 1252 [1]

Walter Shiryngton, appointed 1407 [3]

[40] Pat. 3 Edw. III, m. 14.

[41] Ibid. 22 Edw. I, m. 6 d.

[42] Ibid. 23 Edw. I, m. 7. Alexander occurs in 1309 (Pat. 3 Edw. III, m. 14).

[43] Ibid. 4 Edw. II, pt. 1, m. 13.

[44] Close, 7 Edw. II, m. 5.

[45] Pat. 7 Edw. II, pt. 2, m. 15.

[46] Close, 12 Edw. II, m. 11.

[47] Ibid. ; Pat. 12 Edw. II, pt. 2, m. 18.

[48] Pat. 4 Edw. III, pt. 1, m. 38.

[49] Ibid. 23 Edw. III, pt. 1, m. 13.

[50] Ibid. pt. 2, m. 9.

[51] Ibid. 2 Ric. II, pt. 1, m. 41.

[52] Ibid. The mastership was granted to him for life by Edw. III, and confirmed by Ric. II. Thomas occurs as master in 1365 (Chan. Misc. bdle. 20, No. 4), and 1387 (Pat. 11 Ric. II, pt. 1, m. 29 d.)

[53] Pat. 20 Ric. II, pt. 1, m. 17.

[54] Ibid. 2 Hen. IV, pt. 4, m. 16.

[55] Ibid. 12 Hen. IV, m. 6.

[55a] Ibid. 14 Hen. IV, m. 30.   [55b] Ibid.

[55c] Assize R. 1528, m. 32 d.

[56] Cal. Papal Let. vii, 222.

[57] Pat. 6 Hen. VI, pt. 1, m. 1.

[58] Ibid. 12 Hen. VI, pt. 2, m. 23. He was probably a Knight Hospitaller, for he is called Brother Andrew Bircheford, knight, of 'Swynfeld.'

[58a] De Banco, East. 23 Hen. VI, m. 94 d.

[58b] Harl. Chart. 76. A. 25.

[59] Pat. 37 Hen. VI, pt. 1, m. 13. His seal is preserved in Harl. Chart. 77. F. 16.

[60] Pat. 49 Hen. VI, m. 19.

[61] Ibid. 12 Edw. IV, pt. 2, m. 25.

[62] Ibid. 13 Edw. IV, pt. 2, m. 14.

[63] Ibid. 5 Hen. VII, m. 26 (10).

[64] L. and P. Hen. VIII, ii, 169.

[65] Ibid. 4183.

[66] B.M. Seals, lxv, 89.

[67] Ibid. 90.

[1] Feet of F. Kent, 36 Hen. III.

[2] Close, 13 Edw. III, pt. 3, m. 27.

[3] Pat. 8 Hen. IV, pt. 1, m. 3. The king also made the appointment of one of the brethren in 1408. (Pat. 9 Hen. IV, pt. 2, m. 13).

[4] Chant. Cert. 29, No. 108.

[5] Pat. 3 & 4 Philip and Mary, pt. 3, m. 25.

57. THE HOSPITAL OF ST. JOHN THE BAPTIST, ROMNEY

Nothing is known of the foundation of this house, which was under the authority of the jurats of the town. In 1401 the house lent £10 to the corporation,[6] which was repaid in 1408. John Wygynton was chosen master of the house for life on 12 February, 1406, with a corrody from it of 8d. weekly; and he agreed that if he should die in office the house should have 40s. of his goods.[7] On 19 January, 1434, Stephen Pocok, master, leased to Richard Glover of Lydd 8½ acres belonging to the brethren and sisters of the house in the parish of Lydd.[8] In 1413 John Ive paid £11 6s. 8d. for a corrody of 26s. from the house to the behoof of his daughter Joan.[9] In 1458 Simon Maket was admitted to the rule and governance of the hospital by the name of prior, taking for his wages and soap for washing the vestments of the hospital 20s. yearly; and on the same day John Porter was admitted steward for the management of its lands, taking for his labour 15s. yearly.[10]

In 1495 and afterwards the corporation received money for the rent of the house of St. John the Baptist;[11] and it seems likely that it had then ceased to exist as a hospital.

MASTERS OR PRIORS OF ST. JOHN THE BAPTIST'S, ROMNEY

John Wygynton, resigns 1399 [12]
John Halegood, occurs 1402 [13]
John Wygynton, appointed 1406 [13]
Thomas Rokysle, occurs 1408 [14]
Stephen Pocok, occurs 1434 [14]
Simon Maket, appointed 1458 [15]
Robert Bernyngham, occurs 1480 [16]

58. THE HOSPITAL OF ST. STEPHEN AND ST. THOMAS, ROMNEY

Adam Cherryng founded a hospital in honour of the martyrs St. Stephen and St. Thomas, in Romney, for the maintenance of lepers and of a chaplain celebrating divine service there, endowed it, and obtained charters of confirmation from Baldwin, archbishop of Canterbury (1184–90), and various archbishops and popes. In 1322 it was said that there should be at the hospital fifteen, or at least thirteen, brothers and sisters, each receiving from Michaelmas to Christmas half a bushel of wheat weekly, and from Christmas to Michaelmas 4d. weekly instead, with a hundred of faggot-wood at Michaelmas or 8d.[1]

But in the middle of the fourteenth century no lepers were found to live there, and the hospital became almost derelict; and in 1363 John Fraunceys, the patron, ordained that in place of the lepers there should be there two priests, one of whom should be master or warden. The master was to be resident, and should be appointed by the patron, or in default by the jurates of the town; and he was to appoint the other chaplain and pay him 40s. yearly, or in default to distribute 23s. 4d. each quarter of a year among the poor of the town. This new foundation was sealed by the barons of Romney, and confirmed by the archbishop, the chapter of Christchurch, Canterbury, and the king.[1a]

Sir Reginald de Cobeham and Agnes his sister, as patrons of the hospital, in the first part of the fourteenth century leased to John de Holdesdon, chaplain, a chamber in the close of the hospital and lands in Romney, Old Romney, and Dymchurch.[2]

Indulgences to benefactors to the chapel were granted by various bishops in 1375, 1379, 1391, and 1451.[3]

The patronage of the hospital passed from John Fraunceys to his daughters, and from these through feoffees to William Waynflete, bishop of Winchester. In 1481 it had come to ruin and its buildings had collapsed, and on 22 November it was annexed to Magdalen College, Oxford, founded by the bishop.[4]

MASTERS OR WARDENS OF THE HOSPITAL OF ST. STEPHEN AND ST. THOMAS, ROMNEY

Stephen, at the foundation, *circa* 1180–5 [4a]
Richard Scherewynd, occurs 1378 [4a]
Elias de Postlyng, appointed 1364 [5]
Nicholas Chamberleyn, appointed 1385,[5a] resigned 1386 [4a]
Adam de Cokermouth, appointed 1386 [5a]
John Harard [4a]
John Frebody, occurs 1400 [5b]
John Hale, appointed 1409 [6]
Robert Haddelsay, resigned 1419 [7]
Thomas Morton, appointed 1419,[8] resigned 1421 [9]
Thomas Stodyer, appointed 1421,[9] died 1435 [10]
Andrew Aylewyn, appointed 1435 [10]
Richard Berne, appointed 1458 [5a]

---

[6] *Hist. MSS. Com. Rep.* v, App. 536.
[7] Ibid. 536.   [8] Ibid. 537.
[9] Ibid. 539.   [10] Ibid. 544.   [11] Ibid. 549.
[12] Ibid. 535.   [13] Ibid. 536.
[14] Ibid. 537.   [15] Ibid. 544.   [16] Ibid. 545.
[1] W. D. Macray, *Muniments of Magdalen College, Oxford*, 131.

[1a] *Lit. Cant.* (Rolls Ser.), ii, 436–42; Pat. 38 Edw. III, pt. I, m. 30; Dugdale, *Mon.* vii, 641.
[2] *Hist. MSS. Com. Rep.* iv, App. 427.
[3] Ibid. 464.
[4] Ibid. 459; *Lit. Cant.* (Rolls Ser.), iii, 307.
[4a] W. D. Macray, op. cit. 7.
[5] Cant. Archiepis. Reg. Islip, fol. 363.
[5a] Dugdale, *Mon.* vii, 640.
[5b] Pardon R. 1–14 Hen. IV, m. 17.
[6] Cant. Archiepis. Reg. Arundel, ii, fol. 53b.
[7] Ibid. Chicheley, i, fol. 116.
[8] Ibid. 116b.   [9] Ibid. 128b.   [10] Ibid. 210.

59. THE HOSPITAL OF ST. BARTHOLOMEW, SANDWICH

The date of the foundation of this hospital is not known, but one grant of rent to it belongs to the year 1227, and some others may be earlier. It appears to have been from an early date under the governance of the mayor, jurats, and commonalty; and according to the custumal of the town they visited it every year on the feast of St. Bartholomew. The master rendered an account before the mayor and jurats whenever they thought proper. Three priests should officiate constantly in the chapel, with a stipend of 5 marks each; and the allowances of food and lodging for the brothers and sisters were prescribed in detail.[1]

Edward III on 9 July, 1349, granted all manner of profits of the passage over the water between Sandwich and Stonar to the brethren of the house of St. Bartholomew, Sandwich, in aid of the alms of the house.[2] It was found in 1537[3] that they had neglected the maintenance of certain groynes, which was probably a charge in connexion with this.

In the certificates of colleges and chantries the gross income of the hospital, including profits from the ferry, amounting to £16, was returned at £42 0s. 4d., and the net income as £39 19s. 1d. yearly.[4] The hospital survived the Dissolution, and Archbishop Parker says of it in his return[5] of 1562

It is of the first foundation of one Sir John Sandwich, knight, and now of the foundation of the mayor and commynaltie of the town of Sandwich. And by the said mayor ther are placed from time to time the number of twelve brothers and four sisters, who are releaved only of the revenues of the said hospitall, amounting to the yerely value by estimation of £40. The said hospitall is charitably used to God's glory, and the same surveyed from tyme to time by the mayor of Sandwich and kept in godlie order. It is not taxed to the perpetuall tenth.

The state of the hospital, however, does not seem to have been entirely satisfactory in 1587, when several persons deposed that although the number of brothers and sisters was maintained, and most were old and impotent, still some were young, some had property outside, had paid large sums for their places, or had let out part of their lodgings.[6]

King James I in 1620 at the suit of James, Viscount Doncaster, made a grant of the hospital and all lands belonging to it to Sir John Townsend and others; but the corporation successfully resisted this.[7]

The Charity Commissioners reported in 1837 that there were in the hospital a master and sixteen brothers and sisters, and described its property in detail.[8]

MASTERS OF ST. BARTHOLOMEW'S, SANDWICH

John Coperland, occurs 1347 [9]
Richard Pyneham, occurs 1383 [10]
John Herdeman, occurs 1402 [11]
Richard Delver, occurs 1408 [12]
Thomas Cryhton, occurs 1418 [13]
Thomas Parker, occurs 1437 [14]
John Dowle, occurs 1445 [15]
John Harnes, occurs 1550 [16]
Robert Kite, occurs 1552 [17]
John Terry, occurs 1553 [17]
John Jarman, occurs 1557 [17]
Francis Hook, occurs 1696 [16]

60. THE HOSPITAL OF ST. JOHN, SANDWICH [1]

This hospital, like that of St. Bartholomew, appears always to have been under the governance of the mayor and jurats, but the year of the foundation is not known, though one deed belonging to it is dated 1287. The custumal of the town describes the regulations for the brothers and sisters in detail.

In the certificates of colleges and chantries the gross income of the hospital is given as £5 1s. 7d., and the net income as £5 1s. 3d. yearly.[2] It survived the Dissolution, and Archbishop Parker reported[3] of it in 1562

This house is charitablie founded, maynteyned and provided by the mayor and jurates, and they have no possessions, and there are releaved twelve poor people.

In 1837 the Charity Commissioners reported[4] that there were there a master and six brothers and sisters, and the right of appointment belonged to the mayor and jurats, but had long been given up to the mayor. The property was described in detail.

MASTERS OF ST. JOHN'S, SANDWICH

John Baker, occurs 1371 [5]
John Wilkins, died 1516 [6]

---

[1] A long account of the hospital is given by William Boys in his *Hist. of Sandwich*, 1–102, where a chartulary and several other documents are set out in full or in abstract.   [2] Pat. 23 Edw. III, pt. 2, m. 22.
[3] *L. and P. Hen. VIII*, xii (2), 136.
[4] Chant. Cert. 29, No. 51. Printed in Boys, op. cit. 90–4.
[5] Cant. Archiepis. Reg. Parker, fol. 237b.
[6] Exch. Dep. Easter, 29 Eliz. No. 20.

[7] Boys, loc. cit.   [8] *Charity Com. Rep.* xxx, 566–9.
[9] Boys, op. cit. 37.   [10] Ibid. 44.   [11] Ibid. 45.
[12] Ibid. 50.   [13] Ibid. 52.   [14] Ibid. 40.
[15] Ibid. 54.   [16] Ibid. 75.   [17] Ibid. 81.
[1] A long account of the hospital is given by Boys in the *Hist. of Sandwich*, 119–45, where abstracts of a register and other documents are given.
[2] Chant. Cert. 29, No. 56; Boys, op. cit. 137–8.
[3] Cant. Archiepis. Reg. Parker, fol. 237b.
[4] *Charity Com. Rep.* xxx, 569–71.
[5] Boys, op. cit. 133.   [6] *Arch. Cant. Wills*, 296.

61. THE HOSPITAL OF ST. THOMAS, SANDWICH

Richard II on 28 June, 1392, granted licence for Thomas Rollyng and William Swan, clerks, John Godard and Richard Benge to grant a messuage and 132 acres of land in Woodnesborough to twelve poor inmates of a hospital to be founded by them at Sandwich in honour of St. Thomas the Martyr.[1] It appears from the deeds of the hospital that they were the feoffees of Thomas Elys of Sandwich, the real founder, and so the hospital is sometimes known by his name. Its property and management have always been vested in trustees.

In 1481 it was found by inquisition that Henry Grensheld, then deceased, on 12 January, 1471, enfeoffed Herman Riswyk of 15 acres of land in Woodnesborough, and the latter on 3 May, 1472, enfeoffed John Aldy, John Swan, Thomas Norman, chaplain, and Nicholas Burton, wardens of the hospital of St. Thomas the Martyr, Sandwich, of the same to the use of the twelve poor persons in the hospital, and these received the issues, contrary to the statute.[2]

In the certificate of colleges and chantries the gross income of 'Ellys hospitall' is given as £13 6s. and the net income as £12 0s. 4½d. yearly.[3] It survived the Dissolution, and Archbishop Parker reported[4] of it in 1562

It is first founded by one Thomas Ellis, and yt is now of the foundation and patronage of the mayor and jurates of the same. Ther be placed, for tyme of life, eight brothers and four sisters, and they are releaved by almes and the revenues of the said hospitalls, amounting to £12 by yere. The hospitall is very charitablie ordered, and serveyed by the mayor. It is not taxed to the tenth.

Regulations[5] for the management of the hospital were drawn up by the governors and trustees on 17 July, 1725, because they could not find any then existing. The twelve persons were to be eight men and four single women.

The Charity Commissioners reported[6] in 1837 that there were in the hospital eight brothers, one of whom was annually appointed master by the trustees, and four sisters; and described its property in detail.

62. THE HOSPITAL OF SEVENOAKS

Peter de Crouland, vicar of the church of Sevenoaks, had licence[7] on 16 April, 1338, to grant 100s. of land and rent to a chaplain to celebrate divine service daily in the free chapel of St. John, Sevenoaks, for the soul of Thomas de Somerset, chaplain, deceased; but he died before doing so, and his kinsman, Peter son of Walter de Crouland, had a similar licence[2] on 26 January, 1340. This chapel appears to be the same as the hospital of St. John the Baptist, Sevenoaks, the wardenship of which was granted in 1349 to John de Tamworth by the king, into whose hands it came by the vacancy of the archbishopric.[3] In the archiepiscopal registers it is sometimes called the hospital of St. John the Baptist of 'Quenebroke,' in the parish of Sevenoaks.

The advowson of the hospital, chantry, or chapel of St. John in the parish of Sevenoaks was granted in exchange by the archbishop of Canterbury to the king in 1538;[4] and the hospital was dissolved soon afterwards, a pension of £8 2s. 10d. being granted to John Cleyton, master, on 10 March, 1540.[5]

MASTERS OR WARDENS OF SEVENOAKS

John de Tamworth, appointed 1349 [6]
Ralph Leghton, resigned 1383 [7]
Robert Toller, appointed 1383 [7]
Reginald Brita, appointed 1385 [8]
Robert Cokeyne, appointed 1386 [9]
John Kyngman or Kyneman, appointed 1412,[10] died 1434[11]
Robert Toft, appointed 1434 [11]
James Radich, resigned 1454 [12]
John Eylmer, appointed 1454 [12]
William, died 1517 [13]
Thomas Baschurche or Bastlet, appointed 1517,[13] resigned 1523 [14]
John Roydon, appointed 1523 [14]
John Cleyton, the last master [15]

63. THE HOSPITALS OF SITTINGBOURNE

It was found by an inquisition[15a] taken in 1288 that one Samuel, a clerk, by the grant of King John built a little chapel and hospital at 'Schamele' in the parish of Sittingbourne for the lodging of poor people, and after his death they fell to the ground. Afterwards another chapel in honour of St. Thomas the Martyr was

[1] Pat. 16 Ric. II, pt. 1, m. 32. A detailed account of the hospital is given in Boys, *Hist. of Sandwich*, 149–71, with abstracts of several documents relating to it. [2] Inq. p.m. 21 Edw. IV, No. 27.
[3] Chant. Cert. 29, No. 54; Boys, op. cit. 156–8.
[4] Cant. Archiepis. Reg. Parker, fol. 237b.
[5] Boys, op. cit. 161–4.
[6] *Charity Com. Rep.* xxx, 571–3.
[7] Pat. 12 Edw. III, pt. 1, m. 13.

[2] Pat. 14 Edw. III, pt. 1, m. 47.
[3] Ibid. 23 Edw. III, pt. 2, m. 14.
[4] *L. and P. Hen. VIII*, xiii (1), 1519 (68).
[5] Ibid. xv, 555.
[6] Pat. 23 Edw. III, pt. 2, m. 14.
[7] Cant. Archiepis. Reg. Courtenay, fol. 251.
[8] Ibid. fol. 259.   [9] Ibid. fol. 264
[10] Ibid. Arundel, ii, 64.
[11] Ibid. Chicheley, fol. 204b.
[12] Ibid. Bourchier, fol. 59.
[13] Ibid. Warham, fol. 363.
[14] Ibid. fol. 377b.   [15] See above.
[15a] Inq. p.m. 16 Edw. I, No. 59.

built by the alms of the passers-by and other men of the hundred of Milton, and Henry III granted [16] it to a chaplain named Silvester, who lived there for sixteen years. On his death the vicar of Sittingbourne seized the chapel and carried off the marble altar, and one of its bells was carried off into the county of Essex and the other to the church of Sittingbourne.

In 1225 the master of the hospital of St. Cross, 'Sweynestre,' had a grant of a fair yearly on the vigil and the day of the Invention of the Cross at his chapel during the king's minority.[17]

In 1232 the lepers of the hospital of St. Leonard of 'Sweynestre' by Sittingbourne had a grant of protection.[18]

The chantry certificates mention a free chapel in Sittingbourne called Thomas Becket's chapel,[19] which was dissolved in 34 Henry VIII.

64. THE HOSPITAL OF STROOD

The hospital of the New Work of St. Mary of Strood by Rochester was founded by Gilbert de Glanville, bishop of Rochester; and must date from the years 1192–3, for the bishop states in his foundation charter that he has in mind the restoration of Christianity in Jerusalem and the liberation of King Richard. He granted to it the churches of Aylesford, St. Margaret (Rochester), and Halling, a small prebend from the tithes of his knights in Halling, Holborough, and Cuxton, the church of St. Nicholas, Strood, tithes in Dartford and Wilmington and other possessions; and these were confirmed by a charter of Hubert, archbishop of Canterbury, and a charter of Richard I dated at Worms, 14 August, 1193. The same king also on 20 April, 1194, granted to the hospital two parts of the wood by Malling pertaining to the manor of Aylesford. All these charters were confirmed by Edward III in 1332.[1] Confirmations were also granted by Popes Celestine [III][2] and Innocent [III].[3]

The monks of Rochester strongly resented the foundation of the hospital and its endowment out of the revenues of the see; and in 1239 a dispute about the churches of Aylesford and St. Margaret's was referred to arbitrators, who decided that the monks should have the church of St. Margaret and 18 marks from the church of Aylesford in addition to 2 marks which the sacrist of Rochester already had.[4] But this

did not settle the matter, and in 1256 Pope Alexander IV ordered that the prior and chapter should have the church of St. Margaret and the hospital should be free of the payment of 20 marks out of the church of Aylesford.[5] In 1291 some of the brethren of the hospital resented the passage through the grounds of the hospital of a procession of the chapter, and a fight followed.[6]

In 1277 it was found by inquisition [7] that the founder granted to the master and brethren some houses next the bridge of Rochester for the repair of the west end of the bridge and that they received the rents from the houses and repaired that end of the bridge until the siege of Rochester, when part of the houses were burnt, and afterwards they carried away the unburnt timber to their own house. They also received the wharfage from a quay at the west end of the bridge.

The hospital was allowed exemption from taxation on several occasions [8] in the fourteenth century, on the alleged ground of poverty.

Bishop Hamo de Hethe visited the hospital on 18 September, 1320,[9] when several documents belonging to it were exhibited to him and transcribed in his register. He made new ordinances [10] for it on 4 July, 1330, in consequence of its depression and the neglect of the masters. The master was to be professed of the rule of St. Benedict and appointed by the bishop, from the college if possible or else from another college of the same order; and was to have with him four brethren, priests professing the same rule. They were to have a common chest in which the muniments and precious goods of the house were to be kept under three keys, and the common seal was also to be kept under three keys. They were to give no corrodies or pensions and cut down no trees except for necessary repair. The details of their clothing and daily life were also prescribed.

In 1402 the bishop took the administration of the goods of the hospital into his own hands, on account of the neglect of the master and brethren, and committed the same to John Hoke, his registrar.[11] The hospital was again sequestrated in 1443 on account of dilapidations and because no accounts were forthcoming.[12]

In the *Valor* [13] of 1535 the spiritualities of the hospital, consisting of the rectories of Aylesford and Halling, the vicarage of Strood and the chapel of St. Blaise, Malling, were valued at £40 9s.

[16] Pat. 39 Hen. III, m. 14.
[17] Close, 9 Hen. III, m. 14.
[18] Pat. 16 Hen. III, m. 2.
[19] Chant. Cert. 29, No. 106.
[1] Pat. 6 Edw. III, pt. 1, m. 19. Printed in Dugdale, *Mon.* vii, 666, and also with several other charters and documents relating to the hospital in Thorpe's *Registrum Roffense*.
[2] *Reg. Roff.* 642.   [3] Ibid. 643.
[4] *Flores Hist.* (Rolls Ser.), ii, 235; *Anglia Sacra*, i, 349.

[5] *Cal. Papal Let.* i, 329.
[6] *Flores Hist.* iii, 73; *Anglia Sacra*, i, 353.
[7] Inq. p.m. 5 Edw. I, No. 31.
[8] e.g. Close, 13 Edw. III, pt. 1, m. 49 d.
[9] Roch. Epis. Reg. vol. 1, fol. 5.
[10] Printed in *Reg. Roff.* 637.
[11] Roch. Epis. Reg. vol. 2, fol. 176 d.
[12] Ibid. vol. 3, fol. 187 d.
[13] *Valor Eccl.* (Rec. Com.), i, 105.

and the temporalities, including the manor of Hawkyns in Strood, at £22 4s. 6½d. yearly; and deductions of £9 13s. 8d. brought the net income down to £52 19s. 10½d.

The hospital and its possessions were surrendered by the master and brethren on 8 July, 1539, to the prior and convent of Rochester;[14] and they were granted in June, 1541, to the dean and chapter of the cathedral on its re-foundation.[15]

MASTERS OF STROOD

Thomas, occurs 1243 [16]

Edmund, occurs 1267 [17]

John de Hallingeberi, occurs 1293 [18]

Roger Wygayn, occurs 1306 [19]

John Blondell, occurs 1318 [19a]

John de Rodeswelle, appointed 1318 [19a]

Richard de Novo Castro, appointed 1319,[19a] resigned 1322 [20]

Robert de Thorpe, appointed 1322,[20] resigned 1323 [21]

W. de Langeford, appointed 1323 [22]

John de Raddeswell, appointed 1323 [23]

Roger de Stowe, appointed 1325,[24] died 1345 [25]

Richard de Strode or Scheftling, appointed 1345,[26] deserted 1352 [27]

William de Basynges, appointed 1361,[28] died 1383 [29]

Thomas Bromlegh, appointed 1383,[30] occurs 1390 [31]

John Swan, occurs 1391, 1395 [32]

John Longe, appointed 1397 [33]

Philip Mongomery or Morgan,[34] appointed 1399,[35] resigned 1403 [36]

William Batteford, appointed 1403 [37]

John Marcham, occurs 1418,[38] resigned 1425 [39]

William Hebbeng, appointed [39] and resigned 1425 [40]

John Gorewell, appointed 1425,[40] occurs 1434 [41]

Thomas Thowe, occurs 1444,[42] resigned 1465 [43]

Richard Brakynburgh, appointed 1465,[43] occurs 1470 [44]

Edmund Lychefeld, occurs circa 1480,[45] resigned 1493 [46]

William Barker, appointed 1493,[47] deposed 1507 [48]

Robert Aunger, appointed 1507,[48] died 1508 [49]

Richard Cotenden, appointed 1508,[49] resigned 1512 [50]

Thomas Hobson, appointed 1512,[50] resigned 1517 [51]

John Wilbore, appointed 1517,[52] surrendered 1539,[53] the last master

The seal [54] of the hospital (1400) is a pointed oval of red wax, measuring about 1½ by ⅞ in., representing the Virgin crowned, standing on a carved corbel in a canopied niche, pinnacled and crocketed with tabernacle work at the side, holding the Child on the right arm and in the left hand a sceptre fleury. The Child carries an orb and cross in the right hand. Legend :—

SIGILL' COE OSPIT BE MARIE DE STRODE

[14] *Reg. Roff.* 651.

[15] *L. and P. Hen. VIII*, xvi, 943 (42).

[16] Feet of F. Kent, 27 Hen. III.

[17] *Reg. Roff.* 259. [18] Ibid. 152. [19] Ibid. 636.

[19a] Roch. Epis. Reg. vol. 1.

[20] Ibid. fol. 55.

[21] Ibid. 54 d. [22] Ibid. 59.

[23] Cant. Archiepis. Reg. Reynolds, fol. 22b.

[24] Roch. Epis. Reg. vol. 1, fol. 69b. He was master of Milton.

[25] Close, 20 Edw. III, pt. 1, m. 19.

[26] Roch. Epis. Reg. vol. 1, fol. 218b.

[27] Ibid. 256b.

[28] Cant. Archiepis. Reg. Islip, fol. 225.

[29] Pat. 6 Ric. II, pt. 2, m. 8; 7 Ric. II, pt. 1, m. 29. He and his successor were often employed as clerks of the king's works in the neighbourhood of Rochester.

[30] Pat. 6 Ric. II, pt. 2, m. 4.

[31] Pat. 13 Ric. II, pt. 1, m. 39.

[32] Roch. Epis. Reg. vol. 2, fol. 23, 64.

[33] Ibid. fol. 99.

[34] Cant. Archiepis. Reg. Arundel, vol. 1, fol. 464b.

[35] Roch. Epis. Reg. vol. 2, 130 d.

[36] Ibid. vol. 3, fol. 35d. A corrody was granted to him.

[37] Ibid. 36 d. [38] Ibid. 1 d. [39] Ibid. 49.

[40] Ibid. An exchange with the rectory of Ickford.

[41] Pat. 12 Hen. VI, pt. 2, m. 23.

[42] *Reg. Roff.* 151, 650.

[43] Roch. Epis. Reg. vol. 3, fol. 243.

[44] Pat. 10 Edw. IV, m. 9; Early Chan. Proc. bdle. 64, No. 496.

[45] Early Chan. Proc. bdle. 60, No. 194.

[46] Roch. Epis. Reg. vol. 4, fol. 8. A pension of £22 was assigned to him.

[47] Ibid. 8 d. [48] Ibid. 44 d. [49] Ibid. 48 d.

[50] Ibid. 60. [51] Ibid. 76.

[52] Ibid. He was vicar of Lamberhurst and Hartley and had a papal dispensation to hold the mastership as well (B.M. Stowe Chart. 586).

[53] *Reg. Roff.* 651. [54] Harl. Chart. 44. D. 14.

COLLEGES

65. THE COLLEGE OF BREDGAR

Richard II on 19 July, 1392, granted licence for Master Robert de Bradegare and others to found at Bredgar a college of one chaplain and two clerk scholars who should serve God and celebrate divine service in the parish church of Bredgar at all times except when the said scholars were busy with their studies ; and also to grant in mortmain to the chaplain and scholars messuages, lands, and rents in Hollingbourne, Hucking, Bredgar, Wormshill, Borden, Tunstall, and Bicknor.[1]

Robert made an ordinance[2] for the management of the college on 7 April, 1393. The chaplain was to celebrate daily for the souls of the archbishop and others in the church of Bredgar or in the chapel of the college, the details of the service being laid down ; he was to be nominated by the scholars within fifteen days of a vacancy, and was to receive 12 marks yearly, to reside in the college and not to hold any other benefice with a cure. One of the two scholars was to be of the founder's kin and the other of the parishes of Bredgar, Hucking, or Hollingbourne ; and each when he could read and sing competently was to be nominated fellow and scholar by the master until he completed his twenty-fifth year or was promoted, married, or removed for just cause, but was not to be nominated until he was seven years old and had received the first tonsure, and was not to have any voice in the nomination of the chaplain until he was fifteen years old. Each of the scholars was to receive 40s. yearly for his maintenance, and the residue of the goods of the chantry was to be applied to its repair or otherwise to its use. Further detailed instructions were given as to the life of the scholars and the management of the property of the chantry.

On 3 April, 1398, an agreement was made between the prior and chapter of Christchurch, Canterbury, and John Promhelle, chaplain, and Thomas Webbe and Thomas Monk, clerks and scholars of the college, by which the prior and chapter bound themselves under a penalty of £100 to maintain for ever in their almonry school two poor clerks to be nominated by the chaplain and scholars.[3]

The founder made fresh ordinances[4] on 12 August, 1398, revising and adding to the earlier ones. The chaplain might absent himself for one month of thirty-two days from the college in each year, and might have a servant to assist

him at mass and otherwise serve him ; he was to have the northern chambers of the college and 40s. at the end of each quarter during the life of the founders and £10 (yearly) after their death. The clerk scholars were each to have 10d. weekly and a southern chamber of the college, and they were to take the order of sub-deacon at their twentieth year. In the first week of October in each year the anniversary of the founders was to be kept by the chaplain and the four scholars, and an account made up of the goods of the college. The chaplain and scholars were to retain a lawyer of the counsel of the archbishop of Canterbury at a fee of 6s. 8d. yearly. The books of the college were not to be lent out. At the same time John atte Wyse, 'the newest of the founders,' ordered that after his death 6s. 8d. yearly should be distributed by the chaplain to the vicar, churchwardens, parish clerk, sexton, and poor parishioners of Bredgar.

In 1403 Robert de Bradegare and others had licence[5] to add a messuage, lands and rents in Borden, Bredgar, Stockbury, Bicknor, Aldington, Hollingbourne, Hucking, Wormshill, and Milsted to the endowment of the college of the Holy Trinity, Bredgar ; and further small additions were afterwards made.[6]

In the Valor of 1535 the gross value[7] of the possessions of 'the primary chantry of Bredgar,' given in the certificate of Sir Walter Dowle, chantry priest there, was £32 14s. 8d. yearly, and deductions of £4 18s. 5½d. reduced the net value to £27 16s. 2½d. In 1546 the gross value[8] of 'the late chantry in the parish of Bredgar' was £39 15s. 4d. yearly and the net value £36 12s. 7d. ; and the return mentions a chalice of silver price 26s. 8d., a bell price 10s., and two old vestments and albs price 10s., 'all which stuff came into the hands of Walter Dowle, late master there.'

The 'chauntery house' of Bredgar came into the possession of George Harper and was granted back by him to the crown in exchange in 1542.[9]

CHAPLAINS OF BREDGAR

John Promhelle, occurs 1398 [10]
John Parterych, died 1490 [11]
Thomas Denway, appointed 1490,[11] died 1491[12]
Thomas Colley, appointed 1491 [12]
Walter Dowle, occurs 1535 [10]

[1] Pat. 16 Ric. II, pt. 1, m. 24.
[2] Printed in *Lit. Cant.* (Rolls Ser.), iii, 15–21.
[3] Ibid. 68–70.
[4] Printed in Dugdale, *Mon.* viii, 1391–3.

[5] Pat. 4 Hen. IV, pt. 2, m. 13.
[6] Ibid. 13 Hen. IV, pt. 1, m. 18.
[7] *Valor Eccl.* (Rec. Com.) i, 68.
[8] Chant. Cert. 29, No. 107.
[9] *L. and P. Hen. VIII*, xvii, 283 (48).
[10] See above.
[11] Cant. Archiepis. Reg. Morton-Courtenay, fol. 145b.
[12] Ibid. 148b.

66. THE COLLEGE OF COBHAM

Edward III on 18 November, 1362, granted licence for John de Cobham to found a chantry of five chaplains, of whom one was to be master, in the church of Cobham, and to grant to them in mortmain the manor of Westchalk, and lands and rents in Chalk, Cobham, and St. Werburgh.[1]

The founder made these grants to the chantry or college in 1363; and several more grants were made by him and others under a licence by letters patent, dated 29 March, 1367, for the master and chaplains to acquire in mortmain lands and rents to the value of £40 yearly.[2] On 24 November, 1376, the king granted licence for the founder to grant to them the advowsons of two churches[3]; and the church of Horton by Dartford was appropriated to them in 1378.[4] The church of Chalk was granted to them by the prior and convent of Norwich in 1380.[5] The church of Rolvenden was granted by Richard de Ponynges and John de Clyntone in 1383, and appropriated in 1389,[6] the bishop then ordaining that in addition to the seven chaplains then in the college there should be two chaplains temporal; and Walter Schudham, master, John Moys, under master, and the five fellows formally agreed to this. On 10 November, 1389, John de Cobham had licence to grant to the college the advowson of the church of East Tilbury in Essex[7]; which was appropriated to them accordingly, the number of nine chaplains being increased by two.[8] All the above letters patent and grants and some others were confirmed by Richard II in 1390.[9]

Indulgences to penitents visiting the college at certain times were granted by several popes[10]; and the appropriation of the churches of Rolvenden and Tilbury confirmed.[11] Pope Innocent VII in 1405 granted licence for an alteration in the costume of the master and chaplains.[12]

An inventory[13] is preserved of the books, jewels, vestments, and ornaments of the college, made by the undermaster and sacristans in 1479.

The oath of acknowledgement of the royal supremacy was taken on 27 October, 1535, by John Bayly, master, John Norman, fellow, and Thomas Webster, William Wharffe, and Stephen Tennand, brethren.[14] In the Valor of that year the whole of the possessions of the college were valued[15] at £142 1s. 2½d. yearly, with deductions of £13 19s. 5d., leaving a net income of £128 1s. 9½d.

The college was not dissolved in the ordinary way, but privately surrendered by the master and brethren to George Brooke, lord of Cobham, whose possession was secured by Act of Parliament.[16]

Sir William Brooke, Lord Cobham, who died on 6 March, 1597, left by his will[17] to Sir John Leveson, Thomas Fane, and William Lambard, the site of the college and other lands, as well as sums of money, bricks and timber, to make a college to be called the New College of Cobham. This was completed on 29 September, 1598, and statutes were made for it. The wardens of the lands contributory to Rochester bridge were to have the management and to be called the presidents of the college, and the college was to consist of twenty poor persons, each of whom was to have a lodging and 6s. 8d. monthly. One of these, a man, to be nominated by the Baron Cobham, was to be warden, and another man, nominated by the presidents, sub-warden; and the remaining eighteen were to be chosen by various parishes, three each by Cobham and Hoo, two each by Shorne and Strood, and one each by Cooling, Cliffe, Chalk, Gravesend, Higham, St. Mary's, Cuxton, and Halling.

The college exists thus to the present day.[18]

MASTERS OF COBHAM

William de Newton, resigned 1371[19]
Edward de Stanlake, appointed 1371[19]
John Wetewang, occurs 1378[20]
Walter Shuldham, resigned 1390[21]
William Tanner, appointed 1390,[21] died 1418[22]
John Gladwyn, occurs 1420,[22] died 1450[22]
William Bochier, died 1458[23]
William Hobson, appointed 1458,[23] died 1473[22]
John Holt, occurs 1473[22]
John Bygcrofte, occurs 1481[23a]
Thomas Lyndley, occurs 1491[23b]
John Sprotte, appointed 1492,[22] died 1498[24]
John Alan, appointed 1498,[24] died 1502[25]

[1] Pat. 36 Edw. III, pt. 2, m. 16.
[2] Pat. 41 Edw. III, pt. 1, m. 27.
[3] Pat. 50 Edw. III, pt. 2, m. 13.
[4] Thorpe, *Reg. Roff.* 431; Pat. 3 Ric. II, pt. 1, m. 28.
[5] Pat. 4 Ric. II, pt. 1, m. 21.
[6] *Reg. Roff.* 234.
[7] Pat. 13 Ric. II, pt. 1, m. 1.
[8] Newcourt, *Repertorium*, ii, 595.
[9] Pat. 13 Ric. II, pt. 3, m. 42–32.
[10] *Cal. Papal Let.* iv, 42, 61, 62, 396; vi, 27.
[11] Ibid. iv, 226, 390; vi, 28. [12] Ibid. vi, 49.
[13] Printed in *Reg. Roff.* 239.
[14] *L. and P. Hen. VIII*, ix, 692.

[15] *Valor Eccl.* (Rec. Com.), i, 104.
[16] 31 Hen. VIII, cap. 13; 1 Edw. VI, cap. 14.
[17] The will, statutes, &c., are printed in *Reg. Roff.* 242–57.
[18] Some further details are given and documents printed in an article by Mr. A. A. Arnold, in *Arch. Cant.* xxvii, 64.
[19] Roch. Epis. Reg. vol. 1, fol. 348.
[20] *Reg. Roff.* 431.
[21] Roch. Epis. Reg. vol. 2, fol. 10.
[22] *Arch. Cant.* xxvii, 75.
[23] Roch. Epis. Reg. vol. 3, fol. 230.
[23a] Harl. Chart. 44. C. 42. [23b] Ibid. 44. C. 44.
[24] Roch. Epis. Reg. vol. 4, fol. 23.
[25] Ibid. 33 d.

John Bald, appointed 1502 [25]
John Baker, occurs 1502 [22]
George Crowmer, appointed 1512,[26] resigned 1532 [27]
Robert Johnson, appointed 1532,[28] resigned 1533 [29]
John Wylbor, appointed 1533 [29]
John Bayly, occurs 1535 [30]

The seal [31] (1415) of the college is of red wax, measuring 1¾ in., and represents the Virgin full-length with crown and nimbus, holding in the left hand the Child, also with crown and nimbus, and in the right a branch. On the right beneath a tree is St. Mary Magdalen kneeling in adoration. In base a shield of arms: on a cheveron three lions rampant. Legend :—

[SI]GILLUM . . . RIE DE COBEHA[M].

67. THE COLLEGE OF MAIDSTONE

The hospital of Sts. Peter and Paul called 'le Newerk of Maydeston' was of the foundation of Boniface, archbishop of Canterbury, for the finding of one chaplain. The master should make continual residence, and there should be ten poor persons maintained there, but in 1375 there were only five.[1] The churches of Sutton by Dover, Linton, and East Farleigh, were appropriated to it; and its temporalities were valued in 1384 at £5 10s. 5d. yearly.[1a]

Pope Boniface IX on 25 June, 1395, authorized William Courtenay, archbishop of Canterbury, to make the parish church of Maidstone into a college of a master and twenty-four chaplains and clerks.[2] Richard II on 2 August, 1395, granted licence for this and for the incorporation into the college of the hospital and the churches appropriated to it [3]; on 10 February, 1396, he granted licence for the master and college of All Saints, Maidstone, to acquire in mortmain lands and rents not held in chief, to the value of £40 yearly [4]; and on 28 May, 1396, he granted to the master and chaplains in frankalmoign the advowson of the church of Crundale, and the reversion of the manors of Tremworth and

Fannes on the death of Henry Yevele.[5] Henry IV confirmed this grant in 1400 [6]; and in 1407 he granted licence for them to acquire the manor of Wittersham and lands in Maidstone, Loose, Boxley, and Hoo.[7]

In June, 1396, the archbishop was allowed to take twenty-four masons called 'fre maceons,' and twenty-four masons called 'ligiers' for the works of the college [8]; and after his death the pope, in 1398, confirmed the foundation, his executors testifying that he had erected the college, appropriated the hospital and its churches, appointed John Wotton to be master, added to the four clerks who previously served the parish church twelve chaplains and eight clerks, to say the day and night hours, and made statutes for them.[9] His successor, Thomas Arundel, founded a chantry of three chaplains, two in the cathedral of Canterbury and one in the college of Maidstone, to pray for himself, the late archbishop, and others.[10] The advowson of the college belonged to the archbishop of Canterbury until it was sold to the crown in an exchange in 1537.[11]

Archbishop Warham, after a visitation in 1511, when William Grocyn was master and Giles Rede sub-master and there were five other fellows, issued orders on 6 October that the prior and officers should make full accounts and inventories, and that the college should show its right to the appropriations of the churches of Sutton, Linton, and Farleigh.[12]

In the Valor of 1535 the gross value [13] of the possessions of the college, including the manor of Shillington and the chapels of St. Faith, Detling and Loose, was £212 5s. 3¾d. yearly, and the net value £159 7s. 10d. The deductions included corrodies of £2 to each of five poor persons, a survival of the old foundation. In 1546 the gross value was given as £208 6s. 2d., and the net value as £187 3s. 9d. yearly,[14] and a later certificate [15] gave the gross value as £211 4s. 1¼d. yearly, out of which the master received £31 as his stipend, and the sub-master and sacrist each £5 13s. 4d. The plate amounted to 52¼ ounces gilt, 26 ounces parcel gilt, and 38¼ ounces white.

The college was suppressed in the first year of Edward VI, and granted to George Brooke, Lord Cobham, in fee on 10 May, 1549.[16]

[26] Roch. Epis. Reg. vol. 4, fol. 68; L. and P. Hen. VIII, i, 3215.
[27] Roch. Epis. Reg. vol. 4, fol, 166 d. He was then bishop of Armagh.
[28] Ibid.   [29] Ibid. 179.
[30] L. and P. Hen. VIII, viii, 1037; ix, 692.
[31] B.M. Harl. Chart. 43. I. 31; 56. I. 42.
[1] Inq. p.m. 49 Edw. III (2nd Nos.), No. 46.
[1a] Twysden, Decem Scriptores, 2169. Several documents relating to it are given in the History of the College of All Saints, Maidstone, by Beale Poste (1847).   [2] Lit. Cant. (Rolls Ser.), iii, 45.
[3] Pat. 19 Ric. II, pt. 1, m. 11; Dugdale, Mon. viii, 1394.
[4] Pat. 19 Ric. II, pt. 2, m. 37.

[5] Pat. 20 Ric. II, pt. 1, m. 17; Dugdale, Mon. viii, 1395.
[6] Pat. 1 Hen. IV, pt. 6, m. 32.
[7] Pat. 8 Hen. IV, pt. 2, m. 13.
[8] Pat. 19 Ric. II, pt. 2, m. 4.
[9] Cal. Papal Let. v, 96.
[10] Ibid. vi, 133, 313; Lit. Cant. (Rolls Ser.), iii, 109, 123.
[11] L. and P. Hen. VIII, xiii (i), 1284, 1519 (68).
[12] Cant. Archiepis. Reg. Warham, fol. 43b.
[13] Valor Eccl. (Rec. Com.), i, 75.
[14] Chant. Cert. 29, No. 1.
[15] Ibid. 28, No. 1.
[16] Pat. 3 Edw. VI, pt. 4, m. 7.

MASTERS OF MAIDSTONE

William de la Sele, appointed 1282 [17]
Michael de Wydewode, appointed 1304 [17a]
John de Eghtham, appointed 1311 [18]
Thomas Jordan, appointed 1312 [19]
John de Waltham, appointed 1324 [20]
William de Malden, appointed 1326 [20a]
Martin de Ixnyngg, appointed 1334 [21]
Richard de Norwico, appointed 1349 [22]
William de Leghton, appointed 1357 [23]
Simon de Bredon, appointed 1357, [24] died 1372 [25]
Thomas Yonge, appointed 1372 [25]
William Risynge, appointed 1377 [26]
Thomas Crosser, appointed 1378 [27]
John Ludham, appointed 1380 [28]
John Wotton, the first master of the college, [29] died 1417 [30]
John Holond, appointed 1417 [30]
Roger Heron, appointed 1419, [31] resigned 1441 [32]
John Drwell, appointed 1441 [32]
Peter Stackley, appointed 1444 [32a]
Robert Smyth, appointed 1450, [33] died 1458 [34]
Thomas Boleyne, appointed 1458 [34]
John Freestone, resigned 1470 [34a]
John Lee, appointed 1470, [34a] died 1494 [35]
John Comberton, appointed 1494, [35] died 1506 [36]
William Grocyn, appointed 1506, [36] died 1519 [36a]
Thomas Penyton, appointed 1519 [36a]
John Leffe, occurs 1541, [37] 1544 [38]

The seal [39] (1543) of the college is of red wax, measuring 2⅝ inches.

Obverse.—Within a carved and traced Gothic panel, the two lower cusps terminating with flowering sprigs, a shield of arms : per pale,

[17] *Reg. Epist. J. Peckham* (Rolls Ser.), iii, 1058.
[17a] Cant. Archiepis. Reg. Winchelsey, fol. 297.
[18] Ibid. 50.   [19] Ibid. 50*b*.   [20] Ibid. 254.
[20a] Ibid. Reynolds, 262*b*.
[21] Pat. 8 Edw. III, pt. 1, m. 41.
[22] Pat. 23 Edw. III, pt. 1, m. 1.
[23] Cant. Archiepis. Reg. Islip, fol. 258*b*.
[24] Ibid. 278*b*.
[25] Ibid. Whittlesey, fol. 90.
[26] Ibid. Sudbury, fol. 121*b*.
[27] Ibid. 123.   [28] Ibid. 133*b*.   [29] See above.
[30] Cant. Archiepis. Reg. Chicheley, vol. 1, fol. 95*b*. His will is printed in *Arch. Cant.* iv, 225.
[31] Cant. Archiepis. Reg. Chicheley, vol. 1, 103*b*.
[32] Ibid. 230*b*.   [32a] Ibid. Stafford, 78*b*.
[33] Ibid. 107.
[34] Ibid. Bourchier, 71*b*.   [34a] Ibid. 113*b*.
[35] Ibid. Morton-Courtenay, 158*b*.
[36] Ibid. Warham, 327.
[36a] Ibid. 369.
[37] *L. and P. Hen. VIII*, xvi, 455.
[38] Ibid. xix, p. 171.
[39] B.M. Harl. Chart. 86. G. 45.

dexter the see of Canterbury, sinister Archbishop Courtenay. Legend :—

SIGILLUM CO . . . . . . OMNIUM SANCTORUM DE MAYDENNYSTONIE

Reverse.—The Trinity, in a canopied niche with tabernacle work at the sides. Inner border engrailed. Legend :—

IN NOMINE PATRIS . . . . II ET SPIRI . . . . .
MEN

68. THE COLLEGE OF WINGHAM

The foundation of the college of St. Mary, Wingham, was completed by John Peckham, archbishop of Canterbury, who made statutes [1] for it on 18 February, 1287. In these he states that the scheme originated with his predecessor Robert, who obtained a bull from Pope Gregory X on 23 December, 1273 ; and he himself took it up and finally came to an agreement with Tedissius de Camilla, rector of Wingham, in the time of Pope Honorius IV. The college was to consist of a master or provost and six canons, all to be appointed by the archbishop. The provost had a portion assigned to him and houses near the rectory for his habitation ; and of the six canonries two were to be priestly, with prebends at Chilton and Pedding, two diaconal, with prebends at Twitham and Bonnington, and two sub-diaconal, with prebends at Retling and Womenswold. The provost and canons might all appoint vicars under them, who were to be either priests or deacons, and the altarages of Ash, Nonington, and 'Goodwinstone,' were assigned for the maintenance of these. One of the canons was to be appointed steward for the administration of the common goods, and was to pay a daily portion of 12*d*. to each resident canon, reserving the rest for the common needs. The conditions of residence were prescribed. The foundation and statutes were confirmed by Edward I on 7 June, 1290. [2]

Pope Nicholas IV in 1291 granted indulgence to penitents visiting the church at certain times ; [3] and in 1292 he gave licence for the archbishop to grant land in Wingham to the canons to build houses upon. [4] The canons had licence in 1306 to acquire land in 'Goodwinstone' to build houses upon ; [5] and in 1441 they received lands in Preston, Ash, Staple, Wingham, and Stourmouth for a chantry for William Cokkowe. [6]

The archbishop in 1287 appointed Peter de Geldeford provost and also filled all the canonries

[1] Cant. Archiepis. Reg. Peckham, fol. 32 ; Dugdale, *Mon.* viii, 1341.
[2] Pat. 18 Edw. I, m. 26.
[3] *Cal. Papal Let.* i, 543.   [4] Ibid. 548.
[5] Pat. 35 Edw. I, m. 46.
[6] Pat. 19 Hen. VI, pt. 3, m. 28 ; Pat. 7 Edw. IV, pt. 2, m. 12.

except Twitham.[7] The vicarage of Wingham was appropriated to the provostship, and Peter was granted licence for non-residence until he should receive all the fruits; and he was also allowed to retain the church of Bishopsbourne for life.[8] In 1298 he had a grant of protection for one year while going to Rome.[9] He was deprived of the provostship shortly afterwards by the archbishop, who appointed James de Gobeham; but when Peter died at Rieti the pope appointed Amedeus de Sancto Johanne provost. A struggle followed, James protesting that Amedeus was only seventeen years old and not in orders, but the latter secured a dispensation from the pope in 1301, and retained possession.[10]

William de Handlo, provost, had an indult in 1306 to enjoy the fruits of his benefice and of the churches of Wootton and Hasely though non-resident for seven years for the purpose of study;[11] and in 1313 he had a further licence of non-residence for three years.[12]

In 1328 the provost had become too feeble to perform his duties, and the rector of Monkton in Thanet was appointed to act as his co-adjutor.[13]

In 1344 John de Bourne, provost, had licence of non-residence for three years while studying at a university.[14]

Bernard Berardi de Montegasino and Thomas de Clipston obtained papal provisions to the provostship in the middle of the fourteenth century, but neither appears to have secured possession.[15]

In 1374 John Fordham, provost, was allowed to hold a parish church for two years together with the provostship;[16] and in 1391 William de Wyndesore, provost, who had spent much on the repair of the church, was given leave of absence for three years;[17] and was also allowed to hold another benefice for one year, as Wingham was near the seaport by Sandwich and so he was put to excessive expense in hospitality.[18]

Archbishop Warham made a visitation[19] of the college on 16 September, 1511. Henry Ediall, prior, said that the foundation was for eight vicars choral, but now there were only four; each canon had to give an ornament to the house at the end of ⸗is first year of residence, and also to serve his term of residence in his own house and at his own table, but none observed this. The house of one of the canons was very ruinous. The prior held two incompatible benefices, and was ordered to show a licence for this. The chaplain of Ash was a monk of Boxley, and one of the vicars a monk of Evesham, and both were ordered not to cease wearing the monastic habit.

Richard Benger, one of the canons, got into trouble in 1535 for upholding the cause of the pope, but the matter seems to have been dropped.[20] About the same time the parishioners of Ash complained to Cromwell that the canons had usurped the vicarage to their own use for the last twenty-two years and let it to farm to temporal men, who put in the cheapest curates they could obtain. Within a quarter of a year they had seven curates. By their complaint to the archbishop the canons were compelled to appoint a curate, but kept from him the tithes of wool and lamb.[21]

In the Valor[22] of 1535 the gross income of Master Edmund Cranmer, provost, was given as £65 6s. 8d.; from which deductions had to be made of £9 to the resident parish priest, £3 to the sexton of Wingham, and £22 to Master William Warham, late provost, for life. The gross income of the six canons was £143 7s. 8½d. and their net income £84 5s. 11d., the deductions including the salaries of five priests serving the cures at the chapels of Ash, Overland, Richborough, Nonington, and Womenswold, and two priests, two choristers, and a sexton in the church of Wingham. In 1546 the gross income of the college was given[23] as £209 12s. 4d. and the net income £170 18s. 7d. It was suppressed in the first year of Edward VI, and the gross income was then said to be £187 15s. 8d.; and it possessed 40 oz. of gilt plate, 6 oz. of parcel gilt, and 89¼ oz. of white.[24]

The site and possessions of the college were granted on 16 June, 1553, to Henry Palmer, knight, and his heirs.[25]

PROVOSTS OF WINGHAM

Peter de Geldeford, appointed 1287,[26] occurs 1298 [27]

James de Gobeham [28]

Amedeus de Sancto Johanne, occurs 1301, 1305 [29]

William de Handlo, occurs 1306,[28] resigned 1317 [30]

[7] Cant. Archiepis. Reg. Peckham, fol. 34b, 35.
[8] Ibid.; Cal. Papal Let. i, 497.
[9] Pat. 26 Edw. I, m. 15.
[10] Cal. Papal Let. i, 593.
[11] Ibid ii, 4.   [12] Ibid. 115.
[13] Lit. Cant. (Rolls Ser.), i, 268.
[14] Cal. Papal Let. iii, 124; Cal. Papal Pet. i, 50.
[15] Cal. Papal Let. iii, 483, 484, 516; Cal. Papal Pet. i, 239, 261, 320, 338.
[16] Cal. Papal Let. iv, 199.
[17] Ibid. 357.   [18] Ibid. 370.
[19] Cant. Archiepis. Reg. Warham, fol. 37.

[20] L. and P. Hen. VIII, viii, 386–7.
[21] Ibid. ix, 1110.
[22] Valor Eccl. (Rec. Com.), i, 36.
[23] Chant. Cert. 29, No. 15.
[24] Ibid. 28, No. 15.
[25] Pat. 7 Edw. VI, pt. 4.
[26] Cant. Archiepis. Reg. Peckham, fol. 34 d.
[27] Pat. 26 Edw. I, m. 15.
[28] See above.
[29] Pat. 33 Edw. I. pt. 1, m. 11.
[30] Cant. Archiepis. Reg. Reynolds, fol. 19.

Walter de Kemeseye, appointed 1317,[30] occurs 1318[31]

John de Bruton, occurs 1321 [32]

John de Bourne, occurs 1344,[28] resigned 1351[33]

Robert de Solbery, appointed 1351,[34] died 1359[35]

William de Tratynton, appointed and resigned 1359[36]

John de Severley, appointed 1359,[36] died 1365[37]

William Reed, appointed 1365 [37]

John Fordham, occurs 1374 [38]

William de Wyndesore, appointed 1374,[39] resigned 1401 [40]

Andrew Yonge, appointed 1401 [40]

Matthew Assheton, occurs 1434 [41]

Thomas Moonie, occurs 1436 [41a]

Thomas Rotheram, occurs 1467 [42]

John Coppyng, died 1495 [43]

Thomas Morton, appointed 1495 [43]

Henry Ediall, occurs 1511,[44] died 1520 [45]

William Warham, appointed 1520 [46]

Edmund Cranmer, occurs 1535,[47] the last provost [48]

69. THE COLLEGE OF WYE

Henry VI on 27 February, 1432, granted licence for John Kemp, archbishop of York, to found the college of Sts. Gregory and Martin in the parish of Wye, in which he had been born; and for the master or provost and chaplains of the college to acquire in mortmain lands, rents, and churches to the value of 100 marks yearly, and also to acquire the advowson of the vicarage of Wye from the abbot of Battle, and to appropriate the vicarage.[1] The design was not carried out at once, and on 28 March, 1439, in consideration of a deduction of £200 from a debt owing to the archbishop, the king granted to him the advowson and rectory of Newington by Hythe

with the grange of Brenzett and lands in Newington and Broomhill, lately belonging to the abbess of Guines in Artois, with licence for him to grant the same to the master and chaplains of the college, when founded, and for them to appropriate the church.[2]

The archbishop founded the college accordingly by the cemetery of the parish church, and appointed Richard Ewan the first provost on 14 January, 1448.[3] The vicarage of Wye was appropriated to the college by the archbishop of Canterbury on 9 November, 1449;[4] and the master and chaplains had licence in 1450[5] to acquire and appropriate the church of Boughton Aluph, and in 1451[6] to acquire lands and rents in Canterbury, Wye, Boughton Aluph, Crundale, Godmersham, Bethersden, and Postling. Edward IV in 1465 granted to them the churches of Newington, Brenzett, and Broomhill, formerly of the abbess of Guines.[7]

The prior of Christchurch made a visitation [8] of the college during the vacancy of the archbishopric in 1454; when everything was found in good order except for a hole in the churchyard wall and a few other trifling matters. The statutes could not be produced, as the copy belonging to the college was still in London, but they were explained to the visitor. The foundation consisted of a provost, two fellows, a minister or parochial chaplain, seven choristers, and two clerks. At each vacancy of the provostship the fellows submitted several names to the abbot of Battle, who selected one; and no one was eligible unless a doctor or scholar of theology and a member of Merton College, Oxford.

Archbishop Warham made a visitation [9] of the college on 25 September, 1511, when John Goodhew was master and Thomas Rogers fellow. Thomas Penycoke, curate, William Gowlaw (a Scotchman), and Thomas Martin also belonged to the house, as well as four clerks and four choristers. The master showed his letters of institution to the parish church of Staplehurst, but had no papal dispensation for two incompatible benefices. He frequented in a suspicious way the house of John Stephens of Herne Hill in the deanery of Ospringe, and it was noted that there were other charges against him.

The oath of acknowledgement of the royal supremacy was taken in December, 1534, by

[31] Pat. 11 Edw. II, pt. 1, m. 5.

[32] Ibid. 14 Edw. II, pt. 2, m. 9.

[33] Cant. Archiepis. Reg. Islip, fol. 257. He joined the Friars Minor (*Cal. Papal Let.* iii, 483; *Cal. Papal Pet.* i, 261).   [34] Ibid.   [35] Ibid. 338.

[36] Ibid. 281–2.   [37] Ibid. 503.

[38] *Cal. Papal Let.* iv, 199.

[39] Pat. 48 Edw. III, pt. 2, m. 6.

[40] Cant. Archiepis. Reg. Arundel, vol. 1, fol. 276.

[41] Pat. 12 Hen. VI, pt. 2, m. 23.

[41a] *Cal. Papal Let.* viii, 615.

[42] Pat. 7 Edw. IV, pt. 2, m. 12.

[43] Cant. Archiepis. Reg. Morton-Courtenay, fol. 159.

[44] Ibid. Warham, fol. 37.   [45] Ibid. fol. 370.

[46] Ibid. He was archdeacon of Canterbury and had a papal dispensation to hold the provostship in addition without residence (B.M. Stowe Chart. 590).

[47] *Valor Eccl.* (Rec. Com.), i, 36.

[48] Chant. Cert. 28, No. 15.

[1] Pat. 10 Henry VI, pt. 1, m. 6; pt. 2, m. 9; Dugdale, *Mon.* viii, 1340.

[2] Pat. 17 Hen. VI, pt. 1, m. 12; Dugdale, *Mon. ut supra.*

[3] Wharton, *Anglia Sacra*, i, 380. A copy of the statutes is preserved among the archives of Merton College, Oxford.

[4] *Lit. Cant.* (Rolls Ser.), iii, 198.

[5] Pat. 28 Hen. VI, pt. 1, m. 5; Rymer, *Foedera.*

[6] Pat. 29 Hen. VI, pt. 2, m. 4; Dugdale, *Mon.* viii, 1432.

[7] Pat. 5 Edw. IV, pt. 1, m. 8.

[8] *Hist. MSS. Com. Rep.* ix, App. pt. i, 105.

[9] Cant. Archiepis. Reg. Warham, fol. 40.

Richard Waltare, provost, and three others.[10] In the Valor of the next year the gross income of the college was given as £125 15s. 4½d., and the net income £93 2s. 0½d.; the deductions including £3 6s. 8d. in payments to poor people, and £3 3s. 4d. in obits for the founder and other benefactors.[11]

The college was surrendered on 19 January, 1545, and an inventory of its goods was taken on the same day, these being valued at £7 1s. 10d., besides a silver salt and its cover, weighing 18 oz. and valued at £3; ten silver spoons weighing 8¼ oz. and valued at 27s. 6d., and two old masers valued at 6s. 8d. The debts owing to the college amounted to £21 6s. 11¼d., and it owed £51 6s. 2½d. to the king for first-fruits and tenths. Pensions of £26 13s. 4d. to Edward Bowden, master, £6 each to William Dodding and Thomas Sotheby, fellows, and £10 to Richard Clyfton, master of the grammar school, were given.[12]

The site and most of the possessions of the college, including the manors of Perycourte and Surrenden, and the rectory and advowson of the vicarage of Broomhill, were sold on 13 March, 1545, for £200 to Walter Bucler, the queen's secretary.[13]

MASTERS OR PROVOSTS OF WYE

Richard Ewan, appointed 1448 [14]

Thomas Gauge, occurs 1450,[15] resigned 1462 [16]

Nicholas Wright, appointed 1462,[16] occurs 1470 [17]

John Goodhew, occurs 1511 [14]

Richard Waltare or Walker, occurs 1525,[17a] 1534,[14] 1535 [18]

Edward Bowden, surrendered 1545,[19] the last master

The seal [20] of the college is a pointed oval measuring 2⅜ in. by 1½ in. In two carved niches, with heavy double canopies and tabernacle work at the sides, on the left St. Gregory with triple tiara, seated, lifting up the right hand in benediction, and holding in the left a cross or crosier; on the right St. Martin, seated, lifting up the right hand in benediction and holding in the left a pastoral staff. In base, under a round-headed arch, between masonry, the master or provost, three-quarter length, turned slightly to the left, in prayer. Legend :—

[SIG]ILLŪ C͞OE COLLEGII S͞COR GREGORII T MARTINI DE WY I C͞A.

ALIEN HOUSES

70. THE PRIORY OF FOLKESTONE

Eadbald, king of Kent (616–40), is said to have built here for his daughter Eanswith a monastery dedicated to St. Peter. Nothing is known of the history of this house, but it would seem to have been the earliest nunnery in England, with the possible exception of Barking. In 927 King Athelstan made a grant of Folkestone to Christchurch, Canterbury, describing it as the place where there was formerly an abbey of nuns, and where St. Eanswith was buried, and adding that it had been destroyed by the Danes.[1] The account [2] of the life of St. Eanswith says that the site of the church was swallowed up by the sea.

In 1095 Nigel de Munevilla, lord of Folkestone, and Emma his wife granted the church of St. Mary and St. Eanswith, Folkestone, and all the churches of their demesne pertaining to the honour of Folkestone, with various other posses-

sions, to the Benedictine abbey of Lonlay in France, thus founding a new monastery. Their daughter and heiress Maud married Rualo de Abrincis, and later William de Abrincis, lord of Folkestone, granted a charter of confirmation to the monks.[3] In 1137, with his permission, they moved from the castle of Folkestone, where they were founded, to a new church outside. Pope Innocent III on 26 May, 1204, confirmed the possessions of the priory, including the churches of Hawkinge and Alkham.[4]

In 1294 a grant of protection was made to the prior while going beyond the seas.[5]

Folkestone, being alien, was taken into the king's hands during the war with France, but generally granted at farm to the prior, who paid £30 yearly for it in 1338 [6] and £35 yearly in 1342.[7] In 1390 the priory was granted [8] during the war to the prior, bailiff, and sacrist of Westminster Abbey at a yearly rent of £20; and in

---

[10] L. and P. Hen. VIII, vii, 1594 (9).
[11] Valor Eccl. (Rec. Com.), i, 38.
[12] L. and P. Hen. VIII, xx (1), 68.
[13] Ibid. 465 (37).   [14] See above.
[15] Pat. 28 Hen. VI, pt. 1, m. 5.
[16] Cant. Archiepis. Reg. Bourchier, fol. 84b.
[17] Harl. Chart. 45. A. 54.
[17a] Ibid. 86. H. 29.
[18] Valor Eccl. (Rec. Com.), i, 38.

[19] L. and P. Hen. VIII, xx (1), 68.
[20] B.M. Seals, lxvi, 22.
[1] B.M. Cott. MS. Tib. A. ii, fol. 12b.
[2] Nova Legenda Angliae.
[3] Exch. K.R. Mem. R. Mich. 4 Hen. IV, m. 10 d.
[4] Cal. Papal Let. i, 17.
[5] Pat. 22 Edw. I, m. 24.
[6] Close, 12 Edw. III, pt. 1, m. 20.
[7] Pat. 16 Edw. III, pt. 1, m. 16.
[8] Ibid. 13 Ric. II, pt. 2, m. 27.

1393 a monk of Westminster was appointed prior by the king.[9] In 1399 the priory was restored to him under the condition that during the war he should pay to the king the tax paid of old to the abbey, and should properly maintain the priory and pay tenths and other subsidies.[10] Folkestone appears afterwards to have been made denizen, and it escaped the dissolution of alien priories, though the tax of 6 marks yearly was paid regularly to the king.[11]

Prior John brought an action in Chancery in 1433 against Robert Walton and others, with William Clerk, vicar of Folkestone, for assault at mass in Folkestone church.[12]

Archbishop Warham visited[13] the priory on 22 September, 1511, when apparently there was no prior, but James Burton had been appointed administrator. He was ordered to make a full account and inventory. Nothing else was noticeable except the curious fact that the other three monks had originally been professed in different houses and orders, William Weston in the Augustinian monastery of St. Mary Overy, Thomas Seale in the monastery of Bermondsey, and John Carter in the Premonstratensian monastery of St. Radegund.

In the Valor[14] of 1535 the gross income of the priory, including a disputed annuity from the college of Wye, amounted to £63 0s. 7d. and the net income to £41 15s. 10d.; after deductions of £21 4s. 9d. in rents and fees, the old tax of 6 marks being paid to Eton College pending a lawsuit.

In the same year Folkestone was visited[15] on Friday, 22 October, by Richard Layton, who reported that there were there a prior and a sick monk. The priory was in the gift of the archbishop of Canterbury, and Lord Clinton was the patron. The parish church belonged to the priory, and with the glebe formed almost its whole revenue. The house was in utter decay; it consisted of one hall, one chamber, a kitchen, and a little parlour underground, not meet for a monk; the barns were well filled with corn, and there were a few cattle, but no household stuff. The prior and monk were both guilty of serious offences. This unfavourable report was probably one of the reasons why the priory was surrendered[16] on 15 November, before the Act of Dissolution was passed in the next year; though Thomas Bedyll, who received the surrender, describes it as a little house well repaired, and the prior a good husband and beloved by his neighbours.[17] It is difficult to say which of the two versions is correct. The prior complained[18] at first that he had nothing given to him but a bed lacking both pillows and blankets; but on 20 March, 1537, he received a pension[19] of £10, dating from the preceding Michaelmas.

The priory was at first leased[20] to Edward, Lord Clinton; and on 9 January, 1539, it was granted to him in fee simple.[21]

PRIORS OF FOLKESTONE

Peter, occurs 1296 [22]
Robert de Stokeyo, occurs 1326 [23]
William Medici[24] or Waterham,[25] appointed 1344,[24] occurs 1345 [25]
Thomas, died 1361 [26]
James de Suessione, appointed 1361 [27]
John de Husceu, occurs 1370 [28]
Sampson Sennys, appointed 1372,[29] resigned 1376 [30]
Nicholas Barbarot, appointed 1376 [31]
Nicholas Chiriton, appointed 1393,[32] resigned 1426 [33]
Richard Longe, elected 1426,[34] died 1427 [35]
John Ashforde, elected 1427,[35] resigned 1446 [36]
John Combe, elected 1446 [37]
Thomas Banys, occurs 1467,[37a] deprived 1493 [38]
Thomas Sudbury, occurs 1502–3 [38]
John Thornton, appointed 1513,[39] died 1516 [40]
George Goodharst, collated 1516 [41]
Thomas Barret, the last prior [42]

The seal[43] of the priory (fifteenth century) is a pointed oval, measuring 2⅛ by 1¾ in., representing St. Eanswith standing crowned in a niche with round-headed arch, holding in the right hand a book and in the left a sceptre or palm branch.

[18] Ibid. xi, 1437. [19] Ibid. xiii (1), p. 577.
[20] Ibid. p. 585. [21] Ibid. xiv (1), 191 (10).
[22] Pat. 24 Edw. I, m. 21.
[23] Exch. K.R. Alien Priories, bdle. 5, No. 4.
[24] *Cal. Papal Let.* iii, 214. By the abbot of Lonlay.
[25] Close, 19 Edw. III, pt. 2, m. 22 d.
[26] Cant. Archiepis. Reg. Islip, fol. 292. [27] Ibid.
[28] Exch. K.R. Alien Priories, 10, No. 10.
[29] Cant. Archiepis. Reg. Whittlesey, fol. 90b. He is also called Sampson Senis (*Hist. MSS. Com. Rep.* ix, App. pt. i, 355), and in a list of aliens is called Sampson Veillard, and said to have two monks under him (Chan. Misc. 18, file 3, No. 32).
[30] Cant. Archiepis. Reg. Sudbury, fol. 118b.
[31] Ibid.
[32] Pat. 16 Ric. II, pt. 2, m. 9. He was a monk of Westminster, and was appointed by the king.
[33] Cant. Archiepis. Reg. Chicheley, fol. 46.
[34] Ibid. [35] Ibid. fol. 46b.
[36] Ibid. Stafford, fol. 23. He became prior of St. Martin's, Dover. [37] Ibid.
[37a] Exch. of Pleas, Plea R. 7 Edw. IV, m. 64.
[38] Cant. Archiepis. Reg. Morton, fol. 32.
[38a] Early Chan. Proc. 262, No. 22.
[39] Cant. Archiepis. Reg. Warham, fol. 353. He was prior of St. Martin's, Dover. [40] Ibid. 361.
[41] Ibid. [42] *L. and P. Hen. VIII*, ix, 816.
[43] B.M. Seals, lxv, 65.

[9] Pat. 16 Ric. II, pt. 2, m. 9.
[10] Ibid. 1 Hen. IV, pt. 2, m. 13.
[11] Ibid. 6 Edw. IV, pt. 2, m. 4.
[12] Early Chan. Proc. bdle. 12, No. 226.
[13] Cant. Archiepis. Reg. Warham, fol. 39.
[14] *Valor Eccl.* (Rec. Com.), i, 52.
[15] *L. and P. Hen. VIII*, ix, 668–9.
[16] Ibid. 816. [17] Ibid. 829.

In a smaller niche above with ogee arch, pinnacled and crocketed, is the Virgin standing crowned, holding in the right hand the Child and in the left a sceptre. Tabernacle work at the sides. In base, under a flat arch, the prior half-length in prayer. Legend :—

SIGILLŪ CŌMUNE PRIORATUS DE FOLKESTON.

71. THE PRIORY OF LEWISHAM

Elstrudis, countess of Flanders, with her sons Arnulf and Adelulf, on 11 September, 918, granted Lewisham, Greenwich, and Woolwich of her inheritance to the abbey of St. Peter and St. Paul, Ghent, for the good of the soul of her lord Baldwin and herself and her sons.[1] Edgar, king of the English, in August, 964, at the prayer of his friend Dunstan, under whose governance the abbey was in the time of his brother King Eadwi, granted to the abbey Lewisham and its appurtenances of Greenwich, Woolwich, Mottingham, and Combe to hold as fully as he had held them in demesne, and as formerly Elstrudis had given it to the abbey. Later the English possessions were taken away from the abbey ; and in 1016 Edward the Confessor, son of Ethelred, being kindly received at Ghent by the abbot, vowed that if his father's realm were restored to him he would restore its possessions to the monastery ; which he did accordingly in 1044, granting a charter of liberties.[2]

William I granted a long charter of confirmation and liberties in 1081. Henry I also granted a charter of confirmation, which was confirmed by Henry III in 1229,[3] and again by Edward II in 1317 ;[4] and other charters were granted by William II, Henry I, and Stephen, and by John in 1209.[5] Gervase de Cornhell at one time claimed to hold Lewisham and Greenwich of the abbot, but eventually (about 1165) withdrew his claim.

The church of Lewisham[6] was appropriated to the abbey by G. bishop of Rochester, and the church of East Greenwich[7] by Bishop Richard in 1239. The temporalities belonging to it in Lewisham and Greenwich were valued in the Taxation of 1291 at £70 18s. yearly, and those in London at 16s. 10d. In 1293 and again in 1313 the abbot claimed and was allowed various liberties in Lewisham and Greenwich.[8]

In 1275 the abbot of Ghent and the prior of Lewisham were ordered[9] to appear before the king with all the muniments relating to the priory, so that the king might then cause what should seem fit to the council to be done touching any defaults or withdrawals there might be, as it pertained to him to provide that in houses of his patronage the distributions and alms established by him and his predecessors should be observed without diminution or deceit. The abbot and convent had licence[10] in the same year to sell the manor of Lewisham to the bishop of Rochester, though this appears not to have been done ; and it seems probable that they had already begun to find their English property troublesome, and wished either to dispose of it or to evade the charges on it. In 1330 the people of Lewisham and Greenwich complained[11] to the council that the barton of Lewisham had been granted to the abbot for the maintenance of four chantries, and distribution of alms on every Thursday and Friday for the souls of the founders of the priory, but that these had been withdrawn for sixteen years.

In 1298 a charge of robbery was brought against the prior.[12]

In 1299 the abbot was amerced in £40 by reason of a toll which the prior of Lewisham had taken without warrant in the king's highway at Greenwich ; but he was pardoned this at the instance of Amadeus, count of Savoy.[13]

Lewisham, being a cell to Ghent, was of course alien ; and in 1295 a clerk was appointed to the custody of the priory, as the number of foreigners staying there constituted a danger to the realm on account of the situation of the priory on the River Thames.[14] It was taken into the king's hands during the war with France, and generally let to the priors at farm, the amount paid in 1338 being 10 marks yearly.[15] In 1415 the alien priories were definitely confiscated by Act of Parliament ; and Henry V in that year granted Lewisham to the Carthusian monastery newly founded by him at Sheen in Surrey.[16]

PRIORS OF LEWISHAM

Sigo [17]
Arnold, occurs 1229 [18]
John, occurs 1298 [19]
James de Doura, occurs 1317 [20]
William Seregotz or Segrotis, occurs 1343,[21] 1345 [22]

[1] For these charters see *Cal. of Doc. in France*, 500-5.
[2] Carte Antique, T. 10. Printed in Dugdale, *Mon.* vii, 988.   [3] Chart. 13 Hen. III, m. 12.
[4] Chart. R. 11 Edw. II, No. 83.
[5] Ibid. 10 John, m. 2.
[6] Thorpe, *Reg. Roff.* 470-1.   [7] Ibid.
[8] *Plac. de Quo Warr.* (Rec. Com.), 316, 356.
[9] Close, 3 Edw. I, m. 10 d.

[10] Pat. 3 Edw. I, m. 26.
[11] *R. of Parl.* (Rec. Com.), ii, 49.
[12] Pat. 26 Edw. I, m. 7.
[13] Ibid. 27 Edw. I, m. 26.
[14] Ibid. 23 Edw. I, m. 5.
[15] Close, 12 Edw. III, pt. 1, m. 20.
[16] Chart. R. 3–4 Hen. V, No. 8.
[17] Thorpe, *Reg. Roff.* 470.
[18] Chart. 13 Hen. III, m. 12.
[19] Pat. 26 Edw. I, m. 7
[20] Cant. Archiepis. Reg. Reynolds, fol. 22.
[21] Close, 17 Edw. III, pt. 1, m. 33 d.
[22] Ibid. 19 Edw. III, pt. 2, m. 22.

72. THE PRIORY OF PATRIXBOURNE

John de Pratellis, who founded the priory of Beaulieu, in the forest of Preaulx, in Normandy, about the end of the twelfth century, granted [1] to it the manor of Patrixbourne, of the inheritance of his wife, and a cell was established there. The prior and canons of Patrixbourne were afterwards dispossessed by King John, but were allowed to have the land again in 1207 for a payment of 30 marks and a palfrey.[2]

On the death of Simon, prior of Beaulieu, in 1332, the king took the manor of Patrixbourne into his hands, but at the complaint of the next prior an inquisition [3] was taken by which it was found that the king had no right in it, and the king accordingly on 4 October, 1333, ordered the escheator not to meddle further.[4] During the war with France the manor was taken into the king's hands with other lands of aliens and committed to the custody of the proctor of the prior of Beaulieu, at a rent of £10 yearly; but in 1340 it was surrendered by him on the ground that he could not pay the rent, and committed to the custody of the abbot of Langdon on the same terms.[5]

On 7 June, 1390, Richard Altrincham had licence to acquire the manor from the prior and convent of Beaulieu for sixty years, on condition that he rendered to the king as much as they then did.[6] He sold his estate in it to the prior and convent of Merton, in Surrey, on 3 October, 1409;[7] and on 11 August following the king granted licence for the prior and convent of Beaulieu to grant the manor to the prior and convent of Merton in mortmain under the condition that the latter should pay 100s. yearly at the Exchequer during the war.[8]

PRIORS OF PATRIXBOURNE

Walter, occurs 1297 [9]
Ralph de Valle, occurs 1326 [10]

73. THE PRIORY OF NEW ROMNEY

The Cistercian Abbey of Pontigny in France owed its possessions at Romney to its connexion with the archbishops of Canterbury. Thomas Becket was received at the abbey while in exile,[1] as was also Stephen Langton; and the latter in 1222 granted to the abbey 50 marks yearly from

the church of Romney,[2] the grant being confirmed by the convent of Christchurch, Canterbury,[3] and Pope Honorius III [4] in the same year. Archbishop Edmund, who was afterwards buried at Pontigny,[5] added 10 marks in 1238,[6] the convent of Christchurch confirming the grant in 1245.[7] Archbishop Boniface in 1264 granted [8] the whole church to the abbey, reserving a vicarage; and Romney thus became a cell to Pontigny, though it is doubtful whether there was ever any regular settlement of monks at it.

During the war with France the possessions of the abbey were taken into the king's hands and let at farm. In 1342 John de Wymbourne held them at a rent of 40 marks yearly, but was unwilling to pay more, and they were let to Joan de Bare, countess of Warenne, and William de Wath, clerk, at a rent of 45 marks.[9] The advowson of the vicarage was also seized by the king.[10]

The possessions of aliens were finally confiscated by Act of Parliament in the reign of Henry V; and Henry VI on 20 May, 1439, granted 'the priory' of Romney to the warden and college of All Souls, Oxford.[11]

74. THE PRIORY OF THROWLEY

The alien priory of Throwley, a cell to the abbey of St. Bertin at St. Omer in France, was founded about the middle of the twelfth century. Hugh de Chileham, son of Foubert of Dover, by a charter [1] near the end of the reign of Stephen granted the church of Chilham to the abbey; and William de Ipra by another charter about the same time granted the churches of Chilham and Throwley. The grants were confirmed by Stephen, Pope Anastasius IV, and Theobald, archbishop of Canterbury; and afterwards by Henry II and Richard I and by later archbishops.

Sir Nathanael de Levelande claimed the chapel of Leaveland against the monks, but yielded when the abbots of Faversham and Boxley were appointed to settle the dispute. Richard, archbishop of Canterbury, then claimed it; but Pope Alexander III ordered the bishops of Exeter and Worcester to hear the case, and it was proved that the chapel was one of those belonging to the church of Throwley, as granted to the monks by Archbishop Theobald.[2] About the same time Henry de Insula endeavoured to withdraw himself from the parochial jurisdiction of Throwley,

[1] *Neustria Pia*, 917.   [2] Fine R. 9 John, m. 13.
[3] Inq. p.m. 6 Edw. III (2nd Nos.), No. 48; Dugdale, *Mon.* vii, 1012.
[4] Close, 7 Edw. III, pt. 2, m. 6.
[5] Pat. 14 Edw. III, pt. 1, m. 35.
[6] Pat. 13 Ric. II, pt. 2, m. 8.
[7] Pat. 11 Hen. IV, pt. 1, m. 21.
[8] Ibid. pt. 2, m. 5.   [9] Prynne, *Records*, iii, 707.
[10] Exch. K. R. Alien Priories, bdle. 10, No. 10.
[1] Edmund Martene, *Thesaurus Novus Anecdotorum* iii, 1874.

[2] Ibid. 1246.   [3] Ibid. 1247.
[4] Ibid. 1248.   [5] Ibid. 1767.   [6] Ibid. 1250.
[7] Ibid. 1251.   [8] Ibid. 1254.
[9] Fine R. 16 Edw. III, m. 28.
[10] Pat. 5 Ric. II, pt. 1, m. 21.
[11] Pat. 17 Hen. VI, pt. 1, m. 2.
[1] For these charters see *Cal. of Doc. France*, 483–491.   [2] Ibid. 487–8.

but was forced to submit to the abbot. The property of the priory consisted almost entirely of spiritualities, its temporalities being valued at only £1 0s. 6d. in the Taxation of 1291. In an extent [3] taken in 1324, the temporalities were valued at £5 5s. 4d., and the churches at £83 yearly.

The priory, being alien, was taken into the king's hands during the war with France, but in the reign of Edward III it was divided, the abbot of Langdon paying £40 yearly for the church of Chilham with the chapel of Molash, while the prior paid £32 yearly for the remainder.[4]

The abbot and convent of St. Bertin had licence in 1385 to grant the manors of Throwley, Chilham, and Molash to William de Hoo, knight, and his wife, brother and sister for their lives, these rendering £81 yearly at the Exchequer, performing all the works of charity established there, and paying tenths and other quota with the clergy.[5] In 1386 a commission was appointed to inquire about wastes committed in the priory and its possessions.[6]

The priory and its possessions came into the hands of Henry V by the Act of Dissolution passed in his reign; and he granted the manors, rectories or churches of Throwley, Chilham, and Molash to Thomas, duke of Exeter, and others, who on 13 July, 1424, granted them to the abbess and convent of Syon in Middlesex, the grant being confirmed by Henry VI in 1443.[7]

PRIORS OF THROWLEY

Peter, occurs 1297 [8]
Walter le Blok, occurs 1326 [9]
Giles de Ardenburgh, occurs 1356 [10]
Bartholomew, occurs 1370 [11]

---

[3] Carte Misc. (Aug. Off.), 8, No. 1.
[4] Close, 11 Edw. III, pt. 2, m. 37; 12 Edw. III, pt. 1, m. 20.

[5] Pat. 8 Ric. II, pt. 2, m. 1.
[6] Pat. 9 Ric. II, pt. 2, m. 18 d.
[7] Pat. 22 Hen. VI, pt. 1, m. 9.
[8] Prynne, Records, iii, 707.
[9] Exch. K.R. Alien Priories, bdle. 5, No. 4.
[10] Close, 30 Edw. III, m. 9 d.
[11] Exch. K.R. Alien Priories, bdle. 10, No. 10.

ADDENDA

75. HOSPITAL OF ST. MARY, CANTERBURY

In his list of hospitals in Kent, Mr. Arthur Hussey mentions the hospital of St. Mary at Canterbury, founded in 1317 by John Maynard or Mayner, called the Rich, for three brothers and four sisters. He endowed it with £3 7s. in rents in Canterbury and with six acres of wood in Fordwich. The hospital survives as almshouses.[1]

76. HOSPITAL OF ST. KATHERINE, ROCHESTER

The hospital of St. Katherine in the suburb of Eastgate was established under the will of Simon Potyn, living in the inn called the Crown, in the parish of St. Clement, dated Christmas, 1316. It was founded for men and women of Rochester suffering from leprosy or other disease that caused impotency and poverty. It was under the rule of the vicar of St. Nicholas, the heirs of Simon Potyn and John St. Denys, and the Bishop of Rochester, who were to appoint the prior.[2]

77. HOSPITAL OF ST. ANTHONY, SANDWICH

The leper hospital of St. Anthony upon Eche Wall is mentioned occasionally in wills from 1472 to 1496.[3]

78. HOSPITAL OF HOLY CROSS, SWAINESTREY, IN MURSTON

This hospital was probably founded in the 12th century by a member of the Murston family, lords of the manor of Murston. The earliest dated reference to it is in 1225, when the master received royal licence to hold a fair at the chapel of the Holy Cross of Swainestrey, on the vigil and day of the feast of the Invention of the Holy Cross. The hospital was endowed with several small parcels of land in Murston, Rodmersham, Sheppey, and elsewhere in the neighbourhood. The head of the house was the master or proctor, and the inmates are described as ministers or servants of the hospital. The chapel of Holy Cross seems to have been connected with the hospital but had a separate endowment. Master

Simon de Wenge, described as proctor of the hospital, is the only head of the house whose name has survived. The lands of the hospital were apparently acquired by William of Wykeham for the endowment of New College, Oxford.[4]

79. HOSPITAL OF ST. LEONARD, SWAINESTREY, IN MURSTON

Of this small hospital for lepers very little is known. It was endowed with a few acres of land in Bapchild, Swainestrey, and Murston, but must always have been very poor. In 1232 it received letters of protection and in the same year the king confirmed the various small grants previously made to it. This is the last reference to the hospital which has been found. It would seem probable that poverty overtook the house, and its possessions were apparently handed over to the hospital of Holy Cross (q.v.), when its use as a leper hospital diminished. In this way its lands eventually went to New College.

80. HOSPITAL OF ST. NICHOLAS BY THE WHITE DITCH, STROOD

Little is known of this leper hospital. It was in existence in 1253 when the lepers of St. Nicholas *de albo fossato* had a grant of protection.[5] In 1432 the wardenship was granted to Thomas Hikkes in place of George Berchwode.[6] Ten years later, Arnald Knight, falconer, a leper, and Gerardine his wife, had a grant for life of the hospital, he having built a house on the site of the hospital, which had been burnt.[7] Bequests were made to the hospital of White Ditch in 1493 and 1523.[8]

---

[4] The accounts of this and the following hospital are taken from a paper by Mr. Ralph Griffin, F.S.A. (*Arch. Cant.*, xxxiv, 63–78). Mr. Griffin suggests that the two formed one establishment, and that the hospital was dedicated to St. Leonard and was attached to the chapel of Holy Cross, but the deeds he quotes do not bear this out, for in them the hospital of Holy Cross is repeatedly referred to both before and after the date of the references to the hospital of St. Leonard.

[5] Pat. 37 Hen. III, m. 10.

[6] Duchy of Lanc. Misc. Bks., xviii, fol. 12d.

[7] Pat. 21 Hen. VI, pt. ii, m. 16.

[8] *Testamenta Cant.*, 12, 64. Mr. Arthur Hussey gives a short history of a leper hospital of St. Katherine of Strood (*Arch. Cant.*, xxix, 266) at White Ditch which had a chapel dedicated to St. Bartholomew. It is possible there may be some confusion between this house and that of St. Nicholas.

---

[1] *Arch. Cant.*, 'Hospitals in Kent,' by Arthur Hussey, xxix, 260.

[2] Ibid. citing S. Fisher, *Hist. of Rochester* (1772), 211–13, and *Testamenta Cant.*, West Kent, 61–4.

[3] *Testamenta Cant.*, East Kent, 294.

ADDITIONAL HEADS OF HOUSES

The following additional heads of religious houses have been discovered since the foregoing article was written :—

Higham Priory (p. 146) : Alice Heron, prioress, resigned 1489 (Pat. 4 Hen. VII, m. 12 (20)).

Malling Abbey (p. 148) : Joan Baude, late abbess in 1414, and Isabel Ruton occurs as abbess at same date (De Banco, Trin. 2 Hen. V, 354).

Sheppey Minster (p. 150): Joan Cobbeham, prioress, occurs 1435 (De Banco, Trin. 13 Hen. VI, 410).

Boxley Abbey (p. 155): William, abbot, occurs 1336 (Carte Misc. Bdle. 21, No. 242), and Robert in 1430 (Close, 9 Hen. VI, m. 19*d*).

Lesnes Abbey (p. 166) : Mark, abbot, occurs 1219 (Fines, Essex, 4 Hen. III).

Tonbridge Priory (p. 168) : D., prior, died in 1279 and John was elected (Worcs. Epis. Reg., Giffard, p. 107).

Langdon Abbey (p. 171) : Stephen, abbot, occurs 1358 (Exch. K.R. Acc., Bdle. 462, No. 19).

St. Radegund's Abbey (p. 174–5) : John de Retlyng, abbot, occurs 1354 (Exch. K.R. Acc., Bdle. 462, No. 17), and William in 1427, who is described as late abbot in 1437 (De. Banco, Trin. 15 Hen. VI, 128).

Swingfield Preceptory (p. 176) : Wuilherm Hulles, preceptor, occurs 1406 (Pat. 1 Hen. V, pt. 5, m. 29).

Mottenden Priory (p. 208) : John, minister, occurs 1452 (De Banco, East. 30 Hen. VI, 463).

St. James' Hospital, Canterbury (p. 210): Isabel, prioress, occurs 1437 (De Banco, Mich. 16 Hen. VI, 507).

St. Thomas' Hospital, Canterbury (p. 215) : John Neel, master, occurs 1437 (Pardon Roll, 15 Hen. VI, m. 24).

Chatham Hospital (p. 216) : Walter, prior, occurs 1414 (Exch. K.R. Acc., Bdle. 214, No. 5).

Milton Hospital (p. 222) : John Markhamstede, master, occurs 1414 (De Banco, Trin. 2 Hen. V, 339).

Ospringe Hospital (pp. 223–4): Ellis, son of Hervey, appointed master 1263. Roger Lindested described as late master 1263 (Pat. 47 Hen. III, pt. 1, m. 1); William Gamyn resigned 1413 and John Fakenham appointed (Pat. 1 Hen. V, pt. 4, m. 16), and John Fakenham described as dead in 1418 (Pat. 6 Hen. V, m. 11*d*); William Palmer appointed 1418 (ibid. m. 20) and resigned 1422 (Pat. 9 Hen. V, pt. 2, m. 8); James Jerkevylle appointed 1422 (ibid).

Hospital of Strood (p. 228) : John Blundell, master, occurs 1316 (Registrum Roffense, 113).

Wingham College (p. 234): Mathew Assheton, provost, occurs 1414 (Pat. 2 Hen. V, pt. 2, m. 28*d*).

MARITIME HISTORY
(to 1688)

THAT Kent always has been, and in some respects must remain, the most important county in England militarily is due to its position in regard to the continent, the North Sea, and the English Channel, and, in particular, to the existence of the arsenals in the Thames and Medway. Directly fronting the continent, for good or ill, in friendship or enmity, linked historically as well as geologically with the north-eastern coast of France, the highway to the capital, and offering the shortest sea passage to an invader, it furnished, in early centuries, the most tempting objective to any central European enemy. The dockyards, factories of Empire in themselves, and no small element in the military and political importance of the county, are also a source of danger to it as inciting an enemy to raids even if he has no hope of success in invasion. The command of the Straits of Dover and the adjacent waters was formerly necessary to prevent invasion, and is now indispensable to national existence. The retention of that command was assisted by the situation of the Kentish naval bases in relation to the continent, occupying, as they do, an interior position to a large extent of continental coast and thus enabling fleets concentrated at them to strike swiftly at a chosen point while an enemy must be prepared to receive the attack everywhere over a large segment of a circle. On the other hand, such bases are only valuable while menacing during peace, or actual founts of offence during war; experience shows that naval bases which for any reason, temporary or permanent, cannot be used offensively are sources of weakness to their possessors.

The situation and physical features which have given Kent its historical weight through the centuries also render it vulnerable to attack if the English Navy be defeated. The estuaries of the Thames and Medway, the East Swale, and in early times the Wantsum, while favourable to commerce and maritime occupations generally, all afforded easy entrance into the county, and the Isles of Grain, Sheppey, and Thanet were natural points of advantage for an invader preparing for a further advance. Ports like Sandwich and Dover, especially Sandwich, were, if they fell into an enemy's hands, sufficiently capacious to serve as bases for mediaeval fleets; besides ports and estuaries there are many spots on the coast of Kent where a landing on the beach is possible. In more recent times, when the speediest possible sea passage was the essence of the French plan of invasion, and when the power of the British Navy rendered impracticable a formal attack from the sea on Dover, or in the Thames and Medway, while that Navy was undefeated, this beach landing became the equivalent of the mediaeval attacks on ports. Threatened during the last quarter of the 18th century, it was considered an imminent possibility between 1798 and 1805; in those years the flat shore east and west of Dungeness was the pivot on which the fortunes of empires were balanced. A beach landing, however, requires many favourable conditions, some of which are altogether absent at Dungeness and in its neighbourhood.   For Napoleon it was, even if possible, a counsel of desperation at the best, but the conditions of modern maritime war now practically preclude such an attempt by a properly equipped force of any strength.

External to the cliffs and beaches of Kent are the sands which, directly or indirectly, belt two-thirds of it and have had an important influence on local and national history.   Those at the mouth of the Thames and along the north coast of the county have, in view of the danger attending their navigation, checked by their presence the tendency to attack along that portion of the shore they cover; the Downs were not only a refuge for merchantmen but formed a strategical centre from which, under favourable circumstances, war fleets could command the North Sea and English Channel.   Ashore, Dover, with its castle, discharged functions in land war corresponding to those which the Downs enacted at sea; commanding the road to London, and flanking the movements of an enemy who landed on either side of it, any force there must be destroyed or contained before an invader can move forward. In early centuries the Andredes Weald was practically impassable for an army, therefore an invader was compelled to move northwards along the Watling Street.   For naval war the new harbour at Dover will, if successful, take the place of the Downs, which have become useless since the introduction of the torpedo, but Dover itself retains all its importance in military operations on land.

The frequent communication which, we know, existed before the Roman era between Britain and Gaul necessarily involved the employment of something approaching the type of a sea-going vessel, and there is no reason to suppose that all such belonged to the Gallic side.   Recent ethnological research suggests that the Pechts (Picts) of the North of Scotland, akin to the Pictones of the Gallic coast south of the Loire, were a seafaring piratical race at least two centuries before the arrival of the Romans.   Certainly whatever progress in ship construction had been made in Britain would have attained its highest development in the south-east, both because all maritime traffic of consequence must have been concentrated in that quarter and because communication with the continent must have led to the adoption of improvements.   The maritime importance of Kent stands out so pre-eminently during the Roman era that we may infer a relative, if obscurer, importance before the appearance of the Romans, for the historical consequence of the county has always been connected with situation and natural features rather than with men.

Within the historic period the naval history of England and of Kent commences with *Classis Britannica*, the Romano-British division of the Roman fleets, which had its headquarters at Gessoriacum (Boulogne).   And with *Classis Britannica* begins that Dover Patrol which for nearly 1,900 years, through good and ill-fortune, has held the Channel Gate until its history culminated, and perhaps terminated, in the glory of Zeebrugge.[1]

The Saxon pirates were making their presence felt in the North Sea and the Channel a century and a half before the departure of the Romans; as seamen, although not equal to the Northmen, they were skilful and daring

[1] There is a still earlier naval history of the neolithic and bronze ages of which archæologists are slowly gathering the scanty indications.   In the future these will probably cause the present versions of the origin and development of shipping to be re-written.

enough to be terrible to the Romanized provincial, and no unequal match at sea for Roman officers themselves. The landing of the Jutes under Hengist at Ebbsfleet, in the Wantsum, implies previous local knowledge gained at the expense of the Britons, for the space between the North Foreland and Dover was no doubt as favourite a cruising ground then as it continued to be until the 19th century. Experience shows that a river, or arm of the sea, while useful as affording the assailants temporary shelter and choice of time and place of attack, gives no real protection to the side which holds itself on the defensive. In this case, also, the vessels at the command of the Jutes furnished a decisive advantage, so that when they and the Britons eventually fought the Wantsum formed no barrier to their advance into the mainland. Thenceforward, until the appearance of the Northmen, Kent is only connected with the history of the period by military and political events occurring by land.

During the last quarter of the 8th century the northern pirates had appeared along the coastline of Charlemagne's empire, and it was probably a party of these marauders who landed in Dorset in 787. Other raids fell upon Northumbria before the close of the century, but then England had a respite of more than thirty years until in or about 835 a force ravaged Sheppey. England was now between two fires, being attacked in the west by the North-men from Ireland, and in the east by those who came from the Frankish coast or direct from the Baltic. No attempt is known to have been made to meet them at sea, which is significant of their recognized superiority, and perhaps of English degeneration in sea affairs. Probably the West Saxons, who had attained supremacy on land, and on whose tenacity now depended the success or failure of the resistance to conquest, had never been the leading maritime race among the conquerors of Roman Britain; when, during the 9th and 10th centuries, we read of any effort made by sea it seems to be the Jutes and Engles —Kent and the east coast—who take the lead. But as an island kingdom can only retain its independence in virtue of its ability to repel its assailants by sea, the final result of the Northern invasions was certain if the new enemy were sufficiently advanced in political and military organization.

Between 835 and 841 the pirates visited continuously the coasts of Flanders and Normandy; in the last year they crossed the Channel and, after raiding East Anglia, fell upon Kent, where in 842 they sailed up the Medway and plundered Rochester. In 851 came an attack upon Sandwich, where the Northmen were repulsed with the loss of nine ships, but that Sandwich should have been selected is evidence of its prosperity. According to the ' English Chronicle' this body wintered in Thanet, which shows that the Stour was still an effective water-way, but in 853 they or another band were attacked in their stronghold by the English. In 855 a force wintered in Sheppey, a still stronger position. The Danes left when it suited them, and then there was a pause of some years while the Vikings were occupied in wasting Northern France. In 865 the Danes, who were now in the forefront of the attack, entrenched them-selves in Thanet, and this force was the forerunner of the ' Great Army' of the following year which set about the conquest of England. We have only to notice here that the men of Kent were cowed and, far from fighting the raiders of 865 at sea, did not even attempt to fight them on land but tried to buy them off. Between 866 and the Peace of Wedmore in 878 the Danes were con-tinuously reinforced from oversea, and probably many of these detachments raided Kent, especially when the position of the main army made the Thames a line of communication; but the chief events of these years occurred in central England. For the Northmen, as for the Saxons, Kent and its water-ways had been the gate of entrance into England.[2]

The twelve years' struggle here had not resulted in complete conquest and the Vikings passed to the continent for six years. There was now more fighting than plunder in France, so that in 884 a force crossed over from the mouth of the Somme to the Medway and besieged Rochester from which Alfred repulsed them. The year is noteworthy for the first explicit mention of Kentish ships. Guthrum's men of the Danelagh gave help to their kindred before Rochester; when these had fled Alfred sent a fleet from Kent to East Anglia to punish Guthrum's Danes. The squadron fell in with sixteen pirate ships off the mouth of the Stour and captured them, but in coming home met a large Danish fleet and was in turn defeated. It is evident, however, that both heredity and the stimulus of geographical position had combined to preserve some of the Jutish aptitude for the sea, for the Kentish sailors must for centuries have worked most of such communication as was carried on with the continent other than that direct from London. We have no means of deciding when the Kentish men first joined in the North Sea herring fishery, but if, as is probable, it was in the 10th century, or even earlier, they must have had long years of previous experience off their own coast to embolden them to their wider flight. In any case their North Sea experiences made them the hardiest and most daring seamen of the south coast, while the profits from the fishery enriched the towns and increased their importance yearly. Whensoever it may have begun, it was perhaps in this common meeting of men from the Kent and Sussex ports at Yarmouth on what was to them a foreign shore, with the sense of unity thus forced upon them, that was first evolved the consciousness of the advantage of joint action, which afterwards took form as the confederacy of the Cinque Ports. This feeling would be greatly strengthened in the case of Kent by the welding effect of the Danish incursions which fell upon the county far more than upon Sussex; the tendency of the ports to help each other militarily, besides being a common interest and a national duty, would be intensified by their mutual friendship and recognition of benefits gained from united action against their competitors in the North Sea fishery.

Civil war in Norway drove out the defeated to join their countrymen fighting in western Christendom; these last were finding Germans and Franks no such easy prey as they had been in former years. Strengthened by the new arrivals from Norway, and disheartened by defeat in Flanders, an army of Northmen crossed in 250 ships to the landing-place under Lympne, and eventually entrenched themselves at Appledore, while another division, in 80 vessels, entered the Swale and occupied Milton. They soon left the water, abandoning Milton and Appledore, and the subsequent campaigns extended through five years, but the fighting was outside Kent. The conquest and settlement of Normandy by Hrolf then attracted the Danes abroad, and England was relinquished to minor struggles with those of the Danelagh. There is an

[2] Sir James Ramsay (*Foundations of England*, i, 230) considers that the Danish line of approach, whether the objective was the south or east coast, was by navigation along the continental shore until the raiders were opposite the coast of Kent. In this case Kent would receive many minor attacks, by the way, as it were. Sir James Ramsay thinks that the Norsemen, steering for Ireland or the west coast of England, went north.

obscure statement, under 911, in the 'English Chronicle,' which may mean that 100 ships were collected in a Kentish port, and if so the county without doubt supplied its share. There is little of maritime interest to note before the renewal of the Danish raids in 980 beyond the ravaging of Thanet in 968, by order of Edgar, perhaps as a punishment for the practice of wrecking.[2a] If this be correct it implies a customary traffic by sea large enough to provide a considerable proportion of wrecks. William of Malmesbury describes Edgar as cruising with eastern and western fleets which, if true, would indicate an extraordinary revival of English naval energy, but William wrote in the reign of Henry I, and his division of the fleets bears a suspicious resemblance to that which came into practice during his lifetime.

In 980 the Danes appeared again, and Thanet, among other districts, was swept by them. About 991 Olaf Trygvason, whose squadron had been long in English waters, landed and ravaged both at Folkestone and Sandwich; in 994 he joined Swein, King of Denmark, who entered the Thames with a fleet. When they left the river it was to sail down Channel, and the Kentish coast suffered from their passage. The alliance between Swein and Olaf was broken, and they departed, but new bands of pirates took their place, although the turn of Kent did not come again until 999 when they went up the Medway to Rochester. King and Witan decreed the levy of a fleet and an army, but no result followed, and the inaction of the fleet was attributed to jealousies and delays of the army leaders. Swein, now bent on the conquest of England, appeared again in 1003 but did not come in force to Kent until 1006 when he attacked Sandwich. It was quite certain that if the English had not produced ships nor seamen good enough to meet the Northmen in the preceding centuries no artificial effort would provide them now. The attempt, however, was to be made; in 1008 it was determined that every 310 hides of land was to supply a ship, and the resulting fleet was to be ready every year after Easter.[3] In 1009 the first fleet under this law, larger than any that had ever before been seen in England, was collected at Sandwich, where it was to lie ready for movement, ' but we had not the good fortune nor the worthiness that the ship force could be of any use to this land any more than it oft had before been.' It was not the first, nor was it to be the last time, that a machine-made navy betrayed the hopes of its creators. Ethelred himself was at Sandwich, and on his departure the fleet, disheartened by several disasters which had happened, sailed round to the Thames; with an effective irony its place at Sandwich was taken by the Danes who harried Kent. In 1010, and for several following years, a force was encamped at Greenwich; their ships must have been able to stop all traffic in the river.

Swein, with his fleet, came to Sandwich in 1013; the frequent use of the harbour, both by the English and by their enemies, points to an established reputation and, in fact, all through the mediaeval period it was a far more valuable port than Dover.[4] Cnut took up the task of his father, Swein, and he also brought his fleet to Sandwich in 1014 and 1015. The town cannot have been destroyed year after year if it proved useful as a Danish base; if not destroyed it would have grown in prosperity with perhaps an infiltration of

---

[2a] Green, *Conquest of Engl.*, 350.

[3] *Anglo-Sax. Chron.* (Rolls Ser.), i, 259; ii, 114; Thorpe, *Ancient Laws*, i, 310.

[4] At this time most of the passenger traffic went through the Sussex ports.

Danish settlers to quicken Saxon maritime enterprise. The *Encomium Emmae* calls it 'the most famous of all the English ports.' In 1029 Cnut granted, or restored, to Christchurch, Canterbury, certain dues of Sandwich haven and such wreck as might be thrown up on the strand, so that, clearly, the Danish visits had not ruined the town. The North Sea herring fishery was certainly now pursued regularly from Sandwich, for Harold (1035–40) retained, we are told, the profits of the town to himself, 'wellnigh two herring seasons.' Of Dover we hear less, but its situation must always have rendered it a frequent port of transit to the continent, although its harbour was not so well fitted as that of Sandwich to receive fleets. Rochester may have had some trade, but such places as Hythe and Romney must have been entirely occupied in the fishery.

The Danish conquest brought England a long peace. About 1045 danger threatened from Magnus of Norway, therefore a fleet of such strength 'that no man had seen a greater' was collected at Sandwich. Shortly afterwards the town was raided by northern pirates, who then went to Thanet where they were routed. The days were past when a small raiding party could work its will along the coast; after the initial advantage of surprise had been used and lost the pirates were no match for the strength, born of unity, now brought to bear upon them. Besides the concord due to the fishery and identical interests of self-preservation, the Kentish and Sussex ports were now subject to another agency acting in the same direction in the influence of Earl Godwin, their powerful over-lord, as earl of Wessex. If it was Godwin's aim to obtain the throne for his own family, supremacy could only be attained by annexing for himself or his kindred all that was most useful for taxable or militant purposes. As one step towards his object he made himself loved by the seamen, and so far as possible obtained a hold on the coast towns even where, as at Folkestone, it had to be done by fraud.[5] The sailors of Kent and Sussex were the best in his earldom, their shipping the most important along the south coast, and the ports themselves inherently valuable by reason of their situation. Domesday tells us that Dover and Sandwich were both required by the Confessor to provide 20 ships, with 20 men in each, for 15 days' service once a year in return for endowment with rights of sac and soc; for Romney a similar 'service at sea' is alluded to, and the Confessor's charter to Hythe is referred to in that granted by John in 1205. It was essential for Godwin's object that he should be able to rely on the maritime assistance of these ports and on the affection of the men who dwelt in them; subsequent events showed that he succeeded in his design.

It is evident that before the Conquest, and perhaps for long after it, there was no perfected system, either of duties or privileges, among the ports, but it is possible that in the reign of Edward the first decided movement towards confederacy was due to the policy of Godwin. The bond of union was their duty to the same over-lord, intensified by the fact that Godwin was the chief and representative of the national party opposing the Norman intruders. If the earl first drew together the threads which were afterwards to unite the ports into a confederation, he must have found that a like situation and like interests among them

5 Pearson, *Early and Middle Ages*, i, 240.

—their common interests on the North Sea and at Yarmouth—rendered his work easy, and, in fact, only hastened a progressing process. The geographical situation of the ports, from the North Foreland to Beachy Head, was one which rendered all of them almost equally liable to attack from three out of the four quarters of the compass, and the same conditions that had enforced the fortification of the Littus Saxonicum ashore and its defence at sea were reproduced then and have been reproduced to the present day. The first weight of any assault from seaward was most likely to fall upon them, and the incessant Danish attacks would have speedily taught the Kentish ports the advantages of united action when that was possible, while, as between Kent and Sussex there was, besides the common motive of defence, a common commercial interest in the North Sea fishery drawing them together. It was a necessity for continued existence that the Kent and Sussex ports should hold their own coasts and territorial waters; it was almost as necessary, and was certainly to their profit, that they should have the command of all that portion of the Channel fronting them. To do either was out of the power of any one or two ports, but not out of the power of a group when they had learned, or been taught, the wisdom of combination. The motive for association, therefore, came from within and was the product of centuries of stern experience; the deciding impulse may have come from without, and of the two men, Edward and Godwin, whose political position rendered them able to lay the foundation of co-ordinate action, only the latter showed political capacity in his career, while his personal interests coincided with an innovation of national utility. In the 'English Chronicle,' under the year 1046, we find Godwin sailing from Sandwich with two of the 'king's ships,' and 42 'people's ships';[6] it is the first occurrence of such a phrase, and, happening where and when it does, may well be the first indication known to us of the new coalition.

If it be asked whether Edward would have been willing to assist in the consolidation of Godwin's power the answer is that, throughout the reign, the earl made ' a dexterous use of Edward for the succession of the house of Godwin to the throne,'[7] and that he was no more likely to find any difficulty in employing the king to help forward his views in connexion with the ports than he found in other affairs. That these chartered ports looked to Godwin rather than to the king is shown clearly by the events of 1052. In 1051 the earl fled the kingdom temporarily, his immediate difficulties having arisen from his refusal to punish ' his own people ' of Dover.[8] He took refuge in Flanders, and while he was there seamen from Kent and Sussex either went over to serve him or sent word that they would ' live and die with him.' His sons, Harold and Leofwin, had gone to Ireland, but in September 1052 they met their father off Portland. Both fleets moved eastward, and it is significant that in Hampshire, Dorset, and Sheppey Godwin and Harold plundered and burnt as in an enemy's country, while in the intervening district—practically that of the Cinque Ports—they were received, and behaved, as friends and were joined by sailors and ships from Romney, Hythe, Folkestone, and elsewhere.

---

[6] ' Landes manna Scipa,' translated as ' ships of the country people ' in *Anglo-Sax. Chron.* (Rolls Ser.), ii, 139.

[7] Green, *Conquest of Engl.*, 499.

[8] *Anglo-Sax. Chron.* (Rolls Ser.), i, 315 ; ii, 144.

In 1053 Harold succeeded Godwin as earl of Wessex and also in the affections of the Kentish men, as was shown in 1066 when the Sandwich sailor Tostig, impressed during his raid on the south coast, deserted as soon as possible. For the fleet collected to intercept William of Normandy the port of concentration was Sandwich, but the circumstances of its inaction and dispersal belong rather to the history of Sussex.[9] Part of the Conqueror's fleet is said to have put into Sandwich.[10] After the battle of Hastings William marched straight on Dover, valuable in his eyes as a fortified base for his advance, or at the worst to secure his retreat and perhaps still leave him a foothold in England. Even after Senlac the ultimate issue of the campaign must have appeared doubtful to him, but the possession of Dover would enable him to renew his attempt at any time, and, in the interval, to interfere in English politics. He passed by Romney and destroyed it in revenge for the slaughter of some of his troops who had landed there by necessity or mistake. As the chronicler tells us that there had been great loss on both sides, Romney must have been a flourishing and relatively populous place.[11]

William committed Kent to the charge of his brother Odo, bishop of Bayeux, whose tyranny goaded the people of Dover and the neighbourhood to invite Eustace, count of Boulogne, to make an attempt on the castle. Eustace was repulsed by the garrison, but we see that neither Dover nor Romney had much reason to love the Conqueror. Yet the policy of the crown and the self-interest of the portsmen outweighed ill-will due to the feudal tyranny of inferiors, and the Conquest was the deciding factor which made the development of the Cinque Ports certain and rapid. For nearly a century and a half the English Channel no longer separated powers more or less hostile, but was a sea-road uniting territories subject to the same sovereign. From the point of view of domestic policy it was to the advantage of the king to have, in what was the strategic centre of the Channel at that date, subjects on whom he could rely either for a quick and sure passage between England and his continental dominions, or for a speedy concentration of ships and trained seamen in the event of revolt or other urgent necessity. It was, further, the king's aim so to bind to himself by grants of favours and privileges the people holding the gate opening on the vital centre of his new kingdom that they could be relied on not only to refuse to join an enemy but also to repulse him. Thus we find both military reasons and motives of State policy for the charters granted by William and his sons [12] which established the position of the ports and conduced to a closer union between them. On their side, the men of the Kent and Sussex ports bore no such rancorous hatred to the Norman kings as would impel them to refuse services, which they had been accustomed to render before the Conquest, when the reward enabled them to escape all that was most galling in the new institutions. There may also have been an immigration of Norman settlers into some of the ports, especially Dover. Therefore the circumstances in which these ports were placed after the Conquest fostered a continuous growth in wealth and strength. Their privileges gave them commercial

[9] *V.C.H. Sussex*, ii, 128.
[10] Knighton, *Chron.* (Rolls ed.), i, 54.
[11] *Ord. Vitalis*, Bk. III, cap. xiv.
[12] A Roman maritime *colonia*, e.g. Terracina (Anxur), owed much the same duty to the State as the chartered ports to the English crown, and, like them, was exempt from military service on land. Probably it was a case of recurring conditions producing recurring results rather than of imitation.

advantages which, used profitably, resulted in an increase of men and ships, the instruments of maritime power; their strategical position for war was more potent than it had ever been, now that the central region of the north coast of France was ruled by the same monarch, for, with doubled strength, they and the Normans could close the sea passage of communication between north and south Europe and dominate the hither portion of the North Sea.

In 1069 William was taught the inconvenience of the want of a fleet by his inability to attack a Danish force lying in the Humber after it had been driven off from Dover and Sandwich. By 1071 the deficiency was remedied, and in this and the following year the Cinque Ports no doubt contributed effectively to squadrons acting in Scotch waters. Between the last threat of an invasion from the Baltic, in 1083, and the loss of Normandy in 1204, there were few occasions for great maritime levies, but the Kentish ports must have been required to assist in the squadrons raised to take part in the desultory dynastic wars of the period and to provide for the passage of the sovereign and his troops between England and Normandy. Those demands cannot have overtaxed their resources; the strain began with the appearance of France on the Channel coast, and was intensified when the wars of expansion, initiated by Edward I and continued by Edward III, were carried on. The fact that charters were granted by the Conqueror and his sons is sufficient to prove that the Ports gave services in return; there is one indication of their prosperity in the ability of those of both Kent and Sussex to furnish a contingent of ships and men for the crusading fleet of 1147, which took Lisbon from the Moors and founded the kingdom of Portugal. The Kentish division was under the command of Simon of Dover. The prosperity of Dover was largely owing to its privileges when, later, it became the principal passage port for the continent; in 1229 it supplied twenty-one ships out of the Cinque Ports 'service' of fifty-seven, Romney, Hythe, and Sandwich sending five each, and the three Sussex ports twenty-one. For the crusade of Richard I, in 1190, Sir James Ramsay remarks that the Cinque Ports squadron of thirty-three vessels was 'practically the whole English contingent' in the fleet of about a hundred ships. But as these ships were paid by the year the chartering must have been independent of the 'service.'

In 1202 the Cinque Ports ships were sent to sea against the French,[13] and in 1205 we have the series of charters confirming their privileges which bore evident relation to the efforts expected of them after the loss of Normandy. In the same year there is a list of fifty-one galleys belonging to the crown[14], of which three were at Sandwich, four at Romney, and two at 'Neuweiheia,' probably New Hythe.[15] In March 1208 the bailiffs of the principal English ports were directed to cause the ships belonging to their towns to return to England in time to join the king's fleets during the summer;[16] the Cinque Ports were, as well, to select their best men to serve in the king's galleys. This is not the only instance of men to serve in the royal fleets being demanded from the Ports, although the requisition was not textually authorized by their charters even if the 'service,' either in part or wholly, was not in commission at the

[13] Pat. 4 John, m. 12.
[14] Close, 6 John, m. 10.
[15] Cf. Admir. Ct. Libels, xxxvii, 245.
[16] Pat. 9 John, m. 2.

moment. In 1213 a great fleet, said to be of 500 sail,[17] was collected at Dover and subsequently crossed the North Sea to win, on 30 May, the victory of Damme, which destroyed the French fleet collected for invasion. Here, the Cinque Ports 'service' did not at most form more than a tenth of the total number, and probably much less than a tenth of the tonnage. Earlier in the same year a smaller force, probably made up entirely of Cinque Ports ships, had burnt Dieppe and destroyed shipping collected in the Seine, thus delaying French preparations. It must be remembered that, although the deeds of the Cinque Ports show up bravely for two centuries, their exploits were usually performed within a limited area and under special conditions; when royal fleets were constituted on a large scale for important operations they were made up of levies drawn from the whole of the English coast. The particular value to the crown of the Cinque Ports aid was, that although the Portsmen were entitled by prescription to a warning of forty days when the full number of fifty-seven ships was required, probably for some urgent object, a small squadron could always be relied upon at a few days' notice. When large fleets were collected the Sussex and Kent ships formed only an inconsiderable portion of the whole. An order of November 1214[18] directed that a list of all ships of 80 tons and upwards, belonging to the ports throughout England, should be sent to the king by Christmas; so far as the Cinque Ports were concerned this standard of size points to a fact of which we shall meet other evidence, namely, that although the ships they were bound by their charters to supply for the 'service' were very small, most of them possessed others much larger.[19] But if, which was usual, the Cinque Ports only sent vessels of the size that had been required before the Conquest, while ships, generally, were steadily increasing in tonnage, the value of their squadron, as a component part of large fleets, decreased yearly although still useful enough for minor operations.[20]

After signing Magna Charta in 1215 John visited Dover and Sandwich, among other places, for the purpose, it is said, of assuring himself of the assistance of the Portsmen in his effort to free himself. Some time in this year Folkestone was assailed by Eustace the Monk, who had until recently been in John's service but had gone over to the French. The king's attempt to enlist the sympathy of the Kentish ports could not have been successful, although he offered them especial rewards to return to their allegiance,[21] for in 1216 French vessels swarmed in the Straits of Dover and no resistance was made to the passage of Prince Louis of France, who landed at Stonar on 21 May 1216. Louis left England under a truce which continued during the early months of 1217. He returned on 22 April with a considerable force, when, his landing at Sandwich having been resisted, he is said to have burnt the town. Except Dover Castle, which was held by Hubert de Burgh, south-eastern England fell easily under the sway of Louis, who had lost no time in besieging the castle in 1216. After an investment of four months he was compelled to raise the siege, and his failure led to

[17] Roger Wendover, *Flores Hist.* (Rolls Ser.), ii, 79.

[18] Close, 16 John, m. 16.

[19] In 1212 there were two Hythe ships of 100 and 120 tons

(Close, 14 John, m. 6). Probably the town possessed considerable shipping at this date; in 1215 Simon Grim obtained a licence to sell his ship to a foreigner (Pat. 17 John, m. 24).

[20] In Domesday the crew of each of the Dover ships is stated as 20 men; the number was seldom exceeded, at any later time, when the full service was required.

[21] Pat. 18 John, m. 3.

the total overthrow, a year later, of any possibility of success that he might have had.

In August 1217 Eustace the Monk left Calais, intending to make the Thames, with nearly a hundred vessels conveying reinforcements for Louis. He was seen from Dover, where Hubert de Burgh was still in command, and after some hesitation about forty English ships put out after him. They must have been all, or nearly all, Dover vessels and manned by Dover men; the French were caught off the North Foreland and the resulting sea fight is the first one in English naval history in which English seamen are known to have manœuvred for position in such a way as to bring superior force to bear on a portion of the enemy's fleet. It is not without significance that the men who did this were the Portsmen, who must at that time have been the only seamen in England accustomed to work in some sort of combination and orderly co-operation. The French were completely defeated and the immediate effect of the battle was that Louis was compelled to accept terms and leave England.

The naval history of the reign of Henry III is not important, but the services of the Cinque Ports were in continual request for secondary duties. More than once the Ports as a whole were required to find crews for the king's ships,[22] but during this reign, and later, the Sussex division seems to have been of more use to the crown than that of Kent. The patriotism of the Ports did not go unrewarded either in praise or in more material recompense; early in the reign Henry thanked them for their services, and added that he was sending two of his servants to examine the plunder lately taken, secure their share according to their rights, and receive that to which he was himself entitled.[23] But of course it was always difficult to restrain a nearly irregular force such as that of the Ports; complaints of their piratical proceedings were frequent, and in 1220 all but Rye and Hythe were called upon to answer for depredations.[24] In 1224 war was threatening and the barons of the Ports were ordered to fit out a squadron for the defence of the Channel Islands, to remain there between July and September.[25] Various other measures were taken but no maritime action followed. In 1227 the king again proposed active proceedings and was profuse in his expressions of reliance on the loyalty and energy of the Ports; another attempt and failure occurred in 1229, but in 1230 Henry did actually reach Brittany although he did nothing there. This uneasy state of semi-war must have been delightful to the Portsmen; in 1235 there is a notice of the plundering of French ships, notwithstanding letters of safe conduct which were forcibly taken from the crews, who were sometimes 'violently thrown out.'[26] In this instance the offenders were Winchelsea men, but it is quite safe to reason from the Sussex to the Kentish ports.[27] The king had a navy of his own although history seldom records any use made of it. In 1235 we have the stations of eighteen of the king's ships, of which three were at Romney and two at Yantlett Creek; in 1242 three were being built for him in some of the Cinque Ports, and in 1244 there were others at Romney and Sandwich. The Portsmen were impartial; an order of 1246 forbade them to sell ships or ship timber to any

[22] Pat. 10 Hen. III, m. 5; ibid. 17 Hen. III, m. 1; Close, 10 Hen. III, m. 16.

[23] Pat. 1 Hen. III, m. 4.

[24] Close, 5 Hen. III, m. 18d.

[25] Pat. 8 Hen. III, m. 6.

[26] Pat. 19 Hen. III, m. 11.

[27] Ibid. 20 Hen. III, m. 6.

French subject,[28] but there had been, from 1189, a general order for the whole country to the same effect.

The Cinque Ports were carrying on a war with the Bayonnais on their own account, and it was probably in relation to this that in April 1237 each of the head ports was directed to send representatives to the king, who negotiated a peace between the combatants.[29] In 1235 and 1253 delegates from the Ports met for the discussion of naval affairs, but in each case Winchelsea took the lead; in 1235 six came from Hastings, eighteen from Winchelsea, and twelve from each of the other head ports.[30] During this century writs to the Kentish Cinque Ports seem to be synonymous with writs to Kent, no other but the head ports being usually addressed in the county. In 1226 an order not to allow any vessels to sail to French ports is directed to Faversham,[31] but in 1229 Faversham is given as a member of Dover, the others being Folkestone and Margate. The members of Sandwich were Fordwich, Reculver, Sarre, Stonar, and Deal; of Hythe, West Hythe, and of Romney, Broomhill, Lydd, Dengemarsh, Old Romney, and Oswaldstone. Thus, except the Medway and the south bank of the Thames, practically the whole of seafaring Kent was included, directly or indirectly, within the Cinque Ports, and such places as Gravesend and Greenwich are not mentioned until the fourteenth century.

In 1242 the Ports were let loose to ravage the French coast with order to spare only the churches; a fifth of the spoil, 'which ye know belongs unto us,' was to be reserved for the king, and they were especially warned to behave discreetly towards the Bayonnais.[32] For this war there was an arrest in the Ports of all ships capable of carrying sixteen or more horses, which shows that there must have been vessels available of far greater size than those required for the ' service ' under charter.[33] The Portsmen bettered their instructions, ' cruelly exceeding the limits prescribed by the king,' and robbing and killing English as well as French.[34] At last the whole of the French coast, from La Rochelle to Calais, was, in modern phrase, mobilized against them, and after suffering several defeats they were driven, powerless, to shelter within their harbours. A truce with France in 1243 relieved the situation for them. In 1255 Henry landed at Dover, when the inhabitants presented him with some jewels, but their then loyalty did not prevent the Cinque Ports as a whole joining Simon de Montfort during the Barons' Wars. Sandwich stood by Montfort all through; Dover changed hands several times, but the Ports found their profit in piracy, whoever was supreme, and were sufficiently important to be excommunicated with the city of London and the principal barons in 1264. Their assistance, however, had very little influence on the rise of Montfort and can have but little deferred his fall ; but nearly every contemporary writer notices with horror the bloodthirsty and systematic murder and robbery which characterized their action at sea.[35]

---

[28] Close, 19 Hen. III, m. 19*d ;* 26 Hen. III, pt. 2, m. 5 ; 28 Hen. III, m. 12 ; 30 Hen. III, m. 11.

[29] Ibid. 21 Hen. III, m. 9; Rymer, *Fœdera*, i, 373.

[30] Close, 19 Hen. III, m. 20*d.*

[31] Ibid. 10 Hen. III, m. 27*d.*

[32] Rymer, *Fœdera*, i, 406.

[33] Pat. 26 Hen. III, m. 11.

[34] M. Paris, *Chron. Maj.* (Rolls Sec.), iv, 208.

[35] ' Depredantes omnes . . . homines crudeliter ejecerunt in mare, nulli parcentes, tam anglicos quam alienigenas ' (Liber de Ant. Legibus, *Cronica Maiorum* [Camd. Soc.], 73.) It was the same story as in 1242-3. It may be noticed, however, that to throw prisoners overboard was in accordance with recognized international maritime law—or customs—and was defended as a lawful proceed-ing as late as 1603 by the Archduke Albert. Reprisals by Prince Maurice softened the Archduke's practice, but there is no doubt that he was right legally. The custom was very ancient, and probably had its origin in the difficulty of keeping prisoners in subjection in the confined spaces of galleys or mediæval ships. Had it been possible it would have been much more profitable to sell prisoners as slaves, or

After the battle of Lewes, when the queen and the exiled foreign favourites were collecting forces at Damme for an invasion, the Cinque Ports were asked by de Montfort to patrol the Straits vigorously, and it requires little imagination to picture the methods of their vigour. Within what a narrow area the movements of oversea trade were then confined is shown by the fact that their cruising stopped the transit of merchandise to such an extent that the prices of many commodities rose considerably. No doubt commerce would have adjusted itself to the new conditions had they continued, but this immediate result of an intensive outbreak explains how profitable the normal condition of subacute piracy must have been. In 1265 Prince Edward received the Ports into the king's grace, confirming their liberties and forgiving all homicides and depredations; the pardon was needed, for before this a Cinque Ports expedition had burnt Portsmouth which was royalist.

A feature of the maritime history of the 13th century is the appointment of one or more persons, sometimes for a single county and sometimes for a group of counties, as keepers of the coast, a step towards the organization of systematic defence. As the Warden of the Ports was in control in east and south Kent and in part of Sussex the keepers had little authority in these counties, but they should be mentioned here seeing that, historically, they were the ancestors of the conservators of truces instituted locally by Henry V and of the later vice-admirals of the counties established by Henry VIII. The duties of the keepers were both military and judicial in guarding the coast from attack and the prevention and punishment of crime at sea; possibly much of the licence affected now and later by the Cinque Ports was due to the fact that the only direct restraint, nominal and ineffective, to which they were subject was that of the Warden, and that they escaped the government of the king's keepers and often of his admirals. In 1234 the king nominated two of his officers to have the care of the coast of Kent and of an extensive region on either side, but it was to be with the advice and assistance of the barons of the Ports.[36] As might have been expected, there are fewer especial keepers for Kent than for any other county, although these officers were sometimes associated with the Warden.[37] A part of the system of defence under the care of the keeper, or under the Warden, was the line of beacons, corresponding to the modern coastguard stations, which encircled the coast. They were usually placed on the hills nearest to the shore and in war time were guarded by a watch from the neighbouring parishes.[38] South of the North Foreland, with the Cinque Ports ships always more or less at sea, surprise by the French was less likely than elsewhere. To the north, the one at Sheppey, answering to that at Shoeburyness, was the most important; there were others at Cliffe and Gravesend, and the watchers on seeing an enemy were, besides lighting the beacons, to make a loud noise ' de corn et de cri.' The men of Lydd kept watch on Dungeness from time immemorial; the custom was still in full force in 1470, when it was agreed that one man from each boat's crew belonging to Lydd should be detailed for the duty under penalty of a fine which was to go towards maintaining the guns

---

hold them to ransom as was done on shore. In the Mediterranean, where galley slaves for the oar were always at a premium, prisoners were kept alive, while they were drowned in the North Sea.

[36] Pat. 19 Hen. III, m. 14*d*.

[37] Close, 12 Edw. III, pt. iii, m. 33.

[38] ' Signa consueta vocata *beknes* per ignem.' See Southey, *Lives of the Admirals*, i, 360 (quoting Froissart), for the method of constructing them.

there.[39] In 1590 there was a dispute between the Lydd men and their neighbours of the 'Seven Hundreds' as to the responsibility for the Dungeness watch;[40] the obligation of the people of the 'hundreds' seems really to have been connected with Broomhill.[41] In 1580 the only Kentish beacon kept in readiness was that at Upnor,[42] no doubt in relation to the ships lying up in the Medway; for 1588 we have the well-known plan of the Kentish beacons given by Lambarde. After falling into desuetude the beacon system was again established in 1803.

The Welsh wars of 1277 and 1282, and the Scotch war of 1295, were mainly fought by the feudal armies, but squadrons of Cinque Ports ships assisted in all the campaigns, and the services rendered in 1277 were so strategically important as to be rewarded by the charter of incorporation of 1278. In August 1277 Edward granted the Portsmen all plunder taken from the Welsh, and the ransom of all prisoners except those desired by himself, but with the proviso that the grant was not to be a precedent.[43] In 1277, however, out of the total number of twenty-seven ships with Edward only eighteen came from the Cinque Ports;[44] in 1282 there were forty, most or all of which came from the Ports, the barons being ordered to send out vessels to deal with Channel piracy 'from the remainder' of those due from them.[45] They had been also for some time at war with Bayonne whence proctors came in 1276 authorized to make a 'perpetual' peace with the Ports.[46] This, by the mediation of Edward, was concluded in the following year, the king helping it on by paying £100 to the Bayonnais.[47] The business of the Ports was not entirely confined to war and piracy, as is shown by their joining with their new friends of Bayonne in complaining that foreign merchants who chartered their ships for purposes of trade were making innovations in the contracts to their injury.[48] Either Romney was failing or the barons of Lydd must have performed some particular service deserving reward, for in 1290 they were given the same liberties as were enjoyed by Romney on condition of finding one ship towards the five of the head port.[49] In 1291 the Portsmen had the not unusual experience of answering to a commission of inquiry concerning their robberies of French merchantmen during time of peace.[50] Most of these commissions were directed to the Warden; there was more than one reason why it was not to his interest to find the Portsmen more guilty than he could help. Both Edward and Philippe le Bel tried to restore peace by bringing together representatives of the belligerents, but racial passions and greed were too strong for royal powers as yet too decentralized.

The year 1293 was signalized by a sea battle, the outcome of a long series of provocations on both sides, fought at a prearranged spot in the Channel between the Cinque Ports with their Irish, Dutch, and Gascon allies and the Normans, Flemish, and Genoese.[51] The English won a complete victory and prizes were brought into Dover, Sandwich, and Romney, among other places.[52]

[39] *Hist. MSS. Com. Rep.* v, App. 528.
[40] *Acts of P.C.* 10 Mar. 1589-90.
[41] Close, 8 Hen. IV, m. 8.
[42] *Acts of P.C.* 17 April 1580.
[43] Pat. 5 Edw. I, m. 6.
[44] Morris, *Welsh Wars of Edw. I*, 128, 173.

[45] Ibid. ; Close, 10 Edw. I, m. 4.
[46] Close, 5 Edw. I, m. 7*d*.
[47] Rymer, *Fœdera* (ed. 1816), i, 542.
[48] Pat. 5 Edw. I, m. 14*d*.
[49] Ibid. 18 Edw. I, m. 35.
[50] Ibid. 19 Edw. I, m. 17.

[51] Over 400 vessels were engaged on the two sides. They met on 15 May, off the Point St. Mathieu, coast of Brittany.
[52] " The V Portes thorgh powere the se had so conquerd, That Normans alle that yere durst not be sene for ferd." —PETER LANGTOFT.

War with France, really the beginning of 150 years of war, followed and general preparations for offence and defence were made in 1294 and 1295 while Edward himself was engaged in a Scotch campaign. The French king had collected troops and a large fleet wherewith to invade England. He had also the assistance of a traitor, Sir Thomas Turberville, who in 1295 undertook to persuade Edward to place him in charge of some part of the Kent or Sussex coast, where he would admit the French. The fleet of Philip IV was to await, off Dungeness, a preconcerted signal, but Turberville failed and the signal was never made. After waiting some time a reconnoitring party landed at Hythe, where most of them were killed. The French then proceeded to Dover, where a landing in force was effected and the greater part of the town burnt. The details given by the chroniclers are very inconsistent with each other but Dover must have suffered severely because, when called upon in 1297 for their 'service,' the inhabitants petitioned to be allowed to hire ships in consequence of their own having been burnt in the recent attack, so that they had none left.[53]

On 22 August 1297 Edward, with an army and a large fleet collected by a general arrest of shipping,[54] sailed for Sluys and his arrival there was marked by an outburst, more than ordinary in its violence, of the hatred always existent between the Cinque Ports and Yarmouth. As far back as the reign of King John the men of Yarmouth had resented the use of their shore by the Cinque Ports fishermen; in 1219 Henry III, then a boy, had been made to say that he heard that there were quarrels every year between the Portsmen and the Yarmouth burgesses, and that the former, who seem to have been regarded as the aggressors, were not to interfere with the rights or disturb the peace of their unwilling hosts. The order was repeated, in almost the same words, in 1221 and 1222;[55] in 1252, 1254, and 1264 other troubles are known to have occurred. As Yarmouth grew in wealth and strength the burgesses became more and more impatient of the dictation, none too gently exercised, of the Cinque Ports bailiffs; although we have only occasional notices of the constant friction, its existence is proved by the necessity Edward was under in 1277 of issuing a long and carefully worded award defining the respective rights of the jealous rivals.[56] In reality it was a triple quarrel, for Yarmouth was detested as bitterly by her neighbours on the east coast as she detested the Ports. Edward's award not only settled nothing but probably intensified, indirectly, the enmity existing, so that in 1289 and 1290 both parties were directed to send deputies to argue out their grievances before king and parliament.[57] For all we can tell the meetings may have been considered a success, since the Portsmen were only accused, formally, of attacking nine Yarmouth ships between 1295 and 1297; Sandwich, Stonar, and Hythe were three of the offending towns.[58] The quarrel was transferred to the south coast in 1297, when the fleet was lying at Winchelsea ready to sail; five of the townsmen were then killed by men of the eastern squadron.[59] It was only when exceptionally large fleets were collected that the Cinque Ports and Yarmouth levies were required to work together, for

---

[53] Close, 25 Edw. I, m. 14d. However, the French chroniclers considered the attack a failure.

[54] Ibid. m. 18d. In the case of the Cinque Ports they were required to send all ships of 40 tons and upwards, as well as their 'service,' but the king allowed that it was not to be a precedent.

[55] Pat. 3 Hen. III, m. 2; 5 Hen. III, m. 2; 6 Hen. III, m. 2.

[56] Pat. 5 Edw. I, m. 17. Walter of Hemingburgh also refers to the ancient hatred existing between Yarmouth and the Ports.

[57] Pat. 17 Edw. I, m. 8; ibid. 18 Edw. I, m. 42.

[58] Exch. Misc. Bdle. ii, Nos. 8, 16.

[59] Assize R. 945. For the references to the Assize Rolls I am indebted to the courtesy of Mr. L. F. Salzmann.

usually the employment of the latter was confined to the east coast and North Sea. In this case both appear to have sailed to Sluys (five days) peaceably, but then a street brawl occurred which kindled latent passion into flame. The Cinque Ports squadron fell upon that of Yarmouth and nearly annihilated it; thirty-two vessels, of which sixteen were burnt, were destroyed or plundered and nearly 200 men were killed in twenty of them.[60]

Whether the Kentish ports took a large or small share in this deed we do not know, but it is distinctly stated that all the Cinque Ports were concerned in it. The king required letters of submission from both Yarmouth and the Ports touching 'the disputes that have lately arisen . . . after the king's arrival in Flanders,' and insisted that both sides should observe a truce to last for three months after his return to England.[61] The task of inquiring into the affray devolved upon Prince Edward, and the two adversaries were called upon to send deputies to London to state their case.[62] It may have been in consequence of this inquiry that the king took into his hands the liberties, at Yarmouth, of the Cinque Ports and, no doubt to prevent more bloodshed, they were not restored until 1299.[63] Edward issued an award in 1298, which the master and two superior officers of each ship of the Cinque Ports or Yarmouth were to swear to observe and to keep the peace, before going to sea.[64] This attempt to enforce at least neutrality clearly had little effect, for in 1301 and 1303 there were other awards following commissions of inquiry. At this time both sides made out returns of their losses in men and money, the Cinque Ports of Kent showing 180 men killed and £12,953 10s. 8d. in commercial injury.[65] It is evident that the political and military importance of the maritime levies of the two contending powers made it impossible for Edward to deal with them as he would have dealt with ordinary law-breakers. So far from meting out real punishment, the king granted both the Cinque Ports and Yarmouth further privileges in 1298, including that of being quit of all tallages and aids on the hulls and gear of their ships.[66]

In March 1297 the Warden and others were ordered to equip ten ships to watch Calais and the neighbouring ports, and in July a cruising squadron of twelve others was provided from Kent and the adjoining counties.[67] A body of Londoners, horsed and armed, marched into Kent and Sussex to defend the coast during Edward's absence and obtained, in 1299, a promise that their action should not prejudice them as a precedent.[68] The accounts show that Cinque Ports ships, independently of those employed to perform the 'service,' were frequently taken up by the crown in the same manner as those from the non-privileged ports; in 1297 all the head ports, as well as Folkestone, Faversham, and Strood, furnished vessels in this way.[69] Edward and his troops returned to England in March 1298, and from the Thames to Southampton there was a general arrest of ships for his passage.[70] Both this and the levies of March and July 1297 are examples of the application to the privileged districts of the system in use throughout the rest of the country; of the franchised Ports, Winchelsea was the only one excepted in 1298. A two-years truce with France was made in 1299, but the Scotch war continued and the Cinque Ports were

---

[60] Exch. Misc. Bdle. ii, No. 8.

[61] Close, 25 Edw. I, m. 5; ibid. 26 Edw. I, m. 17.

[62] Ibid. 25 Edw. I, m. 6.

[63] Ibid. 27 Edw. I, m. 9d.

[64] Ibid. 26 Edw. I, m. 11d.

[65] Assize R. 395.

[66] Pat. 26 Edw. I, m. 17.

[67] Pat. 25 Edw. I, pt. i, m. 9; ibid. pt. ii, m. 14.

[68] Ibid. 27 Edw. I, m. 29.

[69] Add. MS. 7965, fol. 89 et seq.

[70] Pat. 26 Edw. I, m. 26.

represented, in 1300, in the north by a squadron; of these, eight came from Dover, four from Sandwich (with Lydd), four from Hythe, two from Romney, one from Faversham, and one from Folkestone.[71] William Charles of Sandwich and John de Aula of Dover were in command of the Kentish division, receiving each one shilling a day. In March 1301 orders were given to the ports all round the coast to send ships into Scotch waters by midsummer, and this levy is noticeable for the fact that for the first time some of the smaller Kentish ports are named;[72] Northfleet, Clyve (Cliffe), and Gillingham were each assessed at one ship. Evidently the usual Channel war continued irrespective of any more distant service; in 1304 an order issued for a joint inquiry by English and French commissioners into the fights between, and the robberies committed by, the men of the Cinque Ports and Calais.[73]

The 'service' of the Ports was in request every year; in 1306 it was reduced to twenty-seven ships on condition that they carried as many men as the fifty-seven would have had.[74] In 1303 there was a commission to inquire into the desertion of Kentish sailors, who were to give security to answer for their contempt. No doubt both shipowners and seamen found piracy or privateering more attractive than the royal service, but there was no general disinclination to respond to the demands of the crown. The constant levies of ships and men would seem to be destructive of commerce, but in reality were not nearly so injurious to it as they appear; in the case of the Cinque Ports their privileges and the average of gains from prizes must have represented a pecuniary equivalent far in excess of the profits of trading voyages, which involved great risk of loss from wreck, piracy, privateering, or in the sale of the cargo. The incessant embargoes that harassed trade—then much increased—under Edward III were not yet common, and the alacrity with which most of the ports answered the demands made upon them shows that the assistance required was neither oppressive nor unwelcome, especially as those who contributed to the sea service were freed from any aid towards that by land. There was no permanent naval organization at this time. The king possessed some ships of his own and the commanders were usually charged with their maintenance under the control of the Clerk of the Ships, when there was such an official. When a fleet was to be raised from the merchant navy a certain extent of coast was allotted to one of the king's clerks, or to a sergeant-at-arms, who acted with the bailiffs of the port towns in selecting vessels and men and seeing them dispatched to the place of meeting. Even within the jurisdiction of the Warden he was sometimes associated with officers named by the king for the levy of ships, but usually the writs went direct to the mayors or bailiffs of the head ports. If a ship did not appear, or if the men deserted, they or the owner might be required to find security to come before the king, and although there was as yet no statute dealing with the offence,[75] they might be punished at the pleasure of the king or his commissioners.

Wrecking was of course as prevalent in Kent as in other counties, and piracy, undisguised by any pretence of seizing an enemy's goods, was an ordinary proceeding for Cinque Ports crews, although only the worst cases appear in the records. In 1227 a Spanish merchantman, while lying at

---

[71] *Wardrobe Accts. of 28 Edw. I,* Lond. 1787, p. 271 et seq.
[72] Pat. 29 Edw. I, m. 20.

[73] Close, 32 Edw. I, m. 16d.
[74] Ibid. 34 Edw. I, m. 25.
[75] The first statute was 2 Ric. II,

st. 1, cap. 4, by which deserters were fined double their wages and imprisoned for a year.

Sandwich, was plundered and her crew killed;[76] but notices of such events become more common under Edward I when the arm of the law was strengthening. In 1286 a vessel was lost near Dungeness; much of the cargo was saved but was carried away by the men of the coast who also killed one of the owners.[77] Again, in 1291, a king's ship, returning from Gascony with wine, was lost somewhere on Thanet and the cargo divided among those who could seize it.[78] In 1298 another wreck occurred on the coast of Thanet and the cargo was stolen; here, the right of wreck belonged to the Abbey of St. Augustine, Canterbury, and the abbot was ordered to inquire into the case.[79] It will be obvious that between the men on the shore, the lord of the manor with rights of wreck, and sometimes the crown with the same claim, the owner had little chance of recovering anything. In 1304 three ships bound from Flanders to Bayonne were driven ashore near Romney; the survivors of the crews were assaulted by the country people and cargo to the value of £10,000 plundered.[80] A year later the *Snake*, of Sandwich, was cruising, by the king's order, in the Straits of Dover for the security of merchantmen, but while on this duty her officers boarded a London trader off St. Margarets, from which £250 in money and some goods were taken.[81] After the truce with France there were at least two commissions of inquiry into damages inflicted on the French by the Cinque Ports, but in 1304 Edward agreed to lend Philip twenty fully armed ships for service against the Flemings, which ships were to be equipped by the Portsmen, who must have found it difficult to keep step with the sudden changes of politics.[82]

If Edward I was unable to repress the lawlessness of the Portsmen it is not strange that they took more licence under his successor. There are many complaints during the early years of Edward II of foreign ships being boarded and plundered by them, although it is true that some of these cases were, there is little doubt, only those of the seizure of enemy's goods in neutral vessels and would, later, merely have provided work for the Admiralty Court. For example, an accusation of 1312 that Cinque Ports ships were taking cargo out of Flemish vessels on the Breton coast may belong to either class.[83] But there was much that can have had no excuse of pseudo-legality, and in 1314 the Warden was directed to inquire into robberies committed under pretence of attacking the Scots.[84] In the same year a Portuguese ship ran ashore near Romney; the owners went to the town and agreed there, and at Lydd, for salvaging to be done for one-fourth of the value of the cargo. But when the Lydd and Romney men had got the property ashore they demanded a third, and, being refused, helped themselves to half the cargo.[85] A year later people belonging to Romney joined with those of Rye and Winchelsea in riotously preventing the Warden from making an inquiry into the robbery of the cargo of a wreck on Dungeness. They came to Winchelsea and broke up his court.[86] In 1322 a foreign merchantman was attacked in Orwell Haven by two ships belonging to Winchelsea and Greenwich; the crew were driven ashore, some being killed and wounded, and the ship carried away.[87] At the end of the reign there was a peculiarly flagrant instance of piracy; and it may be considered certain that for

[76] Close, 11 Hen. III, m. 1.
[77] Pat. 14 Edw. I, m. 23*d*, m. 20*d*.
[78] Chanc. Files, N.S. 1689.
[79] Close, 26 Edw. I, m. 12.

[80] Pat. 32 Edw. I, m. 25*d*.
[81] Ibid. 33 Edw. I, pt. i, m. 3*d*.
[82] Ibid. 32 Edw. I, m. 22.
[83] Ibid. 5 Edw. II, pt. ii, m. 15*d*.

[84] Ibid. 8 Edw. II, pt. i, m. 21*d*.
[85] Ibid. 7 Edw. II, pt. ii, m. 18*d*.
[86] *Rot. Parl.* i, 329.
[87] Ibid. 397.

every such case in which the magnitude of the loss made it worth while, or the position of the victims made it possible, to appeal to the king there were dozens where the sufferers were too poor or too powerless to take any action. In this last case a Fleming was boarded by Sandwich and Winchelsea men; they took cargo to the value of £600, brought the ship to the Downs, forced the owners to sign a declaration that they sought no redress in respect of the goods seized, and then put them in a boat to find their way home.[88] Manners were softening to some extent for, half a century earlier, instead of being given a chance in a boat they would have been thrown overboard without more ado.

The enmity between the Ports and Yarmouth still continued if only because the fight of 1297 was yet remembered on the east coast and remained unavenged. In 1316 the smouldering fire seemed about to break into flame again, for Yarmouth ships were sinking and burning those of the Ports off the coast of Sussex. The Ports prepared for war, and the challenge was readily taken up by Yarmouth; the king addressed an inhibition to the Cinque Ports, including one to Faversham, with a threat that if they put to sea they would be proceeded against as rebels. Then he called delegates from both sides before him to dilate on their wrongs, with the result that the Portsmen were assured that they might go peaceably to Yarmouth Fair, the east-coast men being ordered to treat them amicably under penalty of life and property. Moreover the Yarmouth men were ordered to pay £1,000 to the Portsmen they had injured.[89] There was consequently no outbreak but the animosity that continued between the East Anglians and the southern men is shown by the necessity the king was under in 1319 of issuing an especial warning to both, when they were to come together in a fleet raised for service against the Scots, admonishing them not to attack each other as heretofore, ' whereby the affairs of the king and his progenitors have been frequently retarded.'[90]

Leland relates a story, assigned by him to the next reign, of the Fowey men refusing to ' vail bonnet ' to the Portsmen, fighting them off Rye, and earning the title of ' the gallants of Fowey.'[91] The quarrel appears to have been of the reign of Edward II, and arose from a Fowey crew taking a man accused of murder—the culprit or the victim being a Cornishman—out of a Cinque Ports ship and killing some of the men on board her; in consequence of this the Portsmen were attacking all vessels hailing from Fowey.[92] How long the warfare had continued is not known, but in January 1321 the Cornishmen appealed to the king for protection; the Cinque Ports must have disobeyed the inhibition which followed for another was necessary in August, and from this last it is evident that they were also fighting, and holding their own against the coast towns of Hampshire and Dorset, with all the corollary of ' homicides, robberies, and ship-burning.'[93] It is not unlikely that these two counties, and perhaps Devon, had been drawn or forced into the broil by the performances of the Portsmen, who would draw little distinction between any west-country ships

---

[88] Pat. 1 Edw. III, pt. ii, m. 6*d*.

[89] Ibid. 10 Edw. II, pt. i, m. 35, m. 32, m. 2; Close, 10 Edw. II, m. 30*d*, m. 24.

[90] Close, 12 Edw. II, m. 5*d*. See also *post*, p. 265.

[91] *Itinerary*, iii, 22. The bonnet was an additional sail which was laced to the foot of the mainsail for use in fair weather; the word was also in general use as meaning a head covering. In either case Leland implies a refusal to salute, and it has an inferential bearing on the English claim to the salute from foreign ships. The later form of the salute at sea was to lower a topsail. Any personal salute must have been that common to civil life. A hat upon a pole was a demand that the ship thus signalled to should give an account of itself.

[92] Pat. 14 Edw. II, pt. ii, m. 24.

[93] Close, 15 Edw. II, m. 32*d*, m. 31*d*.

which they could find an excuse to plunder. Cornish writers, relying on the complimentary title won by the Fowey men, have taken for granted that they fought on at least equal terms with the Cinque Ports; they may have won an initial success, but the phrasing of the Letters Close implies that it was they, and not the Portsmen, who were yearning for an end to the strife. The latter had also on their hands a quarrel with the Flemings and the men of Wissant,[94] and had been ready to resume hostilities with Yarmouth, therefore they must have felt themselves quite equal to a continuance of the war with the western counties.

The first call upon the Cinque Ports after the accession of Edward II was to provide vessels for the king's passage to France to bring over his bride Isabella. He and his queen landed at Dover in February 1308, and in June the whole 'service' was required for the Scotch war, but this was countermanded in August. The Portsmen showed an inclination to employ their leisure in assisting the Bayonnais, with whom they were friendly for the moment, in a war the Gascons were carrying on with the four Basque towns which formed a confederation somewhat similar to that of the Cinque Ports. This was forbidden by royal order, as was also the seizure of fish, without payment, from Dutch fishermen, which seems to have been another occupation of leisure moments.[95] An order of 1309 to twenty-eight ports to prevent the passage abroad of fighting men during the Scotch war, is addressed, in Kent, only to Dover, Sandwich, and Faversham.[96] For many years during this reign the ports round the English coast were called upon to supply ships for the Scotch campaigns, but as, from the maritime standpoint, the Cinque Ports practically included Kent we seldom find any others mentioned in the county. Obscurity was to the advantage of the poor and undistinguished places not within the liberties of the Ports, for Edward's extravagance soon forced him to call upon the wealthier towns to provide ships, for a longer or shorter period, at their own expense, a proceeding which must have been exceedingly distasteful to owners accustomed to the punctual payments of Edward I.

In 1313 Edward left Dover for Gascony and returned, in July, to Sandwich, where a fleet was collected during the summer. Since Edward's accession there had not been a year when the coast towns had been free from the necessity of preparing naval aid; the pressure on the Cinque Ports was increased by a demand, which was becoming frequent, that they should send their ships manned by crews of double strength. This, no doubt, proceeded from the small size of the ships of the 'service,' and the opportunity it afforded of filling up gaps in the crews from other places. For this or some other reason there was a failure on the part of both the Kent and Sussex ports in the summer of 1315, and pardons were subsequently granted to the barons of Romney, Lydd, Sandwich, and Hythe for the non-appearance of eight ships with double crews.[97] Perhaps they had enough occupation at home, for in November there were twenty-two fighting ships from Calais hovering off Thanet, and it may not have been the first time in the year.[98] In 1316 the Warden was directed to persuade the Ports to set out as much shipping as they could, to serve as long as possible at their expense, 'for the better keeping of the English sea,' and to put down piracy.[99] From requests the step was short to commands, so that in 1319

---

[94] Pat. 11 Edw. II, pt. ii, m. 3.
[95] Close, 2 Edw. II, m. 18d; 3 Edw. II, m. 23.
[96] Ibid. 3 Edw. II, m. 19d, m. 16d.
[97] Pat. 8 Edw. II, pt. ii, m. 9, m. 8.
[98] Close, 9 Edw. II, m. 22d.
[99] Ibid. m. 13d.

Sandwich, Romney, Faversham, and Hythe were ordered to send ships to serve at their own cost for three or four months.[100] Such an exaction was a clear infringement of the privileges of the Ports and could only be defended as a national necessity consequent to the exhaustion caused by the long war. The official Cinque Ports levy was working on the south coast in 1319, but there were a few extra ships from the head ports, and one from Greenwich,[101] with the fleet, which included ten king's ships acting against the Scots.[102]

The Scotch war was renewed in 1322 but ceased a year later in virtue of a thirteen years' truce. During 1321 the younger Hugh le Despenser, the Warden, was at sea with the Cinque Ports ships committing piracy on a large scale. In 1322 Edward sent letters to all the most important ports begging them to do their best in supplying as many ships as they could at their own cost, but in Kent no demand was made on any place outside the Cinque Ports; it must have been known that there were no other towns able to render assistance. The Ports' levy of 1323 was countermanded by reason of the truce, but the king, professing to wish to spare them as much as possible, had informed them that he would be satisfied with twenty-seven ships if they carried the same number of men that the full service of fifty-seven would have had.[103] But the truth was that as vessels of from 150 to 200 tons were becoming common the men of the Ports were now of more value than their ships.[104] The accession of Charles IV to the French throne brought the probability of war with France. An army was sent to Aquitaine in 1324 and many of the ports were called upon to send their largest ships to serve as transports, Sandwich being assessed for four and Faversham for one. In addition to this the Cinque Ports, as well as all other coast towns, were directed to prepare every ship of 40 tons and upwards.[105] The Sussex members of the confederacy were assessed in the same way as those of Kent, and it was possibly because it was a supplementary and unusual service that the king 'agreed' with them that they were to have three-fourths of all prize goods, reserving the remaining fourth for the crown.[106] Two persons were appointed in September 1324 to act as keepers of the port of Sandwich during the absence of the Cinque Ports fleet, as 'on account of its ample size a very large number of vessels can put in at the same time and this is a danger to the town.' [107]

In 1325 Isabella travelled to France to negotiate a peace between her husband and her brother, but it soon became apparent that she was going to sacrifice the interests of the former in favour of her son. The year was one of troubled expectation but in 1326 matters came to a crisis and invasion was seen to be imminent. In August a survey was ordered of all vessels in England of 50 tons and upwards. The list of ports is very full; in Kent we find Romney, Hythe, Dover, Sandwich, Faversham, Gillingham, Maidstone, Strood, Cliffe, Greenwich, and Swanscombe (i.e. Greenhithe).[108] The order for all ships of 50 tons and upwards from places south of the Thames to concentrate at Portsmouth is addressed to all these places, although it is clear that there could have been no expectation of obtaining vessels of that size from some of the

---

[100] Rot. Scot. 12 Edw. II, m. 3.

[101] Probably West Greenwich, i.e. Deptford.

[102] Add. MS. 17362, fol. 25 et seq.

[103] Close, 16 Edw. II, m. 9d.

[104] In a fleet of 1324, sixteen ports sent 37 vessels of from 100 to 200 tons, but not one of these came from Kent or Sussex. There was a 300-ton ship from Yarmouth.

[105] Close, 17 Edw. II, m. 11d, m. 9d.

[106] Ibid. 19 Edw. II, m. 26.

[107] Pat. 18 Edw. II, pt. i, m. 24.

[108] Pat. 20 Edw. II, m. 21.

smaller of them.[109] In September it was decided to strengthen the royal fleets still further by calling upon those who had not been affected by the first levy to contribute towards the equipment of more ships. Faversham was rated for one ship and twenty-nine men, Sandwich for eight ships and 255 men, Hythe one ship and twenty-seven men, and Romney one ship and thirty-three men. Twelve ships, to cruise off the North Foreland, were also to be fitted out in the proportion of three from London, one from Faversham, two each from Hythe and Dover, and four, jointly, from Maidstone, Strood, Rochester, Gillingham, Cliffe, and the small places on the Medway.[110] Greenwich does not appear in these lists but it had afforded maritime assistance in some form.[111] It will be observed that in these levies the legal liability of the Cinque Ports in the matter of size and number of ships is entirely set aside. So far as the remaining evidence enables us to judge, the reign of Edward II was the period of the Ports' greatest prosperity, but in this, and the preceding two reigns at least, Sussex had always taken the lead of Kent, in which Sandwich was the wealthiest commercial port. The continental passenger traffic was then, as it always has been, the mainstay of Dover,[112] for the others there can have been little but the fishery and piracy.

One of the first acts of Edward III was to order the Warden to survey all the king's ships lying in harbours within his jurisdiction and to repair those in bad condition. From the reign of John, and probably earlier, all the kings had possessed ships of their own; it is likely that then, as later, such vessels especially built for fighting formed the backbone of fleets collected for important enterprises. The Ports were required to provide their 'service' for a short war with Scotland, but peace was made in 1328. This levy from the Cinque Ports is noticeable because Waresius de Valoignes, the admiral of the western fleet, was pressing men within their liberties both for their own squadron and for the ships taken up along the south coast.[113] Later, the Cinque Ports claimed that the Admiralty, who represent, historically, the early admirals of the west and north, had no power of impressment within their jurisdiction and that the central authority could act only through the Lord Warden, but it is evident that precedent, and this is not the only one, was against them;[114] it also destroyed their contention that their liability to serve was confined to their own squadron.[115] An interval of peace abroad was turned to account for a renewal of the broil with Yarmouth, necessitating a warning to both to keep the peace pending an award from Edward who, with the optimism of youth, had 'undertaken to terminate the matter in a friendly way.'[116] This occurred in 1330, but in 1336 another conference was needed and relations between the east and south were so strained that the admirals of the north and west were directed to keep the Yarmouth and Cinque Ports crews in their respective commands well apart when the fleets met in that year.[117] Again, in 1337, when a Yarmouth contingent was coming south to join a fleet for Aquitaine the Warden

[109] Close, 20 Edw. II, m. 11d. Those of under 50 tons were only embargoed.

[110] Close, 20 Edw. II, m. 8.

[111] Ibid. m. 9d.

[112] Calais, as a port, only came into existence during the 12th century. During the Roman period an inlet of the sea extended inland as far as St. Omer, and only gradually dried up from marsh to solid ground. For many centuries Calais was non-existent, or only existed as a few unnamed fishing huts at the western point of the gulf. Henry II was continually crossing the Channel—probably more often than any other English king—but I have not found that he ever used Calais. He left, or arrived at, Wissant several times.

[113] Close, 3 Edw. III, m.

[114] Another instance is of 1337 (Pat. 11 Edw. III, pt. i, m. 37d).

[115] See also ante, p. 253.

[116] Close, 4 Edw. III, m. 39d.

[117] Close, 10 Edw. III, m. 21d.

was directed to make proclamation that no harm should be done to them by the Portsmen, the king having heard that fighting might occur ' if these ships chance to meet upon the sea.'[118] But when there was profit in view the sometime enemies could work together for the moment; in 1343 a Genoese carrack was plundered off the Isle of Wight and there were seven Yarmouth and three Sandwich ships among the fourteen that stopped her.[119] There are indications, too, that the old quarrel with the western counties had recommenced. In 1348 the king caused delegates from Dartmouth and the Cinque Ports to meet him at Porchester, when he arranged terms of peace between them and the agreement was solemnly sealed by the corporations on both sides.[120]

The reign of Edward III is the period of decline of the Cinque Ports, and as their power failed we hear less of their quarrels with the other counties. The quarrels were due, to a certain extent, to their privileges which eventually excited jealousy in other ports rising into importance, but more perhaps to the ingrained habits of piracy which rendered them a scourge to commerce and to which their own countrymen, as well as foreigners, were victims. The late Sir Harris Nicolas, than whom no one had a more profound knowledge of the sources of English naval history, described them as ' nests of robbers;'[121] their latest serious historian[122] ignores, as far as possible, that side of their story, but it was one that must have contributed to their decadence in the 14th century, as sovereign and subjects recognized that the evil done for their own profit far outweighed any good done for the kingdom, and that they were, indirectly, a most expensive form of defence. For instance, in 1336 Edward paid 8,000 marks compensation to the Genoese owners of a ship the Portsmen had taken in 1321.[123] In 1338 the king had ordered the restitution of certain goods of which Spanish and Portuguese merchants had been plundered, but the Portsmen, sheltering themselves under the pretence of their liberties, refused to appear before the Warden, concealed the booty, and protected the criminals.[124] Here, a curt threat to annul their privileges was necessary. Coincidently with characteristics which may be called anti-social there were political causes for their descent from their former estate. One feature of the Hundred Years' War was the rise of a French navy which was, at times, able to hold its own—or more—against that of England. In the shock of contending fleets which represented the maritime strength of two nations the Cinque Ports squadrons no longer held the place of former centuries when, in material strength, they were equal or superior to their immediate enemies in the Channel. The growth of commerce among the English ports had caused a steady increase in the size and tonnage of ships, and this alone considerably minimized the relative value of the Cinque Ports' contribution to the national armaments.[125] Moreover, while the coast towns elsewhere were rising in wealth and

---

[118] Close, 11 Edw. III, pt. ii, m. 8d. The same proclamation was made at Yarmouth.

[119] Pat. 16 Edw. III, pt. iii, m. 1d.

[120] Ibid. 22 Edw. III, pt. ii, m. 15.

[121] Hist. of the Royal Navy, i, 357.

[122] Burrows, The Cinque Ports, Lond. 1888.

[123] Rymer, Fœdera (ed. 1816), ii, 948, 1011. This Genoese was one of le Despenser's prizes (ante, p. 263). While he was Warden piracy was open and unashamed.

[124] Close, 12 Edw. III, pt. ii, m. 36. But the Portsmen are not to be blamed for maritime procedure which almost incited to piracy, e.g. letters of marque. If A. lost goods he obtained a licence to take those belonging to the innocent B. who, in his turn, would victimize C. and D., and so the game would go on with little regard to the amount specified, say £200, in the original letters. Add to which drowned, hanged, or mutilated crews: sometimes men were sent adrift with hands and feet cut off.

[125] Cf. ante, p. 263; post, p. 267.

consequence those of the Cinque Ports were stationary or decaying, and the French raids on Kent and Sussex, after the middle of Edward's reign, still further reduced their resources. The steady deterioration of the harbours, of which we see the results to-day, must also have been progressing.

War with Scotland, followed by general arrests of shipping, broke out again in 1332; in January 1335 writs were directed to Stonar, Folkestone, and Reculver, outside the accustomed ports, and in the same year Thomas de Maidstone was captain of the Cinque Ports squadron.[126] A document of this year gives some valuable information about the possible strength of the Cinque Ports.[127] It is an account of the expenses of preparation of a squadron of thirty ships of 3,340 tons manned by 60 officers, 1,915 men, and 93 boys; it was paid for by the crown as additional to, and independent of, the charter 'service.' Here, Sandwich sent six vessels, one being of 160 tons, four of 100, and one of 90 tons; Dover, one of 140 tons, one of 80, and two of 60 tons; Hythe, one of 120 tons, one of 100, and one of 80 tons; Romney, one of 120, and two of 100 tons; and Faversham, one of 50 tons. Thus, five Kentish ports provided 1,660 tons as compared with 1,680 tons from Rye and Winchelsea, there being no ship from Hastings. In 1335 and 1336 there were signs of restiveness in the port towns under the continual embargoes and arrests which injured trade, but Edward dealt tactfully with the difficulty and in December 1336 sent John de Watenhull to the Cinque Ports, and other places westward, to take the townsmen, in appearance at least, into his confidence by explaining 'certain things near the king's heart.'[128] At the same time the coast towns were requested to send representatives to Westminster to discuss matters;[129] in Kent they came from Sandwich, Romney, Dover, Hythe, Reculver, Faversham, and Folkestone. It was no doubt the desire to soothe the impatience of the Portsmen that led the king to give one of three prizes recently taken to the men of Dover, and another to those of Faversham;[130] in 1338 two more were presented to the burgesses of Hythe and Romney.[131]

Between 1337 and 1340, when France, officially or unofficially, was helping the Scots, the balance of maritime war went against England until the victory of Sluys in 1340 restored our supremacy for many years. The importance of Sluys was that it made possible the campaign of Crecy and ensured that the war should be fought on French ground. Portsmouth was burnt in March 1337, and in the same year Dover suffered, the Priory being plundered and the town charters carried off.[132] In May and August 1338 keepers of the coast were appointed all round England; in Kent and Sussex the Archbishop of Canterbury, the Abbots of St. Augustine, Battle, and Faversham, and the Priors of Christchurch, Dover, and Rochester were associated with the Warden.[133] Another arrangement, which applied to all the counties, was an order that within seven miles ('leucas') of the coast only one bell of any church was to be used for ordinary purposes, while, in the event of danger, all were to be rung.[134] Such precautions were necessary although powerful fleets were at sea; that of the summer of 1338 contained 338 ships, of which ten came from Sandwich, four from Hythe, and one each from Romney, Maidstone, Faversham, Greenwich,

[126] Rot. Scot. 8 Edw. III, m. 1; 9 Edw. III, m. 31.

[127] Exch. Accts. K.R. Bdle. 19, No. 22.

[128] Close, 10 Edw. III, m. 4d.

[129] Rot. Scot. 10 Edw. III, m. 3d.

[130] Close, 10 Edw. III, m. 4.

[131] Ibid. 12 Edw. III, pt. i, m. 13.

[132] Pat. 12 Edw. III, pt. i, m. 31.

[133] Close, 11 Edw. III, pt. ii, m. 28d; 12 Edw. III, pt. i, m. 2d, pt. iii, m. 29d.

[134] Rot. Aleman, 12 Edw. III, pt. ii, m. 6d.

Strood, and New Hythe.[135]   In the spring of 1339 French squadrons cruised along the south coast; late in May or early in June they appeared off the coast of Thanet and then threatened Dover and Folkestone but did nothing very effective.   In July a large fleet of seventy or eighty vessels came to Sandwich, but are said to have been so far intimidated by the preparations made to receive them as to draw off and go on to Rye, whence they were chased back to Boulogne.[136]   At this time the maritime preponderance of the French was so effectual as to necessitate large plans of defence ashore; these cost money, of which the provision fell upon the townsmen along the coast.   Their patriotism seems, in some cases, hardly to have been equal to their ability; at Sandwich people were leaving in order to avoid the charges rated upon them for the defence of the town, and a proclamation was requisite threatening forfeiture of land and goods to those who did not return by a fixed date.[137] The barons of Sandwich had called upon Sarre to send its contingent to the help of the head port; the men of Sarre refused on the plea that they were wanted for the defence of Thanet, but eventually it was decided that a part of their force should go to Sandwich and a part remain at home.[138]

The strain of continuous loss was telling on the national reserve of shipping, therefore, in 1340, the sheriffs of the maritime counties were ordered to prevent any sale of ships to foreigners; they were also to certify the number of vessels belonging to each port and the names of the owners.[139]   Before the battle of Sluys was won it was necessary, in consequence of the poverty of some of the coast towns, for the crown to come to their assistance; for a Cinque Ports squadron of twenty-one ships the Council promised to pay half the cost 'as an especial grace.'[140]   Both the small number of vessels and the aid given by the crown point to exhaustion.   In the case of Hythe and Romney there is direct evidence of enfeeblement; in July 1341 the king threatened that unless they supplied their quota of five ships each he would annul their liberties and tallage them like the rest of his subjects, but the Warden reported that there was no suitable ship at Hythe and only one belonging to Romney.[141]   However, in 1340, when there was a national levy of shipping of 100 tons and upwards, the Cinque Ports undertook to provide 30 of 100 tons or more for themselves and the Thames.[141a]   The inclusion of the Thames is perhaps significant; it may mean that London found the ships, and the Ports a large proportion of the crews.   I believe that this levy of 1340 is the first in which 100 tons was the lowest limit for hired ships.   In 1341 another advisory council from the port towns was convened at Westminster; the more important places, among them Sandwich, sent two delegates; one came from Dover, the only other place in Kent called upon.[142]   A treaty of alliance between the Cinque Ports, whom circumstances were now rendering less pugnacious, other outside ports, and Bayonne, was also in negotiation.[143]   The plan of holding a council of those principally concerned with shipping may have been found successful in offering opportunities for conciliation and persuasion so that it was repeated in 1342, 1344, and 1347.   In 1342 Rochester, Maidstone, Hythe, Faversham,

---

[135] Misc. Bks. of Exch. Tr. of Rec. 203, fol. 288b. New Hithe is probably that on the Medway, above Rochester.

[136] Knighton, Chron. (Rolls Ser.), ii, 9.

[137] Close, 13 Edw. III, pt. ii, m. 28d.

[138] Ibid. m. 27d.

[139] Rymer, Fœdera, v, 210.

[140] Rot. Parl. ii, 108.

[141] Close, 15 Edw. III, pt. ii, m. 24d.

[141a] Rot. Parl. ii, 104, 107.

[142] Rymer, Fœdera, v, 231.

[143] Pat. 15 Edw. III, pt. i, m. 44.

Sandwich, Dover, and Romney sent representatives; in 1344 and 1347 only the last three received a summons and in both years two men came from Sandwich and Dover, and one from Romney.[144]

In 1342 Edward intervened in the question of the succession in Brittany, the duke having died without direct heirs. A large fleet and army were despatched in March under Sir Walter de Mauny, and the king himself crossed from Sandwich later in the year. In one fleet alone—that with which Edward sailed—there were 357 vessels, and of these sixteen came from Sandwich, nineteen from Dover, three from Romney, four from Smallhithe, four from Maidstone, two each from Hythe, Faversham, Margate, and Northfleet, and one each from Strood, Higham, Greenwich, and New Hithe.[145] After Edward's arrival many of the ships deserted from Brest, leaving the king and his troops ' in very great peril,' therefore writs were directed to the bailiffs of the ports to arrest the culprits and seize their property.[146] Altogether, from all the counties, 293 ships and their masters were scheduled,[147] and it is certain that, at least in some cases, the owners were heavily punished by fine or confiscation. Three ships of Sandwich, two of Margate, and one each of Strood, Greenwich, Maidstone, Faversham, Dover, Romney, and Hythe are in the list; the masters and mariners were to be committed to Newgate.[148] Two Hythe owners were fined £36, and one of Northfleet £20; the sum of upwards of £3,000 was levied in amounts varying from 6s. 8d. to £180, but most of it was devoted to recompensing those whose ships had been lost or damaged in the campaign.[149] Usually, although threats were frequent and the possible penalties only limited by the pleasure of the sovereign, owners escaped lightly, the shipping interest being too powerful and important to be offended without serious consideration.

Edward, more than his predecessors or successors, favoured Sandwich as a port of concentration; he again sailed from there in July 1345, returning to it from Sluys towards the end of the month. For the campaign of Crecy and the siege of Calais a huge armament was collected—from 1,000 to 1,600 sail according to the chroniclers. The Roll of Calais, which purports to be a copy of a Wardrobe Account of the reign of Edward III, shows that the fleet gathered for the siege included 22 ships and 504 men from Sandwich, 16 ships and 336 men from Dover, 15 ships and 160 men from Margate, 4 ships and 75 men from Romney, 6 ships and 112 men from Hythe, 2 ships and 23 men from Faversham, 2 ships and 51 men from Maidstone, 5 ships and 49 men from New Hithe, 2 ships and 24 men from Aylesford, 2 ships and 24 men from Hoo (Cliffe-at-Hoo), 2 ships and 59 men from Hoope (Hope), and 2 ships and 24 men from Motme or Moeme. All the existing copies of this Wardrobe Account[150] are of the late 16th or early 17th century, and the nature of the discrepancies in the figures attached to many of the ports affords internal evidence that the original record was in some places nearly or quite illegible when it was transcribed. Here, in the six sources available,[151] only three of the preceding places—Aylesford, Maidstone, and Margate—have figures in agreement in all the

---

[144] Rymer, *Fœdera* (ed. 1816), ii, 1193, v, 405, 548.

[145] Chan. Misc. Bdle. ii, No. 35.

[146] Pat. 17 Edw. III, pt. i, m. 17d.

[147] This number included not only those who had left the king, but also others who had sailed

with the Earl of Northampton, in July, and had failed to return to England.

[148] Close, 17 Edw. III, pt. i, m. 4d, m. 3d.

[149] Pipe R. 21 Edw. III, m. 29; Pat. 22 Edw. III, pt. i, m. 19d.

[150] They do not conform to the

character of Wardrobe Accounts, and are not really copies but compilations.

[151] Cott. MS. Titus F. III, fol. 262; Harl. MS. 3968, fol. 130; ibid. 246; Stowe MS. 570, fol. 230; ibid. 374, fol. 28; Rawlinson MS. (Bodleian), C. 846, fol. 17.

MSS.; in the rest there are more or less serious variations and two of the place-names given are difficult to identify. 'Motme, or Moeme,' occurs in the Cotton MS.; in Harleian MS. 246 it is Montormont; in Harleian 3968 'Morve or Morne'; in Stowe 570 Motene; and in the Rawlinson MS. 'Motne or Mone.' In Harleian 3968 Hoo, which is Ho in the Cotton MS., is entered 'Hoo alias Morne'; if this be accepted, Hoo and Motme are identical and have been set down twice. Hope, again, is a vague name and may possibly refer to both the Essex and the Kentish shores of the Thames below Gravesend. The number of ships and men assigned to Margate is suspicious although all the MSS. are in accord; certainly neither before nor afterwards is the town known to have helped the crown to such an extent. On the other hand the crews are very small, so that the vessels can have been but little more than fishing boats, and the men may have been drawn in from neighbouring places. Omitting Motme as doubtful, sixty-seven ships came from the Kentish Cinque Ports and their members, being ten more than the full 'service'; from Kent and Sussex together the number was nearly double that of the service by charter. There can be no doubt that, whatever the total number of vessels employed during the siege, they came in reliefs.

After the fall of Calais—and it should be noted that Calais increased the naval value of Dover enormously—Edward landed at Sandwich in October 1347. The battle of L'Espagnols sur Mer was fought and won by the king in person off Winchelsea on 29 August 1350, and although most of the vessels engaged were royal ships there were no doubt many Portsmen from both Kent and Sussex among the crews. The war continued until 1356, and fleets were raised year by year from the coast towns, but no incident of importance occurred. But it brought shipping business to Dover and Sandwich and no doubt to other of the ports; in 1355 the mayors were authorized to press carpenters and others to build and repair the ships the king had ordered to be built there, and in 1358 a 'dyke' (dock) was made at Sandwich that the king's ship *La George* might be repaired there.[152] After Poictiers the Black Prince, with his prisoner the King of France, landed at Sandwich on 4 May 1356 and then a truce until 1359 was concluded. When hostilities recommenced the French raided Sussex; Kent and the other southern counties fully expected to undergo the same ordeal and Sandwich was supposed to be especially threatened.[153] Although the English fleets were in command of the Channel and no resistance was, or could be, made to the transport of Edward's armies the coasts were constantly harassed by French incursions or the fear of them, and the sense of helplessness was aggravated by the losses suffered from privateers and the exhaustion of the shipowning classes. The experience was not singular, for in former times the almost invariable consequence of the destruction of an enemy's military fleets was an increase in raids and privateering. The large number of ships used for the transport of troops helped the French, for it left no reserve for the protection of the coasts and trade routes. But notwithstanding such checks some of the smaller ports were coming to the front if we may judge by letters directed, between 1350 and 1360, to Greenwich, Margate, Gravesend, and Rochester, on subjects connected with passenger traffic abroad (which was still to be confined to Dover by Stat. 9 Edw. III, c. 8) and the export of certain articles. Romney appears in 1353 in connection with a wreck, when those fortunate

---

[152] Pat. 25 April; 10 May 1355; dyke or dock cf. The Royal 24 Mar. 1358. For the mediæval Dockyards.   [153] Rymer, *Foedera* (ed. 1816), iii, 471.

enough to secure plunder took the precaution of removing the owner's marks from the bales of cargo.[154]

An unstable peace existed between 1360 and 1369; the renewal of the war in the latter year caused the king to convoke another council of provincial experts at Westminster to which Canterbury, as well as the Cinque Ports, sent representatives. The complete loss of the English control of the Channel followed the recommencement of hostilities. Levy followed levy without result; the Commons represented to the king the causes to which they attributed the decay of shipping, and in 1372, after the extermination of the Earl of Pembroke's fleet before Rochelle, the crown was reduced to issuing commissions of array for the maritime counties instead of defending them by fleets at sea. The ordinary rate of hire for ships taken up by the crown was 3s. 4d. a ton for every three months, but now both that and wages were left unpaid in contrast to the liberality Edward displayed thirty years earlier when he made extra and unusual payments to help the equipment of the fleets. The French were strong at sea and used their power energetically, while the English ports were enfeebled and such resources as the country possessed were not employed effectively. The Earl of Pembroke's overthrow caused the collection of another great fleet at home with which Edward sailed from Sandwich in August, but nothing was achieved by it. Raids or invasion were considered probable and Thanet was supposed to be a likely objective; in July and August there were orders to the keepers of the coast to have an especial care of 'Thanet,'[155] to the Abbot of St. Augustine to repair there and undertake its defence, for all the inhabitants to remain in their dwellings on the coast and combine to secure it, and to several of the local knights and landowners to return to their estates in Thanet and Sheppey and stay there to organize measures for the safety of that part of Kent.[156] Another great maritime disaster happened in 1375 in the shape of the capture or destruction in Bourneuf Bay of thirty-nine merchantmen, but there was no Kentish ship among those lost.

Edward III died 21 June 1377, and within a week of his death the French fell in force upon the south coast. The weight of their attack came upon Sussex, for the two 'ancient towns' were by far the most formidable members of the Cinque Ports confederacy, and the Normans had many old scores to settle with them. If, as is possible, they appeared off Dover they were deterred from active measures by its strength and readiness to repulse a landing, but they entered the Thames and burnt Gravesend. Towards the end of 1377 the need for ships was so great that it was agreed in Parliament in November to call upon many of the inland towns, as well as the ports, to build vessels by the following March; as an encouragement the burgesses were promised that, after the necessity had passed away, the vessels should be returned for private use to those who had paid for their building and equipment.[157] The Cinque Ports, as a whole, were charged with the provision of five balingers.[158] The dread of invasion was unceasing, and Thanet was regarded as particularly inviting to the French; evidently the inhabitants thought so, for in March 1378 the keepers of the coast were directed to compel those who had left in fear to return and

---

[154] Pat. 27 Edw. III, pt. ii, m. 4d.

[155] The present hundred of Ringslow was anciently the hundred of 'Thanet'; that is, that part of the island outside the jurisdiction of the Cinque Ports (Add. MS. 34148, fol. 102b). The order, no doubt, applied to the hundred.

[156] Rymer, *Foedera* (ed. 1816), iii, 953, 961.

[157] Close, 1 Ric. II, m. 22.

[158] Pat. 1 Ric. II, pt. iii, m. 6.

take their part in the defence.[159]   Notwithstanding the fleets fitted out here the French, assisted by Spain, still remained in the ascendant at sea; in 1379 or 1380 they were still in control of the Channel.[160]   In September of this year the Warden of the Ports was directed to convoke a meeting of the mayors, barons, and leading seamen, point out to them the disastrous consequences of the loss of the command of the Channel, ask their advice as to the measures expedient, and induce them to contribute towards the cost.[161]   Except when their misfortunes come under notice we hear little of the Cinque Ports during these years and they were probably in no condition to contribute money, or even to provide their full service.   The days were past when their squadrons were strong enough to turn the scale in a coastal war; the struggle was now between nations, and any recovery was dependent on statesmanship which could organize and wield successfully the whole maritime strength of England.   A writ of 1382 directing a general press of seamen in Sussex and Kent seems to point to a temporary paralysis of the Cinque Ports service and the consequent application of common custom to the counties.[162]

An occasional notice shows that the lapse of time had effected no improvement in the treatment of wrecked ships.   In 1380 a Flemish trader came ashore somewhere on Sheppey and, although not much injured, was first emptied of her cargo and then broken up by those at hand.[163]   In 1381 we have confirmatory evidence of the weakness of the Ports in the fact that Anne of Bohemia, coming to marry Richard, was delayed a month at Brussels because a Norman squadron cruised on the Flemish coast to intercept her.[164]   When she was at last able to cross the Channel it was because the French Council were persuaded to give her a safe conduct and order the Normans back into port.[165] Seeing that it was the especial province of the Cinque Ports to control this tract of sea we may infer complete inability on their part to perform their ancient office.   Another sign of their exhaustion is to be found in the almost entire absence of the Kentish members from the fleet lists of this reign.   In a fleet list of 1394, when the worst was past, there are two ships from Sandwich, the *Michel* of 100, and the *Margaret* of 40 tons, and the *Marie* of Smallhithe of 100 tons;[166] in an undated list, probably of about 1380, from Kent only one ship of Strood of 100 tons, and one of Cliffe (Clyve) of 80 tons, occur in the total of 188 vessels.[167]   No doubt the ' service ' was not wholly remitted, and fishing and trade on a small scale must have continued.   In 1385 we have a reference to the town ship of New Romney.   The possession of a town ship, an early example of municipal trading, was not confined to the Cinque Ports but it was a more usual custom, and continued longer among them than elsewhere.   There were new ships in 1396 and 1401; that of the latter year was built at Smallhithe.[168]   The town ship of Hythe was employed in the fishery in 1378;[169] in 1412 the jurats of Hythe hired a Smallhithe ship for their ' service.' [170]

---

[159] Pat. 1 Ric. II, pt. iv, m. 31*d*.

[160] C. Oman, *Political Hist. of Engl.*, 18, 20.

[161] Close, 4 Ric. II, m. 35. The French were particularly successful in single-ship actions, attributed to the superiority of the crossbow over the long bow for naval fighting.

[162] Pat. 5 Ric. II, pt. ii, m. 17. In 1377 the Warden of the Ports

had been ordered to press ships and crews to serve the captain of Calais (Close, 1 Ric. I, m. 20).

[163] Ibid. 3 Ric. I, pt. i, m. 1*d*. In 1387 the ' Blakedepe ' (Blackdeeps), at the mouth of the Thames, is mentioned (ibid. 10 Ric. II, pt. i, m. 1*d*). Cf. *post*, p. 307.

[164] Froissart, *Chron.* Bk. ii, cap. 86.

[165] The barons of New Romney built a barge for her passage; it was wrecked going into Calais (*Arch. Cant* xiii, 209).

[166] Exch. Accts. Bdle. 41, No. 33.

[167] Ibid. Bdle. 42, No. 22.

[168] *Hist. MSS. Com. Rep.* v, App. 533, 535, 536.

[169] Ibid. iv, App. 140.

[170] Ibid. 434.

In February 1385 Charles VI of France assembled a great army and fleet at Sluys for the invasion of England. Walsingham [171] says that the preparations struck terror here and created a panic during which only submission or flight was talked of; some of the French leaders, however, regarded the adventure with different eyes, and the project eventually came to naught by reason of the politic delays of the Duc de Berri. To throw an army across, unless communications were immune from interruption, would have been madness; and we may see in the hesitation of the Duc de Berri and others an indication that the French maritime superiority, although expensive and annoying to England, was of the nature of successful surprises and privateering, and was not of that stable character which is obtained by the possession of an established marine and the destruction of an enemy's fighting fleets that had enabled Edward III to carry over his armies to France. The attitude here was mainly one of passive expectation, but several small actions were fought towards the end of the year, in or near the Straits of Dover, many prizes being brought into Sandwich. As usual, Kent was held to be the probable mark selected by the enemy and some especial measures were taken for its safety. In February 1385 the jurats and commonalty of Sandwich obtained a grant, for two years, of certain customs to wall the town;[172] a month earlier a fish tax was authorized, primarily to pay for the defence of the Kent and Sussex coasts and, secondarily, for the walling of Rye.[173] The tax was of threepence on every noble's worth of fish landed, and the list of places is interesting as showing that, besides the well-known ports, Reculver, Whitstable, Seasalter, Ringwould, Broomhill, Deal, and Walmer were engaged in the industry. In April proclamation was made that persons living within six miles of Dover and Sandwich, and in the Isles of Thanet and Oxney, should withdraw into the towns for protection.[174] In November the burgesses of Dover were allowed ten marks yearly for five years towards the walling and fortification of the town;[175] in April 1386 power was given to the Warden to press masons and other artisans for the walling of Sandwich.[176]

The French fleet at Sluys had been disbanded for the winter but was collected again, on a yet larger scale, in the spring of 1386. In April the proclamation of the previous year affecting people living near Dover and Sandwich, and in Thanet and Oxney, was issued once more. Troops were levied and every important port from the Humber to the Land's End was guarded; Dover was garrisoned by 500 men-at-arms and 1,200 archers under the Earl of Cambridge, and Sandwich by the Earl of Buckingham with as many archers and 600 men-at-arms.[177] These preparations were not made until August and September when, if the French plan had been carried out as intended, their army would have been in England. The English Government had information that the principal descent was to be made in Orwell Haven, but the Dover and Picard fishermen were very good friends and it seems, war or no war, bought and sold fish among themselves. From the Frenchmen intelligence was obtained that Charles intended to land a division at Dover and another at Sandwich, and this news, whether true or false, must have kept the defenders keenly on the alert. In the meanwhile the Duc de Berri and Oliver

---

[171] *Hist. Angl.* (Rolls Ser.), ii 127.

[172] Pat. 8 Ric. II, pt. ii, m. 29.

[173] Ibid. m. 32d.

[174] Ibid. m. 18.

[175] Ibid. 9 Ric. II, pt. i, m. 17. There had been a murage grant to Dover in 1353 (ibid. 27 Edw. III, pt. i, m. 10).

[176] Ibid. 9 Ric. II, pt. ii, m. 15.

[177] Froissart, *Chron.* Bk. III, cap. 37. Mediæval figures given by the chroniclers must be taken with much salt.

de Clisson, the Constable of France, had not yet appeared at Sluys, and for two months an adverse wind blew steadily in favour of England. Late in October the duke arrived, and then good reasons were found for deferring the expedition until 1387. In May of that year troops under de Clisson were collected at Tréguier, in Brittany, and more at Harfleur; the force at Harfleur, under the Count de St. Pol, was destined for Dover or Orwell Haven,[178] but de Clisson was kidnapped by the Duke of Brittany and his misadventure put an end to the undertaking.

The Cinque Ports do not come under notice much in these events but their ships must have been cruising with occasional success judging from the fact that in 1387 five Spanish prizes were brought into Sandwich, and that in 1388 the Ports were exempted from the payment of 5 per cent. on all goods taken at sea at their own expense.[179] War with France was ended in 1389 by a truce which was prolonged from time to time until the campaign of Agincourt opened; but although official peace existed informal hostilities continued. In 1394 and 1396 the Cinque Ports were required to provide their full service for the king's passage to Ireland and Calais, so that we may suppose that they had somewhat recovered from the effects of the war. But the close of the fourteenth century saw also the close, practically, of the Cinque Ports era; Winchelsea, Rye, and Hastings were in decadence not only on account of the losses suffered through French attacks but also from the deterioration of their harbours; the latter cause was also acting at Hythe and Romney, and probably also at Sandwich and Dover. Hythe was afflicted by fire, pestilence, and misfortune of shipwreck, so that the burgesses desired to abandon the town, from which intention they were diverted by the interposition of Henry IV, who remitted their ' service' for a time.[180] In 1398 John Rone, from ' Flanders,' visited Romney to advise about the maintenance of the harbour, and it appears that in 1401–2 a new one was being made.[181] The people of Hythe had been attempting to improve their waterway in the reign of Edward III.[182]

Open war with France was expected daily for years after Henry IV obtained the throne; although it did not come French and English seamen attacked each other's ships and coasts as though it existed, and but for the fact that royal fleets did not engage under official sanction the conditions were those of active belligerency. In consequence of the uncertainty of the truce many of the inland towns, as well as the ports, were ordered on 11 January 1400–1 to build ships, singly or in combination, at their own cost by the following April.[183] The Cinque Ports, as a body, were not affected; Gravesend and Tilbury were rated together for one balinger, Greenwich for one, and Maidstone for one. When Parliament met it protested against this proceeding, and as Henry's position was too insecure to permit him to insist, as he might have done, on the strict legality of his action the order was withdrawn.

While Parliament was complaining, for many years of this reign, of foreign pirates the French chroniclers say that English seamen were incessantly ravaging the French coast, and not only France but also Portugal, Castile, Flanders, and the Hanse towns were protesting continuously about Channel piracy. The Cinque Ports play little part in these recriminations, although

[178] Froissart, *Chron.* Bk. III, cap. 64, 65.
[179] Pat. 10 Ric. II, pt. i, m. 27; 12 Ric. II, pt. i, m. 21.
[180] Ibid. 2 Hen. IV, pt. iii, m. 22. On 3 May 1400 there were 200 houses burnt, and five ships and 100 men had been lost at sea.
[181] *Hist. MSS. Com. Rep.* v, App. 535, 536.
[182] Ibid. iv, App. 434.
[183] Rymer, *Fœdera*, viii, 172.

there is one reference to 100 Picard seamen being carried away to Thanet, which may mean that they were not inactive.[184] But in consequence of the decline of the military value of the Cinque Ports and the rise of the western coast towns the principal attacks were now directed against Hampshire, Dorset, Devon, and Cornwall. In 1402 Henry Pay, the famous freebooter of the time, who is sometimes described as of Faversham and sometimes as of Poole,[185] was, with some Dover men, before the Council for piracy.[186] In 1406 the Warden was ordered to arrest the crew of the *Falcon* of Sandwich for the same offence.[187] Henry himself, sailing from Queenborough to Leigh in 1405, was nearly captured by French privateers; they did take four vessels with him, and if the king's ship ' had not been very swift he had landed sooner in France than in Essex.'[188] Lord Camoys, the commander of the convoying ships, was arraigned for intended treachery but acquitted, and the account of the affair leaves the impression of superior seamanship on the part of the French. Kentish waters have always been a favourite cruising ground for French and Flemish privateers, and if they were strong enough to attack a royal squadron no doubt the losses of small owners were heavy enough. In 1406 Henry gave one of his ships, the *Holigost*, to John Maiheu of Greenwich in consideration of the loss Maiheu had suffered from them.[189]

The conditions at this date, destructive of the humblest maritime industries, led to a curious arrangement between the peoples nearest each other on the opposing coasts. Apparently the friendly relations of 1385 had ceased or were very local,[190] but to minimize as far as possible the ruinous effect of constant captures an agreement was come to in 1412 between the masters and mariners from Southampton to Thanet and those on the French coast from Harfleur to ' Hendrenesce ' for a fixed tariff for the ransom of masters and seamen on either side and for their weekly board while prisoners.[191] Fishing boats, whatever their size, were to be released for 3s. 4d., and disputes were to be settled by arbitration. The compact did not apply to merchants or gentlemen. In 1407 a squadron under Henry Pay, largely made up of Cinque Ports vessels, took 120 French merchantmen off the Breton coast; the need for larger ships was slowly releasing the Cinque Ports from their responsibilities towards the State and leaving them free to employ such force as they possessed for their own purposes. Since the rise of Winchelsea and Rye, Sandwich had never equalled either town in wealth and importance but, in compensation, had escaped the hatred abroad which brought ruin upon them. Now, it was probably the most prosperous member of the confederacy and the only one with an oversea commerce of any extent. In 1411 a petition in Parliament joined it with London and Southampton as a suitable port of shipment for trade with the Mediterranean.[192] It is obvious that the possession of Calais had greatly increased the naval value of Dover, in view of the relation the two ports bore to the Straits, but there was nothing in the new acquisition to improve the commercial position of the Kentish port except, perhaps, as causing some increase in the passenger traffic.

Henry V had probably formed his own opinion about the scandalous excesses practised at sea during his father's reign. One of his first cares was to

---

[184] *Chronique du Religieux de St. Denys* (ed. 1839), iii, 52.

[185] He was buried at Faversham in 1419 (*Arch. Cant.* xxi, 279).

[186] Close, 4 Hen. IV, m. 31, m. 30.

[187] Pat. 7 Hen. IV, pt. ii, m. 10d.

[188] Grafton, *Chronicle* (ed. 1809) i, 497.

[189] Pat. 7 Hen. IV, pt. ii, m. 37.

[190] *Ante*, p. 272.

[191] *Hist. MSS. Com. Rep.* v, App. 536.

[192] *Rot. Parl.* iii, 662.

pass a statute instituting officials called conservators of truces in every port who, assisted by two legal assessors and holding their authority from the High Admiral, except in the Cinque Ports where they were appointed by the Warden, were to have power of inquiry and punishment concerning all guilty of illegal acts at sea.[193] The infraction of truces and the violation of safe conducts was to be high treason. The conservators were to keep a register of the ships and sea-men belonging to each port, take oaths from ship masters that they would observe the law, and act as adjudicators in such cases as did not go before the law courts. They seem, so far as related to judicial functions, to have been a link on the civil side between the earlier keepers of the coast and the vice-admirals of counties created in the sixteenth century. That the statute was strictly enforced and helped to procure quieter conditions at sea is shown by the fact that two years later the king consented to some modification of its stringency by promising to issue letters of marque when equitable. In 1435 it was entirely suspended, being found 'so rigorous and grievous,' said the Commons, an argument which would appeal to a weak government, but the real reason was to encourage piratical attacks on the Flemings after the rupture with the Duke of Burgundy. In 1451, when Henry VI had to pay for these piracies,[193a] it was brought into force again for a short time, and once more renewed by Edward IV. The statute, when first promulgated and actively executed under a monarch who was determined to make his will obeyed, must have been a further blow to the piratical disposition of the Ports.

Henry V began his reign with the intention of having a great fleet of his own. The custom of general impressment had become unduly expensive both for the shipowner and the crown; it was also slow and inefficient and the con-tinual complaints of the merchant class, as voiced in Parliament, were not safely to be ignored. The system could not be and was not at once abolished, but it became much less frequent during the fifteenth century, and there is quite a modern note in the establishment of cruisers along the coast in 1415, of which four were stationed between the Isle of Wight and Orfordness. In preceding centuries it would have been the specific duty of the Cinque Ports to guard that particular stretch of sea. The large fleet required for the campaign of Agincourt included a contingent from Kent, and Sandwich was one of the ports of concentration, but very many ships were hired in Holland and Zealand, the resources of the kingdom being insufficient or Henry resolved not to tax them to the injury of his subjects. During the siege of Harfleur the Cinque Ports fishermen were ordered to go over and fish on the Norman coast to supply the army.[194] After Agincourt Henry landed at Dover on 16 November 1415, one of the two most memorable homecomings the town has witnessed in its long history.[195] Another large fleet was gathered for the campaign of 1417, but out of 217 vessels of which we have details, 117 belonged to Holland and Zealand. Many of the English ports were unrepresented, and it may be surmised that for political reasons the king preferred to hire foreign ships as transports rather than disturb English trade. But the Cinque Ports were called upon for their 'service' and, in addition, ten hired ships came from Sandwich, four from Dover, two from Cliffe at Hoo, and one each from Romney, Strood, Faversham,

---

[193] Stat. 2 Hen. V, cap. 6.

[193a] See *post*, p. 278.

[194] Devon, *Issues of the Ex-chequer*, 341.

[195] This was written in 1908; the number should now be four.

and Gillingham.[196] In April 1420 the Ports undertook to keep a squadron off the Norman coast until the main English fleet was ready.[197]

Until pilgrims commenced to journey by sea direct to their destination the carriage of such travellers to the Continent was a lucrative business enjoyed almost solely by Dover. In 1389 the barons of Dover petitioned that an ordinance made by Edward III,[198] that none such should go from any other port under pain of a year's imprisonment should be enforced; from the king's answer it appears that the privilege they possessed was shared only by Plymouth.[199] But in the reign of Richard II the custom grew up of transporting pilgrims to one shrine—that of St. James of Compostella—by ship to the nearest Spanish port, and this rapidly developed into an important branch of English maritime traffic. They could only be carried in licensed ships, and nobles and merchants seem to have been equally eager to obtain a share in what must have been a profitable trade. Most of the ships engaged in the traffic belonged to the south-country ports, but those of Kent took no great part in it although vessels from Sandwich and Dover were occasionally licensed. The tonnage is seldom given in the licence, but the ships from the western ports, now growing rapidly in wealth and influence, were larger and in every way more suitable than those from the eastern Channel. There is a contemporary song on the miseries suffered by the pilgrims at sea,[200] and in this Sandwich is named as one of the principal places of embarkation but the records do not support the poet.

One of the first measures taken by the Regency after the death of Henry V was to sell off the Royal Navy by auction, but the loss was not at once felt because there was no French navy to contest the mastery of the sea. There were arrests of shipping, of the usual type, during the early years of the new reign, but there was now a general feeling that in this method 'the long coming together of the ships is the destruction of the country.'[201] Vessels were still impressed for the transport of troops, but the military service was handed over to contractors among the nobles who undertook to keep the sea with a certain number of ships and men for a specified time. No doubt the contractors desired to obtain as much money and to go to as little expense as possible, so that in 1442 Parliament, dissatisfied with the results, prepared a scheme by which a squadron was to be constituted of vessels from various ports.[202] It was composed of ships, barges, balingers, and pinnaces, the names marking the gradation in size; one balinger came from Dover, and one from Sandwich. In 1435 the Duke of Burgundy deserted the English alliance, a warning of stormy times to come. Among the preparations made here was a request from the Duke of Bedford, the Protector of the Kingdom, that the Cinque Ports would raise men-at-arms and archers for service in France. At this time there was no belligerent maritime pressure and troops rather than ships were wanted. The Portsmen did not refuse as contrary to their privileges, but, being seamen and not soldiers, professed themselves unable to find the men; they volunteered, instead, to fit out eight barges and balingers at their own expense to serve in the Channel.[203] Here the privileges were not brought forward as a reason for refusal, but at some earlier date the Lydd jurats had protested against

[196] Close, 5 Hen. V, m. 17; *Rot. Norman* (ed. Hardy), 1835, pp. 320–9.
[197] *Hist. MSS. Com. Rep.* iv, App. 435.
[198] 9 Edw. III, stat. 2, cap. 8.
[199] *Rot. Parl.* iii, 275.
[200] Wright and Halliwell, *Rel. Antiquæ*, pt. i. An English traveller in 1456 saw 80 pilgrim ships, of which 32 were English, at Coruña in that year.
[201] *Proc. of P.C.* (1st Ser.), v, 102.
[202] *Rot. Parl.* v, 59.
[203] Add. MS. 34, 150, fol. 23.

finding archers for the king's service because bound to be always ready to serve at sea.[204]

In and before 1430 the mayor and jurats of Dover were petitioning for help in view of injury done by the sea which they could not repair unaided; they were granted a toll on merchandise for eight years.[205] This is, at present, the first known reference to the impairment of the port and the measures taken to remedy it, which have continued for nearly five centuries and have cost so many millions of money; further relief was given by the crown in 1438.[206] The records of New Romney show that the degeneration of the harbour there, and the efforts to improve it, extended throughout the fifteenth century.

The fall of Rye and Winchelsea had rendered Sandwich the leading Cinque Port after a period of comparative obscurity; its ascent was helped by the destruction of Stonar, more or less a trade rival, by an inundation during the reign of Edward III, and the removal to it, in 1377, of the wool staple from Queenborough.[207] In 1397 it was wealthy enough to lend Richard II 100 marks. Also, it occupied in relation to the Downs the position to which Deal succeeded during the 17th century; the requirements of ships lying for shelter inside the Goodwins must have brought much profit to its tradesmen, and the close association between the anchorage and the town is indicated by the use of the phrase 'the Downs of Sandwich' in 1452.[208] The harbour was not used by the crown so frequently as under Edward III, but fleets were sometimes collected there and in the roadstead outside. But Kent, as a whole, was not holding its own with the other coast counties, most of which, notwithstanding war and bad government, were steadily increasing in maritime strength. There are in existence several lists of ships taken up for the transport of troops between 1439 and 1452; in only one of these are there any Kentish vessels, and while London and some of the western ports possessed ships of 300 and 400 tons, and others of from 200 to 300 tons are common, those from Kent are nearly the smallest of the fleet, one of Sandwich and one of Northfleet, each of 40 tons, being the largest. Altogether, there are six vessels, the other places represented being Deal, Kingsdown, Folkestone, and New Hithe; the smallest was the *Margaret*, of Kingsdown, of 18 tons.[209]

Sea-power played no great part in the Wars of the Roses, but the Cinque Ports as a whole, and those of Kent in particular, were Yorkist in sentiment. Discontent, due to their failing resources, would probably have made them ready to welcome any change, and their dissatisfaction with existing conditions was shown by their sympathy with Cade's rising in 1450. One of the complaints of the commons of Kent in that year was the frequent infringement of the privileges of the Cinque Ports in matters of taxation. The presence, also, of the Earl of Warwick as captain of Calais, and from his position able to make things very disagreeable for enemies at his threshold, must have been an important factor in shaping their political beliefs. For the earl the friendship of the Kentish ports had some value, for although neither side experienced any hindrance to sea transit during the war, the knowledge that an unopposed landing in England was within a few hours' sail, and that he could close the Straits without fear of attack from hostile ports, rendered his position very

[204] *Hist. MSS. Com. Rep.* iv, App. 426.
[205] *Rot. Parl.* iv, 364.
[206] *Proc. of P.C.* (1st Ser.), v, 98.

[207] *Rot. Parl.* iii, 10.
[208] *Proc. of P.C.* (1st Ser.), vi, 119. The name, 'Les Dounes,' occurs in 1316 (Pat. 10 Edw. II,

pt. i, m. 4), and again in 1372 (*Ib.* 20 Sept. 1372), where it is 'the coast of Sandwich called les Dounes.'
[209] *Exch. Accts.* Bdle. 53, No. 39.

strong. For many years England had possessed unchallenged supremacy in the Channel, but after 1435 the conquests of Henry V had vanished as rapidly as they had been gained and invasion or raids here were once more possibilities. As usual any such alarms were first felt for Kent; in 1455 orders were issued for keeping watch against attack on the county.[210] On 22 May of that year the first battle of St. Albans was fought, and thenceforward the coast towns had to attend to their own protection. Some time elapsed before the French were really strong enough to move by sea, and Calais acted as a check on the neighbouring coast, but in 1457 renewed alarm was felt and, as events proved, with good reason. In April Warwick, then at Canterbury, thanked the people of Sandwich for provisioning Calais,[211] and, although various entries on the Patent Roll show the general uneasiness, there was no local prevision of the storm which burst on Sandwich on Sunday, 28 August, when Pierre de Brézé, seneschal of Normandy, took the town by surprise.

According to one contemporary French chronicler[212] the attack took place with the complicity of Margaret of Anjou, or of her advisers, but if that be so it is strange that not one of her numerous enemies in England ever had a suspicion of a fact which must have been known to many in France. De Brézé only held the town for a few hours but it was completely plundered and many of the inhabitants killed. The English accounts say that the seneschal came with a combined Norman and Breton force, but Chastellain says that the Bretons attacked the town eight or ten days previously but did little mischief. De Brézé had not fitted out his armament with an especial view to Sandwich; circumstances brought him there. The walls authorized by Richard II do not seem to have afforded much protection although an additional fort for ordnance had been built in 1451;[213] when calm had been restored a brick bulwark, evidently for cannon, was ordered at the Fisher Gate.[214] In the following year the French were again off the coast, but this time there was warning from Warwick at Calais and measures of defence were taken. At Lydd the townsmen were divided into three watches and guns were placed in position at Dungeness. The French landed at the Ness, but beyond frightening the coast towns of Kent and Sussex they did nothing.[215] In 1451 Henry VI paid £4,666 to the Duke of Burgundy for injury done by his subjects to Flemish shipping, for a share of which the Portsmen were no doubt responsible. This helps to explain the particular attention paid to them by their enemies when opportunity offered. But their share must have been comparatively small, and they could only regard with envious admiration Warwick's piratical successes, with whole fleets, done under their eyes in the Straits of Dover in 1458 and 1459.

In the first weeks of 1460 Sandwich was connected with one of the few humorous incidents of the Civil War. The Earls of March, Warwick, and Salisbury were attainted refugees at Calais, where Warwick was supreme and certain of sympathy, if not help, from Kent. Some of his ships were at Sandwich and the government sent Lord Rivers and his son with 400 men to secure the town and take the ships. Warwick, well-informed, struck rapidly, sending

---

[210] Pat. 33 Hen. vi, pt. ii, m. 19*d*.

[211] *Paston Letters* (ed. 1872), i, 417.

[212] Chastellain, *Chronique* (ed. Kerwyn de Lettenhove), iii, 347 et seq.

[213] Boys, *Hist. of Sandwich,* 674.

[214] Ibid.

[215] *Hist. MSS. Com. Rep.* v, App. 521, 522. The ancestral customs of the Portsmen of course conduced to especial French attention. In 1455 and 1456 nine Sandwich ships were seized, by order of the crown, for piracy (Pat. 3 May 1459; 14 Mar. 1456).

over a force which surprised, or was admitted into, the town at night, took Rivers and his son in their beds, and brought them over to Calais. In that merciless war it was remarkable that they escaped with their lives, but the victors were content with holding them up to ridicule. Rivers was paraded before the three earls ' and then my Lord of Salisbury rated him calling him knave's son . . . and my Lord of Warwick rated him and said that his father was but a squire . . . and my Lord of March rated him likewise.' [216] The Earl of March, afterwards Edward IV, did not know that he was deriding his future father-in-law. A new garrison of 500 men under Osbert Mountford was placed in Sandwich, and again Warwick sent his soldiers across, who captured Mountford and dispersed the Lancastrians; Mountford, less fortunate than Rivers, was beheaded. From the easy way in which these two raids were carried out it is evident that the earl must have had many friends in the town. Nor was Sandwich the only Cinque Port which, from love or fear, was desirous of being on good terms with Warwick; in this or the following year they united to make up a gift of 100 marks for him, ' to have his friendship.' [217]

Edward IV showed himself duly grateful for the support given to his cause by Sandwich. In the first year of his reign he gave the mayor and barons £100 yearly from the customs for the fortification of the town and the improvement of the port; this grant was surrendered in 1465 for one in another form by which the townsmen were entitled to export forty sacks of wool yearly to the Mediterranean, free of customs and subsidy provided that they appropriated an equivalent sum, and £20 a year found by themselves to the same objects. [218] Richard III, in 1484, renewed the first grant of £100 a year during pleasure. [219] The reference to the Mediterranean shipments indicates that the town was still engaged in the oversea trade which commenced, perhaps, with the century; [220] it is no doubt to this prosperous era that we may assign the adoption of Brightlingsea as a non-corporate member, a union in which both places must have had somewhat to gain. [221] Since 1229 Walmer and Ramsgate had also become non-corporate members of Sandwich; and by a mandate of 1424 [222] Margate, Ringwould, Kingsdown, St. John's, St. Peter's, Gore End, and Birchington were annexed to Dover as non-corporate members.

Leland describes Sandwich as defended in part by a stone wall and in part by an earthen rampart and ditch; [223] he notices that much harm had been done to the haven by a carrack that sank there ' in Pope Paulus tyme,' and caused the formation of a shoal. Leland visited Sandwich between 1536 and 1542, and Paul III occupied the Papal throne from 1534 until 1549; the phrasing, however, suggests that Leland referred to Paul II, 1464–71. Boys, [224] who had access to corporation documents, tells us that in 1483 the wreck of a Spanish ship, lying ' outside Richborough,' was to be removed; but in 1487 there is an order to pay the mayor £40 in reward for raising a ship of 120 tons, belonging to Sir John Fortescue, sunk in and blocking up the haven. [225] Sir Thomas More was commissioned some time before 1528 to inquire why the harbour had

---

[216] *Paston Letters* (ed. 1872), i, 506.

[217] *Hist. MSS. Com. Rep.* v, App. 544.

[218] Pat. 5 Edw. IV, pt. ii, m. 23.

[219] Ibid. 1 Ric. III, pt. iii, m. 25.

[220] *Ante*, p. 274.

[221] The late Professor Montagu Burrows considered that the connection of Brightlingsea with the Ports existed long before its formal

reception by Sandwich (*The Cinque Ports*, 249).

[222] Add. MS. 34, 148, fol. 123.

[223] *Itinerary*, iii, 116.

[224] *Hist. of Sandwich*, 678.

[225] Exch. War, for Issues, Bdle. 70.

become 'in a few years so sore decayed.' Nothing was said of a sunken ship, the situation being ascribed by some to the Goodwins and by others to the inning of the marshes. Sir Thomas, however, was not writing a complete account of the inquiry but only referred to it as an illustrative anecdote in his *Dialogues*.[226] No coherent story is to be constructed from these isolated, and in some respects contradictory, data, but it seems that tradition and fact unite in assigning the occurrence of a wreck, or of more than one, to the close of the fifteenth century, and that it was believed that the shoal formed by it was the cause of a marked step forward in the deterioration of the haven which, however, had probably been progressing since the formation of the Goodwin Sands. On the other hand an inquiry in 1565, little more than twenty years after Leland wrote, attributed the mischief solely to the inning of the marshes.[227] Dover also was favoured by Edward, although he punished the townsmen for admitting Warwick (probably in 1469) by temporarily suspending their liberties; but in 1473 he gave a grant for ten years to be expended on the walls of the town, injured by gales.[228] In 1483 a toll on passengers and goods was continued for another ten years by Richard III;[229] it was perhaps from the proceeds of this grant that John Clark, master of the Maison Dieu, built the pier on the western side of the town forming the first artificial harbour at Dover.

The happiest fate for men or towns during the troubled early years of Edward IV's reign was to escape notice, and Kent appears to have been so far fortunate until Warwick quarrelled with the king. In July 1469 he and the Duke of Clarence were at Calais, and when they crossed seem to have landed in Kent, as they had an interview at Canterbury with the agents of their northern allies. The campaign which followed ended disastrously for the earl and the duke who, when they returned to Calais, found its guns turned upon them by the former's lieutenant. The reconciliation of Warwick with Margaret of Anjou, the return of the king-maker, the flight of Edward IV, his return and the battles of Barnet and Tewkesbury led up to the last incident of the civil war in which Kent was concerned. In September 1470 Warwick and his followers were expected to land again in the county, and Edward ordered a force to be collected to repulse them; it was probably due to adverse winds that they made Plymouth and Dartmouth. After Tewkesbury, Warwick's admiral, Thomas Fauconberg,[230] with the ships under his command and reinforced by soldiers from Calais, came over and found no difficulty in raising some thousands of Kentish men to march on London to release Henry VI. He failed to force his way into the city, retreated before Edward, and finally deserted his army, which dispersed, while he went to Sandwich with 600 of the Calais troops. There he awaited Edward's arrival, and as he could so easily have escaped we may infer that he knew that he could come to some arrangement with the king or thought that he could hold the town. Edward thought it well to come to terms; Fauconberg surrendered with forty-seven ships and took the oath of allegiance, but his submission did not save his head shortly afterwards.[231] It will be noticed that although these Kentish ports were Yorkist they were compelled to follow the political changes of Warwick because, as they no

---

[226] *Works* (ed. 1557), p. 277.
[227] Exch. Spec. Com. 1083.
[228] Pat. 13 Edw. IV, pt. i, m. 11.

[229] Ibid. 1 Ric. III, pt. v, m. 5.
[230] Bastard son of William Neville, earl of Kent.

[231] *Restoration of Edward IV* (Camd. Soc.), 39.

longer controlled the Straits themselves, they were obliged to serve whoever held the local mastery of their sea communications.

Whatever discontent may have been felt in the interior of the county the Kentish ports accepted Henry VII loyally. Perkin Warbeck, intending ' to have a town of strength,' landed men at Deal on 3 July 1495 to take Sandwich, but nearly 150 of them were killed or captured by the defenders.[232] When Warbeck again tried his fortune in the west country in 1498, a Hythe man, John Bowes, was rewarded with 20s. for bringing his standard to London.[233] The charter service of the Cinque Ports had fallen into abeyance during the Wars of the Roses, but was renewed when order was restored. In the meanwhile the Portsmen had made what profit they could out of the troubled times and there is more than one reference to piracy, especially by Sandwich ships.[234] In one case, in 1472, a Sandwich crew hired by the people of the east coast for the protection of the herring fishery seized a vessel in Orwell Haven and took her away. By 1488 the Portsmen, like the fishermen of other maritime counties, were paying for convoy appointed by the government for the North Sea fishery.[235] Edward IV required the ' service ' for his war with France in 1475, and it was again demanded by Henry VII when he crossed the Straits with an army in October 1491. We find, in connexion with this levy, the first allusion to an allowance from the subsidies and fifteenths made to the Ports towards their expenses. By an agreement of 12 April 1491 it was not to exceed £500; Jeake [236] says that under Edward IV it had been a still larger sum, and refers to a document relating to the expedition of 1475 by which it appears that Kent was then allowed £455 and Sussex £79 5s. 5¼d. It is clear, from this innovation, that while the Cinque Ports as a whole had become much poorer and weaker, Sussex had declined to a far greater degree than Kent, in which Sandwich and Dover were still strong and prosperous ports. The presumption is that the 'service' of 1475 was the first for which this allowance was made, but it does not follow that the poverty which necessitated it was due to the civil war: it was rather the consequence of a natural and progressive decline. The circumstance that for the ' service ' of Romney, in 1492, three vessels were hired from Folkestone, Snodland, and New Hithe is no doubt a sign of its decay.[237] The importance of holding the Channel gate was recognized as clearly as ever—' it is thought here that the king should have a navy upon the sea to show himself as a king to rule and keep his streams betwixt this and Dover,' wrote the Lieutenant of Calais, but it was not as easy to equip a squadron from the ships belonging to the crown, or to merchants generally, as it had been to send an order to the Cinque Ports to go to sea.

With the reign of Henry VIII the era of general arrests and impressment of shipping may be said to have terminated. The coast towns were still to be called upon sometimes to provide ships, but such towns were usually associated in order to lessen the expense and, eventually, the county to which they belonged contributed as a whole to the cost. The non-privileged portion of maritime Kent naturally fell into line with the rest of England, and the Cinque

[232] *Paston Letters* (ed. 1872), iii, 386.
[233] Add. MS. 7099, fol. 46.
[234] Pat. 4 Edw. IV, pt. i, m. 16d; 11 Edw. IV, pt. ii, m. 11d; *Fœdera*, xi, 673.

[235] Campbell, *Materials for a History of the Reign of Henry VII,* i, 347.
[236] *Charters of the Cinque Ports,* 112, 113.

[237] *Hist. MSS. Com. Rep.* v, App. 548. New Hithe is likely to be that, near Snodland, on the Medway.

Ports were, in time, assimilated to the system. Improvements in building and armament were rapidly differentiating the man-of-war from the merchantman; the latter was of little use in fleets except, as an Elizabethan seaman said, ' to make a show,' and to have required the port towns to furnish real men-of-war would have ruined them. If such places as Southampton, Plymouth, Bristol, and Newcastle were unable now to send true fighting ships to sea it may be imagined that the antiquated ' service ' of the Cinque Ports had become only an interesting survival. Three times during the reign of Henry they were called upon for it but only for purposes of transport; on one occasion, in 1531, it was reduced to ten vessels for horse and baggage transport, as men and ships were away at the herring fishery. In 1556 they, nominally, conveyed Philip from England to the Continent, and in 1562 they answered the old call for the last time, again for transport and not for fighting, when Elizabeth was trying to hold Havre.

It was one of the aims of Henry's statesmanship to create a national navy, and there was not a year of his reign that did not witness some accretion to its strength. Such merchantmen as he required were hired, without the exercise of the prerogative; it is not until the reign of Elizabeth that we find in force the further development of the right of impressment, the demand for fully armed ships at the cost of the ports and counties, the immediate precedent for the subsequent ship-money levies. The first war with France, of 1512-14, was fought out chiefly by the men-of-war, but there were some hired ships in pay, and among them appear four of Greenwich, sometimes as fighting ships and sometimes as store ships.[238] Although called ' of Greenwich ' they were really king's ships, the phrase having succeeded ' of Westminster ' and ' of the Tower ' as an occasional equivalent of the later ' H.M.S.'

The vessels of the Ports were required in 1513 to carry over the king and his army to Calais, the troops embarking at Sandwich and Dover.[239] In reply to an inquiry from the Lord Treasurer the civic authorities of Sandwich informed him that 60 vessels could lie at the quay and 500 or 600 in the haven.[240] Dover supplied one fighting ship, the *Fortune*,[241] and Sandwich a transport attached to the fleet.[242] Uniform also was in use, ' a coat of white cotton with a red cross and the arms of the Ports underneath.'[243] In May 1514 the French raided Sussex, burning Brighton, and it appears that they were also off the Kentish coast doing ' great displeasure at Dover without hindrance ';[244] men-of-war were lying in the harbour but the crews were ashore. Not much damage can have been done. On 23 July 1518 Cardinal Campeggio came ashore at Deal,[245] being the first notable arrival there since the advent of Caesar, if the Roman really landed on that beach. The fact that Campeggio came to Deal indicates that it had already become an alternative to Dover in certain conditions of wind and weather, and was preferred to Sandwich. Charles V landed at Dover 26 May 1520,[246] but departed from Deal; he came again to Dover 27 May 1522 and was received by Wolsey ' on the sands.' The vessels employed in the transport of the Emperor and his suite in 1520 included two of 80 tons, five of 50 tons, one of 45 tons, and four smaller ones, of Dover;[247] in

[238] Chap. Ho. Bks. ii, fol. 63 et seq.; *L. & P. Hen. VIII*, i, 3591, 3977.

[239] *L. & P. Hen. VIII*, i, 4083, 4492.

[240] Boys, *Hist. of Sandwich*, 681.

[241] *L. & P. Hen. VIII*, i, 5112.

[242] Ibid. 3980.

[243] Boys, *op. cit.* 775.

[244] *L. & P. Hen. VIII*, i, 4743.

[245] Ibid. ii, 4333.

[246] *Chron. of Calais* (Camd. Soc.), 28.

[247] *L. & P. Hen. VIII*, iv (i), 398.

1522 there were one of 50 tons, two of 30 tons, and one of 24 tons of Hythe, and one of 40 tons of Folkestone.[248] It is evident that the increasing frequency of landings at Deal drew attention to the open nature of the shore and the possible dangers following therefrom, for when war with France recommenced in 1522 Sir William Haute was commissioned as captain of the coast between Deal and Sandwich.[249] Before war occurred the Cinque Ports were ordered to keep scouts at sea, but when it was in progress the maritime operations were of a minor character. The local squadron, cruising on the coast between Rye and the Thames, consisted of three men-of-war and one hired ship of Sandwich;[250] in former centuries the guardianship of this area would have been undertaken by the ports of Kent and Sussex.

About 1539 Henry expected the formation of a continental alliance against England. The new navy, although a mightier instrument of war than even its creator dreamed it to be, was as yet an untried weapon; it was natural therefore to rely upon land defences in the shape of forts, to prevent a descent or support a defending force. As early as 1535 the idea was in the air of fortifying the strategic points round the coast, for Cromwell then noted in his 'Remembrances' that a small tax, formerly paid to Rome, might well be diverted 'towards the defence of the realm to be employed in making fortresses.' Vast sums were being spent upon Calais and Dover; Philip Hoby was in Spain inquiring about the sea walls and piers of St. Sebastian in the hope of learning how to work successfully at Dover, and when he returned, in 1538, he urged the advantage of fixed defences for the protection of the harbour.[251] In the same year there was a payment of £10 to Antonio Fagion, a Sicilian, for 'devices,' i.e. plans, of bulwarks and blockhouses.[252] Besides the dark political outlook there was more than one case of attacks on each other by belligerents in English territorial waters which were incidents well calculated to arouse the anger and pride of the king. In 1539 some 'sad and expert persons' were sent to inspect the coast, and Henry himself directed the 'devices' for the three new bulwarks in the Downs, 'on the frontiers of the sea,' of which the construction was placed under the superintendence of Sir Edward Ryngeley, Thomas Wingfield of Sandwich, and Antony Aucher, with the master mason of Hampton Court as the actual builder.[253] Fortifications were the natural sequel of the realization of the inviting character of the beach between Sandwich and Kingsdown and of the growing importance of the Downs as an anchorage.

The bulwarks at Dover were begun in the spring of 1539 when the French ambassador, passing through in April, noticed in his correspondence with his sovereign their appearance since his predecessor's departure in February;[254] in August there are payments for those at Dover and in the Downs.[255] At first they do not seem to have been named except from their position in relation to prominent objects; there was (1) 'the bulwark under Dover Castle,' afterwards the Moat Battery; (2) 'the bulwark on the cliff,' afterwards the Archcliff Fort; and (3) 'the bulwark on the hill beyond the pier,' or Black Bulwark.[256] Sandgate Castle was at first called Folkestone Castle,

---

[248] Add. MS. 29, 618, fol. 139.

[249] L. & P. Hen. VIII, iii, App. 45.

[250] Ibid. (ii), 2296.

[251] Ibid. xiii (ii), 974.

[252] Ibid. 1280.

[253] Ibid. xiv (i), 398, 400.

[254] Ibid. (i), 670.

[255] Ibid. (ii), 236.

[256] Ibid. xv, 323; xvi, 456.

Compare the map, Cott. MS. Aug. 1; 22, 23, which shows the Black Bulwark at the end of Thompson's pier, the second pier built. The map is the more reliable.

and the cost of building it was £2,887 14*s*.;[257] it was designed by Stephen von Hassenperg, a German, and as it was similar in plan to Sandown, Deal, Walmer, and Camber Castles, he was no doubt responsible for all of them.[258] He had been in charge of the fortifications of Calais and was brought over in haste for those in England.[259] The prevailing view now is that if a fleet is strong enough to take the offensive and occupy that of the enemy, permanent fortifications, except under special conditions, such as may be required to repulse a raid, are not only needless but are a waste of force; in 1539 the new navy was not yet strong enough nor practised enough for its *métier*, and events were goading the authorities, almost daily, to still prompter action. In April a fleet of 68 sail, which proved to be Dutch, came into the Downs; the Lord Warden was on the spot and prepared to make a stout resistance if there was any attempt to land,[260] and although the alarm proved groundless such an incident hastened the erection of the defences on which so much reliance was placed. Besides the three castles of Sandown, Deal, and Walmer, there were also four bulwarks, or sconces, of earth thrown up on the shore fronting the Downs, two of these being between Sandown and Deal Castles and two between Deal and Walmer.[261] By 1540 Sandown Castle was completed and garrisoned, Thomas Wingfield being captain with 34 gunners and soldiers, but there was as yet no artillery in it, nor in the four earthworks which had four captains and 32 men between them.[262] The Archcliff, Moat, and Black Bulwarks at Dover were furnished with guns, but not Sandgate Castle.

Besides its importance as the highway to London the Thames needed defences to hinder approach to the new dockyards at Deptford and Woolwich. The place chosen was where the river begins to narrow at Gravesend, a fort being built there and at Milton, crossing fire with another at Tilbury. A third battery on the Kentish side, called the Higham Bulwark, was made lower down to command the fairway, probably near Higham Creek as the tide sets on to the Kentish shore there. These North Kent defences were planned by Sir Christopher Morris and ——— Needham; there is one obscure reference to two more bulwarks above Gravesend, but they were perhaps never finished.[263] The three forts were in construction in the spring of 1539, and by February 1540 they were completed and armed, but the garrisons of Gravesend and Milton were, respectively, only nine men and twelve men including the captains;[264] there were eight heavy guns in Gravesend fort, of which the largest were three 9-pounders.[265] In 1547 a blockhouse existed at Sheerness, but the date of construction is unknown.[266] Except within the liberties of the Cinque Ports, where they were under the control of the Warden, the new fortifications everywhere were in the charge of the Lord Admiral. Those under the latter soon passed out of his hands; probably it was considered impolitic to entrust a subject with so much power.

In November 1533 the mayor and jurats of Dover wrote to Cromwell that their harbour had ceased to exist, and that unless some remedy were applied

[257] *L. & P. Hen. VIII*, xiv (ii), 645.
[258] Harl. MS. 1647.
[259] *L. & P. Hen. VIII*, xvi, 269.
[260] Ibid. xiv (i), 728.
[261] Ibid. xvi, 456. See also Elvin's *Records of Walmer* for the exact position of some of these earthworks; and W. L. Rutton in *Arch. Cant.* (xxiii) for details of the construction of the Downs fortresses.
[262] Ibid. xv, 323.
[263] *L. & P. Hen. VIII*, xv, 502.
[264] Ibid. 323.
[265] Ibid. 196.
[266] *Acts of P.C.* 20 Sept. 1547; 2 May 1548.

they would be compelled to forsake the town.[267] A year later they petitioned again, saying that until lately the townsmen had possessed nineteen or twenty ships with small craft in proportion, but that during the preceding ten or twelve years the deposit of shingle (' small stones ') had grown so rapidly that the harbour was closed.[268] Very shortly afterwards the harbour works, which have been carried on with little intermission to the present day, were commenced, or rather renewed, but it was no doubt the strategic importance of Dover and not the woes of the inhabitants that moved Henry to action.[269] By 1543, when war with France and Scotland was renewed, the harbour, although by no means a success, was again available for small vessels. The Cinque Ports ' service ' was required once more for the purpose of transport to which it had descended; Henry crossed to Calais with an army in July 1544, and hoys to carry the troops were taken up along the coast. In June all that Lord Russell, writing from Dover, could find to say about them was ' the ships of the Ports are here and do no service ';[270] but their ability now was confined to transport which, when the time came, was performed smoothly enough. Sir Thomas Seymour, who commanded the king's ships in the eastern Channel, made Dover his base for operations on the Norman coast and in the neighbouring waters. In 1544 England took the offensive, but in the following year France was strong enough to fight for the command of the Channel and, although invasion was not very probable, precautions were taken in Kent. The defence of Thanet was confided to Sir Antony Aucher and other gentlemen, who were provided with artillery and 300 men, apparently a flying column; the Archbishop of Canterbury, who was also concerned, applied for guns to be mounted on the cliffs.[271] The principal movements of the opposing fleets were in the vicinity of Portsmouth and the Isle of Wight, but in July the French appeared between Hythe and Lydd, on their way westward, and ' made two or three descents but all to our advantage,' wrote an onlooker.[272] His letter implies that the descents were in Kent, but it is more likely that those on the Sussex coast were meant.

The Cinque Ports had long ceased to count militarily, and it would appear that their ambiguous position in retaining privileges without being able to render services in return was beginning to provoke question. In 1546 the collectors of the fifteenths were demanding full payment within the liberties as elsewhere. An appeal to the Privy Council caused the matter to be laid before Henry; apparently it was decided that no destructive innovation should be made, for the Archbishop of Canterbury was requested to persuade the Portsmen to submit to the same taxation as the rest of the country, but there was no hint of possible compulsion.[273] It was not the first time that their exemptions had been encroached upon;[274] there is a patent of 1544 releasing the non-corporate members of Dover and Sandwich from all arrears of tenths,

---

[267] *L. & P. Hen. VIII*, vi, 1472. Had the diving bell been known it might have helped in the construction of the foundations of the piers, the weak point, but the earliest use of modern bell was in Italy in 1535.

[268] Ibid. vii, 66.

[269] The townspeople were con-sidered to have misused former grants (ibid. viii, 1085). At a moderate estimate I should im-agine that some £40,000,000, in modern values, have been thrown into the sea at Dover. The latest harbour seems now to be con-demned as a failure (1924).

[270] Ibid. xix (i), 708.

[271] Ibid. xx (i), 671.

[272] Ibid. 1323.

[273] *Acts. of P.C.* 21 May, 11 June 1546.

[274] *Ante*, pp. 251, 257, 264, 276. See also charter of February 1440, reciting that the privileges of Dover had been disregarded (Statham, *Dover Charters*, 199).

fifteenths, and subsidies since 1533-4, so that there must have been a recent instance, if only an attempt, of the application of general taxation within the jurisdiction of the Ports.[275] The relief was granted because the ports of Dover and Sandwich, to which these small places belonged, were 'in ruin and decay.' Of the non-corporate portion of Kent we hear little during this period, but probably the towns on the Thames, the Medway, and the Swale were sufficiently prosperous through the coasting trade and the fisheries. The continual presence of men-of-war laid up in the Thames, the new dockyards, and the new forts were all excellent stimulants of local business activity.

To the needs of the new navy we may ascribe the foundation, or re-constitution, of the Guild of the Holy Trinity of Deptford Strond 'for the reformation of the navy,[276] lately much decayed by admission of young men without experience, and of Scots, Flemings, and Frenchmen as lodesmen' (pilots).[277] It was an attempt to obtain skilled men, practised and technically trained, and English subjects, for the navigation, in the intricate waters of the mouth of the Thames and elsewhere, of the large and expensive ships now built. A charter followed, in 1514, devoted to the charitable side of the work of the corporation and no doubt intended to enlarge its influence by making it advantageous to the mass of seamen to be connected with it. The tradition which assigns the foundation of the Trinity House to Sir Thomas Spert has probably no groundwork of fact and has grown up round the circumstance that Spert was, so far as is known, the first Master. He was never, even in after years, a man of any great influence, and in 1513 was, it is true, attached to the Court as a 'yeoman of the crown,' but was only employed in subordinate capacities. It is much more likely that the reconstruction of an ancient guild was, like every other improvement in naval administration at the time, due to Henry himself, but it is possible that it was suggested by conditions already existing within the Cinque Ports. The earliest volume now surviving of rules and orders relating to the Cinque Ports pilotage system, or Court of Lodemanage, commences at 1550,[278] but there is evidence that there was organi-zation and supervision of some sort long before. The volume itself begins as a continuation, and in or before the reign of Edward IV the Cinque Ports Admiralty was dealing with the defaults of pilots;[279] in 1517 there is a specific instance of such action.[280] How and when the pilotage establishment obtained independent existence it is impossible to say, but it is clear that it was acting as a separate and self-directing body during the reign of Henry VIII, and it is of some significance to find such terms as ' elder brethren ' and ' younger brethren,' ' upper book ' and ' lower book,' which it has been the custom to connect solely with the Deptford Corporation, in use at Dover before they come into evidence in relation to the Thames institution. Except perhaps as a charity the latter body led an obscure and unimportant existence for many years; its historians have asserted that its officials had a large share in the formation and government of the Tudor navy, but they have brought forward no testimony in support of their statements, nor, as a fact, would it be possible for them to find a single item of evidence in official papers to substantiate a claim copied from

[275] Pat. 36 Hen. VIII, pt. xxii, m. 12. Another instance is so far back as 3 Ric. II (Add. MS. 34, 148, fol. 102).
[276] I.e. the *personnel*: " Refor-

formation "=restoration or cor-rection (*New Eng. Dict.*).
[277] *L. & P. Hen. VIII*, i, 3808; 19 Mar. 1512-13; Pat. 6 Hen. VIII, pt. i, m. 10.

[278] Egerton MS. 2118.
[279] Marsden, *Select Pleas of the Court of Admiralty*, ii, pp. xxviii, xxix.
[280] *L. & P. Hen. VIII*, ii, 3541.

each other and repeated without inquiry. Even in the 17th and 18th centuries, when its connexion with the Navy was closest, the duties of the Trinity House brought it into contact with the Navy Board only in one or two subordinate matters, and the relation of the Elder Brethren with the Navy authorities was that of service and not of association. Lyon[281] states that the date of the earliest rules of the Dover fellowship is of 26 February 1527; in 1601 it had a suit at law with the Deptford establishment and, shortly afterwards, was itself known as the Trinity House of Dover.[282]

Through several centuries the right of wreck was coveted by both manorial lords and corporations as a source of profit, but still more as evidence of exemption from the inquisition of the High Admiral. Legally, if man, dog, or cat escaped alive from a ship it was no wreck; but we have seen that if the cargo once came into the hands of those who dwelt along the coast it was practically lost to the owners. Every corporation used what influence it possessed to obtain local jurisdiction in Admiralty matters, not only as a question of dignity and profit but even more with the object of escaping the arbitrary and expensive proceedings of the Admiral's deputies who brought much odium upon their master. The earliest grant known of wreck and other rights in Kent is that of Sandwich Haven in 1029 to the Archbishop of Canterbury;[283] in 1139 the Archbishop and the Abbot of Battle were at law about the claim to wreck on Dungeness.[284] The question of wreck and Admiralty rights is more than usually obscure in Kent and Sussex on account of the complicated relation between private privileges, those of the Lord Admiral, and those of the Cinque Ports.

Queenborough, which was favoured in several ways by Edward III, obtained Admiralty jurisdiction by a grant of 10 May 1368,[285] and Rochester by one of 1 June 1424.[286] As a rule such favours were only given to places whose services were valuable to the crown, but it is unknown why the city was so honoured; these two were the only places in Kent outside the Cinque Ports which obtained such immunities. The Hundred Rolls of 1275 show that the Archbishop of Canterbury, the Abbots of St. Augustine and Battle, and other ecclesiastical dignitaries possessed wreck rights round the coast. How these claims were reconciled with the undoubted exercise of the same rights by the Cinque Ports it is impossible to say, but we find signs of the resulting friction to a late period. In 1543 the bailiff of Dover was in trouble for executing process of the Westminster Court within the Cinque Ports,[287] and in 1546 the Archbishop of Canterbury and the Lord Warden were quarrelling about their respective rights in wrecks.[288] According to the 'Book of Customs' of Old Romney the jurats and commonalty were entitled to a fourth part of all wrecks between Dungeness and Hythe;[289] besides the greater disputes between the Ports and outside powers as to the possession of wreck there were minor quarrels between the towns and the Warden as to their respective shares. There were compositions between the Lord Warden and various places before 1561, but in that year the jurats of Romney agreed that Lord Cobham should have a half

---

[281] *Hist. of Dover*, i, 287.

[282] Egerton MS. 2118, fol. 15, 18.

[283] *Anglo-Sax. Chron.* (Rolls Ser.), i, 290–1; ii, 128.

[284] *Plac. Angl. Norman* (Bigelow), 143.

[285] Chart. R. 42 Edw. III, No. 8. But the Queenborough claim was not undisputed, see *post*, p. 293, and Admir. Ct. Acts, xxvi, 3 Nov. 1606.

[286] Admir. Ct. Misc. 952.

[287] Marsden, *Select Pleas*, ii, p. xxii.

[288] *Acts of P.C.* 12 Nov. 1546.

[289] *Hist. MSS. Com. Rep.* iv, App. 424.

of all wrecks and findings at sea.[290] The only person who, in effect, had no place in these discussions was the owner of the cargo. Ships on the Goodwins were held to be wreck and 'peaseably enjoyed' although the crews got safely ashore and the cargoes were salved.[291]

The limits of the Cinque Ports have been very uncertain. It is said that 'anciently' they extended on the south coast to the Red Nore, or Redware, by Newhaven;[292] to the north they reached in 1525 to St. Osyth, but in 1526 had receded to Shoebury, and in both cases the western boundary was then Beachy Head.[293] The crown had become anxious to restrict, as far as possible, franchises which no longer represented equivalent services to the nation and introduced legal quibbles and inequalities; there is one example of this tendency in 1542 when Dover pier having 'won clear out of sea,' it was ordered that the jurisdiction of the Lord Warden was not to extend to it.[294] The Warden claimed jurisdiction 'half seas over' in the Channel, and here again came into conflict with the Lord Admiral.[295] From a petition of 1577 it would seem that the crown then took all wreck between high and low watermark, leaving the Warden such as came on to the Goodwins or was found floating at sea;[296] but the success of these claims, counter-claims, and mutual encroachments varied with the assertive or non-assertive character of the men who happened to be Lords Warden or Lords Admiral. Another Elizabethan document is a bond by the queen's bailiff at Ramsgate to account for wrecks between high and low watermark there and in all the crown jurisdiction in Thanet;[297] with Elizabeth on the throne and Howard of Effingham as Lord Admiral the privileges of the Ports would be confined within their bare rights. The Ports had their own Admiralty Court, 'the type and original of all our Admiralty and maritime courts,' dating from at least the thirteenth century.[298] There are many instances during early centuries of admiralty courts being held upon the seashore at various places within the bounds of the Cinque Ports, but later the sittings were always held in the church of St. James at Dover. Elizabeth regarded the especial position of the Ports with no kindly eye, and it is expressive of the Portsmen's recognition of the situation and their desire to do nothing that might arouse the crown to action that between 1558 and 1597 only three admiralty courts about wrecks were held.[299] Unlike many ancient institutions the Admiralty Court of the Ports has, nominally, undergone little change, and was the only one preserved when all other local admiralty courts were abolished by the 5 and 6 Will. IV, cap. 76; practically it is obsolete.

The question of piracy and wrecking became prominent during the reign of Henry VIII, not because such offences were more prevalent—there were probably fewer cases than during preceding centuries—but because suppression was taken in hand more seriously. To Henry order and security at sea for commerce were a sign and a means of that maritime supremacy he had always in view. It had been found that the existing system of trial for piracy was

[290] S.P. Dom. Eliz. xvi, 57.
[291] Marsden, *Select Pleas*, ii, p. xxxi.
[292] *Suss. Arch. Coll.* xvii, 148. An Admiralty Court held in 1479 named the Red Nore as the western limit (Add. MS. 34150, fol. 36).

[293] *L. & P. Hen. VIII*, iv, 1820, 2250.
[294] Ibid. xvii, 617.
[295] S.P. Dom. Eliz. ccxxxvii, 12.
[296] Ibid. Suppl. xxi.

[297] K.R. Mem. R. 418, Recog. Kent.
[298] Marsden, *Select Pleas*, ii, p. xxi.
[299] *Hist. MSS. Com. Rep.* v, App. 139.

nearly useless, the offender having to confess before he could be sentenced, or his guilt having to be proved by disinterested witnesses who naturally could seldom be present at sea. By two statutes, 27 Hen. VIII, cap. 4 and 28 Hen. VIII, cap. 15, such crimes were in future to be tried according to the forms of the common, and not as hitherto the civil, law. It was no doubt for the better administration of these statutes and for other reasons connected with international obligations in maritime matters, for the protection of the king's and Lord Admiral's rights in wrecks, for the registration of ships and men available and the levy of seamen, and for the execution of domestic regulations intended to prevent unlawful practices at sea, that it was deemed advisable to have round the coast permanent representatives of the Lord Admiral who should be of higher social standing and armed with greater authority than were the deputies who had hitherto visited each county or district collecting the Lord Admiral's profits or maintaining his rights. The new officers, the vice-admirals of the counties, were, in their civil functions, the successors historically of the keepers of the coast and the conservators of truces of the thirteenth and fifteenth centuries, and there is not one of the duties of the vice-admirals which cannot be paralleled among those performed by the earlier officials. There had been occasional appointments, in some of the counties, of officers who had held posts very similar to those of the vice-admirals; but now, instead of acting temporarily and only in one or two districts, they became a band of crown officials stationed round the whole coast, backed by the power of the Tudor despotism, and continued without any interruption during which their authority might diminish through a period of non-continuance. The patents of appointment were from the Lord Admiral, sometimes for life and sometimes during pleasure; each vice-admiral had a miniature admiralty court of his own and his perquisites were shared with the Lord Admiral.

The scheme did not come into operation simultaneously over all England but developed according to necessity and opportunity. The greater portion of the coast of Kent was already under the jurisdiction of the Lord Warden when the vice-admirals were appointed; for the remainder the judge of the Admiralty Court was acting between 1525-36, it, with Essex, being allotted to him 'for the augmentation of the same office' (i.e. his salary), and perhaps because his position better enabled him to hold his own legally with the Warden.[300] The profitable character of this coast in the matter of wrecks is shown by the curious subdivision at various times among several vice-admirals, an arrangement calculated to produce interminable disputes between them and the Warden and their respective officers. In 1549 Richard Cavendish held the vice-admiralship between Wissant and St. John's Road (i.e. Margate), therefore if the Lord Warden insisted that his jurisdiction extended 'half seas over' no better plan to produce contention could have been devised. In 1550 Sir John Norton was vice-admiral for Kent 'ultra Hallowis,' that is to say, the parish of that name in the hundred of Hoo which included Yantlet Creek; in 1559 the coast eastward from Northfleet was placed under Lord Cobham, but as he was already Lord Warden the appointment simplified matters. In 1587 Sir Edward Hoby, the Lord Admiral's brother-in-law, was nominated vice-admiral of the hundred of Milton; at the same time the Judge of the Admiralty Court was acting for London and the Thames. Here was an obvious source of

[300] Admir. Ct. Inq. i.

strife with the corporation of London and, later, the Lord Admiral was asserting jurisdiction in the river.[301]

After Elizabeth's reign there was usually only one vice-admiral for the non-privileged part of the county; in 1624 Buckingham, then Lord Admiral, bought the Wardenship of Lord Zouch and thus put an end for a time to the vexations suffered by those who were liable to be attacked, fined, or imprisoned by one officer for obeying the other. The great increase in the Navy which marked the second half of the seventeenth century, the decline of piracy, more effective legislation, and administrative centralization all tended to reduce the power and the utility of the vice-admirals until, in the eighteenth century, the post became almost entirely honorary. From the Restoration onwards the holders of the office in Kent were all peers and included the Dukes of Richmond and Dorset, the Marquesses of Camden and Rockingham, and the Earls of Romney and Winchelsea. The last vice-admiral was the Marquess Camden, who died in 1840.

The reign of Mary sent many of the outlawed and discontented to the refuge of the sea, and the nearly continuous warfare in western Europe during her sister's reign tempted many such men, besides more commonplace criminals, to continue their vocation.[302] Therefore the plague of piracy, and its near analogue privateering, was virulent during the second half of the century, although a number of cases that the sufferers called piracy were really seizures of goods in neutral ships and were, justly, questions for the judge of the Admiralty Court. The amount of piracy in the Straits of Dover in 1552 called for measures of repression,[303] but that was exceptional, for as Dover was a victualling station for men-of-war the immediate vicinity was not well adapted for piratical operations. The Maison Dieu had been turned into a victualling office for the king's ships from 1545, or shortly afterwards,[304] but the establishment was evidently not in very good working order, for in 1557 the admiral in command complained that in a whole week he could not obtain from the storekeeper supplies for the crews of two pinnaces.[305]

The peace of 1564 and the protests of the continental powers forced Elizabeth to take more energetic action, and a circular letter to the vice-admirals of counties called their attention to the suggestive fact that, although many pirates had been taken, not one had been executed or punished.[306] This was followed, the next year, by a sharply worded letter to the Lord Warden to the effect that the queen was receiving complaints ' daily ' from the French and Spanish ambassadors about pirates 'vehemently to be suspected harboured, victualled, and maintained by some dwelling in the Cinque Ports.'[307] The

[301] *Coke MSS.* (Hist. MSS. Com.), ii, 38. I am greatly indebted to Mr. R. G. Marsden, to whose learned researches the history of the evolution of the office of vice-admiral is mainly due, for much assistance here, and for valuable references to Admiralty Court papers bearing on this and kindred subjects.

[302] Among them was Thomas Brooke, or Cobham, a notorious pirate and a relative, probably a brother, of the Lord Warden. According to the Spanish story of one of his captures in 1563 he sewed up the captain and the rest of his prisoners in their own sails and threw them overboard. Mr. Froude, quoting from authoritative Spanish papers, was entitled to say (*Hist. of England* (cab. ed.), viii, 30) that the deed ' was no dream of Spanish slander,' but later knowledge enables us to say that it was a deliberate Spanish lie. At the Admiralty Court inquiry the Spanish captain and some of his crew gave evidence and did not deny Cobham's statement that he put his prisoners ashore at Belleisle (see Admir. Ct. Oyer and Terminer 44, and R. G. Marsden in *Engl. Hist. Rev.* xxiii, 290). The examination of this incident is of some importance as bearing on the value of Spanish official statements at that time.

[303] S.P. Dom. Edw. VI, xiv, 69.

[304] Pipe Off. Decl. Accts. 3532; S.P. Dom. Interreg. ci, 32 (i).

[305] S.P. Dom. Mary, xii, 16.

[306] *Acts of P.C.* 23 Dec. 1564.

[307] Ibid. vii, 244 (Aug. 1565).

Spanish ambassador was also protesting about piracies committed at the mouth of the Thames; to meet this Elizabeth commissioned some warships, and the judge of the Admiralty Court was directed to inquire how the offenders obtained their provisions and stores and who supplied them.[308] During the war the queen had shut her eyes to much piracy which was half privateering, or privateering which was half piracy, and, now that the need for them was past, the pirates were not ready to become respectable citizens to suit her convenience. The great difficulty, then and later, was how to deal with the assistance the delinquents obtained ashore from persons who bought their plunder or who sympathized with them, and among those were sometimes people of good social position. The officials themselves were not above suspicion; among the instructions of 1563 is one that vice-admirals were to do nothing except in conjunction with other commissioners to avoid any appearance of connivance ' of which complaints have been made.' [309] As the vice-admirals were selected from the titled or untitled county families this plain speaking implies a great deal. The Privy Council letter of August 1565 to the Warden caused arrests to be made in Dover and Romney; the prisoners, with other accused, were sent to London to be tried, but the Lords of the Council, careful of any legal objection that might be raised, returned them to take their trial at Dover.[310] In November commissioners with large powers were nominated for each county, and they were to appoint deputies at every creek and landing-place.[311]

Her action in 1565 was Elizabeth's first real effort to suppress piracy, but it was not very successful. In a case which happened in 1570 some of the deputies themselves were involved and the personal presence of the Lord Warden was necessary.[312] The question was becoming still more difficult to handle by reason of the appearance of the Prince of Orange's privateers, many of which, sailing under letters of marque from him were, either wholly or in part, manned by English subjects. These Orange privateers were an element of *la haute politique*, in view of the queen's uncertain relations with Spain, and she did not hold it advisable entirely to crush them even if it had been in her power to do so. Then the Spanish Netherlands followed the example of the Dutch and sent out privateers, the beginning of the affliction of Dunkirkers which plagued the coast for more than a century, while Englishmen also obtained letters of marque from the Huguenot leaders in France. The English and Dutch pirates and privateersmen used the home ports, secretly or openly, with an almost complete indifference to proclamations and penalties, and with, it is to be suspected, the connivance of mayors and vice-admirals. In October 1571 the queen sent a small squadron to sea which speedily took pirates in the Straits of Dover, eighty of them being imprisoned at Sandwich and fifty-five at Dover; of these fifteen were selected to be tried at Sandwich and ten at Dover. Special commissioners were nominated to try them by martial law if necessary, but most of the 135 were exiled with tacit permission to take to their occupation again.[313] The mayor of Sandwich did what he could by pleading the privileges of the Ports, but he was told that they would be of no avail against the

---

[308] *Acts of P.C.* 12 Aug. 1565.
[309] *Cecil MSS.* (Hist. MSS. Com.), i, 286.
[310] *Acts of P.C.* 23, 29 Oct., 17 Nov. 1565.

[311] Ibid. 8 Nov. 1565; S.P. Dom. Eliz. xxxvii, 47, 48. The commissioners for Kent were the Lord Warden, Sir Thos. Cotton, Thos. Scott, Thos. Wotton, John Triston, Humphrey Hales, and Wm. Cromer.
[312] *Acts of P.C.* 11 June 1570.
[313] Ibid. 3 Oct. 1571; *Hist. MSS. Com. Rep.* xiii, App. iv, 8; S.P. Dom. Eliz. lxxxv, 57.

commission.[314] Frantic efforts were made, in appearance, to stop the assistance accorded to the Prince of Orange's privateers, who sold their plunder and bought provisions, stores, and ammunition with little difficulty.[315] But almost while Elizabeth was declaring loudly that she would 'no longer suffer those kind of dealings,' the Orange admiral, the Count de la Mark, was living ashore at Dover while his ships lay in the bay. Elizabeth wrote to the mayor to compel him and his squadron to leave,[316] but it is obvious that if she had been really in earnest some more effective measure than a letter to the mayor, who was not the right person to act and could not enforce compliance, would have been used.

The Privy Council held that the Cinque Ports, and Kent generally, were especially addicted to trading with and assisting pirates;[317] the experience of 1571 had naturally not frightened away the latter, so that in February 1573 the queen's admirals made another sweep in the Straits, the prisoners being sent to Faversham, Dover, and Sandwich. In the last two towns there were so many that a special commission to try them was asked for.[318] In November Martin Frobisher was called before the Council from his ship in the Downs;[319] in his early career, before opportunity had shown him to be a great seaman and admiral, the presence of Frobisher anywhere meant that there was plunder in sight and was bad for traders.[320] In July 1576 Sir Henry Palmer, in command of three of the queen's ships, was reprimanded for lying at ease at Dover while the Orange privateers worked their will; he was superseded by William Holstock, who joined with three more ships and was directed to seize every Dutch privateer.[321] But by September the political outlook had changed, and the admiral was told to leave the Dutch ships alone unless they were known to have recently plundered English vessels.[322] The treatment of the privateering difficulty followed no system but altered with the diplomatic situation of the moment; Elizabeth had no objection to other nations, especially Spain, being injured if, as here, the Prince of Orange promised not to interfere with the English flag.

In May 1577 some of the inhabitants of the Cinque Ports offered to send out ships pirate hunting at their own expense if promised 'reasonable recompense' out of the goods found on board the captures, which shows that there was known to be a sufficient number of the freebooters at sea to make it a promising speculation.[323] Later in the year new piracy commissioners were appointed and still more stringent methods of repression were adopted. The aiders and abettors ashore were now to be prosecuted and fined, and the fines were to go towards recouping the victims; the takers of pirates were to have a proportion of the property found on board, and commissions were to be granted to private persons to set out ships to cruise for pirates.[324] There were separate commissioners for Kent and for the Cinque Ports, but the Lord

[314] *Acts of P.C.* 20 Feb. 1571–2.

[315] Ibid. 12, 13, 14 May, 20 Sept., 3 Oct. 1571.

[316] *Cecil MSS.* (Hist. MSS. Com.), 21 Feb. 1571–2.

[317] *Hist. MSS. Com. Rep.* xiii, App. iv, 8.

[318] *Acts of P.C.* 15, 22 Feb. 1572–3.

[319] Ibid. 23 Nov. 1573.

[320] See R. G. Marsden in *Engl. Hist. Rev.* xxi, 538.

[321] *Acts of P.C.* 22 July, 6 Aug. 1576; S.P. Dom. Eliz. cviii, 67.

[322] *Acts of P.C.* 7 Sept. 1576.

[323] Ibid. 14 May 1577.

[324] S.P. Dom. Eliz. clxi, 20; Add. MS. 34150, ff. 61, 64. In 1559 the judge of the Admiralty Court decided that all property found in pirate ships must be re- stored to the owners (S.P. Dom. Eliz. vi, 19), therefore the new regulation must refer to goods belonging to the pirates or un- claimed. There had been some doubt whether accessories ashore could legally be prosecuted (*Acts of P.C.* 6 June 1577), and the opinion of the law officers was obtained before the government took action (Harl. MS. 168, fol. 114).

Warden was a member of both bodies.[325] In April 1578 the commissioners for Kent certified that they could find no pirates nor any aiders or harbourers of pirates, but observed that they had nothing to do with the Cinque Ports.[326] In October the mayor and bailiffs of Queenborough refused to deliver a man charged with piracy on the ground that their own jurisdiction extended to such cases, but the Privy Council informed them that their exemptions 'may extend' to civil cases but not to piratical ones, which were only to be determined by special commissions from the crown.[327] In pursuance of this policy, which sought to avoid the conflict of authority between the commissioners and the officials of the privileged ports, the jurisdiction of the latter, in piratical cases, was suspended for three years by an Order in Council of 16 December 1582. The Cinque Ports' commissioners found harbourers of pirates and purchasers of their plunder in Dover, Folkestone, Hythe, Romney, Thanet, and Lydd, there being ten in the last-named town; they found no receivers at Sandwich, Faversham or Fordwich.[328] Some of the persons fined refused to pay, alleging that they had bought the property in good faith;[329] as a rule such recalcitrancy was dealt with by ordering the offenders to appear before the Council, when they were kept in attendance for an indefinite time. The expense, direct and indirect, of awaiting the pleasure of the Council in London might be made a much more severe punishment than the original fine. Another list of persons fined in Kent contains seventeen names, and the amounts vary from £1 to £33 6s. 8d., but as a rule they ranged between 6s. 8d. and £1 10s.[330]

Speculation in piratical spoil was diversified by wrecking when opportunity offered. In 1578 a Dutch ship was wrecked off Romney and of a cargo worth £2,600, goods valued at £2,300 disappeared;[331] the Council applied the favourite remedy of ordering those who professed innocence to appear before them. There were evidently other bad cases of wrecking following this one, for in January 1579-80 there was a general order, applying to the Cinque Ports, that those who refused to restore property traced to them were to be imprisoned.[332] In 1589 a Danish ship went ashore on Dungeness; 'the inhabitants there coming aboard the said ship under colour to yield assistance fell a-spoiling and hewing the ship,' the bailiff of Lydd being 'a principal instrument.'[333]

The general situation in regard to piracy underwent no improvement. In September 1579 a Hansa ship was held in port at Dover because a pirate was known to be waiting for her off Margate, and the Lord Warden had to provide a convoy.[334] In the following year some pirates carried off a Genoese ship lying at Gore End.[335] In 1580 a proclamation against pirates stated that 'at this day they commit more spoils and robberies on all sides than have been heard of in former times.' The concurrent jurisdiction of Lord Warden and Lord Admiral worked excellently to the advantage of criminals; at Broadstairs one

---

[325] S.P. Dom. Eliz. cxv, 32.

[326] Ibid. cxxiii, 24.

[327] *Acts of P.C.* 31 Oct. 1578.

[328] S.P. Dom. Eliz. cxxiv, 16.

[329] Ibid. cxxix, 18; *Acts of P.C.* 16 Jan. 1578-9.

[330] Add. MS. 12505, fol. 333. It is nearly certain that only a few of the lists now exist.

[331] *Acts of P.C.* 20 Nov. 1578.

[332] Ibid. 12 Jan. 1579-80.

[333] Ibid. 15 Sept. 1589.

[334] Ibid. 7 Sept. 1579.

[335] Ibid. 29 May 1580. Gore End, really Margate Roads (K.R. Mem. R. 356 Hil. R. 350), seems to have been a favourite anchorage among Mediterranean captains.

Leland writes that 'the great Raguseis (i.e. Ragusans) lie for defence of wind at Gore End' (*Itinerary*, vii, 127). The appearance, in these waters, of traders from the Ragusan Republic can have been relatively so rare that Leland must have included Mediterranean ships generally among them.

of the Admiral's officers found the master of a ship, said to be a pirate, whom he had a warrant to arrest, but the deputy constable, when applied to, refused to act without a warrant from the Warden.[336] Of course the pirate did not wait. The deputy constable was called before the Privy Council, but no doubt if he had acted he would have been punished by the Lord Warden. In 1587 the slackness of the Cinque Ports provoked a furious outburst from the queen on the subject of the spoils made by the Dunkirkers. She wrote to the Lord Warden that the Ports had been granted their privileges in consideration of services to be rendered in the Narrow Seas, ' whereof there is at this time no use, neither have they been called upon to perform the same '; she noticed that ' they have never at any time made offer' of aid in putting down piracy, but that if they did not she would revoke their privileges.[337] This threat was probably the result of the hesitation of the Ports when asked in the autumn to set out twelve ships for service in the Channel, not only to check piracy but because the political outlook was so dark. They did not refuse but they formulated conditions, all bearing on their right to the sole profit from captures, assurance that all prize cases should be tried in their own admiralty court, non-interference by the Lord Admiral, and permission to take any ships ' that do show hostility against the queen's majesty's subjects,' or were at enmity with Holland.[338] The last clause was equivalent to open war with Spain, which Elizabeth was making every effort, by negotiation, to avoid, and she may well have felt angry at the placid indifference to national policy and assumption of equality in negotiation shown by a few half-ruined ports whose maritime strength no longer counted for anything in the national fleets. So far as the Lord Admiral was concerned, Walsingham thought their conditions reasonable, but as Howard was a favourite of Elizabeth's and influential with her, that was not likely to lessen her displeasure.

It was decided in 1551 to disarm, as useless and expensive, several of the fortifications built by Henry VIII, and the Lord Warden was directed to report which could be spared of those in Kent.[339] All the earthworks fronting the Downs were disestablished in 1550,[340] and the Sheerness fort [341] had disappeared but was replaced by a new bulwark in 1551;[342] Milton, Gravesend, and Higham were disarmed in 1553.[343] The adoption, between 1550-60, of the Medway as an anchorage for men-of-war not in commission necessitated some fixed protection; in 1560 a fort at Upnor was decided upon, the work being placed under the superintendence of Richard Wattes of Rochester and Humphrey Lock. Four years passed before it was completed and it cost £3,621 13s. 1d., the ground upon which it stood being bought for £25.[344] When Elizabeth came to the throne the crown was still overwhelmed by the debts incurred by Henry VIII and increased by Mary. Economy was a first necessity, but the repair of Dover pier and the Black Bulwark were declared to be so important that although other things were left undone they were taken in hand between July and December 1559. The corporation gave £100 towards the expense, but the government were not grateful, for it was maintained that more had been promised.[345] In 1567 and 1568 upwards of £800 was expended at Dover, on

[336] Acts of P.C. 28 Aug. 1587.
[337] Lansd. MS. 94, fol. 92.
[338] S.P. Dom. Eliz. cciii, 51 (i, ii); Hist. MSS. Com. Rep. xiii, App. iv, 85.
[339] Acts of P.C. 4 May 1552.
[340] Add. MS. 34148, fol. 118.
[341] Ante, p. 284.
[342] Acts of P.C. 16 Jan. 1550-1.
[343] Roy. MS. 18C xxiv, fol. 361.
[344] Pipe Off. Decl. Accts. 2204, 3545; Add. MS. 5752, fol. 372.
[345] Add. MS. 5752, fol. 364.

the three castles in the Downs, and at Queenborough;[346] nothing was done at Sandgate, which was unroofed and ruinous but had eight guns in position. At Archcliff [346a] there were fifteen, at Moat five, at Walmer seven, at Sandown four, and at Deal eight carriage guns, and in Dover Castle sixteen in 1572.[347] The Black Bulwark at Dover followed the fortune of the pier, and when that was ruined by the gales, usually suffered with it; it was reconstructed more than once but disappears towards the close of the reign.[348]

The strained situations with Spain which were continually recurring caused fears that a dash might be made from the Flemish ports with the object of destroying the ships in the Medway. Several times the government received information, true or untrue, that such a scheme was in preparation. Therefore in 1574 a new fortification was authorized. Sir William Winter, the Surveyor of the Navy, and another official examined the *terrain* and rejected Sheerness and the Isle of Grain in favour of a fort at Swaleness, opposite Queenborough, to prevent a raid from the rear by the Swale.[349] Winter, it may be noted, was of opinion that it would be well to remove the ships at Chatham to Queenborough Reach if dock accommodation were made there for them, a suggestion which was an anticipation of Sheerness dockyard. The fort was constructed in 1575, and the precaution was taken of blocking by piles the fairway through St. Mary's 'and sundry other creekes,' by which the Upnor anchorage could be taken in flank.[350] Ten years later, when open war with Spain commenced, came the chain across the river at Upnor;[351] from 1572 small vessels had been stationed at the mouth of the Medway to examine all ships and boats passing.[352] In 1570 and 1571 there was instant expectation of war, and the sheriff of Kent was then ordered to arrange for levies from the adjoining hundreds to guard the ships in the Medway;[353] by 1584 it was settled that 1,400 men from the surrounding country were to concentrate at Rochester on any alarm of danger to the ships.[354]

The subject of coast defences is far too large a one to dilate upon here, but it may be said, generally, that the points selected by Henry VIII and Elizabeth for fortification in Kent were justified strategically by the fact that they were those that an enemy would have attacked or wished to occupy himself. Whether the defences were sufficiently powerful and well-designed to protect the harbours and river passages or to hold out long enough to gain time for an English concentration, is a question which, fortunately, was never put to the trial. The evident approach of war caused a large expenditure on the coast defences throughout England between 1583-5, when upwards of £11,000 was devoted to their repairs; Sandgate was restored to efficiency, Gravesend reappears, and the sum of £730 was divided between Sandown, Deal, and Walmer.[355] For what they were worth it was well to look to the Kentish forts, for if Parma had got across in 1588 his landing would assuredly have been in the county and probably in the estuary of the Thames. Early in July 1588 Sir John Norreys, who had been inspecting the defences and military organization of the south-eastern counties, advised the construction of additional

---

346 Pipe Off. Decl. Accts. 3549.

346a The Archcliff is also described as 'alias Guilforde's' bulwark, from the name of an early captain of the fort. It was completely rebuilt and modernized in 1784, and is now (1925) under sentence of final demolition.

347 S.P.Dom.Eliz.xlvi,77; xc,17.

348 In 1595 it was 'decayed.'

349 *Acts of P.C.* 20 July, 5, 19 Aug. 1574; Lansd.MS.xviii, 77; Pipe Off. Decl. Accts. 2212.

350 Pipe Off. Decl. Accts. 2210. The cost was £100 (S.P. Dom. Eliz. clxxxvi, 44).

351 See 'The Royal Dockyards,' *V.C.H. Kent.*

352 S.P. Dom. Eliz. lxxxix, 8.

353 *Acts of P.C.* 25, 31 Dec. 1571.

354 S.P. Dom. Eliz. clxxvi, 56.

355 Ibid. clxx, 91; Lansd. MS. 48, fol. 47.

batteries at King's Ferry, Canterbury, Little Joy near Sandwich, and at that town itself.[356] The Thames received especial attention. By the advice of Federico Gianibelli, an Italian who had designed the famous explosive ships which nearly foiled Parma at Antwerp, more batteries were thrown up on the river banks and, adopting Parma's conception, an obstruction of booms and lighters was made between Gravesend and Tilbury, as also a bridge of boats to enable the army at Tilbury to cross if necessary.[357]

Like all Elizabeth's decisions this one was made very late; when the military officers were consulting and surveying on 22 July with Peter Pett of Deptford dockyard the English and Spanish fleets were in action off the coast of Devon. New batteries were either made or proposed at Northfleet, Erith and Greenhithe. Leicester was at Gravesend on 23 July and found no platforms fit to bear guns; in his opinion both Milton and Gravesend block-houses were ' built to the least purpose that ever I saw and lie most indefensible.' During the middle of August payments amounting to £600 were made to Pett, Mathew Baker, and Richard Chapman for the bridge over the river and the platforms, etc., at the forts; the total estimated cost was more than £2,000.[358] At the end of August Burghley was examining estimates for the completion of Gravesend which still required £265 to be spent upon it, an occupation for which the admirals had given him the requisite leisure. Lambarde's plan shows a maze of beacons in the western extremity of the county, the southernmost being on Dungeness. This was watched nightly by two men from Lydd, while two others were on duty in the town and a bell was rung hourly, the whole arrangement being overseen by two jurats.[359]

As the chartered ' service ' of the Cinque Ports fell out of use it was obvious that they would have to assist the Crown in some other way during the transition stage which preceded their absorption into the system applied to the rest of the country; the manifest alternative was the provision of men for the royal fleets. Outward respect was still paid to their privileges; in 1552, when they were to supply 250 men, the Lord Admiral's officers had to obtain the Lord Warden's ' letters of attendance ' before they could begin their impress.[360] Technically the Ports were, of course, still liable for their ' service,' especially when there was occasion to convey any of the royal family to and fro. In 1556 they were called upon for 380 men, when Philip was returning to Flanders and Charles V going to Spain, in consideration of which levy they were to be spared as many ships ' that the said Ports ought to set forth ' as that number of men would man.[361] But by this time only large men-of-war were employed in the transport of royal personages, and everyone understood that the reference to the ' service ' was a mere form, nor would such vessels as the Ports could send have suited the luxurious ideas of the age.

Philip II drew England into war with France and Scotland in 1557. The Lord Admiral was in command in the Channel, and he was ordered to secure the Straits of Dover by leaving four ships on the station.[362] His fleet was strengthened by a squadron of armed merchantmen, but Kent was represented by only one small vessel of Erith as a non-combatant.[363] The unexpected danger of Calais at the end of 1557 threw a sudden strain on the Cinque

[356] Acts of P.C. 8 July 1588.

[357] Exch. War. for Issues, Bdle. 121; Hakluyt, Voyages (ed. 1903), iv, 208.

[358] Acts of P.C. 12, 18 Aug. 1588; S.P. Dom. Eliz. ccxii, 79.

[359] Stowe, MS. 857, fol. 16.

[360] Acts of P.C. 18 Mar. 1551-2.

[361] Ibid. 31 Aug. 1556.

[362] S.P. Dom. Mary, x, 64.

[363] Ibid. xi, 2.

Ports. The vice-admiral commanding on the coast was directed to take up every available ship of the Ports and hold the Straits until the queen's ships appeared, and the Lord Warden was told to press men without hesitating about 'any scruple of words in his commission,' that is to say as soldiers as well as sailors.[364] On 17 January came an order to raise 1,000 men in the Ports for the recovery of Calais, but the attempt was soon seen to be hopeless, and the men were dismissed, except 100 retained as a garrison for Dover.[365]

In July 1557 permission was given to all subjects to fit out privateers, the captors being permitted to enjoy their prizes without paying any share to the Lord Admiral;[366] the offer was sufficiently attractive to send many ships to sea, including some from Kent.[367] In June 1558 there was fighting in Picardy between French and Flemings, and there may have been some hope of recovering Calais, for the Portsmen were ordered to be ready for service at an hour's warning.[368] In 1559 Elizabeth cautioned the Lord Warden to have particular care of Sandwich 'and the other four Ports,' against a French raid, as so many of their ships were passing to Scotland.[369] Portsmouth and Rye were the principal places of embarkation for the troops sent to France during the war which ended in 1564, and there was little need of local shipping except for transport; in 1560 Dover and Sandwich each provided one vessel for cruising purposes, and tenders and victuallers came from Erith, Rochester, Maidstone, and Milton.[370] All these were paid by the crown. Henceforward the Cinque Ports supplied ships and men under the same conditions as the remainder of the kingdom. Practically the only privilege of their service left to them was that of being bidden through the Lord Warden instead of through the Lord Admiral, and of dividing their share of the burden according to agreement among themselves. But even the privilege of being directly subject to the Warden, who would naturally have a friendly care for their interests, was not unquestioned. In 1577 the Lord Admiral's officers were pressing within the liberties of the Ports, and at Sandwich were 'not only not assisted but evil used' by the mayor; the Privy Council were unsympathetic, and ordered the Warden to 'correct' the mayor and help the Lord Admiral's officers.[371] It is very certain that the attitude of the Council reflected the known sentiments of the queen. By 1591 the breach in the franchises of the Ports had been widened yet further, for they then complained that men-of-war captains were pressing men within the jurisdiction of the Warden; they admitted that 'of late' seamen, although exempt from anything but the 'service' or its recent equivalent, had been taken up by commission under the great seal, but impress by captains was a new departure without precedent.[372]

When Elizabeth came to the throne there were 65 English merchantmen which the Navy Board officials considered large enough to act with the queen's ships; seven of these belonged to Dover.[373] The bounty system inaugurated by Henry VII, by which an occasional tonnage allowance was made to the builders of new merchant ships suitable for use in war, had, under Elizabeth,

---

[364] *Acts of P.C.* 30 Dec. 1557; 5 Jan. 1557–8.

[365] S.P. Dom. Mary, xii, 22, 43.

[366] Ibid. 24.

[367] Admir. Ct. Exemp. v, 288. The list is probably incomplete.

[368] S.P. Dom. Mary, xiii, 23.

[369] Ibid. Eliz. vii, 23. Commissions were issued for 'repairing, erecting, and watching the beacons' (*Finch MSS.* i, 4).

[370] Ibid. xv, 3; Pipe Off. Decl. Accts. 2358.

[371] *Acts of P.C.* 7 July 1577.

[372] *Hist. MSS. Com. Rep.* xiii, App. iv, 98.

[373] Pipe Off. Decl. Accts. 2358. Another paper of the same date estimates only 45 merchantmen (S.P. Dom. Eliz. iii, 44).

settled into a grant of five shillings a ton on all vessels of 100 tons and upwards.[374] This stimulated shipbuilding in places where there was a deep-sea trade to employ such vessels, and tended to the construction of ships of heavier tonnage than heretofore. From at least the reign of John it had been customary to call upon the officials of the ports for returns of the ships and men available for service with the royal fleets, and these returns were required still more often as the bounty system took firmer hold. Most of the earlier returns are lost, but many, complete or fragmentary, remain for the Elizabethan period; usually the details only relate to vessels of 100 tons and upwards, as smaller ships were no longer considered useful, even in theory, for fighting purposes.

The war with France and Scotland was the occasion of the first Elizabethan list of 1560. It was of ships of 100 tons and upwards, and there was only one in Kent, the *John*, of Sandwich, of 140 tons; there were 396 'mariners and sailors' in the Cinque Ports.[375] This return is certainly incomplete for some of the counties, and seems also to be deficient for Kent, at any rate in the number of men, as only that for the Cinque Ports is given; the rest of Kent is not referred to, and in the case of the Ports it gives, probably, merely the men ashore at the date of inquiry. The Cinque Ports were undoubtedly passing through an epoch of commercial depression at this date. A list of 1563 compares their then condition with some vague period called 'within the past 30 years';[376] Romney was 'once a good fisher town, and now utterly decayed, and not one fisher boat remaining'; at Hythe there had been 80 ships and fishing boats, but only eight in 1563; at Folkestone there were three instead of 25 as formerly; at Dover 17 in place of 35; and at Sandwich six crayers instead of 22 'able' ships and fishing boats. Besides Dover, money had been spent on Folkestone and Sandwich harbours during the reigns of Edward VI and Mary in the hope of restoring them; an Italian engineer visited the latter town in 1574 and pronounced its condition hopeless.[377] The year 1563 must have been the worst moment for these towns; by 1566 there was a great improvement. Romney is not mentioned, but Hythe then possessed four vessels of 60 tons, three of 30 tons, 25 fishing boats, and 160 fishermen; Folkestone, 25 fishing boats and 70 men; Dover, 20 vessels, including two of more than 100 tons, and 130 men; and Sandwich, 17 vessels, of which the largest was 40 tons, and 62 men.[378] A number of other places are given in this document :—

	No. of Vessels.	Largest in tons.	Men.		No. of Vessels.	Largest in tons.	Men.		No. of Vessels.	Largest in tons.	Men.
Ramsgate ...	14	16	70	Whitstable ...	19	18	60	Milton by Sittingbourne	26	26	24
Broadstairs...	8	12	40	Faversham ...	18	45	50				
Margate ...	15	18	60	Queenborough	11	16	45	Sittingbourne	3	24	—
Halstow ...	14	7	21	Rainham ...	13	35	12	Upchurch ...	12	14	14
Rochester ...	6	70	27	Maidstone ...	5	50	22	Gillingham	27	20	43
								Dartford ...	7	15	14

[374] Henry VII was following the example of Spain. The Spanish jurists and politicians, searching for means to spur on lagging Spanish maritime enterprise, had probably thrown back to legislation of the Emperor Constantine early in the fourth century A.D. designed to encourage Mediterranean traders; legislation which in the interval had been copied intermittently by other Mediterranean states.

[375] S.P. Dom. Eliz. xi, 27. The distinction between mariners and sailors is obscure and unnecessary to discuss here.

[376] Ibid. xxviii, 3.

[377] Ibid. xcix, 41.

[378] Cott. MS. Julius B iv, fol. 95. Here, again, the register of men is probably only of those at home at the time of the survey.

Another, undated, Elizabethan list gives Sandwich 40 ships and fishing boats, the largest being of 60 tons, and 102 masters and men; Deal, five fishing boats and 35 masters and men; and Walmer, four boats and eight men.[379]

There was an embargo in July 1570 with returns from the counties of the ships and men stayed in the several ports, but there is no list for the Cinque Ports nor for the rest of Kent. In 1572 Thomas Colshill, surveyor of customs at London, compiled a register of coasting traders belonging to the ports of the kingdom.[380] The Kentish section is :—

	100 Tons and upwards.	From 50 to 100 tons.	From 20 to 50 tons.	Under 20 tons.		100 Tons and upwards.	From 50 to 100 tons.	From 20 to 50 tons.	Under 20 tons.
Deptford ...	—	—	I	—	Margate[381] ...	—	—	3	2
Erith	I	I	I	—	Gillingham ...	—	I	—	3
Sandwich ...	—	2	15	19	Faversham ...	—	I	11	10
Dover	—	2	11	5	Mill Hall ...	—	—	3	—
Rochester ...	—	I	5	3	Milton (Gravesend)	—	—	3	7
Whitstable ...	—	—	4	I	Queenborough ...	—	—	I	2
Gravesend ...	—	—	I	—	Rainham ...	—	—	I	2
Sittingbourne ...	—	—	I	I	Broadstairs ...	—	—	—	3
Strood	—	—	—	2	Thanet	—	—	I	I
Frindsbury ...	—	—	—	I	Herne	—	—	—	I
Chatham ...	—	—	I	I	Halstow ...	—	—	—	4
Maidstone ...	—	I	5	I					

In 1576 there was a list drawn up of ships of 100 tons and upwards built since 1571, but it contains none of any Kentish port. A year later another return of vessels of 100 or more tons shows 135 in England; of these, one, which just reached the standard, belonged to Dover.[382] Of the same year is another certificate of 'ships, barks, and hoys,' as well as of men, but probably only of those at home at the time. At Faversham there were 12 vessels and 31 'mariners and seafaring men'; at Sandwich 29 and 118 men; Dover 34 and 110 men; Hythe 5 and 25 men; and Lydd 2 and 20 men. For 1581 we have a Trinity House certificate of the increase of fishing boats in the various ports since 1576, an examination undertaken to find out how the Acts of 5 and 13 Elizabeth, intended to encourage the fisheries, were working. At Sandwich and Folkestone there had been no increase, but in the Medway there were 5 more than in 1576, in 'Thanet' 15, at Dover 6, at Hythe 1, and at Lydd 3;[383] these boats were all of from 15 to 20 tons each. By 1582 the number of ships of 100 tons and upwards in England had risen to 177, but none of them belonged to Kent, nor were there any of between 80 and 100 tons. In the county, outside the Cinque Ports, there were 99 vessels of from 20 to 80 tons, of which 20 belonged to Whitstable, 17 to Milton, 11 to Rainham, 5 to Upchurch, 10 to Halstow, 3 to Sittingbourne, 1 to Tonge, 9 to Queenborough, Minster, and Leysdown, 8 each to Gillingham and Dartford, 3 to Rochester, and 4 to Maidstone.[384] Even in this division the limit of tonnage was not nearly reached, for the largest was only of 40 tons. In the Cinque Ports there were, of from 20 to 80 tons, 33 belonging to Sandwich, 5 to Deal,

[379] Cott. MS. Otho E ix, fol.160.
[380] S.P. Dom. Eliz. Add. xxii. He excluded fishing craft and, inferentially, vessels engaged in oversea trade.

[381] The name of one of the Margate vessels is *Try the Sea Truly.*
[382] S.P. Dom. Eliz. xcvi, fol. 267. In this paper Faversham,

Rochester, 'and the creeks belonging,' are said to be 'contained in the river of Thames.'
[383] Ibid. cxlvii, 21.
[384] Ibid. clvi, 45.

3 to Walmer, 13 to Ramsgate, 6 to Broadstairs, 26 to Dover, 1 to Margate, 2 to Ringwould, 12 to Hythe, 27 to Faversham, 4 to Folkestone, 11 to Lydd, and 1 to Fordwich. Here, the largest was one of 60 tons of Dover, and the next in size, of 55 tons, was owned at Sandwich. It will be noticed that Romney is absent from all these lists. In men the survey was more favourable; there were 243 masters and sailors in the non-privileged portion of the county, and 952 in the Cinque Ports, which would, therefore, include part of Sussex, but the larger proportion would belong to Kent. In February 1580 there were impress warrants out to take up seamen in many of the counties. Kent, Sussex, Dorset, and Norfolk were each required to find 150, Essex and Hants 100 each, but Devon 400;[385] the ratio no doubt represents the relative strength of the counties in seamen.

The information obtained from these lists often seems contradictory, because the key to apparent discrepancies is now lost. Thus, in the foregoing list of 1582 Margate is credited with only one vessel of between 20 and 80 tons, but in 1584 we find that it possessed eight, of which one was of 70, one of 60, and three of 40 tons; there were also six fishing boats and 45 men, of whom eight were pilots.[386] At Birchington there were no boats and only three men, who were employed at Margate. In 1587 the number of Sandwich ships had risen to 43, of which one was of 100 and two of 60 tons, with 108 men;[387] the figures for Ramsgate, Folkestone, Hythe, Deal, and Walmer remain nearly the same, but at Deal there were 40 men available, at Folkestone 44, at Hythe 73, and 19 at Walmer. Dover had risen to 33 vessels, including one of 140, one of 90, and one of 70 tons, with 130 men; Faversham had fallen to 20, and Lydd to 8, barks, all small; at Lydd it was customary for artisans—carpenters, shoemakers, weavers, etc.—to go out in the boats. At Romney there were, we are told in this report, neither boats nor seafaring men. Another return, of October 1587, allots 26 ships to Dover, with 176 masters and men; at Faversham there were 57 men.[388] The campaign of 1588 showed that the armed merchantmen were of no fighting value, and this conclusion was supported by the experience of the subsequent naval expeditions, therefore the authorities became less desirous of obtaining these returns. The Kentish vessels were hardly large enough to serve as tenders; the men were all that the county now had to give. Henry VIII constructed at least one large man-of-war at Smallhithe, and some small shallops at Dover; although the Smallhithe ship was built in Kent it was probably by shipwrights from Rye, and there is no trace of any shipbuilding trade in the county during the reign of Elizabeth. There are still existing many warrants for the payment of the bounty of 5s. a ton on new ships during the Elizabethan period, but not one of them was built in Kent or for Kentish owners. Dover, it may be noted, was the only one of the Cinque Ports considered of sufficient importance to have a Spanish spy stationed at it; his duties, besides making the usual reports, were to suborn government officials and weave plots to burn stores and storehouses.[389]

When Philip II drew up his instructions for the Duke of Medina Sidonia he expected a decisive battle to be fought off the North Foreland, and that the Armada would cover Parma's landing in the Thames or Medway. To the

[385] *Acts of P.C.* 19 Feb. 1579–80.
[386] S.P. Dom. Eliz. clxxxv, 85.
[387] Ibid. cxcviii, 5, 6.
[388] Ibid. cciv, 25.
[389] S.P. Foreign, Spain, Eliz. II, 26 (? 1584).

very last the English Government failed to penetrate the Spanish plans, although it was obvious that the invasion depended upon Parma's army and that, crossing in small vessels and open boats, he would be forced to choose the shortest possible sea passage. On 23 July, when the Spaniards were half-way up Channel, the Privy Council expected the landing to take place in Essex, but the bridge of boats at Gravesend was intended for the rapid trans-ference of the army into Kent if occasion arose. Whether the transference of a half-trained, unsupplied, and badly officered force across a river would have been rapid may be doubted, even if the bridge had proved substantial and Parma had not interfered. In December 1587 and April 1588 Sir John Norreys reported on the military situation and preparations in Kent, but the plans of the responsible authorities were altered almost from week to week. The queen's ships had been commissioned, paid off, and again commissioned during the early part of 1588, but the first measure of local provision was an embargo of 31 March on all shipping, intended not so much to retain the shipping as the men. This was followed, the next day, by orders to the port towns to furnish ships at their own expense;[390] all were to be of more than 60 tons. Five ships and a pinnace were required from the Cinque Ports; the remainder of Kent was unaffected. Unlike most of the other coast towns, which, under various pleas made desperate efforts to procure lighter assess-ments, the Ports set about providing their share with hardly a murmur, and on 15 April resolved that Romney and Lydd should send one ship of 60 tons, Dover and its members one of 100 tons, Sandwich and its members one of 120 tons, and Hythe a pinnace of 25 tons.[391] The unanimity was a little marred by an appeal in May to the Privy Council from Old and New Romney, whose jurats complained that, although Lydd was now far wealthier than they, only the rate of contribution due by precedent could be obtained from it. The Privy Council, perhaps not regretting an opportunity for overruling the Cinque Ports' customs, ordered that the Lydd men were to pay according to ability and 'not as in times past or to any accustomed composition between the Ports and members.'[392]

The Dover ship was the *Elizabeth*, or *Elnathan*, 120 tons, Captain John Lidgen, or Legent; Sandwich sent the *Reuben*, 110 tons, Captain William Cripps; Hythe, the *Grace of God*, 50 tons, Captain William Fordred; and Romney and Lydd, the *John*, 60 tons (? Captain Reynold Veysey).[393] The *Hazard*, 38 tons, of Faversham, Captain Nicholas Turner, also came with the others. The Cinque Ports vessels were at sea by the beginning of May and were attached to the fleet under Lord Henry Seymour cruising off Dunkirk and Gravelines and in the Straits of Dover. Seymour's base was in the Downs, so that the crews of the four ships were almost at home, more fortunate than their fellows pressed to serve with Drake and the Lord Admiral to the westward. Elizabeth had allowed the Maison Dieu to fall out of use as a victualling establishment, so that provisions had to be sent by water from Rochester and London, although Nature had plainly intended Dover to be the supply port for any fleet acting from the Straits. In the intervals of cruises Seymour, like the other admirals, wrote plaintive, discursive, or monitory letters to the ministers; on 20 July, after expressing fears about the Isle of

[390] *Acts of P.C.* 31 Mar., 1 April 1588.
[391] *Hist. MSS. Com. Rep.* xiii, App. iv, 87.
[392] *Acts of P.C.* 6 May 1588.
[393] S.P. Dom. Eliz. ccx, 34 (1).

Wight and the Thames, he added that Sandwich was a place that might prove tempting to Parma, and that he was anxious about. Presumably he meant that, after having won the essential sea victory, the Armada might anchor in the Downs and such troops as it carried occupy Sandwich. However, on 23 July Seymour received a dispatch from Drake saying that the western fleet was in action with the Spaniards, and thenceforward theory gave place to practice. It is characteristic of the slipshod incompetence of the central government that at this last moment Seymour was 'humbly praying' the Council to send him powder and shot, necessaries he had begged 'divers times' previously.[394] When it was known for certain that the Armada was here courtiers and soldiers came galloping down to Dover for the chance of a shot at the Spaniards; among them was Sir John Norreys, second in command at Tilbury, to whose good offices Seymour owed some of the munition of war he required so urgently.[395]

On 27 July, when the Armada was off Fairlight, Seymour had 20 vessels with him instead of the 78 his fleet had been intended to contain;[396] there were eight queen's ships among the 20, and his whole reliance was in these, for he evidently thought the merchantmen of little or no value. A galley, the *Bonavolia*, the only ship of her class in the Navy, was detached to the mouth of the Thames partly to guard the entrance and partly because too unseaworthy for the Channel; it was intended to send some London merchantmen to assist the galley. On the 28th Seymour was ordered to meet the main fleet under the Lord Admiral; when he joined, off Calais cliffs with the Armada in sight in front, he had not one day's victuals in his ships.[397] More distinguished visitors, in the shape of Leicester himself and Robert Cecil, in training to succeed his father Burghley, came to Dover where, no doubt, they did their best to send out provisions, powder, and shot even if the last were in the form of the plough-chains the English gunners were reduced to using.[398]

Everyone knows that the employment of fireships on the night of 28–29 July was the turning-point of the campaign, and that the rout of the Armada was the direct consequence. At a council of war held on board the flagship on the morning of Sunday the 28th, it was resolved to send fireships among the Spaniards. Sir William Winter, Seymour's second in command, claimed that he made the suggestion the previous evening when the Lord Admiral sent for him, but there was nothing novel about the plan, which had been recommended by William Bourne, of Gravesend, in his *Devices* published in 1578, and had been practised in classical times. After the Council, Howard sent to Dover for suitable vessels, brushwood, pitch, and other necessaries, but as it was soon seen that they could not arrive in time for use that night eight vessels belonging to the fleet were prepared and sent among the enemy. Seymour took part in the battle of Gravelines on 29 July, but reserves his praise for the men-of-war and makes no mention of anything

---

[394] S.P. Dom. Eliz. ccxiii, 12.

[395] Ibid. 30. That the second in command of the disorganized militia at Tilbury should so cavalierly leave his duties even if, which is doubtful, it was with the consent of the Council, is another illustration of the lack of controlling intelligence and discipline visible in the civil administration and combatant branches. Sir Roger Williams, who commanded the cavalry of the army, came with Norreys.

[396] Ibid. 50.

[397] Ibid. 64. According to another paper he had provisions for three days on board (ibid. ccxiv, 7).

[398] Ibid. ccxiii, 69. It is obvious that Leicester's proper place at such a moment was Tilbury, but, considered as a general, it was perhaps hardly material where he was.

done by the merchantmen; whether the Ports' ships were with him then we do not know, and he probably did not care. On the 30th he was ordered to lie off the mouth of the Thames while the main fleet chased the Armada northwards; on 6 August all the Kentish ships were with him, having come safely through the campaign.[399] By 8 August Howard was back at Margate and Gore End with such of his ships as had not been scattered by storm; 800 musketeers, from Holland, were also in the town, there being still some fear that Parma would attempt to cross with or without the Armada. Such an adventure might have tempted the generals of the Privy Council, but Parma was far too great a soldier for such follies.

When Howard landed at Margate on the 8th he wrote urging the need of provisions and other relief for his worn-out men; always careful of their welfare he rode off, himself, to Dover and Sandwich to obtain what supplies he could. In London Burghley was drawing up schedules and annotating returns which proved conclusively that the fleet was, and always had been, well supplied; in the meanwhile the seamen were dying of starvation and disease. On the 10th the Lord Admiral had returned to Margate, which was becoming a charnel house; 'it is a most pitiful sight to see here at Margate how the men, having no place to receive them into here, die in the streets . . . it would grieve any man's heart to see them that have served so valiantly die so miserably.'[400] It was not so much want of understanding and sympathy in the ministers that produced these conditions as want of capacity; Burghley, who next to the queen was chiefly responsible, was old and ill; even if he had been in his prime he would have found it difficult to work with the machinery at his disposal. On 22 August Howard, then at Dover, wrote direct to Elizabeth concerning the forlorn condition of the crews there, but on the same day he received official information that the Spaniards were coming back, which gave him other matter for thought. His attempt to get necessaries ashore at once brought into relief the absurdity of the divided jurisdiction for, although Lord Admiral and commander-in-chief, he was, within the jurisdiction of the Lord Warden, practically on foreign ground; 'without his warrant they will do nothing, for so Mr. Barrey sent me word.'[401] It was no wonder that Elizabeth, Privy Council, and Lord Admiral bore with impatience the anachronism of such an *imperium in imperio.*

By the end of August the great fleet was paid off, only a squadron of queen's ships being left in commission in the Channel. The captains and owners of the two ships from Dover and Sandwich petitioned that they had served two months at the cost of the towns and then another two months at the request of the crown; for the second service they begged their pay.[402] After the danger had passed away the civic authorities in most of the coast towns found a great deal of difficulty in collecting the assessments for the payment of the ships sent to sea under the order of 1 April. Both at Dover and Sandwich there was such recalcitrancy, and the subject was brought before the Privy Council who directed that the malcontents were to appear before them.[403] It is possible, however, that the trouble was connected with the second period of two months just noticed; the crown tried, everywhere, to

---

[399] S.P. Dom. Eliz. ccxiv, 39 (i).

[400] Ibid. 66.

[401] Ibid. ccxv, 42. Richard Barrey was the Lieutenant of Dover Castle.

[402] Ibid. ccxvi, 67.

[403] *Acts of P.C.* 30 Sept. 1588.

throw as much as possible of the expense upon the country, and in this case the townsmen of Dover and Sandwich would naturally rebel against an additional outlay which doubled their contribution. In October the Ports were again asked for a small squadron for local service, but of course there was now no intention of putting the cost upon them. Five ships came from Dover, including the *Grace of God* again, the *Ruby* of 140 tons, and three small ones; from Sandwich came four, of which the largest was of 55 tons, and Faversham again sent the *Hazard*.[404]

In 1589 Norreys and Drake led a fleet and army to Portugal to place on the throne Don Antonio, the claimant of the Portuguese crown, and thus dismember the Spanish empire and end the war. The failure of the expedition was due, primarily, to the fact that instead of being undertaken with the whole strength of the crown it was a private adventure on the part of the leaders and their associates to which the queen gave assistance. Consequently the coast towns were not called upon officially for ships, but many were hired by Norreys and Drake on the usual terms of 2*s.* a ton per month. Only three ships are known to have come from Kent—two from Dover and one from Chatham. On 16 March 1589 Drake sailed from Dover for Plymouth to complete there his final preparations; as he left Dover, always a convenient eyrie for such proceedings, he pounced on a fleet of 60 Dutch merchantmen coming through the Straits and seized them for transports.

Dover was again a centre of activity in April 1595 when Calais, held for Henry IV by a French and Dutch garrison, was suddenly besieged by a division of Spanish troops. Ships and men were hurriedly concentrated at Dover, and the Earl of Essex came to take the command, but English help was too slow and Calais was lost. The fear here was that Calais would become another privateer base like Sluys, Dunkirk, and Nieuport, and harass commerce passing through the Straits, but it proved of very little value to the Spaniards during the three years they held it before restoring it to France at the peace of Vervins in 1598.

The failure of the 1589 enterprise deterred Elizabeth from further attacks on a large scale until 1596, when Cadiz was taken and sacked. In December 1595 the Cinque Ports were warned that they would be required to furnish four ships, to be manned, armed, and provisioned for five months at local charge, to serve with the fleet when it went to sea in the spring of 1596;[405] the objective was not then decided but in any case would not have been announced. As in 1588, nearly all the shipping towns, except London, protested that they were assessed beyond their capacity, and this time the Cinque Ports joined in the cry. The levy was reduced to two ships and two hoys; they resolved among themselves that Sandwich, Dover, and Hythe should provide two ships of 160 tons each, while Romney was annexed to the Sussex section to help with the hoys.[406] There was a subsidiary arrangement about the payment of any additional expenses which finally brought the whole matter before the Privy Council to settle the quarrel which ensued.[407] Of the Sandwich ship Fordwich paid for 20 tons, Deal and Walmer together 20, Ramsgate 6, and Sarre 4 tons; the head port borrowed the money necessary for itself at 10 per cent.[408] and Faversham paid £300 towards the Dover

[404] Add. MS. 35831, fol. 1.

[405] *Acts of P.C.* 21 Dec. 1595.

[406] *Hist. MSS. Com. Rep.* xiii, App. iv, 356.

[407] *Acts of P.C.* 8 June 1597.

[408] Boys, *Hist. of Sandwich*, 700.

ship.[409] The Cinque Ports vessels, like all the other merchantmen, were only used as transports, and many independent privateers or traders accompanied the fleet on the chance of plunder or freight from Cadiz. There were, of course, many Portsmen among the crews of the men-of-war; a petition of 1598 states that in 1588 and 1596 the Cinque Ports sent 1,200 men for the royal service.[410] After the return of the Cadiz fleet Philip II prepared an expedition which was to avenge the attack made on Spanish territory. It never got farther northward than Finisterre, but the expectation of its coming led to precautions being taken along the coast; the Medway was to be especially guarded, beacons were to be ready at Chatham and at Barrow Hill, and four batteries (' sconces ') were thrown up near Upnor.[411] The Portsmen offered six ships for service on condition of having prizes without account to the queen or Lord Admiral.[412] Between 1596 and 1599 some £1,400 was expended on the fortifications at Dover, Sandgate, in the Downs, and at Queenborough ;[413] nothing is said at this time of those on the Thames beyond a reference to Gravesend and Milton as ' two silly forts which can do little.' [414]

In men Kent was no doubt fully represented in the Islands Voyage of 1597, but we have no details ; the merchant ships used were hired by the crown, and not provided by the coast towns at their own expense. Another of the many alarms of invasion, which Elizabeth took so seriously, occurred in 1599. No Spanish squadron was ever nearer England than Coruña, and Spain was bankrupt and exhausted, lacking men, ships, money, and hope, but the preparations made to resist its dying efforts were, relatively, greater than those of 1588. The alarm came in the middle of July, and hasty orders were issued for the preparation of a fleet to be concentrated under Lord Thomas Howard in the Downs ; eventually he had there 16 men-of-war and five large merchantmen, besides hoys and tenders. Kent was again held to be the storm centre, it being supposed that the object of the Spanish admiral was to cover the transport of the Archduke's troops from the Low Countries ; to meet this some 10,000 or 12,000 men were collected at Canterbury and Sittingbourne. On 2 August the Privy Council wrote to the Lord Warden that a landing might be expected in the Downs or at Margate, and suggested the construction of entrenchments.[415] The Thames was held to be another danger-point, and Gravesend and Milton were hurriedly placed in a state of defence.[416] The guardianship of the Thames was entrusted to the Earl of Cumberland, assisted by the engineer Gianibelli, and they set about the preparation of another barrier across the river at Gravesend similar to that of 1588, but within a few days the idea was dropped in favour, instead, of sinking ships in the fairway if necessary.[417] To cool observers at the time all these frantic measures, affecting the whole of England, to repel a phantom invasion appeared rather discreditable in the want shown of any sense of proportion ; towards the end of August the government began to realize its mistake, and a naval and military disbandment quietly followed. In 1601 and 1602 the *Mayflower*, 240 tons, of Gillingham, was one of six merchantmen acting with the queen's squadron

[409] *Arch. Cant.* xxi, 281.

[410] *Cecil MSS.* (Hist. MSS. Com.), viii, 543.

[411] S.P. Dom. Eliz. cclx, 102. On 30 March 1595–6 the jurats of Hythe petitioned for munition and carriages for the three guns they possessed (Add. MS. 34, 148, fol. 181).

[412] *Hist. MSS. Com. Rep.* xiii, App. iv, 111.

[413] Pipe Off. Decl. Accts. 3575.

[414] S.P. Dom. Eliz. cclxvi, 67.

[415] *Hist. MSS. Com. Rep.* xv, App. v, 76.

[416] Ibid. 87.

[417] Ibid. 73, 74, 90; *Chamberlain's Letters* (Camd. Soc.), 59.

on the coast of Ireland; this was the last formal assistance given by Kent during the reign of Elizabeth.

By 8 Eliz. cap. 13 the Deptford Trinity House corporation was authorized to erect, at its own cost, beacons and seamarks on the coasts and rivers, and given general control over such seamarks as were then existing. This Act, although it had no immediate effect, was the basis of the future development of the Trinity House; but at the time the privilege of erecting beacons and seamarks at their own expense, without any power to charge tolls, was not of much practical value to the brethren. Moreover, the exercise of such authority was very likely to have brought them into conflict with the vague, but farspread, rights of the Lord Admiral in the matter of beaconage and buoyage. This latter aspect of the question was settled in 1594 by the Lord Admiral's surrender to the crown, in favour of the Trinity House, no doubt for some consideration which does not appear, of all his rights in beaconage, buoyage, and seamarks everywhere, and of ballastage in the Thames, with the fees appertaining thereto, the last item of ballastage being a very profitable one.[418] The work of the Trinity House hitherto had been connected almost solely with the Thames and its pilotage; this grant brought the river entirely under the control of the corporation, and formed the foundation for future extension. The right of the Trinity House to license pilots appears to have been in full operation from the middle of the sixteenth century, and their duty to supply pilots for 'the conduction' of the queen's ships is mentioned in the Act of 8 Elizabeth. One of the grievances of the Hansa in 1540 was that they could not choose their own pilots, but were compelled to take those assigned to their ships.[419] A draft grant of 1582, to a private individual, of the right to pilot foreign ships expressly excepts the Thames, or any displacement of pilots acting under the Deptford establishment.[420]

The use of natural features, such as hills and clumps of trees, as seamarks must have been coeval with the first attempts at navigation. As soon as churches were built those visible from the sea, such as the Reculvers, became of universal utility for the same purpose. Then must have followed the marking of river mouths and the entrances of harbours by signs recognizable by the local fisherman and pilots. Buoyage and beaconage came comparatively late; the earliest one known in connexion with the Thames is the Shoe beacon on the Maplin Sand, which is mentioned about 1542. There must have been others in the river itself, for there is a grant of 20 August 1536 to William Broke as keeper and conservator of buoys and beacons in the Thames, with the accustomed fees.[421] In 1556 the only outside beacons were those of the Shoe and on the Spaniard sand; the Spaniard beacon, opposite Herne and some six miles out, is still represented by a successor, but the Shoe has been replaced by the Maplin lighthouse.

About the beginning of Elizabeth's reign those concerned with navigation came to the conclusion that owing to 'the decay of Margate steeple,' and changes in the sands, more buoys and beacons were required, therefore Richard Barrey obtained a grant from the Lord Admiral of the office of beaconer of the Thames; in 1575 his grant was renewed, with power to levy higher fees than heretofore—from one to three shillings on one to three-masted

[418] Privy Seal, 11 June 1594.
[419] L. & P. Hen. VIII, xvi, 392.
[420] S.P. Dom. Eliz. clv, 111.
[421] Admir. Ct. Misc. Bdles. Ser. II, 224, No. 62.

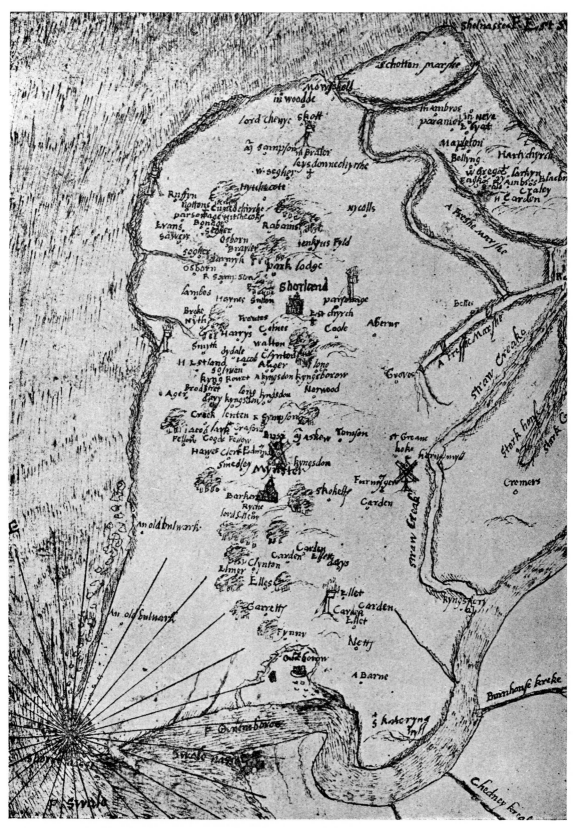

ISLE OF SHEPPEY, *temp.* ELIZ.
(from Cotton MSS., Aug. I. 1, 51).

ships—on account of his trouble in marking out the New Channel.[422] Spanish subjects from the Netherlands were not to be charged. The Red Sand, Long Sand, and Snouts are named in 1345,[423] the Girdler (' Grillere ') in 1361,[424] and the Black Deeps in 1387.[425] The last seems to have been the ordinary, and perhaps the oldest, passage into the river ; in 1540 an annuity of £20 a year was given to John Bartelott for piloting the king's ships through the Black Deeps and for the discovery of a safer channel in part of it.[426] Thomas Spert, the first master of the reorganized Trinity House, was given the succession to Bartelott; and these especial pilots, evidently the *doyens* of their class, were nominated continuously, certainly as late as the reign of James I.[427] After 1594 the whole responsibility for buoyage and beaconage came upon the Trinity Corporation, and their field of action was gradually extended; buoys were placed off the Red Sand, the Spell or Spile, and the Last Sand before 1603, and a beacon on the third named.[428] The existence of beacons in connexion with the Kentish Knock, and the Swallowtail between Margate and Reculver, is implied.[429] The date of establishment of the buoy of the Nore is unknown ; it is constantly mentioned from 1652 onwards, and perhaps was placed in consequence of the frequent presence of squadrons at the Nore at that time.

The Dover Trinity House was incorporated in or about 1606. Emulating their Deptford rivals the brethren agreed in 1568 that the channels between the South Foreland and the western end of the Nore should be examined yearly and alterations certified.[430] For the expenses of this, and for the relief of the poor, two shillings were deducted from every turn of duty of an elder brother and one shilling from that of a younger brother. The management of the Dover institution became so dishonest that in 1616 the Warden considered the advisability of placing it under the control of the Deptford house; but as an alternative it was set on a wider basis by giving the pilots of Deal and Sandwich a share in its government.[431] Unlike the Deptford foundation, that at Dover never willingly supplied pilots to men-of-war, and in the reign of Elizabeth and later the captains were always made to apply through the Lord Warden. It has been noticed that the two Trinity Houses were at law in 1601, and although the subject of dispute is unknown, it was probably due to what were considered encroachments by the London house. After the accession of James I the Deptford corporation came into closer communication with the Government, and occupied an altogether more important position which inspired its members with confidence and pretensions. Cases, involving the customs of the sea, which came before the law courts, were referred to it for an opinion by the judges ;[432] the Navy officials began to ask for the views of the elder brethren on improvements in shipbuilding intended to be applied to men-of-war, and the inauguration of the modern lighthouse system, which

[422] Admir. Ct. Misc. Bks. 970, Nos. 220-1. In 1582 one of these buoys went adrift, eventually fetching up in Dunkirk harbour, and from the resulting documents in relation to its recovery we find that the New Channel in question was by then sometimes called the Queen's Channel (Admir. Ct. Exemp. xxi, Nos. 104, 105). It still retains the same name.

[423] Pat. 19 Edw. III, pt. ii, m. 20d. The Snouts cannot now be identified under a modern name.

[424] For. Accts. No. 24, m. 15; Close, 34 Edw. III, m. 4.

[425] *Ante*, p. 271.

[426] *Rymer Fœdera*, xv, 245.

[427] S.P. Dom. Jas. I, viii, 12 May 1604.

[428] Admir. Ct. Libels, 170, No. 159; ibid. Exam. 37, 5, 6 July 1604; S.P. Dom. Eliz. cclxxxviii, 67.

[429] S.P. Dom. Eliz. clxxvii, 56.

[430] Egerton MS. 2118, fol. 5.

[431] Lyon, *Hist. of Dover*, i, 294.

[432] *Hist. MSS. Com. Rep.* viii, App. i, 236. Cf. pp. 286, 318.

began with the seventeenth century, brought them into prominence either as projectors themselves or as opposing the projects of others. In 1630 they erected a beacon at Kingsdown, as a leading mark through the Gull Channel;[433] this was within the territory of the Dover Trinity House, and shows how quickly the authority of the other at Deptford had extended. In 1624 there was a beacon on Sandwich Flats, opposite the south end of the Brake, but it is not known which body erected it.[434] At the same date a lantern on the middle tower of Deal Castle was ' one of their main seamarks,' and could be used as ' a fire lantern upon occasion.'[435] The twin spires of the Reculvers church formed a famous seamark, but it did not come into the possession of the Trinity House until 1810. As the church fell into disuse and ruin the responsibility for the upkeep of the spires was repudiated on all sides ; such a question arose in 1637 when the Privy Council solved the difficulty by a peremptory order to Archbishop Laud to undertake the necessary repairs without delay.[436] Again, in 1663, the Trinity House, perhaps relying on precedent, certified the Archbishop of Canterbury that the spires were in urgent need of restoration.[437]

In 1580 a certain Gawen Smith proposed to the Government to erect a beacon on the Goodwin Sands to be 20 ft. or 30 ft. above high-water mark and capable of sheltering 30 or 40 shipwrecked men; by night it was to show a light visible 20 or 30 miles.[438] For this he asked a toll on passing ships and a further reward of £1,000 when he had made grass and flowers grow upon the Sands, to be increased to £2,000 when there was a stable foundation for a fort there. By this time the Downs anchorage was frequented as much, relatively to the tonnage afloat, as it was two centuries later, and far more than it is to-day. An indication of this is the ' multitude ' of lost anchors which had made the anchorage unsafe, and that two Deal men, acting under a licence, had recovered between 1599 and 1615.[439] Another phase of shipping life in the Downs was exemplified in the experience of the *Abraham*, a Flemish trader which went on the Sands in December 1615. She was no sooner aground than the Deal boatmen were alongside asking whether the master desired help. He requested that three or four of them should come on board, but they all swarmed up and took charge. For the work of salvage they demanded a third of the cargo, but eventually accepted the master's proposal to leave the amount of arbitration and ' shook hands ' on the agreement. But when the cargo came up many of the packages were opened and the contents divided among the boatmen, while others disappeared by being transferred from one boat to another and could not afterwards be traced.[440] Everyone has heard of the meritorious, and often heroic, work of the Deal and Walmer boatmen in saving life; nevertheless, accusations of plundering, of which this can hardly be an early example, and of extorting high terms for salvage have been brought against them.[441] At the worst, however, the nefarious conduct has never retarded the heroic, which has become almost proverbial. The lighter side of the dangers of the Goodwins is to be found

[433] *Hist. MSS. Com. Rep.* viii, App. i, 244.

[434] S.P. Dom. Jas. I, clxxx, 61 (1).

[435] Harl. MS. 1326.

[436] S.P. Dom. Chas. I, ccclxxiv, 63.

[437] *Hist. MSS. Com. Rep.* viii, App. i, 251.

[438] S.P. Dom. Eliz. cxlvi, 97. The same man also proposed to maintain a packet service between Dover and Calais; the vessel was also to attend wrecks on the Goodwins, and persons saved were to pay fees according to their social position (*Cecil MSS.* xiii, p. 187).

[439] Ibid. Jas. I, xxvii, 56; lxxxi, 110 (i, ii).

[440] Ibid. lxxxvi, 2.

[441] Cf. Defoe's *The Storm*, Lond. 1704.

in the charge of groundage fees made by the Lord Warden—in one instance, in 1624, £15 [442]—from ships which had gone on the Sands and been fortunate enough to get off again. The underlying principle, feudal in origin, was that of compensation to the Lord Warden for use made of his Sands and damage done to them by the ship.

The peaceful reign of James I gave little occasion for military or naval levies, therefore there are few references to the Ports. Dover and Sandwich were two of the three places within the Cinque Ports licensed to allow passengers to pass to and from the 'Continent.' [443] From very early times the king's messengers, carrying despatches abroad, must have passed through Dover, but one of the first references we have to a packet boat is of 1514, 'a boat of Dover which was sent over for the conveyance of the budget;' [444] as in very many later cases, both in peace and war, the boat was taken and the mail consequently thrown overboard. Dover was by no means the only channel of postal communication, Rye, in especial, being a competitor, [445] but in 1636 an agreement was come to with the French authorities that letter carriage should be confined to the Dover-Calais route; [446] notwithstanding this Dunkirk was often an alternative to Calais. In consequence of the numerous attacks on the packets by privateers, under any or no excuse, armed vessels of larger size, carrying six guns, were provided in 1637, the first of the long line of packets intended to fight or run.

London and the other great ports were now monopolizing ocean trade, and there was only a coasting traffic left for the smaller towns which had formerly a share in such foreign trade as then existed; the decline of several of the Kentish ports was also hastened by the failure of their harbours. Mr. R. G. Marsden has compiled a list of trading vessels whose names occur in legal and historical MSS., as well as in various printed sources, during the reign of James I, in which 4 of Broadstairs, 2 of Dartford, 37 of Dover, 11 of Faversham, 5 of Gillingham, 5 of Gravesend, 1 of Hythe, 4 of Maidstone, 10 of Margate, 16 of Milton, 1 of New Hithe, 2 of Northfleet, 1 of Queenborough, 3 of Rainham, 15 of Rochester, 30 of Sandwich, 1 each of Sittingbourne, Strood, Tonbridge, and Whitstable, and 2 of Woolwich are mentioned. [447] There must have been many others that sailed through an uneventful career without attracting the attention of the law, the Admiralty officials, or the Customs, but even as the numbers stand they point to a flourishing coastal trade. Besides the shipbuilding necessary to meet local needs there was also some on a larger scale. Lists exist of some 380 vessels built, mostly for London owners, between 1625 and 1638, the certificate of building, with certain details, being necessary to obtain a licence for ordnance. [448] Of these, three, of 300, 180, and 160 tons respectively, were built at Dover, one other at Strood, and another at Rochester, and the *Royal Katherine*, of 500 tons, by Edward Stevens at Deptford. Stevens was a government master-shipwright who also possessed a private yard. A foreign visitor of this period who came up the Thames noticed that above Gravesend, ' on ne voit des deux costés qu'atteliers de navires et tout fourmille des charpentiers qui en bâtissent . . . c'est une chose etonnante que le grand nombre qu'il y en a.'

---

[442] S.P. Dom. Jas. I, clxxv, 77.
[443] Ibid. xxxviii, 14.
[444] *L. and P. Hen. VIII*, i, 3659.

[445] See *V.C.H. Sussex*, ii, 154.
[446] Add. MS. 6344, fol. 40.

[447] *Trans. Roy. Hist. Soc.* xix, 311.
[448] S.P. Dom. Chas. I, xvi, xvii.

The first naval armament of any importance in the reign of James I was that under Sir Robert Mansell intended to act against Algiers. The western ports were the greatest sufferers from the Mediterranean pirates, but the king thought that all the coast towns, as more or less interested, should bear the expense; in fact, the expedition was called 'the merchants' fleet,' and a committee of merchants controlled the accounts.[449] A circular letter from the Privy Council, in February 1618–19, dwelt on the misdeeds of the Algerine and Tunisian pirates; but in reality the undertaking was more immediately occasioned by the condition of European politics than by the sufferings of James's subjects, and the fleet was a factor in the king's foreign policy. From the Cinque Ports the Council desired £400, payable within two years, of which £200 was to come from the Ports as a whole, and £200 from Sandwich and Dover independently.[450] The waning prosperity of the Ports made it difficult for them to give the same prompt response that had been customary in former years, and it is remarkable that from counties so far apart as Devon and Kent came the same bitter comment—that London having engrossed the trade of the country should pay proportionately for its success. The London trading companies were assessed at £40,000, of which the Trinity House had to provide £4,000 in two years; this was to be obtained by a rate levied on merchantmen, finally settled at eighteenpence a ton for those sailing to the Mediterranean and threepence for others working in northern seas.[451] The Trinity House only negotiated the tax which was to be collected by the Customs officers.[452] In July 1620 the levy was altered to £1,000 a year, from the Trinity House, while the fleet was at sea;[453] but there was, to say the least, some misunderstanding, for in October, when Mansell at last sailed, the Corporation maintained that £1,000 of the original assessment had been remitted.[454] When, in January 1621–2, the London companies were asked to keep the fleet at sea for three months longer the Trinity House was one of the three which made objections;[455] as the merchants' committee was threatening to sue the elder brethren for the disputed £1,000, the latter may have thought it well to get quit of a responsibility which brought no profit.[456]

The representatives of the Cinque Ports met at Romney to consider the demands of the Privy Council; although they arranged to raise some money, it was subject to a protest through the Lord Warden that all the vessels belonging to the Ports were small, and that, in the whole of the confederacy, there was only one ship of 50 tons, belonging to Dover, which traded to the Mediterranean going as far as Malaga. London, they said, had absorbed all their maritime traffic, leaving them only a few coasters sailing to Newcastle and the west of England and some passage boats to France and Flanders.[457] The Ports voted at first only 200 marks, of which one-third fell upon Dover, but the Council insisted upon the £200;[458] even in their semi-ruined state the Ports gave less trouble to the Council than did many other more prosperous places. Notwithstanding their decay the Cinque Ports still affected to be ready to perform their ancient 'service,' and in 1614 based a claim to exemption from payment of subsidy on their willingness.[459] There was some difficulty now in obtaining

[449] S.P. Dom. Jas. I, cxxvii, 42.
[450] Ibid. cv, 88, 89.
[451] Ibid. cv, 44, 46, cxvi, 10; *Hist. MSS. Com. Rep.* viii, App. 242.

[452] Ibid. cxv, 11.
[453] Ibid. cxvi, 4.
[454] Ibid. cxxiii, 13.
[455] Ibid. cxxvii, 42.
[456] Ibid. cxxx, 27.

[457] Egerton MS. 2584, fol. 67; *Hist. MSS. Com. Rep.* xiii, App. iv, 152, 153.
[458] Egerton MS. 2584, ff. 71, 154.
[459] *Suss. Arch. Coll.* xvii, 137.

men as well as ships from the Ports. In 1623 the Council informed the Lord Warden that the punishment of deserters would henceforth be severe, but the bad treatment and privation suffered by man-of-war crews sufficiently explain the hatred felt for the royal service without supposing any deterioration of the sea instinct. Their miseries began before they set foot on board ship, for, in 1620, the Council directed the Warden to raise 100 men, the ordinary press-masters not being employed on account of the distress caused by their oppression and corruption;[460] from this it would appear that it was not yet invariable to act through the Lord Warden in impressing men. A return of 1623 shows that there were 95 seafaring men of between 18 and 60 years of age dwelling in the parish of St. Peter's (Broadstairs), 21 at Ringwould, 43 at Ramsgate, 62 at Deal, 203 at Dover, 70 at Margate, 83 at Sandwich, and 45 at Hythe;[461] for Lydd, Romney, and the rest of Kent there is no report.

The coast fortifications had been neglected for many years, especially since the death of Elizabeth. After 1588 there seemed to be less likelihood of their being put to use and little was done to them until the panic of 1599 brought renewed fears for the safety of Kent. In that year nearly £800 was expended on Upnor, a ditch 32 ft. wide and 18 ft. deep being added to the defences.[462] The contemptuous estimate of Gravesend has been noticed;[463] in 1600 it contained east and west gun platforms and £88 was assigned for their repair.[464] Of Deal Castle we hear in 1603 that the beach had been swept away and that the sea was eating into the foundations;[465] in 1615 it was in much the same condition, and Sandown and Walmer were suffering from similar sea erosion.[466] The ordinary garrison of these Downs castles was 15 soldiers and gunners, with a captain, lieutenant, and two porters;[467] a curious light is thrown on the discipline of the garrisons by 'presentments' to the Lord Warden in 1619, in which the soldiers returned their officers and each other as frequently absent from duty.[468] The men of the Moat Bulwark, at Dover, 'presented' their officers but not each other because, as there was no lodging for them in the fort, they could not be there continuously, but averred that they had not quarrelled, hunted, nor trapped game.[469] At Sandgate, in 1613 there were ten guns, of which five were serviceable, and in 1616 it was said to be in a dilapidated condition.

The approach of war with Spain caused the issue of a commission in 1623 for the inspection of all the coast forts with directions to raze those considered useless and repair and improve those it was considered advisable to maintain.[470] None of the Kentish defences came in the former class. The resulting survey showed that there were 7 guns at Sandgate, but that the sea had undermined the principal battery and that part of the containing wall was down. At the Archcliff and Moat bulwarks at Dover there were, respectively, 13 and 6 guns; both of them were in fairly good condition according to this report,[471] but another of 1625 states that Archcliff had not been repaired since the reign of Elizabeth, and that although there were 11 guns there was no gun platform.[472]

---

[460] S.P. Dom. Jas. I, cxvi, 54 (i).

[461] Ibid. cxl, 64, 65, 66, 67, 68, 69; cxlii, 25, 39.

[462] Add. MS. 5752, ff. 374, 378. The engineers were permitted to take 'serviceable stones' from Rochester Castle.

[463] *Ante*, p. 305.

[464] Add. MS. 5752, ff. 386, 391.

[465] *Hist. MSS. Com. Rep.* vii, App. 253.

[466] S.P. Dom. Jas. I, lxxxii, 129; lxxxvi, 12; lxxxvii, 19.

[467] Eg. MS. 2584, fol. 318.

[468] Ibid. ff. 42, 233.

[469] Ibid. fol. 92.

[470] S.P. Dom. Jas. I, cxlix, 104; cli, 89.

[471] Harl. MS. 1326.

[472] S.P. Dom. Chas. I, vi, 13.

In Dover Castle there were 32 guns, but many repairs were required. At Walmer there were no guns and the sea flowed into the moat; Deal had 4 guns, and Sandown 17, but the latter was in need of renovation. On the Medway, Upnor was armed with 14 heavy guns, including two 32-pounders and three 18-pounders, but the drawbridge was immovable and there were other defects; the river was also defended by two sconces—Bay and Warham—the former with 4 and the latter with 5 heavy guns, but in Warham the tide had washed away the foundation of the gun platform, and there was no breastwork to shelter the men working the guns. At Gravesend there were 16 guns, but Milton is not mentioned and had probably been disestablished for some time.

During the war with Spain, and that with France which from 1627 accompanied it, there was no real expectation of invasion, neither of the two powers being sufficiently strong at sea to undertake offensive measures on a large scale. Such fears as were felt were for raids on the east and south-east coasts from the Low Countries, and it was necessary to protect the roadsteads from the 'Dunkirkers' who swarmed in the Channel and North Sea. The state of the castles in the Downs was amended to some extent in 1625, but in the same year there was not a gun at Sandgate.[473] Little, however, could have been done to the former, for in 1626 the captains of Deal and Walmer reported that the sea was destroying the foundations of Walmer and had several times filled Deal moat with shingle.[474] Charles had no money for land fortifications, which were practically needless if his fleets could keep the enemy occupied, therefore in 1627 we find that Sandgate was falling down and indefensible, and that the Deal and Walmer captains were repeating that if something was not done their respective commands would be swallowed up by the sea.[475] Sandown was in little better condition, but as in 1630 the garrison of Gravesend had been unpaid for six years it may be imagined that there was nothing to spare for rebuilding even after the restoration of peace.[476] The captain of Gravesend had been for twelve years in vain asking for repairs.[477] He redressed his want of pay by demanding fees from shipmasters passing the fort, an abuse which continued off and on for two centuries and was flourishing at least as early as 1625.[478]

Whatever defensive value Sandown, Deal, Walmer, and Sandgate may have had was diminishing because the era was commencing when men-of-war were never long absent from the Downs, and they formed the best defence for the anchorage and adjacent shore as geographical and strategical conditions compelled them to be there in any case.[479] Moreover, if originally intended to stand a siege the castles were now, and probably always had been, too weak for such a purpose and would hardly have checked an enemy's advance into the interior. The defences of Dover, the Medway, and the Thames were of a different character, being intended, in the one case, to deny a strong base and harbour to an enemy, and in the other to protect cities and dockyards from direct and sudden attack by water. Besides want of money, the corruption and

[473] S.P. Dom. Chas. I, iv, 77; xi, 6.

[474] Ibid. xxv, 82.

[475] Ibid. lx, 86; lxv, 62.

[476] Ibid. clxii, 80.

[477] Ibid. dxxx, 122.

[478] Cruden, *Hist. of Gravesend*, 365. Any shipmaster passing Greenwich Palace, while any one of the royal family was in residence, without striking topsail and firing a salute was liable to summary arrest (S.P. Dom. Chas. I, clxxxviii, 78).

[479] In 1635 there is a payment of 10s. to a man for a year's service in making signal fires on Deal beach to give notice to men-of-war captains that despatches had arrived (Aud. Off. Decl. Accts. 1702–76).

favouritism which helped to stultify all the national enterprises at this period were also at work in reducing what small utility the coast defences may have possessed. Officers were appointed not as soldiers but as court parasites; in 1632 John Philpot, Somerset Herald, petitioned not to be removed from the post of Lieutenant at Gravesend because he performed his duties by deputy, and illustrated the position by referring to John Hervey, one of the king's footmen, who held the like post at Sandgate.[480] When the governors were efficient men they had duties which prevented their personal attendance. Sir John Penington and Sir John Mennes were the captains of Sandown and Walmer; but both were seamen of reputation and, in the event of war, when their presence at their commands would have been essential, their services would have been required afloat. In 1635, after a survey, there was an estimate that each of the Downs castles would require from £1,200 to £1,500 for its repair, Walmer being in the worst condition and with no guns in it.[481] After this a wall was built at Walmer to keep out the sea, but by 1641 it was undermined and fallen; in that year the Ordnance Office reported to Parliament that the three castles needed £5,000 spent on them but that the outlay would be of no use without £3,000 more for sea defences.[482]

The outbreak of war with Spain was followed by the preparation of the Cadiz fleet of 1625; it was made up of men-of-war and hired transports, the counties not being required to provide any armed ships. One ship of Dover and three ketches of Milton are named as hired for service, but the port of origin is not given in many cases;[483] from another source we find that Dover lost three ships in the voyage whose crews left 227 widows and orphans.[484] In the fleets of 1627 and 1628, under Buckingham, Denbigh, and Lindsey, only one Dover vessel and a ketch of Milton can be traced. In July 1626 the Privy Council directed the Lord Admiral to send in returns of the ships and men available throughout the country; those for Kent show that very few vessels, of the size now necessary, were to be found in the county. Dover stands at the head of the list with 29 'great ships' of 40 tons and upwards, 11 of from 30 to 40 tons, and 19 smaller vessels; of the 'great ships' one was of 350 tons, one of 240, and eight of from 100 to 130 tons.[485] There were 18 pilots in the town, but few seamen, and the ships lay idle, 'there being not sailors in this town to man a third part of them,' men from the Thames being hired when necessary. At Sandwich there were 11 vessels of 100 tons and upwards, of which one was of 240 and two of 180 tons, 14 of from 50 to 100 tons, and 10 under 50 tons.[486] At Broadstairs there were 65 men and 11 vessels of which the largest was of 20 tons; Hythe, Walmer, Deal, and Ramsgate also possessed nothing but fishing boats, one of 56 tons at Ramsgate being by far the largest in the group.[487] It is noticeable that 17 pilots dwelt at Deal for service in the Downs, but otherwise only 34 seafaring men, and at Walmer there were no pilots, only two fishing boats and 14 men. Another return, of January 1628-9, deals with Kent outside the Cinque Ports. Seventeen places are mentioned but the names are only those we are accustomed to see; the largest vessel was of 35 tons and there were 395 men.[488] Greenwich, Gravesend, Erith, Woolwich, and Deptford are included in the port of London; at Gravesend

[480] S.P. Dom. Chas. I, ccxxvi, 5.
[481] Ibid. cclxxxvii, 33.
[482] Ibid. ccclxxxi, 55

[483] Pipe Off. Decl. Accts. 2263.
[484] S.P. Dom. Chas. I, dxxx, 26.
[485] Egerton MS. 2584, fol. 375 (Oct. 1626).

[486] S.P. Dom. Chas. I, xxxiv, 110.
[487] Ibid. xxxiv, 109; xxxix, 28.
[488] Ibid. cxxxii, 19.

there were 121, and at Greenwich 128 watermen.[489] The Cinque Ports were again surveyed at the same time.[490] Dover had fallen to 36 vessels, of which the two largest were of 260 and 240 tons; there were five of from 100 to 160 tons, and the remainder were under 100 tons; of fishermen and sailors there were 179. Sandwich had only 16 ships and 10 hoys; six were of from 100 to 200 tons, but all the others were under 100 tons and there were 78 men. Margate possessed 14 vessels, including one of 60 tons and three of 40 tons each; Ramsgate had one of 46 tons, but Hythe, Faversham, Folkestone, Lydd, Deal, Walmer, and Broadstairs had nothing but fishing boats. In 1634 there were 13 vessels of from 100 to 260 tons in the whole of the Cinque Ports;[491] in this connexion the Cinque Ports means, practically, only Dover and Sandwich.

Although it had few ships for the royal fleets, Kent bore its share in the supply of their crews and in the terrible loss of life from disease, exposure, and semi-starvation which dishonoured Charles and Buckingham. Such local troubles as were experienced were due to the ' Dunkirkers,' a generic term for the privateers from the ports of the Spanish Netherlands, who thronged the Channel and the North Sea, and who sailed too fast to be caught by the king's ships. Moreover many of them were piloted by English seamen whose knowledge of the coast made the privateers doubly dangerous. In March 1624 the mayor of Sandwich wrote to the Warden about the losses suffered by shipowners of the town, and a few months later the Council were told that the Dunkirkers were infesting the mouth of the Thames.[492] In December of the same year they took a ship out of Dover Roads, there being not a gun mounted in any of the forts with which to fire upon them, and three months later seven merchantmen were taken in one haul near the Goodwins.[493] This kind of thing soon roused some of the old spirit of the Portsmen, and Sir John Hippisley, the Lieutenant of Dover Castle, organized a raid to burn the Dunkirk ships in their harbour; the plan was taken up with spirit, but a gale dispersed the little expedition and Hippisley could not animate the Dover men to another attempt. The packets suffered frequently, but Dover was not the only Kentish town which experienced loss; in December 1625 the people of Gore End were leaving their homes and moving inland in fear of the marauders.[494]

In June 1626 Charles, on the brink of war with France, resolved to follow the precedents of Elizabeth's reign and called upon the maritime shires for 56 ships to join the royal fleet. The Cinque Ports were charged with four ships, each to be of 200 tons and stored and provisioned for three months, but this was subsequently reduced by two being placed upon the non-chartered portions of Kent and Sussex.[495] The Ports sent their two at a cost of £1,500 and made the best of the necessity by petitioning that the ships might guard their own coast, that they might appoint their own captains and officers, and have letters of marque.[496] Of the other two we hear nothing; if they went to sea one at least must have been hired from London or elsewhere. Charles had required the ships for what he would have described as purposes of imperial policy, and had neither thought nor money to spare for such a small necessity as clearing the sea for commerce. But Kent was really better off than most of the coast counties exposed to the Dunkirkers by reason of the many men-of-war

[489] S.P. Dom. Chas. I, cxxxv, 4.
[490] Ibid. 31.
[491] Ibid. cclxx, 64.
[492] Ibid. Jas. I, clx, 85; clxx, 72.
[493] Ibid. clxxvi, 74; clxxxv, 126, 127.
[494] Ibid. Chas. I, xi, 50.
[495] Ibid. xxx, 81.
[496] Ibid. xxxiii, 50; xlviii, 40.

and the many well-armed ocean-going London merchantmen passing to and fro who afforded some sort of protection. They had little to expect from the crown; every penny that could be raised went to maintain foreign war, so that in 1627 Buckingham to protect himself, although he was largely responsible for the existing conditions, procured a protest to be entered in the Council register to the effect that though he had been ordered to equip six ships for the guard of the coast, he could not do so because no money had been assigned for the purpose.[497]

In February 1627 the mayors of Hythe, Folkestone, and Margate asked for guns to protect their roadsteads;[498] the request of Margate was attended to at once, five being sent there, but Hythe and Folkestone did not receive two each until 1629.[499] In July 1627 the Ports petitioned that they were exposed ceaselessly to ' the force and fury ' of the Dunkirkers, who had taken, plundered and sunk their ships within sight of the coast, and who had stopped their herring and cod fisheries in the North Sea; their strength, they added, was diminished by 200 men having been impressed for service in the king's fleets.[500] In 1628 they joined with Yarmouth, Norfolk, and Suffolk in another and similar petition. Dungeness was a favourite station of the privateers, and there are many references to ships being taken off it. Shipowners were encouraged to apply for letters of marque and thus recoup themselves to some extent.[501] Between 1625 and 1628 three ships of Sandwich and three of Dover sailed with them;[502] the largest was of 180 tons. In the year ending with February 1629 there were four Dover vessels and one of Sandwich thus employed.[503] Even after peace with France in 1629, and with Spain in 1630, the malpractices of the Dunkirkers persisted because the Thirty Years' War continued and Spaniards and Dutch fought out their quarrel on the English coast with a supreme contempt for territorial waters, and, as neutrals, English ships were exposed to search which was often only the first stage of robbery. In 1631 there were two cases in which Dunkirkers chased vessels ashore on Sheppey, got them off, and took them away;[504] in 1632 another took an English ship off Dover but, being chased by Dutch men-of-war, ran into the harbour, where she was seized as a pirate.[505] There were four Englishmen on board who were held for trial. A year later four Dutch and four Dunkirkers fought in the Downs; the captains of Deal and Sandown Castles ordered them to desist, which they did for the moment, but the next day the Dutch, probably knowing that the castles were impotent, again attacked the Dunkirkers, taking three of them.[506]

Charles had intended an issue of ship-money writs in 1628 but, alarmed at the feeling aroused, he withdrew from the first trial. Forced, at last, to choose between facing a Parliament and raising money by this method, the writs of 20 October 1634 were sent out addressed to the ports and maritime places of the kingdom. The Cinque Ports of Kent and Sussex, together with Rochester, Maidstone, and the Isles of Thanet and Sheppey, were called upon for a ship of 800 tons, with 260 men, victualled, manned, armed, and stored for 26 weeks' service. The Kentish bank of the Thames, as far as Milton, was attached to Westminster and London, exclusive of the city, for a 500-ton ship.[507]

[497] S.P. Dom. Chas. I, lviii, 66.
[498] Ibid. lv, 19.
[499] Ibid. lviii, 9; ccxlv, 49.
[500] Ibid. lxx, 8, 9.
[501] Ibid. lxii, 1.
[502] Ibid. cxv.
[503] Ibid. cxxxvi, 79.
[504] Ibid. clxxxviii, 42; cxci, 9.
[505] Ibid. ccxviii, 21.
[506] Ibid. ccxxxvii, 16.
[507] Ibid. cclxxvi, 3, 64; cclxxvii, 59.

As the ships required were larger than those possessed by any port except London, it was provided that an equivalent in money might be paid to the Treasury for the equipment of a king's ship—in the case of the Cinque Ports £6,735. Some of the assessments for this writ were : Deptford £43 6s. 5d., Greenwich £120 4s. 10d., Erith £12 8s. 10d., Woolwich £14 15s. 6d., Dartford £27 7s. 6d., Northfleet £21 18s. 8d., Gravesend £23 3s. 6d., Milton £23 0s. 5d., Charlton £13 10s. 8d., Swanscombe (Greenhithe) £13 7s. 6d., and Sandwich and members £285.[508] There seems to have been but little trouble in collecting the money; some difficulties had occurred, the sheriff wrote, but ' now pacified by mild persuasions.'[509] The second writ, of 4 August 1635, was general to the inland counties as well as those of the coast; a ship of 800 tons or £8,000 was demanded from Kent and the Cinque Ports.[510] A meeting at Sittingbourne on 7 November assessed Canterbury at £280, Sandwich and its members at £250, Dover and members £330, Romney and members £180, Hythe and members £40, Queenborough £10, Rochester £70, Greenech or Grench £10, Bekesbourne £35, Tenterden and Orwellstone £90,[511] Fordwich £32, Faversham £70, Folkestone £12, Lydd £110, and Gravesend and Milton £35.[512] There was some local quarrelling; the Faversham men thought that £100 of the Dover contribution laid upon them was too much and appealed to the Warden, Ashe objected to help Sandwich, and Maidstone desired to tax Boxley which was also assessed by the Sheriff.[513] Still, on the whole, there was little hesitation in paying, and by the end of November the sheriff had sent in £4,950.[514] The king was so well pleased with the general response to the first writ that he ordered the Council to send a circular letter to the sheriffs expressing his satisfaction and inviting delegates from the counties to London to see and examine the accounts for themselves.[515] In August 1635 the arrears of Kent and Sussex on the first writ were only £70 13s. 2d., but on the Westminster and North Kent ship £582 7s. 9d. remained unpaid.

The third writ of 9 October 1636 was of the same character as the second, but as it became evident that ship-money was to be a permanent tax the tide of resistance was rising. There were large arrears still owing on the second writ, but Kent was not one of the counties thus passively recalcitrant, because in July 1636 the sheriff was £200 in surplusage, which a court of Quarter Sessions decided to devote to the repair of the high road at Boughton Blean.[516] But it was much less easy to collect the money due under the third writ; in July 1637 the Privy Council wrote to Sir George Sandys, the sheriff, accusing him of ' great slackness and remissness,' and warning him that if the whole amount were not paid by the end of August he would have to attend before them.[517] The end of August came and he did have to appear before the Council when he promised settlement by the end of September.[518] By 5 October he forwarded £300 on account.[519] The Cinque Ports petitioned, begging some consideration, saying that people were leaving the towns in

[508] S.P. Dom. Chas. I, cclxxviii, 21; Boys, *Hist. of Sandwich*, 707

[509] S.P. Dom. Chas. I, cclxxxii, 14.

[510] Ibid. ccxcvi, 69.

[511] Bekesbourne and Greenech were attached to Hastings from the Norman period, and Tenterden to Rye from 1449. See *V.C.H. Sussex*, ii, 129, 130, 143.

[512] Add. MS. 33918, fol. 24. Assessments made in August (S.P. Dom. Chas. I, ccxcvi, 73) differ somewhat from these.

[513] S.P. Dom. Chas. I, ccxcix, 22, 56; *Arch. Cant.* xxiv, 240.

[514] S.P. Dom. Chas. I, cccii, 53.

[515] Ibid. ccxcviii, 74.

[516] Ibid. cccxxix, 17.

[517] Add. MS. 33918, fol. 25.

[518] S.P. Dom. Chas. I, ccclxvii, 22.

[519] Ibid. ccclxix, 78.

consequence of the heavy ratings, and pointing out that formerly, when their ' service ' was required, an allowance out of the tenths and fifteenths had been made to them.[520]   They also alleged that there was not a single fishing boat at Romney or Lydd, and only a few at Hythe where they were beached a mile from the town, while Sandwich Haven was silting up, the port having only a coal and corn trade to London.   Between the hammer of the Council and the anvil of the active or passive opposition of the people, the situation of the sheriffs was becoming a very unpleasant one.   In January 1638-9 Sandys wrote to the Council complaining of the perverseness of the collecting officers; there is a paper of about this date showing arrears of upwards of £900 and giving a long list of parish constables who took no notice of warrants; Sir Robert Pettie of Otford utterly refused to pay anything.[521]   Several of the constables were called before the Council; the collector for Snodland and Paddlesworth asserted that he could only obtain £1 12s. out of the £13 assessed, but it was supposed that there was collusion.[522]   The fourth writ of 1639 was, originally, similar to its predecessors, but the county was afterwards given the option of paying £6,400 at once or the full amount in ordinary course.[523]   Subsequently the assessments were greatly reduced, but two-thirds of the tax were never received.

Local history shows even more clearly than general history the feeble inefficiency with which the ship-money fleets, which cost Charles his throne and life, were handled.   While they were parading pompously and uselessly, the Dunkirkers took their prey as usual within English waters.   The Dover packets were stopped, searched, or robbed as often as before the fleets were commissioned, Dutch fishing boats were taken close in-shore off the east coast, and in 1635 two Dunkirkers attacked a Dutch ship in Dover Roads, under the bulwark where guns should have been but where there was only one serviceable.[524]   A few weeks earlier a ' freebooter ' had blockaded the harbour for some days until assistance came from the Downs; she had carried off one ship, ' we having very small means of resistance,' because the forts and castle were unarmed and useless, and their condition was known to strangers who presumed upon it.[525]   In 1635 a boom was placed across the entrance to the harbour, against the wish of many of the Dover townsmen;[526] it is possible that this was connected with the Dunkirkers, although it may also have been a precaution necessitated by the king's unstable foreign policy, the consequences of which were always uncertain.   In 1636 Charles built ten small ships—' Lion's Whelps '—out of the ship-money, to deal with the Dunkirkers, but they proved too slow to be of any use for the object intended.   In 1639 a Spanish fleet carrying troops to Flanders was caught by a Dutch fleet in the Channel.   After a running fight the Spaniards took refuge in the Downs, where they were followed by Tromp, and where an English squadron under Sir John Penington was lying to enforce neutrality.   Charles hoped to sell his protection to the highest bidder, but while he was intriguing Tromp settled the matter by attacking and destroying the Spaniards.   Dr. Gardiner writes : ' his boasted sovereignty of the seas had been flouted in his very harbour '; as an

[520] S.P. Dom. Chas. I, ccclxxvi, 140.

[521] Ibid. ccclxxvi, 97; ccccx, 129

[522] Ibid. ccccxxi, 29; ccccxxviii, 86, 88; ccccxxix, 63.

[523] Ibid. ccccxli, 52.

[524] Ibid. ccxc, 38.

[525] Egerton MS. 2584, fol. 395. (Anth. Percival to the Lord Warden.)

[526] S.P. Dom. Chas. I, cclxxxviii, 61

object-lesson in the value of the ship-money tax, with which they had been oppressed for years, the occurrence can hardly have failed to impress observers.

A few events in the history of the Trinity House during this period require notice. Such departmental connexion as it had with the Navy began in 1621 under an order of 26 May by Sir Henry Marten, the judge of the Admiralty Court, that no one should hold the office of master or pilot of any ship belonging to the Thames without a certificate of competency from the corporation.[527] The effect of this was that the masters of men-of-war required the Trinity House certificate, and eventually naval men who aspired to that rank were sent to the elder brethren for examination. This was the only permanent association they ever had with the Navy besides the supply of pilots. The system was not successful at first apparently; in 1633 a man-of-war captain wrote that in his opinion the masters recommended by the Trinity House were ' altogether unworthy of his Majesty's service,' being of a class grown untrustworthy by long residence ashore.[528] Subsequently, when the candidates for a master's warrant were trained men-of-war's men nominated by the Navy Board, subject to passing the Trinity House examination, they became one of the most meritorious and skilful classes of officers in the Navy. Pilots continued to be supplied to the king's ships as heretofore, and formed very convenient whipping boys for the captains. For very many years whenever a ship went ashore or was lost with a Trinity pilot on board, the court-martial almost invariably found the pilot guilty and sent him to prison, although in many cases the loss or accident was due to the captain's interference with him. It was probably this risk that made the Downs pilots so unwilling to take charge of men-of-war, and the Dover Trinity House had not the same reasons as that of Deptford for enforcing compliance.[528a] Moreover, complaints and threats filtering through the Lord Warden and the Lieutenant of Dover Castle became attenuated in effect by the time they reached the elder brethren and the offenders.

Another point of affiliation, although only a very temporary one, between the Deptford institution and the Navy is to be found in an order of 1634 that the plans and dimensions of new ships were to be settled by consultation between the dockyard master-shipwrights, the brethren of the Trinity House, and the leading men of the Shipwrights' Company.[529] For the short time this worked the results were wholly unsatisfactory; if the advice of the elder brethren had been attended to there would have been no improvements in shipbuilding during the reign, and, as far as the evidence of the State Papers goes, events very quickly showed them to be egregiously wrong in their opinions on every subject referred to them. A striking illustration of this is to be seen in the discussions which preceded the construction of the *Sovereign of the Seas;* the elder brethren maintained that it was beyond ' the art or wit of man ' to build a three-decker, and described in a prose rhapsody the impossibility of finding any safe place in which to moor her if built. Three years later she was afloat and proved one of the most successful ships of the century, earning from the Dutch, who met her in action, the respectful title of the ' Golden

---

[527] *Hist. MSS. Com. Rep.* viii, App. i, 240.

[528] S.P. Dom. Chas. I, ccxxxiv, 40.

[528a] E.g. In March 1708-9 pilots for the blockading squadron off Dunkirk were badly wanted, but no one would go from Deal or Dover although the men there must have known the shoals of Flanders as well as they knew the Goodwins. Therefore the London Trinity House had to supply them. See also *ante*, p. 307.

[529] Ibid. cclxvii, 62.

Devil.' The explanation of this and other blunders was that the elder brethren were seamen and not shipwrights, and had been thrust into a false position. There was little confidence felt in the professional shipwrights but, whatever their defaults, they were better qualified than professional seamen who did not possess even empirical knowledge.

In 1629 there were 31 elder and 254 younger brethren, which number must have included the majority of shipmasters sailing from London.[530] By a by-law of 6 Henry VIII there was a charge of 10 per cent. on pilots' wages for the relief of the poor, but only 5 per cent. was taken.[531] In 1618 there were 160 pensioners; the growth of shipping and a desire to extend their own influence led the elder brethren to propose, in 1639, the formation of a fund for merchant seamen, similar to the Chatham Chest for Navy men, of which they should have the control and distribution.[532] As the corporation could not obtain power to compel subscriptions the scheme came to nothing. During the Civil War the Trinity House was on the side of the Parliament because its employers, the shipowners, supported the Parliament, because the seamen were generally anti-royalist, and because its interests in the matter of lighthouses had for years past been in antagonism with the claims of the crown. When the rising of 1648 occurred some of the members of the corporation showed signs of sympathy with the revolters, if only by petitions to Parliament, and, although a commission of May of that year praised them for their good service during the preceding civil troubles, the result was that the independent powers of the brethren were suppressed during the Interregnum, and the Trinity House was administered by a Parliamentary Committee. So much confidence had been placed in them that in 1647 the forts of Gravesend and Tilbury were assigned to the care of the brethren.[533] The pilots and others worked under the superintendence of the Parliamentary Committees; in 1653 they, with the Cinque Ports pilots, found a new channel between the Spell and Woolpack sands which they reported to be better than the old one between the Spell and Last. The new channel was to be marked by white buoys, the old one remaining buoyed for the use of small vessels.[534] The investigation was performed somewhat unwillingly, for while it was being done the Trinity House men protested against being compelled to undertake such searches at their own expense.

The people of the seaboard had been the worst sufferers from Charles's naval incapacity, and in Kent, as elsewhere, they mostly took the side of the Parliament. Dover Castle was taken for the Parliament, 21 August 1642, and the three castles in the Downs about the same time; in 1644 they, with Sandgate, were under survey for repair.[535] Sandwich was so far enthusiastic as to petition for fortification, and £330 was assigned for the purpose.[536] In 1645 the County Committee represented the need of a fort at Dungeness, but Parliament regretted that there was no money available to build it.[537] In 1642 the guns at Gravesend were removed to Tilbury, in February 1647 a committee was considering whether it should be maintained; in the following July it was reported on as scarcely tenable, and in July 1648, after the lesson of the revolt,

---

[530] *Hist. MSS. Com. Rep.* viii, App. i, 238.
[531] Add. MS. 31149, fol. 383.
[532] *Hist. MSS. Com. Rep.* iii, App. 79.

[533] *Com. Journals,* 31 July 1647.
[534] S.P. Dom. Interreg. xxxix, 63; xl. 15.
[535] *Com. Journals,* 23 May 1644.

[536] Ibid. 16 May, 13 July 1643.

[537] S.P. Dom. Chas. I dvi, 11 Mar. 1645.

the Kentish Committee was directed to consider whether Gravesend and Queenborough could be made tenable, and if so to rearm them.[538]   Nothing of importance happened on the Kentish coast during the Civil War because the royal armies were too far away for supplies to be pushed through to them even if a base could have been seized and held.   Moreover, although inland Kent was not undivided in its allegiance to the Parliament, the coast was loyal to it and offered no foothold for a landing or for the equipment of royalist privateers.

There was a general reaction in favour of Charles in 1648, and in May the Kentish men rose for the king.   Rochester, Sittingbourne, Faversham, and Deptford were occupied; at Sandwich a pseudo Prince of Wales, who landed, was received with enthusiasm, but Dover Castle was held successfully for the Parliament, and though besieged was relieved on 6 June.   Deal, Walmer, and Sandown Castles were taken by the royalists; the squadron lying in the Downs declared for the king, not at all out of love for him, but out of jealousy of the army and hatred of their new vice-admiral, Thomas Rainsborow, an army officer and a fanatical Independent, the feeling in the fleet being Presbyterian.   Fairfax's victory at Maidstone crushed the revolt by land, and the reappointment of the Earl of Warwick as Lord Admiral stopped the spread of the mutiny in the fleet.   After relieving Dover Castle, Colonel Rich proceeded to besiege the Downs castles.   A royalist detachment sent by the Prince of Wales attempted to relieve the forts on 5 July; they succeeded temporarily with Deal and Sandown, but failed at Walmer which surrendered on 12 July.[539]   On the 15th some of the royalist ships appeared off Deal and cannonaded the Parliamentary troops with little effect; about the 23rd they were joined by the Prince with the main body of his fleet.   He set about frightening London by stopping merchantmen passing through the Downs, and, after two slight attempts on the 4th and 10th, landed a relatively large force on 14 August to raise the siege of Deal Castle; it was repulsed with a loss of 140 killed and wounded and 100 prisoners.[540]   Deal surrendered on 25 August, and Charles left the Downs on the 29th, professedly to seek and fight Warwick's squadron off the mouth of the Thames, but the two fleets were separated by a gale.   Warwick came into the Downs on the 2nd, and Sandown yielded on 5 September.

The Civil War had not brought any chance of good fortune to Dover if the statements in a petition of 1649 be true that the townsmen had lost 50 ships within the past seven years, that their harbour was ruined, and that they had paid the Parliament £35,000 in various ways.[541]   The war of 1652-4 with the United Provinces was to give Dover and the whole of Kent a new insight into what it meant to be in the midst of a great maritime conflict under modern conditions, for, as the county fronted the enemy, contained the principal dockyards, and provided roadsteads and anchorages, its waters and those adjacent were not only the prize of battle, the winning of which had to precede ulterior operations, but were the centre from which the English fleets acted and to which the enemy's attacks were necessarily directed.   With the exception of 1588, Kent had ceased to be in the forefront of danger since the close of the Hundred Years' War; with 1652 commenced another era during which it was

[538] *Com. Journals,* 22 Nov. 1642; 26 Feb. 1646–7; 31 July 1647; 3 Aug. 1648.

[539] *Thomason Pamphlets* (B.M.), E. 451 (86).

[540] Ibid. E459 (3).

[541] S.P. Dom. Interreg. iii, 1, 2

more or less continuously faced with the possibility of raids or invasion, under new tactical conditions, culminating in the long menace lasting from 1798 until 1805. The first Dutch war was fought, on both sides, with fleets of a fighting strength such as had never hitherto been seen afloat; but in a generation hardened by nearly ten years of civil conflict there was curiously little fear of land attack even when doubtful strategic dispositions seemed to render a raid possible. As long as the English fleets were able to seek and meet the Dutch on terms of equality no territorial attack was practicable for the enemy; but there is a hint of what might have happened on a large scale after a crushing defeat in the trifling landings in Kent which followed the Dutch victory off Dungeness in November 1652.

Trained in warfare, and commanded by self-reliant and capable men, the navy of the early years of the Commonwealth, the finest both in its civil and combatant branches that had yet existed in the history of the world, was used even before the war began in a very different fashion to that of Charles I. Kent had suffered long from the Dunkirkers who were now sailing under commissions from Charles II; in August 1649 an English squadron appeared off Ostend and Dunkirk to demand redress, 'and let them see that this Commonwealth will not be destitute of means to have justice.'[542] As a corollary of these minor operations, Dover became a victualling station for the cruisers working near it, and remained a subsidiary establishment until the nineteenth century. The first Dutch war was very popular among the seamen, but Kent took little part in it beyond the provision of men and the experience of being often in the heart of the struggle. The era of the armed merchantman had not yet passed away, but the minimum limit of such ships was now at least 200 tons, and the county had few or none of that size for the fleets;[543] the customs officers of Dover were, among those of other places, called upon to report whether any 200-ton vessels were owned there.

As the English men-of-war were brought forward for service they were concentrated in the Downs, and the first collision between Blake and Tromp took place off Dover on 19 May 1652. Some volunteers came off from the town to join Blake, and others were in readiness when it was supposed that Tromp was returning to the attack. On 27 May the Council of State ordered a letter to be written to the mayor conveying their appreciation of the patriotism displayed, 'which the Council have a very great sense of,' and directing that the men should be rewarded out of the prize tenths. The mayor of Sandwich was also thanked for his alacrity in promoting the public service.[544] Within a week came an order to press all able seamen between 15 and 50 years of age; troops were moved down to the coast, the garrison of Dover Castle was increased, and the townsmen of Sandwich were 'to be encouraged' to defend themselves against any attack that might be made there. The lack of seamen, of whom there were not sufficient in England to man the war fleets and carry on commerce, soon forced the Government to send soldiers to complete the crews. Towards the end of June, Blake went northward to intercept Dutch trade coming home round Scotland, and to stop their fishery; he left Sir George

[542] Royalist prisoners were being allowed a penny a day subsistence money at Dover; Captain Amy wrote from Dunkirk to the mayor that he would starve in the same way such Dover men as were his prisoners (*Popham MSS.* [Hist. MSS. Com.], 40).

[543] S.P. Dom. Interreg. 13, 23 Mar. 1651–2.

[544] Ibid. 27, 28 Mar. 1652; Add. MS. 29,623, fol. 35; Boys, *Hist. of Sandwich,* 715.

Ayscue in the Downs, with 14 or 15 ships, to await the arrival of 20 armed merchantmen fitting in the Thames. On 8 July, Tromp, with the main Dutch fleet of 100 sail, appeared in the Downs. Ayscue could do nothing but place his squadron as much as possible under the protection of the guns of Deal Castle; additional batteries were thrown up on the beach, and the Council of State, as soon as they heard the news, ordered a troop of horse to Deal, and gave a general authority to raise the county if necessary.[545] Fortunately a week of calms, or of foul winds, foiled Tromp, and when the wind did come round it was fair for, what the States General considered, his more important duty of seeking Blake. So Ayscue escaped. When Tromp went round the east coast he took a ketch of Rochester and a vessel, probably a fisherman, of Dover, in the North Sea.

By the middle of August Blake had returned to the Downs which he left again to destroy a French squadron sailing to relieve Dunkirk, and to go westward in search of Ruyter. He missed both Ruyter and the main Dutch fleet under Cornelius de With, who came down Channel behind him driving half a dozen merchantmen ashore between Folkestone and Hythe as he passed; it was said that de With's flagship stood so close in-shore as to be fired upon from Sandgate Castle. De With joined Ruyter, and he and Blake did not see each other until the latter was back in the Downs, when the appearance of the Dutch was followed by the battle of the Kentish Knock some 20 miles from the North Foreland. Dover was a very busy place during the war in view of the succession of prizes and prisoners and supplies of stores passing through the town, and the sick and wounded who remained there. Thomas White, who was mayor in 1655 and 1656, was the naval agent and had charge of all the administrative business and minor repairs connected with the fleet, the prisoners, and the sick and wounded; the quarterly accounts sometimes reached £700 or £800. Many of the prisoners were sent inland to Canterbury to relieve the pressure at Dover, but in October those in both towns were sent home in exchange for English captives.[546] After the defeat of de With and Ruyter on 28 September, Tromp was recalled to the command; on 24 November his great fleet was seen from Margate, and on the 29th he was off the South Foreland while Blake was lying in Dover Roads. The battle off Dungeness and Blake's defeat followed on the 30th. Blake retreated to the mouth of the Thames where Tromp, hampered by responsibility for a large convoy and without pilots, could not follow him, but the Dutchman landed plundering parties who gathered 200 head of cattle from Romney Marsh.[547] As soon as the Council of State were informed of the Dungeness disaster they pushed troops down to the seaboard and ordered immediate attention to be given to the Downs castles, so that as Tromp had no landing force he was unable to do any real mischief although in command of Kentish waters. According to a newspaper account one of his detachments ashore was cut off in its entirety by Colonel Rich's troopers.[548]

Tromp hovered for some time off the coast between Folkestone and the Downs, and on 10 December unceremoniously anchored in Dover Roads, but there appears to have been little or no nervousness ashore. The military

[545] S.P. Dom. Interreg. 9, 11 July, 4 Oct. 1652; *Thomason Pamphlets* (B.M.), E. 769 (1).

[546] S.P. Dom. Interreg. 6 Oct. 1652.

[547] *First Dutch War* (Navy Rec. Soc.), iii, 108.

[548] Ibid. iii, 135.

officers in places of trust were veterans of the Civil War who were not likely to lose their heads merely because an enemy was in sight and without regard for his capacity of doing harm. There was a ' hot press ' to man the reinforcing ships for Blake; at Dover 50 men were impressed but only 20 appeared to receive their travelling money, and, of the 20, most refused when it came to the point of departure.[549] The cause was not dislike of the war but the low pay in comparison with the superior attraction of privateering. On 15 December the mayor of Dover wrote giving the names of some seamen of the town fitted for the command of ships, and asking that the town might be honoured by having one of the new frigates named after it.[550] It was not advisable to assist Tromp's navigation, so on 16 December the Council of State directed a commissioner of the Trinity House to visit the coast and extinguish or alter the lights at the Forelands and elsewhere, as he should judge fitting.[551] He decided that Dungeness light was to be extinguished when the Dutch were in sight; the South and North Forelands were to be lit dimly, but altered about 8 or 9 o'clock ' as agreed,' in a way which is not described and was to be kept secret.

The need for more men led to important improvements in the position of the seamen in the form of increased pay, prize money, and regulations for their welfare when sick or wounded. The immediate effect of this was to bring in a number of men who had previously hung back, and the authorities at both Dover and Deal reported that sailors were joining willingly.[552] During December, January, and February Tromp was in control of the Channel; then Blake got to sea, and on 18, 19, and 20 February 1653 was fought a three days' battle which began off Portland and ended in the Straits of Dover. It was an English victory, and 14 merchantmen of Tromp's convoy, with 700 prisoners, were brought into Dover. Blake's losses were heavy, and Tromp was the first at sea again in May; towards the end of the month he was off Dover, where he took some small vessels in the Roads and, standing close in chasing a ship, cannonaded the Castle and forts. A battle was fought on 2 and 3 June near enough to the shores of Kent to allow the sound of the cannon to be heard inland. That was the end of the war locally, for the last battle of 31 July was fought, despairingly, by the Dutch on their own coast. As the struggle progressed Dover became more and more crowded with sick and wounded English and Dutch seamen; one shilling a day was allowed for the board, lodging, and medical attendance of the English, and sixpence for the Dutch. On 20 June 1653 the mayor wrote to the Navy Commissioners that the sick men were put in private houses, there being no hospital, and that unless the rate was raised he could not compel people to receive them.[553] There must have been many Dutch for £114 8s. was paid on their account for the two months ending on 30 June.[554] However, when the books came under examination at the end of the war the civic authorities of the town experienced some scathing criticism. The total amount was £1,227 16s. 5d., and the commissioners reported that not more than a sixth of that sum had been actually expended for the men, the balance having gone ' in charges ';[555] an enclosed paper giving illustrations of the ' charges ' has unfortunately disappeared.

[549] S.P. Dom. Interreg. 11 Dec. 1652.

[550] Ibid. xxvi, 29. The *Dover*, launched in 1654, was built at Shoreham.

[551] Ibid. 34; xxx, 46.

[552] Ibid. xlv, 66; *First Dutch War*, iii, 340.

[553] S.P. Dom. Interreg. xxxvii, 115.

[554] Ibid. lv, 163.

[555] Ibid. lxvii, 80.

Hostilities with Spain in the West Indies followed the Dutch war, but Spain did not declare war until 1656. This gave a free hand to the Dunkirkers, of whose proceedings complaints came in from all sides; one privateer landed some men at Dungeness who plundered a house.[556] The alliance with France, and the consequent blockade, siege, and occupation of Dunkirk in 1658, was a staggering blow to their industry. There was much trouble in obtaining men to serve in the West Indies, and the same difficulties as existed in other counties occurred also in Kent. The sailors ran away and the local authorities sent whom they could; at Dover, in February 1656, the 26 who came from Romney, Lydd, and Tenterden were all boys or landsmen, and six 'hedgers and ditchers' had been pressed at Dymchurch.[557] On the other hand there were 20 volunteers as well as 18 pressed men from Dover, but it was very exceptional for volunteers for the West Indies to come forward. At the same time Sandwich was required to find 180, Deal 140, and Ramsgate 80 men;[558] of the quality of these we hear nothing. The weak government which preceded the Restoration had to fear royalist risings or landings from abroad; thus in September 1659 the officer commanding in Kent was enjoined to watch the coast vigilantly.

In 1660 the Dover packet service to Flanders was performed by four vessels supplied under contract by some of the customs officers of the port, of whom James Housman, the surveyor, was the chief. In view of the official position of the owners there was something Gilbertian in the fact that not only were the packets known to carry smuggled and prohibited goods inwards and outwards, but Housman was said to receive a yearly payment not to search the vessels.[559] Not only, also, were the mails delayed while the boats waited at Dover for passengers and cargo, but they discharged on the other side according to the business requirements of the freighters—thus a packet would go to Ostend to unload while the mails were waiting for her at Nieuport.

We have seen above that Deal provided 140 men in 1656, which shows how the place must have grown under the stimulus of the traffic through the Downs; during the Commonwealth storehouses had been built for the delivery of provisions and gear to men-of-war calling at the anchorage.[560] A survey of 1660 shows the garrison of Dover Castle and forts to have been 150 men; Upnor, Sandgate, and the Downs castles had each 20 or 30 men.[561] There were guns at Margate, and there is a reference to mounting them in the fort there in January 1664-5.[562] When the second Dutch war commenced Thomas White was reappointed naval agent at Dover.[563] The Admiralty wrote to the mayor that they hoped that fourth-rates would be able to come into the harbour as in the former war;[564] in November 1665 a surveyor of victualling, at a salary of £100 a year, was appointed to act with White. A return of December 1664 of men available gives 350 in the Cinque Ports, but it is obvious that this number only represents those required or still liable. An abstract of the following February, of men actually pressed, assigns 232 to Dover, but this must include seamen from other places who reported themselves to White to obtain their conduct money.[565] The first battle of the war was fought on 3 June 1665 in the North Sea about 40 miles from Lowestoft but the firing

[556] S.P. Dom. Interreg. cliii, 134.
[557] Ibid. cxxxiv, 59.
[558] Boys, *Hist. of Sandwich*, 716.
[559] S.P. Dom. Chas. II, v, 126.
[560] Ibid. xxiii, 31.
[561] Ibid. xxxviii, 47.
[562] W.O. Ord. Warrants, iii.
[563] S.P. Dom. Chas. II, cxvi, 51.
[564] Add. MS. 9303, fol. 171; ibid. 9311, fol. 26.
[565] Add. MS. 9316, fol. 79; S.P. Dom. Suppl. Chas. II, 27 Feb. 1664-5.

was heard in Dover. Both fleets were at sea again during the year but no big battle happened; in October 80 Dutch war vessels appeared off Margate and cannonaded the town, ' breaking chimneys and maiming most of the vessels in the harbour.'[566]

In May 1666 the Dutch were in the Straits of Dover; the great Four Days' Battle, between Monk and Ruyter, which began off the coast between Ostend and Dunkirk and ended in the mouth of the Thames, ensued. By one of those curious flaws of continuity which are not uncommon in the transmission of sound the firing was heard plainly in London and Greenwich, while in the Downs and at Dover people were quite ignorant that any battle was proceeding. Evelyn was at Sheerness on 17 June and saw the bulk of the English fleet in the Medway 'miserably shattered . . . appearing rather so many wrecks and hulls, so cruelly had the Dutch mangled us.'[567] France was bound by treaty engagements to help the Dutch, and on 26 January 1666 Louis XIV declared war against England. After Monk's defeat a French invasion would have been quite possible had Louis intended really to help his ally, but he was looking forward to a league with England at the expense of Holland. Expectation of descent, however, was keen and the militia was embodied, a strong force being moved into Kent which would almost certainly have been the point of attack. The plague was rife in Deal, Dover, and Sandwich during the greater part of the year, which must have been an anxious one on the coast. The English cruisers made the French feel some of the effects of war; on 18 September one of their 70-gun ships was taken off Dungeness and brought into Dover. The beginning of 1667 was less fortunate, for the *St. Patrick*, a new ship, was taken in February off the North Foreland by two Dutch men-of-war.

The Dutch were at sea again towards the end of June 1666, but the English not until July when they won a battle in the North Sea. It had been very difficult to recruit men; on 27 June an Order in Council authorized the impressment of ' all such loose and unknown persons as have not been inhabiting there (Kent) for the space of three months at the least.' In the middle of July de Witt sent over the embalmed body of Sir William Berkely, killed on 1 June, and an informal exchange of views took place soon converted into definite negotiations at Breda. Both powers kept fleets at sea during the remainder of the year but nothing of importance happened. Charles, relying on the certainty of a settlement, and desirous of applying the money voted by Parliament for the Navy to the formation of a standing army, resolved in 1667 not to fit out battle fleets but to trust to some squadrons of cruisers, land troops, and coast fortifications for safety.[568] A consultation was held at Sheerness on 20 March when it was decided to mount a battery of twelve 18-pounders at Garrison Point. The survey of 20 March was in compliance with an order which had been ignored since 27 December 1666; the fort was not begun until the end of April, and then there were seldom more than ten men at work.[569] For the fact that so little was done Charles must be held personally accountable. On 25 March orders were given that two additional fireships were to be placed at Sheerness and two within the Upnor chain; two Dutch prizes were to be moored so that their broadsides would bear on the chain, and the first and

[566] S.P. Dom. Chas. II, cxxxiv, 102.

[567] *Diary*.

[568] The responsibility is invariably placed with the king, but there is some evidence—second rate— that he desired to treat sword in hand, but allowed himself to be overruled by the opinion of the majority of the Privy Council.

[569] Harl. MS. 7170, fol. 43.

second rates within it were to be taken as far as possible up the river.[570] As these orders involved, in the main, only a change of position of the ships they were, in part at least, carried out. Early in June, after the English government had had long warning, the Dutch fleet was at sea and off Dover where an attack was expected—'what the issue will be God knows.'[571] The beacons flamed up,[572] but Ruyter moved northward to put in execution a raid in the Thames and Medway which the Dutch had designed for July of the preceding year [573] but the English concentration at the Nore had prevented.

On 7 June Ruyter was off the mouth of the Thames, and on the 9th a squadron under Admiral van Ghent went up the river as far as Holehaven intending to capture or destroy some West Indiamen and men-of-war lying near Gravesend. These ships retired above the town and, as the wind failed him, van Ghent returned on the 10th to his chief. Moreover, he was perhaps unaware of the helpless state of Tilbury and Gravesend which were, nominally, to bar his passage. After having been dismantled Gravesend fort had not been restored under the Commonwealth; the blockhouse field had been sold, but possession was resumed at the Restoration.[574] The Duke of Albemarle stopped in the town for a few hours on 10 June on his way to Chatham; he found only a few guns mounted and that the governor of the fort had hardly a dozen men, while the inhabitants were removing their property and themselves as fast as possible. Albemarle, before going on to Chatham, left orders that an artillery train following him from London should stop at Gravesend. Pepys, who was also there on the 10th, says that the fort could not have answered the Dutch fire for half an hour.[575] On 13 June Prince Rupert was directed to superintend the construction of the batteries at Woolwich which had been ordered six months previously, and, eventually, 60 guns were mounted on the river front of the Warren.[576]

On 10 June Ruyter decided to strike at Chatham, and as a preliminary attacked the uncompleted fort at Sheerness. Some beginning had been made there in accordance with articles of 6 March 1667, for work to the value of £1,360, between Sir Bernard de Gomme, the military engineer in charge, and two contractors.[577] Of what happened we have an account by Edward Gregory,[578] then clerk of the cheque at Chatham, years afterwards Sir Edward Gregory, a member of the Navy Board and Commissioner at Chatham, who is several times mentioned in the article on the royal dockyards. Sir Edward Spragge, a capable seaman, was in command of the ships and forts of the Medway; he sent, on the 9th, for the only regiment of regulars in the neighbourhood, which marched towards Sheerness, but the movement was countermanded and only one company came. Spragge also sent for 100 seamen from Chatham, but the small craft carrying them went ashore coming down the river and only 44 appeared at Sheerness. On the 10th, just before the attack, a company of the trained-bands came in; the fort itself had 16 guns but only seven were serviceable. The Dutch opened fire about 5 o'clock in the afternoon, and as soon as one man had been killed and another wounded

[570] S.P. Dom. Chas. II, cxcv, 15.
[571] Ibid. cciii, 111.
[572] Ibid. cciv, 43.
[573] Ibid. clxi, 1.
[574] Pocock, *Hist. of Gravesend*, 163.

[575] *Diary*.
[576] S.P. Dom. Chas. II, ccv, 13 June 1667; Vincent, *Records of Woolwich*, i, 313.
[577] Sloane MS. 2448, fol. 44. The Dutch illustrations of these

events show a strong and finished fort at Sheerness.
[578] J. Copland, *Taking of Sheerness*. From Gregory's narrative in the Bodleian.

the garrison ran away, except Gregory and six others who remained to be taken prisoners. The strength of the Dutch landing party—800 men—may well have brought home to the tiny garrison the excellence of discretion; it was under the command of Colonel Dolman, said to have been an English soldier of the Commonwealth army, who also led the assault on Landguard in July.[579] A council of war was held to discuss whether Sheerness could be held permanently;[580] it was decided to be impracticable, therefore the enemy destroyed the fort and took away such naval stores as were to be found. The Dutch estimate that their value was nearly £40,000 must be pure imagination.

Ruyter had upwards of 70 fighting ships, besides fireships, transports and nearly 3,000 troops; when Albemarle arrived at Chatham on 11 June he found no order, system, discipline, or leadership. Of the dockyard men he could not find a dozen for service, the rest being occupied in removing their belongings; to do this they were using the river guard boats which should have been employed in towing into safety the big ships lying near Upnor chain. According to the duke, and the articles of impeachment against Commissioner Peter Pett afterwards framed upon his report, the Commissioner himself had set the shameful example of using some of these boats to transfer his own property. Pett denied this, and on the whole it would seem that he was a commonplace man, fitted for routine and peace duties, who was made to suffer for the defaults of his superiors. Albemarle found the chain, which must have been a light one since it only weighed between 14 and 15 tons, in position between Hoo Ness and Gillingham; this was much lower down than the situation of the Elizabethan chain, and outside any protection from Upnor, but the alteration had become necessary in consequence of the greatly increased number of ships within it. Albemarle's first preoccupation was to throw up two batteries, one at each end of the chain, but of course they were only weak ones. Two ships were sunk outside the chain, then others were called for; Albemarle knew nothing of local fairways and soundings, and appears to have been unable to obtain accurate information, so that he resolved to hold other vessels ready to sink inside the chain. This order, which would have enabled him effectually to block the channel if it had been obeyed, was not properly executed.

While Albemarle was using his respite of 36 hours between the 10th and 12th in the arrangement of these hurried measures of defence, the Dutch were slowly sounding their passage up the Medway. About 10 a.m. of the 12th the leading ships bore down on the chain; it is uncertain whether it broke, was forced under water by the weight of the ships, or was cast loose by some Dutch seamen sent ashore, but it checked the advance only for a moment. The *Royal Charles*, a first-rate (the *Naseby* of the Commonwealth), was carried off, other ships were burnt, and Albemarle sank three more first-rates to save them. There is little doubt that, had the attack been pushed home with more vigour this day, the dockyard and every ship in ordinary might have been destroyed. The Dutch anchored when the tide turned and did not resume operations until the next day; in the interval Albemarle planted guns in suitable positions, and threw up an 8-gun battery at the side of Upnor. When the enemy came

---

[579] See *V.C.H. Suffolk*, ii, 233. If the man of 1667 be the Dolman several times mentioned in the Nicholas and Clarendon Papers his nationality is obscure. Cf. *Nicholas Papers* (Camd. Soc.), ii. 1, 287.

[580] Brandt, *Vie de Michel de Ruiter*, 412.

forward again, on the 13th, they were exposed to a heavy artillery and musketry fire from Upnor and the earthworks thrown up; their fireships, however, succeeded in burning the *Loyal London, Old James,* and *Royal Oak* sunk the previous day, but whose upper works were not under water. With this success the Dutch were content and retired to Queenborough, where they remained at anchor for some days, a detachment landing in Sheppey on the 19th to collect sheep and other necessaries. By the end of the month, when the Dutch were far away, there were 60 or 70 guns mounted in the old and new dockyards at Chatham; on 24 July a belated royal warrant ordered that Upnor was ' henceforth ' to be kept up as ' a fort and place of strength.'[581]

Ruyter separated his fleet into three divisions of which one, under himself, remained in the embouchure of the Thames; a reconnaissance up the river showed little to tempt him to run the risk of a passage, for Gravesend and Tilbury were being strongly armed, and ships were sunk in the fairway of Gallions Reach and at Blackwall Point, these situations having been selected by the elder brethren of the Trinity House.[582] In obedience, later, to express instructions from the States-General a squadron entered the Thames, but by that time there were 80 guns and several companies of foot at Gravesend and Tilbury.[583] The Dutch went up to the Hope on 13 July to attack some English frigates and fireships lying there; after an indecisive action the English came up under the protection of the guns of Gravesend and Tilbury. There was more fighting on the 14th and 16th, but on the 18th the enemy retired to the Nore. They maintained a blockade of the river, and on 23 and 24 July came again to the Hope; there was some fighting in which both sides used up their fireships without much result. One consequence of these events was that in October the Trinity House assistants were ordered to prepare a chart of the Medway.[584]

All these occurrences caused a panic in London and elsewhere, but in some places the effect was only to rouse the people to fury. When the news of what had happened at Chatham was known at Deal, ' the common people and almost all other ran mad,' saying exactly what they thought of the king and government; the official writer of the letter feared that if more such news came there might be a rising.[585] At Dover guns were being mounted on the pier heads ' and at all convenient places '; at Sandwich ' the mayor and jurats have commanded all to rise and man the decayed turf walls about the town,' while young and old from Deal went to work to make Sandown Castle defensible.[586] The naval agent at Deal wrote that there were not 300 men available for the defence of the Downs castles and the coast; perhaps one reason was that at the time sailors at Deal were trying to sell their tickets, for wages due, at 40 or 50 per cent. discount. On 23 June there were 14 or 15 Dutch ships in Margate Roads, but notwithstanding this hint by proximity the ardour at Deal had slackened, ' the chief magistrates of Deal keep to their old trade of disagreeing and have left off fortifying themselves.'[587] Late in July, Ruyter, sailing westward, was off Dover; there was alarm in the town and preparations to withstand an assault, but Ruyter was bent on, what he hoped was, more profitable business and he passed on.[588] Prince Rupert had been enjoined to

[581] Mil. Entry Bks. xx, 162.

[582] S.P. Dom. Chas. II, ccv, 110; Add. MS. 5752, fol. 395; *Hist. MSS. Com. Rep.* viii, App. i, 253.

[583] S.P. Dom. Chas. II, ccviii, 155.

[584] Order in Council, 7 Oct.1667. The report is in Sloane MS. 2448.

[585] S.P. Dom. Chas. II, ccv, 77.

[586] Ibid. 4, 77.

[587] Ibid. ccvi, 157; ccvii, 28.

[588] Ibid. ccviii, 149.

superintend the defences of the Medway in case the Dutch returned, but when a division of their fleet did appear on 23 July there was no ammunition and only one gun mounted at Sheerness, although it was hoped to have 12 or 14 more available by the same night.[589] The peace of Breda was signed on 31 July and ended the war. The sum of £10,000 was immediately borrowed from the city of London in order to construct fortifications on a large scale at Sheerness; £7,612 6s. 8d. was spent there, £1,801 5s. at Gravesend, and £655 14s. at Woolwich.[590] On 22 January 1667-8 a committee of the Privy Council, appointed to deal with the fortifications, decided that Sheerness and new batteries below Upnor were to be finished, and the latter connected by an entrenchment for musketeers, that another was to be constructed at Gillingham, and that the one at Woolwich was to be completed.[591] The batteries below Upnor, on the left bank of the river, were those at Cockham Wood and Bird's Nest; later, probably during the third Dutch war, Middleton's battery was thrown up between Upnor and Cockham Wood.

John Evelyn, the diarist, was one of the commissioners for the care of the sick and wounded, Kent being his district. His correspondence teems with lamentations of his inability to do his duty to the unfortunate men depending upon him, on account of lack of money. He estimated that £2,000 a week was necessary; if the dockyards were almost at a stand for want of stores, and the fleets unable to keep at sea for want of provisions, it will be understood that disabled men, for whom the crown had no further use at the moment, fared badly. In September 1665, when the war was yet young, he wrote 'one fortnight has made me feel the utmost of miseries that can befal a person in my station and with my affections—to have 25,000[592] prisoners and 1,500 sick and wounded men to take care of without one penny of money and above £2,000 indebted.' Again, a month later, he appealed for help for men who 'die like dogs in the street unregarded.' He proposed the erection of a hospital at Chatham to contain 400 beds and corresponded with Pepys on the subject, but in the circumstances, whatever may have been the merits of the proposal, there was no chance of its adoption. By March 1666 he had had 7,000 sick and wounded in his district, of whom 2,800 had been lodged in Chatham and Rochester, and incidentally mentions that 30 of them had been placed in a barn at Gravesend which accommodation, rough as it may have been, was better than the 'nasty corners' of the town. During the war the total sums paid were £13,000 at Rochester and Chatham, £6,100 at Gravesend, £1,300 at Faversham, £961 at Milton, £5,600 at Deal, and £2,262 at Dover;[593] prisoners at Dover cost £341, and at Leeds Castle £4,200. Chatham and Rochester were, as the accounts show, the most crowded; in September 1665 the Commissioner, Peter Pett, wrote that hundreds more than the towns could hold were coming ashore, and that such men 'daily perish in the streets for want of quarters.'[594] Gravesend and other places were similarly thronged, so that the sick went 'from place to place and die on the way.'[595] Were there space such testimony might be multiplied infinitely.

Evelyn was again Commissioner for Kent during the third Dutch war of 1672-4 when the same conditions recurred. On 16 July 1673 he wrote to the

---

[589] S.P. Dom. Chas. II, ccx, 99.
[590] Pipe Off. Decl. Accts. 3611.
[591] W.O. Ord. Warrants, iii.

[592] Sic.
[593] Pipe Off. Decl. Accts. 1820-483.

[594] S.P. Dom. Chas. II, cxxxiii, 22.
[595] Ibid. 63.

Navy Commissioners about 'the sad state of the sick men sent into quarters without a rag to cover their nakedness,' and enclosed a letter from the agent at Deal to the same effect.[596] Queen Catherine sent 100 suits of clothes and 100 hammocks for the Dutch prisoners.[597] Both now and later serious charges of mismanagement, or worse, were brought against the Commissioners of Sick and Wounded, so that the advisability of establishing a group of permanent hospitals was under discussion. The first of such proposals dates from May 1673, when Dover and Chatham were two of the towns in which it was proposed to place such institutions.[598] Nothing was said against Evelyn, but some of his colleagues did not escape accusations of embezzlement, and at Deptford and Dover Evelyn's subordinates were called to account.[599] As this did not happen until 1677 it is evident that there was always a very fair chance of escape for the incriminated. The amounts payable for this war were £10,835 at Chatham and Rochester, £1,400 at Dover, £2,036 at Deal, £5,200 at Gravesend, £1,070 at Margate, and £3,201 at Deptford;[600] but in 1679 £5,300 was still owed at Chatham and small amounts at other places.[601] The bill for the sick, wounded, and prisoners of this third war amounts to little more than half of that of the second, and is one indication of its milder character.

Kent had little connexion with the active operations of the third war, and was mainly used to supply men and receive those disabled. The Cinque Ports still looked vigilantly to their rights and when, in December 1672, it was whispered that men-of-war captains in the Downs intended to send press parties ashore at night there was warning that such a proceeding would lead to armed resistance and bloodshed.[602] In the ordinary course the Kentish seamen were willing enough to serve; from the Downs district there were more than 200 men from Deal alone serving in the fleet shortly afterwards.[603] Some other parts of the county were not so earnest; Dover was 'over-run with schism and faction,' and the governor of Sheerness reported that many seamen had run away into the weald ('wild'), who were recovered by laying heavy penalties on those harbouring and concealing them.[604] By these means 1,500 men were regained.

The garrison of Sheerness was but 60 men, of whom ten were sick or dead,[605] but there was little risk of a repetition of the experience of 1667. As a precaution beacon stations were arranged in April 1672 in Suffolk, Essex, and Kent, those in the last county being at Shurland, Herne, Birchington, Margate, the North and South Forelands, and Dungeness.[606] Early in May the Dutch appeared off Margate, where there were guns but no powder, and then at Dover where the queen, before leaving for Canterbury, came to the Castle to see the enemy's fleet.[607] The centre of action shifted to the North Sea where the battle of Solebay was fought in May; the immediate consequence was an influx of sick, wounded, and prisoners into Kent for whom the government had neither money nor charity.[608] Margate was again affrighted in June because the crews of two tenders, after an evening's carouse together, fired their guns in salute, after the fashion of the time, when separating at 1 a.m.; within eight

[596] Admir. and Navy Bd. 283.
[597] *Lond. Gaz.* 24 June 1672.
[598] S.P. Dom. Chas. II, cccxli, 183.
[599] Add. MS. 11684, fol. 76.
[600] Pipe Off. Decl. Accts. 2549.
[601] Add. MS. 9316, fol. 280.
[602] S.P. Dom. Chas. II, cccxviii, 145.
[603] Ibid. 18 Mar. 1672–3.
[604] Ibid. cccxxii, 180.
[605] Ibid. cccvi, 16.
[606] Ibid. cccxiii, 34.
[607] Ibid. 126.
[608] Ibid. cciv, 29; ibid. 27 Aug. 2 Sept. 1672 (Evelyn to Pepys).

hours the country, as far inland as Canterbury, was up in arms.[609] The Dutch were now struggling not so much for victory as for existence, but they were still able to hamper English commerce by their privateers. The mayor of Sandwich reported the loss of 30 merchantmen off the haven in one week, but one reason for the Dutch success may be read in the action of the captain of the *Dover* who refused to weigh after a privateer because he was commander-in-chief in the Downs.[610] In May 1673 Ruyter came over intending to block the channels leading into the Thames by sinking stone-laden ships in them, but he was compelled to retire without effecting anything. Thenceforward the operations of war were on the Dutch and not on the English coast.

The war of 1672-4 was fought in alliance with the French, which was one reason for its unpopularity, both political foresight and popular instinct recognizing France as the real enemy of the immediate future. Relations between England and France grew so strained that by 1677 a rupture was considered imminent, and the preparations made here obtained the name of 'The Sham War' for the critical period; as a corollary certain fortifications at Tilbury, Sheerness, Gillingham and elsewhere were to be put in hand at once.[611] Parliament voted money for the construction of 30 second and third-rates; the only private builders in Kent with a yard of sufficient capacity to build third-rates of 1,000 or 1,100 tons were the Castle family of Deptford, who launched the *Hope* and *Elizabeth*. Other members of the same family possessed a yard at Rotherhithe, but the Deptford firm continued to build for the Navy until the close of the seventeenth century. Edward Snelgrove opened a yard at Deptford before the end of the reign of Charles II and built many men-of-war, but in 1700 he became bankrupt and his two docks were advertised for sale.[612] It was probably this yard, with a double dock near Deptford Green, which was again for sale in January 1734-5.[613] In 1704 John Winter opened a dockyard at Deptford and he built for the Admiralty, as did also West, who died about 1730 leaving £30,000; another John West carried on the business of the latter. Messrs. Bronsden's yard in Grove Street, Deptford, dated from the first quarter of the eighteenth century; later, they became Bronsden and Wells, and they built continuously for the Navy for many years. Bronsden and Wells were probably succeeded by Dudman & Co.;[614] as the demand grew, from the American War period, for the work of private builders another firm started in Grove Street of which the senior was John Barnard who came from a similar yard at Harwich. One, Whiteacres, possessed a yard at Northfleet in 1711, but he obtained no Navy contracts.

Again, in 1688, Kent showed itself to be the natural containing base against a North Sea enemy. The first station taken up to intercept the Prince of Orange was between the Downs and Kentish Knock, from which point the English fleet could act on interior lines against the invader, that is traverse the radius of a circle of which he had to pass over the arc. Treachery or incapacity then sent it to the coast of Essex, and on 3 November the Prince ran safely through the Straits of Dover. The buoys in the Thames were taken up, although, out of consideration for the mercantile interest, they were replaced

[609] S.P. Dom. Chas. II. cccxxvi, 74.
[610] Ibid. cccxiii, 266; cccxviii,69.
[611] S.P. Dom. Entry Bks. xxix, f. 198, 10 Aug. 1676.

[612] *Lond. Gaz.* 23 Sept. 1700.
[613] *Newspaper Cuttings relating to Deptford* (B.M.), 579, l. 12.
[614] Dews (*Hist. of Deptford*,

271), says that Dudman's yard was that founded by Winter in 1704; it is now a coal depot of the L.B. and S.C. Ry. Co.

by small vessels which were to remain until the last moment.[615]   Dover Castle was taken for William on 8 December; it had been proposed that the people of the nearest towns should capture each of the Downs castles, but on the 11th the men of Deal took all three.[616]

A survey of 1689 showed that Dover Castle was in a ruinous and unarmed state, and that the Archcliff and Moat forts were also defective, but Sandgate and the Downs castles had been recently repaired.[617]   Two years later there were 45 guns in Dover Castle, 13 at Archcliff, 11 at Moat's Bulwark, 12 at Sandgate, 30 at Deal, 18 at Sandown, and 17 at Walmer Castles, 8 at Gravesend, and one at Greenwich.[618]   Upnor, like Woolwich and Chatham, held a reserve of guns beyond those belonging to the fortifications.   The increased strength of the armaments round the coast was due to the fear of invasion which was more or less present until Russell won the victory of La Hogue in 1692, but which was acute after Torrington's defeat off Beachy Head in 1690.   To the same period may be assigned a battery on Dymchurch Wall shown on a contemporary map.[619]   In April 1690 three guns were delivered to the mayor of Dover to help the defence of the town,[620] which may have been placed in the Bench Battery although that battery is not shown in a map of 1725.[621]   It was perhaps disarmed during the long peace which followed the treaty of Utrecht.   The defences of the Medway were added to largely during the war. A fort on Hoo Marsh is placed at Folly Point in an undated map probably belonging to the end of the reign of Charles II or to that of James II;[622] besides this, and Upnor, Gillingham, Cockham Wood, Bird's Nest, and Middleton's, now called James's Battery, previously erected,[623] there were, by 1698, also the Middle, Quaker's, and Buda batteries.[624]   These were very heavily armed; Gillingham had 54 guns of which 40 were 18-pounders, the Hoo fort 26, the Quaker's 17, and the Buda battery twelve 18-pounders, while the Middle Battery had twenty-two 45-pounders mounted.   Within less than half a century most of these batteries had ceased to exist.[625]

The modern lighthouse system began in the seventeenth century on the east coast, its priority being due to the needs of the continuous collier traffic passing to and fro.   Kent soon followed, in view of the guidance necessary for the valuable ocean trade converging into the Straits of Dover.   Dungeness was the first danger-point which received attention, as its growth seaward rendered it year by year more perilous to shipping.   A light there was proposed about 1612 by John Allen of Rye;[626] he lacked money and influence, and all petitioners had to face the fierce opposition of the Trinity House, who opposed such applications not on public grounds but in the spirit of jealous trade rivals. Allen may have been the earliest projector, but it was proposed nearly, if not quite, simultaneously by Hugh Bullock and a partner named Bing who interested William Lamplugh, clerk of the royal kitchen, in the scheme.[627] Lamplugh took the matter to Sir Edward Howard, a court favourite, who had just been appointed ' Lieutenant and Admiral of the Narrow Seas ' as an excuse

[615] *Hist. MSS. Com. Rep.* xi, App. v, 207.

[616] Boys, *Hist. of Sandwich,* 758.

[617] S.P. Dom. Will. and Mary, ii, 71.

[618] Ibid. K. Will. Chest, x, 131.

[619] Colepepyr, *Map of Kent,* B.M. 5460–1.

[620] H.O. Mil. Entry Bks. iii, 25.

[621] King's Prints and Drawings (B.M.), xvi, 50.

[622] Add. MS. 5222, No. 5.

[623] *Ante,* p. 329.

[624] King's MS. 43.

[625] During the war of the Spanish succession the garrisons of Dover, Tilbury, Sheerness, etc., were composed of companies of Chelsea out-pensioners.   There was not the least risk of even a raid.

[626] S.P. Dom. Jas. I, clx, 60.

[627] Ibid. clv, 76.

for a sinecure salary, and Howard had no difficulty in obtaining a patent dated 20 August 1615 authorizing him to erect a lighthouse and beacon at Dungeness Point, and to charge a penny a ton on all English shipping passing each way; the grant was for 50 years and was free of rent to the crown.[628] A paper of 1621 says that in the winter previous to the erection of the lighthouse nearly 1,000 seamen had been drowned by wrecks on Dungeness, but that since it was lit there had been no losses.[629]

From a chancery suit in 1623, between the promoters, it seems that Lamplugh and Bing were to have had half the profits, but there was sharp practice all round and the crown of mismanagement was that by a mistake of the Lord Admiral the toll had been made a penny instead of a halfpenny a ton. Shipmasters then complained that the light was so much neglected that there was 'more hazard than safety in depending upon it,' and that, in any case, it was of no use to them when outward bound.[630] Sir John Coke, a Navy Commissioner, also noted the defects of the light, but when the war with Spain occurred in 1625 it was proposed to extinguish it.[631] However, it must have been more effective than would appear from these criticisms, for in 1624 the civic authorities of Rye, who would have liked to have had control of it, confessed that there had been only two wrecks since it was lit.[632] Lydd steeple, a well-known seamark was, they said, deceptive, especially towards dusk, because it looked like the sail of a ship and lured the careless into danger. As Dungeness is steep-to vessels might be in deep water a few minutes before going ashore.

The Trinity House authorities made themselves the representatives of the discontented; an Order in Council of 9 October 1635 confirmed an arrangement come to between them and William Bullock, the owner of the patent, by which the tolls were reduced to a halfpenny a ton.[633] Bullock procured another patent for the remainder of Howard's term which authorized him to erect a new lighthouse, and the crown now took a rental of £6 13s. 4d. a year.[634] He conveyed his interest to Edmond Winstanley who, in turn, obtained a licence empowering him to pull down the old lighthouse and erect another nearer the sea;[635] that this change of position was already an advantage or a necessity shows how rapidly the point was extending seawards. There was another lawsuit in 1656 in which the earl of Thanet, of the family which afterwards obtained possession of the lighthouse, appears as a claimant in virtue of owning the ground, and tried to obtain an injunction forbidding the light to be shown. A petition to Cromwell brought an immediate order that it was not to be interfered with.[636] In 1662 there were more complaints about the insufficiency of the light; but the original patent was then nearing its term and the proprietors were probably not anxious to spend more than was absolutely essential. In 1664 Sir George Marsh obtained a lease for 31 years from the Duke of York at a rental of £100 a year,[637] but a patent of 1676 [638] recites that Charles had in 1661 already granted the reversion of the light to Sir Abraham Shipman by a patent of 12 January of that year. Although a grant from the

[628] Pat. 13 Jas. I, pt. xxiii, m. 11. The patent is the only one known to the writer which also directs a beacon to be set up.

[629] S.P. Dom. Jas. I, cxix, 118.

[630] Ibid. clv, 76; Hist. MSS. Com. Rep. viii, App. i, 246.

[631] Coke MSS. (Hist. MSS. Com.), i, 151.

[632] Hist. MSS. Com. Rep. xiii, App. iv, 166.

[633] S.P. Dom. Chas. II, ccxcix, 39.

[634] Pat. 11 Chas. I, pt. xxiii, No. 4.

[635] Ibid. 31 Chas. II, pt. v, m. 7. The licence has not been found.

[636] S.P. Dom. Interreg. cxxx, 69.

[637] S.P. Dom. Chas. II, 16 April 1664.

[638] Pat. 28 Chas. II, pt. v No. 12.

Duke of York, as Lord Admiral, could be of no avail against an earlier one from the crown, his daughter and heiress, Elizabeth Shipman, was kept out of possession by the heirs of Sir George Marsh under colour of some legal quibbles. Elizabeth Shipman then procured the new and stringently worded patent of 1676 which authorized her to build another lighthouse if she could not obtain possession of the existing one, and ordered the Customs officers to collect the dues for her and for no one else. Probably she obtained peaceable possession, and it was no doubt by arrangement with her that in 1679 a new patent passed in favour of Richard Tufton in whose family the interest remained during part of the eighteenth century.[639] Tufton's lease was to run for 31 years from the expiration or surrender of Elizabeth Shipman's term, at the same annual rental of £6 13s. 4d.

If a light was necessary on Dungeness the need was as great or greater for one in connexion with the Goodwin Sands, and, in fact, a proposal to deal with them preceded Dungeness. The first one known is that of Gawen Smith in 1580.[640] No other steps were taken until 1623 when Sir John Coke, who was Buckingham's right hand in naval matters, interested himself in the subject. His idea was that the Lord Admiral, Buckingham, should erect and maintain lights on one or both of the Forelands, but in this scheme it was indispensable that the Dutch should consent to pay a passing toll, and over this difficulty the plan collapsed.[641] The Dutch wanted the light for the benefit of their shipping but were not ready to pay for it. Both Buckingham and Coke had more urgent matters to occupy them, and they allowed the question to drop. Some years later Sir John Sackville and others expressed their willingness to maintain a light 'in the Main on or near the Goodwins,' and also to keep salvage vessels and crews ready to assist ships in distress; they asked for a patent to run for 40 years.[642]

The successful applicant did not appear until 1635 in the person of Sir John Meldrum, who was already the proprietor of other lighthouses and who seems to have had influence at court. His success evoked a storm of protest; the Deptford Trinity House of course opposed, as they opposed every private grant, and they drew the Dover Trinity House and the shipowners of Margate, Sandwich, Dover and other places at hand into the league of resistance. The local shipowners wished to escape the charges, the pilots saw a possibility of decreased demand for their services, and many others had no wish to lessen the number of wrecks.[643] Meldrum had obtained a certain number of local signatures to the petition for the light, but the mayor of Dover asserted that many good seamen were adverse, and the Trinity House of Dover wrote that the opposition of Sandwich had been silenced by an undertaking to free the shipping of that town from charges.[644] The Deptford Trinity House said that the lights were unnecessary and would be useless, for reasons 'too tedious (i.e. lengthy) to state' except before the Privy Council;[645] then they offered to establish the lights themselves for one-fourth of the tolls asked by Meldrum.[646] Their opposition was assisted by an unfavourable report from the Navy Board, who simply repeated the selfish and prejudiced reasons of the Dover Trinity

[639] Pat. 31 Chas. II, pt. v, m. 7.
[640] *Ante*, p. 308.
[641] *Hist. MSS. Com. Rep.* xii, App. i, 134, 150; S.P. Dom. Jas. I, clv, 28.

[642] S.P. Dom. Chas. I, cliv, 30. Calendared conjecturally under 1629.
[643] Ibid. lxxxix, 27 (calendared

erroneously under 1627); ibid. cclxxxiii, 1.
[644] Ibid. 73; cclxxxiv, 13.
[645] Ibid. cclxxxiii, 1.
[646] Ibid. cclxxxv, 41.

Dungeness Lighthouse, c. 1702
(from Admir. Ct. Prize Papers, 51, 'Bdle. of Grapes').

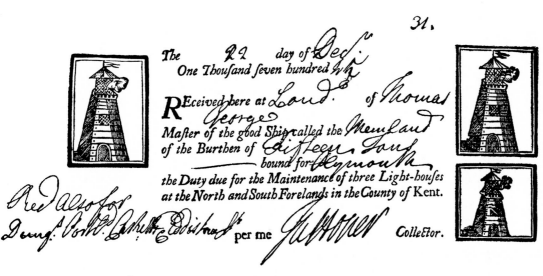

Lighthouses at North and South Forelands, 1745
(from Admir. Ct. Prize Papers, 125, Bdle. 'Jupiter')

House, the fishermen, and the pilots. These last committed themselves to the courageous statement that no wrecks, within their memory, had occurred for want of lights, and said that the project originated with a Dutchman living at Sandwich because it would be of value to Dutch shipping. Meldrum's caustic comment on the Thames Corporation was that ' the Trinity House claim a sole power yet never do anything and oppose everyone else.' [647] It was true, but mainly because the corporation had no power to exact tolls and was not yet influential enough to obtain licences granting them except in rare instances; if they could have obtained them systematically they would have been eager enough to erect the lights, but as that was not the case they could only oppose the courtiers who were more fortunate.

All these denunciations had little effect; there was some delay in passing the patent, which was not enrolled until 1637, but the licence of 9 February 1634-5 was not cancelled, and under it Sir John Meldrum had already erected two lighthouses on the South Foreland, an upper and lower light showing in line over the South Sand Head. That on the North Foreland was, it appears from the wording of the patent, not built until after its issue.[648] The toll allowed was a penny a ton on ships passing each way, and double that amount on foreigners; the term was for 50 years at a rental of £20 a year. In direct contradiction to the pilots, the patent gave as a reason for the establishment of the lights the many wrecks on the Goodwins that had happened for the lack of them. We hear nothing of the Forelands lighthouses for many years, but as commerce grew there were, as in other cases, complaints of the inefficiency of the management. In 1668 the South Foreland lights were said to be so negligently kept that some vessels had run into danger and others had been compelled to lie-to all night because they could not be seen.[649] These lighthouse monopolists were not absolutely independent of criticism because the Deptford Trinity House kept them under watchful and hostile observation, therefore it may be supposed that, in many cases, if the lights could not be seen the default was as likely to be due to the inadequate appliances and methods as to indifference. John Evelyn visited the North Foreland lighthouse in 1672; he describes it as ' built of brick and having on the top a cradle of iron in which a man attends to a great sea coal fire.' [650] This tower was burnt down in 1683, and for some years only a beacon showing a light was used.[651]

In February 1668 Captain John Poyntz proposed to Pepys to build a lighthouse and castle on the Goodwin Sands ' and make the Sands a firm island above high-water mark . . . if I did not complete them this summer I would be bound to lose my life.' [652] In view of the results of certain less ambitious attempts in the same direction in the nineteenth century, it was fortunate for Captain Poyntz that he was not requested to stake his life upon the success of the undertaking; but his offer was perhaps the outcome of general knowledge that the lights at the two Forelands were not very effective. As late as 1693 it was customary to moor a small vessel, as a sailing mark, at the South Sand Head when battleships came from the Nore to the Downs.[653] In 1670 John Smith was the owner of the residue of Meldrum's lease and he obtained a new one, by patent dated 21 July 1671, for 30 years to follow that which he possessed.

[647] S.P. Dom. Chas. I. cclxxxvi, 28.
[648] Pat. 12 Chas. I, pt. xxi, m. 6.
[649] S.P. Dom. Chas. II, clxxix, 37.
[650] Diary, 14 May 1672.
[651] Hasted, Hist. of Kent, x, 357.
[652] S.P. Dom. Chas. II, ccxxxiv, 111.
[653] Lords MSS. (Hist. MSS. Com.), i, 260.

The North and South Forelands were the subject of a lawsuit and appeal in 1688-90.[654] Smith's grant determined in 1717, and the subsequent history of the lighthouses is beyond the scope of this article.

* * * * * *

The later history of Kent is the history of the dockyards, of military arrangements to repel invasion, of the Downs anchorage, of smuggling, wrecks, and the general incidents of maritime history as distinguished from the purely naval which, during the eighteenth century, was overshadowed by the supposed military risks and preparations. The county had become welded with national maritime life and had ceased to have an especial naval history of its own. With 1914 commenced another chapter of its long story when the conditions, political and geographical, which will always render Kent a vital nerve-centre, came into play again causing a renascence of its individuality and naval importance; but the time has not yet come for that chapter to be written.

[654] *Hist. MSS. Com. Rep.* xii, App. vi, 415.

THE ROYAL DOCKYARDS

Topographical writers have arrogated for Woolwich the title of 'mother dockyard' of England, but no claim of the kind could have less foundation of fact. In the Middle Ages, Southampton, Bursledon, Portsmouth, Rye, and Winchelsea were all dockyards of the type to which Woolwich conformed at its inception; in Kent itself Henry V built men-of-war at Smallhithe, on the river Rother, before 1420. If the claim be amended to signify the existence of a dry-dock it is equally ill-founded, for the one at Portsmouth, the first in England but of Italian *provenance*, was built in 1496, nearly twenty years before the rudimentary enclosures of ground which were the beginning of Woolwich. If any place be entitled to be called the 'mother dockyard' it is Portsmouth, not on account of the dock of 1496, but because storehouses and some sort of basins or wet-docks were in existence there in the reign of John.

A fleet may be defined as a mobile extension of the offensive power of its base, therefore the capacity to carry on offensive naval action depends upon efficient bases—ports in which ships and fleets can be built, repaired, stored, and generally prepared for war—and from which an enemy's base can sometimes be masked or destroyed, or his shores and communications attacked. This is particularly true of modern fleets with their many complex equipments, but it is relatively true also for early fleets which also had specialist requirements, although of a more elementary character. In the mediæval period the Channel was the principal scene of maritime operations, and the Norman and Breton ports the English objective, therefore our naval bases were on the south coast. Such places became commercial ports originally by reason of the excellence of their harbours or of some advantage of position; their success in commerce enabled them to undertake dockyard work because magazines of naval necessaries were requisite for their own shipping as well as for that of the crown. The Thames and Medway make no figure in early English naval history after the Conquest, for, although the former was a centre rich in capabilities of supply, neither conformed to what was then another essential of a naval base, that of affording opportunity of getting at once to sea, and of a short line of communication with the French coast.[1] Thus, while there is evidence that shipbuilding was a customary trade in the London district,[2] we find no purely military proceedings associated with it as with the towns on the south coast. Deptford was certainly an early shipbuilding centre; in 1420 the *Thomas of the Tower*, a man-of-war, was brought from Wapping to be put on 'stokkes' at Deptford to be rebuilt there. Of two more of Henry's ships, the *Katrine* came from Greenwich to be put on the stocks in a 'dook' at Deptford for the same purpose, and the *Trinity Royal* was lying in a dock at Greenwich—perhaps in Deptford creek—while under repair. The term dock is in common use from the end of the fourteenth century, but it must not be understood in its modern sense or we should have to admit the existence of many between London and Southampton. The fifteentth-century dock only meant that the vessel was hauled up on the mud of the foreshore with a brushwood fence, perhaps puddled with clay, round her aft to keep out the tide until she was cleaned or repaired.

The ships built at Deptford by Henry V cannot have been the first; it is probable that a search in the records would show others in earlier reigns and that a shipbuilding industry there is of an unknown antiquity. The first reference, as yet discovered, to the pond at West Greenwich, or Deptford, which afterwards became the basin of the dockyard, is of the time of Edward I, when it was the subject of a suit at law in connection with fishing;[3] it was open to the Thames, but the fishery was preserved, and there is no allusion to any use made of it to receive shipping. An order of 1326 instructed the local authorities not to trouble the men of Greenwich for any contribution towards the land service as they had set out ships to serve with the king's admiral;[4] this, no doubt, includes both East and West Greenwich and is evidence that the people of Deptford possessed shipping.

After the death of Henry V the political conditions for many years were not favourable to the formation of Government establishments, so that the nascent foundations of Bursledon and Southampton, which might have developed into permanent naval yards, soon faded out of existence. When Henry VII turned his attention to the reconstruction of a navy he inclined at first towards the Hampshire ports, but one drawback to their use is exemplified by the necessity his officials were under of sending shipwrights and caulkers from Deptford to rig and repair his ships.[5] That they should have been drawn from there shows, incidentally, that the place must have become noted for its shipbuilding and have possessed a settled population of skilled artisans, for workmen were, of course, available locally at Southampton and Portsmouth. No long time elapsed before some of the king's ships were brought round to the Thames and laid up off Erith; this necessitated the hire of a storehouse at 'Greenwich' to receive their gear,[6] and if the house was situated at West Greenwich it marks the commencement of Deptford as the first of the modern

---

[1] Early fleets could not have been collected in the Hope, or at the Nore, on account of the difficulties of supply and correspondence.

[2] Pat. 26 Oct. 1354 : warrant to take trees from Guildford Park and send them to Redeclyve (Ratcliff), for the repair of the king's ships.

[3] Assize Pleas, 7 Edw. I, R. 12.
[4] Close, 20 Edw. II, m. 9*d*.
[5] Chapt. Ho. Bks. vii, fol. 12.
[6] Ibid. fol. 21.

royal dockyards in Kent. There is a payment of £5 in 1487 for one year's rent of this establishment.[7]

The reign of Henry VIII was, in every respect, the beginning of a new naval era. The king was a born naval organizer, and realized the imperial possibilities of sea-power to an extent that none of his predecessors, except perhaps Henry V, had done. For him the Navy was to do what their feudal armies had done for the Plantagenets; it was a complete reversal of traditional policy, and only a statesman of the first rank would so soon have recognized changing conditions and set about turning them to the national advantage. From the date of Henry's accession ships were added continuously to the Navy; at first they were built at Portsmouth, but both personal and administrative reasons may have induced him to make more use of the Thames. From the administrative point of view there must have been an economy in every branch of expense in building near London where all naval stores were plentiful,[8] where the cost of transit was largely saved, and where workmen were numerous; the personal element came into play from the fact that Henry was no mere paper organizer, but took a very actual and living interest in his ships, in which some modifications of design were attributable to him. For instance, he introduced the Mediterranean galley into his service, bringing over Venetian shipwrights for construction. He soon recognized their uselessness in northern waters and ordered galleasses to be designed instead. He was fond of visiting his men-of-war and taking foreigners to see them, therefore it was natural that he should prefer to have them in the Thames rather than at Portsmouth or in the Solent. Moreover, the specialization of the fighting-ship had now proceeded so far that, although they could still be built in many ports, it was more economical, and tended to greater efficiency, to construct them in dockyards especially adapted for the purpose and under the management of a staff of trained officers directly responsible to the crown. There was also a strategical reason, which may have had its weight with Henry. France was a more or less constant enemy, and relations were generally friendly with the Emperor Charles V, but there was always a possibility that the conditions might become exactly opposite, in which case the Thames was a far more suitable point than Portsmouth from which to strike at the Low Countries and cut the imperial communications with Spain.

The essential qualities of a man-of-war then, as now, are speed, strength, offensive capacity, and stowage space;[9] then, as now, these essential attributes could only be gained by an increase of size, as each of the four qualities seemed, in turn, more desirable. So far as the writer is able to judge, it was due to Henry's initiative that offensive capacity, or gun-power, became the predominant feature in English warships of his reign, and it was an improvement which had most important results later in the century. The design of using on shipboard guns of a weight only hitherto employed with armies on land exacted the use of bigger ships, and to it we may refer the construction of the *Henry Grace de Dieu*, said to be of 1,500 tons, and in all probability the largest ship then afloat. She was an experiment, and there is little doubt, a failure,

[7] Tellers' Rolls, 61.

[8] Both Henry and Charles V were dependent on the import of naval stores from the Baltic through the Hansa (*Sim. Papers*, 2 Mar. 1544).

[9] In the sixteenth century, and long afterwards, so much of the hold was filled with ballast that the stowage of provisions, etc., was always a difficulty; fuel space is now the equivalent question.

being expensive, of small sea-keeping value, and too badly designed to carry with safety the armament intended for her. Afterwards it was found that heavier guns than had as yet been in use could well be carried on a lesser displacement. But when she was laid down, Woolwich dockyard was founded. It is not known why she was built at Woolwich rather than at Deptford, but it may be that there was deeper water for launching at the spot where she was constructed than could be found at Deptford. It seems likely that there was at first no intention of doing more than using Woolwich for the especial purpose in hand, for while the construction of the *Henry* began in 1513, we find in the same year the appointment of John Hopton as keeper of the storehouses 'lately erected' at Deptford and Erith, evidently intended to be permanent establishments.[10] That at Erith may be discussed here. On 18 Feb. 1514 the sum of £32 was paid to Robert Page, of Erith, for an orchard and garden 'and other appurtenances thereunto belonging,' in all four acres, upon which the storehouse was built.[11] There are frequent references to the storage of masts, gear, cables, canvas, etc., in it, and ships were often laid up off Erith, or in 'docks' there. The term dock, as used in official papers of this date, sometimes only means moorings, and at other times, apparently, a graving place with, perhaps, an earthen dam at the foot to keep out the tide. Erith was probably selected on account of the deep water there, but the storehouse was found to be liable to inundation, not only by exceptional but by ordinary tides; moreover, the anchorage was on a lee shore in N.W. gales, and no doubt casualties occurred there as in later centuries. These may have been the reasons for its abandonment, but, whatever the cause, it ceases to be mentioned long before the end of the reign.

At Woolwich a smithy was put up, a long storehouse built and thatched, and there are entries of payments for many other houses and pieces of ground during the construction of the *Henry Grace de Dieu*.[12] The ground upon which the Long House and other buildings were placed must already have belonged to the crown, but most of the payments to owners of houses, wharves, etc., were evidently for temporary occupation. In some instances the tenancy may have been continued yearly until the king bought the property; this was the case in that belonging to Marion Daniel, who was paid £6 rent in 1513, but from whose second husband, Nicholas Partriche, it was bought for £100 in 1518.[13] In the same way ground was rented from Sir Edward Boughton at £6 13s. 4d. a year for at least seven years prior to 1546, but then it was purchased and added to the yard by means of an exchange of land and payment of money. Sir Edward Boughton possessed two docks, covering an area of two acres, which formed the principal portion of the yard.[14] The completion of the storehouse at Deptford can be assigned positively to 1513, by reason of the discovery in 1828 of some of the original brickwork bearing the date and the cypher H.R. In 1517 John Hopton, then clerk comptroller of the ships, contracted, for 600 marks, to form a basin in the meadow at the west end of the storehouse, capable of taking five vessels named, which were all large ones. It was to have a 'head' and sluices, and to be enclosed with an

---

[10] Pat. 5 Hen. VIII, pt. 2, m. 10.

[11] Exch. Accts. Bdle. 61, no. 31, m. 6. A modern writer (C. J. Smith, *Erith*, Lond. 1872, p. 61) says that 'it stood a little eastward of the point where the road from the railway station meets West Street at right angles; a considerable portion remains.'

[12] Chap. Ho. Bks. v.

[13] Lansd. MS. 16, fol. 120; Close, 10 Hen. VIII, m. 6.

[14] Rentals and Surveys, 371; *Acts of P.C.* 15 Jan.-14 Mar. 1545-6.

oak paling 7 ft. high.[15] From the position this was clearly an adaptation or enlargement of the thirteenth-century pond, and in 1520 there is a reference to 'the great dockhead of the pond.'[16] It must have had gates of some kind, probably resembling those of the dry-dock of the period. Such docks were excavations in the earth, but now, or soon after, lined with wood, with gates whose position in relation to each other is uncertain. The gates were strengthened with an artificial dam at the foot, and the whole structure had now become a permanent one; that at Deptford occupied a site on the east side of the 'great' storehouse, which was retained permanently by its successors.[17]

The war of 1544 involved the hire of more storehouses at Deptford, so that in 1547 £17 18s. 8d. was paid for them during the year, while only £1 6s. 8d. was charged for Woolwich.[18] The total expenses for Deptford for the year amounted to £18,824, as against £3,439 for Woolwich, and £1,211 for Portsmouth, showing that the first had become by far the most important dockyard. The Navy Treasurer's accounts for part of 1544 show that in August and October from 80 to 90 shipwrights and caulkers were in pay at Deptford, and this number is probably nearly the highest reached during the years of war.[19] James Baker, the master shipwright, received one shilling a day, his son, Matthew, who became one of the principal Elizabethan constructors, twopence, and the others varying sums between these extremes; three halfpence a week lodging money was also paid for the men, who were expected to sleep two in a bed. The year 1546 saw the formation of the Navy Board; one reason for its institution must have been the expansion of the dockyard system, which was becoming too large for isolated and occasional supervision.

In 1547 there is a payment of 13s. 4d. for the hire of a storehouse at Gillingham, the insignificant forerunner of the Chatham yard;[20] more storehouses were taken up there and at Rochester between 1548 and 1550, and there were payments of £3,729 made for victualling.[21] It seems that during these three years vessels were laid up in the Medway without any formal order, for an absolute decision was not taken until June 1550,[22] when the Privy Council directed that in future all ships paid off were to be 'herbarowed' in the river Medway. On 14 August they ordered William Winter, Surveyor of the Navy, to go to Portsmouth and bring round to Gillingham all the ships in the southern port, the reason given being the ease with which grounding and graving could be carried on in the Kentish river. There were probably other considerations favouring the measure; Portsmouth was very expensive because naval necessaries of all kinds, except timber, had to be sent from London, while in examining naval papers of the reign of Henry VIII, one is struck by the fact that the authorities never seem to have been able to settle on any convenient spot for permanent moorings for the ships, which oscillate between Woolwich, Deptford, Erith, Limehouse, Northfleet, Greenwich, Greenhithe, Ratcliff, Barking, and elsewhere, as though every place was tried in turn and found wanting. The Medway may have been a satisfactory alternative, and was used freely at first, but conditions of war brought Portsmouth and the Thames, where working yards were available,

[15] Add. Chart. 6289.

[16] *L. and P. Hen. VIII*, iii, pt. I, 1009.

[17] Chap. Ho. Bks. xi, ff. 14, 43, 44, 49.

[18] Pipe Off. Decl. Accts. 2588.

[19] Add. MSS. 7968, fol. 43.

[20] Pipe Off. Decl. Accts. 2588.

[21] Ibid. 2354.

[22] *Acts of P.C.* 8 June 1550.

to the front again for some years. After the peace of 1563 the Navy officers returned to the Medway, so that in 1564 the twenty-three largest ships of the fleet—nearly the whole of it—were moored below Rochester Bridge, while there were six small vessels at Portsmouth, and none in the Thames.[23]

The payments made by the Navy Treasurer show that Deptford continued to be used far more than the other two dockyards. Edward VI, with an English love of ships, often visited it, and there is a charge of £88 for paving the street leading to the yard, the highway being ' so noisome and full of filth that the King's Majesty might not pass to and fro to see the building of his highnesses ships.'[24] New storehouses were also constructed, and it may be said as of general application that small additions, in the way of buildings, were continually being made in all the yards. Chatham does not appear under that name until 1567, when £1,075 were spent there, supplementary to the customary expenditure—in that year £5,182—for victualling at Gillingham.[25] Part of the foregoing £1,075 no doubt represented land, for in 1570 a mast-pond was made at Chatham, and a house, the Hill House, furnished for the use of the Lord Admiral and the Navy officers.[26] A year later more ground was hired, storehouses and a forge set up, and the presence of a certain number of workmen indicated by the purchase of a flag with the St. George's Cross, to call them to work.[27] When so many ships were lying up in the Medway there must always have been work to be done upon them, therefore it is rather strange that there was no suggestion of a dry-dock at Chatham until the reign of James I; a ' grounding place ' (i.e. graving place) was, however, made in 1584. By that year, the last of peace, the ' ordinary '[28] expenditure at Chatham was £3,680, at Deptford £205, at Portsmouth £30, and at Woolwich £18. In 1574 the ' great dock ' at Deptford was re-made, but an entry of 1580 shows that the old method of closing the dock was still in use;[29] it is not known when dock gates nearer the modern type were introduced, but it was probably not long after, judging by the cessation of the old form of entry in the accounts, when ' marshmen '[30] were paid for dealing with the gravel dams which closed the dock heads. In 1580 Drake's ship, the *Golden Hind*, in which he circumnavigated the world, was laid up at Deptford in an especial dock made for her; she remained as one of the sights of London until she was broken up in the reign of Charles II. Elizabeth visited her in state, and knighted Drake on his own quarter-deck. The queen came to Deptford and Woolwich soon after her accession, attending at Deptford in 1559 the launch of a battleship named after her, and being present at a water pageant at Woolwich in 1560.[31]

Eventually gradations of rank were as clearly defined among dockyard officers as in the executive of the Navy, but at first the master shipwright was the officer who exercised chief authority. Several of these men are mentioned in the State Papers of the reign of Henry VIII, but James Baker, who is said to have designed English ships for the carriage of heavy guns, was the only one whose reputation outlived his generation. The dockyards

[23] Pipe Off. Decl. Accts. 2362.
[24] Ibid. 2194.
[25] Ibid. 2203.
[26] Ibid. 2206.
[27] Pipe Off. Decl. Accts. 2207; Add. MS. 9314, fol. 42.

[28] The ' ordinary ' comprised wages of clerks, shipkeepers, moorings, and normal expenses of administration and maintenance.
[29] Pipe Off. Decl. Accts. 2210, 2216.

[30] Originally from the Romney Marsh district, but the name may have been appropriated later by men especially trained to the work.
[31] Machyn, *Diary* (Camd. Soc.), 203, 232.

at a later date like other departments became hotbeds of corruption, and there are early signs of this tendency. In 1512 or 1513 Sir Edward Howard, Henry's Lord Admiral, wrote to Wolsey that one of the ships with him had so many leaks 'by reason of Bedyll, the carpenter that worked in her at Woolwich, that we have had much ado to keep her above water; he hath bored a hundred auger holes in her and left unstopt.'[32] This looks more like malice than dishonesty or incompetence, but there was plenty of all three in later days; what happened to Mr. Bedyll we do not know, but there could have been few offences that Henry was less likely to condone than that of malicious injury to his ships. The Pett family were associated with the Kentish dockyards for upwards of a century; they probably came of a Harwich stock, and a John Pett, the first one mentioned, was working on the *Regent* in 1499. Peter Pett was established as master shipwright at Deptford in the reign of Edward VI, and remained there until his death in 1589. A son, Joseph Pett, also held the same position at Deptford. The principal Elizabethan builder was Matthew Baker, a son of the James Baker previously mentioned, who was master shipwright at Woolwich from 1572, and was the first to devise a method for the comparatively exact calculation of a ship's tonnage. One good judge, John Davis the navigator, considered Baker the first ship designer then living.[33] Richard Chapman, another Elizabethan master shipwright, built the *Ark Royal*, Howard's flagship in 1588; very little is known about him, but incidental references show that he must have been held in high reputation. The wages of ordinary shipwrights varied from twopence to tenpence a day during the earlier part of the reign, but victualling and lodging, or allowances for them, were also provided; the master shipwrights were paid a shilling a day, but this was usually supplemented by an especial fee of from £4 to £8 a year, a pension of another shilling a day from the Exchequer, and the fact that they built many of the ships by contract indicates a further source of profit. How much of actual dishonesty there was in the Elizabethan dockyards it is not easy to say, although accusations were flung about in plenty, but it is quite certain that envy, backbiting, and all uncharitableness reigned supreme in them.

For a war like that with Spain, to the westward and southward, certain disadvantages of position were inherent in the Kentish yards as bases. Little use, however, was made of Portsmouth, and, while all building and repairs were still carried on in the Thames and Medway, Plymouth became the main secondary supply base for the final equipment and provisioning of fleets. New buildings were added yearly in all the yards, but most often at Chatham, where, in 1590, a storehouse three stories high was erected; this was burnt down in 1593, causing a loss estimated at £2,341.[34] New buildings necessitated the acquisition of more ground at Chatham, but much of it was hired at a yearly rent;[35] still no ships were built there, but every other form of dockyard work was in practice. At Woolwich a ropeyard had been founded in 1574 by Thomas Allen, the queen's purveyor of Baltic naval stores, to whom £800 had been advanced for the purpose, which sum he was to repay at the rate of £100 a year.[36] This experiment in independent production seems to have

---

[32] Ellis, *Original Letters* (Ser. iii), i, 146.

[33] *The Seaman's Secrets*, Lond. 1607, p. 3.

[34] S.P. Dom. Eliz. ccxlix, 15; 'the loss is great and heavily taken' (*Hist. MSS. Com. Rep.* vii, App. 523).

[35] Pipe Off. Decl. Accts. 2229.

[36] Ibid. 3553; Exch. War. for Issues, 6 July 1573.

failed after a few years, when entries of purchases from Allen cease. Even before the war fear of treachery caused anxiety for the safety of the ships in the Medway, information having been more than once received that attempts would be made from the Flanders ports to set them on fire. There were already two forts commanding the river passage; in 1574 St. Mary's creek was blocked with stakes to prevent an enemy coming through it and thus evading Upnor Castle.[37] The dockyard was guarded at night by mastiffs, but was only inclosed with a hedge;[38] when the war commenced it was decided, for greater security, to place a chain, an old and favourite form of defence, across the river at Upnor below the dockyard and the ships in ordinary, and under the fire of the castle. In a letter to Burghley, of March 1585, Sir John Hawkins suggested the chain, with two or four pinnaces stationed at it, and a couple of small men-of-war at Sheerness to examine everything passing.[39] In October the work, after some difficulty, was nearly completed; one end was attached to a fixed support, the other worked round 'two great wheels to draw it up,' and, when at the surface, it was supported by five lighters.[40] An Elizabethan drawing,[41] probably earlier than 1585, shows the ships, their lower masts and bowsprits standing, moored athwart stream in three groups between Rochester Bridge and Upnor Castle, the largest vessels being near Upnor.

The unceasing building and repairing going on at Deptford after 1585 made additional wharfing indispensable; some 500 ft. or 600 ft. were put up along the river bank in 1588 and 1589, and this probably implies an enlargement of the yard.[42] Besides Joseph Pett, there were at Deptford, as his assistants, John Adye, William Bright, John Apslyn, Richard Merritt, and William Pickas, of whom the first four became, later, master shipwrights of reputation. Much work went on at Woolwich, but there are few charges for new houses or wharves in connexion with it, which seems to show that it had been established originally on a sufficiently large scale; in 1607 it was inclosed with an oaken paling, as was also Deptford in 1610.[43] In the latter year there are payments for the purchase of implements to be used in making cordage at Woolwich, and this marks the foundation of the Government ropeyard; cordage was being made there in 1612, and in 1614 the ropehouse was enlarged at a cost of £368.[44] Phineas Pett, in his 'Autobiography,' tells us that in 1608 he constructed new gates for Woolwich dock, with a dam outside them, 'so that we wrought always dry.'[45] Evidently gates were not nearly watertight as yet. It may be that about this time the single was converted into a double dry-dock, although there is no reference to it until 1629.[46] In that year Pett wrote to his superiors that it had not been repaired for twenty years, and was in a very bad condition; he mentioned having to build a dam in front of the gates as though that proceeding had become exceptional.[47]

Elizabeth was at Rochester in 1573, but is not known to have inspected the dockyard. James I came there in 1604, and gave great offence to the seamen by his obvious preference for hunting. He came again in 1606 with

---

[37] Pipe Off. Decl. Accts. 2210.

[38] Ibid. 2222, 2229.

[39] S.P. Dom. Eliz. clxxvii, 26.

[40] Pipe Off. Decl. Accts. 2221; Add. MS. 9294, fol. 58. It cost £610 (S.P. Dom. Eliz. clxxxvi, 44).

[41] Cott. MS. Aug. I, i, 52.

[42] Pipe Off. Decl. Accts. 2225, 2226.

[43] Ibid. 2245, 2248. No doubt the fencing succeeded a hedge as at Chatham.

[44] Ibid. 2252.

[45] Add. MS. 9295, fol. 137.

[46] Ibid. 9297, fol. 167.

[47] Ibid. fol. 182.

his brother-in-law, Christian IV, King of Denmark, who examined every ship, dined on board one of them, and enjoyed a salute of 2,300 guns, ' besides the healths at dinner.' After the death of Hawkins, in 1595, the methods of administration had degenerated rapidly; during the greater part of the reign of James every department of the civil branch was seething with corruption, the highest officials being the most dishonest. A commission of inquiry sat during 1608–9, and brought out some startling evidence, but no painful result followed to the chief delinquents, except that of having to listen to ' an oration' from James, and the old practices continued until 1618, when the aged Lord Admiral, Nottingham, was bribed to retire, the principal officers of the Navy were suspended, and the administration placed under the control of a commission. There had been a proposal in 1611 to build a dry-dock at Chatham, to inclose the yard by a brick wall, and, as a supplementary proceeding, to sell Deptford, valued then at about £5,000.[48] The Commissioners of 1618 set about building a double dock, 330 ft. long, which cost nearly £4,000, and a further £7,000 was expended on wharves, mast-ponds, storehouses, etc., and the ropeyard now established.[49] An area of 80 acres of new ground was taken under lease, but only six acres were inclosed for immediate use.[50] The bulk of this land, 71 acres, called the Lordslands, belonged to Sir Robert Jackson, to whom the crown paid a yearly rent of £14.[51] In 1634 Robert Barker was said to have been the lord of the manor, but the lease was then lost;[52] the explanation is that Barker had sold his interest to Sir Robert Jackson. Towards the end of the century the representatives of Sir Richard Leveson, presumably the freeholder of the remaining nine acres, or of a portion of it, petitioned the crown that the Admiralty still retained possession of three acres, although the lease had run out.[53] The law officers of the crown admitted, after inquiry, that the petition was based on fact; storehouses, workshops, and one of the docks were on the ground, and no doubt some compensation was afforded.[54] When Chatham was enlarged it was again suggested that Deptford should be abandoned on account of the expense involved in sending vessels to and from the Thames from the Upnor anchorage. The new dockyard and establishments adjoined the old dock, which became the ordnance wharf; a new road, 137 roods in length, was made from Chatham church to the new yard.[55]

Chatham grew rapidly now. Another dry-dock, the ' Old Single Dock' shown in a plan of 1698, was built in 1623, a graving dock in 1624, St. Mary's Creek was again blocked with piles to hinder a flank attack, and a new boom placed in 1622 instead of the chain.[56] This was destroyed by ice in the winter of 1623, and the fragments swept out to sea, but was quickly replaced. Notwithstanding the hesitation about Deptford it was inclosed with a brick wall in 1619,[57] and the Commissioners recommended that the construction of new ships should be confined to that yard as two could be worked on simultaneously, the dry-dock being a double one, that is to say, long enough to take in two vessels.[58] Evelyn's plan of Deptford in 1623 shows the king's and the dry-docks belonging to private persons as fitted with gates. In pursuance of this

[48] Lansd. MS. 145, fol. 16.
[49] Pipe Off. Decl. Accts. 2259; S.P. Dom. Jas. I, clvi, 12.
[50] Pipe Off. Decl. Accts. 2257.
[51] Ibid. 2260.
[52] S.P. Dom. Chas. I, cclxxix, 20.
[53] Add. MS. 22617, ff. 104–9; Treas. Papers, xxxvii, 54; xcvii, 85.
[54] Exch. L.T.R. Solicitor's Letters, 11 Feb. 1693–4.
[55] Pipe Off. Decl. Accts. 2258.
[56] Ibid. 2260, 2261, 2262.
[57] Ibid. 2257.
[58] S.P. Dom. Jas. I, ci, 4.

policy ten large men-of-war were built at Deptford in five years, and nothing more was heard for a century and a half of the project of withdrawal. William Burrell, who had been in the service of the East India Company, superintended shipbuilding at Deptford, and enjoyed the confidence of the Commissioners, while Phineas Pett was at the head of affairs at Woolwich. From there the *Trade's Increase*, of 1,100 tons, the largest merchantman yet constructed in England, was launched in 1610 for the East India Company, and in the same year the *Prince Royal*, the largest ship yet built for the Navy. In 1618 however, the yard was practically closed for a time, for under Burrell's energetic supervision all the new building could be done at Deptford, while it was no longer necessary to send ships from Chatham round to the Thames to be docked for repairs.

When Charles I came to the throne England was at war with Spain; afterwards war with France followed as well. This meant ceaseless routine work for the dockyards in the way of repairing and fitting ships, all of which fell upon the eastern yards. Neither now nor in the reign of Elizabeth could they have performed the work but for the fact that there was very little winter cruising, and that more or less delay in proceeding to and from the south coast bases of rendezvous was of less importance, in view of the leisurely way war was then carried on, than it became later. But as it was there are indications that too much was thrown upon them, ships being sent to sea in a leaky and rotten state, no doubt due not so much to incompetence as to speed under pressure from the Government and to want of money for the purchase of stores.[59] In 1626 the Navy debt was £100,000, much of it for pay owing to yard workmen to whom, in 1627, eighteen months' pay was due, while materials could only be obtained on credit at ruinous prices and of bad quality.[60] In January 1627 the Chatham men marched in a body to London to obtain some relief from the Navy Commissioners;[61] in February the repairs of the *Defiance* and *Vanguard*, in dock at Chatham, were at a standstill for want of necessaries to the value of £400.[62] All these conditions were not likely to conduce to good work. As the war went on, and the Government became still more poverty-stricken, the yard services, like the other branches, became utterly disorganized. In October 1628 there were 224 men employed at Chatham, and 37 at Deptford.[63] The numbers are not large, but as they were not paid they stole; doing it with unanimity they swept the ships of all movable fittings and the storehouses of everything left that was saleable. After the return of peace an official reported that the number of men at Chatham might well be reduced, if only because there were no stores for them to work with, that ships' cabins and fittings were being broken up for firewood, and that of late whole families had taken to living in the yard.[64]

The master shipwrights were now being paid two shillings a day besides their Exchequer allowances and perquisites;[65] some of them were accused of absenting themselves for months from the royal yards to superintend the business of the private yards many of them possessed. In 1625 a brick wall was built round Woolwich,[66] and wharves added, but it remained only third

[59] S.P. Dom. Chas. I, ix, 15.
[60] Ibid. xxxix, 9; l, 45.
[61] Ibid. xlix, 68.
[62] Ibid. liii, 29.

[63] Ibid. cxix, 31, 60.
[64] Ibid. cxliii, 37.
[65] Audit Off. Decl. Accts. 1699
64. The allowance varied; *e.g.*

Phineas Pett had a pension of £40 a year from James I (S.P. Dom. Chas. I, cclxxvii, 42).
[66] Ibid.

in importance. In 1627 more of the available Chatham land was turned to use for workshops and storehouses; in 1631 Charles came to Chatham, but, as in the previous year there had still been £6,717 owing for wages, he was probably seen with mixed feelings by the men. These arrears were not paid off until the ship-money was levied. In 1633 Woolwich ropehouse was let to the East India Company for three years at a rental of £100 a year, which was to be expended in completing the wall round the yard and in the repair of buildings.[67] Besides the Chatham ropery there was by this time one at Portsmouth, and the two must have been more than sufficient to supply the Navy.

There were estimates in 1634 for an expenditure of £2,445 in wharves and other works for the four dockyards; new buildings of various kinds, but mostly on a small scale, went up continuously during the reign, but the only additional land was a half acre of ground bought in 1639 to enlarge Woolwich.[68] In 1641 the 71 acres leased at Chatham in 1619 were conveyed to the crown in freehold.[69] A brick wall was ordered for the new yard in 1635, and a small battery and barricade placed to close St. Mary's Creek, but the wall was not built until 1637, and then only in part.[70] The boom at Upnor had been allowed to disappear, for, perhaps resting on the river bed when not in use, it caused deposits and shoaling; as it cost £624 a year for repairs and maintenance a chain was recommended in preference.[71] Portsmouth was coming into favour again, but Chatham was pre-eminently the repairing yard; in 1635 the proportion of repairs there was stated to be as three to one compared with Deptford.[72]

Charles visited the yards occasionally, and when at Deptford in the summer of 1633, seeing a Dutch man-of-war anchored off it, he immediately ordered that no foreign warship was to be allowed to come so high up the river; but it was no one's business to see such orders carried out, and the same ship and captain were there again in December.[73] When the king was at Chatham in 1631 he 'went on board every ship, and almost into every room of every ship . . . and into the holds of most of them.'[74] Charles regarded himself as quite competent not only to interfere in administration, but also to alter the designs and calculations of the master shipwrights for new ships. The authorities looked upon Chatham as the show dockyard; in December, 1631, the Duc de Vendôme came there, and was rowed along it at high water 'in full view of the ordnance lying on the wharf, the orderly lying of the anchors, the convenience of the new buildings, and the stateliness and orderly contriving of the storehouses for the magazine and great commodity of the dry docks.'[75] Undoubtedly it was much superior to anything of the kind existing in France or Spain at the time.

When William Burrell came from the East India Company, in 1618, to serve the Commissioners, he was paid £200 a year, a sum which aroused great jealousy among the other master shipwrights, whose salaries and pensions did not reach half the amount. Burrell's supremacy was only temporary, and Phineas Pett, at first master shipwright at Woolwich, and from 1631

---

[67] S.P. Dom. Chas. I, ccxxxix, 43.
[68] Audit Off. Decl. Accts. 1704–83.
[69] Add. MS. 22617, fol. 109.

Leaving 9 acres of the original lease. See *ante*, p. 344.
[70] S.P. Dom. Chas. I, cclxiv, fol. 70; ccclxiv, 54.
[71] Ibid. cccii, 27.

[72] Add. MS. 9302, fol. 12.
[73] S.P. Dom. Chas. I, cclii, 10.
[74] Ibid. cxcv, 6.
[75] Ibid. cciv, 104.

a Navy Commissioner, was the chief constructor of the first half of the century. He was succeeded at Woolwich by a nephew, Peter Pett, who built, under his uncle's supervision, the *Sovereign of the Seas*, the largest vessel yet added to the Navy. Most of the master shipwrights and other officials were guilty of peculations of a more or less flagrant type. In 1634 Phineas Pett himself and the storekeepers at Chatham and Deptford and several other highly-placed officers were suspended for certain malpractices discovered in the sale of cordage, and Pett had to receive a formal pardon.[76] To describe the habits of the workmen would require an article for itself, but some allusion may be made to the notorious subject of 'chips,' which remained a difficulty down to the nineteenth century. Under Henry VIII there had been a 'chip-gatherer' who collected the waste fragments of wood for the benefit either of the crown or of the men. At some later period the custom grew up of allowing the workmen to take broken pieces of wood out of the yards, and this speedily became a gigantic abuse. By 1634 it had grown to such an extent as to become a standing administrative difficulty, and was complicated by the fact that the custom had existed long enough to become a prescriptive right. The shipwrights and other workmen were then described as carrying chips out of the yards three times a day, as cutting up large timber to make chips, and as building huts for themselves in which to store their plunder.[77] About the same time the Surveyor of the Navy wrote that 'the infinite abuse . . . under colour of chips is intolerable'; to emphasize the necessity for action came the seizure of a lighter at Deptford containing some 9,000 treenails, of from one to two feet in length, which the offender maintained, and perhaps actually believed to be, a lawful perquisite.[78] In this case the intended receiver was a Government shipwright who possessed a private yard of his own. An attempt was made to deal with the trouble by an order to pay a penny a day to the men in lieu of chips;[79] but the only result was that they took the penny, and the chips, and all the other small and valuable articles which went out of the yards under cover of the term. There was no branch of the Navy or victualling departments, and no class of officer, civil or executive, free of similar fraudulent practices.

In August, 1642, Rochester, Chatham yard, Upnor, and the two sconces defending the Medway willingly yielded to Parliamentary Commissioners;[80] there is no reference to Woolwich or Deptford, about which, therefore, no doubt or difficulty could have been experienced. The possession of the dock-yards was of enormous importance to the Parliament, for although they would have been useless to Charles, seeing that he had no ships and had earned the hostility of the seamen, his ability to deny them to his enemies, either by holding them or destroying them, would have had far-reaching military consequences, and might well have turned the scale in his favour. Could he have done so the Parliament would not have been able to fit out the cruisers which prevented him holding a port and receiving supplies and aid from abroad.

The first essential for a business establishment is money for wages and the purchase of raw material. It was the want of money that had been mainly answerable for the dockyard disorganization of the previous half century.

[76] S.P. Dom. Chas. I, ccxxviii, ff. 120, 122. In 1634 the store-keeper at Deptford had been un-

paid for 14½ years; he was charged with selling stores (ibid. cclxviii, 32).
[77] Add. MS. 9302, fol. 40.

[78] S.P. Dom. Chas. I, cclx, 29.
[79] Ibid. cclxiv, fol. 47.
[80] Ibid. ccccxci, 125.

The Parliament, although not rich, had more resources available than had been the case with the monarchy, was a better paymaster, and, therefore, won better service. For a time there was more discipline and more honesty in the yards, although the conditions were still what would now be called a public scandal. The new moral element introduced by the Parliament is indicated by an order of 1644 that at Deptford, and presumably at the other yards, a weekly meeting of the men should be held to hear a discourse on ' saving truths.' [81] There is little to chronicle concerning the Civil War, for the yards were never exposed to any fear of royalist attack until 1648, and nothing happened to interfere with routine work. At Deptford a slaughterhouse, formerly attached to Greenwich Palace, was used for the Navy from about 1649; [82] this may be considered the beginning of the Victualling Yard. The most important administrative change was the commencement of the practice of placing a Navy Commissioner in charge of the out-yards. In Kent this only applied to Chatham, for Deptford and Woolwich were kept under the control of the Navy Commissioners in London. Peter Pett was Commissioner at Chatham, a post he succeeded in retaining until 1667. Another sign of the very different spirit now inspiring the government of the Navy was the dismissal in 1651 of John Bright, the chief master shipwright at Chatham, for making expensive alterations, on his own responsibility, in building a ship; [83] he was replaced by Captain John Taylor, who, in turn, was dismissed at the Restoration to make room for a parasite of the Duchess of Albemarle. The two incidents show as clearly as could a volume the distinguishing characteristics of the two eras.

The Kentish rising of May 1648, backed by the presence of the Prince of Wales in the Downs with a squadron of ships, of which the crews had revolted, placed the dockyards in imminent danger. Rochester was a centre of disaffection, and Deptford was, for the moment, in the hands of the royalists; the Deptford people used the opportunity to plunder the naval stores.[84] Pett ascribed to himself, rightly or wrongly, the merit of preserving Chatham yard, but the peril was soon over.[85] Of Woolwich yard we hear nothing, but royalist sympathies must have been strong in the town because many of the fugitives crossed to Essex from there. There is little to record between the suppression of the revolt and the first Dutch war; in 1650 the Admiralty Committee tried to settle the question of ' chips ' by raising wages all round from a penny to threepence a day, according to the class of workmen, but it need hardly be remarked that the measure was fruitless. The men took the extra money and the chips. Shipbuilding went on apace, for not only had Prince Rupert, and privateering generally, to be dealt with, but the Navy was the only barrier between internal disloyalty and foreign aid. Each of the three yards had now a double dock, but that at Woolwich was said to be the only one suitable for ' great ships.' [86] There were also many private yards available, and orders were placed freely with their owners; some of them belonged to the Government master shipwrights, and a contemporary critic pointed out that this led to the master shipwrights' absence from the national dockyard, to the exchange of good Government workmen for bad of his own,

[81] S.P. Dom. Chas. I, diii, 66. [84] Ibid. 26 May 1648. [86] S.P. Dom. Interreg. 14 Aug.
[82] Add. MS. 9306, fol. 2. [85] Hist. MSS. Com. *Portland* 1650; lviii, 108.
[83] S.P. Dom. Interreg. 29 Oct. *MSS.* i, 459.
1651.

to the possible embezzlement of stores, and to an increase of 100 per cent. in the price as compared with the cost of building in the State's yards.[87] The last point is probably a great exaggeration. The predominance of the Pett family, members of which were in control or in office in all the Kentish yards, caused hatred among their rivals and subordinates which showed itself in accusations against them to the authorities in London. In November 1651 the ill-feeling at Chatham exploded in an outburst wherein most of the chief officers were making charges against each other to an extent that necessitated a commission of inquiry, which sat for three months and was empowered to take evidence on oath. The light in which the Petts were regarded is shown by a remark made by one workman witness to another that he dared not speak ' for fear of being undone by the kindred . . . they were all so knit together that the Devil himself could not discover them except one impeached the other.' There are many depositions in the State Papers, but in the result the accused on both sides were ordered to retain their places; it was the beginning of 1652, and no moment to displace experienced officers without very urgent reason.

From the commencement of 1652 war with the United Provinces was held to be imminent; the yards were working at high pressure in fitting out ships but the Government was not satisfied with the results. The Council of State thought, in fact, that there was ' great backwardness,' and directed Blake to inspect Chatham, Deptford, and Woolwich, and report with whom lay the fault.[88] It was organization that was defective, and new subordinate officials rather than space that was required. The eastern yards were, relatively, quite big enough to answer all demands made upon them in a North Sea war; indeed, at Chatham the additions of 1618 were so large that very little increase was needed until the great extensions of 1860 were undertaken. In 1650 the Admiralty had refused to purchase the East India Company's Blackwall yard,[89] which, after several mutations, became part of the Thames Ironworks Company's property, and such defects as the Thames and Medway bases suffered under were those of difficult, and sometimes lengthy, navigation due to their position of security well away from the sea and any sudden attack. Superiority of position for offensive purposes brought Harwich into favour as a new naval base, and the genius of the Navy Commissioner there, Major Nehemiah Bourne, overcame all difficulties consequent to the total absence of every equipment usual in a dockyard. When the war began the Government had raised shipwrights' wages a penny a day; those at the old yards may have thought that they gave honest work in return, but on the Thames and Medway they were commencing now, quite independent of any dishonesty, to show the faults of routine and established sacrosanct methods of management characteristic of permanent departments. In January 1653 Commissioner Pett wrote from Chatham that he had graved nine ships in one spring tide, ' truly it makes me stand amazed at the goodness of God in such unparalleled successes.' The Generals at Sea took a different view of the amount of energy at Chatham and on the Thames; a few months later Monk wrote to the Admiralty Committee ' it is strange that 20 ships should be so long fitting out from Chatham, Woolwich, and Deptford, where there are so many docks,

[87] S.P. Dom. Interreg. 9 Aug. 1652.

[88] Ibid. 11 Mar. 1651-2.

[89] The Company had owned a yard at Deptford which was deserted in favour of that at Black-wall. In 1636 the Deptford yard was occupied by John Taylor (S.P. Dom. Chas. I, cccxxv, 19).

when there have been 22 or more fitted out from Harwich in half the time by Major Bourne.'[90] Again, Captain John Taylor complained from Chatham that if the seamen could be made to assist in rigging and fitting the ships they might be got ready for sea in half the time; Taylor looked to London for help, but Bourne settled the same difficulty at Harwich successfully by himself. It is significant, too, that Portsmouth, which was practically a new yard and under a new man, stood next to Harwich for rapid and efficient work.

In the middle of the war the Admiralty decided that a new dry-dock was necessary at Woolwich, and it was ordered to be put in hand at once;[91] at the same time the East India Company's dock was to be surveyed with a view to ascertaining its fitness for navy work, but apparently it was not found to be suitable. After the war there was an order limiting the number of men to be employed in all the yards to 980; of these 240 were at Deptford.[92] Office regularity was sought by an instruction that there should be 'an exact and punctual examination' quarterly of dockyard accounts.[93] Unfortunately these measures to improve discipline were only taken when the basis of discipline —money to purchase obedient service—became more and more difficult to obtain. In March 1657 the dockyard men were paid their wages to the preceding Christmas, and that was the last punctual payment they received before the Restoration. The financial position of the Commonwealth became worse and worse, until the men were lucky when their wages were only a year in arrear, while the credit of the Government was so bad that no naval stores could be obtained to fit out or repair ships, and in 1659 and 1660 men hung idly about the yards for want of materials to work with. The tendency to theft, only scotched at best, took fresh life in such circumstances. Even before the extreme scarcity of money Commissioner Pett reported that embezzlement was a normal habit at Chatham; the state of things at Woolwich and Deptford may be inferred from the fact that a Greenwich waterman was reputed to have made £5,000 by purchases from workmen at those yards.[94] Another man confessed to have sold 500 barrels of powder in four years on behalf of gunners of vessels laid up at Woolwich and Deptford;[95] in this case one of the dockyard detectives, to use a modern name, was an accomplice in the transactions. In September 1658 a search was undertaken of all merchantmen riding between London and Deptford for stores stolen from the yards or from men-of-war.[96] It is evident that oversight and inspection was very loose; when the officers did much as they liked it was natural for the men to take something of the same licence, if on a smaller scale. It appears from a regulation of October 1658 directing officers not to absent themselves from the yards without the permission of the Commissioner, and forbidding him to leave without permission from the Navy Commissioners, that hitherto they had all acted as was convenient to themselves in that respect.

Besides its activity in building, Deptford held a foremost place as a distributing centre of stores not only to the other dockyards but also to the out-stations, such as Dover and Plymouth, where cruisers put in for small refits. The only additions to it under the Commonwealth were some wharves and a mast pond. The new dry-dock at Woolwich has been mentioned;

[90] S.P. Dom. Interreg. 7 Jan., 20 July 1653.
[91] Ibid. 2 Sept. 1653; lviii, 26, 27, 61.
[92] Ibid. cv, 65; cxvi, 129.
[93] Add. MS. 9304, fol. 206.
[94] S.P. Dom. Interreg. 7, 20 June 1655.
[95] Ibid. cv, 50, 51.
[96] Admir. and Navy Bd. 2507

storehouses were built there in 1656, and in 1658 the yard was enlarged by the addition of one acre of land known as Chimney Marsh 'next to the State's Yard,' on the east side of Ham Creek, which was to be held on a lease for ten years, at £4 a year, from John Rymill, butcher, of London.[97] It is not always clear how or when these leases were converted into permanent purchases, but no land taken into a dockyard ever went out again. In 1657 there was an attempt to deal with the delay caused by contrary winds in the Thames by building two galleys to tow ships up and down the river.[98] At Chatham the only acquisition was the purchase, in 1656, of a wharf and storehouse adjoining the old dock, but it may be that this relates to the Ordnance yard and not to the dockyard.[99] In the same year the representatives of the lessors of the three acres of Leveson land leased in 1618 [100] put in a claim for their return or compensation; the justice of the claim was admitted, but the pecuniary situation of the Government did not allow any settlement.[101] The boom at Upnor had been allowed to disappear during the Civil War;[102] at one time there had been no intention of replacing it but, instead of it, to moor ten small well-armed vessels just out of the fairway and put the Upnor gunners on board them. In 1658, however, another boom was ordered, but there is reason to suppose that it was never made.[103] The size of the yards is perhaps shown by the number of watchmen attached to each; as would be expected, Chatham comes first with 32, while Deptford and Woolwich are nearly the same with 18 and 16 respectively.

On 28 January 1660–1 the new Lord High Admiral, James, Duke of York, issued regulations detailing the duties of dockyard officers, with a covering letter explaining that the delay in publishing them had not been because they were unimportant, 'but that I was informed that the present want of money had so hardened and emboldened many persons' that there was little hope of amendment until the primary cause was removed.[104] It was a perfectly fair warning, and no doubt James, who had the qualities of his defects, who would himself have made a first-class routine official, and who did not anticipate the financial extravagance of the monarchy, or the overpowering social and political difficulties in his way, intended that the Navy of which he was proud should have behind it clean and efficient civil departments. To obtain that he was, by nature and policy, prepared to be merciless.

James commenced his official career with some excellent regulations; the crying need of some method of checking theft led to the plan of marking Government stores by stamping the broad arrow on metal and timber articles, and running coloured threads through cordage and in the texture of sails. A proclamation of 19 November 1661 declared the necessity of such action because, for one thing, shipowners furnished their ships completely with stores stolen from the yards; [105] if such a statement was simple truth it showed that, beyond petty larcenies by workmen, systematic embezzlement on a huge scale was rife among the superior officials. Pepys, who now comes upon the scene, gives us some particulars of what went on, but not so many as might have been expected; nor is his information as valuable as that to be gleaned from

[97] S.P. Dom. Interreg. clxxx, 170; Add. MS. 9306, fol. 197.
[98] S.P. Dom. Interreg. 3 Oct. 1657. Cf. *post*, p. 354.
[99] Add. MS. 9305, fol. 114.

[100] *Ante*, p. 344.
[101] Add. MS. 22617, fol. 108.
[102] Ibid. 9299, fol. 206.
[103] S.P. Dom. Interreg. cxcv, 10.

[104] In August 1660 the yard wages in arrear amounted to £36,000 (Add. MS. 9312, fol. 1).
[105] Ibid. 9316, fol. 19.

official papers. He commenced his official life without any expert knowledge or technical training, but with an open mind, seeing that he had to begin by learning the multiplication table, and with a determination to keep his place and make as much money as he could. Of his colleagues, Sir William Coventry, James's secretary, with 'the power behind the throne' which he enjoyed, was the only one who desired reforms or who had brain and will enough to institute them. Pepys, rather late in the day, seems to have taken his first lesson on 1 July 1662[106] when he talked over the abuses at Deptford, 'in which he did give me much light,' with the clerk of the cheque there; the next day he sat in judgment on the same clerk and other officers and concluded that they did not perform a third of their duties. In August 1662 the Navy Board issued a circular in which they stated that they had been moved to personal inquiry by ' the common scandal' of the management of the Navy; ' the ignorance of some, the unfaithfulness of more, and the remissness of most in the discharge of their trust' was most serious, and they asked what would happen in war time if things went thus badly during peace.[107] The dockyard officers were stigmatized as negligent, lazy, ignorant, and dishonest. The rounded phrase quoted smacks of the best style of the Clerk of the Acts, and the Navy Board seem to have been satisfied in allowing him to use his pen. Of his colleagues, the three principal ones had belonged to the navy of Charles I, the worst possible school of training ; the main difference between them and him was that they—old hands—took all the presents they could while he only took those that he dared.

In July 1663 there were 238 men at Deptford and, in the following February, 324 at Chatham.[108] Smoking in the yards appears to have been allowed until March 1663–4 when a Navy Board order prohibitedit ; this was re-inforced in 1679 by a further regulation that the punishment for a first offence should be a fine of six days' wages, and dismissal the penalty for a second.[109] Usually many years elapsed before the disciplinary rules of the Navy Board became accepted as normal observances, and that against smoking was likely to be peculiarly difficult to enforce among unpaid men. In 1672 some ship-wrights were found smoking, amid shavings and chips, in the *Henrietta's* cockpit at Chatham; the Commissioner put them in the stocks and erected a whipping-post in the yard for future use, but the men pulled it down and threw it into the river.[110] In this and other matters the unruliness of the workmen was largely due to the fact that they were always more or less unpaid, but they were to some extent protected from the consequences of debt by the rule that the permission of the Admiralty was necessary before they could be sued at law, while the certainty of eventual payment enabled them to procure credit. This custom dated from the reign of Charles I but fell into desuetude under the Commonwealth and did not at once become invariable again. It must be remembered that the presence of shipwrights in the dockyards was often involuntary, impressment being applied to them as well as to the seamen. By a warrant of 18 March 1631–2 the yard officers were exempted from the liability to serve on parish offices ; this was confirmed, and extended to the executive officers of the Navy, by an Order in Council of 27 August 1663.

The working hours in the dockyards were from 5.30 a.m. to 6.30 p.m. between March and September, and from daylight to dusk during the remainder

[106] *Diary.*
[107] Add. MS. 9311, fol. 83.
[108] S.P. Dom. Chas. II, lxxvii, 68; xciii, 36.
[109] Add. MS. 9315, ff. 7, 14.
[110] S.P. Dom. Chas. II, cccxxix, 63.

of the year;[111] in 1678 the Chatham Commissioner proposed that they should work only from 8 a.m. to 4 p.m. between 5 November and 2 February considering 'the roguery and villainy they commit when it is beginning to grow dark.'[112] Time for breakfast was allowed between February and November, and always an hour and a half for dinner. The Deptford men mutinied in February 1665 because, under stress of work, it was proposed to defer commencing the breakfast half-hour.[113] For mutiny the Navy Board had one punishment the men feared acutely, that of sending them to serve at sea; but this was double-edged because it interfered seriously with the yard work, especially in war time. It was done, however, in 1672.[114] The men were not badly off for holidays, having nine full days, and four others, including Restoration and Coronation days recently added, for which a day's wages were allowed for half a day's work.[115] At the Restoration the salaries of the master shipwrights were £104 10s. a year at Chatham, and £114 10s. at Deptford; at Woolwich a master shipwright was only occasionally in office, the building and repairing being usually controlled by the master shipwright of Deptford. The assistants to the master shipwrights received £70 at the three yards.[116] The next responsible officer at Deptford, the storekeeper, had £144 18s. 4d. a year, and at Chatham £106. Salaries went up and down, but with a general tendency to rise, so that in 1686 the Chatham master shipwright was obtaining £131 5s. with an additional £30 for a clerk.[117] The cost of rat killing at the three Kentish yards stood at £17 a year.

The first mention of Sheerness by Pepys, in the *Diary*, is on 18 August 1665, but the subject must have been under consideration long before that date, because on 8 August the Navy Board ordered that Chatham yard should equip Sheerness with the requisites for cleaning ships' hulls and supply the men to work there.[118] In July the plan of a dockyard had been drawn out; that was dropped in August, to be renewed on a larger scale in September, when it was intended to include an acre and a half of land with a 26-gun battery at the Point, but whether it was to contain a dry-dock was left undecided.[119] Commissioner Peter Pett of Chatham, who was in charge of the details, recommended that nothing should be done until the whole matter had been thoroughly examined; but it was the first year of the second Dutch war, and if Sheerness was needed at all the need was urgent. Therefore in November an expenditure of £700 was authorized to fit it for elementary dockyard work,[120] and on the 13th of that month the Navy Board directed that all large ships were to be cleaned there.[121] The reference to the large ships explains why Sheerness was required. The increasing size and draught of men-of-war, the shoaling of the Medway, and the difficulties of navigation for big ships in that river and the Thames, causes which have killed Deptford and Woolwich and are killing Chatham, were already acting and re-acting on each other. Working tides and awaiting winds often meant long delay, both in reaching and leaving the up-river yards, and the intricate navigation was a fruitful source of accident. Sheerness, situated on the sea, easy to enter or to leave in nearly all winds, with

---

[111] Add. MS. 9315, fol. 6; Admir. and Navy Bd. viii, 16 Feb. 1663-4.

[112] Admir. and Navy Bd. cccxxx, 3 Nov. 1678.

[113] S.P. Dom. Chas. II, cxii, 8.

[114] Admir. and Navy Bd. 2886, 16 April 1672.

[115] Add. MS. 9328, fol. 202.

[116] Ibid. 9311, fol. 71.

[117] Harl. MS. 7464, fol. 61.

[118] Add. MS. 9315, fol. 8.

[119] S.P. Dom. Chas. II, cxxvii, 53; cxxix, 87; cxxxii, 5.

[120] Ibid. cxxxv, 4 Nov. 1665.

[121] Ibid. cxxxvi, 121.

a deep water anchorage and in touch with Chatham, compared favourably with its competitor Harwich, the other new yard, where space was limited, water shallow, communication with the supply yards long and circuitous, and where ships were often wind-bound for weeks. There was also the obvious gain that Chatham would be relieved of a great deal of minor work which could be done without sending vessels into dry-dock. The great drawback to Sheerness besides the existence of a bar, not then material, was and is that it is practically indefensible if the British fleet loses the command of the North Sea, and this quite irrespective of any question of invasion. An interesting attempt was made about 1680 to deal with some of the difficulties of navigation near London by the use of 'towing engines.' Admiral Sir Edw. Spragge had invented or adapted these by the use of a paddle, worked by two capstans, the motive power being 96 men. Later the men were replaced by horses, six horses being held as equivalent to 72 men. These tugs soon dropped out of use, but were considered quite successful; the empty hulls of third-rates of 1,000 tons could be towed from Blackwall to Woolwich in an hour against the wind, giving about three miles an hour, but nothing is said about the tide. Fourth and fifth rates were towed with masts and rigging standing.

When Sheerness was established Chatham was stricken badly by the plague, and this may have been one motive for its immediate foundation in order to escape, if possible, infection in the fleet.[122] There were 800 men at Chatham dockyard[123] from whom Sheerness was to be supplied. The ground taken by the crown was unhealthy marsh land of little value, but there is some obscurity about the ownership and the terms of purchase. In the State Papers Alderman Francis Meynell, of London, is the only owner referred to, but some legal proceedings of the eighteenth century, and some later official papers, show that Colonel Edward Vernon, called by Pepys 'a merry good fellow' had a real or pretended interest for which he was extravagantly paid. In 1683 Charles, who perhaps also found him 'a merry good fellow,' conveyed manors and parks, of relatively enormous value, belonging to the Duchy of Lancaster in Derbyshire, Staffordshire, Leicestershire, Nottinghamshire, and Warwickshire to Vernon in return for his interest in the Sheerness land and a payment of £7,000.[124] As soon as James came to the throne the Attorney General was directed to move in Chancery to vacate the grant on the ground that it had been obtained 'in an improper manner . . . for a very inadequate consideration,' and a decree to that effect was obtained, the £7,000 being repaid, but there is no indication that the Sheerness ground was affected. Could we know the inner history of the transaction it would probably throw one more instructive sidelight on the king and court. A document of 1823 describes 40 acres at Garrison Point as having been obtained from Vernon;[125] but another paper states that the whole of the Sheerness ground, and that adjacent, belonged to Sir Michael Livesey, an attainted regicide, whose property was conveyed to the Duke of York who, in turn, sold to Meynell for £500.[126]

The progress of the yard was slow; in June 1666 Sir William Penn, then in superintendence there, reported his inability to do much, it being 'wholly

[122] S.P.Dom.Chas.II,cxxxvi,58.
[123] Ibid. cxxix, 69.
[124] Benson and Whatley v. Capt.

J. Vernon (c. 1743) B.M. 816 M.5/16. Also a yearly rent of £600 a year according to an undated and

unsigned paper (S.P.King William's Chest, xv, 72).
[125] W.O. Ord. *Rents*, xxxviii.
[126] Ibid. *Misc.* vi, fol. 42.

unfurnished.'[127] Then came the Dutch raid of 1667, which completely disorganized the dockyards, already reduced nearly to impotence by reason of the chronic want of money which was the pivot cause of most of the naval maladministration of the period. In August 1667, however, engineers were at Sheerness engaged in planning fortifications, and the necessary appurtenances of a dockyard, on a larger scale than had been designed previously.[128] By the end of the second Dutch war the Navy debt was £1,100,000;[129] in 1670 £459,000 was still owing and, as far as yard wages were concerned, one old quarter due before 1668 was supposed to be paid off concurrently with the one running.[130] Naturally, debt and poverty produced a plentiful crop of misdemeanours among those who felt the pressure most severely, and the cases noticed form no doubt only a fraction of those which actually occurred. High and low were equally unscrupulous. In December 1667 the Navy Board wrote to the clerk of the cheque at Chatham that a contractor claimed payment for stores not entered in the dockyard books; ' it is no small trouble to us to find the negligence of our officers so published to the world.'[131] Negligence was probably a very lenient description of their conduct. In the spring of the year the Chatham yardmen, who had a year's wages due, petitioned that they were starving;[132] as a consequence, ' the people's hands are so inured to stealing' that no half-cut work could be left in the sawpits even over a night.[133] Phineas Pett, the master shipwright at Chatham, was dismissed in 1668 because he was found to be in partnership with a shipbuilder at Gillingham from whom he purchased timber for the king's service that he had first bought himself as a private builder.[134] The partner, John Bowyer, professed ignorance as to how articles marked with the broad arrow came into their yard.

Hardly any additions, and nothing of note, were made to the dockyards during the period 1660–70. Pepys credits Sir Nicholas Crisp with a project for a basin or wet-docks at Deptford to receive 200 sail,[135] but elsewhere the design is attributed to the Duke of Ormond.[136] It seems to have been intended partly for the use of the Navy, but the scheme was killed at once by the opposition of the Navy Board. Notwithstanding the legacy of debt left by the second Dutch war there was an intention, in 1670, of establishing a new dockyard between Erith and Greenhithe. Twenty-four acres of land were bought, plans were drawn for two double dry-docks, a wet-dock, and the necessary storehouses, etc., at a total estimated cost of £63,000, and excavations were actually commenced.[137] That the new yard was to be on a splendid scale is clear from the amount to be spent on it, for in 1688 Chatham, then again enlarged, was valued at only £45,000. Why it was supposed to be required we are not told; it may be that the shoaling of the Medway below Rochester, to which there are several references between 1670–80, resulting in the grounding of ships at low water and delay in navigation, had determined the Navy authorities to close Chatham when it was in working order.[138] We know as little why it was abandoned as why it was begun except that the perpetual want of money would be a sufficient explanation. While it was being discussed

[127] S.P. Dom. Chas. II, clix, 25.
[128] Ibid. cciii, 87.
[129] Ibid. ccxvi, 84.
[130] Add. MS. 11602, fol. 213.
[131] Ibid. 9311, fol. 155.

[132] S.P. Dom. Chas. II, cc, 110.
[133] Ibid. ccxxv, 135.
[134] S.P. Dom. Chas. II, ccxliii, 115; Add. MS. 9311, fol. 83; Orders and Instructions, 27 Aug. 1668.

[135] *Diary*, 25 Jan.; 15, 19 Feb. 1661–2.
[136] Add. MS. 9303, fol. 171.
[137] S.P. Dom. Chas. II, cclxxxv, 88; ccxcviii, 62.
[138] See *post*, pp. 375, 385.

there was a new ship which had been on the stocks in Woolwich yard so long that much of the work had become rotten from exposure to weather.[139]

References to the character of the work done in the existing yards seem to show that the reason for desiring that at Greenhithe could not have been want of space or pressure due to excess of zeal amongst the men. Captain John Cox, who was Commissioner at Chatham in 1670 and who came from a man-of-war, was disgusted to find that both officers and men of any standing were too dignified to work and described them as walking about with their hands in their pockets.[140] In 1673 his successor, Sir Richard Beach, recommended the completion of the brick wall round the yard, as repairing the fence would cost nearly as much.[141] This was authorized, but its construction raised trouble among the shipwrights; the officers desired doors, communicating with their own houses, made in the wall and seem hardly to have troubled to conceal their motives.[142] On the other hand Beach, who was an old Royalist privateer captain of the Commonwealth period, did not conceal his opinion of them, and they no doubt had good reason for their complaints of 'his continual threats and cursing of us.' Beach had little sympathy for the officers who, in various ways, could take care of themselves, but the plight of the men was so bad that almost anything might be forgiven them and he did his best in reporting their condition to the Navy Board. In November 1673 he wrote that they were 'ready to starve and brought so low that they are not able to do a day's work';[143] three months later he wrote that some were actually dying of starvation and that one good workman had gone mad in consequence of 'the necessity himself and family were brought to.'[144] It was the period of the third Dutch war and the men, although they had no voice in calling the tune, had to help to pay for the music.

In June 1673 Prince Rupert wrote that the fleet had been shamefully equipped, 'merely huddled out'; on another occasion he nearly used his cane to some of the Navy Commissioners. But if they were not supplied with money to buy stores or to pay the men they were not morally responsible. Peace was made in February 1674 and then wholesale reductions were in view, it being proposed to discharge 1,616 men from Chatham, Deptford, Woolwich, and Portsmouth, retaining only 424 in pay; £31,600 was owing in yard wages.[145] Discipline became looser than ever under the Admiralty Boards which succeeded James, after the Test Act had enforced his resignation. In 1677 Beach remarked that in one week the master shipwrights at Chatham had given 247 days of leave to the men, who employed it to work elsewhere, and the officers, finding that after suspension they were soon restored to their places, were indifferent to his orders.[146]

The Chatham officers never escaped censure for long; in September 1673 they were told, ironically, by the Navy Board that it was not intended that timber fit for use, taken from ships under repair, should be used for firing.[147] Beach's position did not grow easier with time. In 1677 war with France was expected and a large shipbuilding scheme was put in hand. There were, in May, 232 shipwrights and caulkers at Chatham, 162 at Woolwich, 113 at

[139] Add. MS. 11602, fol. 218.
[140] S.P. Dom. Chas. II, cclxxxii, 57; ccxcvii, 58.
[141] Admir. and Navy Bd. 281, 25 June 1673.
[142] Ibid. 282, 10 July 1673.
[143] Navy Bd. Letters, i, 599.
[144] Ibid. i, 897.
[145] Ibid. 6, 10 March 1673–4.
[146] Admir. and Navy Bd. 321, 16 Aug. 18 Oct. 1677.
[147] Add. MS. 9311, fol. 246.

Deptford, and 15 at Sheerness; the Navy Board proposed to enter 360 more at Chatham.[148] How many more men actually came to Chatham we do not know, but as the plans of the Admiralty always outran their financial capacity we find that by the following March the men were, in Beach's words, threatening to tear him to pieces for their wages, 'if there be a purgatory upon the earth I am in it here.'[149] His relations with his officers were no happier; he complained that the principal master shipwright, Phineas Pett, was away ill most of the winter and absent making holiday most of the summer and, a little later, that since Pett had married 'this last woman,' he had become puffed up with pride and seldom appeared in the yard.[150] In January 1677-8 the Commissioner found further cause of fault with the officers generally, in that their perquisites —casks of tallow, oil, resin, etc.—took up so much room in the yard.[151]

Chatham was perhaps worse than the other dockyards because discipline had been allowed to run slack under Peter Pett, and officers and men revolted against its restoration by the Navy men who succeeded him. After Commissioner Thomas Middleton came there in 1668 he wrote to the Navy Board, 'I used to think those at Portsmouth the worst people in the world, but they are saints compared with those at Chatham.'[152] In 1678, when steps were taken to arm and drill for local defence the men belonging to Chatham, Beach, in addressing them, expressed the hope that they would behave better than their predecessors of 1667, when only one in twenty appeared at the time of trial.[153] About the same time the gate porter was fined for allowing the men to drink and smoke in his taproom during working hours;[154] the yard porters were allowed to keep alehouses for the use of the men, and the man at Chatham at this time was reputed to have made a fortune. But the other yards also had their scandals. In 1675 there were 256,000 treenails missing from Woolwich, which suggests thefts over a series of years suddenly detected;[155] in 1679 the yard was again to the front, and this time badly, for the two most important officers, the storekeeper and the clerk of the cheque, were involved. Bills had been given for stores never received, and the consequence was a new regulation, that future holders of the posts, in all the yards, should give security.[156] Of Deptford there is no definite accusation, but the opinion of the storekeeper there of his brother officers is shown by his statement that he did not believe that they required keys of the gates merely to pass in and out, and that if the keys were given, 'I shall humbly pray that I may have my bonds returned to me.'[157] There was a fire in Deptford yard on the night of 17-18 June 1667, which caused a panic in London, it being thought that the Dutch had come up the river and taken it.[158]

---

[148] Add. MS. 9316, fol. 256. It was supposed that there were 2,724 shipwrights and apprentices in the whole of England.

[149] Navy Bd. Letters, iv, 595.

[150] Ibid. v, 499, 717.

[151] Admir. and Navy Bd. 321, 12 Jan. 1677-8. How they came to be perquisites Beach does not explain; perhaps it was the euphemism of sarcasm. On the other hand, there is some reason to believe that from the sixteenth century dockyard officers had been allowed the condemned stores of their several departments; if so, the custom was now hardly recognized and was put an end to completely shortly afterwards. The Lord Admiral was originally entitled to 'cast' ships, which was the reason why ships were seldom or never 'cast,' but ordered to be rebuilt, and for the continuity of names in the Navy.

[152] S.P. Dom. Chas. II, ccxxxviii, 8.

[153] Admir. and Navy Bd. 330, 1 Nov. 1678. Albemarle said that when he came to Chatham on 11 June 1667 there were not twelve men there out of 800 borne on the yard books (Grey's Debates, i, 24).

[154] Ibid. 7 Aug. 1678.

[155] Navy Bd. Letters, ii, 445.

[156] Ibid. v, 1037; Add. MS. 9303, fol. 22.

[157] Admir. and Navy Bd. 355, 16 Nov. 1681.

[158] Evelyn's Diary (ed. 1884), ii, 27.

The perennial question of 'chips' gave the authorities no rest. The first order after the Restoration, dated May 1662, was to the effect that they were only to be taken out of the yards once a week.[159] This, like most of the Navy Board regulations, became a dead letter, and in 1671 some one at Chatham seemed to find it humorous that the old women who came into the yard to gather the chips were like to carry away men-of-war 'in their laps.'[160] The workmen said, frankly, that they could not live without the perquisite; this may be read and illustrated in the light of the statement of an informer that the chips at Deptford, Woolwich, and Chatham might be estimated at a load of timber a day and that many other things went out with them.[161] In 1674 the Woolwich officers were accused of allowing planks to be carried away as chips,[162] and the ceaseless trouble the matter caused stirred the Navy Board to find a fresh remedy. They ordered that from 1 January 1674–5 the chips were to be collected and sold;[163] this failed because the cost of collection was 8s. or 10s. a day, there was danger of fire and, finally, no one, it was supposed by arrangement, would buy the collected chips.[164] In face of this difficulty the Board directed that large pieces were to be reserved for the tarhouse and other fires, and the small thrown outside the gates for the poor.[165] After a three years' trial the Navy Board, in 1677, gave up the struggle, it having been 'an experiment of great charge and little profit';[166] the men were again permitted to take out 'lawful chips.'

The Upnor chain was not renewed until it was wanted in a hurry in the spring of 1667;[167] it is said to have been a poor affair, but the maker, Edward Silvester, was petitioning for payment for it in January 1668.[168] A new one was placed in 1670 with an arrangement of guard boats, planned by James, in connexion with it.[169] This was the last one used at, or below, Upnor. The question came up again several times but there was no general belief in the need for it and, after the victory of La Hogue, there was no possibility of a local attack in force. In 1688 a new chain was proposed; in 1693, the former one was reported to have been useless for some time, and the Navy Board called for an estimate for a new one, but said that there was no need for haste in the matter.[170] More pressing business claimed attention and the subject dropped until 1698 when the Admiralty drew the attention of the Navy Board once more to the question. That body replied that, although still existing, it was not worth repair and that they attached no value to a chain as a form of defence. Notwithstanding this rebuff the Admiralty still hankered after it and returned to the charge, but only to receive another decided opinion to the same effect.[171] Sheerness and the batteries commanding the Medway were considered a more efficient defence; but the principal reason for discarding the chain was that, in consequence of the great increase of the Navy, it was compulsory to moor many of the ships, and those the largest vessels, below Upnor, and therefore

[159] Add. MS. 9315, fol. 4.
[160] S.P. Dom. Chas. II, ccc, 136.
[161] Navy Bd. Letters, ii, 5; Admir. and Navy Bd. 290, 18 Nov. 1673. The load of timber contains 50 cubic feet; a ton is 43 feet,
[162] Admir. and Navy Bd. 307. 27 Mar. 1674.
[163] Add. MS. 9311, fol. 275.

[164] Navy Bd. Letters, ii, 511, 513; Admir. and Navy Bd. 27, 31 Mar. 1675.
[165] Admir. and Navy Bd. 31 Mar. 1675; Orders and Instructions, 27 Mar. 1675.
[166] Orders and Instructions, 27 June 1677.
[167] Hist. MSS. Com. Rep. xiii, App. ii, 106.

[168] S.P. Dom. Chas. II, ccxxxii, 166.
[169] Ibid. cclxxviii, 170; Add. MS. 9314, fol. 13; Admir. and Navy Bd. xx, 26 Sept. 1670.
[170] Navy Bd. Letters, xiii, 113; xxv, 788.
[171] Ibid. 31 Aug., 30 Sept., 12 Nov. 1698.

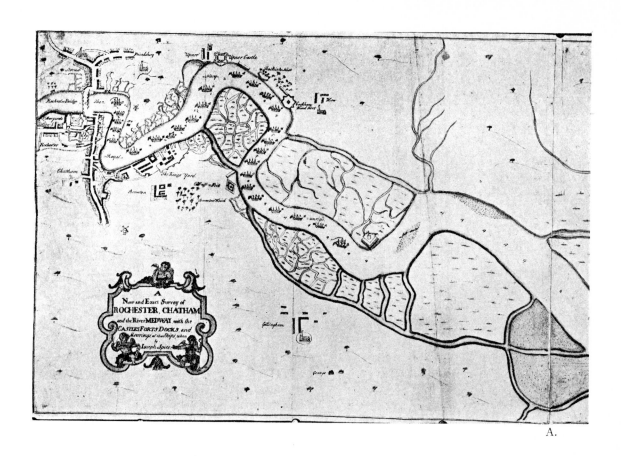

A.

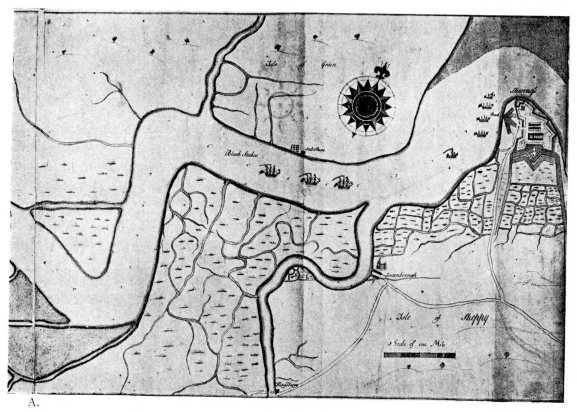

A.

MAP OF THE MEDWAY: LATE 17TH CENTURY
(from B.M. Sloane MS. 5222. No. 5).

beyond any situation where it could have been placed effectively. In war time it would now be represented by a boom between the Isle of Grain and Garrison Point to keep out torpedo craft and nets to entangle submarines.

Sheerness dockyard was used largely during the third Dutch war; in January 1673–4 its officers were ordered the same pay as those of Portsmouth.[172] In May 1673 the clerk of the cheque noted ' the beginning of something like a yard here,' of which the ground, with the storehouse belonging, had been enclosed in 1672.[173] In June 1673 Prince Rupert, commanding at sea, was ordered to send in to Sheerness all ships that would have formerly gone to Harwich for minor refits.[174] After the war it was employed to clean small cruisers but suffered from the lack of appliances and the want of accommodation for the men. The constricting effects of red tape also hindered its growth; it was noticed in 1673 that stores sent from Deptford were carried past it, by water, to Chatham, and then sent back to Sheerness. To the official mind the delay and additional expense thus caused were inconveniences difficult to remedy.[175] The quarters in the fortifications were so limited that in September 1673 two companies of foot added to the garrison were lodged on board a ship in default of room ashore.[176] The shipwrights and other workmen, from Chatham, no doubt lived from the commencement on board hulks grounded on the foreshore, as was the custom there during the whole of the eighteenth century. In 1675 they petitioned that they wanted houses, a market, and a minister, ' living in a manner like heathens ' without the last.[177] Later, in 1689, we find that some houses built for them were occupied by the garrison;[178] for upwards of a century the naval element was always sacrificed to real or imaginary military necessities at Sheerness. There was never any love lost between the two services, and one of the earliest quarrels between them recorded grew out of the beer-selling privileges of the porter of the yard;[179] whatever else was lacking in a new naval establishment its abuses were imported full-grown from the beginning. At one time the utility of the yard seemed so doubtful that it was decided to close it, so that in June 1686, when Pepys, working in association with James, was placing before himself economy and efficiency as the objects to be attained, one step towards them was the disestablishment of Sheerness, which was said to be expensive and of little use in peace.[180] At the moment there was only a guardship and one other vessel there; orders were given to send the workmen back to Chatham and to remove the officers to other yards as vacancies occurred.[181] However, the closure of Sheerness was for so short a time as to make no marked gap in its history.

The Greenhithe scheme of 1670, and the foundation of Sheerness, seem to point to a disinclination to enlarge the older yards. At any rate little more was done during the reign of Charles II than to keep them in a going condition, although some ground on the west side of Woolwich yard is said to have been taken from Dr. Gilbourne on a 17 years' lease in 1663.[182] The only Dr. Gilbourne (Thomas) whose name is known, died in 1638;[183] he is mentioned in

[172] Add. MS. 9314, fol. 22.

[173] S.P. Dom. Chas. II, cccxlv, 47; Admir. and Navy Bd. 2886. 12 June 1672.

[174] Admir. and Navy Bd. 2887, 2 June 1673.

[175] S.P. Dom. Chas. II, cccliii, 14 Oct. 1673.

[176] Orders and Instructions, 17 Sept. 1673.

[177] Navy Bd. Letters, ii, 557.

[178] Ibid. xiii, 969.

[179] Ibid. ii, 495.

[180] Ibid. xi, 763.

[181] Admir. and Navy Bd. 364, 13 June 1686; Add. MS. 9315, fol. 21.

[182] Vincent, *Records of Woolwich*, i, 259.

[183] Munk, *Roll of Royal College of Physicians*, s.v.

connexion with the yard in 1634, but his ground was then outside it.[184]   In 1676 Sir Wm. Pritchard was paid £3,363 for houses and land at Woolwich for the use of the Ordnance Department.   In 1682 and 1683 estimates were drawn up for docks at Chatham;[185] the decision to build was taken in November 1684, and one dock was begun just before the death of Charles.   Ships were steadily increasing in size, and it was said of the existing docks that there was scarcely room enough to swing a caulking mallet in some parts of the largest of them when a first-rate was inside.[186]   There was indecision on the part of the authorities whether to build one double dock to take two ships, or two single docks, the first plan being from 20 per cent. to 30 per cent. cheaper but far less effective for rapid work.   Eventually it was decided to build two single docks, one by contract and one by the Navy Board, on ground adjoining the yard of which part belonged already to the crown and part to the Dean and Chapter of Rochester, this last being obtained by exchange with the Chapter.[187]   It was the ground occupied by one of these docks about which the difficulty subsequently arose with the heirs of the freeholder.[188]   The Navy Board dock was built by Sir Phineas Pett, the other by John Rogers, house carpenter, whose tender was £5,310.[189]   Both were to be 200 ft. long, with an extreme breadth of 54 ft., and of 36 ft. at the apron.   From the plans, to scale, they seem to have somewhat exceeded these measurements, especially by 3 ft. or 4 ft. in the breadth;[190] the old double dock was only 45 ft. wide,[191] although 350 ft. long, but in 1684 it was said to be nearly useless on account of water from springs welling up into it.   Docks were still built of wood, with smooth, sloping sides, and steps at each corner leading down to the bottom; the earliest stone docks, stepped at the sides in the modern way, and with gates of two leaves instead of the triple wicket gates, were those of Portsmouth and Plymouth under construction in 1693. The new works at Chatham were inclosed by a brick wall and fence, and in 1686 a storehouse 660 ft. long was erected; this, with the wharf in front of it, cost £7,362.[192]   Ten new masthouses, each 112 ft. long and 17 ft. broad, were also put up at a cost of £2,020.

In 1682 Sir Phineas Pett proposed the construction of a basin at Chatham large enough to contain 25 second- and third-rates, the advantage being the great saving of time which would follow in several ways; the Navy Board always feared the possibilities of fire, much intensified in such a confined space, and their adverse opinion prevented its execution.[193]   Several slight fires had occurred there before 1671,[194] and the Navy Board evidently had no mind to run risks.   From 1676 Woolwich became permanently 'distinct and separate' from Deptford, a master shipwright having been appointed to it in December 1675.[195]   From 1685 until 1689 Balthazar St. Michel, brother-in-law of Pepys, was Commissioner in charge of Deptford and Woolwich; on 31 May 1686 he announced that the king expected strict discipline to be maintained, and that

[184] Add. MS. 9294, fol. 699.

[185] Ibid. 9312, fol. 70, 72.

[186] Admir. and Navy Bd. 370, 10 Dec. 1683.

[187] Ibid. 61, 28 June 1685; Navy Bd. Letters, x, 525.

[188] *Ante*, pp. 344, 351.

[189] Admir. and Navy Bd. 61, 13 June 1685; S.P. Dom. Entry Bks. lv, 334.

[190] King's MS. 43.

[191] The *Britannia*, 100, the widest ship in the Navy, was of 48 ft. 8 in. beam.

[192] Add. MS. 9317, fol. 34.

[193] Ibid. 9322, fol. 68; Admir. and Navy Bd. 51, 9 Mar. 1681–2; Navy Bd. Letters, viii, 285, 595. The contract with Sir J. Tippets, the Surveyor of the Navy, had been authorized, and the specifications give some interesting details. There were to be two pairs of gates, one pair opening outwards, and the other inwards (Cal. of Tr. Bks. vii, pt. i, p. 425).

[194] S.P. Dom. Chas. II, ccxcviii, 138 (3).

[195] Admir. and Navy Bd. 32, 11 Dec. 1675; Add. MS. 9322, fol. 3.

no one was to be absent without leave from himself or the Navy Board.[196] This was only a renewal of the regulation of 1658 fallen into oblivion;[197] in 1662 the Navy Board had remarked that new regulations were usually only old ones revived.[198] When the improvements of 1686 were in hand six new mast houses, similar to those at Chatham, were made at Deptford, and the sum of £2,430 was spent on the wet-dock there.[199] The yard was somewhat enlarged by demolishing the Navy Treasurer's house and including the ground and garden, but there appears to have been great want of space here and elsewhere. The new Navy Commissioners of 1686, doing their best under the watchful eyes of James and Pepys, reported that their efforts to put down waste and theft were hindered by the fact that while the Navy had increased tenfold the yard accommodation had only grown by one-fortieth.[200] Neither statement can be accepted at face value, but we may note their energy as shown by one small reform in the shape of an order that, in future, no pigs were to be kept in Woolwich yard; a like order for Deptford did not issue until 1698.[201]

Although not of the highest rank in the dockyards the master shipwrights continued to be, in many respects, the most important civil officers of the Navy, for so much depended on them, both as to the conduct, industry, and ability of the men, and the plans, strength, and seaworthiness of the ships built and repaired. Except Sir Anthony Deane, and he had no connexion with the Kentish yards, there was no eminent builder of this period. Pepys, in a paper not designed for publication, laid before the king in 1685 his private and unfavourable opinion of the best known government and private shipwrights, but, for a reason not altogether discreditable to himself, he dwelt only on their faults.[202] On the other hand James must have known nearly as much as Pepys about them, so that there can hardly be much exaggeration. Robert Lee was the senior master shipwright at Chatham, and Pepys described him as ' full of the gout,' and as never having built a ship in his life; his assistant, Phineas Pett, was ' lazy and debauched.' Edmund Dummer, another assistant, was ' an ingenious young man but . . . a mere draughtsman.' Dummer, however, was soon to show himself to be the ablest Surveyor of the Navy that the years had yet produced. John Shish, at Deptford, was ' illiterate, low-spirited, of little appearance or authority '; his assistant, Fisher Harding, ' a very slow man, of no learning, authority, or countenance.' Mr. Lawrence, at Woolwich, had ' never built a ship in his life but the *Little Victory* . . . and when done was found fit for nothing but a fireship . . . a low-spirited, slow and gouty man . . . illiterate and supine to the last degree.' Daniel Furzer, at Sheerness, was ' young and never built a ship.' We need not follow Pepys in his criticisms of the master shipwrights who possessed private yards, but he has something depreciatory to say of all of them. His object was to persuade James that it was necessary to pay any amount to Sir Anthony Deane, for whom he had a sincere admiration, to secure his services on the Navy Board, and that there was no one who could take Deane's place.[203]

In 1688 there was no dry-dock at Sheerness, but only a graving place made in 1673.[204] The yard, which was governed by the Commissioner at

[196] Add. MS. 9328, fol. 17.

[197] *Ante*, p. 350.

[198] Add. MS. 9311, fol. 83.

[199] Ibid. 9317, fol. 34.

[200] Ibid. 9322, fol. 147.

[201] Ibid. 9315, ff. 19, 31.

[202] *Engl. Hist. Rev.* xiv, 63, 64; Pepys, *Memoires of the Royal Navy* (ed. 1906), 29 et seq.

[203] The French also admired Deane's designs, and Louis XIV ordered them to be copied for his men-of-war.

[204] Add. MS. 9315, fol. 10.

Chatham, was very small and inclosed by the fortifications; the hulks, on board which the workmen lived, were all moored on the Blackstakes side of the dockyard. Its value was estimated at £5,393 in 1688, raised to £6,960 in 1698, by small improvements.[205] A building slip was added after 1688,[206] and the first man-of-war built there, the *Sheerness*, 32, was launched in 1691. In 1692 there was much work in hand, and the officers in charge dwelt on the necessity for providing proper housing accommodation for the men, most of whom were still going backwards and forwards between Sheerness and Chatham.[207] In September, a month before the date of this letter, some houses were being built for them,[208] so that it may be inferred that as soon as the buildings were finished they were as usual taken for the use of the garrison. In 1691 there were only 80 men attached to the yard; the number does not rise to over 200 until the commencement of the war of Queen Anne's reign.[209]

At Chatham, in 1688, there were the old double and single docks, a building slip, and the two new docks constructed in 1684–5; no new docks were added for many years, but a mast-dock costing £3,130 replaced, before 1698, the old one filled up in 1686. The new one had 32 brick arches to keep the masts under water. The estimated value of the yard in 1688 was £44,940, and in 1698 £56,059, some new buildings having been built in the interval, e.g. a cordage storehouse in 1692.[210] The authorities were content with the facilities already existing at Woolwich; the single and double docks remained and there were never more than the three there. In October 1695 an agreement was made with John Gregson by which £10 a year was paid to him for the use of Ham Creek;[211] during the war of William III many small accessions occurred in the shape of buildings and restorations, and the walling of the yard was proceeded with in 1692,[212] so that its total value, £9,669 in 1688, was supposed to be £15,801 in 1698. At Deptford there was the old dry-dock and a building slip opening into the basin, of which the area was 38,503 sq. yds. Early in the reign of Charles II Sir Denis Gauden, the victualling contractor of the Navy, had taken a lease of certain ground, westward of the dockyard, from John Evelyn, on which he built the Red House in 1671, later the Navy Victualling Yard, for the better execution of his work.[213] In 1681 Gauden let 2½ acres of this land to the Navy Board, on a 36 years' lease;[214] here, between 1688 and 1698, were made a mast dock, nearly as large as the basin, an anchor wharf, and storehouses for various purposes.[215] The value of the yard, £15,760 in 1688, had increased therefore to £28,641 in 1698. In March 1688 there were 479 shipwrights and caulkers employed at Chatham, 171 at Deptford, and 96 at Woolwich.[216]

The Revolution, with its sequel of foreign war, brought a press of work for the dockyards. It must not be supposed that because Chatham was the only one in which additional docks had been placed that the Admiralty were satisfied with the existing accommodation. The centre of struggle was moving westward, so that while Chatham and Sheerness were sufficient for the North Sea, and Deptford and Woolwich still valuable for building ships, supply and

---

[205] King's MS. 43.
[206] Navy Bd. Letters, lxv, Feb. 1707–8.
[207] Ibid. xxiii, 227.
[208] Add. MS. 10,121, fol. 129.
[209] Ibid. 9324, ff. 27, 51.

[210] Ibid. 10121, fol. 129; King's MS. 43.
[211] Add. MS. 9315, fol. 29.
[212] Ibid. fol. 59.
[213] Admir. and Navy Bd. 2886, 5 Dec. 1671. Cf. *ante*, p. 348.

[214] Navy Bd. Letters, lxi, 8 Oct. 1706; 65 (1708).
[215] Admir. Sec. In Letters, 3637, 13 Mar. 1723–4.
[216] Exch. Misc. Tr. of Receipt, Bdle. 76, no. 12.

repair bases were required nearer the scene of action. Plymouth was founded and Portsmouth was enlarged. Had financial conditions permitted still another yard would have been established on the south coast; but the Admiralty would not consider one in the Thames and curtly rejected the proposal of ' one, Daniel Defoe,' to buy his ground at Tilbury for the purpose. There was no money available for the things absolutely necessary, much less for that which was only advisable. The Navy Debt of 1689 included £75,000 for yard wages; in 1691 this had grown to £116,500, and in 1693 it was still £107,000, the men then having fifteen months' wages owing to them.[217] In one respect they were better off than the seamen, who were sometimes unpaid for three, four, or five years; in another they were worse off, for the seamen had at least food and lodging while the yardmen were often nearly starving. In November 1693 Sir Edward Gregory, the Commissioner at Chatham, wrote to the Navy Board that ' the case of the men is truly deplorable and, since I can but make a shift to live, from my very heart I wonder how they rub through.'[218] A few months earlier he had lectured the Navy Board on the dangerous political consequences likely to follow delay in paying the yardmen, since there were plenty of agents ready to foment discontent;[219] he expected that if the Chatham tradesmen ceased to give credit work would also cease. But even this condition of things seems to have been better than that existing in 1691 when the men, of whom there were 800, were living on bread, cheese, and water, and were becoming too weak physically to do their work properly.[220] No doubt the Navy Board would have been delighted to order payment in full if the Navy Treasurer had held the money to meet their demands; as it was the dockyards were often nearly at a standstill for want of materials for which the Navy Board could not pay cash and could not obtain on credit, and materials were of more immediate importance than wages.

That the men availed themselves of such resources as were open to them to alleviate their position is shown by the payment of £100 to George Everitt in 1696 in reward for information given by him concerning abuses and thefts in the yards, information which must have been considered valuable in view of the large amount.[221] The Navy Board were always ready to pay informers but settled the tariff themselves; fifteen years later two Deptford labourers, who had thrown some light on what was going on in that yard, asked for 150 guineas, but were told that £25 was enough.[222] In 1694 the Commissioners ordered that the men at the yards were to be searched ' when they least suspect it.'[223] Some warning leaked out, but at Woolwich, when the search took place, stolen property was found in 39 of the tool chests;[224] at Chatham there were very many more thieves although the number is not stated.[225] There were several reasons why prosecution was unsatisfactory, so that the Navy Commissioners decreed that those found out were to be fined in treble the value of the articles stolen. The men at Deptford and Woolwich insisted on their right to take out chips three times a day, while once was the custom in the other yards.[226] Experiments at

---

[217] Add. MS. 10121, fol. 111; Navy Bd. Letters, xxiv, 894; Home Off. Admir. vi, 17 May 1693.

[218] Navy Bd. Letters, xxvii, 638.

[219] Ibid. xxvi, 35. In 1699 a plot to burn the ships at Chatham and Portsmouth, arranged by Mathew Wall, a notorious Jacobite agent, was discovered (Bath MSS. iii, 344).

[220] Ibid. xix, 795, 875.

[221] Add. MS. 9314, fol. 43.

[222] Admir. and Navy Bd. 2889, 30 July 1711.

[223] Add. MS. 9315, fol. 28.

[224] Admir. and Navy Bd. 458, 7 Dec. 1694.

[225] Add. MS. 9328, fol. 42.

[226] Admir. and Navy Bd. 555, May 1702.

Chatham showed that once a day there meant many tons. At the launch of the *Restoration* a man 'accidentally' picked up 36 lb. of cordage with his chips; no doubt similar 'accidents' happened, not only daily but many times daily, among hundreds of men. The Admiralty expressed a belief that the yard officers connived at these abuses,[227] and it seems hardly possible that the families of the workmen could have been admitted at Deptford and Woolwich to cut up wood for the men without the knowledge of those in charge.

It should be pointed out that there was also a brighter side in the conduct of dockyard work than that dwelt on here. The sea officers often complained, and often with justice, of bad workmanship and bad equipment from the yards, but it is obvious that for the English fleets to have kept the sea successfully through a series of years, a sufficient standard of excellence must have been consistently reached. Not infrequently the sea officers' complaints were well grounded, but were really consequences of the want of money which enforced the purchase on credit of stores of inferior quality.[228] Even so the dockyards sometimes received praise from the admirals; Russell, in 1691, expressed his satisfaction with the way in which the ships from Chatham had been fitted.[229] In 1693, when some of the flag officers and captains doubted the quality of the work from Chatham because it had been executed so quickly, Sir Edward Gregory reminded them that if the repairs and equipment had not been equally well done the previous year, some of the three-deckers 'would have been left behind' during the winter cruise in the Bay of Biscay, for which they were never designed.[230] Relations between the civil and the executive officers were nearly always very strained. A typical case occurred in 1705 when Captain Jonas Hanway of the *Tilbury* found fault with the material at Woolwich and with the laziness of the workmen, whom it was necessary to bribe to induce them to do anything. The Navy Board retorted that the officers of the *Tilbury* had abused and struck the workmen; Hanway admitted the truth of this, justified it, and delivered himself of some plain opinions of the Navy Board and their subordinates.[231] The Navy Board would never admit to an admiral or captain that there could be anything lacking in the best of all possible organizations, but not long before they had, themselves, reprimanded the officers at Deptford and Woolwich for the dilatory way in which the work was being performed in those yards. The officers replied that the spiritless way in which the men were working was due to the deprivation of privileges to which they had long been accustomed; the answer of the Navy Board was that the men were paid to work and were not to be bribed to it, and that much of the fault must be with the officers.[232] There had been a mutiny at Woolwich on account of an alteration in meal-times and an interference with the chips; the Woolwich men had marched riotously to the Admiralty and their sullen inertness was an aftermath of the rebellion.[233] The administrative weakness of the Navy Board itself was to be found in too much leniency. Officers were sometimes suspended for negligence or dishonesty, but seldom dismissed, and still more rarely prosecuted; the men knew that detection was unlikely and that punishment was uncertain and light. The reasons are discovered in the flagrant political, moral, and pecuniary dishonesty of the period from which the Admiralty and Navy Board themselves

---

[227] Add. MS. 9316, fol. 378.
[228] Ibid. 9328, fol. 83.
[229] Admir. Min. Bks. v, 9 Jan. 1690–1.
[230] Navy Bd. Letters, xxvii, 162.
[231] Ibid. lix.
[232] Add. MS. 9328, ff. 210, 211.
[233] Ibid. fol. 128.

were not free, in the bureaucratism and routine now becoming a marked feature in naval administration, in the fact that the civil side never produced an official of organizing genius, and because it was not easy to replace trained officers and workmen of whom the supply was relatively small in the country.

Throughout these years there is a continuous series of orders concerning the dockyard officers. When Pepys was using the new broom in 1686 he affected wonder in finding that the officers employed the men on their own private business such as working in gardens, making furniture, etc.; there was nothing new in it, but a public notice, to be affixed to the gate of each yard prohibiting such proceedings must have seemed a strong measure to those it touched.[234] In 1692 the Navy Board woke up to the fact that when officers were removed from one yard to another they took away chimney-pieces, locks, fire hearths—in short, all that was movable, the consequences being that the house had practically to be rebuilt for the incoming officer. Worse still, they took with them the official papers of their departments, so that Sheerness documents might perhaps be resting at Woolwich or Portsmouth. For this the Navy Commissioners were primarily to blame; the examination and passing, at the Navy Office, of the dockyard accounts was so slow, being sometimes five or more years in arrear, that when an officer left one yard for another he felt bound to take his papers with him in order to be able to check the Navy Office clerks when the day of settlement came. However, it was forbidden for the future, and also the officers' houses were to be surveyed on a change of occupancy.[235]

In January 1696 salaries were raised all round but the old Exchequer fees were abolished; the chief officers at Deptford, Chatham, and Portsmouth were to have £200 a year, and £150 a year at Woolwich, Sheerness, and Plymouth; the day wages of the men varied from 1s. 6d. to 3s. We find a notice in 1697 of the practice of using the yards as convenient inlets for smuggled goods,[236] and in 1698 certain of the officers were detected in acting as agents for contractors of naval stores.[237] The pay of the officers and of the senior workmen was increased by permission to take 'servants,' or apprentices, who were supposed to be taught trades and whose wages were taken by their masters. This was a fruitful source of abuse, for such apprentices were frequently used as house servants and taught nothing. The accession of George I brought new Admiralty and Navy Boards, which included Russell, Byng, and Wager. They were the only men of weight and experience on the Boards, and it was probably due to their presence that we find new endeavours to purify the civil departments. A circular, to all the yards, of 30 July 1715 dwelt on the irregularities lately discovered at Deptford, from which the master shipwrights had been dismissed, such as 'the shameful practice' of taking money for entering and promoting workmen, entering servants under the names of persons who were not entitled to the privilege, favouritism, and other evils.[238] Once more the back doors, opening into the dockyards, of officers' houses were to be bricked up;[239] and, again, the officers were forbidden to employ the king's workmen or to use the king's stores for their own purposes.[240] From another source there

[234] Admir. and Navy Bd. 2507, 6 Sept. 1686.
[235] Ibid. 18 Aug. 1692; Add. MS. 9328, fol. 27.

[236] Ibid. 2507, 21 Oct. 1697.
[237] Add. MS. 9328, fol. 76.
[238] Ibid. 9315, fol. 41; ibid. 9328, fol. 331; Admir. Cont. Misc. 89, 20 July 1715.

[239] Add. MS. 9315, fol. 41.
[240] Admir. and Navy Bd. 2507, 8 Aug. 1715.

are further sidelights to be obtained on Deptford, for a pamphlet of 1717 shows vividly the enormous waste of timber, of which there were sometimes 14,000 or 15,000 loads in store, which went on there.[241] This publication also dwells upon the bribery rampant in all departments, but no doubt Deptford only reflected the customs prevalent in all the other yards. At Chatham the men were said to waste three-fourths of their time and to convert an unconscionable amount of timber into chips.

A dry-dock was proposed for Sheerness in 1708 and, presumably, made, since it is shown on a plan of 1725,[242] but no other improvements come under notice during the war of the Spanish Succession; it had no history beyond a reference in 1709 to the fact that the storekeeper there was taking bribes.[243] In 1701 the single dock at Woolwich was enlarged to enable it to take in a first-rate, and more ground was bought in 1705 and 1710.[244] In both cases it was obtained from the Bowater family, the lords of the manor;[245] that of 1705 cost £746 17s. 6d. and, abutting on the highway at the back of the yard, was already in use by the Navy authorities before purchase. In 1708 further negotiations were commenced, but were not completed before 1710; in the interval the yard officers were inclined to occupy the Bowater ground as in the previous instance, but Mr. Richard Bowater was watching them and sending to the Navy Board claims for payment. The officers were warned that if they did not confine themselves to the dockyard they would be made to pay any charges incurred. In 1710 the new ground was fenced, and 4,040 yds. of the dockyard paved, for the reason that it would tend to the dispatch of work and be healthier for the men.

Deptford was extended by the purchase of some of the Evelyn ground, including the 2½ acres leased from Gauden in 1681;[246] negotiations were commenced in 1710 but the matter was not settled until 1714, when the freeholder took £2,050, having abated from the £5,000 price and £5 a year rental, for a 51 years' lease he asked at first.[247] A wharf was also bought in 1710 from a proprietor named Hollis, but this must have been a small affair.[248] In 1711 the dock was lengthened, 'a great and difficult work,'[249] the double dock at Chatham having been similarly treated in 1703.[250] It need hardly be pointed out that the necessity for enlarging these docks followed the automatic increase in the size of vessels, which is the unchanging characteristic of ship construction through the centuries. It was in part due to the same cause that, from the end of the seventeenth century, it became necessary to attend to the dredging of the Medway in certain places. The silting of the river had been noticed in 1667,[251] and as early as 1680 the Navy Board were contracting for a 'dredging engine.'[252]

---

[241] Williamson, *Memoir of Mr. Joseph Allen*, London, 1717.

[242] King's Prints (B.M.), xvii, 14.

[243] Navy Bd. Letters, lxviii, 26 Aug. 1709.

[244] Add. MS. 9328, fol. 105.

[245] Ibid. ff. 236, 242, 248, 251, 252.

[246] See *ante*, p. 362.

[247] Admir. and Navy Bd. 2889, 5 Mar. 1710–11; Navy Bd. Letters, lxxi, 17 Nov. 1710, 20 Jan. 1710–11; lxxii, 2 Mar. 1710–11; lxxx, 19 Feb. 1713–14; Navy Bd. In Letters, 689, 6 Aug. 1713; Treas. Papers, ccl, 4; ccliii, 3. In the general overhaul which followed these enlargements the remains of *Royal Escape*, the collier in which Charles II escaped after Worcester fight, and which had been taken into the Navy at the Restoration, were found in the mast dock. The Admiralty ordered that another vessel should be built on her lines, and that the name was to be continued in the Navy (Navy Bd. Letters, lxxx, 19 Feb. 1713–14).

[248] Navy Bd. Letters, lxix, May 1710.

[249] Admir. and Navy Bd. 2889, 25 Sept. 1711.

[250] Treas. Papers, xcii, 25 Mar. 1703.

[251] *Hist. MSS. Com. Rep.* xiii, App. ii, 106.

[252] Navy Bd. Letters, vii, 757. In 1677 Lewis Bayley obtained a patent for 14 years for a dredger working with nets, and for a pile-driving machine, but dredgers had been in use on the Rhône from the beginning of the century.

In the estimates of 1702 the sum of £1,950 was assigned to the object of deepening the river.[253] In 1712 there were 797 men carried on the books at Chatham, 647 at Deptford, 511 at Woolwich, and 162 at Sheerness; of these, 400, 320, 250, and 60 respectively were shipwrights.[254] The figures do not represent the highest numbers employed for, in the preceding June, 400 men had been dismissed from Deptford and Woolwich in view of approaching peace; wages were then fifteen months in arrear. The yard men were 'regimented' through the wars of William III and Anne as in those of Charles II, but as a defending force they must have been quite valueless. From Chatham, in 1696, the Commissioner remarked that the arms had been issued to the Ordnance storekeeper 'with whom, for aught we know, they remain, having never been favoured with the handling of them.'[255] It was noticed in 1715 that the arms in all the dockyards had become useless from want of attention to their condition.[256]

Walpole's long administration was one of peace, and little happened in the dockyards beyond routine work. An order of 25 April 1715 directed that only single men were to be entered at Sheerness who were to live 'in garrison,' as there were stores outside and opportunities for stealing.[257] Probably this means that they were to lodge with the troops, but if so the arrangement did not continue long. The water supply was always a difficulty at Sheerness; till about this time it had been brought in small craft from Deptford and Chatham, but in 1724 the Navy Board sunk a well at Queenborough. They desired to reserve it for the use of the dockyard and the ships, but were snubbed by the Treasury and directed to throw it open to the public.[258] In 1716 the slip opening into the basin at Deptford[259] was replaced by a dry dock,[260] and in 1720 the single dock at Woolwich was rebuilt. In 1716 also, the practice was commenced of making sails in the yards;[261] hitherto they had always been bought, or made by contract from canvas supplied by the Navy Board. Renewed orders issued in 1718 and 1721 in reference to the persistence of the yard officers in employing the workmen about their own private affairs, but the same abuse was still flourishing in the beginning of the nineteenth century.

The ground at Deptford, bought in 1714 and occupied by the mast dock and anchor wharf, was separated from the old dockyard by a brick wall and was traversed by a right of way from Sayes Court. The officials found this arrangement very inconvenient and the yard, as a whole, too small; therefore in 1725, having the opportunity, they took from the Evelyn family another six acres of land extending from the back of the mast-dock to Sayes Court and made another road outside the yard.[262] Commissioner Kempthorne, at Chatham, wrote forcibly to the Navy Board, in November 1723, about the shoaling of the Medway, which had progressed so rapidly within his experience that large ships could only come up now between half-flood and half-ebb tides. He said, 'We find the banks in the river daily increase, especially near the docks'; the Muscle Bank, he remembered, twelve or fourteen years previously, as only dry for ten or twelve yards at low water, whereas it now showed three-quarters of a

---

[253] *Commons' Journ.* 10 Nov. 1704.
[254] Add. MS. 9336, fol. 289.
[255] Navy Bd. Letters, xxxvi, 675.
[256] Admir. and Navy Bd. 2507, 29 Oct. 1715.

[257] Admir. Cont. Misc. 89.
[258] Admir. Sec. In Letters, 3637, 1 Nov. 1723; 3638, 27 Aug. 1725.
[259] *Ante*, p. 362.

[260] Admir. Cont. Misc. 89, 10 May 1716.
[261] Add. MS. 9315, fol. 42.
[262] Ibid. fol. 50; Admir. Sec. In Letters, 3637, 13 Mar. 1723–4; Navy Bd. Min. 2554, 16 July 1740.

mile.[263] A survey followed, but the report was not so unfavourable as Kempthorne's, who, however, was embodying the result of daily experience.

There was trouble in the ropeyards in 1729, especially at Woolwich. For years past there must have been much to seek in the administration, for in 1717 the officer in charge was accused of demanding 3s. 6d. from each man when he gave him work to do. The present difficulty arose from the desire of the Navy Board to enter apprentices, whereas the men were determined to keep their craft a close corporation. Those at Woolwich went out on strike, but the Navy Board brought up men from the provinces and found little difficulty in winning the day.[264] The new plan of making sails in the dockyards soon evolved its own system of theft. At Deptford an informer gave interesting details of the common methods practised. Men made breeches out of the canvas, which were sold to the shipwrights and seamen; canvas and ropes were taken out of the yard and divided into lots which were drawn for out of a hat. He had known 300 yds. of canvas at a time to be taken by the master sailmaker or foreman, and believed that much the same practices were common at the other yards.[265] The Navy Board decided on a sudden and simultaneous search at all the dockyards; Deptford and Woolwich came worst out of the test, much being found on the men and in their lockers, but Sheerness emerged quite innocent from the ordeal. Then came the contractors, who complained that they could not get stores received, nor the bills for them, without bribery, ' all the clerks, and even the watchmen and labourers, do expect and insist upon treats '; the officers required a handsome douceur.[266]

Enough has been said to show the general conditions of work and management at this period, although further examples for nearly every month of every year could easily be adduced. The next extension of the dockyards was at Deptford, where in 1734, six houses adjoining the yard were bought on the recommendation of the officers to avoid the risk from fire; they were obtained for £749, pulled down, and the ground inclosed.[267] In 1744 another small addition was made in the shape of six tenements belonging to Mr. Wickham in a place called the Orchard, adjoining the officers' residences, that is to say, on the south or west of the yard. These were bought for £350.[268] At Woolwich the slip between the docks, shown in the plan of 1698, being ' decayed,' was filled in. During the years which had passed since the scandals of 1729 this yard does not appear to have improved in *morale*; in 1732 the foreyard of the *Falmouth*, repairing there, was found to be sprung, but the responsible superiors only ' covered the wound ' with tar, and in 1735 we find notices of bribery affecting the officers.[269] At all the yards now, the old wooden wharves were being rebuilt in brick as the necessity arose for renewing them. In 1736 £7,000 was allotted for the repair of one of the docks of 1685–6 at Chatham,[270] and in the following year the slip between the old docks, shown in the plan of 1698, was filled up and a new one made in another position.[271] In 1736 Woolwich ropeyard was enlarged by a small purchase from Mr. Bowater, the lord of the

[263] Admir. Sec. In Letters, 22 Jan. 1723–4. The French were suffering in the same way. Brest was silting up during the eighteenth century to such an extent that, while there was depth for 80 ships of the line in 1688, space could only be found for 30 in 1763 by advancing the chain seaward. There was no dredging until Choiseul became minister of marine.

[264] Navy Bd. Min. 2544, 8, 13, 20 Aug. 1729.

[265] Ibid. 20 Oct. 1729.

[266] Admir. and Navy Bd. 2507, 7 Nov. 1729.

[267] Navy Bd. Min. 2547, 5 Sept. 1733; 2548, 26 June, 29 Nov. 1734.

[268] Ibid. 28 Oct. 1743, 10 Oct. 1744.

[269] Ibid. 2546, 8 Nov. 1732; 2547, 7 Feb. 1734–5.

[270] Ibid. 2550, 3 Mar. 1735–6.

[271] Ibid. 2551, 18 May 1737.

manor,[272] and the next extension was in 1743, when he offered ground, apparently 20 acres, at the west end of the yard, for £3,000. After some bargaining his terms were accepted.[273] Shortly afterwards—in 1744—another small property, adjoining Bowater's ground, was bought for £230 and the proceedings were highly characteristic of the Navy Board. The agreement to purchase was made on 30 November 1744, and on 21 January 1745 the vendor, Peter Beardsley, was requested to show the Woolwich officers what had been sold by him as they and the Navy Board were equally ignorant.[274]

In 1738 lodgings were being built at Sheerness for some of the workmen under an Admiralty Order of March 1736, and the difference in dates is a perfectly fair illustration of the normal speed of the Navy Board.[275] A new building slip was made at Chatham, and 'abuses and frauds' there this year were sufficiently marked to induce the Admiralty to call for an especial report on them. A fire occurred in Deptford yard on the night of 6-7 June 1738, extinguished without much damage, but on 5 July 1739, the Red House, which was really a collection of victualling storehouses, was burnt down.[276] On 27 December the joiner's shop at Chatham was on fire; in April there had been a fire at Sheerness attributed to the sale of spirits in the yard by the porter. All that the Navy Board could find to do was to reprimand the officers and direct that the order of 23 August 1694, prohibiting the sale of spirits, should be read to the workmen.[277] Strictly, the porters were only allowed to sell small beer, to be drunk outside the taprooms, but for generations they had been tacitly permitted to sell wine and spirits; the Navy Board contented themselves with reiterating previous instructions when anything occurred which called attention to their infraction and, as usual, it was no one's business to enforce them.

The disabilities of the Thames yards came into evidence more clearly year by year as ship tonnage grew greater; in April 1739 the *Boyne*, 80, of 1,390 tons, was ready for launching at Deptford, but the officers reported that it would be necessary first to dredge in front of the slip to give sufficient depth. War with Spain was threatening during the early part of 1739, and naval preparations were in hand; the shipwrights seized the opportunity to put pressure on the Boards. Those at Chatham did not wait for the declaration of war in October but mutinied in August, the pleas being that they were unjustly fined, and injured in their perquisite of chips. Four members of the Navy Board went to treat with them and the result was a victory for the men.[278] The Woolwich men followed the example set them; in October, within a week of the declaration of war, they struck work stating that they would not resume it until every article of their petition, which the Navy Board had refused to receive while they were idle, was complied with. Twice members of the Navy Board journeyed to Woolwich to persuade the men, who became so riotous that troops were marched into the town. Woolwich was of less importance than Chatham or Portsmouth, and the Board stood firm; warrants were issued against the ringleaders, but as the men slowly came back to work during November, the Navy Board were ready to forgive and forget. They then received the petition,

---

[272] Navy Bd. Min. 2550, 5 May 1736.
[273] Navy Bd. Misc. 983, 29 Aug. 1743; Admir. and Navy Bd. 2559, 12, 31 Aug., 7 Sept., 14 Oct. 1743; Priv. Acts, 17 Geo. II, cap. 20.

[274] Navy Bd. Min. 30 Nov. 1744; 21 Jan. 1745.
[275] Ibid. 15 Feb. 1737-8.
[276] Admir. and Navy Bd. 2553, 10, 28 Dec. 1739.

[277] Ibid. 30 April 1739.
[278] Ibid. 29, 30 Aug. 1739. The timidity of the Navy Board was even more evident at Portsmouth.

and the answers throw some light on the conditions of work. The men said that it was hard to be discharged when worn out, to which the answer was that no useless man could be kept, and that it had always been considered a favour to continue such a one as a labourer. They asked double wages for Sunday work, and this was an innovation that the authorities promised to consider. The request for a whole, instead of half day, on the customary holidays was refused, but that to be allowed to come ashore for dinner when working on board ships in the river was granted. The everlasting question of 'chips' was another grievance; to that the Navy Board replied that they were entitled 'to such chips as shall be split out by their tools.' Other subjects were extra pay for overtime, and the manner of payment, which was now half yearly. After being lectured about their 'enormities,' the deputation retired 'with great submission.' It has been noticed that in 1710 the greater part of Woolwich yard was paved for hygienic and other reasons; it still remained so unhealthy that in 1742, riggers working there were paid 33 per cent. more than at the other dockyards.[279] There was some unrest at Sheerness, soon quieted, and Deptford remained peaceful; in 1740 there were signs of a renewal of disorder at Chatham but it passed off. The Admiralty solaced their troubles by refusing Anson's indent, just before he sailed, for soap for the use of his squadron, soap not being a necessary, apparently, with the Lords Commissioners.

There was an intention, during the war of the Austrian Succession, of establishing naval hospitals in connexion with all the principal naval bases, and Queenborough was noted as one suitable place, but nothing was done there; there had been a small hospital at Chatham since the early years of the reign of William III. The war also caused an effort to be made to tighten up administrative processes; it was usual to send all ships constructed by private builders to Deptford or Woolwich to be rigged and fitted, and the Admiralty now found fault with delays which had passed unnoticed in time of peace, so that the Navy Board warned the officers at the two yards 'on their peril' not to fail in future.[280] There can have been little improvement, for an Admiralty Order of 20 March 1741-2 directed a general inquiry to be held into the competence of the dockyard officers. Deptford was especially under a cloud at the moment on account of the disgraceful quality of the materials sent out for the hospital building at Gibraltar, the responsibility for which was under investigation. Within a week of the Admiralty Order, on the night of 26 March, another fire occurred in Deptford Yard. If the men were unruly they had what would now be considered wrongs in the hours of summer work, which were from 4 a.m. until 8 p.m., with intervals of half an hour for breakfast and one hour for dinner, while in winter they worked by lantern light; the Navy Board might say with truth that it was as much as 'reasonably' could be expected.[281] Sheerness is seldom mentioned, but the dilatoriness there educed unfavourable comment from the Admiralty who were now rousing the somnolent Navy Board.[282] In 1744 the yard workmen were again formed into regiments, as France had become an enemy and the old possibilities again recurred. There was at once a quarrel between the master shipwright and the clerk of the cheque at Sheerness about precedence as captains; as it was proposed to drill only one company of the dockyard levies every other Saturday this playing at soldiers

---

[279] Admir. and Navy Bd. 2555, 16 Mar. 1741-2.

[280] Navy Bd. Min. 17 Nov. 1741.

[281] Ibid. 22 April 1742.

[282] Ibid. 29 Oct. 1742.

could not have been taken very seriously, and there are indications that the Navy Board looked askance at the whole business. It was an Admiralty fantasy, and when, in 1745, the Lords Commissioners desired to be informed whether the Deptford and Woolwich regiments were properly drilled and officered, the Navy Board knew that if they were it was independent of any assistance from them.

Just about this time relations were strained between the Admiralty and Navy Board because the former was not taking the latter at all at its own valuation. The Duke of Bedford and Lords Sandwich and Anson had become members of a new Admiralty Board from December 1744; this is not the place for a political disquisition, but all three were administrators of a very different quality from their predecessors, for even Sandwich, vile as a politician, had merits when political and personal interests were not at stake. As a First Lord, later, he often brought an element of warm humanity into official phraseology and action. Sandwich was First Lord (for the second time) 1771-82, during which period he immortally damned himself in the eyes of historians. Sir Charles Middleton was Navy Comptroller 1778-90, and used to write plainly and talk plainly to Sandwich. Many years later, when Middleton was himself a peer and First Lord in 1805, he noted during a retrospective moment on an old letter that Sandwich was no worse than those who followed him ' in my time and more zealous for the improvement of the service. He was called a jobber, but they are all equally so, and indeed more so than I ever found him to be though more secret in their manner.' The new Admiralty had not been in office long before the Navy Board were showing a ' proper pride ' when exposed to the unusual experience of their lordships' strictures; as early as May 1745 they found it due to their dignity to protest that they were entitled to criticize the orders of the Admiralty.[283] Worse was in store for them. In July they were curtly reprimanded and told not to allow orders given by them to dockyard officers in July 1744 to remain unnoticed until July 1745.[284] All this has a direct bearing on the working life of the dockyards, for as they were under the immediate government of the Navy Board, they at once fell into a slothful and inefficient condition when that body was itself inefficient. In October the junior Board[285] were told that they did not appear to know their own practice in dealing with prizes, and a fortnight later the Admiralty tried the effect of irony, not expecting ' to hear of so much surprised concern at their supposing a possibility of their Board[286] making a mistake.'[287] Other biting censures addressed to the Navy Board by this Admiralty could be quoted, but any effect was only temporary. As a rule the eighteenth-century Admiralty Boards were pliable and negligent because any real reform would have meant the loss of the enormous political and personal patronage in the hands of the First Lord and others. This particular Board was determined to have both power and patronage while it sought a measure of efficiency, but would no more have sacrificed political influence for the sake of efficiency than its predecessors or successors would have yielded it.

[283] Admir. Sec. In Letters, 7 May 1745. In some matters the Navy Board possessed independent powers.

[284] Admir. Sec. Out Letters, 10 July 1745.

[285] Technically junior, but there was always latent antagonism between the two Boards, and under a weak Admiralty the Navy Board was quite independent. Historically, and as a matter of evolution, the Admiralty was its junior, and was never allowed to forget the fact.

[286] The Navy Board.

[287] Admir. Sec. Min. lii, 7, 19 Oct. 1745.

Admirals Matthews, Lestock, and the other prisoners awaiting trial for their conduct in the action off Toulon in February 1744 were interned within the walls of Chatham dockyard and not allowed to go outside them. In the yard and in the town feeling was so strongly shown in favour of Matthews, who had been Commissioner there, 1736-42, that riots were feared and the prisoners were removed to Deptford. The storehouses known collectively as the Red House at Deptford had been used by victualling contractors and commissioners since the reign of Charles II; in 1742 the place was constituted the principal Navy Victualling depot, and a large distillery was added.[288] The Red House property was not, however, bought by the Victualling Commissioners until 1756,[289] and the Navy Victualling department was not finally removed from Tower Hill until 1785. There was more trouble in the yards in 1745, the ropemakers at Woolwich and Chatham going out on strike; picketing and all modern methods were practised, and at Woolwich the position looked so serious that the Navy Board asked for troops.[290] An innovation was introduced by the Admiralty in May 1746 in the shape of printed forms on which the dockyard Commissioners were to report, by every post, the progress made in the work in hand.[291] Sheerness came to the front in 1747 on account of ' the neglects and mismanagements of the officers ';[292] this came from the Admiralty, for the Navy Board had no fault to find. Between 1744 and 1749, the principal war years, there was a Commissioner in charge at Deptford and Woolwich, but he was discontinued at the peace.

When the peace came the dissatisfaction with the administration, which the Admiralty had shown so often and so strongly, led to the adoption of a new measure, a ' visitation ' of the dockyards by the Lords Commissioners, a proceeding which, dropped for a time, has again become a regular institution. This first one was the consequence of the ' slackness of execution which must arise from the remissness of officers or inefficiency of men,' and was probably due to Sandwich's initiative.[293] The first visit was paid to Woolwich, where many of the workmen were observed to be idle, old, or infirm, but the labourers doing piece-work were estimated to be accomplishing as much in 4½ days as those paid by the day did in 10. Many infractions of the Navy Board orders were noticed: the ships in ordinary were in very bad condition, were inhabited by women and children, and were never visited by the yard officers, who had not overhauled the moorings for three years. When the Master Attendant was sent for he was found to be too old and feeble even to be censured and was superannuated on the spot. The storekeeper was the only officer who won any praise. The others were called together and lectured, the Lords Commissioners assuring them that the Admiralty was determined to enforce discipline and efficiency; to help towards this object notices were to be posted at the gates offering rewards for information affecting either the officers or the workmen.

At Deptford there was the same story of elderly and infirm workmen, of whom 95 were marked for discharge. There were various abuses noticed, but on the whole the yard was better disciplined than Woolwich; the victualling storehouses were in very bad condition, ' the roofs being open in many places,

[288] Admir. Sec. Min. 9 Nov. 1745; Order in Council, 23 Mar. 1742. Cf. *ante*, p. 362.

[289] Ibid. 13 Jan. 1756.

[290] Admir. Sec. In Letters, 14, 15, 17, March 1745.

[291] Admir. Sec. Min. 24 May 1746.

[292] Ibid. 14 Dec. 1747.

[293] Ibid. 18 Aug. 1749.

the walls tumbling down, and everything in disorder.' Neither the storekeeper at Sheerness nor his predecessor had sent in accounts for an indefinite period, but in other respects little fault was found with the yard. At Chatham the storekeeper was so old as to be incapable, and his accounts were $3\frac{1}{2}$ years in arrear. Workmen leaving the yard at noon were seen to be carrying out whole timber in the presence of the officers, of whom five were noted as too old for their work. One of the docks was under survey for repair at a cost of £7,800, but when the responsible persons were examined as to how the estimate was arrived at they could only profess that it was based on the cost of the dock when built. There were several other causes of displeasure, one being the bad condition of the ships in ordinary which signified ' great neglect in the officers.' The Hill House[294] was used as a pay office, but the dockyard officers thought that there was some danger of the seamen looting it one day; the Admiralty therefore decided to let it and use another building, less easy to storm, as a pay office. The Hill House was eventually pulled down when the Chatham lines were extended between 1803-5. There are further references in 1749 to the shoaling of the Medway, although that subject did not come within the purview of the Admiralty examination at the ' visitation.'

The inspection by the Lords Commissioners was followed by a luxuriant crop of orders for the better management of the dockyards, but the Admiralty had forgotten to reckon with the passive stolidity of the Navy Board. In November 1751 the latter were called upon to report as to what they had done in execution of the Admiralty orders, and their answer was so unsatisfactory that it drew another rebuke on them from their superiors.[295] That had no effect, so, in June 1752, the Navy Board were paraded before the Lords Commissioners, told that they had allowed four months to elapse before they gave any directions at all in accordance with the orders issued to them, and, besides neglecting other matters, had ignored the ' positive injunction ' to introduce task (or piece) work. The defence was that the time of the Board had been occupied in preparing returns for Parliament, that there were ' insuperable objections ' to task work for shipbuilding, and that ' they were against any innovation. . . it was impossible to put the workmen of the yards on a better footing than they are at present.' [296] In short, the best of all possible dockyard worlds. One of the greatest faults of Admiralty Boards has always been the worship of precedent; but the weakness was far less marked in them than in the old Navy Boards, largely composed of men brought up in an atmosphere of precedent and who turned to it for support and instruction in all circumstances.

The victualling office at Deptford was again burnt on 16 January 1748-9; according to the *Gentleman's Magazine* damage to the amount of £200,000 was done, but this is probably a great exaggeration. There was another fire in February 1761. At Woolwich so much iron was stolen that it was intended to have the smith's work done by contract, but the tenders were so high that the Admiralty considered that it would be cheaper to submit to theft.[297] How Woolwich Yard obtained fresh water before 1753 we are not told, but in that year a contract was made with Mr. Bowater by which he was to supply it for £60 a year; he was to build a reservoir, and the Admiralty laid down pipes into

[294] *Ante,* p. 341.
[295] Admir. Sec. Min. 12 Nov., 17 Dec. 1751.
[296] Admir. Sec. Min. 3 June 1752. Probably the Navy Board thought of the Admiralty as Congreve thought of Woman :—
' The Pains they cause are many,
And long and hard to bear,
The Joys they give (if any)
Few, short, and insincere.'
[297] Ibid. 9 May, 3 July 1751.

the yard.[298] 'Chips' came under consideration again this year, the new rule being that the amount taken out of a yard was not to be more than could be carried untied under one arm.[299] A decision of April 1754, to enlarge Deptford double dock, may be noticed because the new work was to have piers of stone and two-leaf, instead of wicket, gates showing how slowly timber construction and the ancient gates gave place to stone and modern gates in the older dock-yards.[300] In March 1754 there were 801 men in pay at Deptford, 698 at Woolwich, 1,188 at Chatham, and 276 at Sheerness; by October 1761, when the Seven Years' War was nearing its end, there were 1,074 at Deptford, 1,080 at Woolwich, 1,720 at Chatham, and 455 at Sheerness.[301] The dockyard regiments were revived at the beginning of the war; Deptford and Woolwich provided one each, and Sheerness supplied two companies for that at Chatham. Thomas Slade, the Surveyor of the Navy, was colonel, and Adam Hayes, the master shipwright, lieutenant-colonel of the Deptford regiment. The embodiment was, of course, purely for local defence, but these assumptions of military rank and knowledge must have provoked some derision among officers of the regulars. It had been proposed, in 1701, to inclose Chatham dockyard by fortifications, but as there was then no possibility of invasion the project was dropped; the outlook was more uncertain during the Seven Years' War, and the Chatham lines were constructed in 1755-6.

The 'chips' regulation of 1753 provoked discontent which burst out into riots at Chatham in June 1755; the men struck work for a month and the ringleaders were punished by being sent to sea.[302] A new Admiralty was in office in 1757, but they spared the Navy Board as little as their predecessors had spared them. The Navy Board were told that their reports on the progress of shipbuilding in the dockyards seemed intended 'rather to mislead than to inform' the Admiralty, and were directed 'to transmit an account that can be depended upon.'[303] In the middle of the war the Woolwich men took the opportunity of airing their grievances, which were that some had been sent to sea, others discharged for no offence, that they were not paid for working overtime, and that they had no proper medical attendance.[304] Not having received any answer within a week to their petition, or demands, they declared their intention of striking; this brought some members of the Navy Board to Woolwich in a hurry with instructions from the Admiralty to placate the men if possible. They also, to be prepared for eventualities, took a party of the Guards with them; only a few of the shipwrights attended to discuss matters, and the Navy Board decided to press the ringleaders for sea service. This, they thought, might 'occasion some disturbance,' so the soldiers were left at Woolwich, but the measure appears, as usual, to have cowed the men.[305] In October 1758 the Deptford men were 'riotous'; some thirty of the leaders were discharged, but the *émeute* was crushed without the necessity of sending any of the men to sea.[306] In 1759 the fear of invasion was somewhat more acute than usual until Hawke won his great victory in Quiberon Bay. But in June the Admiralty woke to the fact that although the yard men had been regimented

---

[298] Admir. Sec. Min. 23 Aug. 1753.

[299] Admir. and Navy Bd. 2507, 4 May 1753.

[300] Admir. Cont. Misc. 91, 30 April 1754.

[301] Admir. and Navy Bd. 2187, 14 Mar. 1754; 2193, 6 Oct. 1761.

[302] Ibid. 2188, pp. 343, 350, 352, 361, 364, 374.

[303] Admir. Sec. Min. 7 Jan. 1757.

[304] Ibid. 29 April 1757.

[305] Admir. and Navy Bd. 2189, 30 April 1757.

[306] Admir. Sec. Min. 23, 25, 26 Oct. 1758.

at the beginning of the war, 'they have not hitherto had opportunities of being exercised in the use of their arms';[307] they were, therefore, to be drilled twice a week for three weeks ' taking particular care that they be taught to fire.' After that, a drill once a week would keep them sufficiently skilled, it was supposed, to meet French troops of the line. Nothing was said about training the dockyard colonels and their officers.

If the Navy Board had known the state of both the civil and military branches of the French marine towards the close of the Seven Years' War, they would have had a good dialectical answer to the criticisms of the Admiralty. That government was nearly penniless and had no credit; as a consequence the magazines were empty of stores, ordnance and munitions were insufficient and inferior in quality, ships were rotting unrepaired, while the dockyards were idle for lack of materials. On the civil side, therefore, the conditions were similar to the worst days of James I and Charles I, not again possible in England. But in the early seventeenth century, whatever the shortcomings of the administration, our officers and men never, as a whole, lost confidence in themselves. Here, as the result of persistent ill-fortune culminating in the terrible disaster of Quiberon Bay, the French officers' corps, feeling themselves outfought and outskilled, depressed by the little interest in the Navy and its welfare shown by the Court, had completely lost its *moral* and, for the time, had forfeited its own self-respect, that of the social class from which it was drawn, and that of the men. An angry dissatisfaction with themselves, the first stage toward recovery, showed itself in bitter quarrels, often resulting in duels, between the civil and military officers.

The test of the Seven Years' War proved the inadequacy of the existing dockyard accommodation, but there was neither time nor money during the conflict for any important improvements. Beyond the addition of building slips in most of the yards little had been done to increase their utility. When Lord Egmont became First Lord in 1763, he and his advisers determined to spend large amounts on Portsmouth and Plymouth, but the home yards were abandoned, so far as improvements were concerned, on account of the difficulties of navigation. The river in front of Deptford was steadily shoaling; ships could only go down from the yard with the wind in five out of the thirty-two points of the compass, and had been known to be delayed two months waiting for a wind. From Woolwich they had, out of the thirty-two points, seven available, but, as line-of-battle ships were becoming larger, they were finding it difficult to leave the dockyard with their guns and stores on board. A little later it became necessary to send the stores in lighters with the ships and tranship them in Northfleet Hope or at Gravesend, the same proceeding, conversely, being needful when such ships were coming up the Thames. Chatham was disadvantaged by there being only six points of the compass for winds which would take down ships of the line, and ten which would take them up, and that only for a few days during spring tides. The difficulties of navigation in the Medway were to some extent obviated during part of the eighteenth century by placing posts, for warping ships, on both banks; these were discontinued in 1773 when warping buoys were laid down.[308]

Lord Egmont thought that some use might be made of the embouchure of

---

[307] Admir. Sec. Min. 19 June 1759.

[308] Admir. Cont. Misc. 27 Aug. 1773. A beacon was placed on Okehamness Point in the same year.

the Medway, and, Sheerness being on a lee shore, turned his attention to the Isle of Grain and had borings made, but the subsoil was found to be so bad that it daunted the engineers. Then, in 1765, reluctant to abandon the idea of a dockyard on the North Sea, where so much time would be gained in comparison with the river yards, the question of adapting Sheerness was again debated. The yard had been growing river-ward because as the old breakwater ships broke up they served as foundations for extensions of made ground. The yard had been found most useful, during the wars between 1739-63, for docking and supplying cruisers and the North Sea squadron when the ships did not exceed 1,200 or 1,300 tons; probably it was about this period that it gained its Service soubriquet of 'Sheernasty.' Sir Thomas Slade, the Surveyor of the Navy, drew out plans for an entirely new yard with dry docks and accessories; chain moorings were at once put down for line-of-battle ships to lie there in ordinary instead of at Chatham. When this had been done someone found out that the port was infested with the Teredo Navalis, 'which is very singular, being the only port in England where they are known to bite to any degree of consequence.'[309] The plague was supposed to be due to the old break-water ships, full of the Teredo from all parts of the world, and to vessels from foreign waters undergoing quarantine in Stangate Creek. The plan of coppering ships' hulls had just been introduced, but it was still in the experimental stage and was not as yet known to be a remedy. It was also considered doubtful whether, from the nature of the ground, deeper docks could be made at Sheerness; therefore the scheme of a large dockyard was laid aside.

In 1762 the yard wages were fifteen months in arrear, but the men were discounting their pay tickets at $7\frac{1}{2}$ per cent.; that sounds bad enough, but it indicates an enormous advance in the national credit from its condition in the beginning of the century when such tickets could only have been cashed at a discount of from 25 to 50 per cent.[310] The tide of national success rose high in several directions, but particularly in maritime trade; as a result private ship-builders were so busy, and could afford to give such high wages, that it was difficult to keep a proper number of men in the Government yards. The peace estimate was fourteen shipwrights for every 1,000 tons of shipping in the Navy, so that on the then existing 300,000 tons 4,200 of them were required.[311] Lack of space forbids detailed reference to the Admiralty visitations of the dockyards which followed that of 1749, but that of 1764 must be noticed. Lord Egmont was a great favourite with the shipwrights, and justly so, for it was due to him that a superannuation scheme for their benefit was then introduced. The Lords Commissioners had remarked that there were many aged and infirm men among the shipwrights who could not be discharged 'without great inhumanity and a great discouragement to the service.'[312] The Board decided to memorialize the crown to establish a superannuation fund, and it was authorized by an Order in Council of 12 October 1764. The Order sanctioned a pension of £20 a year to ordinary shipwrights, but the number was not to exceed one in fifty of those employed; thus, although there were 105 men suitable for superannuation at the moment, only 66 could be favoured, the others having to wait. It was not very liberal but it was a beginning. In 1771 the privilege

---

[309] King's MS. 44, fol. 20. This was not true: Portsmouth was, or had been, infected to such a degree that it had almost been abandoned.
[310] Admir. and Navy Bd. 2194, 22 Jan. 1762.
[311] Admir. Sec. Min. 18 Nov. 1765.
[312] Ibid. 9 Oct. 1764.

was extended to one in forty of those employed,[313] and in 1792 a large super-numerary list was added; by another Order in Council of 6 October 1802 the possible amount of pension was raised to £28. Ropemakers were not included in the superannuation because they could finish a day's work by 11 a.m. and then either earn overtime or go to work elsewhere.[314] They were also allowed to keep public-houses, a privilege forbidden to the other workmen.

In 1764 the question of 'chips' awoke renewed attention. The Navy Board, in an access of vigilance, wrote to the Admiralty[315] that the men not only cut up good timber but used their working time for the purpose, that small articles were concealed in the bundles, and that to allow 'what is called the Poor' into the yards twice a week to collect chips was equally prejudicial from the point of view of theft. They proposed entire abolition and an allowance in lieu of the perquisite, but nothing was done and the yard visitations of 1767 evoked fresh angry comments from the authorities. Chatham was then the worst, for the men held periodical sales of their plunder, and in the dockyard, as a whole, there was 'sloth and inactivity among the people beyond what we observed anywhere else.'[316] Hitherto, the dockyards had been patrolled by watchmen drawn from among the workmen. This system had always been inefficient, but little trouble was taken during peace to keep strangers out of the yards and there were repeated orders and censures which show that the officials were hardly more successful during war. From the end of 1764 the watchmen were replaced by marines, and the dockyards were to be considered garrisons under the command of the chief civil officer who was given a commission.[317] Every method must depend largely on the intelligence of sub-ordinates and there was still something wanting after the reform. In May 1767 a Comte de Chabrillan, staying at Rochester, landed, from the river front, in Chatham yard and walked through it until stopped by the porter at the gate. The sentry at the river front, who had allowed him to pass, was court-martialled, but what story had lulled his vigilance, if any had been necessary, we are not told. It appears from a circular order of 1768 that it was 'known' that foreigners were in England for the purpose of obtaining plans of men-of-war and of the dockyards.[318] It was evidence of the admitted excellence of the Navy in the last war. In 1770, when war with Spain was anticipated, the marine guard was withdrawn and a new police system, adapted from the ancient one, put in force. Of day warders there were six at Woolwich and Sheerness, respectively, seven at Deptford, and eight at Chatham; at night there were 36 watchmen at Chatham, 30 at Deptford and Woolwich, respectively, and 14 at Sheerness.[319]

Deptford was enlarged in 1765 by ground taken in from the Victualling Office; this permitted the construction of new masthouses, a new mast pond, and a building slip, the last estimated to cost £3,818, and the mast pond, £16,963.[320] The new ground was not enclosed by a brick wall until 1769. Benjamin Franklin's lightning conductors were fitted in Chatham dockyard in

[313] Order in Council, 25 Sept. 1771.

[314] Admir. and Navy Bd. 2201, 11 Dec. 1771.

[315] Ibid. 2196, 5 Mar. 1764.

[316] Ibid. 2198, 5 June 1767.

[317] Ibid. 2196, 21 May 1764; Admir. Sec. Min. 5 Nov. 1764.

[318] Admir. and Navy Bd. 2508, 9 Aug. 1768.

[319] Ibid. 2200, 19 Jan. 1771. In 1776, after 'Jack the Painter' had been condemned for arson at Portsmouth yard, he said in his confession that he had never been challenged while walking about any of the dockyards, including the Kentish ones.

[320] Admir. Cont. Misc. 10 Jan. 1766; Admir. Sec. Min. 28 Nov. 1765, 12 Jan. 1770.

1771. Portsmouth and Plymouth were steadily expanding, but the resolution not to make any enlargement of importance in the Kentish yards considerably restricted the docks available in view of the increasing number of ships, so that in 1772 the Admiralty decided to build and repair all frigates and sloops in private yards leaving the government establishments for line-of-battle ships only. At this date there were 939 men at Deptford, 868 at Woolwich, 1,553 at Chatham, and 439 at Sheerness as compared with 2,228 at Portsmouth and 2,033 at Plymouth; in the home yards rather less than half the totals were shipwrights. In 1773 embezzlements on a large scale were discovered among the storekeepers' clerks at Portsmouth, and this led to an alteration of the system of appointment in all the dockyards. In the early days of the Navy, high officials, such as the Treasurer and Comptroller, had found one clerk sufficient, while the yard officers had none. Gradually, the necessity for a large staff had arisen, and their appointment was a perquisite of the officers, who received a premium of 150 to 200 guineas, while the clerk's salary was usually about £30 a year. It was an incentive to dishonesty, and when not actually thieves the clerks were notoriously open to bribery to expedite business or favour applicants. The Admiralty now decided that they would nominate in future to the storekeepers' clerkships and that the men appointed should give security, but salaries were also raised by £10.[321] To any one not accustomed to the administrative history of the Navy it will appear extraordinary to be told that the order was ignored, and that the Parliamentary Committee of 1788 found that the storekeepers were still taking premiums from their clerks. Another abuse forbidden in 1767 was the demand of fees by dockyard clerks from the workmen before the former would make out pay notes for the work done,[322] but this offence also continued into the nineteenth century.

In 1774 Chatham dockyard covered 68 acres,[323] all enclosed within the fortifications of 1756; in area it had increased from 61 acres 1 rood in 1746.[324] In the time of Elizabeth any ship of the Navy could have been moored above Upnor, but now 74-gun ships were of 1,600 or 1,700 tons; therefore in the four miles between Rochester bridge and the lower end of Gillingham Reach there were moorings for only five such at their ordinary draught; if kept light, which was considered very prejudicial to them, depth of water could be found for twenty. The four docks of the preceding century had not been increased in number, but there were six building slips, three of which dated from the recent Seven Years' War. The Sheerness dry-dock could receive 60-gun ships, but it was difficult to retain workmen there, both on account of the lack of accommodation for them and the reputed unhealthiness of the district. In consideration of these drawbacks the Admiralty granted certain privileges to the men; housing was supplied for a certain number of them and for their families while the others lived on board the breakwater ships. In 1774 there were 425 people living in 192 rooms, and 551 in 258 cabins on board the ships. Water was provided free from Chatham, the Queenborough well of 1725 having failed to give satisfaction. Captain T. Hyde Page, an engineer officer, was entrusted with the task of attempting to find water at Sheerness itself, and he succeeded in obtaining a plentiful supply from a well sunk in Fort Townshend in 1781-2. His success was, in a great measure, owing to the aid of Mr. Cole,

[321] Admir. and Navy Bd. 2508, 8 May 1773. [322] Ibid. 6 Oct. 1767. [323] King's MS. 44. [324] Add. MS. 31323Y.

an engine-maker of Lambeth, ' a very ingenious man.'[325]   Deptford was still held to be the most convenient centre for the receipt and distribution of stores. It contained only the two docks, but there were six building slips, three opening on to the basin, and three on to the river.   Those on the river had from 12 to 14 ft. of water in front of them, and the double dock had from 16 to 18 ft.; ships of any size had therefore to be launched very light.   At Woolwich there was more water, but the most important section of the yard was the ropery which supplied Deptford and all the foreign stations.   The yard had not progressed beyond the original two docks, but there were now four slips. More land, always westward, was taken from the Bowater family in 1779 and used for the construction of storehouses and building slips.[326]

The visitation of 1774 showed, as usual, many abuses existing in the dockyards.   A number of men attached to the ships in ordinary appeared at the muster once a month and followed other occupations in the intervals. Persons ' of all callings in reduced circumstances,' and of any age, had been entered as shipwrights, with the result that after only a few years' service many of them were only fit for superannuation.   In consequence of this discovery there was an order that in future no one of more than 35 years of age was to be entered, but the American war and the resulting demand for shipwrights compelled the Admiralty to relax this rule in February 1778.[327]   When the shipwrights decided to strike it was usually during a war or when one was approaching, and the advent of the American War of Independence gave them their opportunity once more.   The excuse was the introduction of piece-work which the Navy Board had supposed, or wished to suppose, would be to the advantage of the men; these complained, probably with truth, that they were given timber not ready for use and kept waiting for accessories such as bolts, treenails and fittings; others were not permitted to work during the dinner interval, and ' chips ' were again a grievance.[328]   The Admiralty sanctioned a partial reintroduction of day work, but the men were determined, and evidently in communication, so that they struck simultaneously in all the yards; as was customary those at Woolwich were inclined to lawless proceedings and troops again appeared there.   When it was understood that the Admiralty were firm many of the men at once gave in, but three months elapsed before the most obstinate, seeing that their places were being filled up by applicants from the private yards, came back to be re-entered.   The ringleaders were refused, and the occasion was taken to reject those over 40 years of age.[329]   Earnings were said to range from 3s. 1½d. to 5s. 7½d. a day, but these rates, good in themselves, might co-exist with individual hardship.   There had been some serious incendiarism at Portsmouth and, in March 1777, there was an attempt to cause another fire there.   This made the Admiralty reflect that there were ' no established regulations ' at any of the dockyards for dealing with fire; the deficiency was remedied by the promulgation of standing orders as to the

[325] Add. MS. 23655 fol. 89. This MS. states the Queenborough well to have been effective, but expensive; the King's MS. quoted above, also official, pronounces it a failure.

[326] Admir. Sec. Min. 12 July 1779. Also in 1784, according to

Vincent (*Records of Woolwich,* 61, 277).

[327] Admir. and Navy Bd. 2508, 22 July 1774; Admir. Sec. Min. 7 Feb. 1778.

[328] Admir. and Navy Bd. 2203, 3 Feb., 5, 6 July 1775; Admir.

Sec. Min. 17, 25 May, 17, 18 July 1775; *Ann. Register,* 1775.

[329] Admir. and Navy Bd. 2203, fol. 210. American agents tried to induce some of the dismissed men to emigrate to the Colonies where coming events would have made them very useful (Ho. Off. Papers, Aug. and Sept. 1775).

duties of officers and men, and the provision of a proper supply of water, fire engines and appliances.[330]   At Chatham there were to be eighteen large, and twelve small, engines, 'fire poles with hooks,' ladders, etc., and Deptford, Woolwich, and Sheerness were to be supplied in proportion.   The first serious fire, after these preparations, was at Woolwich in 1802 when they did not prevent a very heavy loss.[331]

Notwithstanding the failure of the strike in 1775 the shipwrights refused piece-work, and the middle of the war was not a fitting time to risk further trouble.   The Navy Board did not press the matter but directed the yard officers to see that the men did something like their duty at day work;[332] keeping the workmen to the mark depended on the foremen and quartermen who were most often slack themselves.   When peace returned, the Boards could afford to be more independent, and, although they did not touch the thorny piece and day work question, they made other regulations intended to improve discipline. A new and important one was the introduction of a ' black list,' of which a copy was to be kept at each dockyard, containing descriptions of officers and men who had been dismissed.[333]   There had been occasional orders previously that men dismissed from one yard should not be employed at another, but they must have been dead letters and this was the first systematic attempt to prevent it.   Chips, again, which the men spent ' no inconsiderable portion of their time ' in cutting up, provoked comment ; the general inclination to theft was the cause of a curious regulation that overcoats and wide trousers were not to be worn, and that labourers working in storehouses were not to wear trousers at all.

The American War threw into relief once more the drawbacks of the Thames and Medway.   In 1785, Lord Howe, then First Lord, had the *Brunswick*, 74, built at Deptford on lines which gave her two feet less draught than other 74's of the same tonnage, hoping, if she were successful, thus to introduce a model which would obviate the effects of the increasing shallowness opposite the river yards and in the Medway; the ship, however, was a failure. Lord Howe then planned the enlargement of Sheerness, but nothing was done. Parliament was now beginning to take an inquisitive interest in the civil administration of the Navy, and a committee of 1788 brought to light some odd facts.   In the dockyards fees, or bribes under that euphemism, were the motive power.   The officers received premiums, amounting sometimes to hundreds of pounds, for the appointments of their clerks; the clerks took fees from contractors, for stamping the pay notes of the workmen, for making out invoices and bills, and for every detail of their ordinary daily duty.   Presents of hampers of wine were called ' hampering ' the clerks.   The fees of the men took the form of ' chips '; it was remarked that they stopped work, half an hour before the bell rung for their release, to collect chips or to cut up valuable timber to make chips, and that much copper and brass went out with the wood. In 1786 Middleton wrote to Pitt that ' the dockyards were without discipline or method, and the Board without decision or control . . . the public suffers in thousands for a trifling gratuity received by a yard officer,' but [he continued], as their appointments were due to interest at the Admiralty they were indifferent

[330] Admir. Sec. Min. 22 May 1777; Admir. and N. Bd. 2205, 21 Oct. 1777.

[331] *Ann. Register.*
[332] Admir. and Navy Bd. 2508, 3 Nov. 1779.

[333] Ibid. 2509, 24 June 1783. There was already a ' black list ' of naval officers at the Admiralty.

to censure or criticism. But Pitt himself was criticized by an ex-Secretary of State for his indifference to capacity in his appointments at the Admiralty, seeing that he put at the Board Commissioners 'who do not know larboard from starboard.' Thirty years earlier Henry Fox told Dodington 'capacity is so little necessary for most employment that you seem to forget that there is one where it is absolutely so, viz. the Admiralty.'

The period of the Revolutionary war was a halcyon time of plunder in the dockyards until Lord St. Vincent began drastic measures of reform after he became First Lord in 1801. In the meanwhile the deficiencies of the Thames yards were always goading the Admiralty to resolves to undertake improvements which, however, never came into being. In 1800 the engineers reported to Lord Spencer, the then First Lord, that any money spent on Deptford, Woolwich, and Chatham would be wasted on account of the distances from the sea, difficulty and delay in navigation, shallowness in front of the yards, and want of accommodation for ships within their precincts. At Woolwich the deep channel had shifted to the Essex side of the river, so that the moorings were in five feet less water than in former years. The want of water at Deptford was attributed to the action of London Bridge as a dam in causing deposit, and the foundations of Chatham yard were considered precarious. Lord Spencer fell back on Lord Egmont's idea of using the Isle of Grain,[334] and St. Vincent agreed with him, so that borings were again undertaken, but again the results were unfavourable.[335] No one recommended the enlargement of Sheerness. Besides the unhealthiness of the situation there were doubts whether stable foundations could be obtained, and the inconvenience, or worse, of the exposure of its front to a heavy sea in certain winds would always remain. In 1802 a report was presented to the Admiralty which recommended the formation of a new arsenal farther down the Thames, on a small promontory between Greenhithe and Northfleet. This was approved, not only by St. Vincent and many other admirals, but by Pitt and Lords Melville and Barham. During the last decade of the eighteenth century certain improvements in machinery were adopted in the dockyards, but as the buildings had never been planned with any expectation of the use of steam, heavy engines, or co-ordinated work, they always remained inferior in arrangement to the best private yards. Lord Melville, writing in 1810,[336] said that their equipment differed little from that of a century earlier, and that in 18 years they had not provided more than one-half the cables and cordage, one-sixth of the anchors, and one-fourth of the sails used in the Navy. Yet upwards of £40,000 had been spent at Woolwich between 1791 and 1793 in improving the buildings.[337]

When St. Vincent came into office the Baltic fleet of 1801 was in preparation, and the shipwrights thought this a good opportunity to enforce an increase of wages. The movement was thoroughly organized, delegates from all the dockyards arriving in London to compel the submission of the Admiralty to the demands of their 'constituents.' The agitation, or conspiracy, must have been arranged while Lord Spencer was First Lord, and it seems as if they

[334] *Ante*, p. 376.
[335] Add. MS. 27884, fol. 12.
[336] *A Letter . . . to the Rt. Hon. Spencer Perceval . . .* Lond. 1810, pp. 24, 27.

[337] Admir. Cont. In Letters, i, 15 Feb. 1820. The introduction of chain cables threw a further strain on the machinery of the old buildings. The first man-of-war supplied with them in modern times was H.M.S. *Conqueror,* sent out on the St. Helena station in 1815. They had been tried in 1791 in the French navy.

thought that the change of men would make no difference; if so they must have been very ignorant of St. Vincent's reputation in the fleet. He would have preferred to act on his own responsibility, but thought himself bound to bring the matter before the Cabinet which, much against his wish, authorized certain concessions. The delegates rejected these and 'insisted' on double pay; then St. Vincent, on his side, insisted on being allowed a free hand. The delegates were at once dismissed the service, every mutinous shipwright was threatened with the same fate, and the military arrangements hinted ominously at what would happen if the men indulged in any disorder, perhaps even if they gave any excuse for the use of the troops. The ordinary shipwright was not ready to risk his life nor to sacrifice his position, and the insubordination at once ceased, but 89 men were discharged from the Kentish dockyards of whom 21 belonged to Deptford.[338] A dockyard officer of 1812 notices that the Deptford men were 'very boisterous and unruly in time of war,'[339] and evidently much the same temper was shown in the other yards.

In 1792 the Admiralty, in response to Parliament, had promised an investigation into the civil administration, but the stress of war, or the fear of loss of political patronage in appointments, had prevented the redemption of the pledge. In St. Vincent's opinion the civil departments were 'rotten to the very core,' and nearly every admiral was of his mind. Lords Spencer and St. Vincent were at one in their judgment of the administration, but while Lord Spencer would have reformed the system, sparing individuals, St. Vincent brought to Whitehall the quarter-deck prejudices against the civil officers in many respects justified by experience. One of his colleagues, Sir Thomas Troubridge, commenced his official career with the openly expressed view that the hanging of all the master shipwrights was an urgently needed measure of reform. As soon, therefore, as the Peace of Amiens gave the opportunity St. Vincent directed the Navy Board to commence an investigation. The spirit in which they entered into it is shown by the fact that they arranged for the Surveyors of the Navy to inquire into the management of Deptford and Woolwich; these two yards were under their superintendence so that they were requested to report upon themselves. Lord St. Vincent thereupon took the inquiry out of the hands of the Navy Board and determined that there should be an examination by the Board of Admiralty. The Lords Commissioners discovered such startling malversations and abuses that St. Vincent decided that nothing short of a public Parliamentary inquiry would meet the case. The result of the Parliamentary inquiry was the issue of fifteen reports on all the branches of administration, and the impeachment of Henry Dundas, Lord Melville, who had been Treasurer of the Navy. It is of course impossible to give here even a synopsis of the voluminous reports but, for the dockyards, they demonstrated that all the malpractices, which, as has been shown, had been customary for centuries, had swollen with a tropical exuberance during the opportunities of the war. And this notwithstanding that no witness was compelled to give answers incriminating himself. A London police magistrate estimated that the plunder from Portsmouth alone reached £1,000,000 annually,[340] but the law officers of the Crown thought that the more moderate

[338] *Parl. Papers* (1806), xi, 360. [339] Lang, *Improvements in Naval Architecture*, Lond. 1853, p. 3. [340] Colquhoun, *Police of the Metropolis*, p. 75.

sum of £500,000 would cover the losses from all the dockyards. The scale of robbery can be gauged from one prosecution. In 1803 two men were convicted of defrauding the Government by means of false vouchers procured from the clerks at Deptford and Woolwich; for work of the value of £235 5s. they had obtained £2,415 13s.[341]

In reading these accounts of the dockyards it should, however, always be borne in mind that through the centuries the naval administration was better than any existing among our rivals elsewhere. The safeguard was that, co-existing with the poisonous political element inside and outside the Admiralty, there was always an antidote and a disinfectant in the form of a naval element which usually knew its business, indulged in nepotism and jobbery only in the lower and less important executive grades and, even among the political admirals, put Blake's quintessential maxim of not allowing 'foreigners to fool us' far in front of all political gospels. The seamen had prejudices, but these shams were outside their real lives. The sea is always a hard mistress; harder still in the days of sail, imperfect scientific appliances, and incomplete knowledge. Their lives had been spent in contact with realities, and their daily safety depended on qualities of brain and hand, and a tireless vigilance and foresight which could never be relaxed except at peril of instant destruction. They were hard men, sometimes even bizarre brutes, but they were strong men, and the ceaseless conflict with Nature endowed them with qualities of directness, loyalty, and duty which, combined with their professional knowledge—although often the best of them never reached the Admiralty Board Room—always in issues of real moment enforced their decisions on the politicians.

But they had the defects of their qualities. Their lives were passed in an intellectual vacuum so far as the 'humanities' were concerned, with few opportunities for obtaining culture or knowledge other than such knowledge as resulted from individual observation in their wanderings. Thus the naval officer was frequently ignorant of simple things outside his profession, often prejudiced, dictatorial, and partial. There was also another cause—pathological—explaining the peppery, narrow-minded, imperious admirals and captains of fiction and the drama who were no fanciful creations of authors and dramatists, and whose defects of mind and temper were more often the result of morbid physical changes due to the unhealthy conditions of a lifetime spent at sea than of any original bent of mind or of the habit of command. Man may be defined as an unstable chemical combination, and his mental and physical reactions are the result of chemical processes and changes which may be hindered or helped by the experiences of the race during millions of years as to the best media for obtaining and retaining the maximum of health and strength. The most important of these experiences have been those gained in matters of diet and the physiological or pathological consequences which ensue from errors in food. The diet sheet of the old Navy, mostly made up of salted, dried, and stale foods, originally of bad or indifferent quality, often consumed for weeks or months on end, had, in conjunction with almost sedentary lives, its natural result in inducing chronic constipation with all the disastrous sequelæ which follow, a condition which is one of the most common

[341] *Ann. Register.* In 1814 a 74-gun ship was supposed to re- quire 2,000 oak trees, i.e. 3,000 loads of timber; large oppor- tunities for everyone in one item alone.

yet one of the most serious to which humanity is subject. There is hardly a disease in which chronic constipation is not, if not the exciting, at least the predisposing cause, and it usually conduced to the fatal termination which, whatever the actual complaint, swept off so many crews in the seventeenth and eighteenth centuries. In elderly men it induces, eventually, a condition of intestinal stasis, from which some of the admirals certainly died, and which in any case causes a frame of mind irritable in action yet sluggish in mental processes and lacking the capacity for concentrated thought. I have little doubt that many of the notorious eighteenth-century naval scandals—Lestock and Matthews, Keppel and Palliser, and Byng's fatal hesitations—were really due to the intestines rather than the brain, which was poisoned by auto-toxins inhibiting the higher faculties of self-control and clear thinking which would otherwise have made them prefer their duty to the impulsive gratification of personal feelings and temper. No medical man who studies eighteenth-century victualling records would believe, even if there were not documentary evidence to controvert it, Nelson's 'band of brothers' to be anything but one of his emotional lapses. Most of the captains were very quarrelsome. The world has a classic in 'The Influence of Sea-Power on History'; one nearly as important has yet to be written on the influence of disease on sea-power commencing with the effect of malaria on the Greek thalassocracy.

During the Revolutionary war barracks had been built at Sheerness for the workmen, but they much preferred the breakwater ships where they were free from observation, and where 'there was no species of infamy unpractised.' In 1802, by the orders of St. Vincent and the hand of Sir Isaac Coffin, the Commissioner, they were ejected, but the lawless rabble attempted Coffin's life in revenge. Between 1792 and 1810 the dockyard accommodation was overtaxed so that, in shipbuilding, the government yards had not, in that time, provided more than half the new line-of-battle ships and only one-fifth of the smaller vessels added to the Navy; nor had they executed more than a proportion of the repairs. Dock and slip facilities were limited, the rate of work was slow, nor is it at all certain that the prevailing belief that, although more deliberate, the royal yards turned out better work than the private yards was well founded. Officially, a dockyard-built ship was supposed to have a third longer life than one from a private yard although there is no doubt that at times both of them turned out some very bad work; but as the private-yard ships were built under the inspection of a Navy Board official the departmental responsibility remained. Also the dockyards were supposed to build more cheaply but, if true, the relative prices did not allow for losses by theft and idleness. At Deptford, besides the two dry-docks, there were now only five slips; on the three facing the river first-rates could be built, but nothing larger than 32-gun ships on the two opening into the basin, of which the gates gave an opening of 37 ft.[342] At Woolwich, as well as the two dry-docks there were four building slips; two of them were available for first-rates, and two for 74-gun ships. Chatham possessed four dry-docks and six slips; on three of these first-rates could be constructed, third-rates on two of them, and small vessels on the sixth. The depth of water on the sills of the dry-docks at high-water spring tides varied between 17 ft. 3 in. and 18 ft. 4 in., therefore large ships could not be docked at all at neap tides, and first- and second-rates only with spring tides. At

[342] Admir. Cont. In Letters, i, 26 July 1805; *Parl. Papers* (1805), viii, 271. Cf. p. 379.

Sheerness there were, by 1808, two dry-docks;[343] there were two slips, on the largest of which a 64-gun ship could be built, the other was only suitable for sloops of 300 tons.

The idea of the new dockyard at Northfleet had not been dropped, and as the war continued year after year it seemed to become more and more necessary. St. Vincent would have converted the whole of Deptford into a victualling yard. Woolwich was hopeless; dredging went on there at enormous expense, but the mud accumulated as fast as removed, and it is said that £125,000 had been expended in dredging in ten years.[344] At Chatham, as we have seen, first- and second-rates could only be docked at high-water spring tides, and then with difficulty. The Northfleet site was probably suggested by Joseph Whidbey, Master Attendant at Woolwich; in 1807 John Rennie the elder, with other engineers and assisted by Whidbey, surveyed the ground and sent in a report which, after giving reasons for the decline in value of the other yards, dwelt on Northfleet as the best situation for a new arsenal.[345] Rennie sent a plan of the proposed dockyard which was to have eight building slips and eight dry-docks, basins, and a wet-dock of $87\frac{1}{4}$ acres capable of containing 60 line-of-battle ships and 50 frigates, thus saving the expense of moorings and the delay in working upon them when lying in the tideway. The necessary land, the Wadham estate, was bought, but the estimated cost of the yard was £4,500,000, and every one in authority expected that that sum would be much exceeded. The war was costing so much that it was impossible to lavish money for any purpose not absolutely essential, and perhaps vested interests in the existing yards had some adverse influence. When the war ended retrenchment was the one object in view, and there was a further reason for hesitation in the character of the sub-soil which was said to be as bad as that of the Isle of Grain; the Northfleet project was therefore abandoned, the land being sold in 1831. As an alternative Sheerness was taken up in spite of its obvious disadvantages. In 1808 the Commissioner reported that the foundations were giving way, and that he feared that a heavy gale and high tide, coming together, would destroy the yard; it was made of timber thrown together ' as wanted,' and in 1813 was in such a dilapidated state as to be almost useless, so that entire reconstruction was requisite.[346] John Rennie designed a new yard of granite to cover $64\frac{3}{4}$ acres and containing five dry-docks and suitable basins, machine shops and storehouses. It was commenced in 1815, the dockyard reopened in 1823, and finished in 1826; remarkable skill was shown in overcoming the difficulties connected with the unstable foundation and in dealing with other engineering problems.[347] The dock gates were of cast iron, the first of the kind, and part of the yard was paved with iron blocks, the discarded ballast of men-of-war. There were facilities for dealing with nine sail-of-the-line simultaneously; the total cost was upwards of £2,000,000.

Chatham Yard was enlarged and improved in 1820 and the years ensuing; 188 acres, part of St. Mary's Island, were bought,[348] but the dockyard did not actually extend to St. Mary's Creek. Among other additions another dry-dock was built. An Act was obtained in 1833 authorizing the purchase of the leases of wharves and land adjoining Woolwich with power to buy the freehold.[349]

[343] Add. MS. 31323F². Cf. p. 378.
[344] Vincent, *Records of Woolwich*, i, 288.
[345] Add. MS. 27884.
[346] *Parl. Papers* (1826), xx, 503.
[347] *Autobiography of Sir John Rennie*, 164; Smiles, *Lives of the Engineers*, s.v. Rennie. Only three dry-docks were actually completed.
[348] 1 and 2 Geo. IV, cap. 107.
[349] 3 and 4 Wm. IV, cap. 65

The water conditions had not improved, but they were better than at Deptford, and the introduction of steam enforced the extension of all the yards that were to be maintained. Woolwich steam factories, therefore, were founded in 1839-40, but the ropeyard was disestablished in 1835. Between 1842-6 upwards of seven acres of land were added to the dockyard, and in 1842 it contained 56 acres.[350] In the middle of the century the dry-docks were replaced by modern ones, two being built in 1841 and one in 1848. As years passed on ample appliances for the construction and repair of steam vessels and steam machinery, and for the making of armour, were furnished; but the size of ships was increasing yearly, and machinery, docks, and appliances were becoming out of date almost as soon as completed. In position it became less and less suited to modern requirements, therefore it was closed from 1 October 1869 and handed over to the War Office. Some of the sheds, and much of the machinery, were removed to Chatham.

Sheerness was more than once supposed to be threatened with the same fate, but the fears of the workmen and staff were groundless. The old abuse of 'chips' at last died out here, and at the other yards, after the Great War. In consequence of the recommendation of the Parliamentary Committee of 1805 an allowance had been granted in lieu of the perquisite, but the allowance itself was abolished by an Admiralty Order of 9 January 1830. The Admiralty House at Sheerness was built in accordance with an order of 31 May 1827[351] to please, it is said, the Duke of Clarence, who proposed to reside in it. During the Napoleonic war a 28-gun ship had been hauled ashore to serve as a residence for the Port admiral—'£2,000 was applied for to build a house, but the fitting of this ship at an expense little short of £5,000 was deemed more economical—not to reckon the value of the ship,' wrote an Admiralty official of his superiors. A chapel in the yard succeeded, in 1835, the old chapel over the entrance gate; this was burnt down 26 November 1881. In 1852 Sheerness, with the other dockyards, was connected by electric telegraph with the Admiralty, and in 1854, owing to the demands caused by the Crimean War, a steam factory was established.

By an Admiralty Order of 31 January 1821,[352] Deptford was to be maintained chiefly as a depot for small work; between 1830 and 1844 it was closed, but utilized for breaking up condemned men-of-war. After it was reopened shipbuilding continued there until 1869, but the conditions of modern iron, and then armoured, shipbuilding of heavy tonnage were lessening its utility yearly. The era inaugurated by the *Warrior* of 1861 gave the death-blow to Deptford, but the immediate future had been so little anticipated that, between 1856-9, upwards of 20 acres of ground had been bought for the future development of the yard.[353] In 1864 it covered rather more than 27 acres, with some 2,000 ft. of river frontage, but at most stages of the tide ships could not lie alongside the dockyard wharves. The last warship built there, the sloop *Druid*, was launched 13 March 1869, and the yard was closed on the 31st of the month; it was sold to Mr. T. P. Austin, who disposed of some 21 acres of the ground to the Corporation of the City of London for use as a foreign cattle market. The Victualling Yard had been made more convenient by the erection, in 1780, of many necessary storehouses and buildings for the preparation

[350] *Parl. Papers* (1861), xxxviii, 143. [351] Admir. and Navy Bd. 198. [353] *Parl. Papers* (1861), xxxviii,
[352] Ibid. 206. 143.

of provisions. The establishment of the Gosport and Plymouth Victualling Yards reduced, to a certain extent, its importance, but in 1827 the mast-house and adjoining ground of the dockyard were transferred to the Victualling Yard, to which the business of seamen's clothing was removed at the same time.[354] In 1858 it received the title of Royal Victoria Victualling Yard.

Little requiring notice happened at Chatham during the middle third of the nineteenth century. In February 1845 there was a fire which did damage to the amount of £20,000. In 1847 19 acres of ground, adjacent to the dockyard, were bought, and in 1854 the remainder of St. Mary's Island, 185 acres in extent. It was clear that as Woolwich and Deptford were becoming useless, and Sheerness was not greatly favoured, a huge extension would be necessary at Chatham, practically the only eastern yard. For the time nothing was done beyond commencing a new dry-dock in 1855, the prolongation of the dockyard wall towards St. Mary's Creek, and the embankment of part of St. Mary's Island. A Parliamentary Committee of 1861 urged strongly the importance of proceeding immediately with the extension, and approved Chatham, not only on account of the necessity for a great North Sea dockyard, but also for the security the new defences, just authorized by Parliament, would afford it. By the 24 and 25 Victoria, cap. 41, the Admiralty was given power to acquire and use St. Mary's Creek on condition of providing conveniences in place of certain vested interests destroyed. The works were commenced in 1862, but the plans were not finally settled by Sir Andrew Clarke, R.E. until 1864, while they were carried out under the superintendence of Mr. E. A. Bernays, C.E. The existing yard contained 97 acres, and the extension was to include 380 acres; the site of St. Mary's Creek was to be occupied by three basins communicating with each other, and also with the Medway by one lock at the Upnor side and two opening into Gillingham Reach. The repairing basin, at the Upnor end, 21 acres in area, 33 ft. deep, and with four dry-docks opening into it, was finished in 1871, then followed the middle, or factory basin, and the third, or fitting-out basin, in 1883. Steam appliances, workshops, and other necessary buildings were erected in proximity to the basins; the whole extension was completed by 1885 at a cost of £3,000,000. In 1877 a branch from the London, Chatham, and Dover Railway Co. was run into the yard; a new dry-dock, estimated to cost £450,000, was commenced in 1897 and finished in 1903.

Even in 1883 some skilled observers were regarding doubtfully the prospects of the new yard in view of the growth of the battleship, the tortuous navigation of the Medway, and the insufficient depth of water, except at high-water spring tides, on the sills of the lock gates. Their forebodings have been justified as battleships have reached a displacement of 19,000 tons with no sign of pause in their growth. A still more serious disadvantage, affecting both Chatham and Sheerness, is the bar outside the latter port over which capital ships can pass only just before, or after, high tide.[355] As regards Sheerness itself it does not answer to the primary requirement of an efficient base, i.e. that it must be independent of the protection of a fleet. The purpose of a base is to fit

[354] Admir. and Navy Bd. 204, 1, 3 Nov. 1827.

[355] In 1908 the dredging of Sheerness bar was in contemplation. But if dredged it would only be a half-tide bar and disabled battle-ships might be compelled to wait half a tide to enter, a delay that could be attended by most disastrous consequences.

out a fleet which leaves it to take the offensive; if ships have to stay to protect it, it is a failure. It is more than doubtful whether, if liable to attack, Sheerness could ever be left to rely on its land defences. At present (1908) Chatham is of less value as a dockyard than at any previous period of its history; the absence of a satisfactory battleship base on the North Sea has caused the attention of the Admiralty to be turned again to the Firth of Forth where, as far back as 1710, it was intended to form a dockyard at Rosyth.[356] The development of aircraft has introduced new factors into the situation of dockyards, a question which does not need discussion here.

The dockyard regiments were again formed in 1847 and disbanded in 1857.[357] When completely organized in 1848 Chatham supplied 1,395 men, Deptford 1,057, Woolwich 994, and Sheerness 890.[358] They were then called the Royal Dockyard Volunteers. The men are said to have taken up the work with interest, and to have made capital artillerymen, but the scheme was not regarded with favour by the seamen at the Admiralty, and the organization was allowed to collapse before the battalions were disbanded.[359]

[356] Although Leith was a naval station, Rosyth would have been very useful as a dockyard during the Napoleonic war, but it had then only been for a century under consideration, and the Admiralty has always moved with deliberation. In 1677 the considered plan of an Intelligence Department, devised on quite broad, modern lines, was proposed to Pepys: the Admiralty sat on the idea for two centuries before, assisted by much outside vituperation, hatching it into life. The French started their Naval Intelligence Department, as a section of the Bureau des Affaires Étrangères, in 1766.

[357] *Parl. Papers* (1857-8), xxxvii, 275.

[358] Ibid. (1847-8), xli, 273.

[359] *Life and Letters of Sir J. B. Sulivan*, pp. 117, 397.